T5-BCL-959

Black Characters in the Brazilian Novel

Center for Afro-American Studies
Claudia Mitchell-Kernan, Director

Afro-American Culture and Society
A CAAS Monograph Series
Volume 6

Black Characters in the Brazilian Novel

GIORGIO MAROTTI

Translated by Maria O. Marotti and Harry Lawton

CENTER FOR AFRO-AMERICAN STUDIES
UNIVERSITY OF CALIFORNIA, LOS ANGELES

Library of Congress Cataloging in Publication Data

Marotti, Giorgio.
Black characters in the Brazilian novel.

(Afro-American culture and society, ISSN 0882-5297 ; v. 6)
Translation of: Il negro nel romanzo brasiliano.
Bibliography: p.
Includes index.
1. Brazilian fiction—History and criticism. 2. Blacks in literature.
I. Title. II. Series.
PQ9607.B53M3713 1987 869.3'093520396 86-16041
ISBN 0-934934-24-X
ISBN 0-934934-25-8 (pbk.)

Originally published as *Il negro nel romanzo brasiliano*

Illustrations from the work of the German painter Johann Moritz Rugendas (1802-1858).

Center for Afro-American Studies
University of California, Los Angeles

Library of Congress Catalog Card Number: 86-16041
ISBN 0-934934-24-X
ISBN 0-934934-25-8 (pbk)
ISSN 0882-5297
Printed in the United States of America

Design: Serena Sharp
Typography: Freedmen's Organization
Produced by UCLA Publication Services Dept.

CONTENTS

PREFACE

This book is not a history of slavery in Brazil. This book is simply the history of one of the consequences of slavery, of how the Black was and is represented in the Brazilian novel. It is also the history of how the social structures themselves, beginning with the family, were modified by the presence of the Black element. Finally, it is the history of the altering of the *forma mentis* of those novelists who have passed down to us the deeds and misdeeds of slavery and who most of all, often unconsciously, felt the presence of the Black in Brazil.

The Portuguese discovered Brazil in 1500. Colonization began a few decades later. Brazil remained a Portuguese colony until 1822 when it became independent, and was the only Portuguese-speaking country to establish an empire in the midst of many Spanish-speaking republics in Latin America. Brazil also became a republic in 1889, one year after the abolition of slavery.

Slavery accompanies the history of Brazil right from its birth. In fact, the new land offered only lush vegetation and fertile soil populated by nomadic *índios*, hunters and gatherers. The Portuguese found nothing like the rich empires the Spanish had found in Mexico and Peru or the great reigns the Portuguese themselves had found in India. There was nothing therefore to compensate the daring explorers for the hardships and risks of the long voyage (we note in passing that the Portuguese verb *explorar* means at the same time to explore and to exploit).

There was thus but one possibility, that of commercial agricultural enterprise: to exploit the particularly fertile soil in order to grow on a vast scale products easily and advantageously sold in Europe. But many hands were needed to cultivate the land. The Portuguese were daring men, adventurers and voyagers in a particularly happy moment of their colonial and commercial expansion, but they did not have much agriculture. Slavery, already known in Portugal, was applied on a wide scale in Brazil. As the índio proved unsuitable for work in the fields, Blacks began to be imported from Africa.

Other countries too, such as the United States of America, have known slavery. In Brazil, however, the phenomenon had different characteristics that one must bear in mind if we want to understand the history of the Black Brazilian.

The first of these characteristics is the absolute extent of slavery, which in Brazil was identified with the very structures of the country. The second characteristic dates back to the early days of colonialism when the Portuguese adventurers arrived in the new land alone, their families having in most cases remained at home. The women of these men were *índias* and Blacks. Brazil was born as a country of mixed races right from the start. The third characteristic is a consequence of the second and is the purely economic character of slavery, which is free from any racist formula. Especially in the nineteenth century, when the process of the mixing of the races was already in an advanced phase, there were slaves with almost white skins while certain pure Blacks had succeeded in obtaining their freedom through work and were free citizens, at times occupying important positions in society.

There were certain preconceptions of a social type that made it difficult for free Blacks to assert themselves in society. There existed also a scale of values coming from the Blacks which identified the white man with the highest of values. All this, however, did not prevent the full and total participation of the Blacks in the history of Brazil. Blacks fought alongside the Portuguese in the colonial wars against the Dutch and the French. They fought the Portuguese in battles for independence. The Black slaves who enlisted during the war with Paraguay were automatically declared free citizens.

The aim of this research is, first, to see how Black characters have been described in the Brazilian novel (here I am taking up again and bringing up to date the studies by Raymond Sayers and Gregory Rabassa published in the United States in the 1950s). The second aim is to analyze the Black character in relation to the structures of the society in which he lived, namely, the structures described in the novel. The third aim is to establish the moral position of the writer with regard to his characters, starting from the principle that all Brazilians, Black or white, progressive or reactionary, willingly or unwillingly, have to a greater or lesser extent been conditioned by slavery. The fourth aim of this research is to establish a constant relationship between the authors, the events related, and the historical reality in which they lived.

In the choice of Black characters, so numerous in the Brazilian novel, I have followed the principle of the Black condition, of the importance and the meaning given by the author to the color of the skin of his protagonists. I have left out Black characters where having black skin had no importance in the general context of the work; I have singled out others because their way of being and doing was closely bound up with the color of their skin.

As far as the quotations from various authors are concerned, I have decided to leave the original Portuguese terms when they serve to indicate a person of color. In fact, the words *negro* and *preto*, with their diminutives, are adjectives that indicate the color black and in themselves are without any pejorative connotation. They are used indifferently in the same phrase by the same author to indicate the same characters. The same may be said for the term *crioulo*, which serves to indicate a colored person born in Brazil, or the term *cafuzo*, which literally means off-spring of Black and índio. Finally the term *cabra*, used to indicate a person of low social standing, be he Black or white, can be used in a positive sense.

Slavery was for millions of men a desolating certainty lasting through the centuries. I shall be satisfied if the reading of this book makes one doubt the many certainties through which man continues to abuse his power over his fellow men.

1 THE UNCERTAIN BEGINNINGS

The Black slave has been present in the Brazilian novel since its very beginning. In 1859, *Ursula*, one of the first novels of Brazilian literature, was printed. Even though its plot follows the canon of romantic fiction its author makes it an exceptional work. *Ursula* is a work by a woman, the first Brazilian female novelist and one who lived in Maranhão. Maranhão is one of the northern states of Brazil, a region that supplied numerous writers; yet because of its very geographical nature—the great distance that separated it from the cultural center of the country—the society of Maranhão was particularly conservative and male oriented.

For a woman, Maria Firmina dos Reis, to write a novel in 1859 in the city of São Luís do Maranhão was by itself exceptional. The plot, even though it followed the canonical development of a romantic story of love and death, was designed to shock a public of provincial and conservative readers: the young Tancredo falls madly in love with a young and beautiful cousin whom his mother had brought up as a daughter; Tancredo's father opposes the marriage and manages to send his son away so that he himself can marry the girl, with whom he is in love, as soon as his wife dies; Tancredo is bitterly surprised upon his return to discover that his mother is dead and his fiancée has become his stepmother. Tancredo then runs away in desperation and when he becomes ill he is saved by a young Black man whose name is Túlio; Túlio's owner is in fact Ursula, a young and beautiful woman who lives in poor conditions together with her paralyzed and widowed mother; Tancredo pays a ransom for the good slave Túlio thus giving him freedom; meanwhile Tancredo and Ursula fall in love with each other. But Ursula also attracts her uncle Fernando's passion; Fernando had been in love with his own sister, Ursula's mother, for a long time and now he has transferred his incestuous passion to his niece. The story ends in a slaughter: Fernando, who years before had already killed his own brother-in-law in a fit of jealousy, kills Tancredo, Túlio, and Susana, an old faithful servant; Ursula, who in the meanwhile has also lost her mother, becomes insane and dies. Fernando spends the last years of his life in gloomy remorse behind the walls of a monastery.

In the novel *Ursula* two aspects stand out: more obvious though less interesting is that the plot resembles those of the *feuilletons* or popular romances that were starting to appear in those years. The second and more interesting aspect lies in the author's clear intention to challenge the conservative audience and expose social realities in an accurate way. For example, Fernando's incestuous passion for his sister and his niece and Tancredo's father's passion for his son's fiancée were not merely imaginary fiction. Considering time and place, to deal with these situations was a challenging and shocking act. Dos Reis's challenge consists in presenting in literary form the social reality of the great families of Maranhão. (Writers and chroniclers of a later period have provided us with the evidence of this reality.) These families, because of the distance from any center of progress and change, were ossified in their slaveocratic mentality and restricted by an enclosed family environment while they witnessed their own slow and inevitable decadence. The violence of institutions was thus exerted not only against slaves but also towards those, especially women, who were subjected to the patriarchal will.

All this is present in the novel written by dos Reis, a brave elementary-school teacher in a country where illiteracy was widespread. Slavery is also present in her work, but it is not depicted as an accepted and inevitable fact; slavery is described as an injustice and an eternal crime against man. In her writings, however, she does not suggest any revolutionary solutions; even the novel *A escrava*, written in 1887 on the eve of the liberation of the slaves, tells the very sad story of a mother deprived of her own children, and ends with a legal appeal to a judge for the liberation of a minor. The slaves described in *Ursula* are stereotypes: Túlio is the good slave who even after his liberation decides to remain the servant of Tancredo, his new master; Susana is the good old Black woman, the *mãe preta*, the Black mammy, who sacrifices herself to save her young mistress.

Dos Reis's criticism transcends any mere social solution. In her simplicity and clarity, typical of an elementary-school teacher, she points out the very roots of the contradictions of a hypocritical and bigoted society. The gospel and religion that served as an alibi to justify the slave system had in fact always preached equality and brotherhood among human beings. The events she narrates—the continuous violence, the exhausting and inhuman work, the murders that were never punished—were all part (and now we know it) of those masters' privileges on which the basest injustice was legally founded.

And this good twenty-four-year-old schoolteacher was a young woman who lived in great isolation in a distant province of the huge

Brazilian empire that lived and thrived upon slavery; she dared to state that what daily happened in front of everybody's indifferent eyes was an injustice; it was contrary to what was written in the gospels and to that religion which everybody claimed to follow.

With the typical clarity of simple people, dos Reis denounced the basic conflicts of Brazilian society.

While what she tells can be easily accepted by the modern reader, for her contemporaries it was shocking reality. A comfortable alibi for the vast majority of whites was, for example, the immoral behavior of Black people (according to the rules of the time). In this immorality the whites were often accomplices and partners of the Blacks and moreover the white masters certainly did not set a good example; they were at best only more discreet and more hypocritical. The author emphasized instead that Black people, although treated as animals, did not always act as such, and in fact many among them were able to sustain noble feelings in spite of the hellish life they were compelled to lead.

Ursula is certainly not a great novel but it does provide us with valuable evidence of the level of degeneration slavery had reached in Maranhão. In fact, dos Reis does underline a specific aspect of slavery with which later authors deal. The slave-master relationship, the complete submission of the Black man to the white man, was not limited to the purely economic field that had given birth to the slave trade during the second half of the sixteenth century. Especially in some distant provinces, crystallized in a sclerotic system, slavery had surpassed the purely economic relationship and evolved into a pure expression of the worst instincts. In other words, violence and cruelties were not the punishment inflicted upon slaves who did not perform their requested duties. They became instead a way of expressing and giving free vent to the anger of a class of masters who could commit crimes while remaining inside the law. This was slavery and this was the brave denunciation by Maria Firmina dos Reis.

Yet there was still a long way to go. Two curious episodes happened during the 1975 celebrations of the one-hundred-fiftieth anniversary of the author's birth which can help us understand the peculiar environment of Maranhão. The critic Nascimento Morais Filho in his book devoted to dos Reis, *Fragmentos de uma vida*, praises the woman from Maranhão and connects our writer with Donana Jansen, the literary figure and the political and economic one. Yet, we know from several writers and chroniclers that Jansen was the owner of huge plantations and great riches (her importance in the life of Maranhão derives from that); and we also know that her name was handed down in legends as one of the cruelest owners of slaves. In particular her reputation still survives nowadays in children's stories, and once masters threatened to sell their restless slaves to Donana to keep them in their place. This is a very unhappy comparison, which can only be explained by the fact that in 1975 when Morais Filho's book was written, Jansen was still considered important by many people in Maranhão, important people to whom the critic's words were presumably addressed

The second episode from 1975 refers to a quotation from the introduction to the book *Ursula* by Horácio de Almeida, who writes, commenting on the Black character Túlio, that he is "A slave who thanks to his personality and his white soul occupies an important position in the work as a whole."[1] In 1859 there was still a long way to go if in 1975 there was still someone who talked about a white soul.

Another writer who can be named among the forerunners of the fiction based upon Black people is José de Alencar (1829–1877). He is one of the greatest nineteenth-century Brazilian novelists and the author of numerous works, among which *Guarani*, *Iracema*, and *Ubirajara* comprise a sort of *chanson de geste* treating the mythology of Brazilian *índios*.

The Indians were no longer a problem in the Brazilian world of those years; they were either integrated or destroyed. The few survivors either lived at the borders of an agricultural civilization that was foreign to their culture of nomadic people, hunters and gatherers, or they had taken refuge in the middle of the forest. Since they were no longer a problem for anybody, the Indians were a good subject for mythology and thus provided the historical basis for a country that had no past. The Blacks had historically replaced the Indians by performing work in the fields and thus creating the economic basis of the country. They had entered in the master's family where they performed various manual tasks; Black women were in the white master's bed and had borne illegitimate mulatto children, thus arousing jealousy in the families. No one could be a less appropriate subject for myth than Black people.

De Alencar created a Black character in the comedy *O demônio familiar*, the story of a *moleque*, a Black boy who gets into all sorts of scrapes. What interests us in this comedy more than the plot is the opinion that the author, clearly a conservative, expresses about Blacks and slavery. This is how he introduces his terrible protagonist:

> The ancients believed that each house was inhabited by a family devil upon which the calm and serenity of the people who lived therein was

> based. We Brazilians have unfortunately realized the truth of this belief; in our homes we give hospitality to this family devil. How often he shares with us the endearment of our mothers, the games of our brothers and some of the love and affection of our family! But the day comes when, like today, he, either in his ignorance or in his malice, disturbs the domestic peace; and he transforms love, friendship, reputation and all those sacred objects into a children's game. This family devil is in our homes, we all know him—there he is.[2]

The veiled criticism of the institution of slavery (as if it were the work of gods or of natural forces) serves the purpose of blaming the unhappy young Black boy. What will be the punishment for this public danger with a black skin?

> Take it, your certificate of freedom; it will be your punishment from now on because your guilt will be your sole responsibility; thus morality and law will hold you responsible for your own actions. Once you are free you will feel the need for honest work and you will appreciate the noble feelings that today you do not understand.[3]

O demônio familiar is a comedy. It is not a treatise on slavery, for slavery is mentioned only because slaves were very widespread at the time in Brazil and were part of the life of the family, where they performed countless tasks. The author, however, mirrors in his idea the general opinion that Blacks were not ready for freedom; for Blacks, freedom ended up being a sort of punishment. If we consider the structure of Brazilian society at the time—huge plantations in the hands of large patriarchal families based upon the work of the slaves—then this opinion was partly true. In fact there was very little opportunity for any kind of work that was not coerced. Pedro, the moleque, states that he wants to become a coachman for the two protagonists when they get married: what is the meaning of being a coachman, a free man, in a society where all coachmen were slaves like all the other servants? The problem was in the Brazilian society itself and in its structures, but this was a subject upon which not even the most revolutionary spirits dared tread.

José do Patrocínio (1854–1905) is another writer who describes slaves in his work. He was a dark-skinned mulatto, a journalist, and a great orator who fought a long battle for the emancipation of the slaves. Although personally loyal to his race he was deeply affected by the spirit of the times. In one of his novels, *Motta Coqueiro*, his Black characters follow the most stereotypical clichés. It is worth noting, however, that the novel was directed against the death penalty (Motta Coqueiro is the protagonist who is unjustly condemned to death) rather than against slavery. Although the work was published in 1877, only eleven years prior to the abolition of slavery, two prominent characters are described from a proslavery point of view. The good and the bad slaves oppose each other; the good one is on the master's side, the bad one acts against the masters. The bad Black in this case is a woman; her name is Balbina and she has the ominous reputation of being a *feiticeira*, a witch, and, as we will see later on, the character of the *feiticeiro* always invites the writers' attacks: "She was a tall stocky *preta*; her evil eyes were full of blood, her nose was big and her lips were tumid."[4] Balbina has a very sad background but the author narrates her story without a single comment and spends many pages describing her evil actions. She used to be the nurse of some white children who, once they grew up, decided to sell her. On the new farm Balbina with her reputation of being a feiticeira exerts her influence upon the other slaves. This is already a crime. In the slave system a power other than the white master's was in itself a crime. Moreover she knows the secret of herbs; this is another fault because she is able to do things that the white masters, in spite of their knowledge, are unable to do. To complete the picture the author charges her with other sinister habits such as that of sleeping with snakes.

Motta Coqueiro, the master on the new farm, has her punished cruelly for the purpose of preventing any possible evil action, although she has done nothing wrong; the overseer, in his turn, persecutes her with ferocity. So Balbina, who had been sold by the children she had nursed and who had been whipped without reason, starts to plot to have her naïve master condemned.

My point is that do Patrocínio tells of the poor woman's misadventures as if they were the most normal facts while he describes in gloomy terms her evil personality and Motta Coqueiro's sad destiny. This reeks of the proslavery point of view, as does his description of the good slave Domingos:

> He had a noble character, the *preto* Domingos. His resignation made his flat and black face pleasant. The instinct to obey had matured him, as had his age and his master's strictness. He was like a faithful dog and as passive as a saddled animal. He struggled against those who attacked the *casa grande* and white people; he withdrew indignantly in the face of his fellows' abyss of perversity which they had often revealed to him with their evil suggestions.[5]

We find here a total inversion of values to the masters' advantage, according to which the poor Domingos is meant to inspire our pity. His virtues lower him to the animal level; he is faithful to his master like a dog and he is ready to die to defend his master's life and his properties. He is passive as a mule in the exhausting work through which he increases his master's wealth; he is likable because he is resigned and he is mature thanks to his master's discipline—his beatings—and his instinct to obey, that is, his sad addiction to servility. His supreme virtue, then, consists in avoiding his fellows and in withdrawing in front of that abyss of perversity and those evil suggestions, at which the author hints without explaining but which one can easily imagine: that he run away, that he rebel against oppression, what else?

José do Patrocínio was a cultured man who had led a long struggle against slavery. If this is what he really thought, then we can only imagine how others felt about this problem, those who thought that slavery was an absolutely inviolable dogma.

Maria Firmina dos Reis, José de Alencar, and José do Patrocínio are not only the first Brazilian writers to deal with the theme of slavery in their works. They also present three different ways of facing and describing the same problem, three ways that we will find innumerable times in different shapes displayed by later writers.

Dos Reis embodies the religious aspect; her sincerely and deeply felt Christian faith did not allow her to accept the fact that other human beings should be tortured and should spend their lives in chains. De Alencar is the great romantic writer and the solid bourgeois thinker who creates an Indian mythology and who describes the Black man without ever abandoning the typical prejudices of his time. Do Patrocínio is the intellectual and the political man who claims great principles although he cannot get away from the stereotypes commonly applied to the world of slavery. In fact he is the one who creates the two typical characters who recur again and again: the bad slave, who does not accept slavery and who is generally a sorcerer, a feiticeiro (in this case it is a woman); and the good slave who is, instead, the one who accepts the system in which he lives and to which he adapts himself while cooperating willingly with his white master.

From the second half of the nineteenth century, that is, the time during which these writers lived, up to the time of contemporary authors who have the courage to overturn opinions accepted for centuries, the Brazilian novel constantly reiterates the same themes, although in different ways.

2 JOAQUIM MANOEL DE MACEDO: THE VICTIMS AND THE EXECUTIONERS

Joaquim Manoel de Macedo (1820–1882) is an author who gained remarkable success in the field of the urban novel and in a genre we might want to call *feuilleton*. He was a simple writer and he was aware that he was. The critic Astrojildo Pereira writes about him, "A novelist for young ladies and about young ladies, Macedo places weddings at the beginning, at the middle, at the end of anything. Everything in his novels is centered around weddings, points towards weddings, ends up in weddings."[1] This very simplicity, which mirrored accurately the widespread feelings of the time and the prejudices of the patriarchal society, is the cause of his success. *A moreninha* (*The Dark-Haired Girl*, 1844) was his undisputed masterpiece.

A moreninha can be considered a classic of its kind: Augusto and Carolina meet as children on a beach; they exchange a promise of eternal love; they lose sight of each other; they meet again as adolescents in the charming setting of the Paquetá island where they recognize each other (also thanks to the help of a youngish grandmother, who stands out in the midst of a juvenile confusion created by the other young people); they marry and—as one might imagine—they live happily thereafter. *A moreninha* provides us with a complete and sincere picture of the mores of the time: the fake Bohemian students who lived a life of leisure while being served by their *moleques; o namoro*, that is, the courtship of their sweethearts carried out either through languid glances and conventional signals or through love notes which the everpresent moleque would deliver; the use of French words; the slow pace of a society all dressed up as Europeans (jacket, hat, gloves, ample clothes with trains and half a dozen underskirts and silken stockings); the serene and unquestioned acceptance of established habits and morals; and eventually, underneath all this, the certainty of a system based upon slavery.

In *A moreninha* there are three important Black characters: two moleques and an elderly female servant. The first moleque is Rafael, the faithful servant of the young Augusto who apparently is unable to move around without his young slave: "The good Rafael was at the same time his cook, his shoe-shiner, his barber, his errand boy, and . . . whatever else was needed."[2] But the good Rafael had also another function which, at least for him, was much less pleasant. When Augusto, toward the end of the novel, feels more and more nervous because of his growing passion for Carolina, Rafael will pay for it. "If the innocent *moleque* prepares tea too early he gets half a dozen slaps on the face because he is accused of wanting to go loafing around in the streets; if the following day he is only ten minutes late he gets two slaps on the face so that he will hurry up."[3]

The other moleque is called Tobias and he belongs to a girl with whom Fabrício, another student, is in love. Tobias is the stereotypical lively Black boy, he has a quick tongue and he grasps situations easily. If on the one hand Augusto depends totally on Rafael for his elementary existential needs, Fabrício's good prospects of success in the courtship of his lady lie greatly in Tobias's prompt response. That Fabrício says Tobias is as quick as a monkey and calls him *maldito crioulo* (damned Black) should not be read as disparagingly racist remarks but rather as a sign of his admiration. *Crioulo* denoted a Black person born in Brazil who did not come directly from Africa.

The third Black character, Paula, the elderly female servant who had brought up Carolina, is the center of another episode that was supposed to touch and move the readers. At the end of the elaborate dinner—everything is very formal, young people and adolescents are all dressed up in their ceremonial clothes while the elderly watch them contentedly—one of the guests, a German, invites Paula to drink a glass of wine: the glasses multiply and at the end Paula, almost drunk, is hit by a temporary illness. The four medical students who are consulted (Augusto is among them) suggest a hot footbath without revealing the woman's real physical state. The slave who arrives with a basin full of water shows clearly that she is afraid of scalding her hands; then the beautiful Carolina sends her away and with her beautiful and delicate hands washes her old nurse's feet. The young Augusto, touched by such kindness, replaces her, and this four-handed footbath is the beginning of a great eternal love.

From the episode I have quoted it is clear that the author was untroubled by the fact that Rafael, Tobias, and Paula were slaves. Macedo wrote to please his audience; through his stories he meant to soothe and sweeten the many daily frustrations. Yet this master of triviality and conventions faced, at some point of his career, the theme of slavery and attacked directly the wretched institution in three thesis novels collected under the title *As vítimas-algozes* (*The Victim-Executioners*, 1869). What I find most interesting is that Macedo leads a frontal attack against one of the pillars of Brazilian society at the time and exposes vehemently an untouchable subject while at the same time never altering the triviality of his plots and the conventionality of the situations.

His strategy in its simplicity touches on genius: avoiding historical and moral reasons which were foreign to the Brazilian reality of the time, he shows through three long thesis novels that the evil of slavery consists in the very absurdity of the relationship between master and slave. In fact, they both become each other's victims and oppressors. At the beginning the master is the oppressor and the slave is the victim; owning one or more slaves structures the master's family life in such a way that he ends up depending on his slaves, who often loathe him and who eventually become his executioners.

One of these three melodramatic stories is called *Simeão, o crioulo* (*Simeão, the Black Man*; we have already seen that at the time the term crioulo indicated a Black person born in Brazil). Simeão is a slave who was brought up by his masters as their own son; he was also nursed together with his young mistress; he has all the advantages of freedom, yet he is not a free man and he knows that he could be enchained and whipped exactly as the other slaves. When this happens, through Simeão's own fault, the young man starts to develop a deep hatred toward his master and especially towards the husband of his young mistress. The story ends tragically with robbery and death. Simeão joins forces with other scoundrels against his former benefactors. Even facing death Simeão remains a slave: he is hanged while his white accomplice is only sent to prison.

Another story is called *Pai Rayol, o feiticeiro* (*Pai Rayol, the Sorcerer*). Pai Rayol is a sorcerer, an expert in herbs and poisons; he has already changed many masters and received harsh punishments because of his evil personality. On the farm where he now works he has a lover, Esméria, who is another slave. Pai Rayol induces Esméria to become the master's lover thus taking all power away from the legitimate wife: Pai Rayol's poisons complete the job by eliminating the mistress and her children. When at the end the master is on the verge of following the same fate, the intervention of two other slaves saves him and removes the sorcerer.

The third story is called *Lucinda, a mucama* (*Lucinda, the Mucama*, that is, some sort of lady-in-waiting or Black playmate who was usually assigned to a white young lady, often when she was still a child): Lucinda is given as a present to Cândida, a girl of the same age, to serve her as a mucama. Lucinda and Cândida grow up together. The slave, however, ends up by enjoying a greater freedom than her mistress; both through her example and especially her licentious tales she exerts a negative influence on Cândida. When a young

French adventurer arrives Lucinda acts as a go-between between him and Cândida; she also becomes the Frenchman's lover and helps him become Cândida's lover. The intervention of the police (the Frenchman was wanted for crimes he had committed in France) hastens the final resolution of the story; meanwhile a generous cousin in love with Cândida saves her from dishonor and shame.

These three stories transcend the melodramatic trend intended by the author and demanded by the literary taste of the time. They are absolutely realistic because they refer to real situations. Simeão's case, in which the Black boy shares his master's life and is then relegated to his previous condition of slavery, is real. The sorcerer of Pai Rayol's story, who creates disorders among the slaves and troubles his master's serenity, is just as real as the Black woman who becomes the master's lover and takes away power from the legitimate wife. Finally, the truest case is that of Lucinda in which the mucama, the young mistress's playmate, ends up by exerting a continuously negative influence on her: it is the point where the two worlds converge and clash, the rigid Portuguese morality ruling the mistress's life and the African slave's instinctual freedom.

The facts, events, and situations Macedo describes are nothing more than aspects of the daily life that he continually witnessed.

Macedo is an honest writer, a man who belongs totally to his time, himself a victim and an oppressor, at least to some extent, in a story in which he is the protagonist. In other words, Macedo is not Machado de Assis: he is not a genius, he does not have the talent of irony and he is unable to step back from his environment to give a historical overview and perceptive insight. This makes Macedo more interesting in my view: in Machado's world we perceive the presence of that eternal protagonist who is Machado de Assis himself; Macedo's works, instead, mirror the environment of his time with its prejudices, limits, and drawbacks.

If for a moment we set aside the noble principle inspiring the author, we see that Macedo quite often shows a total lack of understanding towards the slave as human being, as a person with dignity. In *Simeão, o crioulo* the protagonist is brought up as a son of the family and is nursed together with his young mistress; the privileges he enjoys make his condition as a slave even more wearisome, and the sight of other slaves who are whipped—knowing that some day he might incur the same fate—contributes to embittering Simeão's mind. He is simultaneously rejected both by the master's world and that of the slaves. The only entertainment of his life is the *venda*, that is, a trading post where he can drink and play games with occasional friends. It is against the venda that Macedo launches his harshest accusations. Under the pretext of a moralistic attack against the place of perdition the author reveals in fact constant concern about the place where slaves and other derelicts meet and pass around the words of revolt. To go to the venda and thus allow himself the only possible entertainment in his life without future prospects, Simeão commits minor acts of thievery. It is Florinda, his young mistress and foster sister, and a slave girl who discover him; at this point Domingos Caetano, the master, arrives. Here we have a stereotypical situation: the just but strict master, the good young mistress, the rebel slave, and the faithful obedient slave, "Florinda was a saint: she pitied the crioulo and remained silent, the slave, however, obeyed and spoke up."[4] At this point Domingos Caetano, "justifiably angry," whips the slave six times until Florinda, weeping, manages to tear the whip away from her father's hands. It is at this point that the author, totally against his will and his intentions, gives us a magnificent description of Simeão, which turns the miserable little thief into a fully dignified and proud human being:

> While he was whipped Simeão stayed still, he neither moaned nor cried nor uttered a single word of repentance and sorrow. When eventually Domingos Caetano, deprived of the whip, still threatened him, he looked down, with a feverish glance and with solemn eyes, on both the master who had so rightly punished him and the young lady who with so much pity had interfered in order to spare him a greater and well-deserved punishment.[5]

Macedo's position is inevitably ambiguous. On the one hand he feels the historical need of a change—the civil war in the United States had just ended, and Brazil and Cuba were the only two countries that still preserved slavery. On the other hand, his reasons are inspired mainly by the fear of the irreparable damage that slavery could cause to the masters' families, that is, to the white masters. Naturally these were the reasons to which his reading public responded; yet we are left to wonder whether the writer ever faced the problem of the intrinsic humanity of those who lived in the condition of slavery. In *Simeão, o crioulo* there is another deeply meaningful episode: Simeão has a lover, a slave who belongs to Hermano, Florinda's fiancé. Every night Simeão, avoiding the strict surveillance, joins his woman, who lives in Hermano's house. At first sight it would look like the typical case of a comedy of mores: the masters' couple is paralleled by the slaves' couple; yet here the parallelism is purely negative. Let us start with the choice of the names: Hermano means strong and brave man, while Florinda reflects in her name feminine grace and gentleness (*flor* means "flower"). In contrast, we have Simeão (is there here an unconscious racism in the name that reminds one of the disparaging word for monkey, *símio*?) and his anonymous partner ("The mucama did not have the white lady's education: her nature is that of an animal.").[6] What seems mainly to trouble the writer is that these nightly meetings, which were commonplace in the life of the plantation, jeopardized the masters' life and wealth. Luckily, adds Macedo, "Simeão, the slave, went there only as an animal, dragged by his instinct seeking his equal."[7] Eventually Hermano, awakened by a noise, finds the two and, strong and brave, floors Simeão, who had dared fight against the white master in an attempt to run away: "Simeão was recognized and the slave, his lover and accomplice, was immediately punished in front of him."[8]

It is sex, the eternal ancient taboo, that prompts the writer's defense of the masters' world, his world—let us not forget it. Simeão's and his partner's mating might perhaps endanger the master's house but that in itself is only the slave's business: they do it in the house only because she is a domestic slave who lives in the house; otherwise they would have done it in the *senzala* and it would have made everybody happy. There is one revealing episode: at some point Domingos Caetano has a heart attack and Florinda's dress slips aside, exposing her breast. Simeão is present, "He the slave, the animal made of ice and hatred whose evil eyes, the sacrilegious infamous eyes, devoured voraciously the young maid's naked breast, the virginal breast."[9] At this point the author must have had the impression of having gone too far and wants almost to move back to reassure himself and his readers: the Black slave could not mate in any way with his white mistress; these were unthinkable ideas in the Brazil of those years. And the author insists twice, "The badly educated *crioulo* who was unrestrained because of the habit of going unpunished certainly did not even dare dream a criminal and horrible lust for the angelic purity of the white mistress."[10] And shortly afterwards he states again:

> The Black slave never or almost never did dare raise his eyes on his mistress and attempt against her honor; but his depraved imagination often managed to break the sacred veils and expose in vulgar nudity and scandalous postures the body of his master's wife or daughter.[11]

The sexual obsession prevails completely in the other novel, *Lucinda, a mucama*. Here, to make his point, the author does not need dramatic situations: what happens in the three hundred pages of the book was mostly a daily reality in Brazil in those years. The relationship between the young white mistress and her companion, the Black slave, was one of the pillars of the Brazilian family structure during the period of slavery and, in many cases, even afterwards. The Black world, in its origins and as a general rule, did not ascribe to feminine virginity the same importance as did the Western Christian civilization; greater importance was given to fertility. The debasing conditions of slavery, the promiscuity in the senzala, the masters' strong desire to increase the number of slaves, all this made the sexual interrelation extremely free. In the masters' world, in contrast, the rigid Portuguese morality, the strong influence exerted by the Arabs and a life spent in long lazy days, all made the protection of feminine virginity and honor an obsession. Two representatives of these two different worlds, the white and the Black adolescents, are put together: from their meeting an unbalanced and abnormal situation is inevitably born. This is the case of Cândida (again notice the choice of the "white" name), who receives the present of a mucama of her age, Lucinda. Cândida is only eleven years old but she is already an exquisite combination of feminine virtues: she speaks French (a sine qua non for acceptance in high society at that time), she knows English, history, geography, she plays the piano, she sings with a melodious voice, and she is talented in embroidery. Lucinda plants the first seed of doubt in Cândida's mind; she teaches her a thousand little things so that when Cândida has her first menstruation she will hear from her mother, cautiously and tactfully, only half of what she already knows. The separation between the limpid source and the turbid pond has been removed, the author tells us: in short, the turbid waters of the pond will contaminate those of the source. The arrival of Souvanel, a young Frenchman who claims to be a political refugee but who is instead wanted for fraud, accelerates the tempo. Here the author expresses fully his abhorrence of sex by inserting a long indictment against "the vice of the *namoro*" (the namoro is the rewarded courtship); he claims that the honest girl can only receive notes from a fiancé chosen by her parents. Even this behavior is wrong, but it is a minor sin that one can absolve in the name of love and erase by a wedding.

Souvanel is the very embodiment of evil for the author: he has committed crimes against patrimony in his native land, he teases flippantly the Brazilians' provincial curiosity, and commits eventually the worst of all possible crimes: he seduces Cândida after being Lucinda's lover, after having been "in the slave's black dishonest arms, the slave who was her mistress's rival."[12]

In the author's words it seems as if the very contact with the Black woman is impure in itself. When Frederico, Cândida's enamored cousin, sees Souvanel shaking and kissing her hand, his natural feeling of jealousy is overwhelmed by a deep disgust in seeing that the object of his love is touched by hands and lips that "a little before had hugged and maybe even kissed in a brutal impulse the depraved *negra's* face."[13]

It is clear that it would be unjust to view Macedo's work from a modern standpoint. The twenty-year-old Simeão, who is compelled to steal a few coins to have a drink of wine and play with other human beings, who is beaten up when he goes to see his woman, who looks at his young mistress's breast (and where else should he look?), and who utters some onanistic obscenity is the object of pity for us modern readers. We also pity Cândida who pays as if it were a crime to have slept with a man whom she loves. We almost like Souvanel, the beautiful French scoundrel who emptied the vaults of some merchant (here we are reminded of some hideous characters created by Balzac and Molière), who lives exploiting the miserable bourgeois aspirations of some rich slave owners, and who sleeps with equal success in turn both with the beautiful slave and the charming mistress.

Joaquim Manoel de Macedo fought a noble battle against an iniquitous institution; yet he fought without ever overcoming the limits of his petit bourgeois mentality. This is what on the one hand makes us appreciate his courage while, on the other hand, making us find his work interesting from a historical point of view: literary geniuses such as Machado de Assis, who was also the descendant of slaves, did much less than did Macedo.

From this point of view *Pai Rayol, o feiticeiro* is a most interesting book. The author seems to be particularly concerned with the character of the sorcerer. We have noticed already how Macedo expresses his fears concerning the venda, the trading post where the slaves gathered and where they exchanged their ideas; the feiticeiro embodies for Macedo an even greater danger because he is the man who creates the ideas that some day might lead others to revolt; he is a man whose powers might make him a chief capable of replacing the legitimate master. Pai Rayol is such a man, and the author once again in an attempt to give us a sinister description creates a fascinating character. He is physically ugly and his ugliness is enhanced by the signs left on his face by diseases and cruel punishments. He changed many masters because he never adjusted to slavery and never gave up the "scandalous cult of *feitiço* or of *candomblés*."[14] This proud Black Spartacus has taken refuge in a feigned and indifferent docility, in a gloomy and ominous silence since he is aware that his fellows are so degraded by slavery that they are "unable to obey his voice urging them into a horrible conflagration, which many times he had imagined and he believed was possible."[15] From that moment, "disillusioned by his own fellow slaves, loathing that brotherhood which did not provide him with reliable tools of immense evil in the murderous war against the masters, he depended solely on himself and he concealed his true nature inside himself."[16]

A constant terror of the unknown, embodied by the Black world, runs throughout Macedo's work. The Black slaves, who had been eradicated from their own villages and were regarded as things and debased to the level of animals, still kept their beliefs (mistakes and savage prejudices in the author's words). They managed to propagate them in the new land. For the author they are a constant source of corruption: corruption of the language, of costumes, of sacred religious beliefs, which form the base of any immorality. Most frightening of all is the feitiço, witchcraft, the power of occult forces. The master has no control over these, yet they hit him through mysterious diseases. He can perceive them in the night when he hears the somber rumbling of drums.

On this subject Macedo's position is very clear: the evil comes from Africa, "The *feitiço*, like syphilis, came from Africa."[17]—"Organized witchcraft which was institutionalized in repugnant ignoble rituals and mysteries, like a plague, came to us together with the slaves from Africa."[18]

In the fazenda of Paulo Borges, an indefatigable worker and a greedy land and slave owner, evil comes, namely the *zumbi*, the Black ghost (probably another unconscious memory of an actual Black ghost, Zumbi dos Palmares, the legendary leader of the biggest Black rebellion in Brazil). He is embodied by Pai Rayol, the sorcerer. Pai Rayol induces his own lover, Esméria, to become Paulo Borges's mistress. It is the reversal of a historically common situation at the time: the white master who knowingly used the Black slaves without any respect for their family links is seduced by the shrewd and evil Black woman. Esméria is successful in her perfidious goal; little by little she replaces the legitimate wife who, in the author's words, is, however, an interesting woman: "Tereza was not a beautiful lady; yet, even setting aside the physical superiority of her race, she was handsome, her face and figure were graceful and gentle so that any comparison with the *crioula* would have been unthinkable."[19] Naturally Macedo uses hard words against Paulo Borges although it seems that the worst thing for him is not that he had a mistress but that his mistress was a slave. On this point his moral judgment gives way to his social prejudice, "The master who debases himself to the point of choosing his slave as his lover is more than immoral."[20] In a few months Tereza and her two sons die by poison. The youngest son dies of syphilis because he was nursed by a sick Black woman, "Poor little angel who had been deprived of his honest mother's breast in the crib, he drank syphilis and death from the depraved slave's impure nipples."[21]

Paulo Borges's final rescue by two slaves is meaningless. What counts, Macedo tells us, is that "slavery continues to exist in Brazil. And slavery, the mother of the victim-executioners, is prolific."[22]

This is Joaquim Manoel de Macedo: an honest writer who, without ever escaping from the spirit of the time, without ever opposing what was the current moral, and always using that moral and those prejudices, found, however, the courage to face the problem of slavery, the institution on which rested the morals, the spirit, and the prejudices of his time.

3 THE ENCHANTED KINGDOM

The menace of the sorcerer instigating the Blacks to revolt against the masters, the ever-increasing fear of slave rebellion and escapes, which occurred frequently during the second half of the nineteenth century, are the prevailing motifs of Araripe Júnior's novel *O reino encantado* (*The Enchanted Kingdom*, 1878). The novel is inspired by a real incident, the slaughter of Pedra Bonita in 1838. Without ever changing the substance of facts, however, the writer introduces some new elements in the tale which give a completely different historical meaning to the events.

A brief sketch of the events is necessary to examine the author's special perspective: in 1836 a fanatic called João Antônio gathered a group of followers in a place called Pedra Bonita in the region of Flores, in the state of Pernambuco. In his sermons João Antônio promised the coming of the mythic king Sebastião's kingdom: in this kingdom the poor will become rich, the Black will become white, the sick will heal, there will be enough for everybody. A missionary, Father Francisco José Corrêia de Albuquerque, a brave apostle of the *sertão*, convinced João Antônio to discontinue his insane sermons. Two years later, in the same place, another deranged man called João Ferreira, again started the same kind of sermons, asserting that the great rock towering over the place, the Pedra Bonita, would split and from it would emerge Dom Sebastião and his splendid court. João Ferreira was supported in his insanity by another holy man, Frei Simão, and by a certain Pedro Antônio, brother of João Antônio who had initiated the sermons at Pedra Bonita. For the miracle to happen, João Ferreira asserted, numerous human sacrifices were required: the blood on the rock would cause the cleft of the stone and the second coming of the king.

In a delirium of collective insanity the followers of the sect swarmed together to offer themselves as well as their own relatives, especially the children, in sacrifice. João Ferreira himself was killed and the massacre continued until the authorities of Flores intervened. The slaughter was stopped, although both sides incurred many deaths.

These are the facts as they were recounted by the *prefeito* of the *comarca* of Flores to the president of the province of Pernambuco on

May 25, 1838. In this work I do not intend to give a detailed historical analysis of the reasons that caused these events to happen in Brazil. I will only mention briefly that messianism, prophetic expectations, and mystical components, which can be found in various forms among different people, found a fertile ground in Brazil. One should remember first of all that Brazil was colonized by Portugal, a country where the Middle Ages still prevailed while in other European countries the Renaissance had already blossomed. A universe made of frightening legends and obscure fears found a sublimation in a nationalism that had been frustrated by the battle of Alacacer el Kebir when the king Dom Sebastião and the best of Portuguese aristocracy had disappeared: Dom Sebastião's return meant for a long time the return of Portuguese grandeur. This aspiration, which never faded, gave birth to various movements of a messianic kind, called *sebastianistas*. The first navigators brought to Brazil this vague aspiration of a Portuguese Middle Ages. There it found a fertile ground because the old medieval structures were created again in the new land: huge rural properties similar to the ancient feudal estates, the uncontested power of the *fazendeiros* who, thanks to their armed squads, enjoyed the same privileges as the lords of the past centuries, serfdom made legal and transformed into slavery, the absence of a state based upon law and central power, the continuity of a certain form of religion. Specific geographic data must be added to these social structures: the new land with its immensity and its distances—rivers, forests, deserts measurable in months of walking; the natural calamities, droughts, and floods that could annihilate entire regions. All this intensified the imbalance between human beings and their environment. For this reason human rebellion and natural reaction often took various forms that resembled each other: violence and mysticism, rebellion against the world and flight from it.

Messianism and mysticism have had and continue to have a rich history in Brazil as evidenced by the huge masses of people who annually visit Juazeiro do Norte, Bom Jesus da Lapa, and Monte Santo. A terrifying scene of collective fanaticism occurred at Juazeiro do Norte when Padre Cícero, the great healer of the sertão, died. Hundreds of thousands of people were gathered in a frenzy of collective fanaticism while the military airplanes of the nearby FAB (Brazilian Air Force) base flew low over the house of the holy man thus paying a last tribute to the man who had represented for them the only form of truth, the answer to many unanswered questions. Padre Cícero's presence is still so deeply felt in the Northeast that a very popular contemporary preacher, Frei Damião—an Italian Capuchin friar—was prohibited by the authorities from preaching at Juazeiro, lest the large crowd of *sertanejos* see in him a reincarnation of Padre Cícero, whose return to those arid lands nobody ever doubted. There is such a deep and hidden religious continuity in the Northeastern world that in recent years nobody was surprised when political guerrillas appeared in the area of Araguaia: it had been expected for thirty years, Padre Cícero had said so. On the occasion of the recent terrible flood of the São Francisco river even the national press repeated a prophecy of Antônio Conselheiro, another great holy man: the sertão will be transformed into an ocean.

The events of Pedra Bonita are perfectly aligned with the historical reality that had its roots in the Portuguese Middle Ages and continues to the present time in the same area of Brazil. The novel *O reino encantado* is based upon those events. The plot centers on the kidnaping of a fazendeiro's wife and daughter by João Ferreira's followers and on the lengthy hunt of the fanatics up to the final massacre. The new elements suggested by Araripe Júnior are deviations from the historical records of the time: Pedra Bonita's center is defined as a *quilombo* and João Ferreira's fanatics are identified as *quilombolas*. These historically false deviations provide us, however, with an interesting perspective on the problem of slavery. In fact, Araripe Júnior was able to write a remarkable work of art without ever setting aside his slave-owner's mentality. He does not even exhibit the good will shown by Joaquim Manoel de Macedo a few years before in writing *As vítimas-algozes*. Araripe Júnior is from beginning to end a slave owner who sees the events from the perspective of a slave owner and who falsifies facts by identifying the fanatics as quilombolas. He does create a gloomy, frightening image of rebellious and fugitive Blacks.

The story starts with the arrival of the fazendeiro José Vasconcellos and his wife and daughter on their farm. The atmosphere is gloomy, a vague feeling of danger pervades the air. The first news is alarming: some animals have been killed mysteriously, some slaves have run away; a sinister sorcerer, Frei Simão, has been seen prowling around the plantation and apparently he instigated the slaves to rebel. Vasconcellos understands right away that the very basis of the slave system on which his wealth is founded is threatened. He does not even question whether that system is right or wrong: slavery for him means "*Negros* and slaves had lived up to that point in the security of work."[1] Upon his arrival on the farm Vasconcellos becomes furious at the escape of some slaves and deems it necessary to make a memorable example. Following the overseer's advice, he chooses some Blacks who seem inclined toward the cult of *feitiçaria* and has them whipped and then left chained to the pillory.

The author offers no comment, except for a few vague expressions of compassion for those poor people who had been lynched. It seems as if whatever happens is ineluctable and necessary. The very existence of slavery cannot be discussed. No ways are even considered to persuade the slaves to work, except the blindest brutality. Vasconcellos himself lacks the courage to witness the punishment, the description of which the author asserts he wants to spare us.

The scene of punishment suggests another idea: the man who selects the slaves to be punished, who whips them with pitiless ferocity, and who chains them to the pillory is Manuel Velho, the overseer. Yet he is always described as a brave and strong man, the hero of the story who, at his own risk and with unconquerable strength, will save Vasconcellos's wife and daughter from the mob of the fanatics. Vasconcellos himself is described as a good and brave man, an exemplary father and husband. *O reino encantado* is, then, a novel of the time of slavery in which the iniquitous institution is not even questioned. The characters are described and judged without taking into account their attitude towards other human beings who lived as beasts of burden. The author himself does not choose a different position. He views slave labor as the basis of the society in which he lives and whose justice he honors. This moral atmosphere pervades the description of the good Vasconcellos and the brave Manuel Velho who cheers up when the *capitão do mato*, the slave hunter, is preparing to go after fugitive slaves: "The scoundrels must not be very far away. . . . We have here excellent dogs who recognize the *negros*; it will be enough to unleash them and they will start hunting right away."[2]

There are only a few short instants in the text where the author seems to be aware that the slaves too are human beings. One of the Blacks who had been whipped and chained to the pillory succeeds in freeing himself by literally tearing his legs away from the wooden rings that imprisoned him. A slave woman helps him to climb over the wall: "Zigue-Zigue showed his fleshless shin-bones and his flesh in miserable state, 'Is it for this misery that the whites want to have slaves?', Zigue-Zigue said, 'Our Lord Jesus Christ did not shed his blood for this unholy people! Go away Justina: Frei Simão will avenge us.'"[3] Frei Simão is inserted in the words of the unhappy slave to serve the purpose of counterbalancing the impact of the description of the slave's miserable state: Frei Simão is for the author Evil itself, the Monster, the one who will sacrifice innocent victims on the altar of

Pedra Bonita, a man who has obscene designs on the innocent Maria, Vasconcellos's daughter.

The rebel slave is a terrible danger because he threatens the most sacred taboos of the masters' society: property and the family. Inasmuch as he represents a danger he must be either eliminated or deprived of power. At some point Manuel Velho, the good and courageous Manuel Velho, discovers the fugitive slaves' refuge and sees slaves sitting around a big fire eating the meat of the animals they hunted, "Those rascals had a feast at the master's expense! This scene made his blood boil."[4] The brave overseer's indignation is caused by a moral reason, that is, by the violation of the principle of private property. The slaves, themselves property, were destroying another property, the master's beef. It was a double sacrilege. Manuel Velho's anger is sincere because he is not the true owner but only a simple cowboy, one of the master's workers. It is the violation of the principle that causes his anger.

Moreover, Vasconcellos, the master, when he leaves to hunt fugitive slaves is not only inspired by the desire to recover something he owns. He also has the moral force of someone who knows he is fighting for a noble and right cause: "Bernardo de Vasconcellos, while these events occurred in the *fazenda* of Porteira, was on his way to Pau Ferro with the intent of suppressing the insurrection and, trusting his moral force, of compelling the slaves to enter the good path."[5]

The "good path" means necessarily the return to slavery and to coerced work.

In another episode Vasconellos meets one of the fugitive slaves:

> The audacious and vindictive *negro* stared at the master with a hideous hatred. Without paying any attention to that, the *fazendeiro*, whose moral force had never been denied, took a few steps towards him holding the whip in one of his hands and the gun in the other while threatening to wound him.—'No, *nhô* Bernardo!' screamed the slave crouching like a panther and getting ready to jump. 'Be patient . . . here there is no more master and slave. Here he who has more courage wins.'
>
> Before so much audacity Vasconcellos trembled with rage; he did not hold back any more and launching himself against the *preto* struck him forcefully on the face with his whip. The slave moaned in pain and walked a few steps back, conquered by his master's courage.[6]

This episode suggests some remarks about the way the author introduces his characters. In *O reino encantado* good and evil are always clearly separated. This is quite understandable for us if we remember that Araripe Júnior's world was based upon unquestioned moral certainties. And since these moral certainties were created and served the purpose of preserving the slave system, the fugitive or rebellious slave was always viewed as a negative element. In this episode the slave is called "vindictive" and his hatred "hideous"; yet a few lines before the author had said that Vasconcellos had recognized the slave "as one who once used to be a constant object of his master's insolence."[7] The author does not tell us what these insolences were. What enrages Vasconcellos, however, is that the Black man dares face him man to man, declaring that at that moment there were no longer masters and slaves. Considering the direction of the work and the context, the slave must inevitably be subdued. Once this is done Vasconcellos departs, leaving him in good hands, "considering that it was useless to murder him," that is, he decides to spare the slave's life. The author does not add any comment to his sentence, which to modern readers appears quite clear: Vasconcellos spares the Black man because he deems it useless to kill him. Apparently, if he had considered the Black man's death "useful" he would have done it, since he had previously ordered terrible whippings for punishment.

While Vasconcellos is engaged in these adventures, the rebellious slaves, *os quilombolas*, attack the farm. In the description of this attack Araripe Júnior achieves a total and clear-cut separation between Good and Evil: on the one side he puts the respectable slaves, *os dignos escravos*, those who defend the master's life and property and therefore their right to continue to be slaves until the end of their lives; on the other side are the murderers, the wild animals, as *bestas-feras*, the bloodthirsty brutes, *os brutos sanguinários*, who meet their death in the assault on the farm, the place where they had suffered for so many years, the prison to which they have been condemned even before their birth.

The detailed and long description follows of the imprisonment of Clemência and Maria, Vasconcellos's wife and daughter, by the Pedra Bonita fanatics. The adventures and misadventures of Manuel Velho and the two unlucky women are interspersed with scenes of fanaticism and slaughter by the bloodthirsty João Ferreira and Frei Simão. But not all the fanatics are Blacks. The few whites involved are reduced, in the author's words, to the degrading state of the Blacks: "The majority of them were fugitive slaves among which were some mestizos taken away from their small fields and a few whites who through contact with the Africans had become as primitive as they. In general all of them in their aspect showed an expression of indefinite bestiality."[8] Once the artificial barrier created by slavery is overcome, the white who mingles with the Blacks is contaminated by that contact and becomes himself a primitive being. This is the warning the author sends to his audience.

The story of the novel—a work which on the whole is quite interesting to read—ends with the arrival of the good people who attack the fanatics' camp while Manuel Velho accomplishes his last heroic act by rescuing the two women. The author is consistent up to the last scene, since he does not deviate from the principle upon which his work is based. In the description of the annihilation of the quilombolas his sadistic pleasure in the destruction of his own enemy surfaces:

> They, the fugitive slaves, the rebellious murderers were on the verge of being captured, slaughtered, strangled, and dragged to the pillory. It was impossible for them still to have illusions about their future.
>
> Since they were not facing unknown people, however, their fear faded away. The struggle of men against men did not scare them.
>
> To go back to their prisons and suffer incredible punishments was something that they could not endure.
>
> Once they had lost the last hope that the miracle might occur, the only possibility left to them was to shed the last drop of their blood for their own freedom.
>
> This instinctive conviction inflamed all the cruel ferocity that the burden of superstition had removed. The hatred against those whom they called their crucifiers was kindled again in a horrible manner and aroused the dormant energy of their wild souls, pushed them against the crowd who appeared to them with all the dark shades of the life in the *senzalas*.[9]

The author has nothing new to add to what has already been said. Once again, as it happened with Joaquim Manoel de Macedo, the writer intending to give us a negative description ends up by drawing a magnificent portrait of those he meant to present under a gloomy light. In *Simeão, o crioulo* the protagonist bears the whipping by the master without crying, without ever uttering words of repentance; in *O reino encantado* the rebellious slaves prefer to struggle to the death instead of surrendering and accepting their doom. In both cases, to understand the work we have to keep in mind the authors' point of view, taking into account their world and their mentality. They thought slavery was a social institution that was part of the legal order. Therefore they justified morally the punishment given to Simeão and the hunt for the fugitive slaves. Following the same logic they judged in a negative way Simeão's pride while he was punished and the slaves' refusal to surrender. The punishment of a guilty slave and the capture of fugitive slaves were a part of a moral order upon which slavery was based.

It is for this reason that Domingos Caetano, who whips Simeão, is "good" and Vasconcellos and Manuel Velho, who rejoice at the idea of unleashing dogs after the Blacks, are "good."

Joaquim Manoel de Macedo wanted to eliminate slavery because of the negative consequences that, from the moral point of view, slavery had on his world, the masters' world. Yet he never questioned its legal validity and this attitude caused many contradictions in his work. Araripe Júnior is consistent, however, because he has no doubts: there is only one evil in slavery and that occurs when the slaves run away and there is no more slavery; the good is to capture them as soon as possible because when they are free they can only do very serious damage.

Tristão de Araripe Júnior (1848–1911) came from an old family from Ceará; he was a magistrate, a journalist, a very cultured man, one of the better-known literary critics of his time, a positivist thinker. He wrote a work that was an apology for slavery and at the same time it was false from a historical point of view. From the reports of the local authority of the time, we know, and the author must have known it too, that the Pedra Bonita fanatics were just fanatics; they were not fugitive slaves, they were not quilombolas, and Pedra Bonita was not a quilombo.

Why then did he write a novel which falsified the historical truth? I can only suggest some possibilities.

First of all we have to consider that a writer writes for a given audience and Araripe Júnior's audience consisted of the bourgeoisie, a class that always thrived on slavery. Also Araripe Júnior was an intellectual, unlike Macedo, who was a simple writer for young ladies. While the simple writer for young ladies perceives that slavery is evil and struggles against it, the intellectual, the cultured man, is much more deeply affected by the ideas of his own social class and feels that the legal texts that legitimize slavery are important—they are its bread and butter. He does not dare think that those texts which he considers as the purest expression of the universal law are only a set of practical rules through which human beings often justify their control over other human beings. These doubts rarely touch the mind of the intellectual whose task is more often that of giving an elaborate and culturally rich form to the banality of the mass media.

O reino encantado was written in 1878, ten years before slavery was legally ended. The law of *Ventre Livre* (free womb) had already been enacted, which set free all the children of slaves born after 1871. The world of fazendeiros, of the rich bourgeoisie, felt that the foundation of the slave system on which their prosperity was based was reeling. These people from the day of their birth had seen Black slaves around them. They had shaped the existence of those slaves to meet and to serve their purposes: slaves were nurses, waiters, stablemen, coachmen, rural workers; there were even slaves to rent, and those who were free to find a job outside a house so long as they paid part of their salary to their owners. This world which had lasted for centuries was on the verge of disappearing.

In the southern part of the country alternatives to slavery had been attempted: rural colonies of European immigrants, the creation of industry. In the Northeast the rural bourgeoisie guarded their privileges. Tristão de Araripe Júnior is an illustrious son of that bourgeoisie, of that social class which during three centuries had thrived on slave labor. There is then a logic in his choice: he refers to an incident that really happened, Pedra Bonita, and to people who had really existed, João Ferreira, João Antônio, Frei Simão and others. He refers to the quilombo, the fugitive Black slaves' refuge that had existed from the beginning of slavery. He combines two separate realities and transforms Pedra Bonita into a refuge of fanatic quilombolas.

This is obviously the logic of his world, the masters' world. In the history of slavery in Brazil (we need to remind the reader once again) all the documents, or at least the most important documents, come from the white world, from those who knew how to read and write, from those who in one way or another even when their skin was not totally white, were connected to the masters' world. For that world the end of slavery had a more violent impact than the end of the automobile would have for our contemporary world; it meant giving up structural goods that had been considered indispensable for whole generations. That these structural goods consisted of other human beings with darker skin had little impact upon the set of selfish interests that prevailed in the masters' class. That class had also a comfortable historical alibi when it refused to admit the large masses of slaves into its world as free citizens. The slaves whose tribal, linguistic, religious, and often family unity had been destroyed when they had been taken away from their villages and made to live like animals in the promiscuity of the *senzala*, were quite often debased human beings.

We now know that that degraded state resulted solely from social and environmental conditions; it had nothing to do with ethnic qualities. We must remember, however, that the science of the time thought differently about racial differences. The Brazilian bourgeoisie then faced a double problem: on the one hand it had to give up precious structural goods, while on the other hand it had to admit and accept as free citizens, at least on a purely formal level, a mass of people who were considered inferiors.

This set of fears and anxieties gives birth to that paranoia of the besieged citadel of which Araripe Júnior's book is a good literary example. Vasconcellos and his family, besieged in their farm by the cruel quilombolas, lost in the immensity of the sertão, represent the Brazilian bourgeoisie, numerically inferior as compared to the large masses of Blacks ready to abandon the senzalas and swarm into the streets. It was not a baseless fear, for in the South the upper bourgeoisie that pressed for the end of slavery at the same time opened the doors to German and Italian immigration to avoid the danger of a Brazil with a Black majority and control.

As a loyal representative of his class Araripe Júnior gives us in this good novel a wretched defense of an institution and a world that were inexorably doomed.

4 ISAURA

> "Get up, noble and generous woman," said Alvaro gesturing with his hands so that she would get up. "Get up, Isaura; it is not to my feet but rather in my arms, here near my heart that you have to rush because, in spite of all prejudices of the world, I regard myself as the happiest of all mortals in offering you my hand as your husband!"[1]

With these words the novel *A escrava Isaura* (*The Slave Isaura*, 1875) by the *mineiro* Bernardo José da Silva Guimarães (1827–1884) ends. It is a typical romantic drama, bound to touch and make many generations of readers shed tears. *A escrava Isaura* belongs to the canon of works that not only contributed to the struggle against slavery but also offered an interesting portrait of the mores of the time. In fact, while the story of poor Isaura, so beautiful and so unhappy, touched almost everybody in Brazil in those years, the novel showed also ambiguous elements, as later critics pointed out.

We can observe first of all that *A escrava Isaura* is more the story of a character, Isaura, than a novel on slavery. Isaura has the misfortune of being a slave but she has none of the features of a slave. The story is simple: Isaura's mother is a beautiful mulatta, the slave of a rich *comendador*, the owner of a wealthy *fazenda*; the comendador, who is lecherous as well as rich, tries with all his wiles to seduce the beautiful mulatta. Since he is unsuccessful and wants to avoid a fight with his wife, who meanwhile has found out everything, the comendador entrusts the mulatta to his overseer to make her work in the fields; the overseer, who is Portuguese, falls in love with the mulatta and, from their relationship, Isaura is born. The comendador, who besides being lecherous is also evil, takes revenge by sending the overseer away and mistreating the mulatta, thus causing her death. Isaura is brought up by the comendador's wife, a pious lady. She learns languages, she studies, she learns to play the piano, she is virtually a white young lady even though she remains a slave. Meanwhile Isaura's father tries to ransom her but his attempts are in vain because the comendador refuses to let her go. The good wife dies, and the comendador dies too. Isaura is left to Leôncio, the comendador's dissolute son. Although he is married to a beautiful and rich young lady named Malvina, Leôncio harasses Isaura with the same dogged obsession with which his father harassed her mother. One could almost call this a real family tradition against which poor Isaura resists with unconquerable courage. Eventually, when the situation becomes unbearable, Isaura, with her father's help, runs away to Recife where, thanks to her charms and beauty, she shines in society. A handsome, rich, and virtuous young man by the name of Alvaro falls in love with her. The cruel Leôncio, however, finds her and drags her back to the fazenda where he subjects her to continuous vexations and where eventually he compels her to marry a poor cripple. But Leôncio, besides being cruel and lecherous (qualities he inherited from his father), is also a spendthrift, a quality his father had not bequeathed to him. So Leôncio is in debt up to his chin: Alvaro takes advantage of that by paying back all his debts and arrives at the right moment—that is, at the moment of the nefarious wedding. He comes as the new owner of Leôncio's wealth and property: he then also owns Isaura, to whom he offers his hand while Leôncio, fuming with rage, blows his own brains out.

It is clear why a story like Isaura's became immediately very popular all over Brazil and made many female readers shed tears of emotion. Many parents adopted the name Isaura for their newborn babies, for they saw in the beautiful slave a symbol of the struggle against slavery. Or rather they thought they saw that, while in reality Isaura's character owes its popularity mainly to her being a nonslave slave; she is similar in every aspect to any white young lady of the time, whose freedom of action was very much limited by her father and brothers' will and who was often compelled to marry an old and disagreeable husband. Thousands of lady readers saw in Isaura not their slaves but themselves; they recognized their own chagrin as young ladies condemned to long, lazy hours of boredom in the large rooms of the masters' houses while their freedom was under strict control by family authority: they remembered the long, enervating, and often disappointing wait for the *noivo*, the fiancé who would drag them away from one form of servitude and then compel them to enter another form of slavery. Isaura represents the female condition in Brazil at the middle of the nineteenth century, that is, the white female condition of the owners and masters, which had nothing to do with the conditions of the Black slaves who were living either at the *senzala* or who belonged to the group of domestic slaves.

First of all, the author was concerned with making both her origin and skin whiter: her mother is a mulatta, which means she is only partly Black, while her father is a Portuguese, that is, he is one hundred percent white: "Her skin is like shining ivory, of a whiteness that does not stand out, darkened by a delicate shade that one would not know whether to call a slight paleness or a very delicate pink."[2] The fortunate owner of such a skin is "like a Venus who is born out of the foam of the sea or like an angel rising from the vaporous mist."[3]

Isaura's whiteness is acknowledged in the first place by her own masters. Malvina, Leôncio's wife, while talking to the slave tells her: "You are beautiful, you have a beautiful color of skin; nobody would know that in your veins there is a single drop of African blood."[4] Later on, it is Leôncio himself who has a very meaningful talk with his brother-in-law:

> "Then, what do you think of a slave of this kind?" whispered Leôncio to his brother-in-law.
>
> "Isn't she an invaluable treasure? Who would not say that she is an Andaluz from Cadiz or a Neapolitan?"
>
> "Nothing of that kind; but rather something better," answered Henrique full of wonder, "she is a perfect Brazilian."
>
> "No, not a Brazilian! She is superior to all there is."[5]

Later on it is always Leôncio who gives full expression to his gross owner's pride: "Isaura is like a luxury item which has to be always on display in the sitting room. Would you want me to send my Venetian mirrors to the kitchen?"[6]

All this evidence gives a perfect portrait of Isaura. Her skin is ivory, slightly rosy, she is similar both to an angel and a Venus. Obviously any young lady of the good Brazilian society would have wanted to resemble Isaura and identify with her. And if that were not enough, Leôncio's words testify both to a vulgar bourgeois taste typical of that kind of society and to a naïve patriotism. The comparison with an Andalusian from Cadiz or with a Neapolitan, reinforced by the hint of the Venetian mirrors, is a meaningful example of a certain tendency of that Brazilian world which, still without a true cultural identity, saw in the comparison with anything European the canon for beauty or a value unequaled on the national market. The answer of Henrique, who sees in Isaura the perfect embodiment of the Brazilian woman, rescues instead the national pride.

This is the beginning of the literary fortune of the character of Isaura. Bernardo Guimarães's description probably contains many subconscious elements: it respects the canon of both classic and modern beauty—Venus and the Venetian mirrors; it reflects the prevailing taste of the time—the Italian and Spanish beauty. It was enough to provide dreams for the audience of the time (let us not forget that the romantic period was in full bloom), which saw in Isaura either a model to identify with or the woman-angel to protect and conquer.

The main point I want to make clear is that Isaura is not a slave: the color of her skin and her upbringing might at the most make of her an extreme case and an exception. *A escrava Isaura*, then, is not a direct novel on slavery; it is only partly so because of the setting of the story rather than because of the tearful adventures of the protagonist.

First of all we notice that the author shows no sympathy for the world of the Black slaves, the authentic ones. In fact, the persecution of which Isaura is a victim stirs no compassion in the Black women who live in the kitchen: their sentences betray their envy of the privileged situation the young woman enjoys. They rejoice, and tell her so, when Leôncio's dogged obsession compels her to seek refuge among the other slaves. If on the one hand, the Black women do not pine away for Isaura, she, on the other hand, does not waste her affection and her words to show compassion for her fellow sufferers. We can instead assert that Isaura—and, with her, Bernardo Guimarães—never faces the problem of slavery per se but rather the very personal problem of her own slavery. At some point in the development of the story the protagonist, in a moment of distress for her sad state, gives vent to an expression that reveals what the author really thought of the Black slaves: "My God! since I was so unlucky to be born a slave, it would be better for me to be born ugly and deformed like the basest of all the *negras*."[7]

The Black world cannot be any better than that of the whites: when Isaura is not harassed by Leôncio it is André, the Black page, who makes her unhappy. The author finds a way to have André utter some unfortunate sentences: "I feel bad for you when I see you here, mingled with this rabble of stinking and slobby *negras*."[8] André is a clownish character, the Black man who apes only the external aspect of whites and who tries gauchely to imitate them, bragging about it with a childish naïveté: " 'I go around always with a tie, gloves, and good shoes, all starched up, decorated, and perfumed, and what matters even more,' he added, patting his pocket with his hand, 'with my pockets always full of money.' "[9]

For Bernardo Guimarães the Black slaves are caricatures of human beings or deformed and stinking creatures. And while I point this out I also emphasize that Guimarães was among those who fought actively for the abolitionist cause. In fact, though they struggled against slavery—and this is true for most writers of the time—the abolitionists did not necessarily face the issue of the true human dignity of the Black slaves. The problem is one we witness with monotonous recurrence in our time: the acceptance of an idea on a purely theoretical and universal level does not imply at all the commitment to live that idea on a daily basis, taking personal risks and making practical choices. To recognize the principle of the abolition of slavery is one thing; to recognize that "the rabble of stinking and slobby *negras*" and a slave who is "ugly and deformed, like the basest of all *negras*" have real human dignity is another thing. These inconsistencies between enthusiastically asserted ideal principles and the practical realization of those same ideals are among the most common events reported in the mass media, especially of our time. Let us then not blame the Brazilian intellectuals of the nineteenth century because they were not better than we are. Let us try instead to understand, without showing outrage and hypocritical attitudes, how some intelligent and sensitive men conceived and propagandized the idea of abolition of slavery, which was the historical opposite of the slave system in which they were born and had lived.

Bernardo Guimarães came from the state of Minas Gerais, the most traditional in Brazil, the state that owes its wealth to the slave labor in the diamond and gold mines. A historical reality based upon slavery was incompatible with an idea—a hypothesis or a theoretical principle—imported from Europe. Abolitionism was in fact fashionable among the intellectuals; it was an idea that came from France. It made Brazil appear to be very far ahead of other civilized nations. There remained the practical problem of finding a profit to replace that coming from the slave labor. Brazilian intellectuals, however, did not perceive that the problem was more theoretical than practical: the large European proletarian masses at the time, free on the legal level, lived in conditions that were not very far from those of the Black slaves in Brazil.

This is why Guimarães builds a literary model, that of Isaura, who is not a slave but rather an extreme case of a young lady of good family reduced to the slave state. Thus, he could struggle in the name of a principle without being compelled to accept the human reality in which the same principle was embodied. Guimarães asks for freedom in Isaura's name—and probably only in Isaura's name—and not in the name of those "stinking and slobby *negras*" who would not know what to do with their freedom.

A escrava Isaura is the story of a young lady, not the story of a human condition. The author is very careful not to hurt sacred institutions; this attention stands out through various episodes. Let us take the example of Miguel, Isaura's father: his woman has been dragged away from his arms and murdered by the comendador, Leôncio's father. Yet, this episode is described with delicate euphemisms: "He subjected the mulatta to such hard work and to such a cruel treatment that in a short time he sent her to the grave."[10] Leôncio spends all his time harassing Isaura; yet Miguel, who in our opinion would be justified if he used extreme means to take revenge against the crucifiers of both his wife and daughter, does not display any sign of rebellion. The only thing he does is to collect through many years of hard work the exorbitant sum of money requested for Isaura's ransom. He visits Leôncio's house to ransom his daughter with the same respect he has displayed when he had visited the comendador many times in vain. It is only when he faces the most absolute refusal, and when he understands that his daughter has no way out, that he dares do the unthinkable, that is, to abduct the slave from her legitimate masters.

Once again we notice the author's extreme caution in dealing with the problem of slavery. He never faces the problem of the virtue of the institution in itself. Instead he provides us with a series of extreme cases: the slave Isaura is an exceptional case and so is her awful situation, which is certainly quite uncommon. It is only when he faces the inevitable that poor Miguel can risk the fatal step of helping his daughter run away. It is not an act of rebellion against the institution, which is never questioned on the theoretical level, but rather a simple practical solution, a way out in the face of an exceptional danger:

> He was quite aware that, in the world's eyes, to abduct a slave from her master's house and help her run away, besides being a crime, was a dishonorable and shameful act for an honest person; but the slave was his beloved daughter, the pearl of purity, on the verge of being soiled and destroyed by the hand of her murderous master. This thought justified him in his own conscience.[11]

In other words, when the most sacred of principles, that of private property, becomes incompatible with the principle of the inviolable rights of the human being (especially in the case of a beautiful and pure young woman), one can make an exception, one can find a justification to one's own conscience.

In contrast, the love story between Miguel and Isaura's mother (the author never gives her name and calls her only "the mulatta") is hurriedly defined as "the fatal, but very understandable weakness" that cost the Portuguese his job and the woman her life.[12] After all Miguel is a clumsy Portuguese immigrant: he commits the "weakness" of loving a woman whom he should have worked to death and commits the "shameful act" of helping his daughter run away, his daughter who was on the verge of ending up like her mother.

The situation goes from bad to worse. If Miguel tries to find justifications for himself to assuage his conscience for having helped his daughter run away, she feels something we would call a real guilt complex for the freedom she won in such an *illegal* way. When Isaura is the midst of a party in the city of Recife, what troubles her is not so much the reasonable worry of being recognized but rather the sacrilege of finding herself, a slave, close to free people. That is, she feels that slavery is not a purely technical fact but rather a moral indignity which prevents her from sharing life with free people:

> What do I come here for, I, a poor slave, in the midst of a party of the rich and the masters! This luxury, this life, these homages all around me upset my senses and make me dizzy. I am committing a crime by putting myself in the middle of such a brilliant society; it is a betrayal, my father; I acknowledge it and I feel guilty. . . . If these noble ladies could only guess that a miserable slave who ran away from her master is enjoying herself and is dancing alongside them![13]

The author adds no comment, either directly or through his character, concerning an aristocracy that could afford to be brilliant and enjoy its leisure, thanks to slave labor, and that, from a purely human point of view, was inferior to the slave's beauty and charm. This slave continues to torture herself in her relationship with Alvaro, with whom she is in love, because she conceals from him her real condition (as if she were a criminal or had syphilis):

> It was too much to take advantage of the noble and generous young man's ignorance! A fugitive slave showing up at the ball and hanging proudly on his arm in front of the most brilliant and distinguished social class of an important capital! It was a way of paying back with the darkest ingratitude and the most degrading disloyalty the services that he had given her with such delicacy and amiability.[14]

And when, at the end, the usual bad guy—but it is a very special bad guy, one who does not really belong to that *brilliant* society—recognizes Isaura, she is "annihilated by grief and shame," she asks humble forgiveness from the people witnessing the scene:

> "You do not need to touch me," she exclaimed with an anguished voice. "My ladies and lords, forgive me! I committed an infamous act, an unforgivable indignity! But God is my witness that a cruel fatality pushed me to do this. Gentlemen, what this man said is true. I am . . . a slave!"[15]

As I said, Alvaro is in love with Isaura. He is rich, young, and handsome; in other words he has everything. He is also an abolitionist; and this quality, which in our eyes would be very commendable, compels the author to play with words to save the popularity of a character who claims such brave ideas that might offend the susceptibility of some readers. Alvaro is on the whole "liberal, republican, and almost socialist"[16] (let us note the delicacy of the *almost*). The author defines his ideas at the same time as "eccentric and reformist."[17] For this reason the author places at his side another character, a slightly older friend called Geraldo, who is endowed with common sense. Geraldo succeeds in counterbalancing Alvaro's impetuousity and brings him back to the more respectable path of social conventions.

The concern that law, established rules, and social conventions be respected is the author's constant preoccupation even to a greater extent than is the struggle against slavery. For example, when Isaura is recognized as a fugitive slave, Alvaro, thanks to his social prestige, succeeds in obtaining the official custody of the woman he loves while waiting for her legal owner to appear. To avoid that eventuality, Alvaro bribes Martinho, the scoundrel who denounced Isaura, so that he will not warn Leôncio. It never occurs to Alvaro that he might want to help her run away because that, even though it would free Isaura forever, would make him guilty in the eyes of the law. Alvaro himself confesses to his friend Geraldo that he experienced shame and embarrassment in front of the good society when Isaura was unmasked. As we see, respect for conventions and legal order continues unchanged. Even when Alvaro has absolute power over Leôncio, because he has become the legal owner of all his belongings, he is reluctant to ruin the *fazendeiro* (pure goodness or, rather, unconscious class solidarity?); and he considers the possibility of exchanging all the goods he has ransomed, for Isaura, who is legally part of those goods. Through his characters, the author legitimizes slavery. Alvaro is now Isaura's master yet he is ready to pay back Leôncio the equivalent of the wealth he lost to compensate him for the loss of Isaura: he thus explicity recognizes Leôncio's right over Isaura through a natural masters' complicity. Only the discovery of Leôncio's wickedness eventually compels Alvaro to take extreme means.

The author's extreme caution and awareness manage to rescue both Isaura and slavery: Alvaro frees Isaura with complete respect for conventions and laws; Leôncio is punished because he is evil, not because he is a slave owner. The happy ending is perfect. The good readers of that time were able to dream of romantic adventures with

Isaura as a protagonist without having to feel that their properties were endangered by subversive ideas.

Through Alvaro's character, Guimarães expresses his ideas on the problem of slavery. Alvaro, as we have seen, is an abolitionist: he not only proclaims his ideas but he has also freed the slaves whom he inherited. Yet thanks to his philanthropic insight he did not leave his slaves to themselves: he made them work on his fazenda as wage laborers. The author suggests through Alvaro's experiment—always with due caution—that such an example could give good results for the fazendeiros from an economic point of view. To be precise, the author declares that the former slaves, "subjecting themselves to some kind of mutual discipline not only avoided idleness, vice, and crime, but they ensured their own survival and could save some money thus they could also pay back Alvaro for his sacrifice in giving them their emancipation."[18] Immediately after this description the author, almost to counterbalance the impact of the brave ideas he had suggested, defines Alvaro as "original and eccentric like a rich British lord."[19] Yet, in the state of Bahia in 1864 (a few years before *A escrava Isaura* appeared in 1875), the fazendeiro João Garcez dos Santos had freed his slaves; he had made them free workers and for three years gave them a reduced salary (thus he could pay back his own economic loss). The results of replacing slave labor with free labor were excellent.[20]

In fact the end of slavery was a legal act that did not alter the real structures of society: the great masses of rural workers who constituted the backbone of slavery were compelled to accept the low salaries their former owners offered them, because they were deprived both of education and of any kind of property. João Garcez dos Santos's experiment, had it been accomplished on a large scale, could have ended slavery a few years earlier without creating a painful imbalance among the masses of the former slaves. It would also have offered economic advantages to the fazendeiros who, instead, had to face the violent impact of the 1888 law. But the fazendeiros of the time did not understand that. And probably not even Guimarães understood it well: in fact, after describing Alvaro's experiment, he called him "original and eccentric like a rich British lord."

Basically the most authentic character is Leôncio: he is the true and best representative (meaning that he sums up the most characteristic features) of that class of slave owners who lived parasitically upon the wealth accumulated by their ancestors. Leôncio was a spoiled and arrogant child, who made it through school thanks to his father's social prestige; he was a lazy and corrupt teenager and young man.

GENERAL STORE IN RECIFE

VENDA EM RECIFE

Throughout his life he shared two typical attitudes with the representatives of his class: the refusal to identify himself with his own land and the refusal to work. Leôncio repudiates his own land, and he spends long periods in Paris where he lives the elegant and wasteful life of a gentleman; he goes back to Brazil only when his father compels him to return, by cutting his allowance. Because he repudiates his homeland, Leôncio refuses also to work, which is the most traditional way of accepting one's own world. All work seems beneath the dignity of the young self-proclaimed gentleman. The author explains in a quite revealing passage that the "import and export trade, even on a large scale, even the trade of Africans, seemed to him degrading and improper speculations for his high position and his refined upbringing."[21] Since he could not engage in great stock market speculations, because his father with some common sense forbade him to do so, and since he had no interest in his farm, Leôncio led a lazy and parasitic life. He was the proper representative of a class ineluctably doomed to disappear.

5 SEX UNDER THE SUN OF THE TROPICS: *A CARNE*

"All these Brazilian naturalists . . . are obsessed by the problems of the flesh, much more than their European brothers: it is not, however, a withered and mortified flesh in urban cellars, but rather a liberated flesh, exposed to all temptations under the sun of the tropics." Thus Luciana Stegagno Picchio comments in her *La letteratura brasiliana.*[1] Júlio Ribeiro (1845–1890), the author of *A carne* (*The Flesh*, 1888), belongs to the literary movement of Brazilian realism. This movement, which Zola inspired, had many followers in Brazil; among them, in addition to Júlio Ribeiro, were Aluísio Azevedo, Inglês de Souza, and Adolfo Caminha.

Again quoting from Stegagno Picchio, "*A carne* never becomes art: it is only pornographic melancholy, which is never rescued by the very positivist wish to show patterns of human physiology in their crudest aspects."[2]

A carne, instead of being a true literary work, is an interesting document. It reminds one of the romantic Indianism of Gonçalves Dias, José de Alencar, and Gonçalves de Magalhães. These writers, who lived in a Brazil that was still inhabited by Indians who often ventured to the borders of big cities, created a literary model inspired by the myth of the good savage from French literature—Montaigne, Rousseau, Chateaubriand. Similarly, Júlio Ribeiro creates in *A carne* a story that, though it is part of the naturalist movement, does not depict Brazilian reality.

This is the plot in its essence: a beautiful young woman called Lenita is brought up by a widowed father. From her earliest years she shows an interest in any kind of science. She learns then with optimal facility Italian, German, Latin, Greek, physics, mathematics, social sciences, and so on. Beautiful, cultured, and wealthy, she is not interested in the men surrounding her and she rejects many marriage proposals. At her father's death, unable to bear any longer either her solitude or the company of various suitors, she finds refuge in the house of her godfather, a *coronel* who lives with his wife on a *fazenda* in the interior of the state of São Paulo. Here, Lenita, after a period of rest, starts to suffer from disturbances that lead to sadism and erotic obsessions. One day the coronel's son, Barbosa, an eccentric, arrives at the fazenda. He is forty years old, separated from his wife. He has spent long periods in Europe and currently spends his time, rather misanthropically, studying and hunting. The young and excited Lenita sees in Barbosa, in an ever increasing familiarity, the true object of her anxieties and of her erotic fantasies. They become lovers. It is Lenita who is the seductress, and who then makes herself the man's slave. They love each other madly at night in the alcove and during the daytime in the fields. During a short business trip Barbosa takes, Lenita discovers among her lover's papers a journal in which he talks about three women whom he had loved in previous times. Lenita then understands, or rather she thinks she understands, that she was only one of Barbosa's many women, an adventure among others; she was not the unique woman she thought she was. She runs away from the farm and, since she is pregnant, she finds a former suitor willing to marry her and pretend he is her baby's father. She writes a cruel and impersonal farewell to Barbosa, without ever mentioning that she found out about the three past lovers. Barbosa kills himself, scientifically, with a curare injection.

As we said already, this confused melodrama is realistic mainly in the author's intentions. The recurrent motif, the appeal of sex—the FLESH written almost always in capital letters—ends up by being too obsessive to be credible. It could be credible only if one thought that the protagonists were in a continuous hysteria, something the author never mentions. Where the story becomes most improbable is in the description of the protagonist. Lenita, in the midst of a deeply patriarchal society such as that of Brazil, becomes the perfect specimen of high education (while the young ladies of the good society lived in their placid ignorance). She controls with total autonomy her own life in the midst of a society that legally limited the freedom of women to the advantage of male authority. She seduces and abandons a married man after becoming pregnant, thus violating abruptly all the taboos of her time. She is a rather unlikely character in the Brazilian reality at the end of the century.

The comparison we have made with the romantic Indianists brings us back, however, to a very common tendency in Brazilian culture: the perennial crisis of identity that always pushes men of letters toward the other side of the Atlantic and renders them less authentically Brazilian in spite of their repeated affirmations of nationalism. Just as the *índio* is featured as a literary European model, the reality to which Ribeiro makes his appeal is a reality imaginable only in the dynamic and brilliant Paris of the end of the century. Thus, Lenita, the suffragette and feminist *ante-litteram* in the sleepy Paulista province, can at best be the result of the author's wish fulfillment.

Joaquim Manoel de Macedo is much more real, if not realist, with his various Cândidas and Moreninhas who, although idealized, correspond to some human examples found in the Brazilian world of that epoch.

All of *A carne* is a continuous escape from Brazilian reality. It begins with a dedication to Emile Zola which is full of false, provincial, unctuous modesty: "Une chandelle n'est pas le soleil et pourtant une chandelle éclaire. . . . Les rois, quoique gorgés de richesses, ne dédaignent pas toujours les chétifs cadeaux des pauvres paysans."[3] (The dedication concludes with a "St. Paul," followed by a date, which disorients the reader temporarily until he understands that it refers to São Paulo.) Now let us consider the foreign terminology: *A carne* is a continuous flowering of foreign terms and scientific citations (the names of scholars of that epoch, Latin names of plants) which clash in a strident manner with the peasant environment that is the setting of the story. Is the author trying to confirm his Nordic origins (he was a son of a North American) or is he trying to show off his culture? It is a boring succession of *étagères, netskés, vide-poches, huit-ressorts, pur-sang, kirchwasser, black town, bric-à-brac, choke-rifled, struggle for life* that nourishes a story which has as its sole foundation a sugarcane plantation in the hinterland of the state of São Paulo. And to make the story all the more unbelievable the author describes *realistically* and *positivistically* Barbosa's laboratory in the great room of the farm:

> Leiden bottles, machines of Ramsden and Holtez, compartmental batteries of Cruikshank and Wollanston, energy batteries of Grove, Bunsen, Daniel and Leclanché . . . Planté accumulators, Ruhmkorf spools, Gleisser tubes, Foucault and Duboscq regulators, Jblonchokoff spark plugs, Edison lamps, telephones, telegraphs . . .[4]

One does not know if the author intended to make a caricature of the Massachusetts Institute of Technology ante-litteram or if he was imitating the science-fiction novels of Jules Verne. All this was constructed by Barbosa and Lenita in a gaudy scientific-sexual communion in the farm of the old coronel (it is useless and superfluous to ask if it was possible to construct such a laboratory in an agricultural zone of a still preindustrial Brazil). And as the crowning touch we note a letter Barbosa sends to Lenita that closes as follows: "I continue to look forward to the day in the near future when I'll give you a strong and energetic English-style handshake."[5] Waiting restlessly for a vigorous handshake is a rather depressing prospect: evidently literary realism is badly reconciled with a sense of humor. Incredibly, Júlio Ribeiro succeeds in being a realist author in spite of himself when he forgets the complex of cultural origins affecting his prose, and describes what happens in the fazenda. They are generally secondary descriptions, functional with respect to the principal events, but for this reason are much more genuine and interesting; they are not weighed down by foreign constructions.

The first of these episodes concerns a Black fugitive and serves to introduce us to a series of pseudo-orgasms of sadistic origin that disturb Lenita, and disturb even more those poor unhappy victims of Lenita's desires (but this the author does not consider worth underlining). One day the protagonist meets a Black man of the plantation who has an enormous ring of iron around his left ankle, and who asks her to request that the master remove it because the leg is now one big wound.

> And he showed the ankle ulcerated by the chain, wrapped in filthy stinking rags.
>
> "What did you do to end up suffering like this?"
>
> "A sin, *sinhá*; I ran away."
>
> "Were you mistreated? Did you have fear of being beaten?"
>
> "Not at all, *sinhá*: *negro* is only an evil animal, at times he loses his head."
>
> "If you promise not to run away then, I will ask the coronel to take off the iron."
>
> "Promises, *sinhá: negro* promises, word of God!"[6]

We can observe certain subtle hypocrisies in the conversation that do not come up in successive comments. The admission of guilt by the Black man followed by Lenita's question about the mistreatments must have given the public a sufficiently valid excuse for such mistreatments, further justified by "*negro é mesmo bicho ruim.*" In this way the author avoids posing the problem of slavery and of the escape from slavery, limiting himself to insinuating that the Black man was not mistreated and therefore mistreatment was not the reason he ran away. Note that the Black is always anonymous. In fact the imagination of the author disappears when he tries to name a Black slave. It must be a conditioned reflex, considering that the phenomenon is repeated by other authors. The response of the coronel to Lenita's interceding for the Black is a concoction of clichés, a summary of the *fazendeiros'* reasons against the abolition of slavery. Worst of all is the silence of the author, who is always attentive and precise when he comments on the erotic anxiety of Lenita and the existential dilemmas of Barbosa:

> These philanthropists, these modern crybabies of abolition with their talk of equality are full of nonsense and delusions. The *preto* always needs a whip and chains just as he needs cornmeal and blankets. What a sorry state agriculture would be in if these people did not stay in the fields and were not subjected to a good whipping given by a boss who knew what he was doing.[7]

We repeat once again that these words are perfectly natural in the mouth of a coronel, but it is rather strange that Ribeiro, always inclined to a comment or a direct participation in the events, does not feel the need to comment here as he did in other similar occasions.

After this episode the Black runs away but is quickly captured and chained at the pillory. The coronel promises him a good beating and swears never to release the iron even upon divine orders. In the meantime Lenita has begun to show her sadism more often: she gives tremendous pinches to the Black female slaves, and tortures the little birds that have the misfortune of falling into her hands. All her culture, her humanistic and scientific preparation, gives in to the desire to see with her own eyes the application of the *bacalhau*, the whip of twisted leather, this "legendary torture, humiliating, atrociously ridiculous" (and this is precisely all that the author has to say, which makes one wonder what he means by ridiculous).[8] The punishment ceremony is described in detail in a continuous crescendo, which must lead Lenita, the hidden spectator, to near orgasm. Here, there is no compassion for the Black, who is presented to us in a way that does not exactly elicit sympathy: we have then the arrival of the boss, accompanied by the *caboclo* armed with a whip; the terrorized Black just liberated from the pillory; and the two torturers, who joke and rebuke the disgraced one with gross irony for having run away:

> The *negro* got up lividly, trembling,
> miserable.
> Under the stimulus of fear his features almost
> dissolved.
> He fell to his knees with hands joined, his
> fingers knotty and twisted.
> It was the ultimate expression of human baseness,
> of animal cowardice.
> It was infused with pain and disgust.[9]

The Black remained prostrate on the ground and was compelled to lower his pants showing "the dry buttocks of a thin *negro* already full of cuts and scars."[10] A detailed description of the punishment follows, the caboclo using the whip with professional and calm skill, "to prolong the satisfaction it gives, like a good gastronome who savors a delicious dish."[11]

The caboclo is satisfied, Lenita, hidden behind a wall, is satisfied and, at this point, we may suppose that the author is also satisfied, because he gives us a horrendous description without uttering any comment as if it were a pure accident, occupied as he is by the gushing forth of the main character's orgasm.

Ribeiro had wanted to write a realistic novel, not a novel on slavery. For him, and not only for him, the reality worth portraying was similar to the world described by the sacred masters who lived on the other side of the Atlantic. Having to give a Brazilian setting to the story, he accepted slavery as an accidental fact, something that was part of the social or natural order, such as a war or calamity, both of which are often described without recourse to philosophy, and which are always secondary to the main characters in the structure of a novel.

Júlio Ribeiro belonged to the world of masters, and the manner in which he saw and confronted the presence of slavery is typical of slave masters (because for him it is a question of a pure presence and not of a problem). One episode, almost isolated in the context, is that of the dance of the slaves. It is a night with a full moon, the Blacks in a circle sing and beat their drums "with an agitated rhythm, nervous, ferocious and wild."[12] At the center of the circle a Black man dances the *samba* with a velocity and an expenditure of energy—stressed by the author—that would have wiped out a white man in less than five minutes.

The Black man sings:

> The voice of the singer, fresh, modulated with a timbre both gloomy and profound, had infinite sweetness, and inexpressible charm.
>
> Closing one's eyes one could not believe that these sounds so pure could emanate from the throat of a *preto*, filthy, disgraceful, depraved and repugnant.[13]

The author never described the Black; neither before nor after presenting the scene did the author ever give an individual description of the Black. Of him we know nothing else than his melodious endowments. That the author tells us he is "filthy, disgraceful, depraved and repugnant" can only mean that these are the inseparable attributes of being Black. That he was depraved could be proven logically only after a presentation of the behavior of the character; and that was not done. Disgraceful and repugnant are attributes that need a description which did not appear (repugnant to whom? With the tastes the author attributes to his characters . . .). At worst he could be dirty because of the dance on the dusty threshing floor, and only because of this, given the frequent washings that are the daily practice of the inhabitants of the tropics in Africa as well as in Brazil. Of course these terms apply only because he is a Black and necessarily this makes him "filthy, disgraceful, depraved, and repugnant."

If these are the attributes of a single Black, can you imagine what those of a group of Blacks are? "The scent of the trampled earth and that of the *cachaça* and the cigars was overwhelmed by a harsh human odor, as garlic, very strong, a stench of African sweat, undefinable, which hurts one's nose, which damages the nerves, which stupefies the brain, suffocating, intolerable."[14]

Despite such a display of scientific knowledge, Ribeiro ignores not only the fact that different human races emanate mutually disagreeable odors but also that the whites at that time in Brazil were accustomed to the smell of the numerically dominant Blacks. From the above quotation it almost seems that the Nazi gas chambers were experimented with on the farms of Barbosa half a century before and, moreover, in the open air.

But all these descriptions are nothing more than the prelude for the appearance of public danger number one, the sinister character, the *feiticeiro*, the sorcerer. This is Joaquim Cambinda, an eighty-year-old slave who is useless for work. (Here the author means probably that a man who has reached eighty years should still be able to work in the fields):

> This *preto* was horrid, bald, deformed, had enormous jaws, with yellow eyes, furrowed by bloody scabs on the very dark skin. Bent by age, slow, limping, when he got up, wrapped in his blanket of grey wool, and he made several steps, he resembled a hyena, gloomy, slow, cowardly, ferocious, repellent. He had dry sclerotic hands; his toes were twisted inward and without nails, frightening.[15]

Evidently the author does not recognize at all that this is only a state to which an old one who spent all his life in slavery has been reduced. For him Joaquim Cambinda is the evil one and more than once he defines him as a monster. The description of an initiation ceremony then follows in which the author emphasizes the more macabre and repugnant aspects of these "horrendous mysteries": the *mandinga*, the black witchcraft that does evil, that gives illness, that kills; toads cooked alive on a slow fire; hands of a dead unbaptized baby, bones of the deceased one; kissing the horn of the statue of Satan, the testicles of an African idol; and finally the most terrifying thing, the scene of possession of a Black woman, with Cambinda who directs and participates as the leading actor.

And so here we have our clever Júlio Ribeiro, with his beautiful positivist culture, with his style so European, with his million boring citations in French, German, English, and Italian, who, as soon as he returns—in the literary sense—to earth, discovers the witches, the sorcerers, and falls back into those Middle Ages from which he thought he had escaped; he too is a poor white in the besieged citadel, trembling at the gloomy nocturnal beatings of the drum; a poor sorcerer's apprentice who is not able to dominate the force he has unleashed, unable to break his pact with the Devil, with the slavery that has served him and which now persecutes him.

In Joaquim Manoel de Macedo's *Pai Rayol, o feiticeiro*, the monstrosity of the sorcerer is decisively tempered because the author sees the origin of all evil in the institution of slavery itself. Ribeiro, however, does not comment on slavery; his interest focuses on the noble part of the story, on a more-than-transparent desire to scandalize the public with the details of the relationship between the two lovers. Slavery for him is something that exists, something that is there and one does not question; it is also something that discomforts him, not because he does not like the institution but because he does not like the Blacks, who for him are depraved, dirty, and evil.

Although his scientific knowledge does not enable him to understand the Black world, it does allow him to create the rational structure which reduces the impact of the people of color to a conflict between Good and Evil, between Light and Darkness. If Cambinda is the evil one, who will be then the Angel of Extermination? Barbosa walks with an air of dignity preceded by the perfume of Legrand soap and Havana cigars. (Recall by analogy the *catinga*, the stench of the sweat of the Blacks.) His features are fine and regular, his mouth Saxon style (remember the lips and the enormous jaws of Cambinda), the hair slickened according to the latest fashion (remember Cambinda's baldness and the *carapinha*, the black curly hair pasted by dirt and sweat of the whipped slave), a "gentleman in the true sense of the word" (compared to "the ultimate expression of human baseness of animal cowardice," referring to the punished Black).[16] Joaquim Cambinda walks wrapped in his blanket of grey wool while Barbosa "wears a light silk suit with a cream-colored tie, an immaculate white shirt and, in the button of the vest, he had a large perfumed rose."[17]

It will be this sexy dandy who puts an end to all the diabolical plottings of Joaquim Cambinda and who liberates the farm from the nightmare and the mystery. Barbosa discovers and proves scientifically that the death of a young female Black is by poisoning. There have been also other mysterious deaths since Joaquim Cambinda came to the plantation. For Barbosa there is no doubt; the old sorcerer is guilty. Dragged in front of his masters and threatened with being whipped, Cambinda admits his guilt and tells all his crimes: he killed men and women because they were enemies, he killed slaves to damage the masters, he killed babies to take revenge on their mothers, he caused rheumatism in the old coronel, and he caused paralysis in the old mistress. The coronel has Cambinda enclosed inside the pillory, but the furious Blacks lynch the old sorcerer, burning him alive. Justice is done without the white gentlemen ever having dirtied their hands.

Only after the description of this episode does the writer express a comment on what has happened. He admits that from a legal point of view in the fazendas the Middle Ages survive and that the master's desire is the only existing law: it is of no consequence that Cambinda was burned alive; the authorities preferred to ignore the whole matter. Everyone lived better in the fazenda after the sorcerer's death. The coronel and his son, being good and pious men as the author insists, were used to the rigors of slavery; and since the lynching had been done it was better not to think about it and to continue to live.

Ribeiro, like Araripe Júnior in his *O reino encantado*, can consider the coronel as a good man even though he has slaves whipped. Having accepted the reality and necessity of slavery, the goodness of a man must be considered independently of the drastic decisions that he is compelled to take as a slave master, just as in a war a man may commit actions that in daily life may lead him to imprisonment.

Ribeiro maintains his slave master's mentality to the end of the novel. There are some minor and purely functional episodes, and there are notes, little phrases, but the conclusions are always the same. One episode concerns a little Black boy (always anonymous, naturally) who loses his arm in the gears of a machine that pulverizes sugarcane; the child's father, seeing his son dragged by the saw-toothed wheels, blocks the mechanism by throwing a bar of iron into it, thus saving the son but breaking irreparably the machine:

> The *negrinho*'s life was saved but the gears were broken beyond repair, wheels, axles, levers, everything was broken. It was bad luck, it was the work of the devil himself, this disaster, said the enraged coronel. Not certainly for the *crioulinho* for he was born free, one of the September 28th people; it was a trifling damage that he was crippled. The mishap, however, caused the interruption of the work when everything was going so well, with the weather never having been so good.[18]

The author adds nothing to what we have transcribed. The episode serves only to give a reason for Barbosa's trip; he must procure a new machine. The cold and detached tone with which the author describes the incident, focusing the attention on the disaster of the broken machine, is, however, appalling, especially when one compares it to the dramatic tone with which he describes the scene when Lenita is bitten by a poisonous snake.

We have two more examples. The first one refers to Barbosa and Lenita's affair. No one in the house is aware of the affair (also because in the house there are only two ill, elderly people), but in the *senzala*, the affair "had already started to be a juicy piece of gossip for the slander characteristic of the *negro* race: the *pretos*, especially the *pretas*, murmured, made comments on the unproductive huntings, pointed out sentences, dared to utter obscenities."[19] There is clearly an almost inborn malevolence on the author's part: a frantic relationship such as the one he describes would have provoked juicy comments in any small town in any part of the world at any time and not necessarily in an area inhabited by Blacks. Maybe what offends him is that Black people are making comments on a white people's story; this is only the corollary to the complex of the besieged citadel.

The other episode is that of Barbosa, who, having been seduced and abandoned by Lenita, decides to commit suicide: "He had given himself away with his hands tied to the whims of a hysterical woman who had offered herself to him, who had given herself to him just as she would have offered herself and given herself to anybody else, to a *negro*, to a slave."[20] Let us avoid any comments on this last embellishment, which reveals to us other minor, yet not negligible, obsessions.

What else are we left to say on a work like *A carne*? First of all we should repeat that in Júlio Ribeiro there is no contradiction on the topic of slavery. We cannot find then that inconsistency noticeable in other authors where ideal principles are solemnly claimed while thousands of revealing sentences say exactly the opposite. Although not a concern of this work, one should wonder instead why Ribeiro chose such unlikely characters for a novel intended to be realistic, while he neglected choosing instead those very interesting subjects that the Brazilian situation of the time offered him.

It seems almost that he wrote *A carne* for the purpose of proving something. The initial dedication to Zola, the story, and the construction of the characters who are so non-Brazilian, the continuous and almost obsessive use of foreign terms, and the long geographical explanations give the impression that the whole work was written to provide the reader with a certain idea of Brazil. The readers are then asked to consider normal what is instead an extreme case. The author wants to project the image of a white, cultured, and scientifically evolved Brazil where the characters create a story that might have happened in very civilized France. It is a Brazil where slavery is only a disagreeable but rather minor fact, a historic heredity that one cannot discard, and with which one is compelled to deal.

Yet the author's intentions are for us secondary and marginal. What matters is how he faced (or rather how he avoided facing) the problems caused by the existence of slavery. His constant contempt for the Black race, the indifference he shows concerning the problems of slavery combine with what we called the complex of the besieged citadel. All this clearly shows that Ribeiro belongs to that species of people who believe they can solve problems by denying their existence and by pretending they do not see them. The strangest thing is that the novel was published in 1888, the year when slavery was officially abolished, the year when the most violent and heated demonstrations against slavery took place. Maybe his work simply expresses the masters' reaction—never mind whether it is conscious or unconscious—against a solution that they were eventually compelled to accept.

6 ALUÍSIO AZEVEDO

The Maranhão and *O mulato*

When Aluísio Azevedo (1857–1913) published *O mulato* (*The Mulatto*, 1881) readers in the peaceful and somnolent São Luís do Maranhão reacted so violently that the writer was compelled to run away lest his life be in danger. Yet it was the same audience who had received with great enthusiasm his previous work, *Uma lágrima de mulher*, a sentimental novel for young ladies set in Lipari on the background of a stylized Italy. What was it that caused the citizens' wrath against Aluísio Azevedo to the point of compelling him to abandon his native city?

It was certainly not the fact that the protagonist of his novel was a mulatto. In fact, this character was not a particularly representative mulatto, just as Bernardo Guimarães's Isaura had little to share with the real Black and mulatto slaves. Even as a protagonist, Raimundo, the mulatto, is not a very representative or controversial character; he is instead a rather dull and unbelievable character. In the novel's description of his native province, however, Aluísio Azevedo creates a magnificent picture: with masterful ability he exposes all its deficiences, hypocrisies, and conflicts. He treats it as a city and a whole region that had entered an irreversible phase of decadence.

What then were São Luís and the Maranhão like in 1881? Dunshee de Abranches in his *O cativeiro* (*The Prison*, 1941) and Graça Aranha in his *O meu próprio romance* (*My Own Novel*, 1931)—both writers belonged to illustrious families from Maranhão—give interesting descriptions, full of meaningful details. Their opinions often converge and often they even quote the same examples, although de Abranches is generally more critical than Graça Aranha concerning their homeland.

Maranhão, an isolated province in the northern part of Brazil, adjacent to Pará with its great Amazon forest, had entered upon, as we have said, a phase of splendid decadence. The growing coffee boom had brought to the states of the South both capital and energy, and the great *fazendeiros* of the North had nothing better to do than to sell their slaves to the big landowners of the South, especially to those of the state of São Paulo. The big *fazendas* of Maranhão remained in complete abandonment and the old fazendeiros moved en masse to São Luís, the capital, where they led a well-to-do and spendthrift existence. In the words of de Abranches, in the years immediately preceding the period of decadence, one lived in grand style in São Luís: the concerts of Margherita Ponchielli, the great Italian soprano, the French dressmakers and hairdressers, and the splendid European jewels all contributed to give a particular style to the life of the capital of Maranhão. The intellectual life there was one of the most lively in Brazil, and its inhabitants had baptized São Luís the Brazilian Athens. This is one of the contradictory aspects of a spirited people like the Brazilians: this absolute lack of modesty explodes in hyperbolic comparisons such as that made by Bernardo Guimarães in naming Recife as the Venice of Brazil because of the marsh canals that the two cities have in common.

But great dangers were building up on the horizon: the law of the *Ventre Livre* of 1871 had signaled irremediably the end of slavery despite the fraudulent attempt of some fazendeiros who, in league with parish priests, registered newborn Black slaves with a date previous to the real one. Still more serious was the menace represented by the new generations of European immigrants who were revolutionizing the work market and did not tolerate close contact with the Blacks. For that reason the fazendeiros, even before the decree that officially abolished slavery, "chased away from their land the Blacks and mulattoes like rabid dogs so as not to lose the skilled help of the foreign farm hands."[1]

The story of Maranhão is a bit special, marked by a strange destiny. The province that in the years before the end of slavery represented the more obscure aspects of conservatism and racism had had in the previous half century some authentically revolutionary moments. The struggle for independence, for the separation of Brazil from the metropolis, had seen Black slaves actively participate alongside their white masters. The explanation furnished us by de Abranches is very interesting. According to this writer the life of Maranhão was founded on slavery, and on the contribution of the Black farmhands (family mail carriers, love messengers for young couples, thugs in the fights between various familial and political groups, spies in the service of jealous husbands and wives, confidants of delicate affairs, or even of the crimes of their masters). When the young Brazilians—the Jacobins, as they liked to call themselves—and the representatives of the *partido nativo* began to plot against Portuguese domination they had to seek the help of their Black slaves. This may seem absurd, but to make a revolution the good bourgeois Brazilians had to enlist their slaves! The slaves formed the mass of the revolutionary force that besieged São Luís. The houses and the fazendas were abandoned by the slaves because independence meant the automatic end of slavery. Naturally, when the first Brazilian government became installed its first job was to return the Black fugitives to their former masters. Many Blacks fled into the *quilombos* while others requested asylum on the ships of Lord Cochrane, the English admiral who had come to accelerate the advent of independence to the advantage of the British crown, which was anxious to find a new commercial partner in South America. And the English admiral "gathered them chivalrously aboard the liberation squadron and then a few days later, on the open sea sent them to be sold again in other places as war booty."[2]

The Black slaves were present in the failed liberal revolution of 1831 and above all they were a determining part of the great revolt of the *balaios*, the famous *Balaiada* that bloodied Maranhão from 1838 to 1840. The term *balaio* means a straw basket; it is a nickname for a certain Manoel Francisco dos Anjos Ferreira, who manufactured these baskets. The violence perpetrated by an official and a group of soldiers against the sons of a balaio pushed the latter to a revolt, helped by neighbors and relatives. It was an authentic social revolt, one of the few true social revolts: "It was a protest against the barbarous conscription, against arbitrary prisons, against the arrogant rich, against all the violence that befell the poor without protection, *negros*, Indians, and poor whites."[3] In these few lines, Capistrano de Abreu has captured the essential motives of the revolt. In this struggle of the poor against the rich, in this social revolution, there appears a different element: the Black fugitives of the quilombo of Cosme, or better Dom Cosme Bento das Chagas, *Tutor e Imperador das Liberdades Bemtevis* (Guardian and Emperor of the Bemtevis Liberties). Although unable to achieve a true and proper alliance, Blacks and whites had a common objective, the struggle against the rich, against the great landowners. But what lost this revolution and decreed its end was the fact that the revolutionaries belonged to different ethnic groups. The future duke of Caxias, who commanded the repression force, knew how to divide easily the two groups, which had never really been united, and how to push the whites of the balaio against the Black bemtevis. When rebels of the balaio found themselves in difficulty and on the verge of surrender, they received an offer of amnesty, provided that they first join in combat against the Black quilombolas. Very significantly, the chief of the repression force, Colonel Luiz de Lima e Silva, future duke of Caxias, tried whenever possible to save the lives of the slaves, attracting them to the fazendas with the promise of pardon because "slave labor represents the greatest wealth of the country."[4] At the same time they advised the rich to eliminate the mulattoes and the *cabras* pitilessly so as to avoid future revolts.

It was just these revolts, the quilombo of the Black Cosme and the class struggle of the balaio, that determined the reactionary structure of Maranhão, as did irreversible economic decadence. The master class's fear was tremendous. Masters saw themselves as white gentlemen stranded in the cities, deprived of the only source of wealth and of life because they knew only a life parasitically based on Black labor; they imagined themselves confronted and beaten by those poor whites whom they had always regarded with proud disdain and by those Black slaves whom they never even considered as human beings.

The masters' revenge expressed itself through the cruelest behavior towards the slaves. For example, a young white girl, abandoned by her father in the fazenda during the revolt, had fled together with a mulatto, her foster brother; they were recaptured after the end of the war. The girl's father, after having savagely beaten his daughter, wanted to compel her to stab her lover in the heart with a knife. "Since she refused to do this he had her stripped and tied to the body of her lover, already dying from numerous blows received; then he hung her on a tree and later threw the two corpses in a field as a meal for the crows."[5]

De Abranches refers, moreover, to the episode of babies born from adultery or violence perpetrated during the revolt. These babies were thrown during the night on the beaches or in deserted streets. Yet, it is easy to perceive at times in de Abranches, as well as in Graça Aranha, some strange reticence in judging facts and persons, almost as if both writers, although sincere in their support for the struggle against slavery, realized that the end of servitude would coincide with the end of their class and their world. This is why de Abranches says that the girl in the episode just cited was not brought up by her father as she should have been. Does this mean that had she been well educated she would not have coupled with a "dark mulatto" (in the words of the author)? It is perhaps the old taboo of the white woman and the Black man that the author fears confronting, in admitting that in the "dark mulatto" the woman had seen, first of all, a man, certainly a better one than her own father who, unlike the daughter, had received a fine and delicate education.

Graça Aranha recalls the episode of the wife of a fazendeiro who had been caught by her husband in flagrant adultery with a Black man. The Black was killed, his body was salted and dried; and the woman, locked in a room, was forced to eat the meat of her lover for survival until the husband had her killed and thrown to the crows for food. (A similar episode is related by Monteiro Lobato in the short story, "Bugio Moqueado.") Almost as if he wanted to counterbalance what he just said, the author adds: "Slavery in Maranhão did not consist of many horrible facts such as this one. Generally the *maranhenses* lived with their slaves in great and easy familiarity."[6] Right afterwards he cites the case of the public minister Celso Magalhães who was suspended from his job for having dared bring to trial a noblewoman accused of having killed with a bayonet the son of one of her slaves. De Abranches refers to this episode, however, with the version in which two children were killed, and adds that

> the criminal, however, accompanied by her relatives, was silent during the trial and was amazed at seeing herself dragged to the bench of the accused when in the interior of her province so many slaves were beaten to death by their masters and chained to the pillory without anyone being disturbed in their property for this reason.[7]

De Abranches, who also brings up the true case of the Black man Amaro, maintains that the good families of São Luís were not cruel to their slaves. In this case, Amaro was caught in adultery with the master's wife and was tried by a whole family council and, after having been whipped, was covered with honey and left for the insects as food while the master's wife was sent back to the paternal household. He blames this kind of cruelty on the people of the fazendas who were accustomed to the vices and violence of the *senzalas* rather than to the refined and cultured society of São Luís.

It is necessary to understand de Abranches and Graça Aranha. Their memoirs passed through the hands of their fellow citizens before ending in the hands of posterity. Because their fellow citizens would recognize themselves in the writing, problems of friendship, relationships, political connections, and sincere affections made their discussion more circumscribed than the writers would have wanted. But we can say that they, especially de Abranches, had achieved their goal perfectly: it does not matter for us whether the families who mistreated their slaves came from the old maranhense stock or whether they did not. What matters is that de Abranches has handed down to us the testimony of an old slave about the time when the slave trade was flourishing: "At that time, my *sinhô-moço*, the slaves were such a bad thing that we couldn't even have a grave in the cemetery of the Holy Mercy: they buried us outside the walls."[8]

There is an episode in which de Abranches, without making accusations, describes a scene that prompted his clear antislavery choice and, at the same time, implicated many important figures of the "good" society of Maranhão. The author then relates that when he was a child, Emília, a mulatto slave of a noble family, had been his wet nurse; she had a very beautiful daughter named Amélia, already free, who lived by selling typical food in the streets. The daughter had decided not to have a family until she could free her mother; to such a purpose she had worked very hard saving the necessary sum. To overcome the resistance of Emília's mistress, who was not willing at all to lose such a precious slave, Amélia had devised a strategy: the day of São Benedict was a day in which the noble families liberated a slave; Amélia would then pay for her mother's liberty and her mistress would grant that liberty as if it were an act of spontaneous munificence. Young de Abranches, then six years old, would have given the sum to the mistress who, however, refused once again on the grounds that she had to move to Rio de Janeiro with the family and needed Emília's help very much. In the face of this the courageous and beautiful Amélia also went to Rio de Janeiro. She went directly to the senate to find Senator Nunes Gonçalves, an illustrious relative of Emília's mistress, and obtained her mother's ransom.

This episode decided de Abranches's antislavery vocation. His phrases about the illustrious and noble senator and his noble relative sound either bitterly ironic or purely ceremonial, for example: "A Maranhão lady with a well-formed and charitable heart, native from a traditional family of São Luís and aunt of the great abolitionist Joaquim Serra."[9] A few years later de Abranches found a way of taking revenge on the "magnanimous liberal and generous" Senator Nunes Gonçalves. When the illustrious senator was bound for Rio, accompanied by nine of his best slaves whom he meant to sell to the fazendeiros of São Paulo, de Abranches told the strong abolitionist groups of Fortaleza in Ceará where the boat would stop. Thus the illustrious senator, "liberal of heart and of principle," had the pleasure of seeing with his own eyes nine precious slaves escape, taken away by force by the young *janqadeiros*, the rough and generous fishermen of Ceará, who then tranported them to safe asylums. De Abranches's excellent book of memoirs concludes with the funeral of Emília, his sweet *mãe preta*, the Black mammy as he always called her, who had nursed him with her healthy milk and who was compensated by a long and sincere struggle for the liberty of the Blacks.

In those years one lived in São Luís do Maranhão in what was left of an opulent past even though, as we said, the real wealth was transferred to the south. Having abandoned the cultivation of cotton on which the wealth of the country was based, and having sold most of the slaves to the great cultivators of São Paulo, the fazendeiros of Maranhão came to live their last season in São Luis. They brought their families and their habits with them, which greatly irritated the old inhabitants such as Dunshee de Abranches and, above all, Graça Aranha. Double families had become common: in addition to the legal family *teúdas* and *manteúdas* (literally "kept" and "maintained"), the splendid mulattoes constituted the second nuclear family, which many times ended by becoming the first family. The bastard children often were the school companions of their "legal" brothers. Priests were the first to give a bad example with their concubines (there was one, according to de Abranches, who was well noted for having more than two hundred children by his concubines), and many rich men had authentic harems.

A society so dissolute in customs was, however, very fanatical as regards the purity of blood. According to de Abranches, "at São Luís the ladies of the good families fought desperately to avoid bastards and to conserve pure blood among their children."[10]

On the same subject Graça Aranha insists further:

> In the family of my paternal grandfather the preconception against *negros* and mestizos was aggressive. They sought purity of race with furious zeal. The Maciéis Parentes and the Aranhas families never mixed with the Indians. Mating with *negros* and mulattoes would have been an abominable thing. In the interior of the province I often met these relatives of mine, in extreme poverty, barefoot, simple workers employed in the *fazendas*, but totally preserving the purity of the white blood. They were generally blond with blue eyes with the same features that one could find in most of the sons of my father and also in two of my brothers. My paternal aunts, like hunting animals, sniffed and discovered the mestizo elements no matter how hard one tried to hide it. Tireless fanatics in the name of this prejudice, if they knew of some marriage plan of some relative, they started to investigate the entire pedigree of the suitor and if they discovered even the smallest drop of *negro* or Indian blood they would not give up until they saw the unhappy alliance destroyed. Poor aunts, the last representatives of this family prejudice to which I owe the fact of being white; they managed to die just in time, before the invasion of the mestizos in the old family.[11]

In this city and this province, so closed and backward, it was not only the slaves and the people of color who suffered from discrimination and violence. Women too, because they were weaker and less protected, ended by being reduced to a situation of semislavery. Dona Emília Branco, Aluísio Azevedo's mother, told de Abranches of her own odyssey: Young and beautiful, endowed with rare talent, she had come from Portugal to São Luís with her family when she was a child. Still very young, she was compelled to marry an uncouth and brutal Portuguese, a well-to-do merchant. This was one of the most solid Portuguese traditions in São Luís do Maranhão, the most primitive expression of that racist and nationalist complex we have seen expressed by Graça Aranha's words: the children of Portuguese married only Portuguese or children of the Portuguese. Among the merchant class (very strong in São Luís as it was in the rest of Brazil) the custom prevailed that the first daughter had to marry the first clerk, and the second daughter married the second one, and so on. This allowed the fortune to be kept intact (the dowry remained in the family), and allowed the firm to be reinforced with the help of employees seriously motivated to give their best and, above all, to preserve whole the much-valued and vaunted racial purity. The daughters who dared to rebel against the despotic paternal will were treated as slaves, confined to a room, beaten to death, or chased out of the house and driven, therefore, to prostitution. Dona Emília Branco did not escape her destiny, at least for some time: she lived years of hell with an uncouth and brutal husband until she found the courage to run away to a friendly family. There, she lived as a perfect recluse. The doors of the good families of São Luís were closed to her, until her marriage with the illustrious Portuguese consul put an end to what was considered the greatest scandal in Maranhão society.

Again, we have de Abranches relating this episode: while the elderly lady was narrating her whole life to him, her son Aluísio Azevedo came in to talk to her about the novel, *O mulato*, that he was writing at the time. And his mother told him pointedly: "In any case, don't be too cruel to Ana Rosa, don't forget that she was one of the last victims of domestic slavery of the Maranhão women."[12]

It is the Maranhão, where in those years one of the major Brazilian poets, Gonçalves Dias, was inexorably rejected by the family of the woman he loved because he was a mulatto, which provides the setting for Aluísio Azevedo's *O mulato.*

The plot of the novel is the following: Raimundo, the main character, a young twenty-six-year-old man, comes back to his native town, São Luís, which he had left as a child. In São Luís an uncle, Manuel Pescada, a Portuguese merchant, waits for him, as do the shadows of a tragic family past, which he ignores. His father had a relationship with a slave named Domingas, his mother; later his father married a white woman of a good family, but did not manage to rescue Domingas from his legitimate wife's anger. While he was away, his wife had Domingas tortured with red-hot irons until she became insane. He took Raimundo to safety to São Luís and upon his return found his wife in the arms of the parish priest, Diogo. He killed his wife and lived a brief time full of remorse until he was killed by Diogo. Raimundo was first sent to Rio de Janeiro by his uncle, then to Portugal, where he grew up, until he graduated in law; after an educational trip to the rest of Europe he returned to Brazil and decided to settle down in Rio de Janeiro, where he planned to open a commercial house. First, however, he intended to liquidate all that he owned in São Luís. He knew nothing of his shadowy past; he ignored his mother's slavery, and even the fact that he was a mulatto.

This is the background. Upon his arrival in São Luís his uncle, Pescada, gives him cordial hospitality; he has a young and beautiful daughter, Ana Rosa, who according to tradition should marry her father's first clerk, the ugly and dirty Portuguese, Dias. Raimundo finds the setting and the atmosphere in São Luís absurd: he cannot understand why he is treated with so much coldness. He is the only one who ignores that he is a mulatto and therefore a pariah for the good society of São Luís. Although the parish priest, Diogo, had killed his father, no one knows about it, and in fact Diogo is considered a saint. Diogo pours oil on the fire of Maranhão's slander against poor Raimundo. The rest of the story follows a linear trend interrupted at times by some excellent environmental descriptions. Ana Rosa falls in love with Raimundo and practically seduces him. Poor Pescada cannot give his daughter to a mulatto, although he is his nephew, because he cannot oppose Maranhão society and his own family. There follows the revelation of his origins, which upsets Raimundo; the decision of the two lovers to marry in spite of everyone and everything; and the death of Raimundo by the hand of Dias, who was armed by the always-wicked parish priest Diogo. The epilogue: Ana Rosa's marriage to Dias is crowned by economic success and the birth of several children, and Diogo dies, still considered a saint by everyone.

O mulato is an early work by Azevedo. For this reason it suffers, on the one hand, from a certain *feuilleton* style (which the author retains in less committed works); on the other hand, it is too simplistically one-sided: the evil ones are all on one side and they are always and totally evil, without any possibility of redemption. We have already said that the first criticism of *O mulato* is that the main character is not a mulatto, or at least not much of a mulatto; his racial characteristics are subdued to the point that he himself ignores that he is a mulatto. This is undoubtedly true. One should recognize, however, that *O mulato* is a typically oppositional work. The target is not only slavery but the entire slave structure, including the lifestyle in São Luís. The author assumes that the people in Maranhão are hard and often cruel to their slaves. What he attacks is a hypocritical and intolerant world that lives in luxury off of slavery, although it does not tolerate Blacks.

O mulato is an anticlerical, anti-Portuguese, and antislavery novel. In practice all of Maranhão is being accused. That it is a problem novel explains the weakness of the main character, his lack of consistency as a human being, and the lack of credibility of many of his actions. Since Raimundo is bound to be the victim of prejudice and intolerance, his behavior must not be identified with that of an adversary who could be defeated. Raimundo is always truly himself, all he wants is to liquidate his business as soon as possible and leave São Luís, where he is bored to death.

So we find poor Raimundo walking in the streets of São Luís: his presence brings on embarrassment wherever he goes, conversations come to a standstill, the atmosphere is cold. He is never invited to a party or a reunion. So he lives in isolation at home.

> One circumstance, however, was not quite clear to him: while the heads of the families shut the doors in his face, the girls did not shut their hearts to him; in society they all rejected him, this is true, but in private they invited him to their bedrooms. Raimundo saw himself titillated by various ladies, single, married, and widowed, whose advances reached the point of sending him flowers and messages that he pretended not to receive because in his educated character he found this very ridiculous and silly.[13]

Raimundo's situation is very forced and unrealistic: he is a young twenty-six-year-old, bored to death in a provincial city. He does not take advantage of the many invitations of so many women, among whom there must have been a pretty one worthy at least of a light affair.

Even Raimundo and Ana Rosa's encounter includes scenes that are amusing to the modern reader. Ana Rosa is in love with Raimundo and, while he is away, she spends her time in her cousin's room rummaging morbidly among his things. One day Raimundo surprises her and reprimands her; the girl bursts into tears and declares her love to him. Raimundo is torn apart between the embarrassment that the scene causes him and the affection for the beautiful cousin which inflames his heart; eventually he is practically compelled to declare his love to her and promise her that he will ask her hand in marriage as soon as possible. At this point, Ana Rosa throws herself into Raimundo's arms:

> She embraced him fully and warmly putting her head on his shoulder and puckering her lips in anxious expectation. The young man, having no way out, gave her a timid kiss on her lips. She reciprocated immediately with two passionate kisses. Then the young man, despite his moral energy, was in a commotion—was on the verge of giving in—the heat went to his head, his temples throbbed. On his congested and red hot face, he felt Ana Rosa's cold nose breathing excitedly. But he managed to regain his composure: he freed himself from his cousin's arms with great tenderness, he kissed her hands respectfully, and asked her to leave.[14]

Ana Rosa will have to do more in order to seduce Raimundo!

Manuel Pescada is compelled to reveal his past to Raimundo in order to justify his refusal to grant him Ana Rosa's hand. Even then, however, Raimundo does not rebel against that prejudiced world which forbids him to realize his love dream. Instead, he ends up by accepting, even though deeply troubled, the sad reality that surrounds him and decides to go away as soon as possible, giving up Ana Rosa forever. Again it is the latter who, at the moment of his departure, dashes into Raimundo's room. Defying any prejudice and even the moral code in which she has been brought up, she offers herself to him, compelling him to seduce her and therefore stay. In the melodramatic scene Ana Rosa, faced with Raimundo's continuing resistance, goes as far as to place herself between him and the door through which the young man tries to leave to avoid, this time in vain, having to make love to her.

As I have said, Raimundo's crystal purity makes him undoubtedly a rather unlikely character. Yet, his behavior cannot only be ascribed to the author's youthful inexperience; it has rather a precise function in the structure of the novel. If Raimundo had accepted the invitations by the Maranhão women—so needy of affection—he would have done nothing wrong; yet his behavior might have justified to some extent the solid antipathy that the world of São Luís had shown him from the very beginning. If he had seduced Ana Rosa—or rather if he had let her seduce him—he would have trespassed the laws of hospitality toward Manuel Pescada, who had received him in his house. If, upon discovery of his origin, he had rebelled against the hypocritical and bigoted world of São Luís and he had said, to hell with it, defying it and taking Ana Rosa with him, he would have done a commendable thing. But he would have violated one of the most solid social taboos of the time and he would have placed himself in an antithetical position to the Maranhão world, thus providing an explanation, if not the justification, for the hostile attitude that everybody showed toward him. Instead, poor Raimundo thinks only of leaving and if, in the end, he makes love to Ana Rosa it is because he has no other alternative: either love her or literally walk on her, because the passionate cousin had blocked the door with her own body. He would have to walk over her if he wanted to get out.

Raimundo is hardly incisive and credible as a character, because he must be more of a pretext than a main character. He must be living proof that even the best of men ends up by being suffocated and annihilated by a world like that of São Luís do Maranhão. The true main character is, then, the Maranhão world, the narrow-minded and shabby province, eternally tied to the symbols of the past, closed to any intellectual progress, unable to renew itself and find alternatives to the inexorable and approaching decadence.

The author, who is ineffective in describing Raimundo, creates pages of rare power when describing the environment and especially the people. In this novel and in the following one, *O cortiço*, Azevedo reveals his talent as an authentic writer of social problems. His pages are genuine works of art and interesting environmental reconstructions.

We have said that *O mulato* is an oppositional novel, anticlerical, anti-Portuguese, and antislavery. The more decisive and even violent elements are the first two; the third is almost a consequence of the first. Slavery as it is presented in these years is a consequence of a world created and perpetuated by the Portuguese and accepted and sanctioned by the clergy. The clerk, Dias, is one of the first Portuguese whom we meet, except Manuel Pescada, who is himself the victim of the prejudice of his mother-in-law and of the parish priest, Diogo.

> Dias, adding to the staff of Manuel Pescada's house, was an uptight type like an egg, like an egg gone bad which hardly shows its rotten interior. In his jaundiced face, however, in the disrespect for his own body, in the patient silence of his exaggerated parsimony, one perceived a fixed idea, an objective toward which the acrobat walked without looking sideways, preoccupied, as if balanced on a tightrope. He did not disdain any means that might get him as soon as possible to the goal: he accepted without examination any path that at the moment seemed shorter. Everything served, everything was good, as long as it took him as rapidly as possible to the desired goal. He would walk on mud or red-hot coals to get to his objective—to get rich. His physical aspect was repugnant: thin, emaciated, rather short, relatively bent, a sparse beard,

> a low brow with sharp eyes. The constant use of clogs had made his feet monstrous and flat: when he walked he threw them clumsily to the side with the same movement that web-footed birds make when they swim. He hated cigars, walks, and meetings where it was necessary to spend some money; someone close to him smelled immediately a pungent stench of dirty clothes. Ana Rosa could not understand how a woman of a certain class could tolerate such a pig. Eventually talking with her friends when she wanted to give them the right idea of what Dias was like she would sum up her idea by saying: "There is a man who does not have the courage to buy a toothbrush."[15]

The main motives of the anti-Portuguese controversy in Brazil are summed up in the description of Dias. The marked antipathy toward the Portuguese in Brazil is a particularly interesting phenomenon because Brazil was discovered and colonized by the Portuguese and Portuguese is the language spoken. It is all the more remarkable if one thinks that the Brazilians are a very hospitable people. The various foreign ethnic groups, even in massive numbers of immigrants such as the Italians and the Germans, never caused an antipathy similar to that triggered by the Portuguese.

The causes of such an attitude can be varied. The golden age of colonization was characterized by the bureaucratic and administrative attitude with which the Portuguese conquerors always approached the new land; therefore, they always opposed those colonists who had settled in the new land and had become Brazilians. Then followed a period during which Portugal, which had itself entered a phase of decadence, mainly sent merchants to Brazil. These merchants, though they ultimately settled in Brazil, initially came to enrich themselves and then return to the motherland. They adopted a life-style exactly the opposite of the Brazilian: they worked themselves to exhaustion and closed themselves to any form of external life. In contrast, Brazilians were always lovers of anything new and always considered work with a certain detachment. On the one hand were people who refused to spend and enjoy themselves and, on the other hand, were people who loved the good life and had a remarkable capacity for spending even beyond their means. It is natural that these two diametrically opposed life-styles would lead inevitably to the Brazilians dispersing their wealth while the Portuguese increased theirs. This evoked and built up a natural feeling of envy that might be the hidden reason behind the writings of Aluísio Azevedo and others.

One of the characteristics that Azevedo emphasizes more than once is that of bad odors. Brazilians, as a tropical people, love water, and we do not know how much the Indians and the Blacks, with their frequent washing, contributed to creating this healthy attitude. The European immigrant, however, was used to another climate, and especially if he came from a poor and rural class, had little acquaintance with water and personal hygiene. The new land, with its eternally humid heat, typical of the tropics, had always compelled the foreigner to adopt the local attitudes with regard to hygiene. The most reluctant were always those groups that lived closed in their own clan and therefore adopted with great difficulty the habits of the place: this applied to the Portuguese, toward whom many accusations of uncleanliness were addressed.

Azevedo describes at length an episode in which Dias ends up by being sick because of his continuous dirtiness. The doctor, after having examined him, prescribes a cure based on baths. Manuel Pescada, seeing that the doctor's advice was not being followed, visits the sick one and tries diplomatically to make him understand that the Brazilian climate requires a different type of personal hygiene. The author takes advantage of this occasion to give us a grotesque picture of two Portuguese merchants who, sitting side by side, recall nostalgically all the dishes of the Portuguese cuisine. It is one of those scenes in which, by criticizing Brazil and exalting Portugal, the characters are bound to make themselves disliked by the Brazilian public. And even the character of Pescada, always depicted as a good and fatherly person, is compromised by his ignorance and prejudice when he plans to marry his own daughter to a man like Dias, whom he should avoid—if not for esthetic reasons, at least for hygienic ones.

Azevedo's attacks are addressed not only against the Portuguese but also against a world and a mentality created by the Portuguese. The character of Maria Bárbara, Pescada's bitter and cruel mother-in-law and Ana Rosa's grandmother, exemplifies this; she made her son-in-law promise her that he would not marry his daughter to any one but a Portuguese, or at least a descendant of a Portuguese, one hundred percent white.

> Maria Bárbara was the true type of the old maranhense brought up in the *fazendas*. She talked a lot about her grandparents, almost all Portuguese; she was very proud and full of blood prejudice. When she talked about the *pretas* she called them "filth" and when she referred to a mulatto she would call him *cabra*. She had always been like that and for piety no one was her equal: at Alcantara she had had a chapel devoted to Santa Barbara where she compelled her slaves to pray every night, in chorus, with their arms open, sometimes in chains. She sighed over the memory of her husband, "her João Hipolito," a fine Portuguese

> with blue eyes and blond hair. Maria Bárbara had a great admiration for the Portuguese, feeling an unlimited enthusiasm for them and preferring them over all Brazilians. When Manuel Pescada, who at this time was just starting his business in the capital, asked for permission to marry her daughter, she said "At least I have the certainty that he is white."[16]

Needless to say, Maria Bárbara is of course very cruel with her slaves: every day the house resounds with the old lady's screams and the beaten slaves' cries.

An even more hideous character is Quitéria, Raimundo's father's wife, the one who tortured Domingas and drove her insane:

> The rich Brazilian widow, Dona Quitéria Inocencia de Freitas Santiago, very religious and blood conscious; for her the slave was not a man and the fact of not being white was the same as being a criminal. She was a beast! Under her hands or under her orders many slaves died under the whip, or the pillory, by hunger, by thirst, or with red-hot irons. But she never stopped being devout, full of superstitions: she had a chapel in the *fazenda* where the slaves each night, their hands swollen by beatings or their shoulders ripped by the whips, prayed to the Holy Virgin, the mother of the unhappy ones.
>
> At the side of the chapel there was a cemetery for the victims.
>
> She had married José da Silva for two simple reaons: because she needed a man and there wasn't much of a choice, and because they had told her that the Portuguese were one hundred percent white.[17]

As we can see clearly from these pages, Azevedo's anti-Portuguese argument was not addressed against the Portuguese as such, but it was rather a struggle against a world built on prejudice, on absurd social stratifications, on sordid interests, on rigid racism, on the attachment to a past world in which the Portuguese element prevailed. Quitéria and Maria Bárbara were not literally Portuguese, yet they admire the Portuguese because they represent that world tied to the slave system with which they identify.

Two personal facts played a part in Azevedo's attitude. He was a son of a Portuguese diplomat who had been his country's consul at São Luís, an authentic aristocrat; but his mother, to whom the writer was very attached, had suffered a long time during her previous, unhappy marriage to a Portuguese merchant. In the second place, Maranhão was isolated geographically from the center of power and bound to economic and cultural decadence. Here, all the struggles that the progressive and liberal elements had often supported in vain, from independence to the latest journalistic arguments, had been directed against the reactionaries, who were often Portuguese or at least nostalgic of the world created by the Portuguese. Both personal and political reasons created Aluísio Azevedo's attitude.

O mulato is an interesting testimony of a world and an epoch. The author also criticizes the representatives of a petty nationalism against the Portuguese, who nonetheless accept the same system created by the Portuguese. For example, Sebastião Campos, Maria Bárbara's other son-in-law, is "a typical type of the Maranhão." He always speaks badly of the Portuguese and does nothing but exalt the products of his province against all the imports and he is at the same time a representative of rabid racism. He cannot even explain to himself why he is a racist, he just repeats the usual commonplace sentences such as "*preto* is *preto*; white is white; *moleque* is *moleque*; boy is boy."[18] One of his precious ideas is that Brazil's greatest disgrace was having won the war of Guararapes, in which the Portuguese defeated the Dutch who were their competitors in the colonization of Brazil. In the taverns, the same people who criticize the Portuguese show the most fanatical racism against the Blacks. Even a mulatto, very proud of being half white and of his tacky elegance, commenting on Raimundo's misfortune, says: "That's the way to do it to keep the *pretos* in their place!"[19]

All the gossip in the various meetings that take place in the houses of Manuel Pescada and his friends is always centered on the nostalgia of the good old times and on complaints about modern times and the Blacks who do not want to work. It is the perfect picture of the maranhense province, unable to renew itself, enclosed in itself, and continuously repeating the same old clichés.

The gloomiest representative of this type of maranhense life remains, however, the parish priest, Diogo. In him are summed up all evils, his personal ones as well as those he shares with his contemporaries. It is he who, as Quitéria's adviser and lover, is guilty of Raimundo's father's disgrace. It is he who killed Raimundo's father. It is he who, as Pescada's adviser and Ana Rosa's confessor, has plotted against Raimundo. It is he who turns Dias against Raimundo and incites him to murder.

As we have already said, one of the faults of *O mulato* is that it is a one-sided novel in which the good people are always good and the evil people are always evil. The candor of Raimundo, who resists all temptations of the flesh and who never rebels even against the most glaring injustice, is set up against the satanic wickedness of Diogo, who seduces married women and who villainously kills his enemies, even when they, like Raimundo, have not wronged him in any way. The lack of credibility of one character is paralleled by that of the other. If Raimundo is a pretext to denounce the evils of Maranhão,

Diogo is a summary of all possible evils that might have afflicted Maranhão at the time.

Diogo is a priest, and the author's choice reflects obviously anticlerical ideas. Thanks to the testimony of both Dunshee de Abranches and Graça Aranha we have already seen the conditions of absolute immorality of the clergy in São Luís at the time. It is not a question of an occasional and understandable weakness of the flesh, but rather of a corrupted life-style. The clergy found in slavery the opportunities to satisfy their lechery as well as the economic security that allowed them to live in idleness. The priest, whom de Abranches mentions, who had fathered more than two hundred children from his slaves must have been remarkably wealthy, considering that he educated all of them. Such a clergy must naturally be one of the bulwarks of slavery and one of the fiercest opponents of any innovation or progress that might encroach on the privileges they enjoyed.

What Azevedo attacked most vehemently was the hypocrisy of those who preach the virtue they do not believe in and are the first to violate. Diogo is a devil, but he has the reputation of a saint; Diogo is dangerous because he is intelligent. The racism of the merchants and the old fazendeiro families is limited by their obtuseness; Diogo is dangerous because his voice is followed by many.

> He was a handsome old man, he must have been at least sixty, yet he was still strong and well preserved: lively eyes, erect body, but masked by a saintly sweetness. He used to wear elegant shoes, always shiny; he had his socks and special collars bought in Europe, and when he laughed he showed his beautiful teeth all plated with gold. He had graceful movements, white hands, and snow-white hair that was a beauty to see. Diogo was the confidant and the adviser of the good and slow Manuel, who would do nothing without consulting him. He had graduated at Coimbra, whose marvels he related; rather wealthy, he never gave up his trips to Lisbon, where he used to go once in a while "to get the years off his back" as he would say, laughing.[20]

Wealthy, cultured, and elegant, Diogo is the representative of a clergy able to exert a remarkable charm and influence upon those who listen to him. There is a moment in which even Diogo, despite his perfect self-control, lets his feelings come through and shows himself for what he really is. It is when, talking about Raimundo, who is going to arrive, the good Manuel in his simplicity says that it would have been better if his nephew had become a priest, the career he had initially planned for him. At this sentence, Diogo bursts out:

> "And after all we see increasingly more priests who are blacker than our cooks! And is this just? The government," the priest emphasized

LANDING OF THE SLAVES

DESEMBARQUE DE ESCRAVOS

the words, "should take serious steps! They must prohibit the *cabras* certain offices!"

"But Father . . . "

"They should stay in their place!" Then the priest transformed himself with anger. "And it seems that this *moleque* was born just to spite us," he screamed. And he showed the letter, crumpling it: "One can count on the fact that this is an intelligent man! They should all be morons! morons whom we could use only to serve us! Wretched!"

"But Father, I don't think it is right . . ."

"Of course it is, my friend, don't be silly! Would you like to see your own daughter confessed and married by a *negro*? Would you like to see Ana Rosa kiss the hand of a son of Domingas? If you had grandchildren would you like to see them slapped on their hands with a ruler by a teacher who is blacker than my own dress? My dear friend at times you seem stupid!"

Manuel lowered his head, defeated.[21]

The last words of Diogo contain a striking contradiction that clearly exposes both his and his contemporaries' guilty racist position and deprives it of any scientific or sociological support. It is not a question of keeping other individuals at a distance or in a subservient position because they are incompetent; it is rather a question of excluding them just because they are intelligent and competent, while in the words of the priest, they should have been born morons, able to perform only servile labor. The rest of the reasons, so to speak, are typically visceral and prompted by visualizing in a position of privilege, such as that of a priest, a group of individuals one was accustomed to seeing normally in a subordinate position.

The prejudice against the mulatto was rather widespread. The same prejudices expressed by Diogo are attributed by the writer to an anonymous group of people conversing in a commercial house (often the commercial houses functioned as a meeting place for various people not necessarily connected by economic interests):

And the conversation took another direction leading on to celebrities of dark race; important people of the maranhense society who had a rather suspicious dark color were cited; all the distinguished mulattoes of Brazil were mentioned: the celebrated anecdote of the emperor and the engineer Rebouças was told emphatically. A person, to the general amazement of the group, mentioned Alexandre Dumas and swore that even Byron had *negro* blood.

"And so what? Is there anything to be amazed at?" said one roughly. "We have had a president who is as black as the porters who are carrying the barrels of alcohol out there!"

"No . . . ," grumbled an old man who among the merchants enjoyed the reputation of having good opinions. "You cannot deny that they have great ability, especially as far as music is concerned."

"Ability?" whispered another with the air of mystery of one who tells something forbidden.

"Talent! I tell you! That mixed race is the shrewdest of all Brazil! Poor whites, if they are allowed to get some instruction and decide to have their say. Then everything is going to go topsy-turvy! Luckily they don't have many chances!'"[22]

One must keep in mind that the reality described by Azevedo refers to the last years of slavery when the racial mixture had already given excellent human products who were well established in many branches of Brazilian life. Racial prejudice at this point became the pure cliché of those who were afraid of dangerous competition.

The debate over the mulatto, or rather against the mulattoes, is typical of a multiracial country where, moreover, the meeting point among the different races had such a tragic genesis as slavery. The mulatto who became educated and lived as the white proves that slavery is founded only on the violence of man over man. And in a world that did not want to give up slavery and the advantages deriving from it, the presence of the mulatto was like the ghost of a bad conscience from which one flees by denying its existence.

The mulatto character is part of a definite historical reality. We have already met the character in Raimundo's comments: "It is the way to do it to keep the *pretos* in their place." In this respect, Dunshee de Abranches's testimony, citing the words of an aristocratic maranhense lady, is very relevant:

> Do not forget to verify what I am telling you, and that is that the worst enemies of the *negros* are not the whites. And when you examine the tragedies of slave owners persecuting and slaughtering their slaves, look carefully and you will see that the authors of these crimes used to scratch their ears when they were small. It is true as the poet Euclides Faria writes in one of his satires, that the mulatto, being a mixed race, always carries in his soul and blood the *negro* fighting against the white.[23]

At his friend's words de Abranches observed:

> Suddenly certain well-known characters of *negro* and mestizo women came to my mind who, having become the mistresses of very wealthy men of the place, led a very leisurely life and kept a large number of slaves. In particular, two among those had become very popular—Caterina Mina, a dark *negra* who used to go out only with her entourage of *mucamas*, and Evarista, always covered with jewels, the heir of the

capitalist Malaquias Gonçalves. Both were considered generous and charitable, but they never gave up their slaves. Other mulatto women, however, wanted at any cost to pass for whites. Their cruelty with their slaves and their race was without equal. And they were ready to do anything and ready for any sacrifice to infiltrate pure-blood families. These women, on their part, were rigorously traditional; and when it came to marrying their children they investigated their suitors up to the fourth generation.[24]

This is the sad heritage of slavery. While racial prejudice persecutes even those who are definitely free from the chains of servitude, the mechanism of the society itself transforms the former victims into the torturers of their former brothers. Yet there is no other possible choice. Being free and economically independent led them inevitably to being owners of slaves who, at the time (let's not forget it), were a practically indispensable commodity. And in a society that identified being white with owning slaves, what kind of behavior could one expect from uneducated former slaves who had suddenly become ladies, thanks to their position if not the ambition of owning slaves, and who wanted to become related to whites? Former slaves at least had no other models to imitate except the good people of the place, the great local ladies. Like dona Ana Jansen, the most famous of the maranhense matriarchs, these ladies walked on their slaves' bodies, spread on the ground, in the fashion of Roi Soleil in the provincial version, so they would not soil their feet through contact with the ground!

There is still another character in *O mulato* who deserves critical attention. This character is among those who are most easily verifiable in real life, perhaps the only character in the novel who does not have a polemical function and did not evoke controversy. The Black mammy, a mãe preta, whom Abranches exalted in his memoirs, was a well-loved and familiar character whom the white and wealthy Brazilians would at the time have recognized easily. When Ana Rosa comes back home, her former wet nurse waits for her to help her undress and go to bed, or rather to the *amaca*, as was the custom in the Maranhão. (One of the recurrent aspects of slavery is that it is not necessity that creates the role and therefore the employee in charge of the role. It was rather the presence of many possible employees that created new roles; thus a healthy young woman like Ana Rosa needed a slave to get undressed):

Mônica was about fifty years old; she was fat, healthy, and very clean; had large breasts which hung inside her calico. At her neck was a necklace with a metal cross, a coin of 200 *réis*, a *cumaru* bean, a dog tooth, and a piece of wax embedded in gold. From the time she had breast-fed Ana Rosa she had devoted to her a maternal loving affection and an unconditional dedication. Iaiá had always been her idol, her only "I love you" because her own children had been taken away from her and sold to the south. Once she would never come back from the well, where she spent her days washing, without bringing her fruits and butterflies which for the little girl were the greatest pleasure in this life. She would call her "my daughter, my prison" and every night and every morning when she would go and come back from work she would always bless her with the same words: "May God make you a saint, may God help you, may God bless you." If Ana Rosa committed some mischief at home which her *mãe preta* did not like, she would immediately reprimand her with authority; when, however, the accusation or reproach came from somebody else, even if this was the father or the grandmother, she would take sides with the little girl against everybody else.

She had been free for six years. Manuel had freed her at his daughter's request, of which many people had disapproved. "You will be paid well!" they said. But the good *preta* had stayed at home with her masters and continued to take care of her own young mistress, better than before, even more a prisoner.[25]

Mônica is a character once easy to find in Brazil: she is a slave (or former slave, it does not make much difference) perfectly integrated in her position. The trauma of the separation from her children, instead of transforming itself into hatred and bitterness, is overcome through a new affection, through the adoption (so to speak) of a new daughter. Characters such as Mônica are to be considered one of the few human sides of slavery, a respite in a world in which cruelty and harshness prevailed.

Beyond the rich gallery of characters, *O mulato* must be remembered for what we would call a detailed typology of merchants, storekeepers, tavern owners, clerks, girls of good families, opulent matrons, and hysterical old women. They alternate in a succession of meetings, encounters, parties, supper conversations deriving suddenly from the frailest pretext, as often happens in the province, where they interrupt at times the somnolent rhythm of work.

Also the group descriptions are remarkable, especially the markets and the parties in which one feels the life and authentic reality of Maranhão pulsate. A good example of this kind of description is the slave market, which is part of the great general market, where, among sacks of onions and potatoes, human beings were sold:

The middlemen examined in the full light the *negros* and the *moleques* whom they found there to be sold: they examined their teeth, their feet, and their thighs; they asked question after question, they tapped with the end of their hat on the shoulders and on the thighs in order to examine the muscular tone as if they were buying horses.[26]

From Family Boardinghouse to Urban Sprawl

After leaving São Luís do Maranhão, where the extreme sensitivity of his fellow citizens did not allow him to stay after the publication of *O mulato*, Aluísio Azevedo had the opportunity to perfect his capacity for analysis and his descriptive technique in Rio de Janeiro. *Casa de pensão* (*Boardinghouse*, 1884) is partly autobiographical. It is the story of a young man from Maranhão and his experience in Rio de Janeiro. The novel is also a very interesting analysis—and maybe an irreplaceable tableau in Brazilian literature—of the so-called middle class that was taking shape in those years.

Being a country of masters and slaves, Brazil always had its weak point in the middle class, or rather in the lack of a middle class. By the middle class I mean that class which arises from the impact of the neocapitalist society on the large working classes. It consists of the laborer who becomes an artisan—even after periods of generations—and ends up by creating a small enterprise; of the peasant who becomes a small landowner and sends his children to study in the great city. That did not happen in Brazil for the very simple reason that the working class consisted of slaves. If it is partly true, as the writers of the time stated, that the European proletariat found itself quite often in worse conditions than the Brazilian slaves, it is also true that certain proletarians had the opportunity to change their social positions, at least through their children. The slave could only generate more slaves. Of course there exists a historically documented evolution of the slaves: an example is the freeman or the mulatto who sometimes reached remarkable social positions, especially through education. What counts in a society is the proportion, however, the number: in this case the number was too small to have any impact during those years under consideration.

For a long time after the period analyzed by Azevedo, it was practically impossible to live in Brazil without being compelled to use slaves, simply because in a preindustrial time most servile labor was done by men. There were no free men available to perform those jobs which formerly had been the exclusive task of the slaves. The last decades of the nineteenth century brought about a slow and decisive transformation; the end of slavery, the beginning of a slow industrialization financed by British capital, and the mass arrival of new European immigrants built the foundation of change that had its final consolidation only in the era of Vargas, in the 1930s. What was left, then, to the meager representatives of the middle class enclosed between an oligarchy—fazendeiros and rich merchants—and the large anonymous mass of slaves? Not much on the whole: public employment, or some menial labor on a newspaper or for some well-established professionals, mostly lawyers, or some parasitic job for the house of some great aristocrat. Raymundo Faoro, in his excellent work *Machado de Assis: a pirâmide e o trapézio*, gives this definition of the middle class (even though Machado de Assis is the author examined in this work, the definition is applicable, in our opinion, to the entire period):

> During the Empire, among landowners and speculators, aristocrats, and parliamentary representatives, the middle class was a purgatory ostracized by the great powers. It did not perform those balancing roles that the future proletariat would evoke. It was not situated between the wage earner and the rich. Its position was that of a class beneath the others. Underneath it there was nothing, the slave. It did not produce the statesmen, the barons, the bankers, and the *fazendeiros*, nor did it give rise to nonconformism and revolution. Its time came only fifty years later: for the time being it was the remains, the residue of less fortunate destinies.[27]

Casa de pensão is a middle-class story, even though the protagonist is the son of a rich merchant of the Maranhão. Amâncio (such is his name) is a young provincial who comes from São Luís to enroll in the medical school in Rio de Janeiro. His "correspondant," where he lodges in the first days in Rio, is a person called Campos, a Portuguese merchant and friend of the family. Campos has a beautiful wife, Hortênsia, whom Amâncio, longing to have fun and many adventures in the great city, starts to court unsuccessfully. Shortly afterwards, Amâncio moves to a pension owned by a certain João Coqueiro, a student who is the son of a well-off but now bankrupt family. He married a French woman twice his age and lives managing a boardinghouse where a varied human fauna exists. João Coqueiro has a sister, Amelinha, twenty-three years old, whom the whole family tries to marry off to Amâncio. The entire novel is the story of the seduction of Amâncio by Amelinha, interrupted by necessary pauses for ritual hypocrisy, and by the young man's useless attempts to seduce Hortensia and another lady, named Lúcia, who lives in the pension. After seducing the poor Amâncio, Amelinha, who with all the family already exploits him ruthlessly, wants to get married. Amâncio runs away, but João Coqueiro has him arrested under the false accusation of carnal violence. In the trial Amâncio is absolved; João Coqueiro, desperate, pursues Amâncio to the hotel where he now lives and kills him. End of story.

The story obviously has a very frail plot. The main theme—the seducer Amâncio being seduced—alternates with the personal stories of the other guests of the pension, all members of that meager and scarce middle class compelled to live in relatively modest lodgings compared to the aristocratic houses. We find there a pair of artists eternally fighting among themselves and with their creditors; an idler with his wife—the beautiful Lúcia courted by and courting Amâncio; an employee in the city commerce; a *guarda-livros*—that is, an accountant; a Portuguese with tuberculosis who later dies in Amâncio's arms; and another pair of rather uninteresting characters.

In *Casa de pensão* the study of the varied characters and their personalities is more interesting than the story itself. The first character is of course Amâncio, the only one who, being endowed with a remarkable family fortune, does not belong to the middle class. He therefore awakens the aggressive interest of women, namely Amelinha and Lúcia. Amâncio is the typical representative of a human fauna that particularly flourished in Rio de Janeiro in those years: young people from rich families who always thought of having fun and enjoying life without ever concerning themselves with any working activity. Here he comes to the capital, the Court, as Rio used to be called, rather clumsy in his provincial elegance. "He wore a white suit, had a brooch with an emerald on his shirt, a diamond ring on his left hand, and a big golden chain on his stomach."[28] He arrived in Rio full of hopes; in his imagination the capital is like an enchanted place, like Dumas's Paris, "full of students and seamstresses where he could have all his adventures without causing scandal as in that damned province." He wanted "a big old city, full of gloomy streets, full of mystery, of hotels, of gambling houses, of suspicious places and capricious women, great enchanting and libertine ladies capable of anything just for a moment of pleasure."[29] His childhood, the world he left behind, was similar to the world of many young people sharing his same conditions: brought up by an excessively severe father ("in the Portuguese way," in the author's words), he lived morbidly attached to his mother and grew up in an environment of continuously sensually excited and disturbed women. The vaguely morbid setting with the constant company of women reminds us of the childhood of Padre Amaro in Eça de Queirós's novel. It reminds one also of the characteristic *menino-diabo*, the devilish child described by Machado de Assis in *Memórias póstumas de Brás Cubas*, because of his continuous mischief, instigated but never punished, and despotic wishes, always satisfied when he goes on vacation with his grandmother. During his childhood there was also a Black wet nurse similar to Mônica, the one who brought up Ana Rosa in *O mulato*:

> They would say she was an excellent slave: she had very good manners, she never argued with the whites, never answered back: she tolerated the hardest punishments without saying a harsh word, without making a gesture of violence. While the whip whistled on her shoulders she would just moan and let her tears run silently across her cheeks.[30]

Casa de pensão is not a novel centered on slavery, just as *O mulato* was not. Both are novels written during the period of slavery; in each the author, though professing liberal ideas, embodies the conditioned reflexes of a man immersed in a world where slavery is commonplace. This absolves him from making any comments on this unhappy woman, whom he does not even call by name—*uma preta*, a Black woman, that is all—and who exists only as a function for the main character. Having bought her for little money because of her shabby aspect and bad health, Amâncio's father cured her with good food and made himself an excellent slave. Of course there is no humanitarian satisfaction in this, but only the pleasure of having made an excellent business deal, "a good bargain," as if he were dealing with a car that he had repaired.

> The *negra* became very attached to the little boy. She stayed up for him during consecutive nights and showed such care that her master, when the son stopped being breast-fed, consented to give her her liberty for the six hundred *mil-réis* that she had saved over the last fifteen years. But the *preta* never abandoned her white masters' house and continued to serve as before; except, of course, for the punishments, because the poor thing, besides being free, was already advanced in age.[31]

There is something worth noting in this passage, something similar to the language of slave owners, even though this was not the author's intention. Amâncio's father bought the slave for a few pennies, *duas patacas* in the writer's words; then he gives her her freedom in exchange for six-hundred mil-réis, thus making a good deal even without counting the services already given and that in practice he continues to have a slave (which perhaps was part of his calculations, for where could an old ex-slave go in that society?). Yet he consents to "give her her freedom" because the poor woman, the "great bargain" fully repaired, was worth—and the author says it—a *conto de réis*, which is more than her master accepts in payment to free her. Azevedo does not comment on this. He creates the character solely to tell us that, since the poor woman who had breast-fed Amâncio was in bad health, she must be the cause, according to the scientific determinism of the time, of the diseases afflicting the young man.

Amâncio comes to Rio de Janeiro with an official excuse: he must attend college, and he picks medical school for lack of any better choice. Naturally, in his simple sincerity of debauchery, he understands that all the time devoted to study is time taken away from fun. Moreover, he knows perfectly well that he will never be a good doctor and that he will always have the money necessary to obtain the services of the best doctors any time he needs one. Yet he understands that in his case it is merely a question of form. "It is not a question here of making a 'physician,' but rather of making a 'doctor,' no matter of what kind. It is not the question of gaining a 'profession,' but rather of obtaining a 'title.' You don't need a job, but rather a position in society."[32] Amâncio's reasoning is very interesting because it reflects the thought of the entire society at the time, for which the charm of a title had a basic importance independent from the work one performed or might eventually perform. The slightest idea of a work ethic and a sense of duty towards one's fellow men and society exists neither for Amâncio nor for his contemporaries who find themselves in the same position. And later on, almost to reinforce this concept: "Medicine would be useful to some poor young man who might need it in order to live, someone who is not in my position."[33] At the end of the novel, when Amâncio receives the news of his father's death, after the first shock the first thought that comes to his mind is that now he can spend whatever he wants without having to account to anyone.

> Eventually Amâncio found himself free and master of his own fortune; he could spend at his pleasure without having to worry about keeping to his monthly allowance. He wasn't even concerned about the risk of exhausting his money because he could still count upon what he could inherit from his mother and grandmother.[34]

Not only does the ethical problem of the responsibility of wealth not cross the mind of our young man, but neither does the more basic and selfish one of investing that wealth so as not to waste it.

Amâncio's position regarding problems of an economic character is, however, shared by many other representatives of the same class. João Coqueiro lives a shabby and dull life as the owner of a boarding house (and to get to that position he had to marry a woman twice his age) because his father, an old-fashioned aristocrat, has squandered all the estate that his wife brought him as dowry.

> Lourenço was already ruined when he got married. Of all he had been and of all he had owned, all that remained was, besides his whiskers, the habit of doing absolutely nothing. In the best groups, however, one always mentioned his distinguished demeanor of *fidalgo* and one talked with benevolence of his personal qualities and his eternally youthful spirit.[35]

This fidalgo, Lourenço Coqueiro, had already squandered a fortune, his own; his marriage to a rich woman rescued him from ruin and one could imagine that the past experience has served him as a good lesson. Instead, Lourenço, although his responsibilities have grown with marriage, repeats only the same mistakes; and it is not even a question of a choice between a life of pleasure and one of work. He could have reconciled both by living wisely, but he was too much affected by a world that did not have an authentic work ethic. Among his fidalgo obsessions it is worth remembering the intention of imparting a rough and inconclusive education upon his son despite the latter's lack of enthusiasm. Finally his fetishism for an old emblazoned revolver, the same one that João Coqueiro later used to commit his crime: "And how many times, trembling with fear, he had seen him discharge that same weapon against an orange which a slave kept still with a raised hand."[36] Again it was always a slave, even for this tropical William Tell who is neither crazy enough to use his son nor unsophisticated enough to use a normal target. Here again the institution creates a role: the slave exists and therefore is used to provide his master with a cheap thrill.

Pereira is of the same mold as Lourenço Coqueiro and Amâncio, although they are separated by different family fortunes. He is a guest of the pension, presumably the husband of Lúcia. Pereira is an absurd character who can only be explained as the product of a certain world and a certain time: he is a mollusklike person, who lives in a continuous rest and never makes any decisions; nothing even alters his tranquility. He lives together with Lúcia, a beautiful and aggressive woman who, after seducing him, practically imposed herself on him—he was the only man available on whom she could blame her pregnancy.

> Pereira accepted her as he would have accepted any other imposition because he was one of those men who prefer the state of disease to the annoyance of the remedy. Only at the end of four days of honeymoon, since Lúcia insisted with her marriage ideas, this easy-going person declared with the greatest calm that he could not make her happy on that account, because since the age of eighteen he had been married to an old witch whose whereabouts Pereira did not know, nor wanted to know anything about.[37]

This eternal sleepyhead lives with Lúcia at the expense of a benevolent uncle, and after the uncle's death he drags himself from one pension to another, always followed by creditors and always dragged by his woman, who is always restless and seeking a man who might free her from the situation she has got herself into.

Lúcia's target is, of course, Amâncio. But Amâncio is Amelinha's favorite hunting ground. The two women unleash a war in which relatives and others participate, with the exception of the always-sleeping Pereira.

If Ana Rosa was quite aggressive toward Raimundo, Amelinha and Lúcia are no less aggressive in their attacks against what is called (God knows why) the stronger sex. Lúcia plays hard, she does not beat around the bush. With Pereira, once she saw that she had exhausted any classic advance, "seeing at the end that the moron was incapable of any action or reaction, she took the initiative and the thing was solved instantaneously."[38]

Two other women insert themselves between Lúcia and Amelinha. The first one is Nini, the daughter of João Coqueiro's wife from his first marriage, a poor girl who is afflicted with a nervous disease and who attacks Amâncio every time she sees him. The other one is Hortênsia, who is similar to Machado's Sofia in *Quincas Borba* because of her continuously offering and then withdrawing herself, giving and denying in a seesaw of never-kept promises that lead Amâncio to despair.

The whole story unfolds in a Rio de Janeiro that conceals its provincialism with a continuous imitation of Paris: the newly arrived Amâncio is astonished by the Parisian demeanor of the waiters, whom his friend addresses in French; when he gets out of prison his colleagues greet him triumphantly at the Hotel de Paris while a musical band composed of Germans plays the Marseillaise. This continuous refusal of a national identity that resolves itself in a perpetual search for what is foreign finds its expression also in phrases such as the following, which João Coqueiro's wife addresses to Amelinha to compliment her beauty and elegance: "You don't even look like a Brazilian!"[39] That may seem rather strange to us, accustomed as we are to the exaltation of a certain type of feminine beauty, of which Brazil produces some splendid examples. But the search for an ideal beauty conceived exclusively in foreign terms led to these aberrations of taste.

Casa de pensão is a good book, a perceptive and interesting description of the life of the so-called *carioca* middle class in the second half of the nineteenth century. The slaves, the Blacks, appear here in the background because they are the condition sine qua non of the very existence of Brazil in those years: the Black boy holds the orange that serves as a target for Lourenço Coqueiro's revolver—and the author does not say anything more, never mentions whether or not there has been an accident in the performance. The former nurse of Amâncio is not even granted a name and is only mentioned to explain the precocious rheumatism of her foster son. Another Black character is Sabino, Amâncio's moleque, his companion of revelry, his accomplice from his first school escapades to his last sentimental adventures. There is also a young anonymous mulatto girl who is Pereira's and Lúcia's slave: in fact the two penniless, debt-ridden good-for-nothings must have a slave to justify their status as petit bourgeois and be helped in their little daily needs, such as taking a glass of water, asking whether dinner is ready, bringing a letter. And the poor slave is the constant target of all her master's creditors who try to get ahold of her to recover their lost money. At the end João Coqueiro succeeds in "confiscating" her as a balance for the last unpaid bill.

With *O cortiço* (*The Apartment Building*, 1890) Azevedo shifts his attention from the adventures of the middle class to those of the nascent proletariat. Those are the years—the story is set in that time immediately preceding the end of slavery and the advent of the Republic—when in Brazil, and especially in Rio de Janeiro, a slow and decisive transformation was taking place. A new class composed of bankers, speculators, and intermediaries, who made large profits with the export of coffee, was developing side by side with the former class of masters, the great landowners. New capital, especially English, provided the basis of this decisive change. The country, the sleeping giant, aroused greed because of its immense unexploited riches. Someone was always ready to awaken it from its dream, which had already lasted too long. The great capital was determined to make Brazil enter a new economic cycle in which there was no room for slavery. Once the slave trade had been abolished in the middle of the century, thanks to the decisive intervention of England, the country had opened its gates to the new labor force consisting of European immigrants, at first Germans and later Italians, who arrived in great numbers following the agreements stipulated among the various governments. The ethnic predominance, which once was Black, was thus decisively changed: racial reasons, either hidden or apparent, as well as obviously economic ones, had impelled the ruling class to want this change that protected it from a possible future ethnic conflict. The white immigrants had brought with them a new concept of work. Although they came initially to substitute for the slaves, they intended to become masters and to enrich themselves, to break that fatal circle of poverty to which the mother country, in its dearth of natural resources, had condemned them. The immigrant came with a different human preparation. Made aggressive by other battles, they came from the Old World where the protection of the master could no longer save them from hunger. The Black slave was doubly unfit for the new forms of neocapitalist labor: the Blacks came from a tropical world where saving, in the primordial sense of accumulating food for the cold season, had no meaning. In the tropics, all that is not immediately consumed perishes rapidly: however, everything also flourishes very rapidly. The very ancient tribal structure, decisively communitarian, was an obstacle to individual saving. As slaves they had been forced to work only for others, for the masters who whipped them. The immigrant, in contrast, came from a world in which saving had been based upon the need to survive long, cold winters, a need confirmed historically by famines, wars, and social transformations facilitated by the proximity of the city to the country; and this proximity had been many times the prelude to social transformation leading to that urbanization which had created the bourgeoisie.

The immigrant had not been brought in chains, although the ships in which they traveled were not any better than the slave boats. They came determined to transform their condition. The only way to do so was to transform the world to which they came. This is how, in essence, neocapitalist Brazil at the end of the century was born, replacing patriarchal, agricultural, and slavist Brazil.

O cortiço is the fictional history of a historical moment, the story of the last slaves and the first proletarians. It is a story of poverty, defeat, resignation, conquest, and victory. It is a bitter story, according to the literary canons of naturalism, where material victory inevitably implies the renunciation of inner happiness. It is also the story of a world upset by a profound identity and trust crisis, where the old values—but were there any?—were negated and replaced by an obscure and gross materialism.

O cortiço is a typical chorus novel with hundreds of protagonists whose stories interrelate and separate continuously. The cortiço, the apartment building, is the place where many human beings drag along their daily existence in the hope of redemption that will never come. The cortiço is an important moment in the history of urban Brazil, a moment destined to repeat itself whenever the capitalist society needs a new underproletariat, which in its turn creates new cortiços.

Because of its structure as a multiple story, *O cortiço* is a novel that does not have a well-defined plot. It does have, however, a connecting thread given by the creator and master of the cortiço, who is the Portuguese João Romão, an ex-farm laborer, a man who, working at a terrifying rhythm, saved all of the surplus and a good part of the necessities, stole whatever it was possible to steal, and became, in the period of a decade, the owner of a cortiço, a tavern, and a rock quarry. In this task he was helped by a Black slave, Bertoleza, with whom he was mated and who gave him all her savings so that he could buy her a *carta de alforria*, the document that gave her her freedom. João Romão took possession of her savings and gave her a false *carta*. This is one of the many intrigues exemplifying his existence. The two work practically in a monopoly: the quarry workers live in the shacks of the cortiço, which they rent; they do their shopping at João Romão's tavern and grocery while their wives, who are usually laundresses, are compelled to pay rent for the various fountains abounding in the cortiço. For all these reasons, combined with the full expansion of Rio de Janeiro in these years, the fortune of João Romão was destined to increase. Bordering the cortiço was a *sobrado*, a masterly house belonging to another Portuguese, Miranda, a wealthy merchant. He is not any richer than João Romão, but he has solid bourgeois aspirations, having married a lady of the upper Brazilian society with a good dowry. He aspires therefore to an aristocratic title, a baronetcy, which he will obtain after the payment of a suitable donation, as was the custom in the last years of the Empire. The two Portuguese are continuously arguing over questions of boundary, and they hate each other passionately: João Romão hates Miranda for his bourgeois demeanor, Miranda envies João Romão for his ever-increasing wealth. A third Portuguese arrives in the cortiço. It is Jerônimo, a serious and honest worker who starts to manage the quarry. He is married to another Portuguese, Piedade, a good housewife, and they have a daughter whom they bring up very well. Jerônimo's misfortune is called Rita Baiana, a beautiful mulatta, the lover of a *capoeira*, a gangster, a mulatto called Firmo. Because of Rita Baiana, Jerônimo is wounded by Firmo during a fight; later, Jerônimo kills him in an ambush; he then abandons work, wife, and daughter, who end up in disgrace. In fact Jerônimo ruins himself; he is always drunk, troubled by remorse, unable to free himself from a state of subjection to the mulatta. The various stages of Jerônimo's degradation are counterbalanced by João Romão's repeated financial successes. João Romão has transformed the cortiço into a petit-bourgeois building and is investing his wealth in various activities. At this point João Romão himself becomes a bourgeois and the best way for him to reach this goal is to marry his former rival Miranda's only daughter: thus he will be able to aspire even to a title—viscount or maybe count—having married the daughter of a baron. Concerning Bertoleza, who has worked all her life side by side with João Romão and has some rights over his wealth, the solution is easily found. She is still a slave, although she is convinced she is free thanks to the fake carta de alforria given her by João Romão; it will be enough then to notify her former master to come and get her. This promptly happens. The novel concludes with Bertoleza's suicide while João Romão receives a delegation of abolitionists who come to bring him a diploma as an honorary member.

As also in previous works, Azevedo is a great master of choral descriptions. Still a classic of Brazilian literature is the scene of the morning hubbub, when the cortiço awakens and the noises, the noises of the world that starts to live again, are born from the various parts to fuse into a roaring crescendo that covers all other sounds:

> It was five in the morning and the *cortiço* awakened, opening, not its eyes, but its numerous doors and aligned windows. It was a happy and satisfying awakening of one who has slept like a log for seven hours. In the meantime heads congested by sleep emerged from the doors; one heard full yawns, strong as the resounding of waves; throats clearing themselves everywhere, cups starting to jingle; the perfume of warm coffee spread all over dominating all the others; the first words, the first "good mornings" were exchanged from window to window; conversations interrupted the night before were resumed; the children started to make confusion while, from inside the houses, came the muffled cry of the babies who could not yet walk. Shortly afterwards, around the faucets, there was an increasing hubbub; a tumultuous swarming of males and females. One after the other, they washed their faces uncomfortably under a thread of water that ran at the height of five palms. The doors of the latrines never stopped, there was an opening and closing at every moment, an entering and going out without truce. They did not waste time there inside and they came out still tying their pants or their skirts.
>
> The noise increased condensing itself; the daily tumult was accentuated; at this point one could not distinguish separate voices, but only one compact noise that filled the entire *cortiço*. They started to do their shopping at the grocery; discussions and arguments interrelated; one heard laughter and cussing; one did not speak any more, one screamed only. One felt in that sanguine fermentation, in that vigorous appetite of wild plants that sink their vigorous roots into the black and nourishing mud of life, the animal pleasure of existing, the triumphant satis-

faction of breathing the earth. The hubbub reached its climax. The Italian pasta factory in the neighborhood started to work, increasing the noise with its monotonous breathing of steam machines. The trips to the grocery multiplied, transforming themselves into the constant swarming of a crazy ant colony.[40]

As a good naturalist—coming furthermore from a solid and well-educated bourgeoisie—Azevedo has a love-hate relationship towards the most primitive manifestations of existence: he is fascinated by them but he cannot sublimate and accept them completely; for him the existential rhythm has no way out, it becomes a prison and ultimately a condemnation. When that cortiço, thanks to João Romão's speculations, improves its structures and takes on a petit bourgeois aspect, a new cortiço will be born immediately to receive the riffraff of the first and the new wave of daily laborers who come attracted by the mirage of easy money. Here is the new cortiço, which its owner has baptized pompously São Romão:

And in that putrid and fuming earth, in that hot and muddy humidity a world begins to swarm, to boil, to increase, something alive, a generation, which seemed to bud right there, in that sea of mud, and which was multiplying like so many larvae in the manure pile.[41]

São Romão transforms itself slowly and becomes a series of dwellings progressively cleaner and inhabited by a new social class: artisans, students, minor public employees, and young clerks. The demand for housing is always higher and the prices become always less accessible to many of the former renters. In the meantime a new cortiço arises, the Cabeça de Gato whose proprietor is a well-off *conselheiro*, a high functionary in the Empire, who is unable to appear himself because of social decorum and uses a Portuguese as his deputy. The new cortiço is presented by the author in a manner decisively worse than the first:

As soon as São Romão enlarged itself, the Cabeça de Gato sank into vulgarity, becoming more and more foul, more and more despicable, more and more *cortiço*, living satisfied with its own garbage and mud, which the other one rejected, as if its ideal was that of preserving unchanged forever the true type of the dormitory by the river, the legitimate one, the legendary one; the one in which there was a *samba* and a fight every night; that in which men were killed without the police being able to discover the murderer; a breeding ground for sensual larvae, in which brothers and sisters slept together in the same bed; a paradise for worms; a quagmire of hot and fuming mud from which life sprang brutally as if from putrefaction.[42]

The first observation is that Azevedo gives here a description still valid for the *favelas* that surround the residential quarters of the great cities and replace the former cortiços. The writer gives here an example of two types of popular dwellings in a city and a civilization in transition. São Romão is one type of residence that accompanies the evolution of the time: the city changes, the inhabitants change generally for the better, and also the houses change. The Cabeça de Gato represents, instead, the other possibility on which both literary fiction and social reality agree: there is and always will be, the author seems to say, in a certain type of civilization a class of men destined to live in the mud, and to be the lower steps in a world that pays attention and admiration only to the top; and if some of them leave the mud and the dirt to go and live in a better place, this is only because others are replacing them in the room they left empty behind. And when they go and live in a clean and renewed São Romão, a thought will always follow them that they are living in a world that does not tolerate the defeated, for whom there will always be a Cabeça de Gato waiting a few hundred meters away.

O cortiço is a solidly constructed novel; it is a great picture in which there is a vast gallery of characters who are placed according to a precise order. Three examples, all valid, correspond to three types of figures easily recognizable in the labor world of Rio de Janeiro in those years. They are, in order, João Romão, Miranda, and Jerônimo. All three are workers and Portuguese. It is clear why they are workers. In a social novel the protagonist must belong to the more humble classes, which progressively replaced the slavehand. It is less clear to us why they should be Portuguese. The reasons are varied and all valid; they must be foreigners because the Brazilian proletariat was numerically scarce in a country where slavery still reigned. The Brazilian proletarians were mostly ex-slaves or descended from slaves; they were people who had no idea, because they had not seen it, of the ruthless, competitive neocapitalist world. The Brazilian proletarians aspired, both in Brazil and in the novel, to the petty prestige of public employment; they were often even condemned to extend their slavery into employment at minimum salary offered by the then arising industry. They must be Portuguese because the other European immigrants, Germans and Italians, had taken a different direction: the Germans were confined to the rural colonies of Santa Catarina (where the use and teaching of German had predominated until President Vargas forbade it in the years preceding the Second World War). The Italians, more assimilated into the Brazilian world, had founded the rural colonies of Rio Grande do Sul or had directed themselves toward the coffee plantations of São Paulo. It is reasonable to suppose that Azevedo was not familiar with this type of immigrant since there were few Italians in Rio de Janeiro at that time. The Italians present in the novel are in fact a small group of street vendors, dirty and noisy, who end up by moving to Cabeça de Gato when São Romão improves and "they are replaced by cleaner people."[43]

The Portuguese were and always have been a constant factor in immigration to Brazil. João Romão, Miranda, and Jerônimo were three representatives of the Portuguese proletariat present at the end of the last century. We will see in detail how these were represented.

We have said that *O cortiço* is the story of the last slaves and the first proletarians. It is first of all the story of Bertoleza and of João Romão. There is a sarcastic Brazilian proverb that says that the best thing the Portuguese created in Brazil was the mulatto: the joke hides a truth, that many Portuguese immigrants mated frequently with the Blacks. The thing is explainable: despite all the racial prejudices, of which we have seen a short survey in *O mulato*, and considering that many of these men had absolutely no economic possibility of creating a regular family, the only possibility they had of a regular sexual life was the *amigação*, that is living together, *more uxorio*, with a slave or with a Black woman who was not in a position to expect any future prospects. This was João Romão's initial condition:

> João Romão had been from the age of thirteen to twenty-five employed by a vendor who had enriched himself among the four walls of a filthy and dark tavern in the alleys of the Botafogo quarter. In those twelve years João Romão had succeeded in saving the little that he had earned so that when his master went back to the homeland he left him, for payment for back salaries, not only the store with whatever was inside it, but also a *conto* and a half.[44]

Saving will be a permanent obsession in João Romão's life; at a time in which devaluation was minimal, and the demand for capital very high, saving had a value unknown in modern times. Having become an owner, the young Portuguese launches himself into work with renewed enthusiasm and, at this point, he meets Bertoleza, a Black slave who had lived with a Portuguese porter who died from overwork. Having obtained the trust of the woman, he proposes that they live together and "she accepted with open arms, happy to live together again with a Portuguese because, as every *cafuza*, Bertoleza did not want to subject herself to *negros*, and looked instinctively for a man of a superior race."[45] (Let us note here briefly that the author did not free himself of the racial prejudice that he shared with his contemporaries.) Bertoleza represents the beginning of João Romão's economic fortune, first, because he takes away her savings by cheating her with a false carta de alforria, then later, because he finds in her a very valuable collaborator:

> Bertoleza on João Romão's side took over the triple role of employee, servant, and lover. She worked hard but always cheerfully; at four in the morning she was already prepared for her daily duties. She started the coffee for the clients and immediately afterwards she prepared breakfast for the workers of a quarry that was behind the field beyond the tavern. She swept the floor of the house, she cooked, she sold at the stall of the tavern when her friend was busy outside; she was in charge of the other sales in the intervals of the other tasks and she spent evenings in front of the tavern where with a terracotta oven she cooked livers and fried sardines that João Romão had bought at the Peixe beach in the mornings, her sleeves pulled up and clogs on her bare feet. And that demon of a woman found even the time to wash and mend her man's and her own laundry.[46]

During the time they lived together, they led a miserable existence. They slept on a straw pallet and they ate products that were unsalable. "João Romão neither took a walk nor did he ever go to church on Sunday."[47] Thus, day after day by cheating people whenever possible, by buying for two bits what the slaves stole from their masters, by stealing at night, with Bertoleza's help, the materials of a nearby construction yard, João Romão ended up becoming the owner of the quarry and of a piece of land on which he built the first three shacks that later on would be transformed into the cortiço of São Romão.

The rest of the story is nothing more than the ineluctable progression of João Romão's fortune. He spends his time collecting money that he is practically unable to spend because he does not know what to do with it. João Romão is, in the context of a Brazil in transition, the new man. Even though he is a rich man, in one basic feature he is different from the other owners: he does not have slaves; he has people working for him, but they are all people living in a state of liberty. This happens not because the sordid Portuguese merchant is prejudiced against slavery—his only idea is to become rich at any cost and he has neither the time nor the capacity to think of anything else; the only reason is that in the new capitalist order there is no room for the slave. The static wealth of the older fazendeiros, based upon the unchangeable value of the property and the constant buying power of money, was being regularly replaced by the dynamic concept of wealth, of money that generates new money, of economic survival tied to the continuous and ineluctable increase of production. In this respect, the rough, mean, and narrow-minded João Romão is a representative of the new times.

In this context Bertoleza's story takes on the sad meaning of a parable and becomes the concrete symbol of the history of the Black slave in Brazil. On a smaller scale João Romão does with her what his compatriots had done over three centuries: he exploits her to the maximum in all ways, as labor power and as a woman; and, when the time comes for him to change social positions by becoming a bourgeois through marriage to Miranda's daughter, he pushes her back into her original condition as a slave. *O cortiço* was written in 1890, two years after the emancipation of the slaves. During three centuries the master class had constructed rural wealth by exploiting Black labor: at the moment of converting this wealth on the industrial plane, the door to European immigration was open and the slaves were given freedom without even attempting a sham of social and rural reform. Incapable of competing with the more aggressive competition, just at the moment in which they could have taken advantage of the labor power and inserted themselves into the new productive system, the Blacks, now formally free, became definitely marginalized in the world of the slave-proletariat. In this Bertoleza's story is symbolic of other stories.

João Romão's relationship with Bertoleza had always been criticized by his enemies, starting with Miranda; mating on a stable basis with a Black woman, living together more uxorio, was considered at the time the lowest social point to which a white man could fall. Obviously the social criticism was much more benevolent, if not even tolerant, when the relationship between a white man and a Black woman was fleeting or occasional and did not evolve into a stable union. In *O mulato*, even the very discreet and highly respected Dias visited a mulatta every Saturday night: but the affair had no social consequences, because it stopped where it started.

João Romão's and Bertoleza's relationship ends naturally the day when the Portuguese decides to become a bourgeois and starts to enjoy the money he accumulated during so many years of sacrifice. This moment of crisis occurs when João Romão reads in the newspaper that his neighbor-rival compatriot Miranda has been granted the title of baron.

Of the three Portuguese characters in the novel Miranda is undoubtedly the least interesting. We meet him at first as a textile merchant with a solid economic position. He is married to a Brazilian woman who betrays him and whom he does not dare leave because his commercial activities are guaranteed by her dowry. He is a solid bourgeois with his sobrado, a distinguished manor, with his good social relations, his upper-class friendships, his financial speculations, and his parties that are amply reported by the newspapers. Now his baronetcy provokes a violent crisis in João Romão. And it is thus that João Romão decides to imitate Miranda to the point, at the end, where he himself aspires to an aristocratic title; this decision is not only expressed in the new types of business in which he is involved—speculations, buying and selling of stocks—but also in his manner of living itself, in his refusal to continue his work in the tavern serving the *negralhada*—as the author defines the Blacks of the neighborhood; in his type of clothes, in the entertainment that he grants himself, and the new habits he acquires. And while João Romão assumes the attitude of the nouveau riche, Bertoleza continues to be "always the same dirty *crioula*, always full of work, without ever taking a Sunday or a holiday off; she had not shared in any way her friend's new life; on the contrary, the more he rose in social position, the more the unhappy woman was humiliated in her slavery."[48] The author naturally omits telling us that Bertoleza did not have any possibility of following her friend in this new social climb; the world of Rio de Janeiro in those years would have not permitted a Black and uneducated woman to leave her kitchen and enter a coffee shop or a theater.

Thus the distance between the two becomes irreconcilable. When João Romão comes back from the party at Miranda's house to face the bed that he shares with his friend, he thinks "he has to lie down, alongside that *preta*, who smelled of kitchen and fish! He, who smelled of perfume and was so beaming, had to put his head on the same dirty pillow in which the damned hair of that *preta* sank?"[49]

There is no more room for Blacks in João Romão and Miranda's life. The two ex-enemies are reconciled in the renewed faith of bourgeois values, or at least those of that particular bourgeoisie who repudiated and abhorred their recent plebeian origins even more because these origins were very recent.

The third Portuguese character is Jerônimo, the pure, serious, and diligent Jerônimo. He is the kind of immigrant who succeeds in the new land solely thanks to his work, without recourse to the cheating or fraud of which his fellow countryman João Romão is a master. He worked on the plantation from which he withdrew disgustedly because "he had to subject himself to the same kind of work together with the *negros* in the same degrading environment, enclosed like an animal, without aspirations and without future."[50] He tries to make his fortune in the big city and shortly afterwards, thanks to his ability and his perseverance, he becomes an overseer. He is employed as such by João Romão for his quarry, which he succeeds in bringing to optimal levels of production, thus winning the esteem of his master, of the workers, and of the neighbors. Jerônimo, as does João Romão, represents the new order: they are both men who have accepted fully the rules of the game of the capitalist world that was then emerging. They believe in work, in organization, in saving, in competition. They differ only in the forms of investments: Jerônimo, within the limits of his salary and honesty of character, limited himself to securing a good education for his daughter.

We already noted in *O mulato* Azevedo's antipathy towards the Portuguese, an antipathy he shares with many other authors. It may seem strange, but the Portuguese immigrant, the direct descendant of those who discovered and colonized Brazil, was the one who did not assimilate into the Brazilian world. He came to the new land to become rich enough to go back to his own land, he usually worked in a store or grocery, and he did not easily assimilate himself into the surrounding world. If he let himself assimilate he would become a Brazilian, he would start spending and enjoying himself, he would let go, he would never go back to his own land. João Romão lives enclosed in his sordid world until the wealth he has accumulated allows him to enter the Brazilian world as a bourgeois. Jerônimo lived solely for his work and his family: and when he came home at night he took his guitar and, seated on the steps of his home, together with his wife, "gave full vent to his nostalgia for his land with melancholy songs, letting his exiled soul return from the torrid areas of America to the sad villages of his childhood."[51] Jerônimo's titanic force consists mainly in his feeling and being an expatriate. Yet, at some point his *fado* crosses the sensual song from Bahia; the white man meets the mulatta and, through the woman, the expatriate becomes acquainted with the new land.

In Jerônimo's story we have a series of antitheses reflecting the dramatic scheme the author meant to give to the whole tale: the initial clash between Portugal and Brazil (symbolized by the two different ways of singing, the Portuguese fado and the Bahian *chorado*) is followed by the clash between Jerônimo and Rita Baiana, with a fight between the latter and Piedade, Jerônimo's wife, and the various clashes between Piedade and Jerônimo himself.

It starts with the contrast on the musical level. Jerônimo's slow and melancholy songs are followed and accompanied by the other inhabitants of the cortiço. The atmosphere of sadness is suddenly interrupted by an eruption of Brazilian music. "The first chords of the *negro* music were enough to awaken the blood of all those people as if someone had whipped their body with wild nettles."[52] Slowly, but strongly, the Brazilian music with passionate and vibrant rhythm asserts itself and involves all those present starting with the poor and naïve Jerônimo. Then the moon rises and Rita Baiana appears with her naked arms and shoulders, and she starts to dance.

> That mulatta contained a great mystery, the synthesis of all the impressions he had received arriving there: she was the ardent light of noon; she was the burning heat of the siesta in the *fazenda*; she was the warm aroma of the tropical plants which had stunned him in the Brazilian forests, she was . . .[53]

Rita Baiana equals Brazil; through this simple equation Jerônimo knows the woman, the Portuguese knows Brazil.

The Jerônimo–Rita Baiana story is the most delicate and the richest in contradictions in the entire novel. First of all the author takes a clear position, solving the eternal identity crisis that has troubled and still troubles Brazilian authors. Rita Baiana is Brazil, Rita Baiana is mulatta, therefore Brazil is a mulatto country. This truth, which is supported by statistics, although not without some dispute, was much less accepted in the period in which Azevedo wrote *O cortiço*. It is and was a courageous position if it were not heavily affected by a series of prejudices typical of the time, which the author accepts automatically. It is true that Rita Baiana represents Brazil, but what kind of Brazil does she represent? First of all, the writer always indicates Rita Baiana as "the mulatta," "the mestiza," as if mulatta were a separate sex, as if Rita Baiana were not quite a woman. Rita is "fickle as any mulatta," has a lover called Firmo, a mulatto himself; but he is an authentic mulatto who has nothing to share with the virginal and Hamletic Raimundo, the unlikely protagonist of *O mulato*. Firmo is a vagrant, a good-for-nothing, with a quick and lively intelligence but with no desire to apply it to any profitable activity and especially to any fatiguing work. He is also a rascal, a capoeira, a hooligan who was employed many times in the electoral fights to intimidate the voters. His dream is to obtain a state job where he could spend all his time doing nothing. He is agile, nervous, energetic, proficient in fighting, in singing, and playing the guitar. He is a credible and well-described mulatto character.

Firmo and Jerônimo are rivals because of the beautiful Rita. There is a violent fight between the two (and among the spectators there is a division of fans, according to the nationality of each, Portuguese against Brazilians) ending in the wounding of Jerônimo; then, in turn, Jerônimo assassinates the capoeira with the help of two accomplices. But Firmo's true defeat occurs when Rita Baiana chooses Jerônimo as her lover. And it is here that the author reveals his prejudices: "the mestizo blood claimed its right to perfect itself and Rita preferred the European male of a superior race."[54] Bertoleza too had seen in João Romão "the man of a race superior to her own." Let us note that this is not understandable social superiority—the well-to-do merchant compared to the Black slaves, the headmaster compared to the vagrant capoeira—but rather racial superiority. Both Firmo and Rita are mulattoes, therefore, inferior; for this reason she abandons him and tries to improve herself through the Portuguese. On his part, the Portuguese,

> yielding to the impositions of the environment, despised his Portuguese wife, and wanted the mulatta because the mulatta was pleasure, it was voluptuousness, it was the golden and sour fruit of these American *sertões* where Jerônimo's soul learned the lasciviousness of the monkeys and where his body started to have the sensual smell of a billy goat.[55]

Rita Baiana is Brazil, but Brazil is seen as the corruption and degradation of the white man. As a result it looks rather catastrophic!

Yet, maybe unconsciously and despite his racial theories, Azevedo describes Rita Baiana's behavior as more correct than that of the other female characters: for example, Ana Rosa who blocks Raimundo on the doorstep, after having involuntarily provoked his death and after some ritualistic faintings, marries that dirty pig Dias. As another example, the various ladies and young ladies of *O mulato* invite Raimundo explicitly into their beds. Moreover, in *Casa de pensão* the hysterical Nini assaults the shabby Amâncio with the grips of a wrestler, and Amelinha slips into his bed while Lúcia tries the same instantaneous seduction of him with which she literally seized the somnolent Pereira. Again, in *O cortiço*, Estela, Miranda's wife, is a greedy consumer of young men, either her husband's clerks or students. Even the sweet Pombinha, the daughter of the Portuguese Isabel who gave her the best upbringing (even French lessons) so that she could make a good marriage, once married, betrays her husband, runs away with a lesbian prostitute, and becomes a prostitute herself.

Compared to all these females in heat who play hard, Rita Baiana is perfectly proper. She only dances and shows her inviting beauty; as far as Jerônimo is concerned she acts only as a good neighbor, offers coffee and *parati*, the national *cachaça*, the tasty sugarcane liquor. As far as seduction goes, after all, these are college coed-level ploys.

Yet the author is strict in his judgment of Rita Baiana, maybe because her behavior destroys all the taboos upon which the society of the time was based and which the author shares at least partly. She is a free woman, she does not need anybody for support, she helps her women friends, she is independent to the point that she does not want to marry Firmo because she loves her own freedom and independence. Even with Jerônimo, when Piedade tries to convince her husband, Rita proudly withdraws, leaving the man free to decide. In fact, Rita has probably shown that she could be a better wife than the white woman, and the author could not forgive her for this. The audience, however, consisted of white men and women and not of mulattos.

The Rita Baiana–Piedade comparison (which ends up with a noisy brawl between the Portuguese and Brazilian fans) enlightens interesting aspects of the life-style of the proletarian classes of the time. There is the problem of hygiene, which we might find amusing but which was very important: the Brazilians, tropical people, wash themselves more than the Europeans. Rita washed herself three times a day and three times a day she rubbed her body with aromatic herbs. Jerônimo himself learns to bathe every day to the amazement of Piedade who, instead, continues to consider water with the usual parsimony of the farmers, thus provoking her husband's emotional disinterest as well as his complaints.

The relationship between Jerônimo and Rita Baiana corresponds to the relationship between Jerônimo and Brazil: the more Jerônimo feels tied to Rita the more he participates in her life, the more he becomes Brazilian (*abrasileirou-se*, as the author says); and the more he becomes a Brazilian, the more he degrades himself as a man. Azevedo's pessimistic view leaves no choice: either one lives like João Romão, who shut himself up in his own work like a beast and later, after repudiating the world represented by the poor Bertoleza, moved directly to a bourgeois world that had nothing indigenous in its gross imitation of Europe; or one opens up to the Brazilian world, accepts its mellow way of life, and then one degrades himself and loses himself, as happened to Jerônimo.

Apparently Azevedo felt the deep crisis of national identity and the dangers in the choice of a man who lives and works in a certain world. What was the true Brazil? Was it the imported world, that of the French novels, of the theaters, of the concerts, of the banks, of European fashion in a tropical country? Or was it rather the world taking shape in the new proletarian masses, the mulatto Brazil, the Brazil of the samba, the tropical Brazil, the Brazil that was creating its own popular soul despite the chains of slavery and the official prohibitions? Let us not be unjust towards a writer by judging him with a modern mentality: Aluísio Azevedo lived in a world, in a society of masters and slaves in which the real, the authentic, and the true corresponded to the official truth, that of the ruling classes who identified Brazil and its interests solely with their own interests. The others were nothing, they were slaves, they were Blacks from Africa, barbarous people without civilization. How could the former recognize that they shared something with the latter? That is Azevedo's "to be or not to be" and the solution he suggests seems ambiguous to us. Bertoleza is exploited and then pushed back in her gloomy condition of slavery; Rita Baiana, mulatta, half white, free, identifies herself with her own land acting, however, a totally negative and destructive role for the white man. It is she who defeats Jerônimo; she is the master while Jerônimo is the slave. Once again, *Graecia capta* . . .

Azevedo's naturalistic and nineteenth-century solution becomes inevitable in the moment of sin, in that biblical knowledge of the new land and the new woman both too beautiful to be loved and too female to be totally possessed.

> A slow and deep transformation occurred in him, day after day, hour after hour, upsetting his body to its depths, and making his senses acute, in a mysterious and insidious work of chrysalis. His energy withered slowly: he became contemplative and amorous. The American life and the Brazilian nature now showed him unexpected and seductive aspects, which moved him: he forgot the old ambitious dreams to idealize new happiness, violent and spicy: he had become generous, improvident, and frank, tending to spend more than to save; he acquired desires, tasted pleasures, and became lazy, resigned, vanquished by the imposition of the sun and of the heat, that fire wall with which the eternally rebel spirit of the last native had defended his homeland against the adventurous conquerors.
>
> Thus, little by little, his simple Portuguese farmer's habits changed; and Jerônimo became Brazilian.[56]

The author could not have been any clearer in his conclusions although they seem quite strange to us because they come from a Brazilian: he identifies the process of degradation with that of becoming Brazilian. Yet there are no doubts; with the taste for detail typical of the naturalist writer, he lists all the progressive changes in Jerônimo in his transition from Portuguese to Brazilian. He gives a list, particularly interesting for us, of all the Portuguese dishes that are abandoned in favor of the Brazilian ones, and especially of those of the Bahian cuisine, which is of Afro-Brazilian origin.

It is worth noting at this point that, in the context of the eternal problem created by the crisis of national identity, the Brazilian cuisine of the upper classes willingly ignored for a long time the local products in favor of a European cuisine, which was rarely suited to a tropical climate. It was a sign of distinction, especially for the less wealthy, to offer a European product to celebrate a special event. The wicked Dias of *O mulato* in his weekly meetings with his mulatta used to bring a bottle of wine from Porto. João Romão and Bertoleza do the same to create the fake carta de alforria. Amâncio in *Casa de pensão* toasts also with an Italian Moscato d'Asti to celebrate the end of his studies. A glass of parati, the delicious local rum, was considered vulgar, and the Bahian cuisine, which today the official propaganda represents as one of the best in the world, and rightly so, was then considered clearly common.

The list of dishes from the Bahian cuisine that Jerônimo embraces in his process of becoming a Brazilian could nowadays make a good show on any tourist menu. But to the readers of the time, such dishes looked like a betrayal of the true culinary habits of European origin, a step lower than the good food they saw usually on the plates of the slaves and the poor.

The process of Brazilianization naturally is not limited to culinary habits. Azevedo goes much further in his condemnation.

> The Portuguese became Brazilian forever; he became lazy, a friend to extravagance and excess, luxurious, jealous; he lost forever his love for saving and for order; he lost the hope of becoming rich and he gave himself altogether to the happiness of possessing a mulatta and of being possessed by her, only by her, and nobody else.[57]

Jerônimo's metamorphosis, which in many ways could be viewed as a further opening to the world and to a more cheerful and relaxed way of life, is condemned by the author especially because it does not correspond to a fixed model of life. As much as these authors, Azevedo and his contemporaries, called themselves modern and careful observers of reality, they missed one simple and obvious fact: Brazil is a tropical country, populated mostly by people—Blacks, Indians and their descendants—coming from a tropical world. The only authentic civilization this country could express and which it evidently expresses, had to be naturally a symbiosis between a civilization of European origin and the tropical world. Ignoring this symbiosis, as it happened, brought these writers despite their repeated affirmation of nationalism to a condemnation of anything Brazilian that did not imitate the European model, even when clearly anachronistic in a tropical country.

Azevedo fought courageously against the prejudice of the master class and the provincial world in *O mulato*; he whipped the mean petit bourgeois mentality in *Casa de pensão*, and denounced the hypocrisy of the laws and people who took their fellow humans from slavery and threw them into the condition of ruthlessly exploited proletarians in the neocapitalistic society. Yet he let himself be affected by the prejudice of the world he struggled against when, thanks to his naturalistic and deterministic pseudo-awareness, he thought he had found a negative element in the tropical nature and in the people who came from it and lived by it. This is the great limitation of his otherwise valuable work; a limitation that prevented him from giving a word of hope or plan of salvation to a world which, among uncertainties, crimes, weaknesses, and errors, has found a way of asserting itself by revaluating and giving an authentic cultural value to those expressions of life that moved millions of Jerônimos to become Brazilians forever.

7 MACHADO DE ASSIS

Vanitas Vanitatum

> This last chapter is all negative. I did not reach celebrity status through the invention of the unguent, I was not a minister, I was not a caliph, I was not married. It is true that apart from these deficiencies, I had the good luck of not having to earn my bread with the sweat of my brow. And also, I did not suffer from Dona Placida's death, nor from Quincas Borba's semimadness. On the average any person would imagine that I neither had too much nor too little. And they would imagine wrongly because once I arrived at this side of the mystery I found myself with a small advantage, that is the last negative element in this chapter of negatives. I did not have children, I did not bequeath to any human creature the legacy of our misery.[1]

The feelings of existential vanity, of the absurdity of human life itself, are the constants that accompany all the literary productions of Machado de Assis (1839–1908). His novels do not have any plot, yet they are wonderful studies of environment and excellent psychological analyses in which the protagonists are moved by a destiny whose inner meaning they do not perceive. His first book *Ressurreição* (*Resurrection*, 1872) is the story of a man, Félix, who "occupies the twenty-four chapters with which the author supplies him not to marry the widow Lívia, his moral opposite and therefore the repository of every virtue and courage."[2] There is no real reason preventing Félix from marrying Lívia, whom he loves and who loves him. The only reason is that the protagonist is a weak man, a being unable to realize himself, externally hindered by the fear of living. The love, the happiness, the conquest of a loved being, far from being incentives, are otherwise impediments which hinder Félix from becoming fulfilled as a human being, probably because fulfillment would make him face that existential void of which he is a timid carrier.

In the other early works in which the author makes concessions to the romantic taste of the epoch, the void is realized by means of external elements, the social structures themselves or complicated games of destiny. *A mão e a luva* (*The Hand and the Glove*, 1874) is

SLAVE MARKET

MERCADO DE ESCRAVOS

the story, fragile in plot but rich in environmental analysis, of a decisive ambition, of the beautiful Guiomar and her irresistible social climbing. There is an underlying and bitter irony in Guiomar's love: she "wanted a man who, together with a youthful heart and capacity to love, felt in himself the necessary strength to raise her where all eyes could see her."[3] She eventually finds and conquers such a man, after having rejected others and having ensured for herself the affectionate attention of her godmother. This man adapts himself to her as the hand to the glove and the protagonists of such a perfect union live happily thereafter.

A mão e a luva reflects two poles of the human and literary experience of Machado de Assis: the moment of the ascent and social conquest, so autobiographical of the man Machado—the poor, the mulatto, the stutterer, the epileptic; and the moment of the philosopher Machado—the bitter, detached observer of the vanity of existence. It is an early novel in which the author is still undecided and therefore lets future choices and commitments surface more clearly than he did in the two later works, *Helena* (1876) and *Iaiá Garcia* (1878), in which the romantic theme prevails with a canonical liberating ending, sad for the first novel and happy for the second one.

Later, as he himself stated to Mario de Alencar, Machado de Assis lost all illusions about human beings. Thus his great masterpieces were born. *Memórias póstumas de Brás Cubas* (*The Posthumous Memoirs of Brás Cubas*, 1881) is a life seen through the recollection of one who dedicated his memoirs to "the worm who first chews the cold flesh of my corpse" and who at the same time rejoices in not having to transmit "to any human creature the legacy of our misery." It is the story, encompassing the entire cycle of an existence, of a man who, born rich and therefore not compelled to work, lives in the most trivial and simple way. He had a thoughtless youth, a mercenary love, went to college in Coimbra; he had an unrealized marriage, an adulterous relationship, and partially frustrated ambitions. Nothing brightens even for a moment the opaque triviality of an existence that goes by without ever an original moment. The novel consists of a slow accumulation of reflections that drag on day after day in the calm serenity of someone who does not expect anything from life and is not ready to give anything to it. The protagonist's life is the frugal flowing of miserable actions that are nullified by doubt and uncertainty even before they are accomplished.

Quincas Borba, ten years later, in 1891, is the story of a provincial, Rubião, made wealthy by an inheritance. He comes to Rio where he lives fully the brilliant existence of a man totally integrated in a brilliant society in transition. Progressing from nullity to nullity, realizing himself as one void after another, never able to conquer the woman he loves and equally unable to detach himself from her, he is deprived of his wealth by an astute speculator and evolves toward a slow, ineluctable insanity. Both *Quincas Borba* and *Memórias póstumas de Brás Cubas* are stories in which the obsessive, morbid fixation of nothingness clashes with what Lúcia Miguel Pereira calls "the one who always tormented him, his great enemy, life."[4] The existential vacuum is the adventure of a life on which the writer despite himself never prevails.

Dom Casmurro (1899)—the word *casmurro* means mumbler or complainer—is his masterpiece; it is a work in which the struggle against life results in the denial of affections. "It is his best novel," says Agrippino Grieco, "it is the implacable and irreversible condemnation of love and of any kind of affection."[5] The tragic element in this condemnation, in this denial of love, is that it is regressive in time; it projects itself not only on possible future happiness but also on the certainty of a past happiness. What is invalidated is the memory itself of what has been lived: love, friendship, and the serenity of hours past surface again only to be completely destroyed in memory. These memories include a large garden as the setting for the love story of Bentinho and Capitu, adolescents who play, the black shadows of slaves in the background, the voices that get lost, muffled in the courtyard and in the great halls. Family life passes day by day. Bentinho is torn apart by a mother who wants to make a priest of him and Capitu who wants him as a husband. Capitu, whose large eyes resemble the ocean tide, like the flighty wave the sea impresses on the beach, has the eyes of a devious and deceptive gypsy. She is the one who manipulates Bentinho even before he is aware of being manipulated by an even crueler destiny. Daily life follows: economic prosperity, the marriage between Bentinho and Capitu, the close friendship with another couple, Escobar and Sancha, the birth of a son. Then Escobar dies—drowned in the ocean tide. Capitu cries, her large eyes resembling the tide: "Capitu's eyes stared at the deceased, similar to those of the widow though without her tears and words; her eyes were large and open like the ocean wave out there, as if they wanted to take away the morning swimmer."[6] This long desolate stare gives birth to Bentinho's implacable and ruthless jealousy. Moment by moment he scrutinizes all his past life, analyzing all the moments, searching for that evidence. Because of the first-person narration, however, we will never know whether that evidence is real or the result of the protagonist's paranoia. Once he has detached himself from Capitu and has rejected his own son, Bentinho lives the rest of his life in the bitter and opaque tranquility of one who once again has denied himself in the fear of being happy:

> While telling Magalhães de Azeredo that Leopardi was "one of the saints of his church," that he loved him "both for his verses and his philosophy and for some moral affinity," he added: "It is likely that I myself have my own little hunchback"—that is his epilepsy, the fact of being a mulatto and a stutterer equaled the hunchback of the Italian poet whose skepticism caused that moral affinity.[7]

Probably Machado's attitude is even something more than simple skepticism. It is the full acceptance of the denial of happiness for human nature, it is the patient but anguished expectation of the return to the great void.

In his last works Machado de Assis's crude pessimism is often attenuated by the serene melancholy of someone who has received a lot from life without ever having hoped for much. A new world springs forth, and with this new men: Machado sees them and describes them but he does not live and resonate with them any more; they belong to a time to which he does not feel he belongs. *Esaú e Jacó* is the story of two twins, divided and adversaries since infancy. The story unfolds in the Rio de Janeiro of the bankers of the first industrial investments. It may symbolize the two contrasting Goethian souls, which Machado de Assis brought along in a world that he never loved. And eventually in *Memorial de Aires* we have the fine and retiring character of the diplomat Aires, the writer's alter ego, whose silent withdrawing at the end of the novel symbolizes Machado's last denial of a possible encounter, his leave-taking from life.

The motif of existential vanity that reaches its highest point in the silent agony of Bentinho and Capitu's love is diluted in smiling irony in the numerous novellas that Machado used to write for the newspapers. These are stories in which hazard, futility, and appearances often prevail, sometimes for a good purpose, over the serious and pondered-upon virtues. We have many examples. In *A chave*, Marcelina, the beautiful daughter of Major Calda, goes every morning to bathe on the Flamingo beach. There is a handsome young man, Luís Bastinhos, who courts her at a distance. But Marcelina dislikes him. Then, as it happens in stories of this kind, one day Marcelina is drowning and Luís rescues her. This brave rescue gains him an invitation to the major's house. At this point the story might slip into banality but it is not so because Luís, who is handsome, intelligent, and rich, is liked by everybody except Marcelina who continues to dislike him. Luís is in love with Marcelina but his courtship does not put an arrow in the girl's heart despite the major's approval of the young man. When the romance is on the verge of ending Luís invites another girl to dance and, at this point, everybody finds out that Luís is an excellent dancer. Because of this futile virtue Marcelina falls in love with him.

O caso da viúva is the story of the desperate love of Rocinha for the beautiful Maria Luísa, who marries Vieira to obey her father's will. Rocinha is desperate and the cousin who acted as a go-between for the lovers is embarrassed. The two continue to see each other and even though they no longer converse frequently their mutual passion continues to be strong and apparent. Then one day Vieira dies. Maria Luísa is eventually free to respond to her former lover's passion; the cousin runs to give the good news to Rocinha who

> hesitated, looked at the ground, twisted the chain of his watch among his fingers, opened a book of drawings, put a cigarette in his mouth and ended up by saying that . . .
>
> "What?" asked the cousin anxiously.
>
> That "no," he had no intention of getting married.[8]

Once again, though in a clearly ironic manner, Machado concludes with a refusal. Vanity prevails: a love is born because Luís dances well, or a love ends because Rocinha got fed up.

With such a prolific author examples could be numerous, but we can stop here. We are left to wonder what can we know about his time from a writer like Machado de Assis. What could he really tell us about the local people and events? Augusto Meyer, one of his best critics, writes:

> I don't think he was a creator of characters in the realistic mode; he was a painter of self-portraits, when it was necessary, able to depict very well certain portraits when it was necessary but nonetheless very introspective. He himself was the material, the object, the body of his work. Just when he seemed to forget himself to give an illusion of prominence to the invented characters he fell immediately back on himself in a spontaneous recovery, and he locked himself in a darkroom with the purpose of looking at the negatives in the light of an implacable lucidity. He depicted therefore the Rio of his time, its people, and the environment of his time for the sole purpose of cultivating freely his passion of psychological analysis—an indirect, unveiled outlet, sometimes even unconscious, of his own pessimism.[9]

It is undoubtedly true, as the author himself admitted, that Machado de Assis is above all concerned with depicting himself and that the study of others is secondary to the study of his own ego. But it is also true that Machado left us not only great frescoes of the society of his time but also a rich series of chronicles. We can say objectively that few writers have been able to tell us so much and so well of the world in which they lived. Raymundo Faoro stressed the importance Machado gave to social conventions, which end up playing the determining role that the naturalist writers would usually ascribe to natural laws:

> Instead of the victory of arbitrary vices and virtues disconnected from environment, space, and time, free in the world of the absurd, a determined vision arises which accentuates the predominance of social conventions. Freedom of conscience, men's creative force capable of breaking up the institutions and destroying the external order, are reduced to a dream, a vague "Virgilian eclogue," powerless and empty, deprived of energy, deprived of a strong will. The absurdity of life continues untouched, despite all, the child of the frail human destiny, the remains of a great dream, injured by the ceaseless movement of the tides. Man—Pascal's "truthful being"—does not create history, does not create the destiny, vague shadow; he reflects, without boundaries, the social relations that rule, impel, and dominate. God, man's father, is only a blind and mute spectator to the vulgar struggle for bread, wealth, and power.[10]

Machado de Assis ends up by depicting his own ego in a world dominated by social conventions. We can undoubtedly say that social conventions and the force of society itself have a predominant and determining role in Machado's entire work.

Lúcia Miguel Pereira analyzes Machado de Assis's behavior toward his stepmother and establishes a comparison with the early works. Machado's stepmother, Inês, a mulatto like himself, acted as a true mother for the future writer, who abandoned her completely once he started his career in literature and, especially, once he married the white Carolina. The two women never met and this was certainly not due to any possible opposition by Carolina, who had a very good personality. The truth is that Machado's life was a struggle to emerge in society, to make himself white in a world that had fixed prejudices. For this reason, according to Pereira, all the female protagonists in his early works struggle to reach a place in society:

> One after the other, Guiomar in *A mão e a luva*, Helena Estella in *Iaiá Garcia*, and Lalau in *Casa velha* reflect the author while they discuss the rights of ambition and struggle against social hierarchy. These . . . books, so different in their plot and final resolution, revolve around the same topic: social climbing.[11]

Ambition, social climbing, and social conquest in the early works are followed by a solid bourgeois respectability and a fixed social framing in the middle and later works where the new men, speculators and bankers, also surface and not always pleasantly. By depicting himself, Machado depicted fifty years of life in Rio de Janeiro, from the flowering of the Empire to the first years of the Republic. Yet society underwent this long transition without really changing, or rather, changing the least possible the hinges on which it was based.

It is impossible to summarize here all the various social motifs that are described and analyzed in Machado's work. We refer the readers to Raymundo Faoro's book *Machado de Assis: a pirâmide e o trapézio*, probably the most complete and rich book on this author. Faoro examines the various aspects of Machado's bourgeoisie, as well as his moral uncertainties, his quest for a noble title. Faoro also deals with Machado's concept of progress solely connected to the external aspects of modernity, of politics as an activity reserved for those who come from the upper classes, of the *fazenda* as the background for urban bourgeois life, of the birth of a new entrepreneurial class and its union with the ruling class against the overcautious class of the landowners, of the social and economic closure towards the petty bourgeoisie, as well as the special kind of Brazilian politics. Faoro analyzes more than half a century of Brazilian life because Machado de Assis—the eternal scholar himself—depicted that society during more than half a century.

Augusto Meyer says: "He lived in a time of appearances, in a society based upon absolute truths, a stratified, slavist and romantic society."[12] The first of these absolute truths was monetary stability: according to data furnished by Raymundo Faoro, "During fifty-four years—from 1827 to 1881—the most flourishing period of the Empire, the index of the cost of living rose only from 153 to 190."[13] Monetary stability guarantees and is guaranteed by political stability founded upon the Empire and its electoral system solidly centralized in a few secure hands. Faoro provides us with other data:

> In Brazil in 1872, with a total population of 9,930,479 inhabitants, discounting the slaves, the minors, women, and illiterates and the people without income, the politically active population amounted to 300,000 or 400,000 people—those were the only people who could read and who had a positive notion of the world and things and who could understand, within the limits of their education, what monarchy, republic, representative electoral system, the right to vote,.and the government were.[14]

From the same author we learn that "in the 1881 election only 96,441 voters showed up in a population of probably twelve million inhabitants. That is, less than 1% of the population voted."[15]

Political and economic security were part of a system connected to the large land properties, which in their turn were based upon slavery.

The World of Labor in Machado de Assis's Novels

> Félix had known work when he had needed it to live but as soon as he had reached the means that allowed him not to have to worry about the next day he gave himself body and soul to the serenity of leisure. But one should understand that this leisure was not that apathetic and vegetative existence of lazy souls; it was, if I am allowed to say so, an active leisure consisting of all sorts of elegant and intellectual occupations that a man in his position could afford.[16]

Félix is the protagonist of Machado de Assis's first novel, *Ressurreição*. His attitude toward work is the synthesis of all the attitudes of the main characters in Machado's novels: work does not ennoble anybody; work is something you do only if you are compelled by external circumstances (and in this case only after you have put up a fierce resistance); work must be avoided as much as possible. The social status that guarantees the individual's position towards others is not given by the activity one develops but rather "by the elegant and intellectual occupations" one can afford.

Machado de Assis was, at the same time, a great chronicler and a great writer. We cannot know with absolute certainty where one ends and where the other begins, which is lucky because nothing makes a work of art more fascinating than a certain amount of mystery surrounding it. We will never know up to which point the author describes the events appealing to the audience's participation, and when the irony and the teasing of the readers starts. In fact the readers at some point feel betrayed and compelled to review their opinions and their unshakable convictions.

How many among the readers of the time recognized themselves in Félix, "the young man without occupation, without ambition"? And how much of Machado was in Félix, in his continuous struggle for the conquest of a social status, eternally in contrast with the Leopardian awareness of the vanity of existence? "His life was spent in a unique mixture of elegy and melodrama; he spent the first years of his youth sighing for flighty things and, when it seemed as if he had been forgotten both by God and man, an inheritance fell in his lap which raised him from poverty."[17] Even in the ambiguity of Félix's personality there is a projection of the author's alter ego, of the two souls Machado carried within himself up to the end, up to the later works, up to *Esaú e Jacó* when he embodied himself in the two protagonists, the two enemies united since the maternal bosom:

> His spirit had two faces and, even though they formed a single aspect, they were different among themselves: one was natural and spontaneous, the other was systematic and calculating. Both, however, merged together in such a way it was difficult to recognize and define them. Everything fused and mixed together in that man made up of sincerity and affection. A journalist of the time, a friend of his, used to compare him to Achilles' shield—a fusion of tin and gold—"but much less solid," he added.[18]

Where does tin end and gold start in Machado de Assis?

How many times does the poet of existential vanity, the philosopher eternally attracted by the voluptuousness of nothingness, compromise and identify himself with the poor and ambitious young man who has conquered wealth through work, or with the young boy who admired the luxurious dwelling of his rich godmother and benefactor?

Guiomar too, the beautiful headstrong and ambitious Guiomar, is poor and has a rich godmother. She addresses her in the hope of seeing herself free from having to work:

> Guiomar had shown then the desire to be a schoolteacher.
>
> "There is no possibility," she said to the baroness when she confessed that aspiration to her.
>
> "What do you mean?" the godmother asked her.
>
> "There isn't," repeated Guiomar, "even though I neither doubt nor can I deny the love you have for me, everybody has a duty to perform. Mine is . . . is to earn my own bread."
>
> These last words slipped through her lips almost by force. A blush came up to her cheeks; one would say that her soul covered her face with shame.
>
> "Guiomar!" exclaimed the baroness.
>
> "I'm asking you a very honorable thing for me," answered Guiomar with simplicity.
>
> The godmother smiled and approved with a kiss—she consented with her mouth while in her heart she responded in a quite different way; that is, that her fate should have been different.[19]

How many poor or simply nonaffluent girls would identify themselves in Guiomar and how many would share her feelings? And how much is there in her of the young Machado's hopes and of his relationship with his godmother? And where does the irony of that exaggerated blush and of those dramatic sentences start?

Always in *A mão e a luva*, among Guiomar's various suitors, besides the headstrong and ambitious Estêvão whom she eventually marries, is Jorge, who resembles Félix in *Ressurreição* in his attitude toward work and life:

> These were Jorge's apparent defects. He had others and among those there was the mortal sin, the seventh. The name he had inherited from his father and his aunt's influence could have helped him make a career in some public activity; yet he preferred to vegetate, passively living on the amount he had inherited from his parents and on the hopes he placed in the baroness's affection. He did not recognize any other occupation.[20]

The portrait of this character marks the pitiless return of Machado, the chronicler who selects and depicts exemplars of the human fauna whom he knew very well and whom he did not like very much.

The author shows a greater liking towards another Jorge, the protagonist of *Iaiá Garcia*, who undergoes a youthful crisis of rejection towards work:

> Valeria had seen it right when she said she did not find in her son any love for the lawyer's profession. Jorge knew a lot of everything that he had learned; he had a quick intelligence, a speedy comprehension, and a very lively memory. He was not deep, he grasped more than he penetrated. He had a theoretical intelligence: for him to follow practical things was barbarous. He owned many goods, which allowed him to live comfortably, and he employed only a small portion of his time in being a lawyer—the minimum that allowed him to keep the name on the door of the office and inside Laemmerh's *Almanaque*.[21]

Even in the major works the protagonists' attitude toward the world of labor does not change. The situation is made even worse by the author himself. The writer prevails, in fact, over the chronicler when he sees in work in general, in practical doing and in human action, one of the many external aspects of existential vanity, the principles of which totally rule his mature works.

In *Memórias póstumas de Brás Cubas* the protagonist, on the verge of getting his degree, plans his future existence as a program of debauchery:

> I had acquired in Coimbra a great reputation as a merry fellow; I was a cheerful student, superficially noisy and petulant, always ready for adventures, exerting always practical romanticism and asserting theoretical liberalism, believing solely in black eyes and written constitutions. The day when the University granted me, on parchment, a degree, in a science that I had hardly rooted in my brain, I confess that

> I felt somewhat cheated even though I was proud. Let me explain myself: the diploma was a *carta de alforria*; if, on the one hand, it gave me freedom, on the other, it gave me responsibility. I kept it, I left the banks of the Mondego and I came away rather disconsolate although already feeling some impulses, a curiosity, a wish to push my way around, to influence, to enjoy life—to prolong University for the rest of my life.[22]

Having always fled any responsibility, having accepted everything life could offer him, having felt useless and unfulfilled ambitions, Brás Cubas comes to the final reckoning when he says, "I did not bequeath to any creature the legacy of our misery."

The perennial and obsessive laziness, realizing itself eventually in madness, dominates the existence of Rubião in *Quincas Borba*:

> Rubião had nothing to do: to kill the long and empty days he used to go to sessions of the courthouse, to the chamber of deputies, to the passing of battalions. He went for long walks, he went to pay useless visits in the evening, or he went to the theater without pleasure. The house itself was a good resting place for the spirit with its sumptuous luxury and dreams floating in the air.
>
> During the last period he spent a lot of time reading; he used to read novels, but only the historical ones by Dumas, the father, or the contemporary ones by Feuillet. . . . Almost always he ended up with the book on the floor, eyes staring at the ceiling, thinking. Maybe some old defunct marquis told him anecdotes of past times.[23]

Félix, Jorge, Brás Cubas, and Rubião are rich because they inherited money; none of them had to struggle to acquire it and none of them knows really how to appreciate it. Otto Maria Carpeaux says of them: "They appreciate money only as a source of comfort and prestige, not as the result of work. Their greatest desire in life is to win more money at a lottery, which is also a frequent theme in Machado's stories."[24] In fact, even in the short stories the rhythm does not change. Each one is as rich as Daniel in "O que são as moças" ("What the Girls Are"):

> Profession: two hundred *contos* in state bonds and buildings insured against fire. He was a spendthrift but he spent with a certain amount of scheming; and this came from experience because the two hundred *contos* were what remained of a fortune of 800 that his father had left him."[25]

Or if one is as poor as João Fernandes of the homonymous short story or as Custódio of "O empréstimo," then there are other solutions, many solutions, except one, work. "João Fernandes" is a short story that describes the vicissitudes of a young man from two to five in the morning: without a job, without a house, dressed up to spit but without a penny in his pockets, João Fernandes has the problem of having to spend the hours of the night without being arrested as a vagrant. He spent his last money to buy himself a cup of tea and a cigar and this kind of spending tells us all about this kind of character: his planning is short term, it does not go beyond the cigar, which he is compelled to light with a coach lamp because he does not own matches. All his mental efforts are focused on how to spend the hours that separate him from dawn, from the return of people in the street, the return of life and sunshine. Not once does he think he could find himself a job and solve in a more definite manner the problem of board and room. Time goes by slowly at the rhythm of the tolling bells and of João Fernandes's ever more whirling thoughts, until five o'clock comes and the return of people in the streets, the sun shining and the reopening of coffee shops, of *botequims*: "João Fernandes ran to the *botequim* where he has had his tea, he obtained a cup of coffee and the promise of a breakfast which he would have paid in the afternoon or the following day. He succeeds in getting a cigarette."[26] To kill time he reads the paper avoiding, however, the job offers until, when the sun is already high, he leaves serene and satisfied towards the new day, towards life:

> He descended along the streets, with eyes on the rosy future: the certainty of breakfast. He did not remember finding any announcement in the *Journal*; he had seen, however, that the minister would be questioned that same day. An inquiry at the ministry! He would have breakfast at 10, at 11 he would go into the gallery of the chamber of deputies. There he would have found a way to mooch a dinner.[27]

Thus the story ends: the certainty of breakfast, the hope for a dinner, no thought for the night which is still so far away.

Custódio of "O empréstimo" belongs to the same kind of penniless optimists without a will to work:

> On the road, walking without having had breakfast, and without a penny, he looked like he was leading an army behind him. The cause was nothing else if not the contrast between nature and situation, between soul and life. Custódio was born with the vocation for wealth, without the vocation for work.[28]

As a vocational optimist he cultivates the dream of the easy enterprise, of the deal that immediately produces money, lots of money:

> Custódio never refused to enter business under the condition of being able to choose and he always chose a business that served no purpose.

> He had the intuition for catastrophe. Among twenty enterprises he always guessed the wrong one and plunged into it decisively with his head down. The bad luck that persecuted him made the other nineteen enterprises prosper and the twentieth blow up in his hands. Never mind, he prepared himself for another one.[29]

Armed with hope and ideas, Custódio goes to see a notary, the *tabelião* Nunes, a rich and intelligent man, to propose a deal, so to speak, but in reality to ask him for a remarkable loan of five *contos* which he needs to become a shareholder in a needle factory under construction. Millions of needles are to be manufactured and distributed over all of Brazil, at an immense profit. Nunes, naturally, refuses kindly but firmly. Custódio lowers his request to five hundred *mil-réis* (the exact half of a conto, and he had asked for five). Nunes responds with a new, courteous refusal to which he adds an offer of a job, barely hinted at because Custódio refuses as if it were an improper proposal. Custódio then goes on to other arguments, economic necessity, contracted debts, stating that two hundred mil-réis would be sufficient. A new refusal comes from the tabelião; not even one hundred, he adds, to avoid new requests. Interspersed by pauses and embarrassed silences, Custódio's requests go down to fifty, to twenty and they are always rejected by the notary. The notary prepares to leave, and at this point, Custódio, in desperation, asks for at least ten mil-réis. Nunes opens his wallet and shows two bills of five mil-réis; he offers one to Custódio:

> Custódio accepted the five *mil-réis*, neither sad nor reluctant, but rather laughing and throbbing as if he had just conquered Asia Minor. It was dinner ensured. He extended his hand to the other, thanking with gentleness, and greeted him with a "see you soon"—a "see you soon" full of implicit affirmations. After that he went out; the beggar disappeared from the office door, he went away like a general walking sure of himself, looking fraternally at the British in trade who walked up the road towards the peripheral quarters. The sky had never been so blue, nor the afternoon so clear; all the men carried in their eyes the soul of hospitality. With his left hand in the pocket of his trousers he held tightly and amorously five *mil-réis*, the residue of a great ambition, which shortly before had launched towards the sun with the impulse of an eagle and now inhabited, modestly, the wings of a strutting chicken.[30]

Machado de Assis's work is full of men like Custódio and João Fernandes. The writer and the chronicler would feed his fantasy through daily observation. The society of his time had found an official occupation for this kind of people: they lived as parasites on the great families, carrying out all those functions that the slaves were not in a position to do and the masters did not want to do: to go into an office, to pursue a chore, to pay or to have a bill paid, to bring an invitation with the due forms to a certain person, to convince the same person to come to a party, to accompany a boy to school, to inquire about the amorous accessibility of a beautiful lady; these were the tasks assigned to the parasite.

Machado's first parasite is found in *Ressurreição*, his first novel:

> Viana was a consummate parasite whose stomach had more capacity than prejudice, less sensitivity than inclinations. One should not suppose, however, that poverty compelled him to such a job: he possessed something that he had inherited from his mother and which he had kept religiously intact, having lived to that moment on the salary from the job he had quit because of disagreements with his boss. But these conflicts between fortune and character are not rare. Viana was an example of that. He was a born parasite as others are born to work. He was a parasite by divine right. . . .
>
> By calling him a parasite I do not allude solely to the circumstance of his performing his gastronomical vocation in other people's houses. Viana was also a parasite of consideration and friendship, the kind and cheerful intruder who, by virtue of obstinacy and art, succeeded in making himself acceptable and loved where, at the beginning, he was received with boredom and coldness. He was one of those meddling and flexible men who go everywhere and know everybody.[31]

The most important parasite is Dias of *Dom Casmurro*. He introduces himself to Bentinho's family by pretending to be a homeopathic doctor; then he reveals the truth. But by this time he is an indispensible character in the family environment. He ends up by participating in all the events as a secondary but necessary protagonist: he directs Bentinho and gives him the first advice; Bentinho confesses to Dias his desire not to go to the seminary because he is in love with Capitu. He is a figure who fits so perfectly in all the events of the novel that one naturally wonders what would have happened to Bentinho and Capitu's story without José Dias. In this novel, which we might well consider Machado's best work, the elements taken from everyday life integrate themselves perfectly into the imaginary story: José Dias is an *agregado*, one who attaches himself to a family, the synthesis and the symbol of all the agregados and all the parasites whom the writer would have known.

Besides the agregado, there are other kinds of parasites of a simpler kind, so to speak, and these are the *convivados*, the eternal dinner guests. Rubião, in *Quincas Borba*, is somewhat the king of the party givers: at his table every evening numerous companions gather. Some are of long standing and some new, all have in common a debt to the master of the house. Once Rubião has a strange reaction towards them: "He found them in the parlor, chatting while waiting: they all got up and shook his hand eagerly. Rubião, at that point, had an inexplicable impulse: to make them kiss his hand. He checked himself in time, frightened by himself."[32] An absurd situation is created: having guests at dinner compels Rubião to reject a series of invitations until he realizes that his guests could sit at his table even when he is not there:

> It happened so. The guests synchronized their watches according to those in the house in Botafogo. At six they all sat at the table. The first two days there was a certain hesitation but the servants had received strict orders. At times, Rubião arrived a little later. And then there were laughs, repartees, and cheerful jokes. One wanted to wait, but the others . . . the others repudiated the first; on the contrary, it was he who had dragged them to the table; he was so hungry that only the plates were left. And Rubião laughed with them all.[33]

The same scene from *Quincas Borba* is described in *Esaú e Jacó*, though with fewer details. Nobrega, the rich capitalist, sees himself compelled to neglect his guests because of his sentimental engagements: "Nobrega, however, had given orders that all would be served and given refreshments as if he had been present."[34]

These men, who spent most of their time far from any work activity, had an excessive passion for titles, for brilliant etiquette to brag about with their friends. According to the data cited by Raymundo Faoro, at the end of the Empire there were in Brazil 7 marquises, 10 counts, 54 viscounts, and 316 barons. All of Machado's characters adore titles in one way or another. The little characters are content with little titles:

> Colonel Macedo had the peculiarity of not being a colonel. He was a major. Some friends driven by a spirit of correction, had started to give him the title of colonel, which at the beginning he rejected but which he eventually saw himself compelled to accept, being unable to spend all his life protesting against it.[35]

The same happens in *Helena*, but there could be many more examples: "Mr. Nicolau Nunes was not a commodore, he was only an officer of the Order of the Rose, everybody gave him the title of commodore and Mr. Nunes could not resist such delicious falsification."[36]

The greater and the more ambitious naturally want more. And here the examples could be numberless starting with Guiomar, who, at the end of the novel, asks her husband jokingly what he is going to give her in return for her support: " 'But what are you going to pay me with? A position at the chamber of deputies? A minister's portfolio?' 'The luster of my name,' he answered."[37]

In *Memórias póstumas de Brás Cubas*, the beautiful Virgília abandons the wavering protagonist for the willful and ambitious Lôbo Neves:

> A week later Virgília smilingly asked Lôbo Neves when he would be a minister.
>
> "According to my will right now; according to others' will, in a year."
>
> Virgília replied: "Will you promise me that one day you will make me a baroness?"
>
> "Marquise, because I will be a marquis."
>
> Then I was lost. Virgília had compared the eagle with the peacock and she had chosen the eagle, leaving the peacock behind with his stupor and his disdain and with the three or four kisses she had given him.[38]

In *Quincas Borba*, the protagonist Rubião lives in a perennial dream of social grandeur up to the point of believing himself a Napoleon III, whereas his associate, Palha, thinks seriously of becoming a baron once he has become rich and has started constructing his palace. In *Dom Casmurro* there is a delicious family scene when Father Cabral receives the nomination to apostolic *nuncio*. In *Esaú e Jacó* the nomination of Santos to baron, which happens on the day of the anniversary of his marriage and which is offered by him as a present to his wife with great scenes of affection between the couple, is considered now one of the classic episodes of Brazilian literature.

These are the people in the world of Machado de Assis, which is a perceptive and truthful mirror of the reality of the time. It would not be right to say that they never work because among them there are some speculators and some merchants. These are the new men whom the writer does not love: Cotrim, the former slave merchant, Brás Cubas's brother-in-law; Palha, who exploits Rubião in *Quincas Borba* in the ambiguous ménage à trois with the beautiful Sofia; Escobar himself, Bentinho's friend in *Dom Casmurro*; Santos, the shrewd and fortunate banker in *Esaú e Jacó*, and the merchant Nobrega. Raymundo Faoro, who so insightfully analyzed the phenomenon of social transformations in Machado, says on this point:

> Machado de Assis after evoking the colonial sources of his heroes, of his merchants, *fazendeiros*, and landowners, feels that at the end of the century his characters have nothing else to achieve, nothing else to say. The new men enter the scene. These are the speculators of the *encilhamento*, the militarists and propagandists of a new faith. They enter

> the stage of real life, but the writer does not accept them: they are the children of a different world which is on the verge of being born. The novelist perceives, when rejecting them, teasing them, and despising them, that they do not belong to the ancient family circle. In the old man's eyes there are only shadows of the decadence, truth of the disorder of the new times, intruders without spirit, manners, or style.[39]

A character who is the alter ego of the writer particularly reflects this attitude. This is the *conselheiro* Aires, who "watches, as silent and skeptical witness, the sunset of the good old times, unconfessed nostalgic, hidden *sebastianista*."[40]

Machado de Assis and Slavery

Was it maybe his love for the good old times, the stubborn attachment to the past which prevented Machado de Assis from entering the struggle against slavery? The writer always chose a time for the setting of his works that was twenty years in the past. Can we interpret this choice as an unconscious attempt to escape the need to face the problem of the servitude of the Black man in Brazil?

For such a complex and inscrutable writer as Machado de Assis there could be several questions and answers. Historical and literary critics had an opportunity to express the most disparate opinions in this respect. Magalhães Júnior maintains that Machado de Assis supported his brothers of color since his first early works. On the opposite side, Lúcia Miguel Pereira draws a perceptive psychological analysis showing how Machado had tried to forget his being a mulatto to the point of interrupting his relationship with his mulatto stepmother, Inês, and of never writing the word mulatto in his works. There are also other critics such as the great scholar and awful backbiter Agrippino Grieco, who hurriedly liquidated the whole matter by saying, "Everything Machado ever wrote on slavery after May 13, 1888, in his usual ironic tone, equals what a humorist defined as an enema in a corpse."[41]

All we can add to what has already been written is that Machado never fought against slavery because he never fought against or for anybody. He was always a very great master of description and of the real and imaginary chronicle. He was a sarcastic writer who led the reader to be involved at the beginning and left him at the end totally confused. We can also say that in his very copious literary production there are relatively few descriptions of the conditions of the slaves. Moreover, it is hard to perceive from our modern standpoint that the entire struggle against slavery had a deeply ideological basis, founded upon both universal and sentimental considerations. There was hardly ever, among the many intellectuals who shed rivers of ink and tears on the unhappy slaves, the knowledge that slavery was the consequence of a system and not its cause. To erase formally a shameful and degrading human condition was the right thing but it was also totally useless if not accompanied by the series of reforms that started to appear only half a century later. To take ignorant, illiterate, and often elderly slaves, accustomed only to humiliating labor, and make them free, often chasing them away from the fazendas where they were replaced by Italians, served absolutely no purpose without reforms in the field of agriculture and in labor legislation.

We can say today, retrospectively, that the official end of slavery in 1888 allowed Getúlio Vargas to create his labor legislation after 1930. Machado saw instead the farce, through the perceptive and disenchanted eyes of a contemporary. And it was just one more farce in grand style for this chronicler of human vanity. To this purpose Faoro says:

> The social incorporation of the free worker in the context of poverty allowed Machado de Assis to weigh the position of the slave from an original standpoint.
>
> He was the only one who insisted on the calamity that the *alforria* could mean for the slave who would be free but without work, without bread, left to beg. The master, and only he, would profit from this act of generosity by getting rid of a useless hand, become old and crippled by work. Freedom under those circumstances was nothing less than cruel rhetoric and a lie.[42]

Several Black people appear in the short stories and novels by Machado de Assis. Among the early works are two short stories, "Virginius" and "Mariana." The former takes up the classical theme of the Roman Virgínia, harassed by the patrician Appio Claudio and killed by her father. The latter is the story of an unrequited love between a slave and a master. In *Ressurreição* we have a short glimpse of a slave, a totally insignificant figure, who fits the author's observation, "the slave whose spirit was accustomed to obedience did not distinguish it from duty."[43] This was the law of those times and places: the white master's will was the only form of duty for the slave. In *Helena*, we have, instead, the typical romantic position of the good young slave who reveals the truth about his young mistress believing that she is in danger. Note the terms the protagonist uses: " 'Let us praise God,' she said, 'because he infused into the vile body of the slave such a noble spirit of devotion.' "[44] This is a typical example of romantic fiction addressed to young ladies of good families.

The slave has no relevance, and Helena's reaction mirrors only the general attitudes of those times.

Iaiá Garcia, however, contains a very interesting Black character, Raimundo. Although this is the last novel of Machado's romantic phase, the figure of the slave is described in such a way that it aroused several observations and debates:

> Raimundo was perfect to serve Luís Garcia. He was a fifty-year-old *preto* of medium stature, strong despite his age, a typically submissive and dedicated African. He was a slave and a free man. When Luís Garcia inherited him from his father he did not want to accept him as an inheritance and immediately gave him the certificate of freedom. Raimundo, nine years older than his master, had carried him in his arms and loved him as a son. The slave interpreted his being freed as a possible way of expelling him from the house. He then felt a rebellious, though generous, impulse, He made a gesture to tear apart the *carta de alforria* but he checked himself in time. Luís Garcia saw only the generosity, not the rebellion, he understood the affection of the slave, he felt his good heart. Between them then there was a pact that united them forever.
>
> "You are free," said Luís Garcia; "you will live with me as long as you wish." From that moment on Raimundo was like the external spirit of his master; he thought for him and reflected his most intimate thoughts in all his actions, always silent and punctual. Luís Garcia gave him orders; he always had everything at the right moment and at the right place. Raimundo, even though he was the only servant of the house, had even the time in the evening to converse with the former master in the garden while the night approached. There they talked of their little world, of the rare domestic events, of tomorrow's weather and of some external event.[45]

In this respect Faoro says:

> Raimundo's rebellious and generous impulse, an impulse truthfully born out of disappointment, says it all: once free the slave lost his house, food, and was abandoned to poverty. The master does not perceive anything: the denial of freedom looks to him like an extreme act of generosity. He was an abolitionist as were all the abolitionists at the end of the nineteenth century who identified themselves with the great liberal movement that had invaded the world, and who were attracted by the ideology but forgetful of the reality. The truth, the naked and crude truth, surfaces in Machado de Assis's call to our awareness, which he launches discreetly between the lines.[46]

What Faoro says is undoubtedly true: Machado's message is clear. A purely formal freedom, incorporated in the system of slavery, has no meaning. There is also a certain amount of satisfaction in the adopted "solution," which will be proposed again in *Memorial de Aires*, written in 1906. *Iaiá Garcia* was written in 1878, ten years before the abolition of slavery. There is a form of recognition of the freedom of the slaves so long as everything else stays the same; masters and slaves remain in their places and everybody is happy. Is this perhaps another way of eliminating the problem, by avoiding it?

Raimundo plays a decisive role at the end of the novel when Iaiá Garcia sends an imprudent note to a man. Raimundo makes an autonomous decision by refusing to deliver the message:

> Iaiá remained still for some moments. Raimundo took the letter from his pocket and remained with it in his hands without having the courage to raise his eyes; when he eventually raised them he said resolutely: "Raimundo did not find it beautiful that Iaiá wrote to that man who is neither her father nor her fiancé," and then he returned to talk to *nhanhã* Estela.[47]

Iaiá Garcia is the last of Machado's romantic works, and Raimundo is an essentially romantic character in his attachment and devotion to his masters: "Raimundo gave her the letter and shook his gray head as if he wanted to push back the years that weighed upon it and go back in time, to when Iaiá was nothing else than a sassy little girl."[48] He is a beautiful background figure, a classic image of the faithful Black man. Raimundo seems to close an epoch in Machado de Assis's life, the time when the author still kept some illusions about human beings.

Once he lost that illusion, he wrote *Memórias póstumas de Brás Cubas*, in which he portrayed life as denial, and gave vent to his bitter irony on existential vanity.

The situation of the Black, like that of any other character, is subjected in this novel to Machado's scalpel, which does not spare anybody. He starts with himself—the protagonist in the first person. In describing Brás Cubas as a child the author certainly did not remember his own childhood as a poor child, but rather the spoiled and arrogant children of that rich bourgeoisie which he had started to visit once he reached success. The following passage is one of the best examples of Machado's prose, as the author avoids taking sides and uttering any judgment while leading the reader along the path of doubt and irony:

> Since the age of five I had deserved the nickname "devil child": and in truth that's what I was; I was one of the naughtiest of my time, malicious, indiscreet, sassy, and stubborn. For example, one day I wounded the head of a slave because she had denied me a spoonful of a coconut

> cake she was preparing, and still not happy about the evil I had done, I threw a fistful of ash in the dish, and still not satisfied with this trick, I went to tell my mother that it had been the slave herself who spoiled the cake for spite; and I was only six.
>
> Prudêncio, a house *moleque*, was my everyday horse; he put his hands on the floor, he got a rope in his mouth as a bridle, I mounted on his back with a whip in my hand, I whipped him, I made thousands of trips on each side and he obeyed—sometimes moaning—but he obeyed without saying a word or at least just a, "Oh, *nhonhô*"—to which I answered, "Shut up, animal!"[49]

Without blaming anybody, without uttering any judgment, without ever taking sides, the author describes—Machado, the eternal chronicler—a piece of daily life, something that happened every day in the gardens of the rich bourgeois households. Many readers of the time probably recognized themselves in this portrait. Few of them, however, realized that Machado was teasing them while depicting this delicious tableau.

What will ever happen to a person like Prudêncio, the man-horse, in a world such as that one? One day the two will meet again, the former master and the former slave, who had become free thanks to an act of generosity from Brás Cubas's father. They are both adults and they meet by chance: Brás Cubas sees a group of people staring at a Black man whipping another Black man. And who is the one with the whip in his hand? No one else but Prudêncio, who at every scream and invocation of the slave answers with a "shut up, animal" just as Brás Cubas used to scream at him when they were both children. The two recognize each other, and Prudêncio, thanks to Brás Cubas's intervention, forgives his slave:

> Superficially the episode of the Valongo was gloomy, but only superficially. I had hardly introduced in it the blade of reasoning when I found in it a malicious, fine, and even deep core. It was a way for Prudêncio to get rid of the beatings that he had received by passing them on to somebody else. Myself, when I was a child, I used to ride him, put a bridle in his mouth and mistreat him without compassion; he moaned and suffered. Now that he was free and he could do what he wanted with himself, with his arms, his legs, now that he could work and rest and sleep free from the former condition, now he vented himself; he had bought himself a slave and paid him back with high interest whatever he had received from me. Look at the shrewdness of that rascal![50]

The conclusions are bitter—and are left always to the reader—in spite of the playful and ironic tone of the author. Slavery can only produce slavery. Prudêncio will never be free from his childhood as a child's horse: the victim must become an executioner to erase the memory.

Memórias póstumas de Brás Cubas is the first of Machado de Assis's mature works. He wrote it, as he himself declared, when he had lost every illusion about life and man. It is a work in which one feels more clearly the impact of disillusionment. Irony here is often ferocious and blasphemous. It is the tool that Machado uses continually in his position as observer and chronicler of the reality he no longer likes. The description of Cotrim, Brás Cubas's brother-in-law, is an example of the subtle and cruel play in which virtues and defects fuse together, apparently subservient to the morals and mores of the times:

> Maybe Cotrim's scruples might seem excessive to those who don't know that he had a ferociously honorable personality. I myself was unjust with him during the years that followed the inventory of my father's property. I recognized that he was a model. They accused him of being greedy and I think they were right; but greed is only the exaggeration of a virtue and virtues must be like estimates; balance is better than deficit. Because he was very abrupt in his manners he had many enemies who accused him of being a barbarian. The only fact alleged on this point is that he frequently sent his slaves to prison, from which they returned all covered with blood. But, aside from the fact that he only sent there the perverse and the fugitive ones, one must also consider that he had smuggled slaves for a long time and so he was accustomed, in a certain sense, to those hard manners that kind of business requires and one cannot honestly attribute to the natural character of a man what is instead the result of social relations. The evidence that Cotrim had pious feelings is found in the love that he had for his children and in the grief he suffered when Sarah died a few months later; this is, I think, irrefutable evidence, and not all of it. He was the treasurer of a fraternity and he was a confrère of various religious societies. He was even an associate in good standing in one of them, which does not fit with his reputation of greediness; it is true that the advantage had not been in vain: the fraternity in which he had been a treasurer had had his portrait done in oil. He was not perfect, it is true; for example, he had the mania of sending to the newspapers the news of some good deed that he had done—a criticizable and certainly not commendable mania, I agree; but he excused himself by saying that good actions are contagious once they are known; and this is a reason to which one cannot deny some weight. I believe (and this is the greatest praise I pay him) that he practiced once in a while those good deeds if not with the purpose of provoking others' philanthropy.[51]

This passage deserves special attention because of that subtle balancing game of which Machado is a master. Note for example the adverb "ferociously" which serves to reinforce the adjective "honorable" for a man who used to have his slaves massacred. The accusation of being a "barbarian" is ironically mitigated by his sending only the "perverse and fugitive" slaves to prison. The "hard manners" are seen as a consequence of smuggling slaves, which was a crime according to the laws of the time; but these laws were imposed under pressure from Great Britain and were badly accepted by public opinion, which thrived upon slavery. The accusation of being avaricious is nullified by parsimony. Good deeds are contradicted by vanity which, in turn, is mitigated by public philanthropy. The love for his children is set against that of selling children, brothers, and parents of other human beings.

Sweetly, ironically, in his usual manner, the author depicts a gloomy Cotrim closed in his concept of honor, a slave butcher, a smuggler of other human beings, attached possessively to his family; greedy, bigoted, tied to the interests of the clans and fraternities, frugal and circumspect in good deeds, vain. "In other words, he might have been lacking in some things but he did not owe a penny to anybody."[52]

In *Quincas Borba*, however, the presence of Black people is very limited, almost nonexistent. Rubião, the protagonist, is a rich urbanized provincial in a Rio de Janeiro that was on the verge of giving up its old *fidalgo* aspect to let itself be conquered by the charm, not a very discreet one indeed, of neocapitalism. All of Rubião's efforts are directed toward taking on a guise suitable to the new social rules. One of these rules, a very strange one indeed for Brazil, was that the sign of highest status was to have white servants; this was a secondary although not irrelevant result of the hasty libertarian ideologies that deprived Blacks of even servile jobs in favor of European immigrants:

> The waiter waited, tense and serious. He was a Spaniard; Rubião had accepted him from the hands of Cristiano not without resistance; as much as he insisted that he was accustomed to his *crioulos* from Minas and that he did not want foreign languages in the house, his friend Palha had insisted, showing him the necessity of having white waiters. Rubião had yielded with discomfort. His good page boy whom he wanted to place in the sitting room, as a piece from the province, he couldn't even leave in the kitchen, where Jean, a Frenchman, reigned; he was degraded to other jobs.[53]

This is naturally a secondary passage but once again Machado does not mince words. This is preceded by another passage in which Rubião contemplates all the things, very expensive and not necessarily in good taste, he was compelled to buy in order to look like a gentleman. It conjures up the impression that the slaves are just objects, and not even very precious ones, to be confined in the least conspicuous parts of the house.

In *Quincas Borba* there is another episode in which a Black man is hanged. He is a criminal, however, and, in spite of the drama of the event, the fact that he is Black does not take on a specific meaning (except perhaps, if he had been white, the author, according to the custom of the time, would have called him "a man" instead of "a white").

The Black presence is even minor in *Dom Casmurro*; the entire work is a painful and insightful introspective analysis of a past love relived and destroyed again through ruthless memory. This rarely allows the author to step aside and take on the chronicler's role. Background figures are necessarily present in that world, including an anonymous Black slave who surprises Bentinho and Capitu in one phase of their idyll. There is only a moment of focus on the Blacks, when Bentinho shows his friend Escobar his slaves. Bentinho realizes only then, thanks to his friend's observation, that their names start with all the letters of the alphabet. Then the slaves return to the background, to their function of exploitable goods, of invested capital: some work at home, some are rented out, some work at the country house. They all have purely economic functions, like the houses Bentinho owns and rents out.

In *Esaú e Jacó*, another minor episode has a strange meaning to our eyes:

> Paulo was the more aggressive, Pedro the more devious, and since both ended up by eating the fruit from the tree, it was the *moleque* who went to pick the fruit up there, either for fear of the beatings of the former or because of the promises of the latter. The promise was never kept, the beating, having been announced was always given and sometimes even repeated after the service.[54]

The fate of the moleque is not worth a discussion here because a few slaps are not objectively such a serious matter; what deserves some thought here is the deep modification of mores created by slavery. According to these mores two seven-year-old children are deprived of one of the most genuine pleasures, that of climbing a tree and picking the fruit. It seems like a trifling thing but it is not. Slavery is also this: thousands of changes occur in the way of being, of facing external reality through intermediaries, of depriving oneself many times of the direct and brutal contact, of the encounter with life.

There were no tree climbings during Pedro and Paulo's childhood. This was shared by thousands of other affluent little Brazilians because custom made them delegate the contact with reality to thousands of intermediaries.

In another interesting scene Santos tells his wife that he has been nominated to become a baron; the masters' party is paralleled by the noisy and sincere cheerfulness of the slaves who felt gratified because the master's noble title distinguished them socially from the neighboring slaves.

Memorial de Aires was written in 1908, the year of his death. In this last of his novels, Machado de Assis talks about the problem of the liberation of the slaves. As in almost all of Machado's great novels, the story is set about twenty years before it was written; the figure of the protagonist, the conselheiro Aires (who is also the protagonist in *Esaú e Jacó*) is the author's transparent alter ego. He is a retired diplomat, an elderly gentleman with tranquil habits who lives observing, as an eternal chronicler up to the edge of death, other people's stories and, to some extent, his own. The story is set in 1888, the year of the abolition of slavery, and it is constructed as a chronicle, or rather a diary; the point of view is not that of the slaves, but rather that of the master.

We have the interesting instance of the baron of Santa Pia who on the eve of the emancipatory law frees all his slaves. Santa Pia is an old-fashioned gentleman who belongs to that aristocratic society to which the author feels quite a few affinities. Santa Pia's action is a form of rebellion against the law that he considers unjust: "I want it to be clear that I consider the action of the government an expropriation since it intervenes in the exercise of the right that belongs exclusively to the owner and which I am going to exert at my own loss, because so I want and so I can."[55] The strange thing is that the author, always inclined because of his own nature as a chronicler to comment on the character's action, does not stress at all that the principle of property is here applied to other human beings, thus violating other principles. The comment this time is uttered by the baron's brother, and it is perfectly in line with the conception of the ruling class:

> My brother believes in the government's attempt but not in its results, unless what one wants is the destruction of the *fazendas*. He is capable of urging all the owners to free their slaves and the day after to propose the collapse of the government which tries to do the same thing through a law.[56]

His position is clearly aristocratic and reflects the fear of the destruction of agriculture. It is also perfectly in line with the way of thinking of the master class at the time, or at least with those masters Machado was familiar with, who, having been accustomed for centuries to slave labor, showed serious concern in the face of salaried labor. Faoro observed on this point that Machado, who had never left Rio, had no experience of the fazendas of São Paulo where salaried labor had been a reality for several years before the law of emancipation.

Santa Pia's conclusion, speaking of the slaves, is also typically aristocratic: "I'm certain that only few among them will leave the fazenda; the majority will stay with me earning the salary that I will determine, and some even for nothing—just for the pleasure of dying where they were born."[57] Even the conclusion of the story is typically patriarchal: once the baron is dead, the beautiful young mistress Fidélia decides to leave and may even sell the fazenda while all her former slaves would like to follow her to town, where she intends to move.

> It took her a lot of pain to make those poor people understand that they would need to work and that she wouldn't be able to find them a job. She promised, instead, not to forget them and, in case she did not come back to the countryside, to recommend them to the new owner.[58]

It is a transparent parable of the former master class that disappears and of the masses of former slaves who are finally free who do not know what to do with themselves; they attach themselves to their former masters as a last refuge against the new, harder slavery of their condition as rural proletarians. Between the two episodes, one with the baron of Santa Pia as protagonist and the other with Fidélia as the protagonist, is the promulgation of the law that frees the slaves. At this point Aires is inserted as a protagonist in a scene Machado de Assis himself probably experienced in the first person:

> Eventually the law. I've never been, nor did my duty allowed me to be, a protagonist of abolition but I confess I felt a great pleasure when I heard of the final vote of the senate and of the sanction of the Regency. I was at the time in Rua do Ouvidor where there was a great turmoil.
>
> An acquaintance of mine, a journalist who found me there, offered me a seat in his coach which was in Rua Nouva and would line up in the organized parade to drive around the royal palace and make an ovation at the Regency. I almost accepted, such was my astonishment, but my quiet habits, my custom as a diplomat, my very nature, and my age kept me back better than the reins of a coachman kept the horses back, and I refused. I refused with displeasure. I left there both my acquaintance and the others who joined and left from Rua Primeiro de Março.

> They told me later that the demonstrators stood up on their coaches, which were open, and made great acclamations in front of the royal palace where the ministers were. If I had been there I probably would have done the same and even now I would have not understood myself . . . no, I would have done nothing; I would have put my head on my knees.[59]

This is the synthesis of Machado's position. The serene initial confession of having never been an abolitionist even though with the reservation due to duty (which duty—that of the diplomat Aires, a well-off white conservative, or that of Machado, the poor mulatto journalist who wrote for the whites and was paid by them?). He refuses to be the protagonist even of somebody else's triumph, to the last denial of that hypothesis of participation, hiding his head between his knees with eyes that refuse to see. And, at the end, he returns to the usual considerations and digressions, the eternal flight from having to face reality:

> It is a good thing that we got rid of it, it was high time. Even though we have burned all the laws, the decrees, and the announcements, we will never be able either to erase the private acts, the contracts, and inventories, nor to erase the institution from history or even from poetry. Poetry will speak of it, particularly in those verses by Heine in which our name will remain forever. In them the captain of a slave boat tells of having released 300 *negros* in Rio de Janeiro where "the Gonçalves Pereira House" had paid him 200 ducats per head. It doesn't matter that the poet alters the name of the buyer and calls him Gonzales Perreiro; it is the rhyme or the bad pronunciation that brings it about. Besides this, we don't have ducats, but in this case it is the seller who changed into his language the buyer's money.[60]

Thus, once again, starting from considerations about the political act that was meant to destroy all the documents of slavery because they were shameful, the writer digresses endlessly toward poetry and irony, still avoiding any form of more involved consideration.

Thus, Aires, the character; in reality Machado's attitude on that day was different and he recalls it in the chronicles of *A semana* of May 14, 1893:

> There was sunshine, great sunshine, that Sunday of 1888 when the senate voted in the law, which the Regency approved, and we all went out in the streets. Yes, I myself went out in the street, I the most closed of all the big snails, I entered the parade in an open coach, the guest of an absent fat friend; we all breathed happiness, it was all a delirium. In truth, that was the only day of public delirium that I ever remember having seen.[61]

In reality the problem of slavery was much more complex than we can imagine and the debate on the subject has continued up to this day. The historian and sociologist Gilberto Freyre declared, in an interview to *Jornal do Brasil* of April 14, 1979, that the end of slavery came too early, under the emotional impact of public opinion, without the existence of adequate structures that could receive the numerous former slaves as free workers. This is true, as we have pointed out already. (Let us not forget, however, that Freyre has his own conditioned reflexes as a descendant of an old family of slave owners.) It remains to be seen, and nobody can prove it, if by delaying the end of slavery by some years the government and the Brazilian society would have created the structures capable of giving employment to the masses of liberated slaves. I have my doubts about it.

Just to give a more pertinent example, we can say that the end of the colonial epoch in the 1960s threw many populations of Black Africa into the precarious situation of having to manage the freedom for which they had not been technically prepared in the context of modern states. Many voices, even in good faith, were raised at the time commenting on the massacres in Biafra and the Congo and criticizing the haste, and especially the lack of preparation, with which independence had been granted. That claim, however, was anachronistic; the international situation in the 1960s no longer permitted delays to provide the preparation that should have been given, and was not given, in the years immediately after 1945. The same is true for Brazil of 1888; the preparation for the emancipation of the slaves should have started twenty years before at the end of the Civil War in the United States and, even in that case, nothing was done. What was worse in the case of Brazil is that the problem, besides being political, was private. The slave in fact was a commodity—excuse my saying that—just as for us the car is today. We know too that the supply of oil will end, yet our cities are still clogged with cars mostly driven by single drivers and utilizing the space that could be used comfortably by four or five people; and our highways are like the Indianapolis Speedway. To give up a slave in Brazil would be equivalent to giving up the car for us. It could only happen, we believe, as it happened: through a drastic change followed slowly and painfully by a transformation of structures that should have changed twenty years before.

Machado had perceived that, however, and had said it in the chronicle of October 1, 1876:

> The law of September 28 is now five years old. God giveth health and life! It was a great step in our life. If it had come thirty years before we

would find ourselves in different conditions. But thirty years ago the law did not come; slaves came, instead, smuggled, and they were sold openly at Valongo. Besides the sale there was a public prison. A man I know sighs, thinking of the whip. "The slaves nowadays have become proud," he says often. "If you give a beating to one there is always someone else who intervenes and calls the police. Ah, the good old days! I still remember the time when the people saw a *preto* all bloody walk by and they would say: 'Keep going devil, you deserve it!' Nowadays. . . ." And the man sighs deeply from his heart, . . . it is touching. *Le pauvre homme*![62]

Machado had understood perfectly well, in 1876, twelve years before the emancipation, that Brazil was thirty years late on the problem of slavery. Probably for this reason, beside his natural inclination, Machado did not struggle vehemently against slavery; he knew that if a change in structure had not occured when it was due, emancipation would have created a dramatic situation.

There are two more chronicles in which Machado deals with the problem of the emancipation of the sixty-year-old slaves (an absurd law passed in 1885 freed the old slaves, who were thus condemned to hunger after a life of work) and that of emancipation in general. The first chronicle is dated June 15, 1877, that is, eight years before the law that freed the old slaves (I am pointing this out because it is evidence that Machado was aware of certain problems and foresaw them even before they actually occurred). In this chronicle Machado tells the story of an anonymous person who gave a very large sum of money to the orphans of the Holy House without letting his name be known by the public:

And I would like the reader to know that the generous action at this Holy House inspired a friend of mine with another beautiful gesture. He had a female slave, sixty years old, who had given him a profit of seven or eight times as much as the original price. At her birthday he freed her without payment. Without payment! This was already a very nice gesture. And now, since only the right hand knew of the case (the left hand ignored it) he took the pen, bathed it in ink, and wrote a simple notice to the newspapers indicating the fact, the name of the *preta*, his own name, the reason of this action, and he added this last comment: "Actions like this deserve all the praise of good souls."

Things done by the right hand!

It happened just then that the *Jornal do comércio* gave notice of the anonymous donation to the Holy House of which the illustrious author had been the only confidant. Our friend stepped backward; he did not send the notice to the newspapers. He just found a way of telling every friend he ran into that Clarimunda was no longer with him.

"Is she dead?"

"Oh! No!"

"Did you free her?"

"Let's talk of something else," he interrupted vivaciously. "Are you going to the theater today?" It would be cruel to demand more.[63]

It is useless to underline the irony: the slave who had already given her master a profit seven or eight times as much as her original price is freed without payment (perhaps only to be sent away to die from hunger), and her master brags about it with his friends after refraining from advertising his gesture in the papers. Machado, detached and bitter chronicler that he was, had clearly singled out the strong ideological component behind the emancipation forces and he had clearly detected the deep structural deficiencies. A successful ideological phenomenon risks becoming a fashionable phenomenon and therefore a comfortable trampoline to launch many mediocre go-getters. How could a sudden enthusiasm for the emancipation of the slaves escape an eye like Machado's?

May 1888 brings the second chronicle, six days after the law passed which ended slavery forever. This is the story of the usual ambitious man who, perceiving that nothing would prevent the abolition of slavery, decides to free his moleque Pancrácio, eighteen years old, more or less. Naturally, to do this he chooses the most pompous way, that is, a dinner in which five people participate (but the newspapers will say that it was a banquet to which thirty-three people were invited—thirty-three was Christ's age when he died) with great speeches, toasts, and Pancrácio rushing in and hugging his benefactor's knees. Later on, letters of congratulation arrive while his friends already think of immortalizing the benefactor in a portrait:

The day after I called Pancrácio and I told him with dreary sincerity:

"You're free and you can go wherever you want. Here you have a friendly house you know already and a small salary, a salary which . . . "

"Oh! my master! I will stay."

"A small salary but one that will increase. Everything increases in this world; you grew up enormously. When you were born you were a little thing like this, today you're taller than I, let me see, look you're four inches taller than I."

"Height doesn't mean anything, no, master . . . "

"A small salary of six *mil-réis*; but it is with one grain after another that the hen fills out her gullet. You are worth much more than a hen."

"I'm worth a chicken, my master."

"Right, so six *mil-réis*, at the end of the year count on eight, if everything goes well eight or seven."

> Pancrácio accepted everything; he accepted even the slap I gave him the day after because he had not brushed my boots well; these are the results of freedom. But I explained to him: the slap, being a natural impulse, could not cancel the civil right he had gained when I gave him his freedom. He kept his freedom and I kept my bad mood; both were natural states, almost divine.
>
> My good Pancrácio understood it all; from then on I gave him a few kicks, I pulled his ears and called him "animal" when I didn't call him "devil's son"; all these things he received humbly and (God forgive me), I believe, even with some cheerfulness.
>
> My plan is done; I want to become a legislator and, in the flyer I will send out to the electorate I will mention that long before legal abolition came along I, in my house, in the modesty of my family, had freed a slave, a gesture which touched all the people who heard about it; and I will also claim that the slave, having (allegedly) learned to read, write, and count, is now professor of philosophy at Rio das Cobras; and I will also state that the pure, great, and really political men are not those who obey the laws but rather those who anticipate them and say to the slave: "You are free," before it was stated by the public powers, which are always tardy, slow, and incapable of restoring justice on earth for the satisfaction of heaven.[64]

Machado de Assis could not help pointing out the other facets of the end of slavery: the usual exploiters capable of using any event to aid their goals. And especially he could not help emphasizing how the end of slavery meant absolutely nothing as long as the structures of a slave society remained. The moleque Pancrácio is luckier than the poor Clarimunda of eleven years before. He is luckier because, in spite of the slaps he gets from his master (or rather his ex-master, if you want to be more precise), he is young and, although he needs a house and work, his master needs a servant; he is lucky because he will be able to see better times as a free man. But how many Clarimundas in those years were able to obtain freedom only to die of hunger?

Because of his detached and nonparticipant attitude, Machado de Assis was vehemently attacked in particular by the demagogue José do Patrocínio, and this might have influenced his bitter reflections on the enforcement of the law. Undoubtedly he saw very far. What did he mean, for example, when in *Esaú e Jacó* he has Paulo say the following words: "Now that the *negro* is emancipated the white has to be emancipated too"?

Black characters are scarce in his stories and they are never protagonists although their actions are always meaningful. For example, in *Vidros quebrados* (*Broken Panes*) the young maid helps her young mistress in her *namoro* with a young man; and, of course, once the

PREPARATION OF MANIOC ROOTS

PREPARAÇÃO DA RAIZ DE MANDIOCA

affair is discovered the young Black is the one who is beaten. Another example is the appalling dialogue among saints in *Entre santos* (*Among Saints*) in which the story is told of a man who was so avaricious that he freed one of his dead slaves to avoid paying the expenses of the funeral. And terrible Nicolau in *Verba testamentaria* (*Testamentary Clause*), when he was in a bad mood, would break the dishes on the slaves' heads and he would kick the dogs. Then he would fall asleep. When he woke up he was extremely kind with everybody, dogs and slaves: "And everybody, dogs and slaves forgot the beatings of the previous day and ran to obey his orders."[65] Finally in *O caso da vara (The Case of the Stick)* there is the story of Damião, who, having run away from a seminary, takes refuge at the house of a lady, who is a friend of his godfather, to ask help from her. The lady helps him. At the end of the day it happens that one of the girls who works in the house, a young slave, had not succeeded in finishing the assigned work. Her mistress wants to punish her and the poor girl runs away screaming; the mistress manages to grab her and, after dragging her by her ears, asks Damião to pass her the stick. Damião had felt a lot of sympathy for the poor girl just a few minutes before and now still feels a lot of compassion for her but he needs the lady's help to leave the seminary. So he gets up and goes to get the stick.

This is Machado's unending game of balance: the usurer who frees the dead slave is a genius at saving money, just as Cotrim's avarice was the extension of a virtue. Damião, the fugitive seminary student, is a good boy who feels compassion for the young Black slave who was not able to finish her work. Even the lady at whose house he takes refuge is a nice person who takes to heart his problem. Yet both of them become accomplices when the time comes to punish the slave. Damião does it unwillingly. He has to choose between his own slavery inside the seminary and the young Black girl's slavery. The lady, in contrast, has neither doubts nor remorse; she just applies the laws of an economic order of which she is an integral part.

During the last years of his career Machado de Assis reached a stylistic perfection in the game of impartial and ironic observation. He manages to stay out of the crowd, and at the same time, he drags the unwary readers to his side before they are able to choose sides. It is no longer the single individual who is on trial, it is the human condition itself which becomes the historical, involuntary, and unaware emancipation of a smiling and monstrous fate. Machado is now an old man, facing serenely his doubts concerning the supreme alternative. "I hesitated whether to go forward or change direction: I stood still some seconds until I withdrew, one step after the other."[66] These are the last lines of his alter ego, the conselheiro Aires. This is also Machado's last testimonial: the return to the most sacred and essential motifs of life, that is, the choice between two slaveries that the seminary student Damião had foreseen and which in *Pai contra mãe (Father against Mother)* is brought to its most tragic consequences.

Pai contra mãe starts with a short preamble on slavery. To be sure, the story is neither against nor for slavery. It is simply about slavery as a historical and social reality. The author takes us directly inside an accomplished fact, a fact whose existence is not questioned and whose function is explained "objectively":

> Slavery brought along offices and apparatuses as might have happened with other social institutions. I will mention some apparatuses only because they are connected to some specific tasks. One of them is the neck-ring and another is the foot-ring; there is also the tin mask. The tin mask cured the habit of drinking by plugging up the slave's mouth. It had only three holes, two to see and one to breathe, and it was locked behind the head. Together with the habit of drinking they lost also the temptation to steal because it was usually with the master's pocket money that they got what they needed in order to quench their thirst. Thus two sins were eliminated while honesty and sobriety were ensured. The mask was grotesque but human and social order cannot always be reached without grotesqueness and sometimes cruelty. The blacksmiths kept the masks hanging on display on the doors of their stores. But let's leave the masks alone for now.
>
> The neck-ring was applied to fugitive slaves. Imagine a big collar with a big handle, either on the right or on the left, coming over the head and closed behind with a key. Of course it was heavy, but the punishment was less serious than the sign. A slave who ran away in those conditions, wherever he went, showed that he was an old offender and he was captured again shortly afterwards.
>
> Half a century ago slaves would run away frequently. They were numerous and not everybody liked slavery. It happened occasionally that they would be beaten up and not everybody liked to be beaten up. The majority was only scolded; there was always someone in the house who took up their defense and even the master was not wicked; besides, the sense of ownership moderated the action because even money hurts.[67]

This is one of the best and most typical prologues in Machado's style. Slavery exists, it is an accepted fact and as such it is presented. The horror awakened by the description of the instruments of punishment is mitigated by the willingly light tone, by the consideration of the positive results, deriving from the use of such instruments and by a benevolent description of the master's attitude. The introduction serves the purpose, at least apparently, of explaining that if the slaves ran away there should be someone in charge of capturing them: "To capture fugitive slaves was a job at the time. It was not a noble thing but since it was an instrument of the force through which law and ownership are maintained it implied a nobility intrinsic to the vindicating actions."[68]

Everything is serenely logical in Machado's universe: men who walk around with their heads enclosed inside instruments of torture, men who run away, and men who capture the fugitives ensure the social and human order that requires grotesqueness and cruelty to continue its existence. Through this serene and detached logic human beings seem almost devoid of any responsibility. They are actors in a comedy whose meaning escapes them.

One of the protagonists is Cândido Neves, Candinho to his friends. A nice guy after all, his job is to hunt down slaves, because it is a vague and sporty job through which he can experience his unstable personality; he is unable to devote himself to a continuous and monotonous occupation. He tried all jobs and abandoned them after a short while. One day Cândido falles in love with a beautiful and good girl called Clara; they marry and live with her aunt Mônica, a nice, cheerful woman. Theirs is a happy family; they play off their names—Cândido, Neves, Clara, the utmost in whiteness—he goes out to hunt down fugitive slaves while she sews clothes, helped by her aunt. They trust God and the Virgin whom they address serenely during hard times; great happiness is coming, a son who will strengthen the happy family even more. There is only one great problem: the number of fugitive slaves diminishes and, consequently, Cândido's earnings decrease just when the needs connected with the child's birth increase. Of course, Cândido does not even think of looking for another job but the author does not insist too much on this. Then the situation gets worse: the baby is born just when the three—Cândido, Clara, and the aunt—are evicted and they find themselves literally without a penny. Aunt Mônica manages to find a room in the house of a charitable lady, but compels Cândido and Clara to leave their son on the doorsteps of an orphanage. There are scenes of heartbreaking despair in which the parents try with every means to postpone the inevitable moment. At the end, when every hope is lost, Cândido makes up his mind, picks up the baby and goes.

Now comes the moment for which Machado was waiting to strike the blow that completely upsets the situation. He brings the reader up to the point of participating emotionally in Cândido and Clara's drama, so much in love and so desperate. Then he throws another character into the setting: Arminda, a fugitive mulatta whom Cândido runs into by chance. The action develops in a flash. Cândido leaves his son at a pharmacy and, then, he pounces on his prey. Arminda screams, struggles, asks for help, she prays to God with the same desperate fervor with which Cândido and Clara had prayed. To move her jailor to compassion she tells him that she is pregnant and he responds with a ''logical'' answer: ''You are the guilty one, who ever told you that you had to have children and to run away?''[69] After a long struggle Candinho manages to drag Arminda to the house of her owner where he receives immediately the promised large reward. Meanwhile, the poor slave, thrown on the floor, has a miscarriage:

> The fruit of a certain time entered this world without life among the mother's moans and the master's gestures of despair. Cândido Neves saw it all; he did not know what time it was. Whatever time it was he had to run to the Rua Ajuda and that is what he did without even wanting to know the consequences of the disaster.[70]

This is another typically sudden change: the appalling despair of the master who loses a new slave concludes the drama of the mother and brings us back to that of the father, namely Cândido, who runs away looking desperately for his own son. He finds him, of course: ''The father grabs the son with the same fury with which he had only a little while before [seized] the fugitive slave; it was a different fury naturally, a fury of love.''[71] The return is a triumphant march, the tragedy evolved into a happy ending:

> And Mônica, once she heard the explanation, accepted the return of the child since it brought back one hundred *mil-réis*. She said, it is true, some hard words against the slave because of the abortion as well as of the flight. Cândido Neves, kissing his son with real tears in his eyes, blessed the flight and did not worry about the abortion: ''Not all children survive''—his heartbeat accelerated.[72]

This is the indifferent Machado's true testimony. It is a story that goes beyond Candinho's responsibilities. The protagonist himself is willingly ignorant. He is himself a slave in a world that did not educate him to work, a world that compelled him to play his own slavery against the life of the newborn. He feels neither shame nor guilt because he only obeyed the laws and rules of his world and society; these are summed up by aunt Mônica's last wretched comments.

With this ''indifferent, objective testimony,'' Machado de Assis says it all.

8 O FEITICEIRO

O feiticeiro (*The Sorcerer*), by Xavier Marques, was written and published in 1897 with the title *Boto & Cia* and republished in 1922 with its present title. This book introduces us to the very heart of Bahia and the most authentic Négritude. Set in the 1870s it has as a background the city of Salvador with its very beautiful baroque churches, its squares, its lanes, its languid and serene atmosphere of decadence, its eternally socially aspiring bourgeoisie, and its noisy, colorful, and friendly people.

The city of Salvador used to be the cradle of Brazilian civilization and was then at the beginning of an epoch of decline. When the novel was written, the city's decline had taken on clear and unmistakable connotations that left no room for hope: the hinterland of the state of Bahia was turned upside down by the Canudos war, and the ancient rural economy of the *senhores de engenho* was in full decadence while the executive power was solidly rooted in Rio de Janeiro. A new economic class was rising and establishing itself in the industries and *fazendas* of São Paulo, which were fed by the continuous new arrivals of European immigrants.[1] Everything helped relegate the city of Salvador to a minor and marginal level. Xavier Marques, a true son of Bahia from Itaparica,must have felt deeply that atmosphere of decadence which his novel mirrors. There, the world of Bahia tries to overcome its crisis by looking into its own past and cultural origins for its strength and values.

O feiticeiro is the story of a family, of a city of the white and Black worlds that meet and unite indissolubly into a new reality. A wealthy merchant of remote Portuguese origin, Paulo Boto, has recently married a young woman called Branca, the orphan of a bankrupt merchant; the couple lives in the house of her widowed mother together with another daughter called Eulália. An old mulatta, Josefa, and her daughter Pomba, who according to the gossips were respectively lover and daughter of the defunct husband of Boto's mother-in-law, are also part of the family. There is also Salustiano, Boto's friend, who is eternally in love with Pomba; he is a poor city clerk always waiting for a promotion that would allow him to marry the girl. One day, during a picnic the whole group meets another friend of Salustiano, Amâncio Neri, a good-looking young man, the son of a rich notable. A romantic affair starts between Amâncio and Eulália, which is, however, opposed by Neri's father who wants his son to marry the daughter of his friend, Dr. Brasilino. Tomásia, Dr. Brasilino's wife, is particularly enthusiastic about this matrimonial plan. Neri leaves for a business trip to the hinterland and, despite his promises, he never writes during the two months he is gone. Because of Eulália's desperation both Paulo Boto on the one side and Pomba and Josefa on the other, each unknown to the others, consult the great feiticeiro, Pai Elesbão, in whose *candomblé* Paulo Boto is *ogã*, a notable. At this point, the story takes on the rhythm of a thriller, deftly built around irrelevant facts and episodes that help clarify occult plots and intrigues. Neri suddenly returns and explains the reason for his silence: he was seriously ill in a forlorn area of the *sertão*. At the same time, the fact is unveiled that someone had requested a *feitiço*, a spell, from Pai Elesbão to have Neri separated from Eulália. For this reason, Neri had become ill until the will of the all-powerful Elesbão, as requested by Boto, made him heal and return to Salvador. The name of the person who requested the feitiço against Neri and the Boto family is also revealed: it is Tomásia, Dr. Brasilino's wife, who would like Neri to marry one of her daughters. Boto and Josefa again consult Pai Elesbão. Tomásia's evil spell must be counteracted and at the same time Neri's father must be convinced to consent to his son's wedding to Eulália. Pai Elesbão will take care of everything: an evil feitiço will destroy Tomásia's nervous system and drive her to insanity, while an amulet hidden in the old notable's bed will induce him to give his son permission to marry in exchange for his renunciation of the presidency of the Republican Club (Brazil was then a monarchy). Thus, Elesbão obtains another victory: he pleases the police chief, who wanted the club to be closed down in exchange for his full protection of the candomblé of Elesbão.

The novel ends with Elesbão's death and funeral. The feiticeiro has given happiness and well-being to his friends, disaster and madness to his enemies; he has ensured tranquillity for his people. His Blacks, all dressed with colorful clothes, accompany him to the cemetery, and cross the "white" town not minding the indifference of the people and the irreverence of the commoners. The feiticeiro is the true winner, the one who controlled the destiny of so many human lives.

I must say above all that *O feiticeiro*, despite the simplicity of the story and the clarity of the plot, is a difficult novel. The main problem arises because the work comes from a world completely different from ours even though this difference seems at first superficial. A feiticeiro is one of the protagonists. But we have already met feiticeiros in the works by Manoel Macedo, by Araripe Júnior, by Júlio Ribeiro. What is the difference, then, between this group of feiticeiros and Pai Elesbão, or rather if we want to be more precise, between Xavier Marques and any of the writers who preceded him? The fundamental difference consists in the writer's position toward the character of the feiticeiro: for Manoel Macedo, Araripe Júnior, and Júlio Ribeiro, the feiticeiro was the other, the enemy, the evil one, the representative of a world one wanted to combat and destroy without even trying to understand it. It was the typical position of the white world, of the master's world that saw the sorcerer as an agitator who endangered the established order. Any recognition, or at least acknowledgment of the intrinsic validity of the character of the sorcerer—as the representative of values different from those of one's own civilization, but not necessarily negative values—would have jeopardized the rights of the white civilization which those writers defended. Xavier Marques takes a different position, even though his position is sometimes ambiguous: he does not reach the total recognition of the Black civilization as Jorge Amado will do in 1968 with *Tenda dos milagres*, but he does nonetheless accept it as something existing and real. The feiticeiro exists and his magic powers are absolutely real and terribly effective.

The impression that comes from the reading of this novel is strange: it is clear that the writer does not even doubt Pai Elesbão's real capacities. Whatever happens in the novel is the work of the feiticeiro's powers: Neri's disease and his state of confusion are induced by the feitiço requested by Tomásia; his healing and return are caused by the opposite feitiço requested by Boto and Josefa; a terrible feitiço leads Tomásia to insanity and causes Neri's renunciation of his political activities (as requested by the chief of police from Pai Elesbão) and Neri's father's acceptance of his son's sentimental choice in exchange for his giving up pro-republican activities (which satisfies at the same time Josefa's and the police chief's desires).

One must be clear at this point about a case as unusual as that represented by Pai Elesbão. The writer could have chosen two paths: he could have described the characters as believers while showing toward them a critical or at least detached attitude, or he could have accepted fully their own attitude. Xavier Marques takes the second road: the protagonists believe in Pai Elesbão's powers and Pai Elesbão performs certain actions because he has the power to do them.

What we have here is not an external description made by a nonparticipant observer; we have, instead, a description made from the inside by a participant who tells the story of other participants.

The great originality of *O feiticeiro* consists exactly in this aspect: the work comes from the other side, from someone who is inside and observes from a point of view that is no longer external; the writer is no longer in a position of false superiority as were the writers who preceded Marques. We can call this work deeply Bahian; it reflects the world of a serene bourgeoisie that is on the verge of accepting on a level of equality the new mixed racial reality. Paulo Boto's family, simple well-to-do merchants, keep in their daily family life those noble habits that were typical of the great senhores de engenho of the Recôncavo of Bahia:[2] a certain modest number of servants; the house always open to friends; some festivities that have to be honored; the regular presence at Sunday mass in the cathedral, always in their best clothes and certain of being continuously observed and criticized. The women of the house are compelled to a lack of activity (except for the duties naturally connected to motherhood) and, therefore, can have long talks, juicy gossip and long-cherished morbid jealousies. The male barber-shop chats are their counterpart while political struggles and elections degenerate every time into heated scuffles and violence of every kind. Students and the children of the good families meet at the Republican Club where they make inflammatory speeches while the wealthy classes, consisting mostly of merchants, look with suspicion at any novelty, especially those that refer to the Republic or the end of slavery. We get great glimpses of provincial life at the end of the last century, such as the amusing scene in Boto's store, when Neri reads some titillating passages from a French novel, that provokes the general indignation of all present for its obscenity. A little later, the same people who indicated their disapproval to the group go individually to Neri to ask to borrow the book or to find out where he bought it. The story is also full of characters like poor Salustiano, who lives his resigned and melancholy city-clerk's life, eternally waiting for a political change that might bring about the promotion which might permit him eventually to marry.

The most interesting and important aspect of the book consists, however, in the character of Elesbão and his impact on the white world, starting with Paulo Boto himself who often has a contradictory attitude. Paulo Boto, in fact, is an ogã, a notable in the *terreiro* where Elesbão's candomblé takes place; yet at home Boto never mentions this activity of his; on the contrary "at home he pretended he has no knowledge of such things."[3] When he lets himself go to a passionate defense of the Black world and of the validity of African culture with his friend Neri, he justifies his knowledge as some kind of juvenile hobby:

> There was a time when I, having nothing else to do, for pure fun I used to come to these fields hunting birds and I happened to know these secrets that were cultivated by some *negros*, who had nearby a *terreiro*. Maybe the mother and father of this *terreiro* are still around. I met them as I met many other Africans. Despite a certain mistrust and suspicion that they had toward the whites they initiated me to their beliefs and rituals.[4]

The author explains Boto's attitudes by saying that the new responsibilities, which came to him because he was the head of a family, made it look improper for him to participate in the African rituals, even though he continued to be an ogã and to contribute his help to the maintenance and development of the terreiro. Eulália herself, when at the end of the story she explains the plot to her fiancé, says only: "You didn't know it yet; now you know it but please be discreet. My brother-in-law, Paulo, has the weakness of protecting these people."[5] As we can see, the protagonists' attitude remains ambiguous from beginning to end: they all believe firmly in the feiticeiro's powers, they use him all the time, but they try as much as possible to keep this attitude hidden. All sorts of racial prejudices against Blacks—or rather social prejudices, since Blacks were mostly slaves and were in the lowest social ranks—are connected to this ambiguous attitude. In fact, Pomba, during the picnic with which the novel starts, shows her knowledge of the existence of a sacred tree and immediately afterwards, in front of strangers, "she disguised in the best possible way this fault which betrayed her African origin."[6] Even her mother, Josefa, who is part Black, always did her best to *limpar a geração*, that is, literally to clean up the generation and keep busy with the *purificação dos descendentes*, that is, the purification of the descendants. The author himself, when describing Blacks, to emphasize the color of their skin compares them with vultures and uses the two forms, the classic one of *abutre* and the more Brazilian one of *urubu*: the crowd of Blacks who accompany Elesbão to the cemetery are called a band of urubus while the head of the slaves, Belmira, who acts as a go-between for Paulo Boto and Pai Elesbão, is compared to an abutre. Even Paulo Boto's juvenile participation in Black rituals has a degrading side: "In that place he had wasted many hours and nights abandoned to the perverse although peculiar pleasures of the *candomblé*, stimulated and dulled by the animal-like odor of the Africans and of the *crioulas*."[7] Josefa herself, criticizing the avarice of Neri's father, adds that, being a widower, he is also guilty of living with a Black woman. Let us point out that it is not the act itself of having sexual intercourse with a Black woman, very common in a racially mixed country, which causes scandal; what causes scandal is the stability and permanence of this relationship, an official concubinage.

Yet, despite all, despite the gossip and the easy irony on the slaves and their supposed freedoms, nobody even dares doubt Pai Elesbão's real ability. Many white ogãs are present at the candomblé where Paulo Boto takes Neri and Salustiano. These men have light skin, *cor limpa*, clean color in the author's words; they are elegant in jacket and tie, know each other, and recognize each other in some sort of mutual complicity. Elesbão bows before them and they are visibly satisfied: they are his official protectors before the established powers, and they are at the same time his protégés against the dark adversities of life. Elesbão is described in terms full of respect: he is an ancient African prince who, once made a slave, conquers his freedom by the *carta de alforria*, thanks to the income derived from his activities as a singing teacher; his deep knowledge of natural forces and magic rituals soon gives him an uncontested power over other Blacks and over many whites. Even physically, his athletic figure, full of majestic dignity, commands respect and fear from those who know him. Paulo Boto is not the only white man who appeals to his powers. Besides Lady Tomásia, whom we have already mentioned, the chief of police appeals twice to Elesbão; the first time as a go-between for his political leader who wants to become senator (and Pai Elesbão satisfies him); the second time, when he wants to destroy the Republican Club without resorting to force, thus avoiding political complications (and Pai Elesbão acts, as we have seen, through Neri's father).

A blind trust in Pai Elesbão's powers emerges throughout the entire novel:

> From that night on under the mattress in the notable Neri's bed, a small marvel was active, without his even suspecting it, introduced there by an intermediate creature. It was a talisman, small in size although extraordinary in its effects. Tio Elesbão, the creator of affections, emperor of destinies, stood there in his mysterious *peji*, tracing the orbit that the hearts were supposed to follow. Modifying, suspending, replacing

> the laws to which the beings capable of love and hatred obeyed in the world, it was impossible that the great father, friend of that house, did not confirm the word of his messenger and believer.[8]

It seems at this point, that men's will and their free choice are nothing but futile shams, and unimportant external expressions, devoid of content: they exist only so long as they are based on a superior will which decides their destiny, the path they must necessarily follow:

> Keeping respectfully still, while he did not deign to look at her, she reflected on the power of the sovereign father who, like a great spider, from the obscurity of his den made the human creatures, just like small insects, struggle while dropped in the invisible web that he wove for them during the course of their existence.[9]

All of them are aware of this power, of this sovereign and determining will, even those who do not have recourse to it. During a talk with Eulália, Neri tries to give her a logical explanation of these fears: "They are the result of the horrid stories that they have told us since childhood—the revolts of *malês* and *hauçás*, the wars of the *quilombos*, the witchcraft. We all live more or less obsessed by these ghosts, by the negro and his feitiço."[10] The correct explanation is helpful in carrying the attitudes of those writers whom we have discussed before and who deal with the character of the sorcerer. This explains the bad conscience of the master class that rapes and oppresses, refusing to understand its victims, and which uses high moral laws to legitimize the law of the jungle. The bad conscience of a world which obscurely perceived the weakness of its position therefore had to have recourse in mystery as a comfortable alibi. But, of course, Xavier Marques goes much further than the other writers who preceded him and, therefore, he has Neri say:

> Behind the sorcerer there is mystery: this enemy entrenches himself inside the most resistant secret of the world. Many laugh about the power of the sorcerer although everybody fears it. This is why I tell you: we are ruled by the sorcerer, how many lives turn around this axis! How many souls live in subjection under this iron hand.[11]

The feiticeiro's power is given an official sanction, a public recognition as if a religious war were taking place. Branca tells her anguished sister Eulália, before she goes to Mass:

> *Breve Santíssimo da Marca* against *feitiços* and misdeeds of the devil and against all the devilish dangers that might occur during life. . . . This is what Branca recommended that her sister read during the Mass.

> The *Breve da Marca* gave strength to Lali's spirit.
> Her religion, the religion of her parents, feared and prevented the misdeeds of the sorceries. If these did not exist why did the sacred books try to exorcise them? And this is why they all believed and they all feared.[12]

This passage is interesting: Eulália's reasoning is quite logical and this way of thinking is not only hers but also is historically rather widespread among many people, not only in Brazil. If there is a God, there is also his opposite, the devil. If the church, God's creature, worries about the feitiço this means that the feiticeiro exists. And if he exists why not have recourse to him at least in case of emergency?

Eulália's reasoning, which gives her strength and hope, is probably based upon the opposite foundation: the reality of evil exists and it is tangible in the pernicious results that cause her anguish. Since everything allows her to imagine that this evil comes from a feitiço, the recognition of the feitiço by such a high institution as the church gives the believer the possibility of detecting it and, therefore, combating it, maybe, by having recourse to its opposite, that is, God.

This is basically the reasoning the author ascribes to Eulália, who, however, ignores how things really are, starting with the true relationship between her brother-in-law and Pai Elesbão. Xavier Marques goes much further: Pai Elesbão, the feiticeiro, is not simply the embodiment of evil, of the devil; he is God and evil at the same time, he is the earthly interpreter of those primeval forces that identify and embody themselves in nature and which the Black world always sees as a divinity, whether good or evil. Exu in the Black pantheon is evil, the devil that before every ritual, before every candomblé, must be removed so that he will not spoil the ceremony. But to remove him one has to adore him, to worship him, to offer him sacrifices and, therefore, to recognize his value. Pai Elesbão's feitiço can be either benevolent or harmful depending on the people for whom or against whom he directs it. In themselves his sorceries are only the expression of those forces of which the feiticeiro is the medium, and which justify themselves only through their existence. The force, the force of nature, the incarnation of natural divinities, is right in itself and because it acts.

Xavier Marques's position is quite different—as we have already noticed—from those of other authors who dealt with the same subject. For Araripe Júnior, Manoel Macedo, and Júlio Ribeiro the feiticeiro was evil and representative of the forces of the Black world, the enemy, and the antithetical world. Xavier Marques accepts the world in its historical reality and in its multiracial setting of Bahia;

he keeps some of the prejudices and reservations of his own world, but this does not prevent him from accepting the other's world. And especially, he does not commit the error of condemning the other's world without having known it first.

The episode of Eulália going to Mass with her *Breve da Marca* follows another episode in which Eulália and her friend Pomba meet each other. The former is full of anguish because of Neri's disappearance and the latter tries to comfort her by telling her what her mother, Josefa, is doing with Pai Elesbão. Of course, it is worth reminding one that Eulália still does not know that her brother-in-law is ogã in Pai Elesbão's terreiro. Pomba's tale is full of colorful details concerning the feiticeiro's dwellings and actions but it is abruptly interrupted by Eulália when Pomba reveals that Josefa, to obtain the sorcerer's help, had to unveil the name of the person involved and, also, had to mention Paulo Boto. At this point Eulália (or rather Lali as they call her) gets upset:

> At this point Lali, discolored from fear, and trembling, exclaimed:
> "Did she mention Paulo . . . your mother?!"
> "Don't be afraid. This is going to remain secret between her and the uncle. It was necessary that he knew . . ."
> "Oh! Pomba!"
> "There is nothing inconvenient; on the contrary . . ." Eulália wasn't even listening any more. So much hardship, so many problems, and so much bitterness and now, even the danger of a scandal; her name, the name of her parents from mouth to mouth, in the circles of the African *negras*, among the street girls and from there to the ears of those who had already fought so much against her family. "What a horror! It would have been better if nobody had ever gone there. I would rather lose everything, despise Amâncio and the Brasilino family. Everything, everything, rather than suffer this shame!"
> Her hands were cold and, trembling, stunned, she held her head with her hands.[13]

Eulália's reaction is typical of a good family girl: she is ready to do anything to get back her beloved yet she is on the verge of fainting or having a hysterical crisis when her name and reputation are in danger of becoming the objects of gossip by socially inferior people. To relieve her, her friend Pomba is compelled to reveal to her what nobody dares say in the family. And that is that Paulo Boto is ogã and therefore his name is the best recommendation to Elesbão, who will certainly be helpful toward the sisters-in-law of one of his affiliates.

As we see, the behavior of the two in-laws parallels each other: Eulália's good-family-girl's fear corresponds to Paulo Boto's cautious reserve as a merchant, father, and head of a family with respectability and a good name to preserve.

Another comparison can be established between Eulália's anguish during a Carnival night and Neri's suffering during his stay in the sertão when he was ill. In both cases, even in the different succession of images, one finds a common aspect: the presence of a majestic Black man who overpowers and rules, who threatens and promises. Once again Pai Elesbão, the master of destinies, permeates even the subconscious thoughts of those who, in one way or another, depend on him.

The novel ends, as we said, with Pai Elesbão's death. What does death mean for a man like Elesbão? Can he really be dead?

> And this morning with a glorious sky, when Pomba was going to take Eulália to Mass in the cathedral, the wonderful creature, the benefactor whom she had never known, had ceased to exist. Her mother had carved his portrait in her soul, line after line, through thousands of stories. As much as she was happy and at peace with herself, she could not remove from her mind the one who had contributed so much to her happiness and who had penetrated the intimacy of her life.[14]

Will his creature ever be able to free herself of him? What will happen to them without Pai Elesbão? Morbidly, Pomba, while she admires her own fresh beauty at the mirror, believes she discerns in her own smile, in the very curves of her own body, the mysterious and gloomy shadow of the African. Pai Elesbão lives because he is Bahia's very soul—Black, white, and mulatto soul. In the squares outside the wondrous baroque churches unfolds the colorful caravan of the Blacks, who accompany the funeral. The court of miracles emerges from the lanes, the hooligans sneer as the young ladies come out of Mass; they all stop and watch. They all are to some extent the subjects of Pai Elesbão, who dies yet continues to live forever in each one of them, in Bahia.

O feiticeiro, besides being a very beautiful novel, is also a document of the history of Bahia. Written at the end of the last century, the novel portrays events set a few decades before, when the city and the province were undergoing some slow but inevitable changes in mores.

Both the economy, based upon the large land estates, and the connected phenomena of slave labor were entering a deep crisis; the abolition of slavery and the Republic were in the air even though nobody dared pronounce these two words except for the hot-headed and liberal students. Despite official resistance, the Black and white worlds were destined to merge together: the white ogãs witness calmly the candomblé of Elesbão, who gives his favors to the chief of police and to certain senators. Neri's father disparagingly associates Black Africans and the Republic, which he considers an utter craziness: yet he lives with a Black woman and his actions are ruled by the feitiço that Pai Elesbão has had someone put under his mattress. A Black woman in his bed and a Black feitiço under it are evidence enough to contradict all his statements. Because of his cautious merchant's attitude, Paulo Boto does not dare admit in public that he is in favor of the emancipation of the slaves, yet he thinks that slavery is unjust and enrolls his name in an abolitionist society. We already mentioned his relation with Elesbão, and we must now mention that his name, Boto, is that of a kind of dolphin in the Brazilian ocean. He chose it to replace his family name, the Portuguese Braga, almost as if he wanted to reject the past that connects him to Europe.

To conclude, it is worth mentioning that among various prejudices against the Black world, one, with which we will deal later on while discussing Jorge Amado, concerns what is now considered the most Brazilian of institutions, the Carnival. In those years, as Xavier Marques attests, the authorities tried to teach the "true carnival"—a carnival, European-style with masks—as opposed to the gigantic Dionysian feast that the Blacks organized in the streets and the squares with explosive energy.

Luckily for all of us, that was a lost battle. Despite all the police decrees, despite the protests by the press and by the moralists, men like Pai Elesbão, the thousand Black Elesbãos, have given Brazil and humankind the most beautiful and most garish feast that ever existed.

9 GRAÇA ARANHA AND THE PROBLEM OF NATIONAL IDENTITY

We have already met Graça Aranha (1868–1931) in the chapter devoted to Aluísio Azevedo and the Maranhão. His autobiographical pages helped us to understand the somnolent and decadent environment of São Luís, where he was born, and to which he remained always emotionally attached even though he left it very early in life. Writer, essayist, diplomat, political man, founder of Modernism, he belongs to a group of uncomfortable characters who could be criticized from various perspectives, but who cannot be ignored especially if one wants to understand the phenomenon of Brazil.

He wrote two novels thirty years apart from each other: *Canaã* (*Canaan*) in 1902 and *A viagem maravilhosa* (*The Wonderful Voyage*) in 1930. They share a common motif: love as a cognitive and conclusive moment for human beings towards themselves and the world, combined with the insoluble search for personal and national identity.

Canaã, more than a novel, is a long dialogue, or rather it is a novel whose plot is very weak and is based upon a rich dialogue through which the characters compare their different conceptions of the world and of life. Milkau and Lentz are two Germans, having come to the state of Espírito Santo in Brazil, searching for a new life. They are not typical immigrants; they are two intellectuals who have abandoned old Europe and with it a certain concept of existence. They meet in a village inhabited by German colonists and decide to ally themselves and unite their efforts the better to build a new life in the new land. Their story, with few episodes, crosses that of Maria, an unfortunate girl of Germanic origin who was reduced to miserable conditions by man's wickedness. Maria and Milkau's encounter represents a final catharsis for both of them, the fulfillment of their lives now devoted to the search for Canaã, the promised land, which can only be reached through the ecstasy of love and a reconciliation with nature.

Canaã is an unusual novel in the vast panorama of the Brazilian novel. It is unusual not only because of the ethical choices that pervade it but also because of the extremely literary and wordy style—at times absolutely unreal—with which the characters express themselves. *Canaã* is also unusual because of the characters, the theme, and the setting.

From a historical point of view, *Canaã* faces the problem of the massive, prevailing presence of rural European colonies—especially Italian and German—in Brazil. How and why were these colonies born? During the second half of the nineteenth century the Brazilian ruling class had to face both the problem of industrializing the country and of the approaching inevitable end of slavery. Brazil was in a hurry to recapture the time lost in the industrial and technological fields compared to other nations of the civilized world. Brazil had neither the time nor the structures necessary to transform the great masses of illiterate and brutalized slaves into colonists, artisans, and workers necessary for the progress of the country. Moreover, the dominant classes, consisting mainly of whites, feared the inevitable moment when, once slavery was ended, they would have to face a Black majority. The coming of European colonists had the advantage of solving several problems at once. It brought into the labor market a cheap supply of ready workers, while it also reestablished the ethnic balance in favor of the whites. Eventually, immigrants also cut off every possibility of reconquest for the large masses of Black former slaves who saw themselves excluded from the new model of development and ended up by constituting an inexhaustible reservoir of labor devoid of any menace and of any contractual power.

Naturally the admission of a new body, such as the immigrants, into an organism with peculiar structures, such as Brazilian society, could provoke dangerous reactions of incompatibility and rejection. The Italians, even though they kept some of their characteristics, especially in the rather isolated rural colonies where they lived, ended by merging easily with the rest of the country, thanks also to many linguistic, ethnic, and religious affinities. The Germans, in contrast, tended to differentiate and isolate themselves. Their colonies, especially during the first years, constituted ethnic groups separated from the rest of the country. They kept their mores, their festivities, their habits, and especially their language; they even refused at times to learn Portuguese. Language became the most important problem, which gave the German colonies their peculiar features, cutting them practically out of any possible communication with the rest of the country and transforming them into independent and isolated nuclei. In the majority of the areas of Germanic colonization, Brazilian ethnic minorities were compelled to learn German. They even forgot Portuguese. It was not unusual that some travelers in those areas who turned to a Black to ask for information were answered in Goethe's language!

The problem took on such serious proportions during the thirties, thanks also to strong pressure from Nazi propaganda, that President

Vargas had to prohibit the teaching of any foreign language in Brazil, especially when it was the first language at an elementary level replacing Portuguese. But this happened many years after the publication of *Canaã*. Besides, Graça Aranha had pointed out this phenomenon somewhere in the novel in the episode when Lentz and Milkau meet a group of German colonists among whom there is a mulatto, Joca, who speaks German even with Felicíssimo, who is another mulatto and friend of the two young men. At Lentz's questions Felicíssimo answers:

> Don't be surprised. That is because of the men who arrived here little over a year ago. There are people here in the colony who arrived here more than thirty years ago who do not speak a word of Brazilian. It is a shame! What happened is that our mule drivers and our workers all speak German. I don't know but I don't think that there is another people like ours capable of learning other people's languages . . . believe me it is a natural gift . . ." Joca nodded approvingly and added that he himself spoke more German than his own language and had even a smattering of Polish and Italian.[1]

Graça Aranha, in choosing Germans as protagonists for his novel, develops a thematic motif. He is interested in the problem of national identity for the Brazilian people: will the blond people who come from far away become the dominators in the near future or will they become absorbed and Brazilian, or mulattos themselves, racially indistinct? These two theses are expressed throughout the novel by the two friends: Lentz foresees the superiority and victory of the white men while Milkau believes in merging through love and symbiosis with nature.

The entire novel is a succession of comparisons and contrasts allowed by the fact that the two protagonists come from an evolved European civilization and find themselves in a rural Brazilian civilization, which in turn is transformed by the determining presence of the German colonies.

Thus the memory of the harmonious European landscape, with its variety and its succession of seasons and colors, is compared to the obsessive and majestic presence of the evergreen *mata* of the Brazilian forest. But, especially, the obsessive comparison is between two human typologies, two ways of facing existential problems. Felicíssimo, the farmer who accompanies the two Germans, expresses in a naive way a pure and simple praise:

> "These Germans have a good eye . . . If it had been up to the Brazilians, we would have a devastation here." And the farmer continued in this tone to praise German virtues for business, economy, capacity of as-

similation, energy in work, contrasting, instead, the Brazilian inferior quality which he pleased himself to proclaim.[2]

Felicíssimo is a simple farmer, a man who spends his existence in touch with peasants and colonists; his naive desire to show kindness and benevolence toward the two young Germans, who for him are important people, is transparent. His opinion then is very relative. There is, however, another character, one of those figures whom the reader is drawn to recognize as the author's alter ego or at least his spokesman: his name is Paulo Maciel. He is a young judge who has come to the village where the story is set, together with other peace officers, to check the inventories of the various inheritances and demand the payment of taxes. He is a cultured and sensitive man, deeply disgusted by the environment in which he is compelled to live and work, and especially by his colleagues, greedy and corrupt functionaries. Paulo Maciel cannot help admiring the excellent organization of the German colonies:

> The order and cleanliness of this colony are admirable. Nothing is missing here, everything is prosperous in marvelous ways . . . What a difference when one travels in the lands cultivated by the Brazilians . . . There you find only carelessness, abandonment and neglect; there is sadness and misery. And there are those who still speak against immigration![3]

Paulo Maciel's observation causes long discussions with his colleagues. A long series of banalities can be found in more recent works, expressing concern for the eternal problem of foreign schemes on Brazil and its wealth.

This was one of the problems that concerned Graça Aranha and other writers of his generation up to the present. The problem was the consequence of a logical although bitter observation that the Brazilian nation did not have the necessary structures in people, means, and capital to manage its own territory. This fact, in many ways true even today, brought Brazil to the creation of its various models of development which have always been based upon the influx and influence of foreign capital. Even before that happened, however, unending discussions and debates developed—ranging from literary and sociological analyses to coffeehouse chats—on the real human capacity of the Brazilian people to manage their own country. Graça Aranha provides us with a long and accurate summary ranging from Paulo Maciel's bitter observations on the nationalistic banalities of his colleagues, up to the dreams of glory and conquest of the proud Lentz.

Even here, however, what matters most is not so much what the author says directly but rather what he allows us to perceive. The presence of Paulo Maciel and the other judges serves the purpose of introducing the theme of bureaucracy and administration of justice in Brazil. This is a fundamental issue for understanding Brazil: the paradox is that a young country like Brazil was endowed from the very beginning with an old soul and structure, deeply bureaucratic, sadly tied to the ancient Portuguese motherland. Portugal, in fact, was a land of merchants and sailors that had come to possess a land like Brazil, which had no already-structured civilization. Because of this, it was impossible, on the one hand, to establish trade, while, on the other hand, it was impossible to populate and transform it into a rural agriculture, since Portugal did not have the men necessary for this enterprise. The Portuguese were then compelled to appeal to an already dead and antiquated institution: slavery became the only way to exploit and populate the immense expanse of the new country. Slavery, however, brought along the reconstruction of a rigidly medieval structure: the castle and the landlord were easily identifiable in the *casa grande* and the large landed estates, while the serfs were recognizable in the Black slaves. An immobile, paralyzed, and paralyzing state existed in which all the efforts were geared toward maintaining the status quo through control and taxation of any productive activity. The state, then, was not based upon production, but rather on control—in other words, it was a bureaucratic state.

Graça Aranha gives us a truthful, although ruthless, description of a predatory incursion, a punitive expedition, namely the visit of "justice" in the German colonies. The comparison stands out too clearly to merit any comment: on the one side, the Germans are devoted entirely to productive activities capable of creating a stable and prolific wealth; on the other side are the inquisitorial, greedy, and corrupt Brazilians. And in their midst is Paulo Maciel, unable to react against the moral depravity of his colleagues. The group consisting of judges and a couple of functionaries does everything possible: they eat and drink at the colonists' houses, they cheat and blackmail as many people as possible, persecuting the defenseless, they harass the poor Maria, and they let themselves be bribed when they cannot bribe themselves. In the meanwhile, Paulo Maciel dreams of running away to Europe, always hoping that Europe will someday conquer Brazil and change it into a white country. Beyond all reason and all contrasting theories, which the book thoroughly summarizes, the author's position emerges clearly, that is, his almost instinctual choice pushes him always on the side of the Germans:

> Milkau and Lentz admired the robustness of those men with the iron wrist, and the Herculian torsos, the reddish beards and the deep blue

> eyes, all alike as if they were brothers. Only a mulatto stood out among them. His face was ruined by smallpox, he was sunburned, had a little sparse and curly beard and his short hair was straight on the forehead. With his bloodshot eyes and the pointed teeth as if in a saw, he often took on the appearance of a malignant satyr.[4]

By reading Graça Aranha's works one gets the impression that the author was troubled by a problem: he was anguished by a serious complex, that of being Brazilian. There is a love-hate relationship with Brazil which Graça Aranha cannot overcome and of which he probably is not even aware. On the one hand, the elitist, Aryan, even racist tendency that makes him admire the Germanic order, organization, and capacity for work is counterbalanced, on the other hand, by the perception that the noisy and mulatto Brazil, the disorganized and corrupt Brazil, whose sensuality seems almost to scare him, is after all more his own than he would like to admit. It is not by mere chance that there are two main protagonists of *Canaã*, and that dialogue is the prevailing form throughout the novel. This unconscious element, obsessing the author, emerges clearly through another episode. It is the description of a festivity at the German colony at which some Brazilians are present, including Felicíssimo and Joca. The orchestra played only European music when, at some point, Felicíssimo, cheerfully drunk, requests, loudly, some Brazilian popular music. He is satisfied and when the orchestra starts a *chorado*, Felicíssimo tries to follow the music with a dance but his drunkenness does not allow him to stand up. He ends up by finding refuge on a chair. Nobody dances; in the large hall there are only these spectators—they are all Germans:

> Suddenly, like an ancient faun, Joca jumped in the middle of the hall and started to dance. His native soul forgot for a moment this painful exile in his own land, among people coming from other worlds. Troubled by the music that spoke to the most remote and eternal essence of life, the mulatto, almost in a trance, liberated part of himself through a proud and extraordinary cheerfulness. His whole body vibrated in a single rhythm; the raised head bore an expression of limitless pleasure, the half-open mouth, with the pointed teeth, smiled; the hair became alive in liberty, now straight and hard, now falling softly on the forehead; the feet flew over the floor and, at times, stopped while the limbs vibrated in a frenzied dance; the hands, now lowered, snapped noisily the fingers that now came out of the extended arms, now spread in the air and, while in that posture, drunk with music, stretched on tiptoes, with his arms open, he looked like he was on the verge of flying. At times, he would run through the hall agitating his body languidly, with

> his feet united, in a short and repeated step. Some other times, obeying the rhythm of the music, he came languidly, swaying his hips, with his head reclined and the eyes ecstatic and he approached some woman almost slitheringly, as if he wanted to drag her in a repressed passion which, however, one guessed to be feverish and dizzy. Then, he launched himself in a tiger-like jump, resumed his madness as if in a gigantic satanic attack; he vibrated all over, trembling convulsively, almost still in the air, in a vibration of all his nerves, imperceptibly swift, almost giving the impression of instantaneous repose in the air like the dance of a hummingbird. In that moment if the orchestra had stopped, and made a pause that would upset everything, Joca would not have perceived the lack of the instruments because he, in his triumphant body, in his rare cheerfulness, in the impulse of his own soul, was living, expending himself in the old dance of his race, his entire being was in movement, was vibration, was music. The scene continued for a while with only this character. Joca looked for someone with whom to dance, a woman who would respond to his appeal, who would respond to his movement. Nobody came, nobody felt the impetus of moving, of vibrating to the rhythm of that dance. Everybody was curious and nothing else. Desolate, caught by a sudden sadness, by a nostalgia of his companions of youth, of the *negras* who felt like him, little by little he became tired . . . His chest heaved, the dark legs did not jerk with the same energy displayed a little while before, similar to the vigorous flexibility of bamboo . . . Exhausted, he collapsed on the floor, his body caved in, and the last interpreter of the national dances yielded the ground to the winners while another music, another dance invaded the scene. It was the Germanic dance waltz, clear slow fluid like a river.[5]

Where is Graça Aranha's heart? At first sight, there are no doubts: everything makes us believe that victory is on the German side, on the side of the European civilization that proceeds with a clear and harmonious rhythm, with its exact proportions, with its serene instincts suggested to the clear force of reason. In contrast, a lot of empathy emerges in the description of Joca, of this cheerful forest elf lost among Germans who are impenetrable and unresponsive to any form of being that is not their own!

We must approach the problem from a historical point of view and try to understand Graça Aranha's perspectives, which must have been quite different from our own. *Canaã* was published in 1902, the same year as the publication of *Os sertões*, and at that time, nobody doubted that the only form of civilization was that expressed in Europe. All the rest was only folklore, which could be judged by the extent to which it approached the model of European civilization. Graça

Aranha feels clearly that he belongs to a country to which he is connected for reasons that go beyond his own origins: he knows that he is Brazilian as few know it, in a way that can be at times even morbid and painful. But he also knows that his country is not the kind of nation he would normally consider civilized: it is a country with a large proportion of Blacks and mulattoes, descendants of slaves, uneducated, noisy, and cheerful people; it is a country with huge landed estates, ruled by a rural oligarchy with a closed and reactionary mentality; it is a country with an immense bureaucratic apparatus that stops and paralyzes everything, a country with thousands of painful contradictions. Yet this is his land . . . What is its destiny going to be? Will it be the integration, the fusion of races with the new European immigrants who have shown such a clear and proven ability in facing the problems connected with the conquest of the land, or will it be the subjugation by these blond people who will create thus a new Brazil, a white Brazil? Let us recall that it is still 1902. Brazil was then going through a particularly apathetic phase of its history, a phase, however, veiled by the anguished awareness of the need to change. In contrast, we can say now that the moral and civilizing force of Europe was a delusion in the light of the two world wars that have drastically changed our way of thinking about Germany, toward which the author shows so much empathy.

The shades of racism throughout Graça Aranha's work responded to the majority of the public opinion and even to a certain scientific and historical conception of the time. During one of the many dialogues of the novel Graça Aranha has Milkau, the idealist foreigner, express the noble apology of the fusion of the races while he lets Paulo Maciel, the Brazilian intellectual, claim his bitterness and regrets at being a white man in a mulatto country. In fact, Milkau says:

> From the very beginning there have been winners and losers under the shape of masters and slaves: during two centuries the latter have struggled against the former. All the revolutions in Brazilian history have been class struggles, the oppressed against the oppressors. The Brazilian people have been for many years just a nominal expression of a conglomerate of separate races and classes. And this state of affairs would have stayed thus for centuries if the strong and imperious sensuality of the conquerors had not demolished the walls of separation that had formed this intermediate race of mestizos and mulattoes which is the tie, the national union that, increasing every day, ended up by conquering the positions of defense of its oppressors . . . and when the army has ceased to be a caste of white people and has become dominated by the mestizos, the revolt has been nothing else than the revenge of the oppressed, which has created immediately institutions bound to remain

for a while, because of the very force of gravity, in temporary harmony with the psychological instincts that had created them . . . This clash of the unconscious was necessary so that what was sought for centuries, through other means, was created: nationality.[6]

The foreigner's apology is counterbalanced by the Brazilian melancholy regret:

> It was necessary that from the conflict of our human species a new type of mestizo be formed, who, adapting himself better to nature, to the physical environment, and being the expression of the average qualities of all of us, would be the winner and would eliminate the extremes that generated him. Perfect . . . let us notice that Pantoja is not an isolated case. Those who rule us and rule us with better consensus and success belong to this kind of mulatto. Brazil is eventually their own . . .
>
> Paulo Maciel thought a moment and, then, while he stared at his own white and slender hands, he continued with an ironic smile: "There is no doubt . . . if I had only a few drops of African blood, I would certainly not be here complaining . . . the balance with the country then could be definite . . . Pantoja, Brederodes . . . do they not proceed strongly and securely? . . . Aren't they the masters of the land . . . Why was I not born mulatto?[7]

Thesis, antithesis. The synthesis comes directly from the writer's comment in a form that, although still indecisive, makes us perceive where his heart is. The author's position is, in fact, clarified by the character of Paulo Maciel, who embodies him spiritually.

> The small world of the colony was present to Milkau's spirit as a clear summary of the entire country. The dominant Brazilians came inevitably from the fusion of the races while the young man with a very fine intelligence, a superior and remarkable sensitivity, was annihilated, vanquished by the others. Was he right? Did he lack that drop of Black blood that would create the right balance in him?[8]

How much of Graça Aranha is really in Paulo Maciel, and to what extent did the writer represent himself? Without going too deep into this problem, which is, moreover, secondary, it will be enough to remember some autobiographical pages by Graça Aranha, some memories and some youthful attitudes in order to find several connections and similarities within the writer and the character he created.

Graça Aranha never achieves a choice and a conclusion. The negative portrait of the Brazilians—the predatory incursion of "justice" in the German colonies—is paralleled by scenes of brutality and violence to which poor Maria is subjected by her own countrypeople.

Shades of racism, which we mentioned above, emerge clearly in *Canaã* when the author refrains from the theoretical discussions he seems to prefer, and shifts to simple description. When the author does not try to prove anything he then shows the conditioned reflexes of the white and cultured Brazilian who does not enjoy seeing himself associated nationally with a country of mulattoes. In one episode, Felicíssimo wants to show off to the two Germans; he starts measurements with the theodolite, an instrument he boasts he knows how to use but which he does not know at all. The scene is a farce in which all the workers are both accomplices and protagonists:

> The workers exchanged intelligent glances. He was playing the usual old comedy of the theodolite. They knew very well that the farmer during over 200 measurements had not succeeded in working with the damned instrument which exerted upon him a satanic influence and which affected his personality, upsetting and causing a terror the signs of which troubled his spirit since the end of dinner. As soon as the theodolite disappeared into the chest, Felicíssimo's soul freed itself from anguish and his youthful good mood came back erasing even the traces of that scientific anguish.[9]

The comments of the hard and aristocratic Lentz toward Felicíssimo are very strict and are summed up in a "these mulattoes," the first time, and by a "that big monkey," the second time.

The author displays an almost morbid pleasure in representing and emphasizing the typical defects of the Brazilians especially when he deals with mulattoes. The representatives of justice who cheat and rob are mulattoes just like Felicíssimo and Joca, who are simple souls, cheerful and clownish. An example is the description of an anonymous mulatta: "A young mulatta sat near the door knocker. She was the embodiment of indolence. Her disheveled hair was pointed like horns. Her filthy shirt fell carelessly on the skinny belly and her flaccid breasts fell flabbily on her belly."[10] The child who guides Milkau is just like the mulatta: "This was a nervous and bony child, he was the rotten product of a race that was extinguishing itself little by little in the deaf and unaware suffering of the species that does not reach a superior flowering and a full expansion of individuality."[11]

Where the author reveals himself most clearly, and probably unconsciously, is when he touches even though momentarily the subject of Black people and slavery. He is not dealing here with the mulatto bureaucrats, swindlers, and cheats, whom the writer might actually have met and whom he describes in the novel; he is dealing here with the other side of the river, that is, with the Black man who was a slave only ten years before. There is a Black man in the first pages of the novel. He is an old man, still physically strong, with a noble and dignified demeanor. When he is interviewed by Milkau all his conversation expresses a painful nostalgia of the "good old times" of slavery:

> Ah, all that, my *sinhô moço* ended . . . what happened to the *fazenda*? Once my old *sinhô* died, his son lived until the government took away his slaves. Everybody went away. The master moved with his family to Vitória where he has a job; my comrades retreated into this great forest and everybody made himself a house, some here, some there, wherever it was more convenient. Myself with my own people I came here in the land of the *coronel*. These are sad times. The government destroyed the *fazendas* and threw us all in the middle of the road, to chase food, to buy clothes, and work like oxen to survive. Ha! The good times of the *fazendas!* We all worked together, those who had to pick coffee picked coffee, those who had to clean the grains cleaned the grains, all together, so many, many people, mulattoes, *cafuzas* . . . The overseer was no big deal . . . nobody ever died of beatings. There was always food and on Saturday, on Sunday's eve, ah, my *sinhô*, the old drums rolled until dawn![12]

Whose nostalgia is this? Is it that of the old Black man who chases the ghost of his own youth or rather that of the writer who cannot free himself from the memories of his youth when he was a slave owner? Maybe the truth is in the middle. Although this might seem absurd, there is some verisimilitude in the Black man's nostalgia; this is not because slavery was a good thing but simply because the end of slavery, without rural reform, meant an even worse evil for many uneducated Blacks, who were unprepared to manage their own freedom and were, moreover, deprived of economic means.

Shortly before this episode, Milkau had run into a *fazenda* in shambles, a nightmarish image, where a *fazendeiro*, having become crazy, wandered among the ruins of what had once been his own dwelling. He was a human wreck who "even in this state, represented the human figure, the superior life involved in the fall of things, dragged into a general disaster."[13] We can say then that if the Black man's nostalgia was likely, then Graça Aranha's nostalgia is certain and it is directed toward his own world and his own class. All this is described in the first pages of the novel when Milkau, the German, travels through the wealthy lands of the German colonists, those who, as the author hopes, will become the new masters of Brazil.

Graça Aranha's repugnance toward Blacks is instinctual and goes much beyond his criticism of the mulatto bureaucrats and the nostalgia for his own lordly past. In his other novel he reveals clearly and repeatedly his substantial conception of existence, and of Love (always capitalized) as a very pure and a very high feeling. Warm and sensuous love, the violent and almost animal sexual encounter, when it is not surrounded and preceded by poetry and intelligence, disgusts and frightens him. We can say simply that his writings give us the impression of a constant sexual phobia.

The love relation, as it was conceived in the Black world, in the context of a different culture, simple and direct and, after all, natural, offended his refined soul. The inevitable state of degradation to which the Black world had been reduced by slavery, accentuated inevitably the animal side of the sexual relation and this increased the writer's repulsion; but he never became aware of his own limitation in this respect. Maria's captivity is the episode in which the writer's hidden taboos emerge clearly: the imprisoned woman is white and her skin is like milk, her hair is blonde; her guards are Black soldiers. And what will these Black soldiers do? Well, they simply do what during centuries the white masters did to the Black slave women on their plantations. It is sad that it did happen then, it is sad that it is happening now to Maria. For the writer, however, it is something else: it is his own ancestral taboo that is violated when Maria's white flesh is soiled by contact with Black skin (and luckily, for all of us, the violence is never consummated). And after all, if Maria is in prison now it is because in the village, inhabited by the blond men, nobody felt pity for her—everybody chased her away as if she were a hydrophobic bitch. But let us see what the writer says:

> During Milkau's absence Maria had known a new torture, coming from sexual persecution. Her whiteness, the rarity of her type in her race, had ended up by exciting for a while the *negro* soldiers. At first the severe bearing of the wretched woman had kept them at a distance, encircling her with respect and protection: almost imperceptibly, however, cohabitation and familiarity allowed an irrepressible desire to arise in them. They tried to seduce her by communicating their lubricity to her through instinct; but when they saw how insensitive and obstinate she was in her rejection of the old prison custom according to which the women prisoners were the lovers of the guards, they became furious, and used terror, force, and cruelty to win her over. Her nights were agitated, always trying to avoid rape by the excited and drunken soldiers. She struggled in their hands and managed to rescue herself either because the two *pretos* fought over possession of her or because her screams scared the two cowards. On days when they let her be it was only to take revenge upon her for the struggles of the night; then they compelled her to work for them as a slave, beating her up and denying her food.[14]

After all these Blacks are really wicked! A close analysis of the above passage reveals all of Graça Aranha's repressed and unrepressed taboos (and not only his, unfortunately, because many of these ideas were shared by his compatriots). The writer, who loves to theorize over everything and who goes from particular to general, does not feel the need here to expand his discussion to the situation of prisons in Brazil. Instead, he emphasizes in a rather melodramatic fashion the black-white contrast. He forgets almost completely, except for a quick hint, that Maria's situation was similar to that of any other female prisoner. It is a sad heredity, handed down to the Black guards from the time of slavery when they were for a long time the victims. (But why were they all Black? Was the job of guard unfit for a white man?) The passage consists of a series of Freudian slips that reveal the author's sexual phobia, his repugnance for the erotic rapport when it is not disguised or at least embellished by verbal refinement, poetry, and spiritual affinity. Examples of this old expression, such as "through instinct, their lubricity" or "*se erguesse*" (which I have translated approximately as "would arouse"), whose literal meaning is "would erect," are immediately followed by the word "desire." These slips tell us what Graça Aranha did not want to tell us.

A viagem maravilhosa takes us to a different time and place. This story is not set in the rural environment of the German colonies of the Espírito Santo, but rather among the good society of Rio de Janeiro. It is no longer the turn of the century but rather the eve of the 1930s. Between the publication of *Canaã* and that of *A viagem maravilhosa* thirty years elapsed. Many things happened during those thirty years in Brazil and in the world. Brazil, having been excluded from the First World War, was dramatically affected by all the problems posed and unsolved by the abolition of slavery in 1888. A series of events shakes the calm and somnolent atmosphere of the great cities. In Rio de Janeiro, São Paulo, and Rio Grande do Sul a series of rebellions—starting with the mythical one of the eighteen of Copacabana—open a crisis in the traditional establishment of the country; in the *sertão* Luis Carlos Prestes starts and accomplishes his long march. In Rio de Janeiro the youth quivers, conspires, debates and, at times, struggles: this is the setting of *A viagem maravilhosa*.

First of all what is this marvelous journey that entitles the book? It is a flight towards love, towards pure ecstasies, even though this flight implies inevitably the rejection of one's own political responsibilities. The story is the long and tormented love affair of Teresa and Filipe, both young, beautiful, and restless: she is married to a wicked fellow, Radagásio (wicked even in his name); he shares the excited and vibrant mood of many bourgeois young people who dislike the gloomy political situation and feel ready to change their country and the world. Their story is entangled with that of many others. The

PICKING OF COFFEE BEANS

COLHEITA DO CAFÉ

happy ending of the love story of Filipe and Teresa involves the abandonment and rejection of any revolutionary ambition. If love is eternal, if only love is worth living, then let the others either change the country or leave it as it is.

The plot is essentially similar to that of *Canaã*: the historical-political problems, which in *Canaã* were connected with the Germans and the almost obsessive comparisons with the mulatto Brazilians, in *A viagem maravilhosa* are replaced by the revolutionary ambitions of the young people against the dominating oligarchy. Milkau and Maria's flight is paralleled by Filipe and Teresa's flight. In both novels the conclusion is always an individualistic refusal to solve the problems.

Despite the thirty years elapsed and despite the writer's active participation in the Semana da Arte Moderna in 1932, his point of view has not changed much. We can say that if Brazil changed in those years, Graça Aranha tried to stay the same. The different historical moment is summed up according to old perspectives. Many of the writer's limitations, which were only hinted at in *Canaã*, emerge here more openly: in *A viagem maravilhosa* he leaves behind any reticence and the work, published posthumously, is violent in its unsubdued problems.

First of all the author's anguished phobia towards sex surfaces even in absolutely secondary scenes such as one when Filipe in his fazenda in the hinterland of São Paulo observes the animals at the fountain: "Once they had quenched their thirst there came sexual cheerfulness. Horses and mules, bulls and cows practice with delicacy the erotic ceremonial. In their movement there was none of the hallucinating human bestiality."[15] As we will have a chance to see later, Graça Aranha perceives a degradation in the practice of the sexual act; whatever side you want to look at it, his is at least a very peculiar position.

Let us proceed with the novel. The characters are inspired in their actions by a quest for an elitist charisma; their natural elite remains in the social field to be later sublimated in an ecstatic purification when they have a chance to meet Love. Teresa, beautiful, dissatisfied, badly wed and very neurotic, dreams of the first classical step of social consecration, the journey to Europe: "And I've never been to Europe! Unbelievable! Everybody comes and goes and here I am, nailed down here."[16] This is exactly like the characters of Machado de Assis, half a century before (but of course without Machado's subtle irony and his ironic feeling of the limits of existence). The fault of all this is, of course, her idiotic husband but also her father who thought only about work: "A worker like nobody else. And he wasn't even a

Portuguese."[17] Here is another snobbish touch: working hard, which in Portugal was *mourejar*, a thing that the Moors did, in Brazil becomes a thing that the Portuguese did, that is, something for the poor immigrants who wanted to become rich. Europe appears again in a comment Teresa passes on a nouveau-riche family: "They have already been in Europe, the family has already made its great entrance in society."[18]

The aristocratic feeling of existence becomes even sharper when we move from pure social conventions to the historical awareness of belonging to the people who contributed to the creation of the country and who are compelled to yield the royal scepter to other, less worthy hands. For example, Teresa and Filipe participate in a solemn mass inside the ancient monastery of São Bento. Swept away by the mystic atmosphere of the environment, the woman allows her imagination to take her far away:

> Teresa's imagination wandered around in the past of that abbey. That had been one of the centers of colonial spirituality. The civilizing force that came from the east and which achieved a better and more fortunate crusade among the American population, spread out throughout the city from that monastery. The monastery indoctrinated and industrialized the *negro* slaves and the Indians. It has become rich thanks to the presence of the great Portuguese families. The most generous donors deserved a burial in the main alley of the abbey or in the lands of the convent. Dona Vitória de Sá came from the founder of Rio de Janeiro. She must have been a very pious lady, the supporter of São Bento, regular in her religious attendance, brilliant in her parties, she was carried around by her slaves in a silk and golden canopy, accompanied by a numerous family and by a clientele of *negro* slaves, *mamelucos*, *caboclos*, *benquelas*, *tapuios*, and of different *minhotos* and *alentejanos* . . . Teresa wandered around in the past, which was also Filipe's past. São Bento had ceased to be the town of Portuguese splendor that it had been once it was incorporated and silently and commercially occupied by German friars. Everything had changed there. Where had the magnificent parties gone and where had Dona Vitória gone in her canopy of crimson, damask, and gold? What had happened to the big eating orgies of the crazy friars and the patriarchal abbots, in the dining halls full of their children, their godchildren and the band of parasites who devoured the best fish and the best meat and who got drunk with the best wine? Now, instead, the Teutonic austerity managed the wealth while it regimented the novices so that they would learn how to exploit the estate of the monastery.[19]

It is a peculiar passage especially because of the lack of any comment from the author (something unusual in Graça Aranha who often supports at the same time two different and opposed theories). This passage is also curious because of its criticism of the German friars. Apparently some time has passed since *Canaã* and the infatuation for the Germans. Teresa's entire vision is clearly visceral: the exploitation of the estate of the convent by the German friars is seen as a moment of decadence as compared to the institution of slavery! German austerity is disparagingly compared to the cheerful debauchery of the friars and of their relatives and parasites who followed them. The crusades are placed on the same level as the "civilizing" activity of the convent which indoctrinated and industrialized the Black slaves and the Indians, and in practice, sordidly traded in human beings!

The presence of the church, the place of worship, seems particularly to excite Graça Aranha's imagination; the church he sees as the center of a long and glorious tradition, of a white past to which a Black presence opposes itself. Even the church, the house of Christ, which should be open equally to all human beings, becomes a pretext for new forms of separation and segregation. This is historically true, however, because the Church in general always fully supported the systematic exploitation of the people of color. The convent of São Bento, as we have seen, prepares the slaves for various forms of work (it indoctrinated them also, thus giving religious consecration to their servile condition). From São Bento we move on to another monument of the glorious colonial past, the church of Nossa Senhora da Glória. In the first passage it was Teresa, while in this second passage it is Dona Isabel, Filipe's aristocratic mother, who rambles:

> Inside the octagonal nave hundreds of electric lamps shone in transparent clarity while hundreds of candles burned with yellowish flames. The silver of the candleholders, of the lamps and chandeliers mixed itself with the gold of the goblets, of the stoles, and of the capes radiating sumptuously. The white altars, the white roses, airy, bands of green leaves enter the meandering harmony of the light. The body of *negros* interrupts the triumphant phosphorescence. The *pretas*, devout, seated on the floor, murmured prayers, while others supporting themselves against the walls of *azulejos*, napped heavily. In the middle of the church the kinky heads floated while the bodies disappeared in the compact mass. The smell of goats, a satanic smell, spread around and gave its distinctive odor to the black devotion. For Dona Isabel all that was nauseating and profane. Her sharp and alert historical sense evoked the devotion of former times, in that small church, a real and courtesan devotion. In that place skeptical emperors had passed in contrition. There, royal princes had been baptized.[20]

The choice of the motif and the gradual evocation are clearly emblematic of the author's aristocratic position: the beauty of the church, the splendor of the ornaments, and the light are used to emphasize the dark mass of the Blacks and the violent smell of their bodies. The fear (which becomes horror) of sex prevails in any of the writer's observations even when he is describing the simplest things such as, for example, the Blacks who dance at the exit of the church, to a music "in which the mestizo lasciviousness swayed."[21]

Brazil is a country where the Blacks played an important and determining historical role. Graça Aranha became aware of this and therefore left behind the German fantasies of *Canaã*. The victory of the mulatto, the affirmation of the mestizo world, already foreseen by Paulo Maciel's gloomy pessimism, is now definite: Aranha rejects viscerally this historic reality. His rejection is mixed ambiguously with the rejection of a certain policy and of a certain Brazil.

On the whole it is very hard to understand what Graça Aranha wants: his solutions are always negative, always full of criticism. He does not provide an alternative. Often the literary aspect, the logical form are only the cultivated and orderly fashion in which he expresses his phobias and his fears; they provide the intellectual veneer for an instinctual position. For example, in describing the funeral vigil of a political leader, the author establishes a comparison between the hunting trophies hanging from the walls and the faces of the people who are present:

> The majority of the people came from the forest, the *senzalas*, from the harbor and the slaughters in the fields. Northeastern people with triangular faces, Portuguese *maranhenses*, *cafuzos* from Bahia, *mamelucos* from São Paulo, *mineiros bisonhos*, *gaúchos castelhanos*, all were underdog Brazilians who came from slavery to slavery. On the walls, on the floors, on the furniture there were the trophies of the *caudilho*. Jaguar heads with the red, wide-open throats, the stupid heads of deer with long horns, picturesque tortoise shells, embalmed hawks . . . from those remains a nauseating odor came, the stench of the *negros* and of any servile stink. It was the odor of the *cangaço*, of the slaughters, massacres, of all the sewers of slavery and death.[22]

Graça Aranha's rejection of Brazil oscillates from visceral positions to historical criticism; what worries him particularly is the problem of the legitimacy of political powers. It is, of course, very dangerous ground because at its origin are aristocratic aspects, strictly elitist, which have been at the base of any political movement in Brazil from independence, to the Republic, to the very end of slavery. The author's criticism, then, never goes very deep; it always stays on the surface and is often entangled in commonplaces:

> The legitimacy of government is fictitious. In Brazil there is no legitimate government. Every government is a usurpation. In order to have legitimacy in representative government one would need legitimate elections. In Brazil the electorate is artificial and elections are a sham. There are only governments of fact, which cannot be disguised as governments of right, legitimate, legal, representative. What is there is nothing but a group of individuals who took hold of the public administration and exploited it for their private interests . . . in Brazil there is only the government that the Army and the Navy allow because these are the only active and armed classes that can modify the institutions without minding the other classes.[23]

From the historical-political commonplace we move on to a commonplace criticism of the ruling class, to which the author adds that share of sexual moralisms which seems always to characterize him:

> They obey the instincts of greed and pleasure. They are adulators, they are slaves, they are cynical. Everything is an adventure. Existence is a game and one expects anything from hazard . . . the breaking up of old ties for the free expansion of lust, money, and position. They are servile and greedy. There is a perversion of sensuality in the greed of indecent voluptuousness, in sodomy, in lechery, and in intoxication.[24]

Graça Aranha spares nobody. After the criticism of institutions and the political class, it is the turn of youth (always, naturally, remaining on the surface and without ever changing the form of the criticism): "They're all indifferent, all vicious in their voluptuousness and greed for money. Selfish skepticism animates them. It is the inner spring of any of these animals."[25] His writings are filled with stereotypical sentences, repeated hundreds of times, which show his rejection of tropicalism: "The triangular face, pale, tropical, sad";[26] he thinks that the mothers are too good . . . "the mother was weak, the Brazilian mother." The list could continue but it would add nothing new. Graça Aranha, when he chooses to be so, can be a master of obviousness and monotony.

Yet the rejection of Brazil goes much beyond visceral positions against Blacks and mulattoes or trivialities against the government, young people, and mothers. The protagonists of *A viagem maravilhosa* share the bitter awareness of belonging to a disappearing world. Brazil changes. The immigrants coming from Europe are giving it a new face, the Blacks assert themselves more every day and assert their presence in every moment of the life of the country. And what does Filipe do, the descendant of the founders of the country, the theoretician of the revolution, the inexorable critic of the national vices?

He abandons the revolution, or rather, he abandons every idea of revolution since he had never surpassed the purely verbal level, and takes refuge in a great, unique, wonderful, and purifying Love. In other words, Teresa's beautiful eyes were enough to deprive Brazil of a revolutionary. Is this maybe Graça Aranha's last message? Can the impossibility of self realization historically and socially be sublimated in the ecstasy of love?

All these young people display a deep sense of fatigue in their vague, repressed, and useless aspirations, in their organistic solipsism, in their absurd incapacity to transform their proposals into practical action.

So much talk and then comes the escape; escape from revolution, and from Brazil itself. Filipe must take a trip into the hinterland of São Paulo to solve some family problems: the family fazenda must be sold, the uncle who was in charge of it wants to leave Brazil, to go and live in Europe. The entire episode is a sequel of symbols: the old family that made the history of Brazil abandons the field, the journey to Europe looks like a return. The fatigue of the uncle who wants to interrupt his long-lasting dialogue with the land is paralleled by Filipe who wants only to return to Teresa. It is the handing over to the new masters, the Americans who arrive full of dollars and projects, and the Italian colonists who have given new life to the land. Graça Aranha does not like the Americans and in describing them repeats the usual commonplaces:

> These individuals are anonymous. They are ephemeral. Life for them is like that of termites; it is a biological mission of the national nucleus, inspired only by economic conquest. They have the awareness of disappearing forever without leaving a trace . . . It is the ultimate assertion of anonymity deprived of any moral finality.[28]

Besides the triviality of the commonplace, he displays the ignorance of one who refuses the most basic information and sees the other, the winner, the new master only in his rougher and less pleasing aspects, which are inevitably connected with power. The pattern of Paulo Maciel's defeat is repeated here—the cultured, the sensitive, the fine—opposed to the mulattoes. Intelligence and sensitivity are handicaps: this is one of the tritest commonplaces. The uncle yields the field to the rough and brutal Americans just as Paulo Maciel in *Canaã* had to yield to the mulattoes. Filipe, in his turn, finds himself in the middle of Italian colonists, a cheerful, festive, lively crowd. He goes away because he is totally unable to participate in any of their simple expressions of joy.

In this episode a character symbolizes the essence of Graça Aranha's vision. He is French. Let us be reminded that France and French people represent for the Brazilian, especially for the Brazilian like Graça Aranha, the best expressions of human civilization. This Frenchman is an old engineer from the prestigious polytechnic school, who has spent almost forty years in the sertão; his language, his way of expressing himself, even the logic of his thoughts, are similar to those of the ignorant caboclos. When Filipe and his uncle speak to him in French, however, he ceases to be the rough and ignorant man and goes back to expressing himself as a cultured and brilliant engineer:

> Filipe was confused by this phenomenon of retrogression of a French polytechnician who, once he penetrated the woods and came in contact with the *sertanejos* had become primitive, rustic, rough, gauche, and deprived of the energy necessary to rise from this inferior level while, instead, when expressing himself in his racial language became again a man of superior intelligence and culture.[29]

The entire conversation with the Frenchman oscillates between these two poles, during the dinner at which French dishes and wines are served: he is, on one side, a cultured and refined man and, on the other side, a rough caboclo; from the Seine to the Araguaia, as the author says: "Filipe pondered long over the ineluctable force of the *sertão*, which made intelligence regress while it eliminated culture and turned men into savages."[30]

What is the meaning of this episode? It is the alibi Aranha uses to justify the defeat of his protagonist, of the man of his caste, of his social class, of those who entered the modern era with a medieval Brazil. The students of the French polytechnic school are always considered the cream of the crop: if a man who came out of that school is defeated by the sertão, his defeat is a justification for Filipe's and his uncle's escape. Cultured and intelligent men are not made to struggle and win agaist this land: maybe the Americans with their dollars and their Western manners will succeed, but the Americans are rough cowboys; maybe the Italians will succeed with their noisy enthusiasm, but the Italians are nothing but rough farmers who come from a poor land to a rich land.

Graça Aranha's aristocratic conception of existence brought him inevitably to a contradiction of the political concepts he had pursued since before he wrote *Canaã*. The renewal of Brazil happened in forms and ways different from those he had dreamt of and, especially, through social classes that were different from his own. He is an isolated figure in his ivory tower. Once he loses the old dream of the renewal of the country thanks to the blond Germans, he sees his land being dominated more and more by the American economic influence, always more and more populated by European immigrants and by Blacks (the Blacks, of course, were there before, but they did not occupy the same social positions).

Given these premises and the author's aristocratic conceptions and preconceptions, his attitude toward Blacks could only become worse in the thirty years since *Canaã* was written. During that period, the decisive transformation of Brazil took place, and the flowering of new ideas connected with Modernism only served to make his way of thinking more closed. This change in attitude can be explained historically, given the rise of the Black world that in *Canaã* was only foreseen but in *A viagem maravilhosa* is in full expansion. Graça Aranha, the citizen and the man, finds himself continuously mixed up with the children of his former slaves, always brash and nagging. For the writer and people like him this must have been very annoying. *A viagem maravilhosa* reflects his intolerance, this annoyance which often becomes true hatred.

When referring to Black people the author uses some specific expressions. The Black nurse Balbina is always referred to as *a peste negra* (the term *peste* corresponds to plague) by Teresa, who feels that she is deprived of her own daughter (while to our eyes Teresa is the one to be blamed because of her lack of interest toward the little girl). The disparaging term *negrada* is used to refer to policemen and soldiers employed in the repression. (There is no understanding that the recruiting was done among the poorest classes, namely Blacks, and that enlistment was for many young people the only way out from death and hunger and the worst forms of exploitation.) The political prisoners were at the mercy of "unleashed sodomizing *negros* who sprang on the prisoners in a beastly and terrifying wrath";[31] the most ferocious among the police chiefs are a mulatto and a Portuguese: "The cruelty of the mulatto was voluptuous, hypocritical, feline" (and here we have again the old sexual taboo against the Blacks that we have already seen in *Canaã* during Maria's imprisonment).[32] The young conspirators commit the unforgivable error of admitting a Black into their restricted circle of upper-class young people. His name is Felismino and he quickly proves himself a coward and a traitor by denouncing all of them to the police. Besides being inferior and vile he shows himself to be also—and how could it be otherwise—a lecher in his enthusiasm toward some prostitutes in the harbor. At the door of the prison criminals are mixed with spies and mulatto soldiers, with Blacks, Arabs, Italians, and Black prostitutes who are their comrades in crimes and debauchery. And so on. Just to be Black or mulatto is in itself a degrading fact in Graça Aranha's prose.

If there is one thing that bothers the author it is the contact between different races: "our unfailing Portuguese who keep the Portuguese characteristics in the *carioca* city and are never tired of procreating mulattoes who then proclaim themselves as the only legitimate Brazilians."[33] This feeling is quite widespread, too, and has been until a few years ago, among white Brazilians: this intolerance towards being fused and mixed with an essentially mulatto people, or at least, with an ethnically mixed people. One of the revolutionaries, equally proud of his own blond hair and of belonging to an old Brazilian family, sums it up:

> You know that I came from the North. I am a Brazilian like nobody else. I am white, I am blond but who cares! To be a Brazilian you don't need to be a mulatto or *caboclo*. These recent children of Portuguese and Black women cannot boast of the Brazilian antiquity as I can. My dear, in this blood three hundred years of Brazil flow. My family like yours, Filipe, created this nation. Brazil is more mine that these mestizos'. I yield only in front of the Indians. To the Africans and their descendants, never. They came after my ancestors, a century after. That's it. Let's stop with this nagging. The fact of having dark skin and kinky hair does not make anyone more Brazilian than the whites. It is just because I'm more Brazilian than anybody else that I'm grieved by all this misery that we fell into.[34]

Monteiro's outburst mirrors at a fictional level Graça Aranha's political and racial anger. He, too, was a blond man coming from an old family, and he, too, was a citizen in a country corrupted by an inept political class and in which Blacks and mulattoes were asserting themselves and were becoming more and more important every day.

The assertion of Négritude is a nightmare for the author. It is again the complex of the besieged citadel which we have noticed in Araripe Júnior and Joaquim Manoel de Macedo: the *macumba*, the *candomblé*, the sorcerer, the magic, the never-hushed rhythm of the drums that expressed during the night a message of anger and hope for the Blacks.

He moves from violent criticism against the Black Balbina to a general attack on everything Black: "The *negra* needs above all a good beating and to be thrown out. We are too weak, nobody ever reacts, neither in the house nor in the streets. This damned police force protects any form of *macumba* and *candomblé*."[35] This statement is historically false: we know very well that in those years there was violent police persecution against any form of Black religion. At best we could say that the persecution had never been strong enough to manage to annihilate Black rituals. But this different issue transcends the historical time of Graça Aranha. In the episode of Radagásio's love affair with Balbina the author gives full vent to his sexual fears and his hatred (because it is true hatred) against Blacks and their cultural expressions, which to him are only forms of beastly superstition.

At some point in the novel Balbina and Radagásio become lovers. Their sleeping together is not, however, a mere chance but it is rather the consequence of Teresa's rejection of her husband. She is, in fact, totally swept away by her passion for Filipe. It is obvious that, as unpleasant as Radagásio is, he certainly is not guiltier than the lovers, Filipe and Teresa, in the double adultery that determines the end of the family ménage; having been rejected by his wife who betrays him, he ends up by finding some consolation with his own servant. It is quite a stereotypical situation: on the one hand are Teresa and Filipe, on the other, Radagásio and Balbina. We do not intend yet to express any moral judgment on the situation but rather to see how Graça Aranha describes the development of the two parallel stories.

We have already dealt with Filipe and Teresa's love affair: Love (always capitalized) is always the moment of supreme truth, of liberation. Love is the ultimate goal to which everything has to be sacrificed, even the noble political passion of Filipe, who abandons his comrades forever.

For Radagásio and Balbina, instead, it is a completely different story. It is not even the simple happy ending of the master who consoles himself with the complaisant young maid. This violates a sexual taboo: Balbina is a Black woman and by joining her, Radagásio lowers himself from his white man's condition, and not only from the social point of view. It seems almost that, in the author's words, the two commit a sacrilege by the simple act of sleeping together! Although parallel to the Teresa-Filipe situation, this story is reversed; now Radagásio is the guilty one since he has a relationship with a Black woman. "All the people of the house will bear witness to your relationship with a *negra*. No judge will ever permit a little girl to be trusted to such a father who abandons himself to a *negra* like Balbina."[36]

The strange thing is that affairs among the white masters and Black servants have always been common in Brazil, at any time. Radagásio's crime, however, is that of having replaced Teresa with Balbina, of having allied himself with a Black woman against his white wife. This is probably the crime with which the author wants to brand the character in the reader's eyes.

Any comment he expresses on Balbina or any aspect of her life has something horrid and sordid. She is a character who causes fear and repugnance and who arouses all of the author's sexual phobias. An example is her scheme of seduction toward Radagásio: Balbina is his foster sister and she is fond of him and she feels sincere anger toward Teresa who despises openly the one who for her is the best of men. Balbina reports to Radagásio his wife's bad deeds and takes advantage of these dialogues to exert her sensuous charm toward the man. Her melodious, sing-song, sexy voice, the strong and sour odor of her body, "the violent stinking lechery of the *negra*" excite Radagásio deeply.[37] But before the man yields totally to the rough and primitive charm of the Black woman, Balbina commits another sacrilege: she will have recourse to the *feiticeiro*, the sorcerer, to have a *feitiço* made against her enemies in order to conquer the man she loves.

We have already noticed the sinister fascination and the unconfessed terror that the figure of the feiticeiro exerted upon most Brazilian writers, with the only partial exception of Xavier Marques. Graça Aranha is no exception: he, too, finds himself inside the besieged citadel; he, too, shows fear of the unknown instead of understanding his own fellow human beings of darker skin. And here is Balbina, who ventures towards the sinister places where the macumba takes place, where the Blacks excited by the *cachaça* dance *samba* to the rhythm of the drums. The old feiticeiro, Pai Jerônimo, appears:

> At the beginning he laughed with his toothless mouth, slowly, encouraging her. The stretched head was covered by hard kinky white hair, the bony face was cheekless, the dark gums surrounded an immense protruding mouth in which a heavy purple tongue smacked. The black back was bent, the stomach was deep, the hips were narrow, the old legs were long, and the arms were large. His naked feet were distorted and the hands were of old iron. All that worn-out and sclerotic carcass became animated by a magic force that came from the supernatural to rule, foresee, guide, protect, and punish. Ogun's force descended on his medium. This force mesmerized Balbina and extracted from her the most obscure and gloomy secrets. The *pai-de-santo* stopped laughing and listened to her confession.[38]

And here follows the description of the festivity: the drums roll, the samba is frenzied, the people are drunk and the naked Balbina is voluptuously caressed by a priestess on her thighs, on her breasts, and on her genitals. Balbina's nudity is not exciting, it creates instead horror and repugnance:

> She was an enormous mass, dark gray, with a bull-like neck, with enormous breasts, and the large stomach which fell on her elephantlike thighs; the expression on her face expressed a state of bliss. The sweet, ecstatic eyes, ajar, and the flat nostrils, which were panting, expired a lucky smile from the half-open mouth.[39]

The horror of mystery embodied by Pai Jerônimo is increased by the horror of sex embodied by the naked Balbina. Graça Aranha unfolds here all his phobias.

And then the *muamba*, the feitiço, the *despacho*, the *mandinga*, the evil eye, in the form of a black hen with yellow *farofa* and extinguished cigars, is placed near Teresa's house in the calm bourgeois quarter of Ladeira da Glória. Tourists and foreigners observe, curious, but for the others it is the moment of fear: rich and poor, white and Black, they all avoid the sinister point, they all fear the object of the curse. Teresa's neighbors, who understand against whom the feitiço is addressed, have recourse to the help of an old Black woman: from an old chest they take out the little statues of Saint Onofrio, of the saints Cosme and Damião, of Saint George, the old amulets; they light candles, they recite placating prayers, and, little by little, the curse is exorcised.

At the end, however, the crime is accomplished: after so many sighs and witchcraft Balbina and Radagásio do the deed and they sleep together. The description of the event is another episode in which Graça Aranha displays his constant phobia of sex. Radagásio is alone in the house, he must prepare a speech, when he discovers Balbina sleeping on the floor, her skirt partly raised. The strong odor that comes from the body of the Black woman, the *catinga*, excites Radagásio; the odor, the body contact are the things that give rise to the greatest horror in the author:

> The strong odor that came from the *negra* held him still and distracted him away from his thoughts . . . His senses were troubled by an anxiety of pleasure which choked him; the *negra* changed position and, because of the movement, the *catinga* came out even more violently. Radagásio felt delight in breathing it in. He came closer—slowly, slowly. It seemed to him that the *negra* had her eyes half open and that she was smiling at him. Radagásio felt like going crazy from desire. He felt a shiver of fear and ran into the sitting room. He wanted some music . . . he remembered to turn on the radio . . . first came a *maxixe*, Radagásio started to dance. He imagined that he was dancing with Balbina who wiggled frenziedly. Next came a *samba*, then another *maxixe*, and all

> that dance, all that music full of *preta* voluptuousness inflamed Radagásio. They met his taste because they agreed with his mestizo blood, which was not very remote. Radagásio sat on the bed, excited by the *sambas* the radio broadcast. Balbina appeared in front of him. Radagásio narrowed his eyes and half closed his lips. Balbina came closer to him with her open mouth, quivering nostrils, and eyes full of heavy lechery. Her raucous, mellow voice murmured on Radagásio's warm face: "*Nonhô*, would you like a little cup of coffee?" Her breath and all the carnal warmth of the *negra* unleashed Radagásio's impulse. He threw Balbina on the bed and, covering her with kisses, answered, panting:
>
> "No, no, I don't want coffee, I want, I want tobacco."
>
> A few minutes later the two brutal, horrendous bodies lay on the bed. Radagásio leaned his dark head on the enormous breasts of the *negra* and little by little he fell asleep.[40]

Discussing the influence of the Blacks upon the sexual life of the white masters, the writer and sociologist Gilberto Freyre said that some white young men, to experience some excitement towards their wives, were compelled to smell a nightgown imbued with the sweat of a Black woman. Only thus were they able to arouse their virility, which suddenly withered at the thought of a sexual relation with a woman belonging to their own race; instead, the memory of the Black women was enough to arouse them. This can be explained historically because white Brazilians, before marrying women of their own race, experienced many sexual encounters with Black women. As a result, the idea of sex was connected to the image of the Black woman. It was some sort of compulsory curriculum vitae.

We do not know how Graça Aranha reached the point of completely rejecting the idea of a sexual relation with a Black woman as something disgraceful. Maybe, since he was unable to love, he felt himself compelled to hate. But he could not ignore the presence of the Black people, either woman or sorcerer, who were always present in his nightmares. In his eyes, everything is horrendous and criticizable in Radagásio and Balbina's relation: Radagásio loves Black music because mestizo blood runs in his veins and this, as racist theories go, is a really good one! Moreover, we know that Balbina's mother once was Radagásio's father's lover (as we see, there was a solid family background); there is then the suspicion that Radagásio and Balbina, besides being foster brother and sister, might be half-siblings. Lecherous and incestuous, that is enough! We are only left with some curiosity about Teresa and Filipe's relation, which the author does not describe for us.

A viagem maravilhosa ends in a rather unusual way. Radagásio takes their daughter away from Teresa, who, after a crisis of despair, finds supreme liberation in her love for Filipe: "They had divine repose, the mystery of mysteries, eternity within relativity. Love solves it all, it can satisfy and give perpetual cheerfulness."[41] A character like Radagásio deserves, however, to be punished; yet his punishment is somewhat peculiar. He is caught, dragged, and tossed around by the mad crowd of the Carnival. For a character like Radagásio, who hates Blacks, and for a writer like Graça Aranha, who not only hates Blacks but also strong odors, violent contacts, noise, and samba, this must have been a real punishment:

> Inside the sounds and the colors the odors move around, *negro* colors, white odors, mulatto odors, all kinds of odors of all the excitements and all the nauseas. Inside the odors there is the movement of touching, violent, brutal, soft, lecherous, sweet, hallucinatory . . . It is the ancestral return to the moon cult, to the night mystery, it is the revenge of the woman. It is the resurrection of the Bacchantes, of the witches, of the devil women. The black mass, the black tragedy, the black magic. The *negra* triumphs, the mulatto triumphs. Music, fanfares, parades, *maxixe, samba* . . . The undulating immobility is crossed by a group of *baianas*, they dance, they sing, they wiggle the heavy *negra* lasciviousness, they are smelled and followed by frenzied gorillas with protruding lips who play tambourines and jump lecherously. The *baianas* have the odor of carnation, of vanilla, of the female . . . The frenzied *baianas* push Radagásio inside the mass. The violent men push him one against the others: *maxixe, macumba, candomblé.* This was Radagásio's *samba.*[42]

Because of his lack of humor and the extremism of his theories, Graça Aranha does not need any further comment. His theories reflect widespread commonplaces. After having dreamt of a white Brazil he rejected Négritude to the very end.

10 LIMA BARRETO: THE PROBLEM OF BEING BLACK

When discussing Lima Barreto (1881–1922) one automatically recalls Machado de Assis. What do these two writers share? They are far apart in mentality, way of living and thinking, and, especially, literary style. They clearly represent two opposite aspects of the same problem, that of the integration of the individual with dark skin in the upper-class urban society at the turn of the century. Barreto was a mulatto just like Machado; both were descendants of slaves, both were writers and journalists, both were public officers. The analogies end here.

The historian Sérgio Buarque de Holanda says: "Despite what they shared, the two *cariocas* novelists diverge on one essential point. While all of Barreto's writings are a somewhat badly hidden confession . . . Machado's are first of all escape and refuge."[1] We might want to say that while Machado apparently forgot his origin, Barreto made out of his being Black a cross to carry with painful obsession, even when it was not necessary. Starting from this premise we can establish a comparison between the series of parallel though opposed characters the two writers created: on one side, we have Machado's upper class, the marquises, the barons, the ministers and the senators, the bankers, the beautiful and elegant ladies; on the other side, we have Barreto's anonymous people, the minor employees, the faceless copyists, the workers, the seamstresses, the failures, the disinherited. Again, on one side, we have Machado's wealthy dwellings, with the beautiful furniture, the vast halls, the large gardens, the elegantly set tables waiting for guests and, once in a while, in the background the presence of a *fazenda* which fed the city from far away. On the other side we have Barreto's *subúrbios,* the outskirts with the small shacks, the back yard with the chicken coops that provide the daily supplies, the small family parties which interrupt the monotony of never-changing days and, at times, the hard and enervating activity of the small farmers.

The comparisons could go on forever. A parallel reading of the works of these two great writers could give us a total picture of Brazilian society at the time, seen from two opposite poles and analyzed and described according to two contrasting ideological principles.

Let us go back to Lima Barreto. As we said, first of all, his works are a badly hidden confession of his life and of his continuously painful defeat. Let us have a look at Barreto's life: his father, a typographer, was a particularly dark mulatto—almost black; his mother, herself a mulatta, had received a good education—she was an elementary-school teacher—from a great family, the Pereiras de Carvalho, who had given her their name and of whom she must have been one of the illegitimate descendants. The tradition of giving their name and educating the children they begot from different slaves was typically Brazilian, as was the tradition of having a *padrinho*, a godfather, an illustrious protector. For Barreto's father this was the senator Afonso Celso, future minister and Viscount of Ouro Preto. Besides being the witness at the wedding of Barreto's father, Afonso Celso was also the godfather of the newborn Afonso Henrique de Lima Barreto.

These data help us to put things in perspective and dismiss those who ascribe the violent and constant anger in Barreto's writings to his condition as a mulatto and an outcast. At his birth Barreto was not privileged but he was far from being an outcast: his father was a technician who worked at the prestigious Tipografia Nacional and who occasionally worked for various newspapers; his mother managed her own small school for children. They could count on an illustrious godfather such as the Viscount of Ouro Preto and on the never-broken ties with the great maternal family. On the whole, he was much better off than Machado de Assis, who was a mulatto, a stutterer, an epileptic, the son of a housepainter and a washer-woman, deprived of great protectors at the time of his birth (although later on he found the generous support of some ladies of good society).

Barreto attended the best schools. His schoolmates were the children of the most illustrious families of Rio de Janeiro. He even enrolled at the famous Escola Politécnica to become an engineer. During his adolescence, however, there were some tragedies. His mother died when he was only seven years old—it was a terrible trauma. For political reasons, his father lost his job although he later was rewarded with the directorship of the insane asylum at Ilha do Governador. Thus, his children had the advantage of living in a large house close to nature. If one wants to look for a cause of Barreto's human tragedy, one might find it in the father figure; the father was an emotionally unstable man who was later driven to madness by daily problems and vicissitudes connected to his work. Before becoming mad, however, the father inspired his son with the burning desire to succeed in society at any cost. Because the father had not succeeded in becoming a doctor, he wanted his son to become an engineer. Probably, Barreto did not have the skills to become an engineer. He failed some courses and was compelled to abandon engineering studies; naturally, this defeat had a great impact on the writer's life. Even though he was quite aware of his weakness in the field of engineering studies, he started to blame all his troubles on being a mulatto among the whites and a poor man among the rich. He had a modest job in public administration and he also worked for various newspapers. In all his novels he attacked everything and everybody; then, of course, he complained that his works were not reviewed by the same newspapers he attacked or by the literary circles he ridiculed. He also criticized public administration and, of course, he never received the promotion he thought he deserved. He became an alcoholic and was often interned in hospitals. He died in 1922 at the age forty-one.

The paradox that affected Barreto's life from adolescence was that of being a rebel, an enemy of all social institutions and, at the same time, having social ambitions. He ended up by ascribing his defeat to the color of his skin, to being a mulatto—which was undoubtedly a drawback in Rio de Janeiro at the time—without realizing, however, that during his entire life he had sought defeat and self-destruction. In fact, not having been able to achieve his goal, he sought final liberation in alcohol. His mother's early death upset him to the point of negatively affecting his relations with women and made him refuse love; his father's madness was a constant nightmare during his whole lifetime, the image of an inexorable doom toward which he walked. (The father lived for twenty years secluded in the house and died forty-eight hours after the son's death.) These family events were Barreto's two tragedies, which he attributed, however, to the color of his skin, while he subconsciously rejected facing his personal reality.

Although affected by a deep emotional charge that distorts the existential vision, Barreto's works are magnificent tableaux of urban life in Rio de Janeiro at the beginning of the century. He depicts the life of the common people, the life of the disinherited, the life of those who struggle for daily necessities, the life of those who do not make the decisions that change history but who, instead, have to adjust the best they can to the continuous changes of situations against which they cannot fight. In other words he depicts the life of many small Lima Barretos.

"It is sad not to be white,"[2] wrote Barreto in his diary, and this sentence is both the leitmotif and the limit of his life and work. It is his leitmotif because it prevails over all and distorts facts and situations. It is also its limit because the author does not overcome the black-white contrast and does not see the existential conditions of the whites who did not belong to the privileged classes. This might account for his dislike of Machado de Assis, the poor mulatto who had forgotten (at least apparently) the color of his own skin, and who had succeeded in making himself accepted by the white world, who had become a high bureaucrat, while Barreto had stayed a junior officer, who had achieved success as a journalist, while he had stayed a simple reporter, who had received all the official sanctions, while he could only count on a few devoted friends. Barreto had even applied in vain to the Brazilian Academy of Letters, of which Machado was the highest member. Moreover, while Machado had achieved a good emotional balance in his marriage with the white Carolina, Barreto had always stayed alone, without emotional entanglements.

Barreto's works are such a complete and total confession that often the reader ends up by confusing the author with his characters. There is an episode in his life—which is transposed into *Recordações do escrivão Isaías Caminha*—which is emblematic of his existential refusal. When he was still a student at the Escola Politécnica, one night, together with some colleagues, he passed by the opera where an Italian company was performing *Aida*. Someone suggested that they could go to the opera for free and immediately the young people jumped over the walls and slipped into the theater. Everyone sneaked into the opera except Barreto, who went back home by himself. His roommate, Nicolao Ciancio, an Italian, also went back home alone, and later on recounted their dialogue:

> "Why didn't you come?"
>
> "Not to be arrested as a chicken thief!"
>
> "?!"
>
> "A *preto* who jumps over the walls at night can only be a chicken thief!"
>
> "And what about us. Didn't we jump?"
>
> "Ah! But you are white, you are 'the boys of the Politécnica.' You are students. That was only a student joke . . . but what about me? Poor me. A *pretinho*. I would have been captured right away by the police. And I would have been the only one to be arrested."[3]

This was typical of Barreto: the fear of a possible rejection paralyzed him to the point of making him withdraw. Foreseeing a rejection, he rejected himself.

One must admit, however, that society in those years was not open to the integration of people with dark skin. These were not insurmountable difficulties (nothing in Brazil is definite; luckily everything is very relative). It is worth recalling here, for a better understanding of this phenomenon in Brazil, that even at the time of the Empire being Black had never prevented André Rebouças from becoming a famous engineer (and Barreto, a student of engineering, certainly knew it). The story goes that at a ball at the court to which he had been invited, André Rebouças had some trouble in finding among the aristocratic ladies one who was willing to dance with him. He ended by dancing with the empress herself, who, once she became aware of this unpleasant situation, invited him herself. This was Brazil. Dark skin certainly created a problem for men like Machado de Assis and André Rebouças, but it was not an insurmountable problem for them. It became so for Barreto because his blackness was at least partly internalized; it gave him the pretext to seek defeat, the destruction that alcohol eventually gave him after he had sought it in vain by requesting success and glory from those men and those institutions whom he attacked ruthlessly.

Another episode confirms Barreto's extreme sensitivity. During the Carnival, in 1906 or 1907, right in the middle of the party he suddenly withdrew even though up to that moment he had been in a very good mood, a rare thing with him. Later on he explained to a friend the reason for his withdrawal, which was solely because the audience and his friends had started to sing a fashionable song:

> "*Vem cá, mulata! Não vou lá não.*" ("Come here mulatto girl! No I'm not gonna come.")

"All that . . . penetrated my ears as an insult. It reminded me of my mother. The offensive invitation seemed directed to her."[4] The maternal figure haunted him morbidly even in the middle of a Carnival ball!

Barreto's works provide an excellent and accurate analysis and description of all the problems and evils of Brazil at the beginning of the twentieth century. It was a rather indefinite epoch: the end of slavery and the advent of the Republic had caused a series of external changes—among which were various struggles for power that almost ended in a civil war—without, however, altering the essence, the solidly rural structure, the large estates, and immense bureaucracy of the country. The changes happened later. The new internal situation in Brazil reflected also the new aspect of the world after the upheaval caused by the war. The first shock occurred in Brazil in 1922 with the eighteen of Copacabana. But 1922 is also the year of the death of Barreto, who thus spent the entire span of his life in that period which was the poorest and the most confused in the whole history of Brazil. We can almost say that the first thirty years of the Republic were an epoch of waiting: Brazil, having lost its ancient aristocratic and imperial soul and not having yet found its new identity, was waiting for the world to give it new laws and new structures to which it would adjust.

Barreto himself had understood perfectly well the purely cosmetic function of the institutional transformation, however. It might seem strange that a rebel and a revolutionary like him would show any tolerance toward the past regime. Yet, Barreto's attitude can easily be explained in that the people who took power at the advent of the Republic had not succeeded in making any changes at all that could be considered progress from a practical point of view. The writer saw the ostentation of power of the new men, who surrounded themselves with policemen and soldiers to protect themselves from possible physical attacks, and recalled the imperial simplicity: "Pedro the Second did not allow himself the luxury of fearing attempts on his own life and he would disembark from a common boat, which, if I remember it well, used to be called at the time the sea tram."[5] He also noticed the difference between the frugality of the emperor and the constant waste of state money under the Republic:

> Dom Pedro the Second, who could boast among his ancestors I don't know how many kings and emperors, had three insignificant houses in Rio de Janeiro which belonged to the crown or the nation; and one in Petrópolis which was his own. Any of our presidents, who has any University degree and who is the son of any *coronel*, owns four or more sumptuous palaces, and receives an income that is almost equivalent to the ancient imperial allowance; the state pays his servants while the emperor used to pay them from his own pocket.[6]

A recurrent pattern in Barreto's work is his attack on institutions, both the traditional ones and the new ones created by the new regime and by the progress of the times. He attacked marriage as it was conceived by bourgeois society, the tragic farce of war, the strident social disparity that had replaced the officially eliminated slavery. He also attacked the obsessive power of bureaucracy, the vanity of the men in the army and the navy, and the new forms of power represented by the newspapers and the greed and incapacity of political men.

Let us start with marriage and the brainwashing to which the girls of bourgeois families were subjected.

> At any moment at any time they would say "because, when you are going to get married . . . "—and the girl ended up by convincing herself that one's entire existence had marriage as the only goal. Education,

> personal satisfaction, cheerfulness, all that was useless; life was summed up by only one thing: getting married. Moreover, she did not find these kinds of concerns only inside her family. In school, in the streets, in the houses of acquaintances, what they all talked about was getting married. "You know, Dona Maricota, Lili got married; she didn't make such a good deal because the husband is not that great"; or then: "Zezé is going crazy to try to get a husband for herself but she's so ugly! My God!"
>
> Life, the world, the intense variety of feelings and ideas, our own right to happiness ended up by looking like nonsense to her young mind; getting married was shown to be a very important thing, some kind of duty, while not getting married, remaining a spinster, looked to her like a crime and a shame.[7]

And so, poor Ismênia (this is the character's name) spends years and years waiting for the moment that is going to give some meaning to her existence. And, instead, after five long years of engagement, her fiancé disappears right on the eve of the wedding day. The poor girl is driven to madness, she goes through a long period of depression and apathy from which she never recovers. It is the inevitable consequence of her upbringing. The parents consult—in vain—doctors, fortune tellers, and sorcerers.

> One could see well of what the girl's despair consisted, but what one could see even better was that the cause of it was that obligation which had been carved into the souls of the girls, that they had to marry at any cost. Marriage was made the pole and the goal of life so that staying single seemed like a dishonor and an offense.
>
> Marriage is not love, is not motherhood, is nothing of all that; it is simply marriage, an empty thing, which is founded neither upon our nature nor upon any of our needs.[8]

Barreto expressed these ideas to the conservative and backward society of Rio de Janeiro. It is easy to imagine that they were badly accepted.

He went even further with another feminine character: he created the kind of woman who is aware of her own dignity as a human being; a woman who does not rebel against social conventions but rather accepts them only for what they are and does not allow them to change her intimate convictions. Olga is the daughter of a nouveau-riche Italian immigrant. She is engaged to a young, ambitious doctor, but she is clearly aware of the act that she is on the verge of accomplishing: she feels that her future husband is not the ideal man who at first he seemed to be, but she also knows that that society would not allow her any other kind of existential solution.

> It was the inertia of society and its tyranny combined with the young woman's natural timidity in the face of possibly breaking up which drove her to marriage. Moreover, she told herself that if it had not been that one it would have been another one just as bad, and therefore it was better not to waste time.
>
> It was for this reason that she did not go to the church driven by her own will although she did not feel the compulsion of an external rule.[9]

Barreto's criticism of marriage as an institution is subtler here: Olga accepts marriage freely only because in her youthful naïveté she is not aware of the subconscious conditioning of social taboos. Although she is not one of the main protagonists she is the character who concludes the last pages of the novel: facing the injustice that has driven her godfather to prison, she decides to go and talk directly to the president of the Republic. She rebels against her husband who tries in vain to forbid her gesture, which to him seems out of place:

> She spoke, now calm and ironic, now rapidly and passionately; at her words her husband experienced a great fright. He had always lived so far from her that he did not deem her capable of such audacity. Was it really she? That graceful jewel? Who had taught her such things? He tried to disarm her with irony and said laughingly: "Do you think you are on the stage?"
>
> She answered right away: "If great things happen only on the stage, well, then I'm on the stage." And she added forcefully: "It is as I tell you: I go and I'm going, because I must, because I want to go, because it is my right."
>
> She picked up the parasol, adjusted the veil, and went out solemnly, sure of herself, high and noble. Her husband didn't know what to do. He was upset and silent as he saw her cross the threshold.[10]

Barreto made clear statements about marriage. Considering the time when he wrote, and the bourgeois environment in Rio de Janeiro with its conventions and hypocrisies, we must think that a character like Olga, who dared revolt against her husband, must have been particularly disconcerting for the various Ismênia's who might have read the book and who spent all their time instead looking for a husband.

In *Triste fim de Policarpo Quaresma* (*The Sad End of Policarpo Quaresma*, 1911), where we found the characters of Olga and Ismênia, there is a violent attack on war and the military caste. The novel is set at the beginning of the Republic when the military was engaged in a long civil war aimed at possession of the new institutions. Barreto insists on the farcical aspects of war, when the opposing factions had come to a stalemate and were wearing themselves out waiting for the other side to yield or to make the wrong move, while they were also maintaining the public appearance of war.

> Almost every afternoon there was a cannonade from the ocean toward the fortress and from the fortress toward the ocean; both the ships and the fortress came out untouched from such a terrible ordeal. Once in a while they reached their target and then the newspapers gave the big news: "Yesterday fort Acadêmico achieved a fantastic shot. With the cannon such and such they centered a cannonade on Guanabara." The following day the same newspaper had to make a correction upon the request of the battery of the Pharoux pier which was the one who had shot the right cannonade. A few days passed and the incident was almost forgotten when a new letter would come from Niterói claiming the merit of the cannonade for the fortress of Santa Cruz.[11]

The war was a show for the taxpayer that the military had to keep alive through a farce, to prolong the state of emergency, the state of siege, which provided so many in the military with privileges. The taxpayer is an audience, however, that, having paid the ticket, wants to enjoy the show from the first row. We recall, by the way, that Machado de Assis himself wrote sarcastically in his chronicles: "For the second time I went down to the Glória beach with the excuse of watching the bombing."[12] But let us return to Lima Barreto:

> At times they came so close to the troops that they created some confusion in the service; at other times a citizen would approach an officer and ask gently: "Would you let me shoot the cannon?" The officer gave in and the assistants charged the cannon, the man aimed and the cannonball went. By and by the revolt became a kind of party, an amusement for the entire city. When a bombing was announced, the terraces of Passeio Público filled up in a second. It was as if it were the night of a full moon at the time when it was fashionable to enjoy it in the old gardens of Dom Luís de Vasconcelos, watching the solitary star shine like silver on the water and fill up the sky.
>
> One would rent binoculars and both old men and young girls, young men and old ladies, followed the bombing as if it were a theater show: "The Santa Cruz burned down! Now it is at the Aquibadã! There it is!" This way the revolt became a daily habit and a part of the mores of the city.[13]

The war appears as carnival and as feast. But during this feast, someone has died, someone is unjustly in prison, someone is chased away from his job. The war is nothing but a pretext to institute power and military dictatorship. But the war continues to be a farce: "The end of the revolt was a relief; the thing was becoming monotonous and the field marshal ended up by taking on an almost superhuman aspect thanks to his victory."[14]

Barreto attacks the military caste deftly: on the one hand he ridicules the false masters of the war while on the other hand he shows the aberrant aspects of the use of power. He avoids the risk that the amusement created by the inefficiency of the men in uniform might make us forget the sinister violence of which they are the bearers. Here is the sad fate of the prisoners, of the simple navy men who took part in the revolt:

> Whites, Blacks, mulattoes, *caboclos*, people of all colors and of all feelings, people who had gotten themselves into such an adventure out of the habit of obeying, people totally estranged from the question that was debated, people taken away by force from their families or recruited in the streets.[15]

There are also the farcical general and admiral. The general talks about the war against Paraguay in which he did not participate because he had to withdraw from the front shortly before the beginning of the operation; the admiral talks about the conspiracies and envies that prevented him from participating in the same war. The admiral's story has some deeply comical aspects, of the bureaucratic military type: his career was ruined because he was once given the command of a ship that was in internal waters, in Mato Grasso; he could never find the ship, however, and upon the advice of some colleagues he started to look for it all over the country until the ministry advised him that the ship had already been sunk during the war. Through this incident the admiral gained the reputation of someone who wanted the command of a sunken ship.

Confused and inefficient, these two are two small employees in uniform, two fathers of families, who are inept at any form of belligerent activity. The two coexist with violent and fanatical militarists—either people who rule in bad faith in the name of their own interest or people who oppress in good faith in the name of God and the motherland.

Lima Barreto's poignant and direct attack against institutions questions their existence while ridiculing the men who are part of them. The image of the superbureaucrat, the model functionary whom Barreto describes, brings to mind the baron of Inhangá in the novel *Vida e morte de M. J. Gonzaga de Sá (Life and Death of M. J. Gonzaga de Sá)*:

> He was an intelligent although idle man who did not understand anything of his office or any other thing. He had started as the head of his section and during work hours his main activity was that of opening and closing the drawer of his desk. They made him director, and as soon as he became acquainted with the new job, he got himself busy in arranging another activity. Lacking something more serious to do for the interest of his country, the baron sharpened his pencil at any time of the day. It was an immense waste of the pencil; but Brazil is a wealthy country and appreciates the service of its children. When he completed twenty-five years of service, he was proclaimed baron.[16]

There is something we have already mentioned and which has to be kept in mind when dealing with Barreto's angry criticism toward society, that is, the direct and deeply negative experience of his life. His experience is at the same time his strength and his limitation: it is his strength because it allows him to describe events he has experienced and it is his limitation because it often drives him to attack institutions and people whom he disguises under the fictional characters. In this case he becomes the failed student who attacks his professors, the little employee who attacks the great bureaucrats, the small reporter who criticizes the director of the great newspapers, the man of the street who nags the politicians, the novelist who defies the literary critics and the literary fashions. It becomes a vicious circle. We have already mentioned briefly what kind of treatment Barreto gave to bureaucrats and to militarists. We can also imagine how uneasy he might have felt in his job as a clerk at the ministry of war and understand why he was never promoted and why he was eventually rejected by the Brazilian Academy of Letters. This was, then, his limitation; and it is impossible for us to know how much of his great criticisms of the mores of the times resulted from his anger towards people whom we do not know.

The list goes on. From his experience as a journalist Barreto finds the means to launch an attack against the great masters of the press, those who, in a country like Brazil, were so sensitive to the news reports and gossip, and had become one of the decisional powers of the country. It is in *Recordações do escrivão Isaías Caminha*, the most autobiographical of Barreto's works, that we find the best descriptions of journalists. Who knows what famous newspaper journalist might have recognized himself in the grotesque description of Raul Gusmão:

> The bloated figure, a mixture of pig and monkey, of the celebrated journalist Raul Gusmão ruled over everything. Even Oliveira, so base and

so beastly, had borrowed something from him, from his fake air of superiority, from his prefabricated gestures, from his search for the sensational sentence, from his quickness to act startled and surprised.[17]

We certainly cannot say that Barreto had a light hand in describing this character, behind whom almost certainly more than one person was disguised. Another piece of gossip concerns a journalist who had the good habit of stealing books from the book store. When eventually he was caught by the clerks he was compelled to pay even the previous thefts to avoid being arrested. Even Barreto's comment at the end of the episode is not one of the lightest:

> The press! What bandits! We should know that if the pirate Barbarossa was resurrected today, with our quick cruisers and formidable battleships, he could only give full extension to his activity if he were a journalist. There is nothing more alike than ancient pirates and modern journalists: the same poverty of means combined with the courage of a robber; rudimentary knowledge of the instrument that they use combined with a sure eye, perception, a capacity to smell the prey, and also insensitivity and a monumental lack of moral sense.[18]

Beyond the gossip, as interesting as that might be, Barreto has given us some deeply modern and realistic pages on the life of the press and its people. Here is the director, a real godfather inside his editor's office:

> During the many years when I was editor at *O globo* I had the chance of noticing the respect, the submission of the subordinates toward the director of the newspaper, that must have had its equivalent only in the Turkish administration. What he does is the work of a saint, what he says are words of wisdom. Nobody knows more or has more power on earth that he. Everybody feels for him a sacred terror combined with fear of losing his favor, and this is true both for the lowest clerk and the editor specializing in literature and in international affairs.[19]

The tyrannical power the director exerts upon his subordinates is nothing more than the reflection of the power that he himself can exert upon the external world. It is worth remembering here that one of the basic features of Brazilian civilization is that of receiving with the utmost facility the most advanced aspects and formulas of the modern and civilized world; this causes a constant clash among different forms of life in Brazil, some of which are connected with the past and others of which are projected towards the future; yet all of them share a constant balance. At the beginning of this century, when Barreto wrote his main works, the urban civilization of Rio de Janeiro displayed strident contradictions: it was the capital of a country that thrived on exporting rural products and importing manufactured goods (the national industry was far from being born) and, at the same time, took on forms of life imported from the most advanced industrial civilizations. The press in Rio de Janeiro, for example, does not reflect the historical evolution of the country, it is not the end product of the evolution of a civilization; in other words it is not the kind of press one could accept from the capital of a big rural country. Rather, it is so essentially because it serves the center of power connected to the interests of the great *fazendeiros* and the great exporters; it is not so in its form and in its techniques, which are imported and adopted in order to imitate the more progressive countries. For example, it suffices to recall that one of the most important elements in the struggle against slavery was the press: two institutions, one typically medieval, namely slavery, and the other typically modern, namely the press, and mass participation through the news, co-existed side by side. This is how in Brazil at the beginning of this century the great games of power connected with the interests of agriculture and export used newspaper techniques that we can find in contemporary political struggles.

To all this one should add a typically Brazilian trait, that is, the enormous importance the public gives to mundane events, to the publicity given to one's own name, which has no equivalent anywhere else in the world. Evidence of this, even in recent times, are the Brazilian newspapers where an enormous number of pages are devoted to mundane events. For all these reasons, the power of a newspaper director in Brazil is something authentic and real. Barreto was right when he stated, talking about the director of *O globo*:

> The terror that he inspired inside the paper radiated even outside. That skinny man, weak in body and intelligence, devoid of culture, scared the entire city and the country. Everybody quoted him. His colleagues who fought against him avoided attacking him directly. Someone in a moment of despair had the courage to face him; but it was only a moment of despair. Once they were attacked and surrounded on each side they would have a fit and they would start kicking left and right. If by any chance someone aimed right and seemed almost able to destroy Dr. Loberant, he ended up by wondering, instead, whether the opposite might happen. Far from making him lose his prestige, these attacks increased it. The people did not want to see his ignorance, his incapacity to write; he was brave and said the truth. There was a debate over a treaty concerning a frontier in which his ignorance of geography was very apparent; the circulation of the paper increased.[20]

At the beginning of the century in a country like Brazil, which was not at the forefront of technical progress, Barreto detected with surprising modernity one of the laws that rule the relationship between newspaper journalists and the public: the reader when he picks up the paper does not expect truth, he rather expects his *own* truth; that is, that form of news which is best adjusted to his own form of intelligence and culture and best responds to his needs and interests. In Brazil twenty years after the end of slavery, with a reading public both ignorant and greedy for news and an immense production of newspapers, this created endless problems. Many tumults and many revolts were caused by news published by the press. Moreover, the lack of precise legislation on the subject permitted these slanderous attacks to destroy many people. Lima Barreto tells us all about that.

He also tells us other things: he tells us how articles on certain events—car races, arrivals of celebrities, and so on—were prepared in advance and often published even when such events did not take place; after all these were news and the public received them willingly. He tells us a story that must have hurt his sensitivity as a man of color: a couple is found, a man and a woman, murdered and disfigured. The press builds up an authentic case on this macabre crime and an illustrious doctor shows off his evidence, based upon Lombroso's theory, that the murdered man must certainly have been a mulatto. The circulation of the paper increases and the doctor is proclaimed director of the Institute for Legal Medicine, until they discover, by mere chance, that the murdered "mulatto" was in reality an Italian, a spaghetti manufacturer from Buenos Aires on his way to Europe.

Barreto's entire work is denunciation. His most beautiful pages, however, those which rightly give him a place of honor in Brazilian literature, are those in which the author forgets his hatred and his bitterness and the complexes that come from his skin color, and in which he addresses his attention, his vibrant and passionate attention, to all his fellow human beings—the poor, the disinherited, and the great mass of workers who endure living in precarious conditions. Barreto has been called the poet of subúrbios, of the extraurban areas, of the subúrbios inhabited by those who cannot allow themselves to live in the city quarters, which are the shelters of the bourgeoisie. Let us recall Aluísio Azevedo and his *O cortiço*. The *cortiço* was a great urban building, shaped like a rectangle with a court in the middle, which sheltered workers and their families, immigrants, and former slaves, at the beginning of the urban civilization and during the industrial era at the end of the nineteenth century. The cortiço did present some advantages: it was usually located in the urban quarters, close to the place of work. The one described by Aluísio Azevedo was in the quarter of Botafogo, close to the ocean and the city center, and bordered upon a rich bourgeois house. Industrial progress and the urban exploitation little by little transformed the cortiços into bourgeois houses while the mass of workers were pushed farther and farther away, toward the subúrbios, the immense districts made of thousands of small houses; two parallel cities grew, thus, in which people led completely different lives. This division lasts up to the present.

The subúrbio is first of all a form of social injustice, the plastic representation of the alienation of the many to the advantage of the well-being of the few: "In this intricate maze of streets and shacks the majority of the urban population lives. The government ignores their existence even though it makes tham pay atrocious taxes which are later spent in useless and sumptuous works in other parts of Rio de Janeiro."[21] Nothing is easy in the subúrbio, not even death: the cemetery is far away and the dead person is carried there by relatives and friends on their shoulders; once in a while they have to stop to have a drink to keep their spirits up and survive the heat and the long trip. There was a case once, Barreto tells, when the friends and relatives arrived at the cemetery almost drunk and without the dead person, who had been abandoned along the road:

> This is more or less how the *subúrbio* is in its poverty and its abandonment to which the public powers condemn it. At the first hours of the day from all those huts, shacks, lanes, hills, crossings, caverns, streets, people emerge and start walking towards the nearest station . . . They are workers, small employees, low-ranking military personnel, state employees, and people who even though honest, survive on shady deals, day by day, earning painfully some *mil-réis*. The *subúrbio* is the refuge of the unhappy. Those who lost their jobs and their fortunes; those who failed in business and all those who lost their positions go and take refuge there; and every day very early they come down searching for faithful friends who might help them, might give them some food for their children.[22]

Lima Barreto is the poet of the subúrbios, the poet of poverty; his prose is not always one of the best, his Portuguese is imperfect, his populist eloquence is often too vehement. Yet in his writing there is a fascinating sincerity, the authentic despair of a man always on the verge of madness and always ready to reject the world even before he is rejected by it. The life of the subúrbios is his life, of the minor ministry employee Barreto, of his family, of his friends and neighbors. The youthful experience in Ilha do Governador helped him describe

ENGENHO DE AÇUCAR

the sad monotony of rural life in *Triste fim de Policarpo Quaresma*. He is the poet of misery, eternally fascinated by the show of human disasters both when they have as a background the city slums and when they unfold among somnolent and brutalized farmers.

The situation of the countryside in those years was worse, in many cases, than that of the subúrbios, which at least were closer to the centers where the slow industrialization of the country occurred. In the rural setting, however, the end of slavery without rural reform (or any other reform for that matter) had increased the negative traits connected to the backwardness of rural life. Those who up to May 13, 1888, had been slaves *de jure* became automatically slaves *de facto*. Ignorant, illiterate, brutalized by three centuries of a degrading situation, they had no other choice than to continue to be slaves in the former fazendas. Moreover, the government had channeled all the financial aids and incentives to the new large colonies inhabited by Italians and Germans, thus declaring the end of the former fazendas. The former slaves, then, could only devote themselves to a survival agriculture. Naturally, all the world that revolved around the former fazendas, caboclos, small colonists, and peasant authorities, was affected by the general abandonment, by the heavy bureaucratic burden that weighed upon everything.

This is how the people of the village appear to one of the protagonists from the city: "Some of those girls from the interior, lymphatic and sad, clumsily dressed, full of ribbons"[23] and later on, "the daughter, very skinny, pale with long skinny arms, observed with faked shyness the dusty ground of the road. When they left, Ricardo pondered on that product of the open air of Brazil."[24] These were the inhabitants of the countryside, some kind of rural aristocracy; Olga's wonder (we have already met this character) is great when she faces the poverty of the farmers and compares it with the apparent wealth of the land:

> What impressed her most during the walk was the general misery, the lack of cultivation, the poverty of the houses, the sad and depressed attitude of the poor people. Having been brought up in the city, she imagined that country people were happy, full of health and cheerfulness. If there was so much clay, so much water, then why were not the houses in brick, and why did they not have roofing tiles? . . . Why around those houses were there no cultivated fields, no yards, no orchards? Wouldn't that be so easy, to work a few hours? And there were no animals, neither small nor big. Just once in a while a goat or a sheep. Why? . . . It could not only be laziness or idleness.[25]

The answer to Olga's question will come later on from Policarpo, the protagonist, himself. The explanation goes beyond the condition of degradation in which the rural masses were left. The origin of everything is to be found at the time of the conquest when alongside the great estates inhabited by slaves grew a tentacular and parasitic bureaucracy, whose task was that of limiting and controlling, exploiting and becoming rich. This bureaucracy continues to exploit to ensure its own survival even now that the golden times of the colonies have disappeared forever.

> That network of laws, rules, codes, and orders in the hands of these little kings and princes was transformed into trestles, wheels, pillories, to torture the enemies and oppress the population while taking away their initiative and independence, disheartening and demoralizing them.
>
> In a blink in front of his eyes all those yellow and worn-out faces passed, who leaned lazily against the doors of the stores. He saw also the dirty children covered with rags, their eyes lowered, who begged stealthily in the streets; he saw those unproductive, abandoned lands, left to the weeds and harmful insects. He also saw Felizardo's despair, a good man, active, and a worker who did not have the courage to plant a seed of corn in the ground around his house and who drank up all the money that passed through his hands.[26]

The character of Felizardo (ironically the name comes from *feliz*, which means happy) is emblematic of the entire rural situation. Felizardo is a former slave, an active man who knows and loves the land; yet, he can do nothing but let himself go, because all of his work initiatives would arouse the suspicion and the greed of the tax man. When the riots start during the first years of the Republic—the beginning of the civil war—Felizardo has to run away and hide in the woods for fear of being recruited forcibly and having to serve a country whose existence he ignores. This doom of passivity and apathy is handed over from Felizardo to his children:

> He lived in constant fear; he would sleep all dressed up and would jump from the window and hide himself in the midst of the vegetation at the slightest noise.
>
> He had two children, but what sad figures they were! They combined their parents' moral depression with a lack of physical vigor and a repugnant idleness. They were two males: the older, José, was about twenty years old; they were both inactive, flaccid, and weak, they believed in nothing, not even in the magic rituals, the prayers, and the exorcisms that made their mother happy and received their father's

> respect. Nobody had ever taught them anything or ever compelled them to do regular work. Once in a while, about every fifteen days, they would pick wood and sell it to the first tavern-keeper for half its value. They would go back again happy and satisfied with some brightly colored handkerchief, a little bottle of eau de cologne, a mirror, and some other nonsense that showed their still rather primitive taste.
>
> They would then spend a week at home, sleeping or walking around in the streets and the stores; in the evening, almost always during festive days or Sundays, they would go out with the accordion to play music, an activity at which they were particularly good so that their presence was much requested at the neighboring balls.
>
> Even though their parents stayed at home during Lent, they would rarely show up there; and if they did, it was only because they were left without food. They were so heedless and reckless about life that they reached the point of not even fearing being recruited. They were, in spite of all this, capable of dedication, loyalty, and kindness; but regular work, day by day, repulsed them like an affliction and a punishment. This lethargy of our people, this kind of morbid, disheartening, and blissful indifference for everything and everybody surrounds our race with a cloud of desperate sadness and takes away the enchantment, the poetry, and the seductive vigor of nature in its blossom.[27]

Because of the ruthless clarity of this analysis, this is one of the best pages ever written on the problem of life in the countryside. The abandonment by the authorities is made worse by the state that is present only through forcible recruitment and taxation. The human typology embodied by Felizardo's young children is particularly interesting because it sums up all the evils Brazil inherited from slavery: once the former structure centering around the plantation terminated, nobody took the trouble to replace it with more modern and valid forms of production. The slaves were accustomed usually to two kinds of production: that to which they were compelled because of their servile condition, and that of survival to which they devoted their free moments cultivating their small yard. Once slavery was over and the plantation was superseded by other forms of production, the only form of activity the slave could conceive of was that connected to pure and simple survival. No external positive change ever directed them toward new forms of activity tied to productive cycles more in tune with the times. In other words, the two young characters described above are totally maladjusted: they have lost—always because of slavery, which had annihilated the former ethnicities—a sense of tribal unity and consequently a conception of work as a form of social activity, of duty toward the group. The end of slavery, while it eliminated compulsory work, never changed the concept of work as a constraint, something that must be avoided as much as possible. The end of slavery marked only the end of a state of affairs but not the beginning of a new era; no new concept of work and no new way of living were introduced which relate the idea of activity to that of improvement, progress, and welfare rather than to that of a useless compulsion for the advantage of others.

One should add to all this that the state left the former bureaucratic structure untouched while it continued its predatory fiscal policy. For that reason the two young characters have in mind their father's example in his fruitless attempt to make his way out of poverty, which was always opposed by an administration that in one way or another succeeded in forbidding him to produce. The two boys' fate was shared by many in Brazil who were constrained between a past that had taken away their roots and their contact with productive reality, and a future manifested only in its negative aspects, in the prohibition to act, and in renewed compulsion through taxation and recruitment.

Lima Barreto had the rare gift of being able to sum up in a few lines the problems and existential drama of that transitional time which, in my opinion, must have been one of the least exciting in the entire history of Brazil. In each of the books he wrote, however, he has also been able to express his own despair, the slow evolution of his anguish. Each book is a confession, and many of his characters can be seen as the author's alter ego.

Recordações do escrivão Isaías Caminha (*Memories of the Copyist Isaías Caminha*, 1908) is his most profoundly autobiographical work. It is the story of a poor mulatto from the province, who arrives in the great city to attend the university and ends up instead, because of hardships and problems, working on a newspaper where, eventually, he succeeds in conquering a job as a reporter. It is a novel in which all the problems connected with being a mulatto are analyzed. And the author identifies himself with these problems throughout the work.

The first lines of the novel bring to the fore the protagonist's father who, as was the case in the author's life, was the one who encouraged him to study:

> The show of my father's knowledge . . . rose in front of my child's eyes as something fascinating. It seemed to me then that his capacity to explain all, his facility in speaking, his ability to read different languages and to understand them, constituted in themselves a reason for happiness, for abundance and wealth as well as a degree entitling him to the superior respect from men and to superior consideration from all people.[28]

Barreto's entire life was made tragic, as we know, by the lack of a social recognition of his talents, by the lack of an official consecration by the very institutions he vehemently criticized. He ascribed this lack of success to the color of his skin. Being a mulatto was for him a stigma as it was for the young Isaías Caminha: "Ah! I could have become a doctor! I could have redeemed the original sin of my humble birth, I would have made sweeter the oppressive torture, the oppressive, mortifying, and boundless torture of my color."[29]

From then on, from the moment Isaías Caminha leaves his native village and goes to the great city, his life is a succession of tests, in which skin color plays a deeply negative role, starting with the journey by train when he notices the different treatment he receives as compared to the whites. Rio de Janeiro, the great city, increases the feeling of isolation of the young provincial, who has problems finding a job even though he knows many people. Isaías, however, is flattered by the friendship of a rich Portuguese baker who always calls him doctor, and he likes that. The color of his skin persecutes him and after a theft occurs in the hotel where he lives he becomes the first suspect; moreover, he is humiliated by being referred to as *mulatinho* by the chief of police. He also resents the way he is treated, since nobody believes that a poor mulatto could be a student. When he finds a job as an office boy at the newspaper *O globo*, he is hurt every time the various editors use the term mulatto to refer to unimportant individuals:

> "What! Felix da Costa! He looks like a foundling! Is he a mulatto?"
> "No, he is whiter than you, sir. He is blond and he has blue eyes."
> "Boy, take it easy . . ."
> He did not understand why I was hurt and suffered.[30]

And Isaías Caminhas keeps on being hurt even after he ingratiates himself with the director and succeeds in becoming a reporter. He suffers because of the envy of his colleagues; one of them during a fight calls him *moleque*, a term that was used to indicate the black children. He is also hurt by the condescension of the director who is surprised by his good manners and his upbringing:

> I understood that he was very much surprised when I told him that I had had a mother and that I was born in a family environment and I had received an education. All this was extraordinary for him. What seemed extraordinary to me in my adventures, he found natural. But the fact that I had a mother who had taught me how to eat using a fork, that was exceptional. I had discovered only later this way of thinking of his. For him, as for the majority of less cultured people in Brazil, men and women who come from the same background as I are all alike, even

more alike than the dogs in their country homes. The men are small thieves, impostors, cheats who have learned something, middlemen for political people, the women (and here the concept is even simpler) are naturally seen only as females.

Their mental idleness drives them to think that and even Dr. Loberant thought along that line. It wasn't difficult for me to make him change his opinion as far as I was concerned. But I was not satisfied. I understood that he saw me as an exception.[31]

We already noticed Barreto's extreme sensitivity on this subject. In his novels he never succeeded, and he did not even try, in dealing with the problems of the relationship between Blacks and whites in rational terms or placing the problem inside a general framework. It is also worth noting that Barreto never considered the problem of Blacks and their integration into Brazilian society. He is only interested in the strictly personal problems of Barreto himself, a mulatto full of social ambition, resentments, and frustrations, compelled to live in a society that places so much value on skin color. The Blacks who appear in his novels are only background figures, and in general they are characters who are confined to the lower levels of the social scale and who never even face the problem of improving. One is a prostitute who confronts the white seducer who ruined her, another is an old woman who comments on her own and other people's disasters; yet another is the poetic memory of an old nurse who used to tell stories:

. . . Aunt Benedita, a poor old former slave of my reverend father. These were naive stories from Europe, delicate tales of passion, of princesses and beautiful shepherdesses, that her savage imagination transformed and mixed together with fights against evil elves, with the witchcraft of some sorcerer, and with a whole series of powerful forces, enemies of the happy life of human beings.[32]

The author never identifies at all with his rare Black protagonists; his alter ego is always either mulatto or white. The black Felizardo and his two children are too far away from him with their somnolent resignation of defeated people, destined passively to repeat their life cycle over and over. It is, instead, Isaías Caminha who embodies him in fiction through his ambitions, his neuroses, and his phobias. It is easy to compare Lima Barreto, who died an alcoholic, and Isaías Caminha, who perceives in alcohol the same strange fascination of the drugs that eventually free him from all evil:

Alcohol was not part of my habits. At home I used to drink it rarely. At that time, however, I felt the need to drink, to get drunk, I was tired of suffering, I wanted a narcotic that would make my tense nerves rest

> from the constant upheaval of these last days. I went into a coffee shop but I experienced a strange feeling of disgust. I only drank a small cup of coffee, and walked sadly towards the ocean and looked enviously at a dockworker who was drinking a big glass of *parati*.[33]

Barreto spent all his life without feminine company except for that of his sister. His biographers have often sought in vain for evidence of a love affair. Similarly, Isaías Caminha constantly avoids women. He withdraws from the sexy girl who sits close to him on the bench at the public park and rejects the Italian upper-class mistress who repeatedly invites him to her home. What he looks for is the ideal woman with whom to withdraw and live in the countryside, far from ambitions, far from the city:

> It has always been part of my personality to run away from what the Bible defines in a manner that is so rigorous for our modern ears . . . Beside wishing for myself and a woman, there would be something more delicate, more spiritual, a sharing that I cannot have with anyone, I harbored inside myself an evangelical thought that forbade me from acting as everybody else, because, in so doing, I would have contributed to keeping a disgrace and to creating some wretched women.[34]

Barreto's desperate confession continues throughout all his books; he creates his spokesmen each time through the most diverse characters.

In *Triste fim de Policarpo Quaresma* another myth crumbles to pieces and is ineluctably destroyed: the myth of the motherland, of the possibility for the citizen to integrate himself and to be part of a larger community in which he can recognize himself and which can help and appreciate him. Policarpo Quaresma is not a mulatto; in this book it is not the racial problem that predominates but rather discrimination and the alienation of the disinherited. Policarpo is a small functionary of the ministry of war, just like the author; he reaches the honorary title of major and after thirty years of diligent service is caught up in patriotic passion. He feels deeply and totally Brazilian and he wants to put to good use all the knowledge he has of his own land—historical, geographical, and scientific knowledge. For him Brazil is the most beautiful, the greatest, the richest country in the world. Caught by this naive enthusiasm, he devotes himself to the study of the guitar so that he can better sing the songs of his land under the guidance of a rustic teacher who is called Ricardo Coração dos Outros (Richard Heart of the Others). This musical passion arouses the gossip and criticism of his neighbors while another passion of his ends up by causing much more serious consequences: Policarpo decides that Portuguese is a language lent to Brazil and that the true national language can only be *tupi-guarani*. Strongly convinced of this, Policarpo sends a request to the ministry in charge. The request is discussed by the parliament and during some weeks Policarpo is made the object of all the possible jokes that the playful temperament of the Brazilians could invent. Unfortunately, one day Policarpo ends up absent-mindedly writing an official letter in tupi-guarani and his director signs it (the usual high-level bureaucrat who signs without reading). The end of the world follows and Policarpo ends up in an insane asylum. When he is released from the asylum, he withdraws to the countryside and devotes himself to farming. The bureaucracy, however, the usual absurd fiscal bureaucracy, persecutes him with unreasonable taxation only because he refuses to be part of the various political fights of the village. When the civil war starts Quaresma goes back to Rio de Janeiro to fight under the orders of Marshal Floriano. Instead of fighting for the defense of the motherland, he ends up by being involved, against his will, in political struggles that have nothing to do with the interests of the nation. Once he realizes that he has become an accomplice of the regime it is too late, and Quaresma becomes once again the victim of the system he helped to create. He even ends up being arrested.

The uselessness of the bureaucracy, the rapacity of the tax men, the tragedy and ideological falsity of the war, the hypocrisy of bourgeois institutions, the ruthlessness of the politicians, all these are the elements of *Triste fim de Policarpo Quaresma*. We are left to notice the rather rare presence of some Black characters, besides Felizardo, whom we have already met. There is the character of an old Black woman, a former slave who lives poorly and remembers, perhaps, the good old times: ". . . and the *preta*, maybe with the great nostalgia of the time when she was a slave and a nurse in some great rich well-provided house."[35] The reality is that the demagogic and superficial way that marked the end of slavery succeeded in making someone even nostalgic of slavery! And then, of course, we have the classic figure of the sorcerer, the *feiticeiro*, to whom even the white masters have recourse when they need something their science cannot give them:

> It was a peculiar situation, that of the African *preto* who certainly had not forgotten the griefs of his long slavery and who, instead, used the residues of his naive tribal beliefs—residues that had resisted with great effort their forced transplant into a land of other gods—using them to

help his former masters. It was as if the gods of his childhood and his race, that bloody fetish of inscrutable Africa, wanted to take revenge for him in the legendary manner of the Christ of the Gospel.[36]

The relationship between the white men, supposedly cultured or at least civilized, and the Black feiticeiro, supposedly always the bearer of forms of barbaric superstition, is always a very interesting topic and it has been dealt with by many writers. The Black man who succeeds in asserting himself and placing himself in a position of temporary superiority toward those who had always ruled over him, achieves some sort of revenge. Barreto describes, with his usual disenchanted irony, the relationship between the village doctor and the *feiticeira*, Sinhá Chica, Felizardo's wife:

Doctor Campos was not at all jealous of that rival. He had armed himself with a vague air of superiority towards the supernatural powers of the woman, but he had not had recourse to the law that forbade the practice of her transcendent medicine. That would have meant unpopularity for him and he was a political man . . .

In the interior, and it is not even necessary to go very far from Rio de Janeiro, the two medicines co-exist without clashes, and they both take care of the mental and economic needs of the population. That of Sinhá Chica, almost free, met the needs of the poor people, those in whose minds, by contagion or heredity, the elves and fetishes still live which can be chased away through exorcism, blessings, and fumigations. Moreover her clientele did not consist only of the local people, those who were born and brought up there; there were also some newcomers from other places, Italians, Portuguese, and Spanish who used her supernatural powers, not only because of the price or because of the contagion of the beliefs of the local environment but also because of that strange European superstition according to which every *negro* or dark-skinned person was capable of penetrating and discovering evil things and of practicing witchcraft.

While Sinhá Chica's therapies were based upon fluids and herbs and took care of the disinherited and the poor, those of Dr. Campos responded to the needs of the more cultured and wealthier whose mental evolution requested the official and regular medicine.

At times, someone went from one group to the other; that happened with serious diseases, complicated and incurable ones which the sorcerer's herbs and prayers could not combat, or when the pills and syrups prescribed by the doctor were just as impotent.[37]

The realism and irony are magnificent. The author establishes a comparison between the two societies, which become equivalent and conjoin when facing things that escape their understanding. He then compares the actions of two saints, the white one and the Black one, the doctor and the sorcerer; the superstitious respect of the poor white before the Black man recreates the dependence among men of different races, reversing, however, their traditional order while leaving the causes and effects unchanged. Blending together the two groups in their common ignorance is an act that reflects the reality of a world in which men, both Black and white, have not freed themselves yet from the misery of their ignorance.

We can imagine the bitter pleasure of Lima Barreto, a mulatto, the descendant of slaves, who watches the Europeans, compatriots of those who reduced his people to slavery in the name of a claimed racial superiority, tremble timidly before an old Black woman, placing her on the same level with the white "doctor" who represents a science that provided a justification for inequality and unjust privilege.

The superiority of science, the superiority of civilization, become empty words at the moment of truth when fear chokes people and makes them equal, no matter what race they belong to. Then everything else—the doctor with a degree from a university, the bearer of official sanctions—is placed on the same level with an old Black man brought in chains from Africa or an old, illiterate Black woman. Which sanction is the most effective, that granted by the society of white men with stamps and official ceremonies or that granted by the fear and ignorance of both white and Black people?

The superiority of both the white civilization and religion is erased. On the one side, the official religion that once provided the justification for slavery by accepting it and by giving an ethical veneer to the violence of men over men now wants to be the only intermediary between man and the unknown through its traditions and rituals. On the other side, another religion in a more confused and maybe more picturesque way places itself between man and the unknown, between man and his eternal fears. Or maybe there is only one religion, a mixture of the two united in the desire to provide an eternally deferred answer.

Sinhá Chica embodies all this: besides being the representative of one of the two aspects of medicine, she is also a religious center for the small community in which she works:

> She did not forget all the saints, the sacred mother church, the commandments, the orthodox prayers; even though she could not read, she was very strong in her catechism and she knew the sacred history fragmentarily, she introduced in it some personal interpretations and added some picturesque details.[38]

Moreover Sinhá Chica not only has knowledge, she also knows how to act, thus becoming some sort of religious authority:

> She was the spiritual power of the place. The parish priest was limited to his role of functionary, some kind of officer of the civil record in charge of baptisms and marriages since any form of communication with God and the unknown occurred through Sinhá Chica. One should mention marriage, but one could also forget it because our poor people used that sacrament very rarely and the simple union, everywhere, replaces the solemn Catholic institution.[39]

Thus, Sinhá Chica embodies in her person the ancestral role of doctor-priest creating a valid alternative to the figures the white civilization had nominated for such roles. The great institutions are once again demystified!

Among the rare and minor Black characters is one who is only vaguely sketched but who deserves to be recalled because this character shows that prejudice against the Blacks was not only a prerogative of the rich whites but was, instead, extended also to the poor whites who used skin color as a pretext to prevail against their rivals. Ricardo Coração dos Outros, the singer who plays the guitar, has a rival who is becoming famous and who is a Black man:

> He loathed his rival for two reasons, first, because he was a *preto*: second, because of his theories. It was not that he disliked *pretos* particularly. The fact was that a famous *preto* who plays the guitar was one of those things that contributed to diminish even more the prestige of that instrument. If his rival had played the piano and because of that he had become famous there would have been nothing wrong with it; just the opposite, the talent of that man who has given luster to his own person, thanks to the prestige enjoyed by the instrument. But since he played the guitar just the opposite happened: the prejudice that surrounded this person ended up by depreciating the mysterious guitar that he loved so much.[40]

What a subtle distinction! The equation of the social prejudice is then the following: the base man who plays a noble instrument well improves himself, thanks to the instrument; a base man who plays a popular instrument well can only contribute to the diminishing of the instrument. This is another one of Lima Barreto's bitter sarcasms, based upon a foundation of truth.

Policarpo Quaresma fails, just as Lima Barreto failed, because he believes that institutions in their various expressions are the manifestations of a general will summed up by the motherland, the most noble of institutions. He finds out too late that the motherland is just a pretext and the institutions are the means of oppression of the many by the few.

Barreto continues his confession: he expresses himself through Policarpo's failure as a farmer, which must have reminded him of his father's similarly disastrous experience. He confesses himself through the failure of Policarpo as a revolutionary and politician who, again like Barreto's father, ends up by losing everything. He confesses himself through Policarpo as a bureaucrat and idealist at the service of his country, of the motherland that becomes an empty word in the politicians' mouths. Barreto continues his confessions.

If we wanted to sum up the writer's production we could say that Barreto knows how to be one of the best Brazilian novelists when he forgets that he is a mulatto. The pathos, the irony, the anger, the bias, and the rancor he vehemently discharges in his writing are true and authentic, even though at times they give the impression of being extreme and of representing a personal vendetta. When he deals, instead, with the theme of the mulatto, the confession borders most often on morbid self-commiseration, on an endless and unchecked self-pity. And what is worse, it is always limited to the purely personal level without ever opening up and placing the problem in more general terms; his descriptions and analysis of Black people are among the truest and the best because the writer never identifies with these characters; he only participates in their tragedies as a human being while he allows himself some distance because of the different skin color.

The figure of the nouveau-riche Italian, one of his many characters, who despite the money accumulated continues to fear and respect any form of authority, is an authentic person whom the author must certainly have met: "Coming from humble and rustic origins he kept at the bottom of his heart that sacred respect of farmers towards the men who were officially invested by the state."[41] This is also true for his other characters, rich and poor, good and evil. Yet his mulatto characters, such as Isaías Caminha, give the impression of being psychopaths who view reality through distorted lenses.

Clara do Anjos, published in 1921, is a work that the author started to write and then edited over and over again. It is the story of a mulatto woman, a simple story in which the protagonist comes from a petit-bourgeois family, is seduced and abandoned by a white young man, a lazybones and a hooligan. It is another book in which the author confesses himself while he identifies himself with many characters.

Clara dos Anjos, the protagonist, could possibly embody the author in her search for and incapacity for achieving a satisfactory emotional life. She certainly represents those mulatto girls of the petite bourgeoisie, who although simple and uneducated, were close to the author in their social condition; he too, despite his culture and sensitivity, was never able to find a companion.

Among the other main characters is one who is clearly an alter ego of the author. He is an alcoholic poet (Barreto himself died as an alcoholic and he was often interned) who has a mad brother (Barreto's father was mad and lived in seclusion with his children). And, of course, he is also mulatto and suffers because of the color of his skin: "I was born poor, I was born mulatto,"[42] thus the story of his life starts, similar in many ways to that of the author:

> In some occasions, Leonardo Flores also appeared; he was a poet, a true poet who had his moments of celebrity throughout Brazil and whose influence had been great in the generation of poets who had come after him. At that time, however, because of alcohol and personal bitterness, the greatest cause of which was his brother's incurable madness, he was a wreck, without memory, almost imbecile to the point of not even being able to follow the simplest conversation. He had published ten volumes, ten successes, which had enriched everybody except him, so that now, he, his wife, and children lived very poorly thanks to a meager state pension.
>
> He went out rarely because his wife tried all she could to prevent him from going. She sent out to buy some *parati* and bought his favorite newspapers to make him stay home. Often he obeyed; but on some rare occasions he resisted, he went out with five hundred *réis* in coins, drank somewhere, slept under the trees of the streets and the least busy roads, and when the alcoholic delirium gave him strength, he undressed and screamed heroically, in a morbid and vain fit:
>
> "I am Leonardo Flores."
>
> The people knew vaguely that he was a celebrity. They called him the poet. At the beginning they would tease him, but when later they learned of his reputation, they started to surround him with a compassionate curiosity.
>
> "A man like this one ending up like this. What a punishment!" said one.
>
> "It is witchcraft! It was envy for his intelligence!" said an old *preta*, "people of our color cannot have intelligence! Immediately the evil ones come and perform witchcraft to ruin the poor guy," the old *preta* added.[43]

This is a clearly autobiographical page, written by Barreto shortly before his premature death; here the eternal motif of persecution is introduced through the Black woman's incoherent talk. It is the motif of the envy of the others which in one way or another has prevented the success and caused Leonardo Flores–Lima Barreto's misfortune.

Clara dos Anjos is the story of a seduction, a novel devoid of a solid plot, which also describes most of Barreto's other novels, although to a minor extent. It is an excellent study of setting and environment, a careful analysis of character, and a ruthless social criticism. Clara's seduction is a pretext that allows the author to transform a rather common act into an example of urban civilization, thus establishing a contrast and a comparison between two social classes, the poor and the rich, the mulatto and the white. Clara is a mulatta and she is the daughter of a poor postman. Her family lives with dignity just above the level of poverty. In contrast, Cassi, her seducer, is white, and he belongs to what we would call the middle bourgeoisie.

Two worlds face each other. Clara lives at home, protected by her parents' affection, which prevented her from having any of life's experiences. She is totally unprepared to face any difficulty. She lives dreaming of the great love and of a good marriage. She is the typical example of that kind of life modeled after the institutions Barreto never tires of attacking.

It is interesting to note, by the way, that Barreto, in the physical description of the girl, a daughter of mulattoes, says that Clara had inherited her father's lighter color and her mother's hair: in fact the mother was a dark mulatta and the father "has the *ruim* hair, evil hair as they say."[44] The evil hair is the kinky hair typical of Black people; and even Barreto's biographer, Francisco de Assis Barbosa, says that our author had evil hair. As we can see some racist prejudice is unconsciously stronger than all the good intentions.

Cassi's case is more interesting. He comes from a middle-bourgeois family of civil servants who live in the subúrbios far from the elegant areas. The father is a nice man, but the mother has all the flaws of the new bourgeoisie: she brags continuously about being the descendant of an English lord who probably existed only in her imagination, and she protects her son in a morbid way, defending him every time he gets in trouble because of women. Cassi's impunity is ensured because his victims are from humble conditions and they have no way of claiming their own rights. Behind Cassi there is always his mother with her own relationships and friendships: "since she had her aristocratic presumptions, she abhorred the idea of seeing her own son married to a *preta* waitress or to a poor mulatto seamstress or to a white girl who worked as an illiterate washerwoman."[45] The sexual motif is thus mixed with class problems, thus perpetuating the dominance of the masters over the slaves, through the support of the institutions once again at the service of the strongest.

The character of Cassi's mother is classic: in her morbid affection she ends up by being her son's accomplice, always finding excuses for his evil deeds. Especially when the son runs the risk of having to work, the mother's despair and indignation reach their climax. This happens twice, the first time when Cassi is an adolescent, and he is expelled from college and his father would like him to learn a trade; the second time is when he is compelled to run away after having seduced Clara. The phrases the mother uses, speaking of the dishonor of the family, quoting illustrious ancestors, are typical of the world that perceived work, especially manual work, as something shameful, to be relegated to the slaves.

The author's description of the character of Cassi is the polar opposite of that of his mulatto alter egos; there is a continuous hatred and an anger that make us think that Cassi impersonates all defects and all evils. Even if we want to look at things from the point of view of the times, we must say that Cassi's character is despicable and contemptible but he is not a criminal up to the point in the novel when he commits a homicide; the homicide itself is rather unlikely because it is perpetrated with the only goal of facilitating the seduction of Clara by eliminating her strict godfather. Cassi never uses violence to seduce his victims and he is generally known in the entire area of the subúrbios as a scoundrel and a second-rate playboy: women who yield to such an individual know what they are going to get, even though, of course, they prefer to delude themselves. Expressions such as "to accomplish his awesome and cowardly crime"[46] and "the suicides, the murders, the filling up of brothels of every kind which his abject actions had caused,"[47] seem exaggerated when we consider that in most cases they are meant to describe the seduction of women who are willing to be seduced.

The fact is that Cassi Jones impersonates the archetype of some young men whom the author must have known and loathed passionately: Cassi is white and uses his skin color as a weapon to seduce Black women or women of an inferior social position. Cassi is well off, he does not work, he only makes some money in some semi-illegal activities, he is ignorant, reckless with women, unable to feel emotions and feelings. He is just the opposite of Lima Barreto who is a mulatto, who works to survive, who is morally honest and rigorous, idealistic, hypersensitive, unable to be successful emotionally.

Cassi's adventures display a characteristic that must have corresponded to the reality of the Brazilian world, that is, the bias and the injustice of people who work in the institutions when there is a conflict between people belonging to different social classes. Apparently this reality must be not only Brazilian, but shortly after the end of slavery in Brazil, it was particularly evident: "Up to that point he counted upon the secret benevolence of the judges and police who intimately judged absurd his marriage to his victims, thanks to the different education, birth, color, and instruction."[48]

Much of Barreto's tragic anxiety is reflected in Cassi's character. See, for example, the following passage, which described, with some exaggeration and naïveté, Cassi's arrival at a party where he meets Clara and where he is expected with frenzy by the young girls present:

> He entered. There was a shiver as if of an electric discharge, which ran through the invited girls. All the girls of different colors, whom poverty and humble origin had there united and merged, admired him immediately in his total emptiness; so powerful is the charm of perversion in the feminine minds. Not even Cesare Borgia, walking all armored into a masked ball given in the Vatican by his father, Alexander the Sixth, would have caused such a commotion. They did not say, "It is Cesare, it is Cesare!" but they murmured, "It is he, it is he!"
>
> When he was introduced to the hosts and their daughter, nobody noticed the greedy glance of gross sexuality which he sent to Clara's well-formed breasts.[49]

The story is quickly concluded. Cassi runs away and Clara is pregnant. The poor girl looks for help from a friend of the family, Dona Margarida, a lady of foreign origin to whom the writer entrusts an exemplary role, that of a good woman who, at the same time, is aware, strong, brave. She is the kind of woman who, without yielding any of her femininity, knows how to live and take care of herself, aware of her own dignity as a human being; she is similar to Olga, herself of foreign origin, whom we met in *Triste fim de Policarpo Quaresma*. Together with Dona Margarida, Clara goes to Cassi's house, where his mother, showing the usual hysterical attachment to her son, offends Clara by calling her "*negra*." The father, who no longer wants to have anything to do with his son, withdraws into a painful stupor, having asked forgiveness from the young woman.

Before the melodramatic ending, however, in which Clara hugging her mother utters the sentence that concludes the novel: "We are nothing in life,"[50] Barreto sums up in a few lines the reality of the social situation and of the injustices to which poor people, "his people," are subjected:

> In the street Clara thought of all that, of the painful sin she had taken part in and of the humiliation she had suffered. Now she knew exactly her position in society. It had been necessary to be hurt without remedy

> in her young girl's sensitivity and listen to the insults of the mother of her victimizer to become aware that she was not a girl like all the others; she was much less in people's opinion . . .
>
> The upbringing she had received, full of affection and protection, was wrong. She should have learned from her parents that her honesty as girl and woman had enemies everywhere, but they should have told her using real examples, clearly. She observed all these men and women . . . nobody among all those people of both sexes would have been indifferent to her misfortune . . . a young mulatto girl, the daughter of a postman! What was needed for her and for those like her was the education of character, through the will, like that of the dignified Dona Margarida, to defend themselves from Cassi and his kind and struggle against all those who opposed, in any way, their social and moral improvement. Nothing made them inferior to others except the general prejudice and the cowardice with which they accepted it.[51]

This was Barreto's last message: never accept your own proclaimed inferiority, and struggle always to assert yourself before yourself and before society.

Barreto's last work is very vast, and I think I have traced his essential lines as far as the problem of blackness is concerned. This whole subject can be divided into two parts: the really Black character whom he observes with an empathetic and compassionate look which, however, he gives to all the disinherited and the wretched; and the mulattoes with whom he identifies personally, with all his chagrin and bitterness. He is a great writer on the whole, although he is limited by an excessive and too-vibrant participation in the story of his protagonists, and by the violent bias with which he attacks his enemies and adversaries whom we recognize as such in his writing but whom we do not know and therefore find less interesting.

Barreto can be viewed as a typical example of those mulattoes whom Gilberto Freyre describes at length and who represent a transitional phase between the traditional servile position of Blacks and the traditional position of whites as masters. Being, from the ethnic point of view, the product of two different races and, from the social point of view, the product of a society in transition, the mulattoes in the passage from rural civilization to the urban and new industrial civilization, tried to progress socially through the new liberal professions connected to the new creation of the great cities. This was the status of many illustrious mulattoes in the history of Brazil. This was what Barreto did and what his father did before him; in Barreto's case, however, the social ascent to which he aspired was blocked less by incidents, such as his failing at the university, than by his painful sensitivity, which made him perceive clearly the injustice and hypocrisy of that society in which he wanted to progress and be successful. His work is at the same time a valid testimony and denunciation, as well as the reflection of a great paradox that made him struggle strenuously to reform the world from which he demanded official recognition.

Barreto never received that recognition he wanted, not because he was a mulatto but because he was a rebel. And he was a rebel so full of complexes that he even ended up by being unjust or at least biased. The situation would have not been so tragic if he had been a mediocre person but, on the contrary, Barreto was a great writer and one who perceived sharply the injustice of which he was a victim.

Machado de Assis was also a mulatto, a writer, a journalist, and a public officer. He succeeded in obtaining all the greatest recognitions in his different careers. Yet, if we compare the works of these two writers we see that Machado mistreated society in his descriptions; and still that same society opened its doors to the great mulatto. The explanation is after all simple. First, Machado avoided all debates of a personal type which make any writer lose credibility; he also never created mulatto characters that might make one suspect his direct participation in the character's story. In the third place, Machado was a sorcerer, as his contemporaries defined him: he described Rio de Janeiro's rich society so well that all his readers recognized themselves in his descriptions, or would have liked to recognize themselves in his characters. He criticized and analyzed that life and society well, showing its defects and hypocrisies in so perfect a way that very few became aware of it; and those few either were not numerous enough to harm him or they were intelligent enough to let it go.

We recall, for example, that monument of ignominy which Machado built in the character of Cotrim, the ex-slave merchant, and the apparently condescending way in which he presented his falsity and hypocrisy: how many fat nouveau-riche bourgeois would have recognized themselves in the superficiality of the description without even suspecting that Machado was branding them forever. We can only imagine the mass of epithets and insults Barreto would have used to describe such a character: and the former slave merchants know bad words very well!

This was Lima Barreto: a poor and brave son of the subúrbios, a mulatinho who, just like his characters, struggled desperately against a society that was so ungenerous in granting to him and to those like him the right to be like anybody else. He led a long and solitary struggle that started when he was a schoolboy fighting with his schoolmates and professors and which he kept on throughout all his life. He struggled for the poor and the disinherited without ever yielding or ever letting himself be corrupted by offers and flatteries. His struggle ended, when he was still young, in the tragic solitude of alcohol and madness.

11 COELHO NETO AND THE BLACK KING

> Ah! African Kingdom, *negro* people, warriors of the *palmares*! If only it could be now! Think of what would become of all that, in a single moment, with the destroyers of the villages! A crowd of people unleashed, hurling themselves indiscriminately down the streets, rolling down the hillsides, warriors with feathers in their hair, brandishing arms, women screaming with children hanging from their waists and assegais in their hands, running like furies, beasts trembling with fear and clouds of hissing arrows, the house surrounded, attacked, brutally invaded with a deafening roar: doors broken down with the blows of axes, walls destroyed and the crowd, in its lunatic fury, thrusting forward, lusting for murder slipping on the blood and destruction: finally the fire, the high red flames wrapping around the house devouring the very air, launching forth clouds of thick smoke; and the triumphant cry of the naked *negros*, the harsh blare of the trumpets, the savage exaltation of the dance around the fire with the wood crackling and the corpses exploding like the green wood of the forest fires of São João. And reigning over it all he stands, lord of the earth, the king! Scattering his people over hill and dale, placing guards on the roads, lookouts in the treetops, and destroying, burning, and avenging his race, his kingdom, Munza, full of hatred and the immemorial suffering of Africa.[1]

So Coelho Neto (1864–1934) imagines the angry and desperate cry of Macambira, the main figure of *Rei negro* (*Black King*, 1914). The son of a Portuguese father and an Indian woman, born in the Maranhão but educated in Rio de Janeiro and Recife, writer, journalist, and a prominent political figure, Coelho Neto in *Rei negro* has made a courageous attempt to create a situation in which a Black protagonist brings to the foreground the drama of the existence of slavery as seen by those who suffered injustice in the very depths of their being.

The tale of Macambira is the classic one of the exiled king. He is not only the slave of a great estate in the province of Rio de Janeiro but also the son of Munza, an African king sold into slavery and dragged to Brazil. Many of the slaves of the *fazenda* are men from Munza's kingdom and show Macambira special respect because of his condition as a captive king. In particular there is an old woman called Balbina, known as *feiticeira*, who keeps the memory alive and nourishes the tradition with her inexhaustible fund of stories. Macambira enjoys great prestige among the other slaves and with his master, who has made him his right-hand man in the management of the estate. He is a model slave, and unlike the other *negros* shows a disdainful indifference to women and never abandons himself to that licentious behavior all too common among the slave population. His master has the highest esteem for him and is afraid lest Macambira buy back his freedom by paying the *carta de alforria* and leave. This was clearly possible in the Brazilian system of slavery, which recognized the slave's right to buy his freedom and to appear before a judge in case of refusal by the master. Manuel Gandra, as the master is called, knows this perfectly well, and to keep his precious slave with him plans to marry him to the beautiful *mucama* Lúcia, with whom Macambira already seems to be in love. Lúcia is almost white, the daughter of a mulatto mother and German father. She accepts the idea of becoming Macambira's wife. The wedding takes place and the newlyweds go to live in a pretty little house that is Manuel Gandra's wedding present to them. Everything seems to be moving towards a happy ending, were it not for the villain Julinho, the boss's son, a typically brutal and violent example of the gentry, always ready to beat and torment the Black workers, and continually on the prowl for women to take off to bed. Julinho rapes Lúcia shortly before the wedding; she is pregnant and does not know who is the father of the child she carries in her womb. In Macambira's absence she gives birth to a child with blue eyes and dies shortly afterward of hemorrhage. Balbina, who has remained close to the young couple, tries to head off the inevitable by warning Manuel Gandra. Macambira returns and finally learns the truth. After a period of time in which he falls into a state of bewildered apathy, he feels a resurgence of pride, kills Julinho, and then takes to the forest where he fights against his former masters.

To clear away any possible ambiguity we must immediately make clear that the creation of a protagonist like Macambira, who is at the same time prince and slave, is by no means (as it may seem at first sight) a literary device or an exceptional case. Many cases of Black slaves belonging to royal families have been authenticated, and their condition was known to the other slaves who continued to show towards them all forms of respect. There were also examples of Black princes whose freedom was bought back by comrades in slavery who regained their liberty. Without going into details, we may add that the flow of Blacks was not always in one direction, that is, from Africa to Brazil. It also went the other way, from Brazil back to Africa. That on one plantation the body of slaves might include the member of a royal family, therefore, is just as credible as the homage we see paid to him by his companions in misfortune.

Rei negro was published in 1914, during what we might call the years of stasis, which extend from the end of slavery in 1888 to the beginnings of the first literary and political movements that succeeded each other after 1922. It is a period in which slavery has been abolished, but the social structure on which slavery was founded remained unchanged. Coelho Neto, however, as a journalist, writer, and politician, was an ardent abolitionist. His novel is intended as a history of slavery, a posthumous history that fits perfectly into the historical context, and has a historical function in a world where de facto slavery continued to exist and where above all among the landowning classes the narrow-minded mentality of the slave owner remained undimished. This, therefore, is a perfectly functional novel, if you consider the day of May 13, 1888 not as the end of an evolution of a historical period ending with the abolition of slavery, but as the start of a real process of liberation whose point of departure was the formal declaration of human rights that was not followed by any real change in the social structure.

Rei negro can thus be considered one of those works written to attack slavery even though the institution had formally been abolished twenty-six years earlier. In this book Coelho Neto adopts an artistic formula that cannot be said to be completely successful, that is, that of a double language. While in fact the language in which the story is told is highly refined, rich in many words that have since fallen out of use, deeply erudite and, frankly, heavy and pedantic at times, the language in which the slaves communicate among themselves attempts to reproduce the rough and ungrammatical style of Black speech. You can say that Coelho Neto commits two sins: an excess of sophistication and erudition on the one hand, which weighs down the text, and on the other an exaggerated coarseness which in turn alienates itself from the true forms of expression of the uneducated. It is nevertheless perfectly valid to attempt to reproduce the manner of speaking of an uncultivated people without forcing it into the mold of correct Portuguese, which is at the same time ascetic and lifeless. It is a decidedly artificial exercise, not only in the exaggeration of many expressions, but also for the simple declaration at the start of his novel, that Macambira spoke his native tongue fluently (let us not forget that we are dealing with a pure-blooded Black of the first generation, the son of a free man, a king sold into slavery). All his conversations with the old Balbina and the slaves from his tribal group therefore take place in their ancient tongue and there is no reason to translate them into an imperfect and ungrammatical Portuguese. Maybe this is one of the ever-present conditioned reflexes of the cultivated white writer, the master of an erudite and refined language, who cannot imagine the Black slaves expressing themselves correctly even when they are not obliged to use a language, in this case Portuguese, not yet their own.

We must not forget that when Coelho Neto, like almost all his fellow Brazilian writers, talks of Blacks and slaves, he is always casting a glance over at the other side, imagining facts, situations, and modes of being he has only seen and never lived. We must also keep in mind that slavery, for members of the well-heeled bourgeoisie, had been fundamental to their lives, something to which they had always been accustomed. And this explains many of their contradictions, certain expressions that they let slip and certain situations they imagine which conflict with the principles they express.

Let us return to the novel and examine in detail the various characters, beginning with the principals. If on the one hand the central figure Macambira corresponds, as we have said, in his status as a slave prince to an existing historical type, his artistic realization is much less credible. In the last pages of the novel Macambira emerges as an avenging champion of the Black race; his is not a flight into the forest, but a triumphant return to his mother earth, a rediscovery of his warrior ancestry and his bloody destiny:

> He turned to look at the mountain chain of the *quilombos*, staring at them for a long time, motionless as a statue. Deep noises echoed through the wood: calls, barbaric cries, strange sounds, and howls. The grasses waved as if moved by a great wind under the purple sky; heaven and earth glowed blood-red.
>
> The *negro* breathed deeply as he observed in wonderment the grandiose spectacle: as announced, the moment of bloody uprising had arrived, the lofty war of the gods, the war of martyrs rising from the earth, with Munza at their head in all his glory. He was in the clouds, in the mountains and on the plain—blood and fire over all.
>
> Over yonder, cirrus and nimbus clouds were gathering in dense groups, while in the fields and hills he could see the tribal chiefs and the fierce warriors, old women and children, their feathers fanned by the wind, their arms gleaming, the trumpets echoing; here was the promised devastation, the revenge of the idols and the *negros*, the victory of their religion and their race. And Macambira, quivering with heroic enthusiasm, brandished his sword, which flashed in the sun, and swiftly, as if unleashing himself for battle, climbed the hill and disappeared into the wood, howling in blood lust, carried away by the vision of slaughter.[2]

It is a fine, deeply epic page, the ideal continuation of the passage quoted at the beginning of this chapter. But it seems forced, something separate from the rest of the novel, a conclusion with little logical connection to the preceding pages. Macambira is a prince reduced to slavery, many of his comrades are fully aware of his condition and pay him the respects due to his rank. But his whole behavior until the moment of the tragedy is that of the model slave, both active and submissive. Thanks to his ability and personal talent he has become the mainstay of his master in the organization of the slave labor on the plantation: he is in practice the steward, the man to whom Manuel Gandra entrusts the day-to-day supervision of the fazenda. He is responsible for making purchases in town, the man to be trusted. The slave order of the whole population rests in a large part on the shoulders of Macambira and it never crosses his mind to try to change the order one iota. And yet in the mountains around the plantation there are many quilombos, and the names of many leaders, all well known.

> *Melchior* lived over there, as well as Barnabé, Felício, Chico Bexiga, Tito. The latter even had a house, cultivated land, a herd of cattle, and armed men to protect him. He was a little king up there. Every so often he would appear at night at Barra to buy provisions at the market.[3]

Who is the true king, Macambira who collaborates with the white slave owner or Tito who lives freely in the hills?

We must try to understand the position of Coelho Neto and all those like him who fought against slavery and struggled for its abolition. To condemn slavery as such could prove unpopular or even counterproductive in that Brazilian world which up to then had lived off the slave order. It was therefore necessary to create some exceptional case, the dramatic moment, the artificially contrived crisis, to paint in darker tints the negative aspects of slavery: all to make the book acceptable to a public that knew only the positive aspects of that slave order, the same public that had permitted the calm and somnolent life of the plantation owners to continue. Macambira does not rebel against the slave order as such (while he complains about the sad condition of his existence) but revolts simply against the son of the man he has served faithfully for years and who has paid him back by raping his wife.

The position of Coelho Neto thus ends up being as ambiguous as that of Macambira in relation to his companions in misfortune.

From the first pages of the novel Macambira is presented to us as a man with a sexual phobia, a fierce moralist, and this unusual attitude is always accompanied by the approval of the author. The explanation of this can be traced to the fact that the agrarian Brazilian civilization emerged at its outset from the encounter (or first the clash and then the fusion) of two mutually exclusive existential concepts: on the one hand the idea of feminine virginity linked to Luso-Arabic sexual obsession codified by the rigors of Jesuit discipline; and on the other, that of feminine fertility linked to the exaltation of sexual relations typical of the world of the Blacks. The white Portuguese, arriving in Brazil after months of long, monotonous sea voyage, at first found in the Indian women an immediate satisfaction of his sexual desires. Once he had become lord of the land and of the slaves, he used and abused the women, who were totally at his mercy. In this Jesuitical hypocrisy he found ways of making them responsible for an act committed only by himself. It is easy to imagine the condition of those wretched women, snatched from their tribal surroundings and deprived of that elementary support represented by the male (husband, brother, or father, the Black man was still a slave and thus unable to defend either himself or the women of his family). The latter, according to a hypocritical moral code, ought to have defended from the lust of the white man something that he did not even consider a virtue. It took Gilberto Freyre, in the early thirties, to demolish the myth of the Black temptress corrupting the habits of the white man when the truth was the precise opposite.

Coelho Neto has tried to give his character the strength of a moralist because he wanted to make him an exception in the Black world that is, on the contrary, seen as degenerate and corrupt:

> Macambira felt offended by the lustful brutality that recalled animals in heat. These were his people, members of his race who allowed themselves to be so depraved, rolling and riding around with the coarse cynicism of dogs. At every step he saw them in their licentious couplings; by the rustling of the leaves he could guess at their disgusting embraces; and he rushed through the forest, shouting curses and putting to flight couples who tripped as they ran.
>
> It was the *negros* from the countryside who, eluding the watchful eye of the supervisors, would slip off into the woods burning with an uncontrollable desire that drove them wild; and then there were the *mucamas* who came down from the hills to meet their lovers in the cool darkness of the wine cellars; he could see them on the river banks, in the damp grass; among the piles of stones, in the caves, in the fields among the animals, and in the woodpiles.
>
> But what really drove him mad was to see the *negrinhas* turning up in the less-frequented areas of the *engenho* cackling with laughter, exposing their lubricious bodies to the brutal gaze of the *moleques*, unaware of any harm done, flirting outrageously with the same casual

indifference in which they hung from the high branches of the trees, leaning out over the abyss, risking their life for an empty nest or an unripe fruit.[4]

In short these Blacks are seen as dirty beasts, but fortunately the omnipresent Macambira serves to try to reestablish morality at all costs.

> Completely committed to his own people on every count, he simply refused to tolerate the corroding filth of lust. He was revolted by the cursed excitement of the senses, which turned men into beasts and caused him to vilify with infuriated hatred all those he discovered locked in sexual embrace. If he came across couples hiding furtively in the woods he stepped in between them and separated them.[5]

It is really a rather improbable description of Macambira who exercises his royal function by playing the role of policeman chasing after young couples who show a public excess of affection. Sincerely, it seems to me rather beneath the dignity of a king, albeit an exiled king reduced to slavery, who might have found a more serious cause to fight for, unless, of course, the author's intention was to underline the strict moral code of Macambira (to be interpreted as a virtue according to Christian ethics) in contrast with the licentious character of the Blacks. Macambira thus becomes a fearless knight of unspotted virtue absolutely immune to the temptations of sex: one beautiful *negra*, in love with him and having in vain offered herself to him, actually kills herself in despair. This attitude of his stirs up ironic and insolent comments from the other Blacks—above all women—who are thus given a chance to give vent to their innate vulgarity.

Here is the basic ambiguity of Coelho Neto: in telling the story of a Black king, he accentuates the absurd character of the hero and the degrading aspects of his people. So the tale itself may provide excellent alibis. Just look, for example, at the book's most repugnant character, Julinho, the master's son, who spends his life beating up the *moleques* and seducing the slave girls. The author makes him the antagonist of Macambira and his moral opposite, and yet the way he is presented—and the handling of his misdeeds—is never left unaccompanied by a series of exculpations. Julinho's mother is almost proud of her son's exploits, particularly when she first perceives the proof of his manly virility and has her confidants tell her all the details; and she is always ready to defend him if any Black father or mother comes to protest about the violation of their daughters:

> For Dona Clara her son had as much right over the life and honor of the slaves as over the fruit on the trees and the game in the woods. She

> could not understand that *negras* would revolt against the rape of their daughters or that *negros* would deeply resent the degradation of their women whom the young master ceaselessly lusted after.[6]

And after this point the writer limits himself to the account of what was extremely common: that it was absolutely normal for masters to dispose of female slaves on their estates as they felt fit; such had been the tradition for more than three centuries. He has, however, already prepared a solid excuse:

> Since Dona Clara was a child she had been used to seeing the slaves coupling together, rolling around in the grass, groaning and panting like animals in heat. She would laugh, throw stones at them, shout and drive them off, at which they would run away like dogs and plunge into the dark of the woods where they would come together again with even greater ferocity. They were like animals who knew no shame and who, on scenting the female, follow her, confront her, attack her, sink their fangs into her, thrust her onto the ground and satisfy themselves with the same natural instinct with which they cut a piece of meat or slaked their thirst in a pool of water.[7]

In short, it is clear: Julinho is the beast that he is, he may violate morality in broad terms, but he certainly cannot offend the Blacks, "who were no more than animals" and who in no way could feel themselves outraged by the behavior of another animal just because he was white and had the advantage of being their master.

Furthermore, the author very cleverly lets it be understood that there is some doubt as to who is seduced and who is the seducer in that commingling of flesh exposed to the sun. The first sexual experiences of Julinho took place, in fact, with the compliant cooperation of the pretty mulattas of the estate:

> He pleaded with them to show him their nakedness, he "wanted to see, just to see." And the most shameless of them complied "just for the hell of it." And the young lad would throw them to the ground, and madly tear off their clothing, sniffing and biting them while they, laughing, would resist, but then, suddenly excited, would grab hold of him, force him to submit, and beside themselves now, brutalized him.[8]

The use of the word brutalize to describe the erotic assault of the mulattas forcing the young master to the ground is clearly a little strong. The only person with the courage to oppose the sexual frenzy of Julinho is, of course, Macambira himself, who appears in the most opportune (or inopportune) moments to separate the couple and send the woman packing. This particular detail is decisively implausible in the context of Brazilian slavery, where no slave would ever have enjoyed such authority with regard to his owners, and where any misguided serf who behaved as Macambira did would probably have been castrated.

We have already referred to the ambiguity of Coelho Neto who, as a writer, must have kept in mind the preconceptions of the public, which, so far as we know, he may have shared. The end of slavery is a fact, the theoretical and judicial acceptance of the Black is also a fait accompli; but the de facto acceptance of those who for centuries had customarily been considered as no more than beasts was well in the future at the time when Coelho Neto wrote *Rei negro*. A Black king, an authentic Black king, a Zumbi dos Palmares, who for decades kept the Portuguese troops at bay, would never have been the darling of the public, that is, of a particular public.

From this point of view Macambira is an idealized character in his complete lack of verisimilitude and the ascetic perfection attributed to him. Let us begin with the moral rigor, or as it may be more accurate to describe it, his sexual phobia. The idea of sin linked to the act of love was born and developed in a completely different climate from that of the Black African population. Without going into details we can say that warfare, hunting, and sexual activity form a single whole that lies at the base of many Black societies: the reward for the leader, for the strongest warrior, and the most skillful hunter, is measured in terms of many women. And thus a leader or king who obstinately rejects women and who declares himself as defender of sexual morality is a complete anomaly. What has happened is that Coelho Neto has injected something into his text, has attributed to Macambira that Jesuitical moral abnegation on which white society, in word only, has modeled itself, and has transformed him into a mythical legendary character, a medieval knight locked in the armor of his purity, snatched from some ancient ballad and tossed into a nineteenth-century Brazilian fazenda. It is a bold and hardly credible transplantation.

What is credible, however, is the response of Black women and men alike to Macambira's attitude (their mocking laughter, coarse sarcasm, and insulting remarks), even if such comments are referred to by the author as further proof of the depraved nature of the Blacks.

Then there is the whole problem of the relationship between Macambira and Lúcia, which poses once again with all its force the old sexual taboo of the relationship between a Black man and a white woman. Lúcia is a slave, the mistress's mucama, the daughter of a mulatto mother and a German father and from the description we have of her—green eyes, chestnut hair with golden highlights, light skin—she is practically white: she is educated, literate, skilled at embroidery. She is, in short, that complex of virtues required of all heroines of the nineteenth-century novel. Macambira, in contrast, is a first-generation Black, his father is an African; he is still the son of the forest while Lúcia is the product of the evolution of civilization. Macambira expresses himself poorly in Portuguese, his language is crude, whereas Lúcia reads novels for the amusement of her mistress and her own pleasure. In short, each is the other's opposite and for that reason they are attracted to each other: a repressed and violent passion in the case of Macambira, an affectionate interest on behalf of Lúcia. The architect of their marriage is, as we know, Manuel Gandra, who wants to keep his precious slave close to him.

The marriage takes place in a double ceremony: the Catholic rites with the priest talking of the duties of the couple and the obedience of the slaves towards their masters, and the Black ceremony by night with all the subjects of King Munza who come to pay homage to the son of their former lord. It is a lovely page, one of the finest in the book, in which all the fears of Lúcia, her fear of her first encounter with the man and the accompanying fear of having hidden from him her violation by Julinho, mingle with the far greater terror she feels as a more-or-less white woman faced with the dionysiac explosion of that Black world created of echoes, sounding in the obsessive rhythm of the drums, of an unknown reality dominated by the motif of the forest and its dark shadows of violence. This is the eternal, obsessive terror of the white man who knows he has conquered the Black body but that he has no power whatsoever over his soul that remains free, notwithstanding the Catholic rites to which it has been forced to submit. His soul now bursts forth in a song of liberation reliving it in memory and the anticipation of the day and the hour, but it will return to its primordial freedom forever under the divine protection of the everlasting forests.

But the true spirit of the Black revolt is not really represented by Macambira, who stands only for the external, the most visible aspect of Négritude, which refuses to accept its sad fate. As a character Macambira is too much a reflection of the fundamental ambiguity of his author: he is strong, handsome, and courageous and at the same time a faithful slave immune to the easy temptations of sex while being open to the feeling of great love. His revolt is too strongly linked to a personal offense not to be shared by the reader, and it is so deeply embedded in his personal, private experience—the rape of his wife, his defrauded paternity—that it cannot count as a political fact in the broad sense of the word. It was out of this that the well-meaning contemporaries of Coelho Neto, on reading *Rei negro*, must have felt reassured in their conclusions: what a splendid slave is Macambira, how easy in one's mind one feels with such a slave; the only thing is, one must go easy in one's treatment of him and not play him such dirty tricks as Julinho did!

The true spirit of the revolt is not in the strong and handsome Macambira, but in old Balbina. And here, fortunately, Coelho Neto ceases to be ambiguous: Balbina is a dirty, old woman, a tough character, almost a witch. It is she who nourishes the strength and courage of Macambira with the memory of freedom and lost dignity. With Balbina the game is swiftly revealed. For her there are no words of sympathy and pity: even when she is beaten first by another slave and later by Manuel Gandra, the author makes no comment, he does not underline the situation. Men like Macambira are assimilable into the system, all you have to do is treat them fairly, but women like Balbina will always be the repositories of rebellion; they represent something that will never die, which passes from mouth to mouth, repeated nightly by the fire, in the pauses between work, in the tales told to children. There are thousands of Balbinas who live on in the nightmares of the owners, locked as they are in their citadels, besieged night and day by the sounds, voices, and signs that they can never understand, but in which one can sense the undying memory of an ancient dignity:

> Old Balbina, a *negra* considered as *mandingueira*, always dressed in rags, filthy and dirty, stinking of pigs and sheep fat. She worked for the pig butcher, and lived knee deep in filth, amid the fat swine, filling their bowls with swill, and sitting with the dirty sheep in their pens. You could hardly make out her bloodshot eyes, which gleamed with suspicion, and if anyone said anything to her, she always shrugged her shoulders high, muttering to herself, kept her eyes to the ground, gesturing to the questioner to go away, and off she went with a coarse guffaw of derision or humming a sort of song that mocked the listener.[9]

Balbina is the soul of Macambira; it is she who reminds him of the kingdom of Africa, the realm of Munza, who fires his hopes of freedom with the memories of the past:

> With an epic enthusiasm she retold the tales of war, described festive and religious scenes, hunting with bow and arrow in the great forest, idylls under the palms, and almost always in the midst of her recital she rose as if inspired and began to sing in a low voice, sometimes swaying her bony body in sinuous movements.
>
> And tears flowed down her time-worn face in contrast with the coarse

CASTIGOS DOMÉSTICOS

> chants of the barbaric song, the lamentations, and the gestures with which she marked her exaltation. And Macambira, captivated by the rhythm, murmured the funeral chant to himself, dreaming of the homeland he had never known as the son of a king in exile and slavery. The two of them sat for hours by the smoky candlelight or by the doorway, opposite the threshing floor, where the *bacuraus* sang, speaking in whispers, humming, or simply sunk in heavy silence: she chewing, he drawing slowly on his pipe.
>
> The *negra* always had something new to tell him, some story taken from the sad storehouse of her memory and Macambira, listening to her, let his mind wander with his eyes fixed on the great low cultivated plane, covered in mist, where he could imagine stretched out before him the huge invincible kingdom of huts and, swarming in readiness, with their arms flashing, the feared heroic warriors of his people.[10]

Unhappiness, anger, and revolt against one's present state are born of the knowledge and awareness that a superior condition of being exists and of the practical impossibility of achieving it. In every form of coercion practiced by man on man, from the simplest to the most complex, from the vassal age of primitive tribes to the concentration camps, the first concern of the oppressors has always been to give a fixed theoretical and immutable value to the system applied at that particular time and place. To justify itself, slavery in Brazil, like a thousand other forms of slavery that have marked the history of mankind from its origins until the present time, had to correspond to an ethical order, to a collection of laws, to a historical situation that justified it, giving it a character of immutability. You are a slave because you were born a slave, because slaves have always existed, because without slaves, who would work the land; how could you work the land without a master to guide you? Slavery is governed by the laws of men and blessed by the representatives of God on earth. In short you are a slave by the will of men and God, in obedience to a universal judgment.

Against the law of slavery, there are only two possible reactions: the hope for a better world or the memory of a better world in the past. To be credible, hope must be nourished by a real possibility; and what concrete hope could be held out to the Blacks in Brazil beyond that of flight into the forest, to the quilombo? The agrarian world, especially that of the large private estates, brings with it the characteristics of something close to immutability. What was there to hope for? That they would all become white, all masters? How could they know that other worlds existed, other civilizations based on respect for individuals, on rewards granted for personal initiative? The only hope they had was drummed into them in the Sunday sermon of the priest, the hope in a better world after death.

But what the white masters could not fully protect themselves against was the memory and the hope that one day the future would be like the past. "And then the old times will be the new times," as the North American Indians sang when they conceived their final hope before the holocaust. It is the memory of ancient times that keeps hope alive in a world that excludes all other alternatives, which forbids all concepts of any reality, apart from that revealed each day in legalized violence and abuse. This is the truest and profoundest sense of Black revolt: *macumba, candomblé, samba*, a new and reconstructed language, a thousand other cultural expressions hastily catalogued as folklore, are nothing but the Black soul finding itself once more in an effort to establish its identity.

And this is the meaning of a character like Balbina and her relationship with Macambira: she exists to keep the memory alive, to teach the young, those who have known only slavery, that there is another form of life, truer and worthier; and that such a form of life is possible inasmuch as it has existed, it was once theirs. It is for this that Balbina "night after night, lightly treading on the leaves, lithe as a jaguar, came through the woods, and sought him out, to speak to him about the lost fatherland, of dead kings and avenging gods."[11]

These avenging gods bring us to the most delicate point of the novel. We must not forget that Coelho Neto is writing a novel about slavery twenty-six years after its official demise, and just two years before the great strike that will bring São Paulo to a stop, another struggle against a new form of servitude. Like any other writer Coelho Neto is writing for his own public, specifically for those who have lived through and off slavery, people who now want to allow themselves the luxury of cultivating a social conscience (especially now that the period is over), but it is always prudent to exorcise the ghosts, not to go overboard, and this is the reason for the creation of a filthy, smelly Black priestess, half-witch, half-mad.

Just look at one of the most interesting scenes in the book, the native celebration organized by Balbina following the Christian marriage ceremony of Macambira and Lúcia. Here we have the three representatives of Négritude, Lúcia being the least interesting, almost white and totally assimilated into the white society. She is more or less a young lady of good family, but without means, a slave by chance and misfortune, another Isaura sacrificed to the interest of the master who has given her in marriage to a Black slave. On the one hand, the author reveals here not only a visible but artistically inept reticence throughout the episode. It is true that the comment he puts in the mouth of Dona Clara, "forcing a pure young girl to soil herself at the hands of a *negro*,"[12] is negated by the petty stupidity of the character herself. On the other hand, the author's own comment on the wedding ("she could still feel on her mouth the press of his hungry kisses, and felt in his warm and acrid breath the broken words that promised and demanded promises, her body still ached from the lustful torture of that night")[13] is a clear indication of a sexual fear rooted in a prejudice that is Coelho Neto's own. Faced with the nocturnal ceremony about to take place Lúcia exhibits a classical white reaction: she understands nothing and is afraid.

The second character is Macambira in his dual role of slave and king. He has been a perfect slave and is now reaping the rewards of his labor, the pretty white wife, the nice house on the hill, security and prestige among his masters and fellow slaves. He is less believable as a king: his royal standing is the result of Balbina's will, her stories and the enthusiasm she has transmitted to the other Blacks for them to come and pay their respects to their former leader, thus stirring in them their former dignity as free men. Macambira is a person continuously at the crossroads, his choice is between the white world, the system, and that of the Blacks. It is a purely hypothetical choice because even though Macambira complains about his condition as a slave, he shows no signs of rebellion either on the individual or the collective level. Nor does he exploit his status as a king to unite his former subjects and drive them to revolt. Now many uprisings had occurred in Brazil organized by slaves belonging to the same tribal group. The authorities as a matter of policy had always kept the groups divided, scattering the members throughout distant regions. Apart from this, it is difficult to imagine that so many slaves from the same tribe would happen to be in the same place for two reasons: the first is that slavery, at the time of the action of this novel, had already been in existence for three centuries and the various tribal groups had totally intermingled, giving rise to new cultural forms. The second is that in that same period the Black slave trade had diminished considerably and it would have been difficult to find recently imported *negros* from the same tribal group living together in the same area. Going back to Macambira, his choice, when it comes, is motivated by purely personal reasons and has nothing to do with his traditional royal function.

Balbina, the third character, is without doubt the most interesting. Between an assimilated Lúcia and Macambira on the verge of assimilation, she embodies resistance to the world around her: she is a slave because she is forced to be so. If she does not revolt it is because she is old, but at the same time she refuses any form of collaboration with the whites. She is instead the sacred guardian of tradition; it is she who feeds Macambira's imagination. Born a slave in Brazil, he must be given an understanding of the freedom he has never known. And it is she who rouses his vanity by drawing towards him the former subjects of the kingdom of Munza, and finally it is she who takes part with Macambira in the final vendetta. And when the nocturnal ceremony begins it is Balbina, between a frightened Lúcia and a childish, vain Macambira, who is the presiding queen.

> Balbina sprang up from the threshing-floor like a creature possessed and began to leap around brandishing her torch in a circle of light. Her skeletal body seemed elastic in her movements and you could hear her harsh panting breath from her cavernous breast. It was that noise, close by, now hollow, now piercing, that could be heard alone over all the other sounds.[14]

Balbina is the connecting thread running through the novel: she is present when Lúcia gives birth, she tries to save the child, she warns Manuel Gandra of the dangerous turn of events, she helps and comforts Macambira in his misfortune. Balbina is Black consciousness, immovable in her tenacity and courage. For this she is also a witch, a feiticeira, or at least believed to be so because of her contemptuous and solitary character. Balbina has to be a witch in a novel such as *Rei negro* because a successful author like Coelho Neto can never bring himself to make the effort to understand another being, especially when that other is a Black belonging to a world forever deemed inferior by that public opinion at which the book was directed. Macambira is a king by chance; his drama arouses sympathy because it is a story of jealousy and passion which can happen at any time in any country. In Balbina's case there are no extenuating circumstances; she is the true face of Black slavery in Brazil, one of those Blacks who have resisted the ultimate shame of handing over their soul to their white masters, of attaching themselves to the system, and who have kept at least one part of themselves free and intact. That is the part that whites refuse to comprehend, regarding it with fear and suspicion and dismissing it hastily as barbaric and inferior. Macambira himself has remained tied to that cultural world, but apart from emphasizing the diversity of the character, the author passes swiftly over this detail in a few lines and never returns to it: "Son of the *minas*, he spoke their language correctly and practiced his ancestors' religion in secret, mingling in the same rites the figures of

Jesus, the Virgin, the saints, and a monstrous idol in the form of a bull."[15] We might see in this a typical example of what today we would call an Afro-Brazilian rite. Balbina, however, in her alleged witchcraft is all Black, all Africa, all forest and wild animals, all mystery and spite. Her fame as a witch comes from her misanthropy, her habit of talking to herself:

> Sometimes she would hum, beating time with her feet, swinging her skeletal hips from side to side, in sinuous movements.
>
> These mysterious incantations, overheard by chance, gave Balbina her sinister reputation as a *feiticeira*. From the fearful report of the first person who had seen her, grew and spread the legend that made her feared, and her cave, already off the beaten track, became even more isolated as a result of the terror she inspired. And what people told each other in the fields and *senzalas* was enough to strike terror into the boldest.
>
> Some *negros* told tales of seeing ghosts and misshapen animals: headless mules, monstrous wild boars with gleaming bristles galloping past, sharpening their claws, and ridden by Black dwarfs or *sacis*; skeletons dragging their winding sheets, toads, owls, and bats. Others swore that they had heard hair-raising shrieks and anguished cries coming from the banks of the marsh and had seen faces wreathed in mist arising from the water, twisted in anguish and groaning aloud the names of the drowned.[16]

As the terror spreads, so does the legend. In addition to the uncontrolled rumors there is the direct evidence of a witness, someone who has seen everything: Marciano, another Black who looks after the animals, gets lost in the woods one night while looking for an English bull that has escaped from the farm. Suddenly a storm breaks out, a mysterious storm, limited to the spot where he happens to be, leaving the rest of the sky clear. What could be happening?

> It was then that he recognized the place: it was the cave near Balbina's hut, he was lost! O Virgin of the Afflicted! He tried to say a prayer, but he couldn't. His arm would not bend to make the sign of the cross. He was lost, totally lost!
>
> Suddenly there was a great roar and things were collapsing over yonder, and the trees were torn up by their roots, and seemed to grow larger, shaking from side to side, as they leapt through the forest as if alive, while stones rained down, crashing against one another, and the fire snaked its way through the trees, the water from the swamp boiled and sputtered like fermenting wine in the vats; and all those animals! Shades with shrouds flapping in the wind, shrieking owls, fat-bellied frogs standing upright like people, each the size of a child, all of them

> dancing to the repetitive rhythm of the thunder punctuated by continuous flashes of lightning.
>
> Suddenly, like a gunshot, the door of the hut blew open with a roar like a ball of fire and Balbina appeared stark naked, with a snake wrapped around her waist, the bones of a skeleton in her hands, and a toad hanging on to each breast, her teeth glistening, flames darting from her eyes, and she threw herself into the middle of the wild chorus.
>
> His terror was such that he fell to the ground in a faint.
>
> He woke at dawn with the cockcrow. Let the Lord God strike him dead if he were lying. He found himself in the middle of the field near the high grass, with the English bull near by, calmly stretched out and chewing his cud. The moon was slipping down behind the mountains in the distance. Our Lady of the Afflicted! What a night! But the old *negra* paid no attention to everything they said. Let them leave her alone. So they talked. Everyone says what he feels like.[17]

The figure of the feiticeiro, as we have seen from other authors, has always stood for a crucial moment in Brazilian literature, the point at which every writer has had to reveal himself. This is simply because the forms of Black religious practice, of which the feiticeiro represents the most sinister manifestation, have always been present in the Brazilian world, assuming a greater visibility in the last few years and bordering on the area of folklore. At the time of Coelho Neto the various forms of Black culture were officially suppressed by the authorities in a last-ditch attempt literally to whitewash all aspects of Brazilian life. Yet even prominent members of the white society still embraced them. At the time of the fictitious action of *Rei negro*, a thorough persecution was not pursued since slavery still existed and the expressions of Black culture and traditions were confined to the senzalas; this did not stop many members of the white class from religiously practicing the forms of a cult that clearly was not sanctified by the Catholic church.

Even in *Rei negro*, every time Dona Clara feels threatened she turns to a feiticeiro to exorcise the curse. But the figure of Balbina has another significance. In his treatment of the figure of the witch, Coelho Neto expresses neither the blind fear of a Manuel Macedo nor the respectful faith of a Xavier Marques. His attitude continues to be subtly ambiguous and he never loses his balance. In fact, he never says that Balbina actually is a feiticeira; instead he says that because of her antisocial and solitary behavior, she had created around herself the aura of a feiticeira in the minds of the Black slaves. The difference is fundamental: on the one hand the author is not obliged to take a position for or against the reality of the witch doctor and her powers;

on the other, he leaves it entirely up to the Blacks in the book to accept the witch and give credit to whatever powers she may possess, be they thaumaturgic or malevolent. It is an elegant way of confronting the problem and evading it at the same time. It is also a means of defining the Black world, attributing to it alone the responsibility of adopting certain ways of life.

Let us try to sum up the position of Coelho Neto with regard to the Black world, bearing in mind, as always, the writers who preceded him and the world in which he lived. Let us remember a major tendency of many writers as they represent Blacks or slaves in general; either they present the Black as he was in the sad reality of the time, above all as they, the writers, saw him at a distance from the lofty position of the white ruling class—in which case the Black becomes a low creature in the broad sense of the word, dirty, ignorant, incapable, ugly, superstitious, and so on. Or they present us with an idealized slave, investing him with all the noble virtues and characteristics taken from the classical figures of the white narrative tradition. In *A escrava Isaura* the major interest was not provided by the condition of a Black woman reduced to slavery, but rather by the lachrymose melodrama of a young woman of good family, and who is virtually white, in the hands of a brutal and lecherous master. In *O mulato* the problem of mulattoes, Blacks, and slaves existed only in the background, and, given that the protagonist was so white he was not aware that he was a mulatto, what was dramatically in evidence was the prejudice that stifled all forms of liberty and thought in the province of Maranhão. In *Rei negro*, the hero has at least one advantage over the characters who came before him. He is a pure Black, of recent African origin, but in the way he is handled, he suffers from a kind of split personality: he is a model slave in the eyes of his masters and, in the pure folkloric moments of the novel, a king in the eyes of his fellow slaves. Not for a moment does he think of exploiting his own status, to assert it by challenging the white overlords: he never asserts it in his conversations with Balbina in which they both accept their wretched fate as something inevitable and inexorable; he never asserts it face to face with Manuel Gandra when the latter comes to see them both after the final tragedy. Even here Macambira still remains the slave talking to his master, feeling confused and humiliated when, following an observation by Gandra, he realizes that he has kept his hat on his head during their conversation.

There are taboos that are not easy to overcome and Coelho Neto never seriously attempted to overcome them; he never thought of abandoning the placid world of respect for the conventions or prejudices of his age. He remains tied forever to the narrow-minded vision of the white master towards his slaves; and thus the African marriage ceremony becomes "more and more chaotic and uncontrolled in its barbaric din and cannibalistic cries."[18] Thus Macambira, at the moment of his revenge, shows a "cannibal's joy,"[19] while the moleques of the engenho "looking dazed and stupid, covered in filthy rags, their eyes running, stretched out their emaciated hands with a simian gesture."[20] Here is the other side of the truth of Coelho Neto: cannibals, that air of idiocy, the simian gestures, without counting other characters in the book whom we have not even mentioned, including a woman slave nicknamed Vaca Brava (Wild Cow), whose name tells everything, all of whom stand for the lowest depths to which humanity can descend. These are the Blacks as seen by the author who makes no effort to comprehend the precise chain of guilt and responsibility that lies behind that air of idiocy of those children left to themselves like wild dogs; and what accumulation of moral wretchedness is at the basis of the cruel and infantile beliefs born around the figure of Balbina; and what a void of desperation lies at the origin of people such as Vaca Brava.

Here is the real limit of Coelho Neto's work despite his statements and actions—by no means without their value on another level—against slavery. This is the explanation for the ambiguities of a character like Macambira, a folkloric king in the slave festivals and his own solitary fantasies, still a slave in his final act of revolt, forced into the revenge of a man driven almost mad with jealousy and grief. A real King Macambira, who might have attempted to avenge not his personal humiliation but the perpetual injustice suffered by his own people, by his tribe in their daily existence in the universal slave state, would have been too strong a character for the tastes of a public that for centuries had slept with the nightmare of a great Black revolt. Such a revolt had been fragmented throughout the course of Brazilian history into a thousand little insurrections, a thousand quilombos, a thousand authentic little kings.

The author attains a much greater credibility and cruelty when he describes, in contrast, the moral wretchedness of the white masters, that Portuguese venality behind the mask of the bonhomie of Manuel Gandra, his acts of bad faith that have become a habit hardened into law, the obese animal stupidity of Dona Clara, the bestial sensuality of Julinho. They, too, are slaves of a degrading system whose fruits they gather for their material advantage, unable to develop their humanity. Like so many members of their class, they remain trapped in the absurdity of their prejudice, whose ultimate offshoots limited and infected the otherwise meritorious work of men and writers like Coelho Neto.

12 FROM *MACUNAÍMA* TO *CATIMBÓ*

The Brazilian literary scene at the turn of the 1930s is rich and varied. Even from the cultural point of view Brazil is a country set apart with its own characteristics without equivalents in North America or Europe. One of the most disconcerting characteristics for us is the disproportionate amount of written material published compared to what is actually read, as compared to the figures available in other countries.

Today Brazil is a land that each day more closely resembles other countries where multinational companies, major industries, and mass civilization are the rule. This you would have found just a few years ago when newspapers, reviews, and even publishing houses proliferated with extreme facility only to disappear in the space of a few years or even a few months, particularly in the more remote provincial cities. Books were usually published in editions of no more than a few hundred copies, to disappear shortly afterwards without a trace.

How can one explain this phenomenon in a country like Brazil where the public at large has never expressed clear cultural interests? It must be explained by the elitist character of Brazilian letters and by the typical nature and background of the writers of the country. Writing poetry, short stories, novels, memoirs, and essays has in most cases served as a form of ornament or cultural distinction whereby the sons of the bourgeoisie added luster to their family name or career as civil servants, professionals, or politicians. All this took place independently of the laws of the publishing market, which today, on the contrary, demands a much more careful selection as a result of higher costs. Once upon a time the Brazilian writer had no need to sell his product since in the first place the book conferred an honorific title on the author, a passport to a more exclusive rank in society. It is for this reason that writers such as Jorge Amado or Rachel de Queirós published their first books so early when their European contemporaries were still struggling with their high school graduation exams. The problem really lies in the fact that not everyone was a Jorge Amado.

To have a rich family or a large *fazenda* behind you (it is said of one writer who later became quite famous that his father had bought him a printing press so that he could give free rein to his talent) was an obvious advantage for the few precocious and talented debutants, but it also thrust on the market a clutter of books destined to be stillborn.

The years that witnessed the Modernist revolution in the fields of art and letters were rich in all sorts of publications. The country was leaving its worst years behind, the years in which Brazil had finally shed its landed-property mentality (even if the majority of Brazilians had failed to notice) but had yet to discover its identity as a modern country. Even in reaction to a mortifying past, the atmosphere of these years was electrifying. It was one of those magic moments in the life of a people when everything seemed possible.

As always happens in these cases, however, history, in the forms of economic difficulty and violent political crises, succeeded in dampening many enthusiasms and dashing many expectations. This gave the opportunity to express themselves to those who had observed only the most superficial aspects of the changing times. That is why the novel in those years is notable for its inconsistent and contradictory achievements. On the one hand we have the work of those who had clearly and intuitively perceived the different pulse of the new age, and on the other, that of honest hacks who absolutely failed to understand the nature of the changes and who sincerely believed in the unalterability of the social structures beneath the superficial transformation of the country's way of life.

We know from our own historical experience that the speed of technological advance cannot be matched by an equal transformation of mentality and habit. The car can take the place of the horse or mule in a few years, but the man at the wheel needs many more years before discarding his horse-and-buggy mentality. And this phenomenon, visible throughout the world, was even more acute in Brazil, where industrial civilization had been directly imported from abroad without the foundations of an established industrial tradition going back for generations.

What happens to the figure of the Black in the novel of those years in which so many came to feel their vocations as writers? Let us say that the period goes from *Macunaíma* to *Catimbó*, from the absurd, brilliant, fantastic, and disconcerting work of Mário de Andrade to the folkloric novel of Sabino de Campos, as rich in information and historical notes as it is poor in terms of plot and ideas. In the words of Luciana Stegagno Picchio:

> A hero without character, part Indian, part African, but white with blue eyes, lazy, lustful, cruel with a soft heart, greedy for money, sly, un-

> trustworthy, capable of every trickery and act of bravery, defeated in his personal life by events beyond his control (the ogre Piaimã), in constant search for his individual grail, the amulet of his lost betrothed, affectionate in a world beset by traps and temptations, Macunaíma belongs to the reverse side of the *ufanista* and Alencarian tradition of the Indian as a noble, spotless knight, and he is an attempt to represent beyond any rhetorical scheme of aprioristic design a multiracial Brazil in its full, social, and linguistic reality.[1]

The product of a searching ethnographic study and a creative effort on the linguistic level when it was published in 1928, *Macunaíma* was not only read as a marvelous work of art that has lost none of its verve today but was and is one of the most serious attempts to create a Brazilian identity.

The very name of the protagonist, Macunaíma, is the result of precise ethnological research. Hitherto, in fact, the name Macunaíma (with the tonic accent on the fourth syllable) stood for God the Creator in the minds of Indians and later for the hero or central figure. Mário de Andrade turns him into a new hero, a negative hero, a man without character in the newly emergent Brazilian race. There is a certain bitterness in this type of choice, a clear indication that the long road followed in constant admiration and imitation of the European model has been a decisive failure and that the great families of old and proud *paulistas* have continued to lose ground in a country where the majority of the population consists of determined immigrants and rowdy Blacks. That is why the hero Macunaíma is a synthesis of all the national vices and why his vices are so emphatic and exaggerated beyond all measure. It is an example of catharsis in the form of caricature, vice so disproportionately inflated that it becomes almost a virtue in its very incredibility.

If Mário de Andrade refers etymologically to native Indian mythology, his Macunaíma is largely Black and hardly Indian at all. When we speak of the native Indian we are certainly not referring to those completely unbelievable creatures created by Alencar, but rather to those tribes that still existed at that time and which were even then moving towards a slow and inglorious extinction against the background of general indifference. The Indian was mythologically a much safer choice, inasmuch as there was no risk of his being confused with reality; whereas the Black was by now an omnipresent and determining reality not always graciously accepted by his former white masters.

Macunaíma is thus Indian by name but Black in fact: "In the depths of the virgin forest Macunaíma was born, the hero of our people. His skin was dark black and he was the son of the fear of night."[2]

The hero sets off on his wild adventure in the company of his brothers, but before reaching adolescence he has already given proof that he has been blessed beyond expectation with all possible vices. Lazy to the point of wetting his pants when it is too much trouble to get down from his hammock, ready to feel up any girl passing within reach of his hands, lecherous and cruel, he is a liar, dishonest, and generally base. His journey is a fantastic flight beyond space and time: "The next day Macunaíma rose early and jumped into his canoe and paddled to the mouth of the Rio Negro, leaving his conscience on the island of Marapatá."[3] Having discarded the useless burden of guilt (perhaps recalling the alibi of the ancient mariners for whom sin did not exist south of the equator), our hero needs a blessing to confront the forest of stone and wild automobiles that is the city of São Paulo: he must change the color of his skin and become white. And here we see again the ancient myth of the origin of the races, the magic spring in which the brothers must bathe. First, Macunaíma, who on coming out of the water is white and blue-eyed; after him his brother Jiguê, who throws himself into the water and washes himself vigorously in the hope of changing color, but the water is dirty and Jiguê only manages to turn into the rust color of copper. Maanape, the third brother, finds only a little water left for his own ablutions after the first two have bathed, and he can only whiten the palms of his hands and the bottoms of his feet; and this is the explanation of the three races that populate Brazil, the white, the red, and the Black.

But if Macunaíma has changed the color of his skin, he has clearly not changed his character and continues to be what he always was. It is always the same Macunaíma who gets lost in the jungle of São Paulo, where at the beginning he always interprets the signals sent to him by the city according to his code of a man of the woods, and where the noises of the machine world are confused with the cries of wild beasts. It is in São Paulo that Macunaíma meets his nemesis, Venceslau Pietro Pietra, a typical figure of the nouveau-riche Italian immigrant with his house in Pacaembu (the smart district of São Paulo populated by the descendants of immigrant families who have made their fortune) and who spends his time doing nothing (or *farniente* in the original text). Venceslau Pietro Pietra is the giant Piaimã, the people eater (the symbol is so obvious that it is not worth further comment). To defeat him, Macunaíma must turn to magic, and since the only magic in Brazil is Black, Macunaíma goes to a *macumba*.

The description of the macumba is very interesting, because this is one of the first literary documents that is the work of a man of culture who has transcended those purely emotional steps that have limited his colleagues through their absurd descriptions to the clichés of the horror story. The scene described is classical: the descent of the saint, the possession of one of the people present, requests made to the *mãe-de-santo*, including Macunaíma's, which is accepted. The new element added by the author, and which does not take place in a macumba, is the curse that works in the case of Venceslau Pietro Pietra and all the plagues brought upon him by Macunaíma, which seem to be suffered by the *filha-de-santo* but which are really transmitted directly to the unfortunate victim.

There are a few observations to make regarding this macumba told by Mário de Andrade. The first is that Macunaíma, to find a macumba, has to take a train and go to Rio de Janeiro. Obviously at that time there were no macumbas in São Paulo, and even if there were de Andrade preferred not to admit it as a proud member of an old paulista family, which he never denies. Second, the place where the macumba takes place is the Mangue, a district notorious for prostitution and crime, a clearly negative connotation. The third consideration regards the public. By now the macumba is by no means an exclusively Black phenomenon and the author repeatedly gives us a list of the onlookers:

> There were many people there, respectable people, poor people, lawyers, waiters, bricklayers—people of no importance, deputies, and con men, all those people and the ceremony was about to begin. A lighted candle was given to everyone who was there, to all the sailors, as to the carpenters, journalists, the rich pigs, the hucksters, the women, the civil servants, lots of civil servants. Tia Ciata sat on a bench in a corner with all those people sweating, doctors, bakers, ushers, policemen, maids, and apprentice murderers, Macunaíma: they all came to put a candle on the ground around her bench, all the people, merchants, bibliophiles, the penniless, academics and bankers, thieves, senators, peasants, *negros*, ladies, and soccer players.[4]

As you can see, there is a very broad following and as a joke at the end of the ceremony Mário de Andrade includes a list of well-known writers. *Macunaíma* is a marvelous fable, a symbolic tale whereby de Andrade has tried to exorcise ancient fears and to demystify long-held principles. It is a vote of no confidence in the Brazilian man in which an excess of irony and imagination would allow readers to recognize themselves without feeling wounded in their vulnerability.

Mário de Andrade, like many of his group, was tied to the structures of an ancient world that was fast disappearing. Modernism itself, of which this author was one of the most distinguished practitioners, from a historical point of view followed the classical designs of Brazil before the age of Vargas. Like the abolition of slavery and the founding of the Republic, Modernism was a movement supported by men who belonged not only to cultural but to a social and economic elite. In other words these were men who were born in the power structure, and behind them lay a long land- and slave-owning tradition that explains why Macunaíma, a Black in all aspects of his behavior and appearance, is presented as the creature of native Indian mythology: because the Indian has by now disappeared and is therefore ennobling, like everything that belongs to the past, and because all the national vices that the author showers on his mad protagonist were the vices that the public (that is, the white public) attributed to the Black population. For this reason the macumba is taken from São Paulo and set in Rio de Janeiro in the red-light district of the city, and, furthermore, this is a macumba designed solely to do harm, according to the belief of the public. This macumba is attended by common people, but also by the rising bourgeoisie of civil servants and professionals whom the older members of the establishment found so irksome, and for this, too, the victim of the macumba is the most irritating character of all. I refer to Venceslau Pietro Pietra, the ex-tinker with his ostentatious riches, the giant Piaimã, the people eater, the voracious swallower of ancient privileges once the monopoly of the aristocratic ruling class.

At the other end of the scale from a writer of worldwide reputation such as Mário de Andrade is Sabino de Campos, a typical example among several of those novelists who proliferated in Brazil when writing was first and foremost an elegant pastime among members of the middle class. A typical representative of a certain small provincial world, Sabino de Campos is interesting for two reasons. The first lies in the mass of information, particularly of a folkloric nature, that he gathers in his books; the second is that these books can be taken as an example of the way of thinking of a certain segment of the middle classes where prejudice and long-standing beliefs find expression unmediated by a cultural apparatus or any critical intelligence. Sabino de Campos describes facts and no more. His approximate analysis, his timorously petit bourgeois comments, might well be those of the man in the street who witnesses the events he relates. His thought is no more than a reflection of that of the public.

His novel *Catimbó* has hardly any plot to speak of and is not worth recounting. Yet it is extremely rich in anecdotal information and curious features of life in the Northeast. This plethora of exotic detail is suddenly exhausted, however, when one turns to the subject of the title of the novel. *Catimbó* is a lesser form of witchcraft closer to the old forms of European magic than to the *candomblé* or the macumba or the Northeastern *xangô*. From the point of view of the ceremony itself, the catimbó is much poorer than other aspects of the Afro-Brazilian religious observances. Well, our author tells us hardly anything of this ritual. And when he does tell of it, he makes it clear that we are not to take it too seriously. Sabino de Campos's thought is no more than a reflection of the petit bourgeois mentality of his fellow provincials who are not interested in dwelling on what, after all, is Black folklore. It reflects the desire not to be confused with an inferior race or to be placed on the same level, especially in the eyes of foreigners who have the tendency to turn mountains into molehills. In short, what is missing from the novel *Catimbó* is precisely the catimbó itself and the *catimbozeiro*, or magician. He is missing as a figure, as a character, and even descriptively. Yet the small amount of dramatic interest in the plot seems to depend only on the evil will of the magician. It is a return of the old formula, "It's not true but I believe it," which the author adopts without seriously coming to grips with the problem of catimbó. At the same time this is the basis of his plot.

The attitude of Sabino de Campos repeats the demeanor of certain characters described by Xavier Marques in *O feiticeiro*: those who never publicly refer to the details of the catimbó, except to dismiss them casually as forms of superstition unworthy of civilized people, but who in private run off to the nearest sorcerer trembling in fear.

The heroine of the story is called Tilde, whose mother has committed the unpardonable sin of offending a certain Meneleu Arruda, known as Socó Panelada, a catimbozeiro, many years ago. All the misfortunes Tilde suffers are the result of this catimbozeiro, even though he is summarily presented to us in the following terms:

> When he cast his spells the *catimbozeiro* used to give those who believed in his powers a weed known as *maconha* to smoke in a pipe or cigarette. It was a powerful drug with the same effect as opium: dreams and marvelous hallucinations.[5]

Is he no more than a charlatan, therefore, although with a good knowledge of drugs and herbs? Not quite, for when Tilde's boyfriend has a bit of bad luck, his first comment is: "For me, it is all because of the *catimbozeiro* Socó"[6]—and when Tilde's boyfriend leaves, again we read:

> When the car started the frightening head of the *catimbozeiro* thrust itself out of the window and the sorcerer, his fingers greased with the *feitiço*, made a mysterious gesture behind the back of the young couple, a gesture imitated by the other *macumbeiras*.[7]

On the journey the two make from Bahia to Rio de Janeiro the memory of the evil magician even pursues Tilde on board ship:

> Seeing the red eye of the Cabo Frio lighthouse, Tilde thought of the fiery eyes of Meneleu Arruda. Perhaps the spirit of the *catimbozeiro*, which traveled far, along the ocean coast, was hovering over the ship? Was that storm perhaps his work? Who knows? Maybe he wanted to sink the ship.[8]

So when Tilde returns to Bahia, again by sea, and this time with another boyfriend, the ship they are on is sunk by a German U-boat. Tilde and her companion save themselves by climbing atop a table.

> Tilde, who was clinging to him, offered up prayer after prayer to all the saints she believed in for their salvation, and when the table rose on the crest of the wave she seemed to see in the horror of that darkness the fearful specter of the *catimbozeiro* Meneleu Arruda, with the two red lights flashing from the orbits of his eyes and a gust of demonic laughter from his voracious mouth, which was as wide as the sea. "*Catimbó, catimbó, catimbó,*" she screamed over the horrifying solitude of the sea.[9]

Apart from the figure of the catimbozeiro, the few references to Blacks do no more than reflect—and how could it be otherwise?—the proverbial racial prejudices of the time. "I will show that a woman like me is not for filthy *negros* with their bestial feet and toothless mouths."[10] The comment comes from a fair young maid boasting of her charms. This is what Sabino de Campos was writing in 1945 and this more or less is what was passing through his readers' heads.

For the purposes of our study there is a more interesting book that was written in 1957 but lacks a contemporary vision. It tells the story of a fierce Black bandit named Lucas who lived in the first half of the nineteenth century. He was an ex-slave who terrorized the area of Feira de Sant'Ana and was finally hanged. Lucas de Feira wa a historical character and still lives in popular memory. His life is evoked by Sabino de Campos more than one hundred years after his death in a novel whose title is most revealing, *Lucas, o demônio negro (Lucas, the Black Devil)*. It is a novelized series of events with no attempt at interpretation, which adopts the usual words of condemnation of slavery and regret for the fate of the slaves. The rest is a long list of commonplaces.

Sabino de Campos never escapes the provincial vision of the events narrated, in which a certain view of life conditioned by centuries of slavery gets the upper hand over the new moral climate of the times in which he lives and over the good intentions that he demonstrates. Let us begin on a note that seems almost comic, the description of Lucas's master. "Padre José Alves Franco, a good and almost saintly man, happened to leave behind several decent descendants represented by a distinguished and prosperous merchant."[11] It is quite common for the Brazilian clergy to have numerous children and equally normal for priests to have many slaves and traffic in human flesh, but it is frankly going a little too far to define such a priest as almost a saint. This virtuous and saintly man, however, leaves the administration of his estate almost completely in the hands of his manager; and the administrator, a robust Portuguese, seduces all the female slaves his energies allow, and uses the whip on the males without pity or respite. Young Lucas in particular bears the brunt of the punishment and demonstrates from his earliest years a decisive and resistant character. The author takes care to remind us that Lucas is physically ugly, cross-eyed, and left-handed. The latter detail is important when you realize that the term *canhoto*, left-handed, is one of the definitions of the devil in popular slang. Lucas grows in courage and physical strength. The author adds that he could climb trees with the agility of a gorilla (how could he miss the chance to compare him with a monkey or an ape?), and one day he decides to escape

> from the land of his old lord, Father José Alves Franco, to the illegitimate and criminal liberty whereby he had freed himself from slavery with his own hands without fear of the rigor of the law and with no regard for anyone. His heart grew ever harder and became decidedly cruel after the creation of his band.[12]

In 1957 Sabino de Campos considers the flight of the slave an illegitimate act, nor does he consider for a moment that the slave in question, hunted and pursued through the woods like a wild beast, may finally start behaving like a wild animal himself. The view of the author is still conditioned by the world of slavery and its laws, in which Lucas's first crime was precisely the desire to be free.

In contrast with Lucas is the good and exemplary slave, a certain Narciso, who manages to capture one of Lucas's bandits.

> It was the brave *negro* Narciso, thc faithful slave of the *fazendeiro* Antônio Pereira Suzarte, who was responsible for the capture. To celebrate this great event, which had unpleasant repercussions among the slaves, Narciso was acclaimed by all those who were anxious to see the whole cursed band wiped out.[13]

Narciso is rewarded with his freedom. But even his freedom is given according to the protocols and customs of the system. The money gathered by public subscription and that offered by the authorities serves to buy the slave's *carta de alforria*. Thus Narciso wins his freedom, the fazendeiro keeps his money, and everybody is happy, all according to the rules.

One notes the different ways in which the author comments on Lucas's crimes. When he describes Lucas raping and assaulting women and girls, Sabino de Campos uses a fiery vocabulary. When, on the contrary, he narrates the amorous exploits of Lucas's enemy, the Portuguese steward, the author describes them as a sort of habit, not the most praiseworthy perhaps, but then not the most heinous either. And only in passing does he hint that the single lesson Lucas has learned from his life as a slave was the lack of respect for life and the dignity of woman.

In the end Lucas is captured after a bloody battle in which he loses his left arm, which for him is the one that counts. His arm was hung on a tree, to the delight of the crowd that enjoyed beating the dead limb with sticks. Then he was taken from one prison to another until he was taken to Bahia, where the crowd insulted him, singing the verses of a popular song that poked fun at Blacks (at least so the author tells us):

O mulato bebe vinho	The mulatto drinks wine
O branco vinho do Porto	The white, port
Caboclo bebe cachaça	The *caboclo* drinks *cachaça*
O negro mijo de porco.	The Black the piss of a pig.

There is another song of the same ilk:

Negro não vai para o céu	The Black doesn't go to Heaven
Nem que seja rezador	Even if he prays
Tem cabelo pixaim	He has wiry hair
Espeta Nosso Senhor.	Which pricks the skin of Our Lord.

There follow several proverbs that openly express the old forms of contempt for anything Black: "The *negro* is bold behind a tree. The *negro* doesn't go into church, he just looks in from the door. Standing up, the *negro* is a piece of wood; lying down, he's a pig."[14]

The last page of the novel is worth quoting without comment as an example of the closed and backward mentality the author embodies. He describes Lucas's journey up to the country's capital at the polite request of Emperor Pedro II, who wanted, as a philosopher and man of letters, to see in person that monster, the Black Devil:

> The reigning emperor, the magnanimous Dom Pedro II, had heard of the exploits of the brigand, and wanted to see him in person. The im-

> pression he received was fearful; Lucas instilled fear even in the soul of the Royal Family. The emperor uttered no word. And the empress, Dona Teresa Cristina Maria, was horrorstruck. Even the pretty little baby Princess Isabel, who was but two years old, and in years to come the one who would sanction the law known as the *ventre livre* [free womb] and afterward the one of the 13th of May 1888 that abolished slavery, even she wept at the sight of the strange face of the Black Devil![15]

Having satisfied the imperial curiosity, Lucas returned to Feira de Sant'Ana, where he was hanged. His cranium was sent to the Institute of Forensic Medicine for the delight of scholars who sought in those bones the reasons for the violence of man against man, which they themselves could see and indeed practiced daily in the domestic tranquility of their families.

As an example of cultural atavism we should add that Sabino de Campos quotes Lombroso, albeit in a very approximate manner, to explain Lucas's innate criminality.

Mário de Andrade on one side, Sabino de Campos on the other: a great writer in contrast with a folklore chronicler. But what lies in between? We have many, many writers in Brazil but nothing really new. Slavery is abolished in Brazil and many Blacks, at least officially, are citizens like anyone else. Many of them, particularly the mulattoes, make their way in public administration and the professions. The colored man is starting to carve out a space for himself in society, starting to integrate himself in the various classes that form the tissue of the Brazilian world, which only now is beginning to separate itself—thanks to a violent push from European immigrants—from the unalterable dualism of masters and slaves that had existed for centuries. Once more, however, the majority of writers play it safe. They turn to the past, they turn to problems that have already been resolved. Nor can we say they are entirely wrong, if we understand that they were writing for an almost exclusively white public or for colored readers affiliated with the white world.

Let us take, for example, Monteiro Lobato, one of the most brilliant and representative writers of the time. In a collection of stories significantly entitled *Negrinha (Little Black Girl)* there are naturally quite a few Black protagonists; but the setting and atmosphere are solidly anchored in the past. The first dates from 1920 and is the title story of the collection whose central figure is a little Black girl: "Negrinha was a poor little orphan, seven years old. *Preta*? Not really, she was a very dark mulatta with ash-colored hair and eyes full of fear."[16] Negrinha, a little nameless Black waif, lives in the house of a rich lady known for her piety and devotion to charity and good work. "Negrinha" exemplifies the sadistic spirit that, along with many other aberrations, flourished with impunity as the result of slavery and continued unabated among the many survivors of the old regime. The negrinha's mistress is just such an example:

> The excellent Dona Inácia was a mistress of the art of tormenting children. She had grown up in the age of slavery and she had had her own slaves; one of those fierce types who likes to hear the swish of the rod and the crack of the whip. She had never got used to the new regime—that indecency of *negros* being treated like whites and the police coming round at the slightest little thing! "The slightest little thing." Maybe a *mucama* burned on the stove because the master had taken a shine to her; or a few strokes of the whip because the servant girl had said, "How nasty the *sinhá* is!"[17]

Let us make it quite clear that Monteiro Lobato was quite right to denounce these forms of cruelty which survived the abolition of slavery because the essential structure of the slave order had not changed. I should like to emphasize, however, that neither Monteiro nor his contemporaries have provided us with a true story of the Black in the paulista society in transition in those years. The story of "Negrinha," written and set in 1920, could quite easily have been set and written several centuries earlier.

The figure of the little Black girl, whose existential function seems to be uniquely that of serving as an outlet for the sadistic instincts of Dona Inácia, risks becoming merely pathetic in the endless series of tortures she is forced to undergo and in the death to which she inevitably succumbs. There is, however, one moment in which the tragedy assumes the dimension of Pirandellian absurdity: when the arrival of two little nieces of her mistress reveals to the child for a moment a childhood she has never known, the first games and the amazing thing that a doll can be. For the first time in her life, the negrinha becomes aware that she is not a thing but a human being, and it is precisely this awareness and the impossibility of returning to her former condition as a domestic object that leads gently to her death—poor little creature, abandoned on a mat, having finally returned to a world of lifeless things.

There follows a horror story, "Bugio moqueado" (1925). The *bugio* is a sort of monkey. The term *moqueado* comes from the verb *moquear*, which is a way of smoking and salting meat to preserve it for a period of time. This is a story, reconstructed through the versions of various witnesses, of a Black man and a white woman (and we well know that this was the most delicate point, the inviolable taboo). The man is flogged to death and his body is salted. The woman, who was the wife of the fazendeiro, is then obliged to eat the flesh of her former, unfortunate lover. Monteiro Lobato's story is merely the fictional account of real crimes such as we have been able to note in the writers of the Maranhão, and therefore offers us nothing new.

The story "O jardineiro Timóteo," ("Timóteo the Gardener," 1920) is, in contrast, a nostalgic story of the good old days: the old patriarchal house, the great garden rich in flowers, the calm flow of time in peace and comfort. Timóteo, the old Black gardener freed by his master even before the declaration of emancipation, represents the continuity of the family whose members are personified in the various flower beds of the garden. The fairest flower bed is naturally that of the Sinhazinha, the master's pretty little daughter.

> The Sinhazinha's flower bed was the most beautiful of all and well represented the image of the heart of a woman rich in all shades of sentiment. Always brilliant with flowers, it immediately attracted the attention of all those who entered the garden. In all it resembled the girl who from her childhood days had immediately monopolized the affection of the family and the devotion of the slaves. Such devotion, in fact, that when the Golden Law was proclaimed, no one had the courage to leave the *fazenda*. Emancipation? What madness! Who, having once become the slave of the Sinhazinha would have ever been able to break the ties of such sweet servitude?[18]

An innovator in the literary world, politically progressive and a socialist, Monteiro Lobato does not escape the rule of those who professed advanced ideas but who are fundamentally solid conservatives, completely tied to their privileges. The old Black gardener continues to mark out the events of the family, *his* family, which is that of his masters, with so many flowers. The years pass, the children grow up, times change, and the fazenda is finally sold. Timóteo alone remains in his garden but his new masters belong to another period. They want to wipe out the past and destroy the garden, for them the symbol of the colonial era which the gardener had managed to save from his old masters' desire for change. But the new owners are brusque and brutal. They use such phrases as "that monkey," and "come here, charcoal face." This, then, is the end of the old times, the end of the memory of a once happy period, the arrival of new and different men, the end of Timóteo buried in *his* garden and his inevitable despair.

The protagonist of the lengthy short story "Os negros" (1922) is once again the past revisited, through the hallucinations of one of the characters during an undesired stop in a haunted fazenda. The love story between a poor Portuguese and the daughter of the wealthy fazendeiro has no Black characters except for the usual mucama who acts as a go-between, and who is eventually whipped to death (while the Portuguese is, instead, buried alive behind a wall and his sweetheart is relegated to a hospice). This is further evidence of the cruelty of the times, and of the use and abuse of absolute power by the large fazendeiros.

To the themes of nostalgia for the property-owning past and the denunciation of violence perpetuated to the present day, Monteiro Lobato adds nothing new to what has already been written by others. If we compare his stories with those written by Carlos Magalhães de Azeredo in *Alma primitiva (Primitive Soul)* in 1895 we can see that the theme of the tale and the tone of the narration are exactly the same. In the first story an old Black man is flogged to death; the second tells of a poor mulatto slave woman who after many tortures is separated from her baby by the order of a cruel mistress. In the case of Carlos Magalhães de Azeredo one can say, however, that he was historically much closer to slavery than Monteiro Lobato.

Those writers who deal with the theme of the Black always show a great prudence in doing so. The general rule is always to play it safe—to emphasize the aristocratic past or scenes of cruelty and violence, on which one could count on universal condemnation—but to advance no new formulas. In 1926 Monteiro Lobato published a book, *O choque das raças e o presidente negro (The Battle of the Races and the Black President)*, in which once again he takes the necessary precautions. The story takes place in the United States in the year 2228. Certainly in some cases you cannot be too careful!

Another example of caution in dealing with scandalous themes is *Preto Eusébio* by Nuto Sant'Ana, a novel that deserves to be remembered solely because it dares to tell a love story between a Black man and a white woman. Naturally the author takes certain elementary precautions, in the first place saving national pride by choosing a non-Brazilian heroine. (However, we do know from various commentators that there had been many cases of white women attracted to dark-skinned men.) So Kati, the protagonist, comes with her husband, King, from an unidentified country in Eastern Europe, precisely from one of those countries from which the number of immigrants to Brazil was of little importance. In short, there is no danger of offending anyone because none of the new immigrants would be able to recognize themselves in the unfortunate couple. With this in mind, the story of King and Kati, foreign immigrants lost in the tumultuous metropolis of São Paulo, and the Black Eusébio, describes a fairly common case in those years but which would not fail to startle a conservative public. There were many Blacks who found themselves better off than many whites. King and Kati are poor like most immigrants—and King shows himself particularly unable to cope—whereas Eusébio is able to live with a certain style. He enjoys the respect and consideration of his neighbors and acquaintances. "Eusébio Diniz, a wealthy *preto*, a white *preto*," as he is described according to the approving formula with its built-in racist stamp.[19]

Conspicuous by its absence from the novel is the reference to any complex problems, reflecting the petit-bourgeois prejudices of the time. The protagonist, for example, is very proud of his social status, which he measures by his approximation to the condition of the white man. "Work is for donkeys and *negros* and I who have been both am now neither one nor the other."[20] Now this is an obsrvation, straight from the colonial period, that comes right from Brazil's neocapitalist industrial heartland in 1932. In the patriarchal rural world, society was divided along clear lines. The white man was identified with the master and therefore with nonwork. The Black was always a slave and thus represented work, comparable in this respect to animals. The passage up the social scale occurs at the moment one passes from work to nonwork. If work is Black, logically nonwork is white. Eusébio's syllogism is basic and reflects a common state of mind. What is strange is that Nuto Sant'Ana sets down without comment this opinion drawn from colonial times, repeated in the São Paulo of the 1930s where modern industrial and neocapitalist labor was transforming the city and the country. The tale quite predictably settles down into a banal ménage-à-trois until Kati realizes she is pregnant and kills the increasingly apathetic King (poor fellow, such an understanding man) and then herself, the author reserving a few consoling words for Eusébio.

It is incredible how time seems to stand still for some writers when they refer to the real changes taking place in the country. Nuto Sant'-Ana deals with the old theme of the sexual encounter of two races with the same sort of caution and fears that had moved Silva Guimarães in 1915 in *Os borrachos (The Drunkards)*, when he described the scandalous concubinage of an Italian peasant and a Black woman in the mystical, religious, and bigoted town of Ouro Preto. Although relations between white men and Black women were very common in colonial and postcolonial Brazil, a public union (this couple dared to walk down the street arm-in-arm under the indignant glare of righteous citizens) was always something rather scandalous. For this reason too the author has kept his distance. The male character seems made to measure to ensure that no reader could possible identify with him. He is an Italian, and thus national pride is saved, but even as an Italian he is a somewhat improbable figure, being both Calabrese and illiterate (two distinctively negative notes). He also talks like a Tuscan, cursing all the time (another negative quality). Finally he even (horror of horrors!) expresses anarchist ideas in clear contradiction to his declared ignorance. Furthermore he is a drunkard and deserves no more than that very dark Black woman with thick lips whom he snatched peremptorily (in this he behaved rather like many of his fellow countrymen) from a wealthy family where she was working as a maid. In short, the Italian in question, even though Brazilianized in the end, has so many faults that he could only be coupled with a Black woman.

In returning to Nuto Sant'Ana, we see that in 1939 he wrote another novel, *Thebas, o escravo (Thebas, the Slave)*, in which we see no change at all in his viewpoint or understanding. To the contrary we must add that 1939 was a year of destiny—the Estado Novo in Brazil and Nazism in Germany—for a lot of people who could calmly express reactionary ideas, making them seem progressive by dressing them up in the new scientific theories.

Thebas is, in fact, the sort of character who had most endeared himself to this group of writers. He is the good slave, obedient, faithful, and hard working, one who by his behavior never questioned the institution of slavery. Once he even saved his master's daughter, as is expected from an ideal slave. And the author can say of him as of Eusébio in the previous novel, "he was, indeed, a white *preto*, a real man."[21] The novel is set in São Paulo in 1750 and the author soon reveals his way of thinking with the following sentence: "The population numbered about four thousand souls. There were a great many Indians, and a great many *negros* also."[22] Obviously the word "souls" embraces only the white-skinned population. Blacks and Indians, according to the point of view of Nuto Sant'Ana, do not possess a soul. And this is the year of grace 1939 when our author delivered himself of such insights.

It is clearly a symbolic tale. Thebas the good slave is in love with the lovely mulatta Maria das Dores, who, of course, is also loved by the steward Gregório, a decidedly nasty character. You can well imagine the quantity and quality of punishments inflicted by Gregório on the good Thebas, particularly since he is a good slave and would never think of fighting back against injustice when this is handed down by one of his white masters. There is, however, a dangerous character called Tião, who speaks only of running away and of *quilombos*. He tries to persuade Thebas to join him but the latter simply recommends calm and patience. Tião frees Thebas when the latter is about to be tortured, and it is Tião who also severely punishes Gregório. In the course of the novel there are two episodes in which the author describes the typical master's reaction, without of course offering any comment. In the first episode Dona Cotinha, the master's daughter, is told by Maria das Dores that Gregório is having Thebas flogged. And what does Dona Cotinha do, not forgetting that Thebas had once saved her life? She gives Maria das Dores a tongue lashing for provoking the men and thus stirring up trouble. The first concern of every fazendeiro, the supreme law of the plantation, was to avoid anything that might disturb the slave order. " 'Well, it's all your fault, missy, and you deserve a whipping yourself,' grumbled Dona Cotinha."[23] Fortunately, adds the author, Dona Cotinha was a good woman and did not order a whipping for her slave, once her old playmate and companion in her childish games, who had turned to her for justice. As an example of myopia in his social vision and in his description of all events linked to slavery, Nuto Sant'Ana has few equals, a fact underlined by the reaction of Cotinha's father, the plantation owner, who would like to have everybody whipped: Tião for talking of escape and quilombos, Gregório for stirring up trouble, Maria das Dores for exciting the men, and Thebas because he lets himself get excited by a girl instead of thinking of work.

Fortunately, all's well that ends well (so to speak), thanks also to the pacific intervention of the local priest, and all are forgiven. Tião is persuaded by Thebas not to run away to the quilombo and takes Gregório's place as a steward, thus organizing the daily labor of the slaves in the name of the master. Gregório, who has taken quite a beating from Tião, repents his previous bad behavior; and Thebas marries his beloved Maria das Dores and then builds the church towers in thanks for the freedom granted to him. They all live happily ever after.

Along the same lines is a series of writers who, never going beyond the narrow confines of folklore, always turn their backs on any serious discussion of social problems, failing to go beyond the nostalgic memories of the good old days. In 1937 Ignácio Raposo published a series of stories about slavery entitled *Mestre Cuia (Master Cuia)*. In the first, the title story of the collection, the *negro* Raimundo is a farcical character, a genial rogue, full of all those vices that are usually attributed to Blacks. He is in fact a pale shadow of Macunaíma but without that violent dose of grotesque humor that Mário de Andrade infused into him. Raimundo obtains his carta de alforria thanks precisely to his vices. His master in fact can no longer stand the sight of him since the slave once even tried to murder him but botched the attempt. When he obtains his freedom Raimundo shows exceptional ability, becomes rich, and returns with a mountain of presents to his former master, who then realizes that his old slave was not so bad after all, but behaved the way he did because he was driven by the spirit of liberty. All this is described by Ignácio Raposo with the greatest seriousness. The story is constructed along the lines intended by the author to give us a purely idyllic view of slavery (the master who frees his clumsy slave instead of selling him or beating him, the ex-slave who returns with presents for his former master—the whole thing is really quite sweet).

The second short story is even more idyllic and brings to the foreground the classic figure of the *mãe preta* or the Black mammy. In "A velhinha do peixe frito" ("The Fried-Fish Seller"), the old woman who sells fried fish gets robbed by a poor, starving, orphaned white boy; and when the boy becomes a rich gentleman the old woman refuses even to be repaid, satisfied with her memory of her act of charity.

But more interesting from our point of view is the third tale, "A rainha Babaô" ("Queen Babaô"), the story of an African queen reduced to slavery whose freedom is immediately bought back by the other slaves. Events of this type really did occur and apart from freeing distinguished persons who had become slaves the Blacks actually had a perfectly legal system of mutual aid whereby the savings of all served to free one of their number who in his or her turn, working as a freed slave, would work for the freedom of another, and so forth.

In the story "Ambrósio missionário" ("Ambrósio, the Missionary") is once again the figure of the incorrigible Black, such as Raimundo. Ambrósio is the slave of a priest. He escapes disguised in priest's clothing and arrives in a little village where he becomes the parish priest and naturally gets into all sorts of scrapes. His identity revealed after a Boccacian adventure, he becomes a slave once again and is sold, but is fortunate enough to come across a master who treats him well. A classical picaresque tale hinging on the adventures of the protagonist, "Ambrósio missionário" serves to underline several characteristics of slavery. The first is a purely economic aspect of the institution. To be Black does not necessarily mean to be a slave. A free Black can occupy any position in society (which actually happened—various Blacks became quite distinguished during the period of slavery), even that of a minister of religion. That Ambrósio is illiterate and manages to pass himself off as a priest gives us quite clearly an idea of the cultural level of the clergy in Brazil at that time.

The stories that follow have for us the same interest as that of Ambrósio because they continue to keep us informed of the various aspects of slavery. In "Os dois cometas" ("The Two Tinkers"), we have further proof that slavery was essentially an economic matter independent of the color of one's skin. If the Black slave Ambrósio manages to become a priest, the white mulatto, a tinker by trade (*cometa* means tinker), becomes a slave again thanks to a dirty trick played on him by a fellow tinker, a Portuguese who steals his documents from him and sells him to a fazenda. Only after a long time does the poor wretch manage to write to his mother and secure proof of his proper status as a free man.

In the following story, "A escrava misteriosa" ("The Mysterious Slave"), we actually have a white female slave, something perfectly possible in a country like Brazil where a white-skinned mulatto has more or less the same skin color as those of Portuguese descent, and where the mixing of the races is the order of the day. In this story a girl of good family is sold by her father because she had lost her virginity. She marries a Portuguese farm manager and returns to claim her rights on the death of her father.

Even more significant is the last story in the book: "De caixeiro a coronel" ("From Servant to Colonel"). The protagonist here is an educated mulatto slave who lives with a family that owns a large fazenda. That he is a man of culture and that he has special duties gives him some privileges. One day, however, he has a row with his master who decides to put him in his place by giving him a flogging. The slave rebels and escapes with a fantastic leap out of the window. Over the course of several years, he becomes a rich and influential coronel, and one day by chance comes across his old master who reveals that he is his uncle. And the author in his final comment lets it be known that "the *senhores de engenho* in Brazil have always shown a great ability in finding half-breed fathers for their bastard sons who happen to be born white."[24]

In the stories of Ignácio Raposo the problem of slavery is not presented; all we have is a description of slavery pure and simple. The author's vision is tied to all those anti-Black prejudices the Brazilian world has inherited from a centuries-old tradition. Exprcssions such as "miserable slaves without honor and without shame"[25] would be more common in the Brazil of one or two hundred years before 1937. Yet these stories are interesting for the clearly nostalgic spirit in which they are written, while the object of the tale itself throws an unequivocal light on the fact that Brazilian slavery was not tied to any principle of a moral character that might justify its existence.

There was no alibi of an ethical or scientific nature, there was no God that obliged the white man to control the destiny of the Black (or if there had been, at least in the beginning, the memory had been lost with time). There was no true science that might justify the dominance of one race over another. There was merely a convention grounded in economic self-interest whereby it was legitimate for some men to exploit others. It is this that marks all the tales of Ignácio Raposo. The white girl of good family sold as a slave, the mulatto tinker reduced to slavery because of his Portuguese comrade's dirty trick, the mulatto slave who escapes and becomes a powerful coronel, the illiterate Black who manages to pass himself off as a priest, the Black who owes his liberty to his own incorrigible character and who gets rich thanks to his native shrewdness, these are all real pages about slavery told to us without comment. And one can finally conclude that slavery like eveything else in Brazil is a variable and permeable system.

Blacks as slaves or free men continue to appear in the Brazilian novel of those years. In *Amanhecer* (*Dawn*, 1938) Lúcia Miguel Pereira tells the story of a well-bred girl who is grievously surprised at the discovery that her father, now dead and whom she dearly loved, had a mulatto mistress who dragged him down the road to spiritism. (These are in fact the years when the various forms of Black religious practice begin to spread among whites.) The girl's reaction is violent: "Papa mixed up his beliefs with his filthy love of that mulatta."[26] Later in the novel the girl's reaction is again provoked by relatives who, to humiliate her, want to make her believe that her mother is a mulatta. "Mama may be a mulatta, but I'm not . . . this was one of Juca's lies. My family was as white as his."[27] We are slap in the middle of the world of petit-bourgeois prejudices, which come to a head when the heroine is forcibly kissed by a young Black. Naturally what provokes her indignation is not that she is forced to submit but that she has suffered violence at the hands of a Black man.

We find many characters from different authors moving through this same atmosphere of lower-middle-class prejudice, even when Blacks are not the central figures of their works. A typical reaction of a jealous girl comes from the protagonist of Rachel de Queirós's *O quinze* (*The Fifteen*, 1930). Informed that the young man she loves has been seen with a colored woman, she uses the expression "soiling himself with a *negra*," and is immediately consoled by another woman who tells her that the girl in question is not a *negra*, but a white-skinned *cabocla*. Obviously the lighter the color of the girl's skin, the less serious the betrayal!

We find an almost identical comment in an analogous situation in *Moleque*, by Athos Damasceno Ferreira (1938), a somewhat weepy tale of a Black child living with white masters who spend their time in nostalgic reminiscences of the good old days. The betrayed wife in this case expresses her indignation with the words "with a *negra*, of all things," while the woman trying to console her asserts that it was a mulatta and not everything Black is necessarily bad.

The Brazilian novel of those years is full of such episodes and expressions: comparisons between Blacks and monkeys, contemptuous phrases, nostalgia for the period of slavery, criticism of the present and colored people who do not know their place, horror and fear at the prospect of the spread of Black religious practice.

Let us briefly refer to the fine historical novel, *A marcha* (*The March*, 1941), by Afonso Schmidt, in which many quite authentic episodes from the last days of slavery are woven into a thin plot; and we conclude this chapter with the assertion that in the novel of the thirties we have evidence that Brazilian writers have finally accepted the reality of the Blacks after the long-held myth that continued European immigration would swamp the Black presence in a white majority. This acceptance of Blacks takes place, but always reluctantly, and not without difficulties and reticence. Mário de Andrade sublimates this awareness in the absurd and grotesque figure of Macunaíma loaded down with vices, while less gifted writers give vent to their phobias by pandering to the prejudices of a narrow-minded public. For all of them, however, there is an awareness that the Black race is a reality with which they will have to come to terms.

WATER CARRIERS

CARREGADORES DE ÁGUA

13 CORNÉLIO PENNA, OR THE DARK SIDE OF NOSTALGIA

> Cornélio Penna has a genuine talent for creating all that is gloomy, dark, and anguished. His evocation of antiquated settings, of strange, abnormal people, of dead cities where families slowly decline and madness always lurks in the wings waiting for new victims, all this is admirably and perfectly achieved. With the soul of a collector who lives in the company of old objects, Cornélio Penna knows better than any of us how to transmute the smell of beauty mixed with secrecy, of degeneration and mystery, which makes an old chest, a music box, a fan so evocative, brimming with the idea of a dark and tragic human survival. One feels his novels are the work of a passionate antiquary who sees fingers, arms, a very life growing from every object, a whole living past which in its own way and mystery still has power over us.[1]

These are the words of Mário de Andrade, author and modern critic, offering us a clear synthesis of the work of this fertile and mysterious writer. His long novels and short stories are linked together by a single plot and have at the same time a single protagonist: mystery. Facts and people never achieve a clear definition. It seems that a secret force always lies behind them, a hidden ''quid'' determining their being, or at least their appearance. A form of religious anguish hangs over everything; existence is nothing but a long sin requiring expiation. But what is this sin, what is the crime that is always hinted at and seems to dominate unopposed every moment described by Cornélio Penna?

Born in Petrópolis, the imperial city, in 1896, of an old aristocratic Brazilian family, Cornélio Penna led a life typical of those young men of his generation who came from a comfortable social background: periods on the paternal *fazenda* alternating with study in the best schools and colleges. Graduating in law in 1919 in São Paulo, he witnessed in that city the most interesting period in Brazilian culture, whose principal organ was the Semana de Arte Moderna (Week of Modern Art) of 1922. These were the decisive years in Brazilian history. The sleeping giant was on the move. Tired of the stalemate that grew out of the suffocating balance engineered by the major landowners, the absolute despots of political power, the young were boiling over with impatience in a country that had obstinately refused to assimilate the great movements of ideas circulating throughout the world since the end of World War I. And if in São Paulo the young intellectuals behind the Semana de Arte Moderna decided to break the ties that bound them to the academic culture of Lusitanian origin, in the same year (1922) in Rio de Janeiro, a group of young officers imprisoned in the fort of Copacabana following an attempted rebellion against the constitutional order cut the Brazilian flag into eighteen pieces, and, each man brandishing his strip of the national symbol, marched against the machine guns of the national police. Sixteen out of the eighteen died. Meanwhile at Recife in 1926 young intellectuals headed by Gilberto Freyre gave birth to the movement of regionalist studies, in an attempt to analyze scientifically the triracial origins of the country. And in that very same year a young captain, Luís Carlos Prestes, led another band of young men on a mad march—lasting two and a half years over twenty-six thousand kilometers—over the inhospitable terrain of the *sertão* to bring the word of revolt to the brutalized *caboclos*.

Cornélio Penna saw all this. He also saw the real revolution, the revolution *malgré soi*, what the generous sacrifice of the young lieutenants failed to achieve, and what the intellectuals of the Semana looked on with aristocratic suspicion: the labor revolution. Right in São Paulo a new force, immigrants, most of them Italians, possessed of a youthful enthusiasm coupled with a robust will to live, are giving the country a facelift. Shopkeepers are becoming bankers, workers are becoming industrialists, colonial sharecroppers, landowners; workers, for the first time in a country that grew up with slave labor, are now going out on strike, seventy thousand strong, marching arm in arm, in 1917. There are new signs of prosperity, flashy in appearance but solidly established, emanating from a new breed of gentlemen with strange accents who spend their money on smart new clothes and shiny automobiles. This is the new São Paulo, which in the thirties starts to show separatist ambitions and a desire for hegemony.

There are really two São Paulos living together: the modern and the Modernist, the force of labor which is transforming Brazil, and the intellectual force which, trying to change only itself, is fast losing an opportunity that will not be offered again: that of establishing itself as the interpreter and spokesman of a gigantic metamorphosis that would launch the country right into the modern era. This is the eternal and recurrent sin of the Brazilian intelligentsia: arriving late on the scene of history rather than anticipating it. The Romantic nineteenth century had idealized an Indian who was really a cultural import from France, instead of paying attention to the native Indians living on the edge of cities and fazendas. The Modernists study the Black and the Indian without noticing that the Italians were turning São Paulo into the leading city in Latin America. Our contemporaries discovered Marxism after it was seen to have failed in more than half the world.

The break with the Portuguese cultural tradition obliges the Brazilian intelligentsia to examine the problems, origins, and survival of racial prejudice which tended to deny or even eliminate the determining contribution of other races—particularly Indians and Blacks—to the establishment of a Brazilian identity. The most notable effort in this direction is represented by the publication in 1933 of Gilberto Freyre's *Casa grande e senzala*. Here is a writer (in the words of Luciana Stegagno Picchio) whose works "cannot be avoided if one wants to understand the mestizo Brazil, the Brazil of African origin, as well as that of the mythical Indian."[2] But side by side with the erudite reflections of Freyre, there were other forms of return to the past, decisively less clear in intention and inferior as cultural expressions. Here the memory of and nostalgia for times past often serve as a model to juxtapose with a contemporary reality that the writer is unwilling to accept or refuses to recognize. We are referring to Paulo Prado and his *Retrato do Brasil* (*Portrait of Brazil*, 1928).

Paulo Prado comes from one of the great *paulista* families, and in his *Retrato do Brasil* has given us a deeply pessimistic analysis of all the evils at the root of Brazilian civilization. (Even Mário de Andrade, also in 1928, offers his contemporaries an album of all the national vices in *Macunaíma*, the hero without character, but the literary form and the knowing, ironical tone manage to smooth out the rough edges of the observation.) Prado's is a bitter work, in which no possibility of revival or redemption is perceived that might transcend the pitiless self-criticism the author aims at his people. Lust, cupidity, and melancholy blossom aesthetically into decadent Romanticism: such are the absolute protagonists, or founding fathers, of a civilization destined to survive only on the vegetable level, without ever asserting itself to the point of dominion or conquest over its native ground. *Retrato do Brasil* is a profoundly dated work. Prado did not see (or did not wish to see?) in those years and in his very own São Paulo the unequivocal signs of the transformation that was to carry Brazil from being a great agricultural fiefdom towards the painful birth pangs of an industrial society. He did not see the changes because from his aristocratic position of leader of a class in retreat he never thought that his *nobreza paulista* was, all things considered, relatively recent. The Portuguese who had come from overseas and the Black man torn from the African forests were as much intruders on the new land as the modern immigrants who, growing more numerous and boisterous each day, were busy transforming the country by vigorously identifying with it. If his analysis of the past is in part accurate, his prophecies for the immediate future have been historically invalidated. In his concern to unearth testimony from archives and libraries, he never saw the skyscrapers and factories going up in São Paulo, which every day seemed less and less *his* as the city assumed the appearance of a great metropolis.

Rather than a historical study of a period, *Retrato do Brasil* is an obituary for a past from which Paulo Prado fails to extricate himself. It is the testimony of one of the last distinguished protagonists of a world well on its way to final extinction. The writer's attitude is perfectly comprehensible, tied as he is by long family tradition to the history of a country whose failure he is obliged to acknowledge. The *bandeiras* of the old paulistas crossed the land from one end to the other, violating it without ever fertilizing it. In the endless spaces of the sertão banditry flourishes, the violent *cangaço* goes unpunished, the great fazendas resemble medieval fortresses. Is this the Brazil preparing to enter the twentieth century? The Northeasterners arriving in São Paulo in ever greater numbers looking for work turn, in their confused memories, shame into glory and defeat into legend. Thus the free and independent cangaço becomes a figure of pride, the symbol of indomitable boldness through whom they react to the torment of a miserable past and the dark, urban geometry of the present. But none of this deceives a man like Paulo Prado, who spots in the recesses of folklore the mythical aspect of underdevelopment. Brazil—his Brazil—is an underdeveloped country in the midst of an industrial revolution.

Retrato do Brasil is at the same time a confession and an act of accusation. As a courageous act of repentance it is valid, but it is less so as an attempt to define the causes of underdevelopment. The accusation starts to lose credibility once the author links slavery to racial mix, placing the blame for the country's social retardation squarely on the shoulders of both.

"The native Indian in his turn was a lascivious creature who lived without restraint in the satisfaction of his carnal desire,"[3] a phrase repeated many times in different forms, singling out the Indian as the primary and most ancient source of the deformation and degradation of the Brazilian male. Then it is the turn of the Black, who has replaced the Indian in the new slave economy: "The dissolute life of the African and the half-breed spread through the highest ranks of society."[4] The mixing of these different races leads inevitably to the organic weakness of the individual and the country:

> Almost all our poets of that period died young, certain in the knowledge that this was to be their fate. Love and Death: the two great themes of Brazilian poetry. The desire for death came to them from an organic failure of will, and the disillusioned melancholy of those who weave romantic dreams day by day. Physically weakened by the abuse of their nervous system, in an instinctive spasm of vitality they sought survival in an almost feminine, dazzling eroticism. Thus they represented the weakness of the race, the vice of our half-breed origins. They lived out their sad existence in a radiant land.[5]

The book had begun precisely with the same sentence, "A sad people live in a radiant land," and closes with the very same words, reflecting the author's fixed idea of the roots of Brazilian melancholy.

Prado revives in entirety the theses outlined years previously by Nina Rodrigues on the evils deriving from miscegenation (and let us remember that Nina Rodrigues was a mulatto whose good faith therefore cannot be questioned):

> The Brazilian half-caste has undoubtedly provided the community with notable examples of intelligence, culture, and moral value. At the same time, this section of the populace offers examples of such physical weakness, an organism so ill-prepared to fight off disease and vice that it is legitimate to ask whether such a situation does not derive from the intense mingling of races and subraces.[6]

Immediately following these clearly racial observations, Prado notes that the Black entered Brazilian society as a slave, and that slavery had a leveling effect on the mentality of the masters. In the daily contact between the races, instead of the elevation of the Black man, we see the white slave owner descending to the level of the slave: "This weakness served as a catalyst in the general social organism: it exposed the deceptive superiority of the slave owner, and placed him on the same level of moral and emotional wretchedness as the *negro*."[7]

Prado adds a long and accurate description of the pitiful condition of the various forces of the state in those days. He writes of agriculture, banditry, and the absence of viable social structures. He also briefly refers to the new ethnic groups from Europe which will finally modify the racial and economic make-up of the country in the future. It is all true, or at least partially true. The fundamental error he has made, however, apart from that already observed (of having failed to take into account the contribution of the immigrants, whom he regards as foreigners in the Brazilian world, rather than accepting them as de facto Brazilians), was to have lumped together the questions of racial mixture and slavery as equal causes of underdevelopment. In so doing, he has placed special emphasis on the former rather than the latter. But the sickness, the real sickness of Brazil was slavery and not the intermingling of the races. If anything, it was a disaster that the mingling of the races came about through slavery, and not among free people. The rot started when the Portuguese came to Brazil, not with the desire to establish colonies but with the open intention to exploit. In the absence of gold and diamonds they turned to intensive agriculture that impoverished the land by the use of slave labor. The evil was that slavery was not merely a means of securing cheap manpower in the context of a precapitalist economy in the process of expansion. The real evil was that slavery was *the* ethical basis of Brazilian society: crime, injustice, and inequality posing as the law of the land.

The remainder of what Prado has to say can be taken as true: his comments on Brazilian melancholy, cupidity and lust, romantic decadence and the inability to create a coherent national identity, the failure to develop the interior and the crumbling of the state. But the author's error is to have seen a typically paleocapitalist problem (development of the country through competition, agriculture tied to foreign trade, the building up of capital for reinvestment) in terms of medieval social structures (slavery as servitude of the soil, the immutability or unalterability of the human mass at the base). The need for progress and continuous growth typical of capitalism was frustrated from the outset by the paralyzing stagnation of slavery. The almost monstrous transformation of São Paulo into an industrial megalopolis results first and foremost from the real collapse of slavery that coincides with the arrival of a new labor force from Europe. It was a purely incidental matter that many immigrants had arrived in rags, that they lived in worse conditions than many Blacks. In the new army of labor—to paraphrase Napoleon—every soldier carried a marshal's baton in his knapsack. Many, indeed, became marshals, captains of industry in a new industrial empire. Many others stopped sooner, but in that war there were many battles to be won.

In vain did the Modernists produce a stream of charming pictures of the recent European arrivals in Brazil, for folklore alone is not enough to confer a mythical imprint on the theme of underdevelopment, as in the case of the Northeast. Here was just the beginning of the transformation of São Paulo into the first city of Brazil and South America.

Let us try to understand the reasons for this attitude. Why is it that the adherents of Modernism limit themselves to the folkloric aspects of the new social reality, while they feel much more deeply about the problems connected to the origins of their country? This probably occurs because, like querulous spectators of a victory, they feel themselves shut out of a reality in which they cannot participate. Their consolation is the past, a return to that world created by their families, by the great *senhores de engenho*: the guilty feel a nostalgia for a world from which they cannot escape.

There is a familiar comparison that people have been disposed to make, a similarity between the works of Gilberto Freyre and of José Lins do Rego. The historical and sociological analysis of the former and the literary myths of the latter focus on a nostalgia for the *Casa grande e senzala*. The same can be said of the works of Paulo Prado and Cornélio Penna. In both we see a return, a retreat into personal origins, a plunge into the past.

Cornélio Penna returns to the great family mansion, revives and recreates through his artist's vision that world gone by. He never leaves it, but is attached to it with every fiber of his being. His is a long, morbid nostalgia for a world perceived through family memories, reconstructed through the conservation of objects and traditions.

The whole of Penna's work vibrates with the counterpoint of a perpetual antinomy: the bonds that tie it to the patriarchal mansion, to the very origins of his cultural identity, are the same that tie it indivisibly to the darkest moments of slavery. To deny slavery would force him inevitably to deny himself; to accept it means putting a black mark against anything referring to his origins.

This may be the crime hidden in the folds of the subconscious, which seems to dominate all the writer's work, giving it the flavor of an unresolved nightmare: Cain, what hast thou done to thy brother?

In few writers does the presence of the Black assume such proportions as in the work of Cornélio Penna. In him the Black is a constant presence, the witness of a whole existence, living side by side with the white protagonists throughout their lives. In *Dois romances de Nico Horta* (*Two Novels by Nico Horta*, 1939) there is the character of the old slave woman who drags out her whole existence in a fearful symbiosis with her masters:

> In the kitchen the old *negra* who had brought them up saw and listened to everything with the fatalistic resignation of her race, for she knew that you always had to be afraid of your masters; it was a sacred fear that she kept hidden in her strong and humble mother's heart, for as a child she had been initiated into the mysteries and punishments of her owners.
>
> "*Negrinha*, pray as you ought to!" her *sinhá-moça* at the time said to her sharply, giving her a crack on the head when she could not make the R-sounds in *fruto* or *espírito*.
>
> She had tears in her eyes, and swallowed them in silence, but she could never say those words of the prayer, and she felt she was tied to a wheel of fire turned by her *sinhá* who had and controlled everything as it was written.[8]

But the sadness of her life can do nothing but exacerbate her ties to her masters and tyrants, pushing beyond the limits of the morbid the wish to be a slave and to tyrannize those who represent her whole reason for being in the world.

> And when one of those godlike children passed by, she knew she had to pretend not to see them, and her immense wish to caress them, to take off their heavy shoes, in sharp contrast with their white feet, so sweet to the touch—but always a hidden touch!—like great white flowers, when she took off their socks as slowly as possible, so as to prolong the delicious fear of a kick aimed casually at her withered belly . . . this, too, had to be craftily concealed.
>
> She knew that she could satisfy this desire during those violent illnesses that every so often toppled them from their altars. And then her vengeance knew no bounds, in a complicated web of cures, jealousies, and precedence that no other servant denied her.[9]

The equivalent of the slave who identifies herself with her masters in a morbid relationship based on shared bondage can be found in the figure of the white mistress who in her turn identifies with the slave. In *Repouso* (*Rest*, 1949) the character of the old Black woman, who is nursemaid, servant, and companion of her young mistress, assumes the exact lineaments of a mother figure, a fixed and unalterable point of reference during an entire life.

> The old *negra* had carried Dodôte in her arms, had been her maid, then her tireless companion, had been with her on all her travels, had seen her through all her changes. She had even been taken with her to college, and had stayed there as a servant, looking after her child.
>
> Dodôte felt that she was a witness to her whole life, the proof of her existence, an affirmation of the logic and consequence of her acts, and

> this feeling frequently gave her a profound pleasure, an impression of relief and comfort, of entry into safe harbor, of a calm cove where she might rest. When she laid her head against that old virgin belly, the womb of a despised slave, and Chica told her her faintly absurd and incoherent stories, Dodôte could feel, even now, her whole life passing before her eyes, even though the episodes were disconnected and did not form a whole, but lived only through the warmth of the broken narration of the old *negra*.[10]

How could Penna free himself from the memories of slavery, how could he avoid that Black world that had always been with him? How could he free himself from himself?

A menina morta (*The Dead Little Girl*, 1954) is, of all of Penna's works, the one in which the Black presence is absolutely decisive. The story, if one can apply the word to a narrative without a true plot, takes place on a large coffee plantation, where the memory of the *sinhazinha*, of the little dead mistress, and her goodness towards the slaves dominates every page of the book. The memory then becomes a nightmare with the return to the estate of the dead child's elder sister, Carlota, to marry a rich neighbor. The finale, with the freeing of the slaves by Carlota who by her act revives the existence of her sister, gives no sense of redemption, of true liberation, of victory, but rather represents the expiation of a long sin, resolved by the death of the fazenda itself.

Among the numerous Black characters who populate the novel, there is naturally, as in *Repouso*, that of the Black woman friend, or confidante. On the plantation, surrounded by relatives among whom she feels a perfect stranger, Carlota immediately turns to Libânia, her *mucama*, or lady's maid. Only with her can she open up, ask her exactly what has happened in the years she has been away from home. When she does not turn to Libânia, her place is taken by Joviana, her former *mãe preta*, her nurse, her Black mammy who had raised her. Both Joviana and Libânia are crucial figures in Carlota's life and that of the fazenda. Only they know the reasons behind certain facts and what has taken place, events the whites prefer not to talk about. Carlota can turn only to them, although as an educated young white lady she has been taught to pay no attention to the *mexericos de negras*, the gossip of the Black women, lest she attract general disapproval.

Libânia and above all Joviana—the Black mammy, denied children of her own, who turns all her affection to the child placed in her care—are authentic figures, easily identifiable as real people, who serve an ambiguous purpose for Penna. The natural ties of affection created between two human beings living together—in this case servants and masters, whites and Blacks—often end up by underlining that "slavery with a human face" which has provided the most convenient alibi to soothe the Brazilian cultural conscience for a long time, perhaps too long.

A menina morta is a story set in the time of slavery, not a story about slavery, and, as we have said, does not go beyond the geographical time and space of the events narrated. Written in 1954, it reflects the way of thinking of eighty years earlier. Is this artistic artifice, or a real inability to cast off the guilty heredity of the Casa Grande? We can never know. What we do know is that in the books of Cornélio Penna the words *Senhores* and *Sinhazinha* are always capitalized, and the Blacks are always described as brutes, capable only of the most primitive emotions and feelings.

Observe, for example, the incoherent state of mind Joviana finds herself in just for having tried to explain to Carlota a few facts relating to the life of her parents:

> Then, having forced her intelligence as far as it would go, she bent her body until her face was almost touching the ground. She began to mutter prayers intermingled with African words, and seemed to be under a spell, carried away by the magic of her own incantations. Evidently for her this was a supreme effort to keep her reason. When she calmed down and looked once more at the *Sinhazinha* her face had resumed its customary look of primitive, generous simplicity.[11]

The most effective descriptions of the affections of the Black workers occur when they are focused on the two sisters: the dead girl who was always ready to intercede on their behalf, and the living one who has made her late sister's mission her own.

At the start of the novel the Black women ask permission to carry the sinhazinha's coffin to the cemetery and, at the inexplicable refusal of the master who wants no one to come to the funeral, are swept away by collective hysteria and rush off en masse towards the cemetery. Promptly rounded up by the plantation steward and his men, they are locked in the senzala's barn to await punishment, not with the *palmatória*, which would have hurt their hands and made them temporarily useless for work, but with a whipping on the back. It is interesting that the feeling the author attributes to these innocent victims is not one of rebellion towards either steward or master (the latter—*o Comendador*, written with a capital *C*—an untouchable figure even in the thoughts of another, protected by the sanctity of his position as *dominus*), but rather one of anger against themselves, each accusing another of inciting this unaccustomed act of disobedience. (It seems almost as if the author cannot conceive the hypothesis that slaves might harbor feelings of hatred with regard to their masters, overseers, the whole established order of the fazenda):

> Their eyes cast murderous looks at one another, and you could read in them wild and pitiless accusations while their thick, dark lips trembled and formed silent curses. Their bodies touched and there was a stifling, bitter odor, but the flesh that united them was bound in implacable enmity, and their hearts and souls joined in mortal battle. Many promised each other bloody revenge, and they yearned to inflict all possible harm on their companions inside, as unarmed and impotent as they! With a knife in hand, and a mad laugh on their fiery lips, they would have done anything, and anything could have happened in that moment of panic! But in the midst of that madness that made their blood boil, those *negras* knew in some, deep, hidden recess of their tormented hearts that they would do nothing when once let out of that inferno, but would continue to live and laugh, united forever.[12]

Once more we note the manner in which Penna describes these women, and the terms he uses—their mad laughter, poor heads, souls in turmoil—to underline the primitive level of their existence with no understanding of what was simply a collective attack of panic, perfectly understandable under the circumstances. Would it be too much to ask of him a brief comment on the brutal violence that had provoked that panic terror?

Even the mulatta Libânia, who as the nurse of the dead girl has a privileged position, rebels when the steward announces the master's order that no slave or Black is to attend the funeral: "I am free! I am *forra*! Here is my *carta de alforria* given by my Master! I'm neither *negra* nor slave!"[13] Just note that "I'm neither *negra* nor slave!" shows us how deep the divisions were among the Blacks, with each one defending his or her color line, tending always towards the white.

Apart from Libânia and Joviana, there is another familiar character, that of the old *negra* who represents the living memory of the fazenda, the recollection of times past, continually evoked and confused with the present. Datate, as the old woman is called, lies paralyzed in her hut, and when she sees Carlota, who has come to pay her a visit, immediately launches into a rambling speech in which, while several times confusing her own sinhazinha with those who had preceded her, she expresses her affection for her white masters, for whom alone she has reserved a little stool, and on which she allows no Black to sit.

The novel includes two choral scenes illustrating the affection of the Blacks towards their young mistresses; the first, already quoted, of the Black women who want to force their way into the funeral and, when harshly punished, invoke their sinhazinha by name during the beating. The second scene, which more or less brings the novel to a close, shows all the Blacks of the fazenda—the women in tears and the men totally bewildered—surrounding Carlota and begging her not to abandon them to their fate after the death of the master, her father.

As we have said, the complete works of Cornélio Penna follow the pattern of a perpetual contradiction. He is perfectly aware that as a man, a citizen, he is the product of a historical situation based on slavery. As a man, as a universal being, as an artist, he cannot fail to note that slavery is the legalization of the mark of Cain. On the literary and philosophical level, his position corresponds with that of Dunshee de Abranches, which we have already examined in detail. Every time the latter found himself having to describe or condemn someone who had assumed a shameful attitude towards slaves, he found he was forced to speak harshly of some relative or acquaintance.

We have thus a whole series of episodes tending to illustrate the good side of slavery beyond the simple ties of affection established between masters and slaves. Let us look at a few of these, and see how, inevitably, the negative, evil side of slavery shows through and gains the upper hand.

Among the slaves genuinely grief stricken by the death of the sinhazinha, there is one, José Carapina, who is particularly saddened because, as the estate carpenter, it is his job to make the little mistress's coffin. His is a typical case of the slave-master symbiosis. He came to the fazenda many years before, sold by his former masters ("dark-skinned landowners, so poor they could almost be taken for slaves"[14]). The affection he felt for his old owners made the separation all the more painful, scarcely lessened by the hope of "eating well and becoming an 'important *negro*' on the *fazenda* of his rich new *Sinhô*, who was always off to Court and knew the Emperor."[15] On the new fazenda, however, he was first tempted to let himself die of hunger, to do what the *negros novos* (those just arrived) did, who ate dirt in secret in order to die, this being the one form of liberty open to them.

> But hunger had won in the end, helped by the smell of cooked beans coming from the enormous pot installed in the corner of the kitchen over the iron tripod red from the ever-burning fire of sweet-smelling wood, helped also by the golden *angu* and the dried meat that was rarely seen in the old house, where more often than not masters and slaves

> sat down to the same mush of *fubá* and vegetables. And he had put on weight and grown, despite the shame of bolting down all that food that his old master would have only eaten on feast days.[16]

Completely integrated into his new surroundings, José Carapina can look with detachment at the years gone by, when he was just a poor slave.

> And the years had passed without him hearing any more of his people and now, even with the greatest effort of memory, he could never be certain which of those *negros* covered with rags, whom he saw in his mind's eye, wearing no more than a pair of pants, or just a piece of cloth tied around their waist, might have been his father, or which of those *negras* in a torn and filthy shift was his mother. Today the wife his *Senhor* had given him, and the children who had been born all wore a white shirt and linen pants, and the *negra* Almerinda made so bold as to put a red collar on her white dress, which opened with a button. . . . But all this, despite the strict goodness of the *Sinhô* and the distant, generous charity of the *Sinhá*, was nothing now without the smiling, merry presence of the child.[17]

There is a constant repetition of the theme of the goodness and generosity of the master, of the theme that the slaves on a rich plantation lived better than poor whites, or better than poor freed men, because the author has told us that the former masters of José Carapina were *morenos*, dark-skinned, although we never learn just how dark. That those in a servile condition, or actual slaves attached to a prosperous plantation, lived better than free but poor men is, however, historically accurate and verifiable.

In another episode the slaves are described as attentive and eager when the master visits the fields, ready to show him the fruits of their labor. They are not driven by fear of punishment but rather by the knowledge that soon the women would be coming with the mules laden with wineskins full of fruit juice, and that their efforts would be well rewarded.

> It was the solicitous attention of the *Senhor* and his paternal presence that kept them in good health, enabling them to maintain that sturdy vigor that was expected from them. But the earth responded generously to their efforts, and gave forth its inexhaustible treasures and bound them all together in a brotherly feeling of power.[18]

It seems almost as if slavery is a pure *accidens* and that the one reality is this profound solidarity uniting masters and slaves in a noble struggle for survival and progress which confers an air of justice and even sacredness on the established order.

Nevertheless there comes a moment when goodness and prosperity inevitably clash with images of cruelty and violence. When Celestina, a poor relative who has grown up on the farm, listens to a tale told by the old Dadate, she is terrorized by the ghostly figures—such as a faceless *negra* who wanders through the rooms of the fazenda—evoked by the old slave.

> Celestina then remembered the terrible legends that circulated around the *fazenda* in the mountains, the stories told of the cruelty of the old masters, and she shuddered at the thought of the picture of calm beauty and fair prosperity which the old paralytic had always described. It was impossible to reconcile that faceless *negra* with that air of prosperous virtue that turned everything into gold. And she was afraid lest all her dreams would vanish like a meaningless lie, a futile and cruel farce. Never more would she be able to listen to that hoarse, monotonous voice reciting scenes so remarkable for evoking the spread and vigor of the estate.[19]

In the novel there are sudden scenes of violence that impress the reader because they are deliberately written as being a part of the daily life of the plantation. To have accepted slavery as socially just and necessary transforms the practice of violence and corporal punishment into a part of the daily routine acceptable to all, be they the well-educated young or pious old ladies. The pious old ladies do not hesitate one moment, as the result of a misunderstanding, to order the steward to thrash a young Black lad. The misunderstanding arises because the ladies did not know that a horse, given to Carlota as a present from her fiancé, was called Satã, or Satan. Hearing the name of the devil on the stable boy's tongue, the ladies grow indignant at what they regard as a lack of respect and, without waiting for an explanation, order the poor boy to be punished. Only after a word with Carlota do they realize they have made a mistake and revoke the punishment. "He's a good *negrinho* after all!"

The well-educated young man, in contrast, is Carlota's fiancé on a visit to the fazenda. The coachman drops a heavy trunk that falls on his own feet, and this clumsiness provokes a violent reaction in João Batista, the fiancé.

> Even more swiftly the young man grabbed the *preto* by the lapel of his jacket, and gave him a series of savage blows with the whip he carried in his right hand. The coachman received these blows that must have scarred his skin, for he was ill protected by the poor livery he was wearing, without any attempt to protect himself, without even trying to run away. He never even removed his foot from under the trunk that was

> crushing it. He kept his eyes open without any expression. He was like an animal that resigns itself to unavoidable pain, and places itself completely in the hands of the master. But he was unmindful even of the primordial instincts of the beast.[20]

The violence of this scene in no way alters the events that immediately follow: the young man composes himself, adjusts his tie, mops the sweat from his face—likewise the slave—and then both of them introduce themselves respectively to the fiancée and mistress as if nothing had happened.

It is only at the end of the novel that Carlota understands the actual reality of slavery, and the contrast between the conspicuous wealth of the white world and the cruelty that supports it. Then she understands what the dead sinhazinha meant to the slaves, and the way she always intervened on their behalf. This moment of truth comes for Carlota when she wakes one morning at dawn and wanders into the barn where they keep the slaves who have been punished chained to the stake.

> But the smile froze on her lips because now she saw what was really happening, the actual consequences of the orders given by her father, and how those old men, the stewards with their long beards and fatherly ways who treated her with such tender affection, applied and increased the punishments to be meted out. Now she knew the real price of her dead sister's prayers, which barely cost her a few softly spoken words. And she felt hatred for that light creature with the dancing step who seemed to make a game of pleading in favor of those bodies that she now saw with their arms and legs all twisted and tied to the stake, with the stifling smell of caged animals rising to her nostrils. The scene seemed monstrous to her, although she had lived it many times in her memory, and as many times heard it told by the wives and sisters of the men who stood in front of her. They probably did not see her, even if they were awake. For them she was probably some shade from hell, or else someone sent to see whether they were suffering as much as had been decreed.[21]

The real protagonist of *A menina morta* is mystery: the mystery surrounding the death of the sinhazinha, the mystery of the hatred that divides the parents, the mystery of those dead figures whom no one wants to talk about, and the mystery of actions referring to events that remain unexplained.

Naturally a fazenda full of Blacks would have to include the mystery character par excellence, the witchdoctor, or local wizard. There is a Black woman, now free, who lives alone and respected by the others who fear her powers. We do not know much about her, except that she has the reputation of being a *feiticeira*. But it is the old Dadate, paralyzed and immobile in her room, who more closely represents the mysterious role of the feiticeira. Carlota, who has gone to see her, senses something odd.

> She could not escape those sibylline eyes that ran up and down her, like those of a strange, voracious animal lying in ambush. The *preta* nevertheless gave no sign of feeling the slightest doubt, the least surprise. She hardly seemed to want to prolong the spectacle that delighted her as well as the secret satisfaction that they were afraid of her and her supposedly harmful influence.[22]

But in spite of her courage and good will, Carlota

> felt a growing repugnance at the old woman's eyes staring at her, and suddenly she wanted to run away, so as not to see the enormous grin of her toothless mouth whenever she paused or waited for her visitor to say something or other.[23]

As always, the description of the witch assumes dark tones. Lacking in Cornélio Penna, as in the case of other Brazilian writers with the exception of Xavier Marques and Jorge Amado, is any effort to understand a reality that requires analysis from a clearly antithetical point of view.

Later on in the novel, Carlota's instinctive fears are confirmed by certain words from Dadate, who complains she cannot rest because of the continuous noise of a large black billygoat tied up outside her hut. The black goat, of course, is a symbol of the devil in popular Brazilian credence. Naturally there is no goat and Dadate's words to Carlota can only increase the latter's fears: "Pardon, *Nhanhã*, . . . no, it's not a goat, no . . . the old *negra* knows it's something else!"[24] When at the end of the novel Carlota runs away from the *casa do tronco*, she will see an enormous black male goat tied up close by the main residence. Are witchcraft and the dark terrors of mystery just a privilege of the senzala, never to enter the main house?

We must allow Penna the courage to have placed himself outside all currents of sociological literature which dominated the years of his literary career, above all when one considers that he was dealing with so crucial a theme as slavery. His is the work of an uncommitted writer, and precisely for this, from our point of view, it turns out to be much more valid and interesting, since it amounts to an artistically successful effort to tie himself to an extinct world without ever judging it.

In *A menina morta* slavery is much more than a literary pretext. It is the very basis of the novel. At a certain point Carlota herself has the feeling that she, too, is a slave, as the result of the continuous limitations imposed on her by family convention, and because her marriage to a man she hardly knows is no more than a crude business arrangement. "O negócio está feito," the contract is signed, is the phrase Carlota hears from those preparing the necessary documents for the marriage. Slavery, too, is just another form of business which, like *feitiçaria*, does not come to a halt at the threshold of the main house.

Slavery lives on in the heart of the protagonists, in the soul of the mulatta Libânia who tears up her carta de alforria in a supreme gesture of sacrifice in the name of her little dead mistress. Of what use to her was that piece of paper now? In the fazenda those Black women who had been freed were subject to the same laws as the slaves, did the same work, and were often whipped.

> There were many who had been freed, buying the certificate of freedom with their own money, but continued under the old obligations, and were often punished, just like their sister slaves.[25]

We have slavery until the last act of purification, the final catharsis, when Carlota first rejects the marriage that would have made a slave of her, too, and then, taking upon herself the complete burden of responsibility handed down to her by her dead sister, frees the slaves. But frees them from what? Liberty catches them by surprise and leaves them dazed.

> One day, without any announcement in advance, the slaves received that evening, from the hands of the surly overseers, their *cartas de alforria*, and returned to the *senzalas* in astonishment, unable to explain to themselves how they had passed from the wretched condition of slaves to that of free men so suddenly and quite without ceremony. During the night some timid fires were lit, and they gathered around them in groups to sing or pray, but their voices died away, or trailed off into a vague murmuring, as if they were afraid of being heard behind the hermetically sealed windows of the main residence. The following morning was a period of complete apathy, the heavy rhythms of the life of the *fazenda* having come to a full stop, as if suddenly struck dead.[26]

The end of slavery seems to coincide with the death of the fazenda itself, in an abandonment to which all seem to yield:

> Everything was closed and silent, the fire was unlit in the outer kitchen which was left dark and smoke stained, as if it had never contained a

> great fire, leaving not the slightest sign of life. There was no communication with the outside world and there were vague rumors of bands of fugitives who had taken to the woods, where they remained in silence, overcome by stark terror, suspecting some inexplicable curse hanging over them, while yet others disappeared in the surrounding territory, never to be seen again.[27]

It seems the author has no desire to follow the life of the fazenda after the end of slavery. And yet something, in spite of everything, slowly starts to come to life again. Little by little some of the ex-slaves return, and after a while life on the plantation resumes its rhythm, or rather "another rhythm without the old strength or power that had gone forever."[28]

But that rebirth, that resumption of life, seemingly guaranteed by the redemption of the little dead mistress and by the voluntary sacrifice of Carlota, no longer held any interest for Cornélio Penna. A masterly poet of anguish and death, he discovered his most fertile source of inspiration in slavery. Beyond that, the slow and fearful nightmare seems to dissolve forever.

14 JOSÉ LINS DO REGO AND THE LONG SEASON OF MEMORY

> An honorary doctor of letters (with the ring to prove it) nominated to the Brazilian Academy of Letters in his last years, he bore with him the proud frustrations of his rank. For he had arrived on the scene of the *engenhos* when their day was finally over, exercising the marginal role of the historical observer or rather that of the true *senhor de engenho*, idealized in the figure of his grandfather.[1]

Thus Luciana Stegagno Picchio summarizes the moral and intellectual position of José Lins do Rego with regard to the world from which he came and which, in various forms, constituted the focal point of his career as a writer. As one reads the works of José Lins do Rego, another name immediately comes to mind from thousands of miles away—one that belongs to quite a different cultural world: Fellini of *Amarcord*. Like Fellini, Rego does nothing but remember, talk about himself, his childhood, his family, his friends, his women, his manias, his frustrations. Obsessed by himself and above all by the world to which he belonged, that of the great *senhores de engenho* now destined to its inevitable eclipse, he recalls Cornélio Penna. But José Lins do Rego's nostalgia is neither dark nor tragic. Undisturbed by specters and remorse, his is a plain and simple nostalgia, veiled with regrets and sweet sadness for a moment and people who will not come back. But it is only nostalgia. Whereas a cloud of guilt hangs permanently over the work of Penna, the sense of obscure sin or unexpiated crime, in the novels of Rego memory is stripped of all moral category and remains no more than the remembrance of time past.

José Lins do Rego Cavalcanti was born in 1901 in the state of Paraíba in Northwest Brazil and died in 1957 in Rio de Janeiro. He came from an old family of senhores de engenho with deep roots in the land and the history of that part of the country. From the point of view of literary history Rego belongs by personal taste and existential choice to the Regionalist movement founded in Recife in 1926 under the guidance and influence of Gilberto Freyre. Regionalism was intended as a continuation of and reaction to the Modernist movement born officially in São Paulo in 1922: a continuation of revolt against an imported literature marked by sterile neoclassical language and the reaction of a rural and folkloric North against a South forging ahead in rapid industrialization. The South, it should be added, was by now decisively denatured or unrecognizable from an ethnic point of view as a result of massive doses of European immigration. A common observation is that the work of José Lins do Rego is the literary and poetic expression of all that Freyre had written in his historical and sociological analysis in *Casa grande e senzala*. And undoubtedly the friendship and collaboration of the great historian of the agrarian civilization of the Brazilian Northwest greatly helped the writer so serenely enamored of his land and people.

From the historical point of view, however, the years of Rego's literary career coincide precisely with the Vargas era. In fact our author's first novel dates from 1932, Vargas having come to power two years previously. To sum up briefly the policies that characterized the Vargas era, we would say the motives that inspired them and the consequences that resulted therefrom were the exact opposite of the principles that form the basis of the patriarchal world of agriculture and slave labor to which Rego belonged. The division between these two worlds was total and was rooted in the very geography of the country. The epicenter of the politics of Vargas was the South or the southern central parts, São Paulo as against the Northeast, which had been the cradle of Brazilian civilization. The Vargas era saw the rise of the new ethnic groups over the rural world of the Northeast. Under Vargas occurred the beginnings of transformation and industrialization against the world of preservation that for centuries had weighed down the agricultural fiefdoms. This was a period of active involvement of the working masses and the politics of populism as opposed to the alienation and oppression so typical of the slave population. Here, in short, was the transformation of the country in a modern sense, its participation in industrial civilization that finally set itself boldly, but not without difficulties and delays, in opposition to that purely agricultural Brazil which for centuries had been the single image of the country. In short, another Brazil was emerging into the foreground and historically overtaking and partially excluding the world to which José Lins do Rego belonged.

Along with many fellow writers, with the exception of Jorge Amado, Rego never intended his Regionalism to serve as a hook whereby he and they might attach their world to the new ideological currents then transforming the country. Nor can it be interpreted as a serene if dolorous confession as to the causes and men that might be held responsible for the historical backwardness of the Northeast. It was on the contrary a poetic return to roots, on the wings of memory and fantasy, in a sentimental and restricted manner but one that never analyzed critical problems, or spotlighted questions of moral justice. Rego, for example, is bothered and tormented by the idea of carnal sin, by guilt associated with sexual habit. But his conscience is not disturbed or even touched by doubt over the eternal sin of injustice inflicted by man on man.

The work of José Lins do Rego, or at least a good part of it, can be defined as a long autobiography retold many times in the first person. It begins in 1932 with *Menino de engenho*, which can be translated as *Plantation Boy*. The *engenho* is a sugarcane plantation possessing only rudimentary machinery to transform its raw material, the cane itself, into the finished product of the sugarloaves. The engenho in question is Santa Rosa where the hero, Carlos de Melo, comes from the city to live after a tragedy has destroyed his family. The head of the plantation is old José Paulino, Carlos's grandfather, a patriarch in the classical sense of the word, who governs his land with justice and firmness. The other characters in the house include his sweet Aunt Maria, who in Carlos's eyes will replace his dead mother; the terrible old Aunt Sinhazinha, whose greatest pleasure is to torture the Black workers; Uncle Juca, who is always ready to make love to all the Black women on the plantation; the women of the *senzala*; the cousins who spend their holidays in the country; the numerous *moleques* with whom Carlos shares a thousand scrapes of a carefree childhood. Carlos de Melo is obviously the writer's alter ego. In fact, when Rego published a book of memoirs, *Meus verdes anos (My Salad Days)*, in 1956 he needed to change very little save the names and the structure of certain episodes from *Menino de engenho*. Carlos de Melo is the main character, but the novel has another protagonist, the plantation itself: its dramas, its stories, its malicious gossip, and its daily routine. And it is also the story of a long defeat, the first chapters of which appear in *Menino de engenho*. Here we witness the initial defeat of Carlos, who in contact with the land manages only to sink toward perdition and to lose that simple childlike enthusiasm. Carlos experiences precocious sexual initiation with animals, with the other moleques, and later with the Black women of the plantation, and ends up with a prostitute who gives him a venereal infection. "*Menino perdido, menino de engenho*, a lost boy, a plantation boy," are the words with which the novel concludes, summing up in a phrase that vocation for defeat that this descendant of these owners of land and men carried inescapably within him.

Carlos de Melo is really José Lins do Rego: both have the asthma that torments them from infancy, the extreme nervous delicacy, the obsessive fear of death and disease, the dark shadow of madness; and it is precisely that delicacy of the nervous system which gives the title to the second novel of the series, *Doidinho* (1933), which means *The Mad Boy*. The story of Carlos de Melo continues in college, a sort of hermitage capable of providing only the rudimentary elements of culture by kicks on the backside, where his miseducation would be complete. The plantation, that carefree world of the senzalas, lives on in the memory of Carlos like a constant recall; the return to the promised land occurs only briefly during his vacations until, finally running away from college, the protagonist returns once again to Santa Rosa.

The third novel of the series, known as the sugar cane cycle, is *Bangüê*, an untranslatable word that indicates the collection of rural machinery which serves to transform the sugar contained in the cane into a finished product. By extension, the word bangüê indicates those engenhos in which the sugar is worked and transformed into sugarloaves. *Bangüê* sees the return of Carlos, who by now is grown up, to Santa Rosa. Old José Paulino is close to death. His Uncle Juca has gone elsewhere, the plantation continues to live according to its peaceful rhythms around the figure of the old patriarch. Carlos de Melo, who until that moment has lived the parasitic and careless life of the rich student, decides to abandon the position of spectator and become involved. He wants to continue his grandfather's work on the plantation but he seems destined to attract defeat. He is a man constitutionally born to surrender, to yield to adversity, or more simply (and this perhaps is the author's message) in him we can see the coupling of exhaustion and inability to generate enthusiasm typical of those who have lived far too close to the organic exhaustion of the human trunk that has run out of sap. To this constitutional weakness we must add the objective difficulties of the historical circumstances of rapid change that required a very different character if they were to be overcome. Carlos tries to find satisfaction in love but only encounters a bitter disappointment. On the death of his grandfather he inherits the plantation; he tries with every means at his disposal to increase production and to earn the respect of his workers but he fails miserably. The external reasons for his defeat are two (without counting his own pathological incapacity for action): first, a tenant farmer, a Black man by the name of Marreira, a descendant of former slaves of the engenho, who, working his fingers to the bone from dawn to dusk, becomes a dangerous competitor and a threat to Santa Rosa; and second, a sugar factory crushes its local competitors one by one with the strength of its technology and the resources of its capital. Carlos de Melo has tried to be a man of the old days like his grandfather. He has tried to apply the rules of a game that is no longer played, and the affectionate support of the other members of his clan, along with the sympathy of his old Black workers who see in him the continuity of those old days, is of little use to him. He leaves, after having made an advantageous sale of the plantation to an international consortium for which his Uncle Juca also works, while the Black workers are forced to move on or to stay put and work for new and more rapacious masters.

These three novels of the sugarcane cycle are, as we have said, essentially autobiographical. They tell the story of the man who sees the decline and fall of his people through the eyes of childhood, adolescence, and youth. The device of describing events in the first person gives the author-protagonist the opportunity to exempt himself from expressing a value judgment. First the child, then the young man, finds himself caught up in a situation, simultaneously historical and personal, and all that can be asked of either is to observe and to react from within, placing each in a position from which it would be difficult if not impossible to offer any form of judgment. And this gives the entire work a greater artistic validity, untarnished by any ideological premise or false moralizing, and at the same time guarantees the authenticity, or objectivity, of the testimony, the memory of a man deeply attached to a historical moment about to disappear forever. The sugarcane cycle, however, consists of two other novels in which Rego tried to see the decadence and the end of his world through eyes that were not simply those of the witness protagonist. It is as if he wanted to give a more spacious if not universal value to a defeat that he did not want to be seen as his alone.

Moleque Ricardo (1935) and *Usina* (*The Factory*, 1936) are the two adult books of the cycle. The first of the two is the story of Ricardo, one of the many moleques on the plantation and one of the numerous Black boys who live in Santa Rosa. Ricardo is tired of his usual life, of the monotonous repetition of those days that seem to resemble one another, of having to do the same thing day after day. He therefore decides to escape to Recife, the big city. The word escape is exact insofar as, even though slavery is over, the moleque still belonged to Santa Rosa and therefore to the *coronel*, José Paulino, according to an unwritten law respected by everybody. In Recife Ricardo first of all works with a railroad worker and then for a Portuguese baker who pays him well and forces him to work very hard. Ricardo leads a very simple existence in the poor district where he lives. A few love affairs, a marriage that comes to a swift end with the death of his wife, Carnival with all of its accompanying rites—getting ready, trying on the costumes, the uniforms, the rows—taking part in collective activity. Ricardo encounters the union. He participates in the first strikes and at the same time makes the acquaintance of Pai Lucas the *feiticeiro* or the *pai-de-santo* of his district. These are the two poles of his life: a return to the African religion of his forefathers on the one hand and participation in the new mass activities on the other. Ricardo chooses to be a member of the union, and much good it does him. After a strike that comes to a tragic end, he is deported along with many companions to the penitentiary on Fernando de Noronha island in spite of the efforts of Pai Lucas to have his sentence overturned.

We shall return later to this novel and to the others for a more detailed analysis. For the moment, let us say that *Moleque Ricardo* loses some credibility and vitality as compared to the other novels, even though it is an excellent book, because of the handling of the protagonist, who far too closely reflects the set of existential problems that belong to José Lins do Rego alone and which he had so evenly transferred to the figure of Carlos de Melo. Once again the writer has told his own story, but the demands of his text have forced him to adopt a Black mask.

In *Usina* we have the conclusion of the failure which the other four novels of the cycle have clearly foretold in their vision of partial defeats. Ricardo returns to the plantation, having done his time, and finds that all is changing, thanks to the transformations brought about by the new financial group for which Uncle Juca works. But transformation does not necessarily mean progress or improvement. Once again it seems that the author is unable to admit possible alternatives to the end of the classical system of the engenho. The usina, or factory, fails, Juca fails as Carlos de Melo fails, and Ricardo fails, killed while trying to help people who are poorer and worse off than he.

José Lins do Rego draws bitter conclusions in his sugarcane cycle but in them there is something more than sad awareness of being the spectator of failure. There is the confession, which never clearly comes to the surface, of being able to belong to no other world than the one disappearing before his eyes. The physical obsession with death and disease, the asthma that tormented the writer and his protagonist, are extended to a world that was historically changing, going through the painful process of renewal, but was not dying. What was dying was the feudal system of the engenho beyond which the writer refused to suggest possible solutions, preferring to imprison himself in the bittersweet memory of time past. He is perfectly consistent when he transfers his personal existential angst, anxiety, and obsession with death to the world, to *his* world that is disappearing; he is less credible, both artistically and in terms of historical testimony, when he thinks he feels the harsh heaving of his asthmatic chest in persons and situations that are much farther from him than he imagines.

The anxious fear of death, the shadow of madness, the whole scene in the impressionistic and undramatic contours of memory return in what is perhaps his finest work, *Fogo morto*, or *Dead Fire* (1943). The title refers to those engenhos in an advanced state of delapidation in which no more work is done and where the fire that allows the furnace or the oven to turn the sugarcane into sugar is no longer lit. *Fogo morto* is also the story of three madmen, or rather three forms of madness. Among the obsessions of José Lins do Rego, with his hypersensitive and extremely nervous temperament, madness was also included. The three characters in question are the saddler, Mestre Amaro, (*mestre* corresponding to master in English or *mastro* in Italian), Coronel Lula and Capitão (or captain) Vitorino. Apart from not being blessed with complete mental balance these three have in common the fact that they are old. They represent even physically three moments of the decadence of the Northeast. Their harmless madness seems to be the alibi or the solution indicated by the author faced with the evolution of a situation that allows no space for those who represent the old system. Coronel Luis César de Holanda Chacon, known as Lula, the master saddler José Amaro, and Capitão Vitorino do not need the attacks of the men of the factory to be victims of defeat. They are already creatures confined to the margins of existence.

The saddest story is that of Mestre Amaro. He has a mad daughter living at home who is prey to continuous fits, and a wife who hates him. Being of a delicate state of health, he lives immersed in the penetrating smell of leather and the malicious gossip of the village where he resides, nurturing a childlike admiration for the leader of the local *cangaceiros*, Capitão Silvino. Mestre Amaro does all he can to help his hero, giving information and news to his informers and preparing things he might need, without fear of the anger and the blows the local police lieutenant Maurício dishes out at the slightest whim. His own state of health, his irascibility, his rather sick appearance, and his nightly wanderings contribute to the local rumor that he might be a werewolf. After various adventures, always linked to the struggles between cangaceiros and the police, Mestre Amaro chooses suicide as the only way out of an impossible existence.

The tale of Coronel Lula is linked to the history of the last decade of slavery itself. It is also linked to the foundation of the engenho of Santa Fé as a result of the courage and the obstinate determination of Capitão Tomás Cabral de Melo who, a few years before, by working hard and forcing his slaves to work to the point of exhaustion, had transformed that territory into a prosperous plantation. The harsh Captain Tomás is succeeded by his son-in-law Lula who, although he is a man of weak character, on inheriting a position of command reveals an unexpected as well as futile cruelty in his treatment of his slaves. Naturally, on the day of abolition not one Black wants to work for Coronel Lula any more, and thus begins the slow decline of Santa Fé. Coronel Lula can do nothing but vent his cruelty on the members of his family and his weaker neighbors like Mestre Amaro, passing the rest of his time wrapped in religious mania in which the litanies are punctuated and interrupted by the lamentations and screams of his mad sister-in-law (madness seems an indispensable ingredient in these families who have lost all their vital spirit).

Capitão Vitorino, on the contrary, is an appealing and Don Quixote-like character immersed up to his neck in all the political feuds that enrich the Northeast. He is always fighting with everybody, beginning with the moleques on the street who insult him, and ending up with the fearful Maurício and Capitão Silvino. (The title capitão, or captain, which for the bandit Silvino was a sign of popular recognition, for Vitorino, however, as for the various *coronéis*, was an honorific title of the national guard.) The amusing thing about all Vitorino's squabbles is that they are absolutely gratuitous. He fights with the cangaceiro Silvino in defense of Coronel Lula whom he hates; he fights with Lieutenant Maurício for the pleasure of fighting, and then in the defense of a few wretched characters of the village. Then he fights with his cousin José Paulino for political reasons; he fights with the *negros*, because they are Blacks; he fights with all, and he loses because he is old and defenseless. A sympathetic character, in short, mocked and loved by all, he is the one positive figure in that saga of decadence and madness which is *Fogo morto*.

Side by side with these works linked to the sugarcane cycle, José Lins do Rego wrote other novels, including *Pedra bonita* (*Pretty Stone*, 1938) and *Cangaceiros* (*Bandits*, 1953) which, although remarkable works, have little to do with the theme of our study, and other minor works that will be considered at the end of this chapter.

As for the Black problem, the most interesting novel of the series is precisely the last, *Fogo morto*. Because it is the least autobiographical this is the work in which the author, while staying within the sugarcane world, the world of the plantation, and describing real characters whom he himself knew, has nevertheless tried to give a historical structure to the reality that gravitates around the Northeastern engenho, dividing the novel into three parts, each of which corresponds to the three principal characters.

Capitão Vitorino takes a fair share of blows from Lieutenant Maurício's men after a successful attempt to release from prison three innocent men, including a Black man. But Vitorino does not like Black men, and not only because the moleques insult him as he passes down the street. Jose Passarinho himself, the Black man for whose freedom Capitão Vitorino fought, has had a series of violent squabbles with the irascible old man. Capitão Vitorino's hatred has different roots. It is something instinctive. It derives perhaps from the fact that Vitorino comes from an old family. He is cousin to Coronel José Paulino, a man reduced to poverty, living on a level very similar to that of many Blacks in the vicinity. The one form of superiority about which a troublemaker like Vitorino can boast with regard to the Blacks is that he is white in an area like the rural Northeast where the color of one's skin has served for centuries to indicate social rank. White equals the gentleman on the one hand, while Black means slave on the other. But Vitorino possesses no more than an old horse and a dagger. His one source of strength is the color of his skin. One of his favorite sayings is the one he continually repeats: "*Sou homem branco*, I'm a white man." And here is one of the typical ways he expresses himself after a row with some moleques:

> I'm a man worthy of respect. I was going down the street and those sons-of-bitches came out into the street to insult me. It's a disgrace. I'm a white man like José Paulino, he's my cousin. These swine won't leave me in peace.[2]

It is interesting to note the sort of relationship established between Capitão Vitorino and Mestre Amaro: the friendship (Amaro is the godfather of Vitorino's son) is based on a reciprocal sense of superiority. Vitorino feels he is superior because he belongs to a great family.

> He was *Capitão* Vitorino Carneiro da Cunha of a well-born family of Várzea in Paraíba. One of his cousins had been a baron and a member of the government of the province. Before going home he decided to have a chat with his relative José Amaro, who was not from a family like his own but was nevertheless a white man.[3]

The color of one's skin is the minimum requirement to be admitted to the presence of Capitão Vitorino, but social differences remain.

Earlier we read, "Old Vitorino regarded his relative as an inferior. He was a saddle maker, a master craftsman whom white people like himself ought not to take into consideration."[4] Here the term white people indicates no racial difference as Amaro, too, is white. It is a pure and simple social distinction. For his own part, José Amaro the saddle maker considers the sort of life led by his relative with contempt, as absolutely devoid of those examples of good behavior that guaranteed lower-middle-class respectability.

> Mestre José Amaro considered him with contempt. He was always rather embarrassed by the company of that poor man whom no one respected. That aimless sort of life, that wandering from one place to another for no real reason, with no purpose, was simply too much.[5]

Both the captain and the saddler show, each in his own way, a deep contempt for Blacks. For Mestre Amaro it is rather a question of an emotional position that is seen in his frequent moments of ill humor in which, furthermore, he is nice to nobody: "The *negro* could only be a slave. No one wants to be free. All wanted to live under the yoke."[6] The saddler is a particularly nervous man and squabbles with many people. Then he has a row with a Black man. He uses the term "*negro*" or even "this *negro*" with profound contempt and with offensive intention. Capitão Vitorino, in contrast, is much more colorful in his insults and in his very frequent rows with people. A perpetual object of his anger is the Black José Passarinho, the same man for whom the captain will do all that is possible to have him released from prison, "Let me deal with this dog, madam. Blacks are meant to be turned into manure. I'm going to kill the swine."[7] On another occasion the captain, responding in anger to a woman member of his family, uses the proverb that manages to be at the same time both racist and antifeminist, a typical reflection of the agrarian mentality: *Negro e mulher não têm que se meter.* (Blacks and women should not interfere.)[8]

Vitorino is a picturesque character who really existed. José Lins do Rego describes him for us in his book of memories, *Meus verdes anos.*

> He introduced himself as a Carneiro da Cunha from Paraíba, and was proud of the fact that he was white. Nevertheless he had married a woman of mixed blood who treated him very badly, as though he was a little boy. He showed a real horror with regard to Blacks. And the *negro* named Mendonça, who had been raised by the Maçanganas, suffered terribly at his hands. When he arrived at the *engenho* and found Mendonça sitting there, no one could convince him to stay. And he would shout, "The only *negro* I accept is Saint Benedict, and that is because he is in heaven."[9]

The business of the Black sitting at the table is a constant source of irritation for Capitão Vitorino; in all the families where a colored person joins them at the table, they know that it is best not to invite Vitorino if they want to avoid a nasty scene.

In *Fogo morto* the part that interests us the most is that regarding the history of the engenho Santa Fé. The story of this engenho is linked to the figure of its founder, Capitão Tomás Cabral de Melo, a man who arrived one day with his slaves and simply had begun to work the land. In the beginning his figure and behavior had aroused scandal simply because Capitão Tomás personally worked his land and took his produce to market together with his slaves, and this was something which in the rural Northeast, where a certain sort of life had crystallized into feudal habits over a period of three centuries, aroused disapproval and amazement. Capitão Tomás is defined as a *camumbembe*, a poor wretch, and rumors begin to circulate concerning his greed and his particularly cruel behavior towards his Black workers. In reality he is a man who works hard in an attempt to forge for himself a place in that rural world composed of engenhos that had been working smoothly for many decades if not centuries.

His wife helps him by taking care of the slaves. This taking care of the slaves is an economic rather than humanitarian attitude. The *negro* is something that costs money and, if intended to produce, he must not be spoiled.

> Overall the slaves were good people. From Ingá she had brought back *negros* of good quality and well made. She had never bought cheap material, walking corpses who would only give problems in the future. She left *negros* of inferior quality sold at a lower price for those who were looking for bargains. What she wanted were people ready for work and *negras* who would produce more and more field hands to cultivate her land.[10]

As you can see, the conception that the good *fazendeiro* has of his slaves is that of the cattle breeder. Treat your animals well for them to give back the maximum service.

There is an episode that deserves quoting because it is indicative of a certain mentality, a certain absurd code of honor generated by slavery. By now Capitão Tomás has achieved his long-desired status of a rich fazendeiro. Santa Fé is an engenho that can even inspire envy among his neighbors. His daughter Amélia has received an excellent education and is about to marry her cousin Lula. But Tomás also has another daughter who has gone mad and is placed in an asylum in Recife. This misfortune has thrown the landowner into a state of frustration from which it seems he will never recover. And then it hap-

FEAST OF OUR LADY OF THE ROSARY, PATRONESS OF BLACKS

FESTA DE N. S. DO ROSÁRIO, PADROEIRA DOS NEGROS

pens that an eighteen-year-old moleque called Domingos escapes from the plantation. This event is like a blow in the face for Capitão Tomás, who is suddenly aroused from his state of apathy and rediscovers all his old energy. Although the escape of the Black slave may be little more than a minor economic blow, it is an offense against the moral order on which slavery is based. If the landowner cannot capture his slave it means that he is unworthy of respect. It means that tomorrow other slaves, too, might be tempted to take to flight in the hope of gaining their freedom. The hunt for the escaped slave is much more a question of honor than it is an economic problem. Capitão Tomás sets off in pursuit, encountering many difficulties on the way. He quarrels with people, he turns for help to his powerful neighbors and finally gets what he wants: the return of the runaway slave. Domingos is punished with the inevitable whiplashing, but for Tomás this represents more of an attempt to reestablish order, which Domingos's flight has damaged, rather than a mere vendetta. Another Black administers the punishments (one of the most atrocious characteristics of slavery is that of forcing other victims of the moral rectitude of the institution to participate in the punishment and help the master against those slaves who transgressed), and in vain Amélia and the victim's mother intercede with Capitão Tomás. The latter seems changed. He seems to have recovered his old strength and energy.

> Capitão Tomás Cabral de Melo was no longer a man saddened by the sickness of his daughter Olívia. The screams of Domingos did not grate on his ears and caused no pain in his heart.
>
> "He will never think of running away again. Amélia, play that sad music that I like so much."
>
> The daughter sat down at the piano. The sunset over Santa Fé was full of sadness. The waltz filled the *casa grande*, and could be heard beyond the door. It spread over the green fields, it went to warm the empty *senzala* where the *moleques* play naked on the dirt floor. It drowned the screams of Domingos spread over the cart with his naked body bleeding under the rough leather of the whip that opened wounds on his back. Amélia's piano playing touched the heart of the old man. Suddenly he rose, went to the door and shouted, "Stop whipping him, Leopoldo."[11]

Fogo morto was written in 1943, and certainly Rego could not have been acquainted with the Nazi experiences of the concentration camps. But does not this scene recall those grotesque and macabre images of the little orchestras of prisoners who accompanied one of their comrades to the gallows, guilty maybe of some minor infraction against the order of the camp? History often repeats itself, and so does the cruelty of man against man, when it can be exercised with impunity in the name of some order or other.

A little later on in the novel Domingos escapes again, taking with him a couple of horses. This time, too, although he is now advanced in years and no longer enjoys the best of health, Capitão Tomás sets out to bring back the fugitive, who is headed toward the *sertão*. The land of the sertão is not fertile like the great plains; there are no big estates there and thus one rarely encounters slaves. The people are poor but free, used to wide spaces and a violent and adventurous life. Capitão Tomás, accompanied by Lula, who in the meantime has become his son-in-law, and by two Blacks, has a verbal clash with a poor but proud inhabitant of the sertão, who, in effect, kicks him off his land, refusing to hand over the slave who probably has taken refuge with him. This is a terrible blow for Tomás. "The *capitão* could not sleep. How could any *senhor de engenho* sleep who had not had the courage to snatch a *negro* of his own from the hands of a horse thief?"[12] After a certain time Domingos is brought back to the plantation by a slave hunter, but this cannot rouse Tomás from the state of deep frustration into which he has fallen. The economic fact of the slave's return is secondary to that of the idea of the violation of the moral order which Tomás has not managed to reestablish.

> Everyone was worried by the state of mind of the *capitão*. After all, the story of Domingos was not a sufficient reason for a man to let himself go like that, living as it were a living death. The *capitão* lived savagely within himself, in his silences, refusing to speak with others. All he could think of was that he had been defeated, humiliated, that he was without honor, that he lacked the necessary strength to look after his affairs. He was a *senhor de engenho* who had lost all respect. One of his *negros* had run away, and he had gone after him as was his right, with reason on his side. And on this occasion he had been insulted by a vagabond of no name and status, the sort of fellow who went around with his shirt outside his breeches and who had come close to punching him. No, he would never in the future be able to raise his voice with any *negro*. He had seen his slave return, tied up. He had seen him whipped by the *capitão de mato*. But it was as though he had seen nothing. For him that *negro* continued to be a fugitive, but stronger now than he had ever been in the past. The *senhor de engenho* of Santa Fé had gone after a *negro* who had escaped and he had not had the strength required to bring him back to his own *senzala*. It was a great humiliation.[13]

What impresses us in the work of José Lins do Rego, apart from his great artistic capacity for bringing his characters and situations to life, is the complete absence of any critical judgment with regard to the institutions that govern the agricultural world of the Northeast. This is perfectly understandable in those that are purely autobiographical, such as *Menino de engenho,* in which a happy childhood on the plantation is revisited with the nostalgic eye of the adult. It is less understandable in *Fogo morto,* where the author comes to grips with the history of a world he has known indirectly through the tales of people he knew. It is probably very difficult to come down a step or two from the casa grande. In *Fogo morto* one has the clear impression that the events involving Blacks are purely functional with regard to the events in the lives of the whites. The flight of Domingos serves merely to explain the state of frustration into which Tomás has fallen. The blows he receives after his first escape have no other purpose than that of breaking the false equilibrium of his master. After his second escape, Domingos disappears as a character because his function ceases with the definitive crisis into which he has plunged his master. We only learn that Tomás's wife has sold Domingos to another fazendeiro, Major Ursulino, known for the cruelty of his treatment of slaves.

> This was the punishment he richly deserved. She had given him away for a hundred *mil-réis* and that was the price he had to pay for what he had done to Tomás. Then she had a moment's regret. God would punish her for that act of cruelty but at bottom she felt no remorse. The *negro* was hers, her property, she had sold him to be rid of the bad example he gave to those who worked with him.[14]

We observe two things here. The first is what we have already written concerning the purely functional value of the Black vis-à-vis his master, emphasized by the words, "what he had done to Tomás." Now we know that Domingos had done nothing to anybody. All he had done was to cut his rope. Thus the consequences of his act had obviously nothing to do with him, but everything, it appears, to do with his master's health. All in all, the escape of Domingos seen through the lens of José Lins do Rego is about as interesting as a fall from a horse. A somewhat restive horse, to be sure, that is then sold so as to cause no more harm. The second thing to be noted is that quick reference to the cruelty of Major Ursulino; because from the slave owner's point of view, which is also the point of view of the novel, the beating to the rhythms of the waltz that had torn Domingos's back to shreds is no indication of cruelty. This is quite logical if you admit the justice of a system, whatever it may be. If you admit that the social system is a reflection of a moral order of things, every violation of the system is a violation of the order and must therefore be punished as a crime, as a sin. In short, Tomás, in having his Black slave whipped, is not avenging himself; he is doing no more than applying the law. Certainly it comes as no surprise that this was the way of thinking of slave owners. What does raise many eyebrows, however, is that when Rego published *Fogo morto* (in 1943), he wrote the novel strictly from the point of view of the owner, without ever apparently having been touched by doubt that if the flight of a Black slave and a fall from a horse can be considered equal in their consequences they are completely different when it comes to the moral evaluation of those involved. As we have said it is difficult to come down from the casa grande and free oneself completely from the brand that slavery leaves on masters and slaves alike.

In the moral code of slavery, to whip a Black is a cruel act when exercised for no reason, without, in short, there being a real wrong or infraction to punish, or when exercised as a sadistic pleasure. Slavery was above all the eruption of the worst in human nature, free nonetheless to manifest itself in dealings with others without fear of reaction, while remaining well within the broad margin of legality that the owners had allowed themselves. In *Fogo morto*, as in the other books of the sugarcane cycle, there are various references to Major Ursulino, a fazendeiro notorious for his open and undisguised cruelty towards his slaves out of pure personal pleasure. The other landowners made use of him as a bugaboo: the threat of selling slaves to his fazenda is the worst that you can deliver to them. It serves to keep order and to maintain the hypocritical face of the benevolence of the other fazendeiros, who thus washed their hands of all moral responsibility. Even if they know that to sell a man to Ursulino corresponds to a lifetime condemnation to perpetual torture, it is not they who wield the rod.

The problem of cruelty appears openly in *Fogo morto* in the figure of Lula, Tomás's son-in-law. Lula is the character who goes from bad to worse as a result of his contact with his new responsibilities as a master. At the beginning he is presented to us rather as a man about town devoted to reading newspapers, strolling around the fazenda with the air of the spectator without taking any initiative. The attitude is worrisome to his father-in-law and astounds the Black workers.

> The *negros* were amazed to see that gentleman with his distant looks, clothed like a city gentleman, never without his cravat, looking at things as though he was simply paying a visit. The *capitão* was not satisfied by his son-in-law's way of life. The *negros* needed a master with open eyes and hard of hand. His son-in-law seemed to him too weak and soft.[15]

Then bit by bit Lula begins to show his true colors and it is he with all his good manners who begins to hand out punishment right and left without any pretext. It is no longer, as the case of Domingos, a question of punishing those who have disturbed the order of life on the plantation. Now the punishments rain down on men who have been model workers. It is nothing more than pure sadism, something all too frequent in the world of slavery. Apparently Lula's mother-in-law is forced to admit the truth. Her son-in-law is a sadist.

> She began to see him as a pitiless man without a soul. The Black woman, Germana, had told her through her tears, "*Sinhá*, Chiquinho has done nothing. *Senhor* Lula likes to beat us Black people, *Sinhá*."
> Those words of the *negra* made an impression on her. To get pleasure from beating Blacks! She knew some people could behave like that without remorse or pity. The daughter of old João Alves always had a new *negra* to torment, her body was always covered in bruises, signs of whiplashes, the marks of blows and slaps. It was no less than killing a living creature.[16]

The practice of indiscriminate violence becomes a habit when Lula becomes the single master of the engenho. A Black named Deodato is appointed steward with the responsibility of punishing the Blacks whenever he feels like it. At the same time Lula is afflicted by two twin manias: that of going to church every Sunday with his family in an elegant coach; the second is to force his Black workers to pray together every day. "The Blacks could no longer pray to their saints Cosme and Damião. That was *feitiçaria*."[17] So Santa Fé acquires a sinister, demoniac reputation. When abolition comes, naturally all the Blacks go away. The first to buy his way out is the steward Deodato. He, too, is an ex-slave who has to stay one step ahead of the others to avoid the wrath of his fellow Blacks. There is one final touch of hypocrisy. The local police chief has given the order for the recapture of the Black Deodato, as though he were responsible for the punishments he administered in the name of his master. Naturally no one dreams of incriminating Coronel Lula himself. Certain forms of complicity remain unchanged. Santa Fé, abandoned by its slaves, in solitude and madness slips into its inevitable decline.

Menino de engenho is the first of the novels of the sugarcane cycle. A clearly autobiographical work, its action is limited to the engenho of Santa Rosa close to Santa Fé, and the author uses the device of telling the tale in the first person singular, thus recreating the world of childhood through the attentive and enchanted eyes of the child who comes from the city to the countryside. Naturally this is a novel in which observation is more important than judgment. Assuming the role of the child, the author limits himself to reporting and describing rather than judgment. And yet if you pay close attention you can see how the author expresses many opinions, not as a child but based on adult experience, whether he deals with his personal situation or weeps for himself and laments the misfortunes that befell him as a result of life on the engenho. Yet he maintains a rigid silence, falsely coated in enchantment and innocence, when he must express a judgment on persons and events that have a bearing on the life of the engenho and its patriarchal structure. It is perfectly understandable that he does not want to pass judgment on relatives and friends as they were in reality. We have noted the same characteristic in other authors who have also dealt with the problem of slavery much more openly and directly than Rego and who found themselves embarrassed when they were obliged to speak, and speak badly, of acquaintances and members of their families.

In *Menino de engenho* there are no precise references to the period in which the action takes place. But we can easily date the story to the years immediately preceding World War I. Slavery had been abolished several decades earlier, at least from the official point of view; but we know very little had changed in the rural Northeast. The land had remained in the hands of the large fazendeiros; there had been no serious progress in agrarian reform. One advantage for the Blacks was that they could refuse to work for people like Lula or Ursulino. For the rest the situation had deteriorated, for the Black no longer belonged to his master, no longer represented invested capital to be preserved. What counted now was only his muscular strength in a world where the labor market was overcrowded. In this sense old José Paulino is quite right when he says that abolition was of no use for all the poor people while it gave greater wealth and opportunity to the rich landowners:

> For poor people, abolition was useless. Today they live on dry flour, hiring themselves out by the day. What they earn isn't even enough to buy dried cod. My Blacks used to fill their stomachs with polenta and dry meat. They never went around naked as they do today, with parts of their bodies showing. I started to make money with sugar only after abolition. Everything my money earned carlier went to buy and clothe my Black workers.[18]

One thing that José Paulino can boast about with pride is that abolition changed nothing on his land. The day after the thirteenth of May, after the great festivities that had lasted all night long, the Blacks on the Santa Rosa engenho reported to work as before and not one of them left the estate.

There are in the novel several defenses of slavery, some in purely sentimental terms. Others are presented in a more logical manner, albeit a logic strictly linked to the narrow point of view of the slave owner, which in the long run can be tranformed into a precise accusation. For example, José Paulino denies that the majority of the fazendeiros were cruel to their slaves:

> The *negros* always had their bellies full. Of course, there were cases when someone might need a taste of leather, newspapers at the time of abolition spoke of landowners who killed their slaves with blows from clubs, but no one today kills an ox with a whipping. You needed a well-fed *negro* for work and to be able to sell him in the future.[19]

It is a type of defense that never goes beyond the blind vision of the slave owner: Blacks as oxen equal capital invested in work for profit at the moment of resale. Will we ever come across a moment of doubt regarding the basic difference between a man with dark skin and an animal?

The candid confessions of Carlos de Melo faced with the wretched spectacle of the tenant farmers who go to work free on the plantation to pay for the right to cultivate their lots is an example of this mentality of the landowner:

> The habit of seeing these people every day in their poverty had made me used to their distress, but when I was a child I found it quite natural that they should live sleeping in a pigsty eating hardly anything, working like beasts of burden. My understanding of their life made me see in all this the hand of God. They have been born thus, because God willed it so. Because God had willed that we should be white and give them orders. We also commanded the oxen, the asses, and the woods.[20]

The major defense of slavery undoubtedly comes in childhood memories of Carlos de Melo from the time he spent on the great plantation where abolition had not in practice changed the ancient order of existence:

> The *senzala* from the times of slavery still remained: about twenty rooms with a sort of roof linking them together with an overhang in front. My grandfather's *negras* even after abolition all stayed in the *engenho*, they didn't leave ''the road'' as they called the *senzala* and they stayed there until they died of old age. I knew four: Maria Gorda, Generosa, Galdina, and Romana. My grandfather continued to feed and clothe them and they continued to work free for him with the same light-heartedness they had known as slaves. Their daughters and granddaughters continued in service with the same love of the *casa grande*, and the same docility of domestic animals.[21]

There are words included in this text that give the passage its authentic tone. The wretchedness of those human creatures condemned to a perpetual form of servitude is presented as the "light-heartedness of slavery," their somnolent victimization or debasement as the "docility of domestic animals." (We have already had cause to note many times that it is always the animal that is used as a term of comparison for these slaves.) The life of the senzala was also degrading from the moral point of view. Accustomed to being treated like animals, to living as their owners' chattels, these women were offered no other satisfaction than the sexual from this sort of life. Hence the facile accusation of immorality and lust cast at Black women. Let us see what enviable lives they lived:

> I never met the husband of any of them and yet they always had a swollen belly, perpetuating the species without taking precautions, without fear. The *moleques* slept in stinking hammocks, the whole room stank horribly like a urinal. Each morning the floor was damp from the night's urine.[22]

These Black women retain a certain moral purity in their language, refusing to speak of certain things in front of the children. When they receive their men, however, they do so in the same room in which they sleep with their children. Where else could they possibly go? And each year they produce a child, "having inherited from their slave mothers this fertility of a bountiful breeding stock."[23] And this paradise continues to perpetuate itself: "The *senzala* of Santa Rosa did not disappear with abolition; it continued, attached to the *casa grande*, with its Black women who gave birth, its good wet-nurses, and the good Black workers in the field."[24]

Independent of the general picture, which turns out to be much darker than the author had intended, Rego has left us some marvelous pages that describe the life of these people and the sincerely affectionate relationships forged between masters and servants, above all between the old women and the children they nursed. For Carlos de Melo, who was not raised on the engenho, there is his mother's old nurse, Tia Generosa, who takes the place of his grandmother, showing him all sorts of little kindnesses and protecting him whenever he gets into trouble.

There are descriptions of old Black women that provide pages that serve as an authentic and a definitive anthology of the Black condition. There is old Totonha, the story teller who goes from engenho to engenho telling fairy tales to the children, fantastic tales in which medieval tradition is mixed with characters from local folklore and events from the Gospels. There is the old Galdina, who was Coronel José Paulino's nurse and was treated with respect by everyone. Her story begins in Africa where one of her brothers had sold her to the slave merchants who had branded her face with a red-hot iron. Then came the long sea voyage: "She was already getting used to that life aboard ship. The sailing boat sped ahead as fast as a steamship. Then one day they touched land. It was a long time before anyone wanted to buy her. The men who came wanted above all big people, girls already grown up."[25] African words mixed with Portuguese make the story of her tragedy, now dimmed in memory and assuming the colors of a fantastic adventure, even more fascinating. Galdina is more or less everybody's grandma; to her nobody can say no: "When they wanted to grab one of us to beat, we always ran to her. She would intercede for her grandchildren with her eyes full of tears."[26]

Granny Galdina, *vovó* Galdina as she was called, was the most important of the Black women and the author remembers her again in *Doidinho*, the second novel of the series, on the occasion of her death.

> *Vovó* Galdina, the good *negra* from the African Coast, was buried in the cemetery of São Miguel. She was more than one hundred years old. And when there were visitors to the *engenho*, they were always taken to see how old she was. She looked at everybody with her gentle toothless smile, delving into her memory and coming up with replies for every question. She sewed without glasses, she dragged herself around on crutches, but all the tenderness and goodness of her race could be seen in that hundred-year-old slave heart. Her long soft lips seemed as though they were about to fall off when she spoke. She would spend the whole day there. The other inhabitants asked for her blessing. The *negra* Generosa called her Auntie Galdina and she was the only one for whom she used that title. She would weep at everything and they used to make a joke of her tears.
>
> "Shall we go and make granny weep?"
>
> "Let's go."
>
> And one of us would approach her pretending to be hurt, twisting his face in pain.
>
> "What is it, what is it, my son?" Her eyes watered in tears of goodness and compassion.
>
> Sometimes she would stay in her little room with her old woman's ailments; the *moleques* would make a paste of herbs for her rusty joints. For years and years she had dragged herself around like this. She'd known grandfather as a child:
>
> "*Ioiôzinho*, I carried him around on my shoulders."
>
> "I carried him around on my shoulders" is an expression an animal would use, worthy of a beast of burden.[27]

Even in those moments when memory is most charged with emotion, José Lins do Rego allows himself certain comparisons with the animal world in talking of Blacks. This must be an example of the duration of the *senhor-de-engenho* complex which remains unsublimated even by a change in historical circumstances and fortuitous events.

Also in *Menino de engenho* there is the Black Generosa, another classic female figure, the one who is in charge in the kitchen and the woman most naturally assailed by requests, above all from the children, requests that she is always ready to grant, as she is always ready to retort to any criticism or attacks on her authority. In the latter case we see her coming out of the kitchen with four stones in her hand, and shouting that the time of slavery was over.

And then there is the sinister character who is simply a Black woman like vovó Galdina, an old African who has refused to be assimilated, who has remained closed in her proud solitude, who has not yielded to the flatteries of the senzala, or to the advantages and the rewards conceded to those who serve readily and to those above all who have tried to forget the outrage they have suffered. With her the author uses no terms like auntie, or granny, with which in general he indicates those Black women who have created an affectionate relationship with their masters. Maria Gorda, as she is called, is herself and that is enough; she does not need any qualifying adjectives.

> You couldn't go into Maria Gorda's room. We had never managed to get close to that old African woman. She could not speak, she babbled a language of her own, and when it was time for lunch or dinner she would come out of her lair and, leaning on a stick, would come and get her food. She shouted at the *moleques* and the other *negras* with her protruding lips and soft, pendulous breasts. She came from Mozambique, and after more than eighty years in Brazil, she spoke a mixture of her own tongue and I don't know what else. I was afraid of this old woman. She was just like a wicked fairy from one of the stories of Sinhá Totonha. Her room stank of rotting flesh. On the night of São João only her door had no fire in front of it. The devil danced with her all night long. I myself thought there was something devilish about her, because I never managed to hear anything human from her, nothing like what one saw and heard from the others. In the *senzala* all were afraid of Maria Gorda. In the afternoons she would sit on a crate outside her door, smoking a long-stemmed pipe; but she always sat alone, muttering who knows what.[28]

We have come across many characters like Maria Gorda, and we have noted that the way the author describes her follows the conditioned reflexes of fellow writers. This is especially noteworthy in a novel like *Menino de engenho*, which is a nostalgic symphony on the theme of the golden age of the past and attempts to stand as a sentimental transcendence of the black-white, master-slave dualism. Such a transcendence is, of course, based on the premise that everyone stays in his place, while the crueler aspects of this division and permanent injustice are obliterated, wiped out by the shared experience of life. In this novel, then, a figure like Maria Gorda represents bad conscience, for she is a living reminder of violence suffered under slavery. The other Black women have become adoptive grannies or aunties, having, albeit out of force of circumstances, accepted the compromise; they have enthusiastically contributed to the creation of a common link with the world of the masters. A slave like vovó Galdina is a permanent alibi for the bad conscience of the owners. They all treat her well, she is a part of the family; she once broke a leg playing blind man's buff with the children. Even her long voyage on the slave ship (and we know what a disaster those journeys were) is made to seem like a holiday cruise, with children scampering about on deck, with never a mention of the stink of hundreds of bodies packed into the hold, nor of the dead, nor of the stench of excrement, nor of the despair and madness. It seems as though they did her a favor to take her away from that barbarous land where brothers sell their little sisters and bring her to live at Santa Rosa where everyone treats her well and shows her affection. With Maria Gorda it is different. She has remained a slave because there was no way out, because she was forced to be. But her soul is still free; she has even rejected her masters' language, shutting herself off from any possible contact with them. She continues to speak her own tongue, to mull over her own thoughts, not to light ritual fires on São João's night so as not to worship the saint of her masters, those who have enslaved her. For this José Lins do Rego says that she danced with the devil the whole night through; but it was not the devil with whom she was dancing. It was perhaps the ghost of her lost freedom, or, for her white masters, it might have been the specter of a crime of which they were all more or less guilty.

Obviously slavery does not exist on the engenho of Santa Rosa, as it does not exist in Brazil, having been abolished at least two decades before the events in this novel begin. And yet the engenho maintains its medieval structure with its feudal overlord in the person of Coronel José Paulino reigning supreme and administering justice and discipline over all his subjects. Compared with other senhores de engenho, Coronel José Paulino could be considered a calm and moderate man. The author recalls how his admiration as a child was drawn instead to other coronéis, violent men not above breaking down a prison door to release anyone under their protection, and who, at election time, did not hesitate to attack election headquarters or burn ballot boxes to install their chosen candidates at gun point. It was common custom for these large landowners to protect criminals seeking asylum; a practice that clearly revealed the sort of justice that prevailed in the Northeast, since the criminal who enjoyed the coronel's protection was more or less safe from the police. In *Menino de engenho* there is, in fact, an episode in which a man on the run for murder comes to ask for protection from José Paulino, who, instead, tells him to give himself up.

Another episode illustrates how justice is administered on the estate. A Black man is put in a sort of stocks, with his feet locked into two wooden rings, on the orders of the coronel. This man (actually here the author uses the insulting term *cabra*) is accused of having seduced a mulatto girl, and must stay in the stocks until he decides to make up for the wrong done by marrying the girl. The man has a bad name, and no one, Black or white, believes in his innocence with the exception of Carlos. The poor wretch spends more than twenty-four hours in that painful position, until the too-narrow holes stop the circulation of the blood, leaving his limbs numb. And yet he refuses to marry the girl, insisting it was not he who made her pregnant. Finally the coronel forces the girl to confess, and she admits that she was seduced by the coronel's son, Doctor Juca. The coronel simply gives the order for the innocent victim to be released. The latter can barely walk on account of his swollen limbs, and can only mutter with regard to his master's son, "Now Doctor Juca can add another victim to his list."[29]

It is a very clear illustration of the prevailing logic of the engenhos of the Northeast. The girl could hope for no form of compensation from Juca, and when we talk of compensation we are not talking of marriage but something much more basic: the admission of the fact of paternity, and financial help. Three centuries of slavery had created two categories of human beings, with different laws, and each with a different moral code. Even after the abolition of slavery, the mulatto woman had no practical chance of forcing Juca to marry her or even acknowledging his child; and this was not because José Paulino had any doubts as to his son's responsibility. Quite simply the question never arises because of the class difference, an ancient habit whereby the frequent sexual contact between whites and Blacks went unrecognized. But by accusing a man of her own rank—who in addition already had a bad name—the girl might hope to repair the damage by marriage thanks to the intervention of the coronel himself, who does no more than scold his son for the embarrassment he has caused in front of all the workers on the plantation. And naturally, in the name of that solidarity between relatives and masters, the cabra who has been so unjustly punished does not even have the right to an apology. Furthermore Carlos de Melo knew that his Uncle Juca had lovers among the mulattas and Black women of the senzala. The boy had even seen him in one of these encounters. And old José Paulino was very understanding in the case of such peccadilloes, even when his grandson contracts a venereal infection when he is little more than a child. Such an understanding could only come from a bad conscience:

> In these cases the old man raised his eyes to Heaven. His life, too, had been full of such irregularities. When he had a row with his Uncle Juca over the mulatta Maria Pia, I heard the *negra* Generosa in the kitchen: "Who's talking! When he was younger he was like a stallion with all the *negras*. Master Juca gets it from him."[30]

The tolerance white men show each other for these escapades is matched by the disapproval they reserve for the white who dares marry a woman of color. In *Doidinho* there is the following episode:

> I knew who this particular *senhor de engenho* was. He was a relative of mine. At Santa Rosa I had often heard of this relative who had married a mulatto woman with whom he was living. There, inside the church, I found that my cousin was a man of respect, a man of parts. Why live in sin? What a sacrifice, to give up his proud position as a *senhor de engenho* for this contact with the poor on his plantation! It seemed an extraordinary thing to me. The virtuous rich man who took into his matrimonial bed the *negrinha* who washed his feet.[31]

For centuries the white gentry had had children from their female slaves, giving rise to the multiracial population of Brazil. But they had rarely recognized their progeny. The theme of paternity in this part of Brazil, and throughout the rural areas, is very problematical thanks to a combination of different factors. First, there is the clear determination of the masters to exercise their absolute right over their female slaves, without assuming any responsibility. Second, the very culture of many African ethnic groups was matriarchal, linked to the mother and the idea of the extended family, the tribe, rather than to the figure of the father. Third, there was the endemic immorality and promiscuity of the senzala and the world of slavery. In *Menino de engenho* we have already seen that the women produced a child a year, always from different fathers. In *Moleque Ricardo* the hero has a mother and several brothers, but we never know who his father is, nor who fathered his numerous brothers. In *Doidinho* there is an observation on the amatory activities of the men of the family.

> The catechism told you to hold on to your chastity. My people regarded this injunction with nothing but derision. For example, there was Uncle Juca, a good man who treated his workers well, who worked from morning till night, and always had a bottle of quinine in his room for anyone who fell sick. And yet he was always spending time with those light-hearted girls at Pilar, in Santa Rosa, and reading dirty books. And not only that, he was always urging me to make love.—"You ought to go outside for a little stroll."—Old José Paulino must have been like him. Wasn't *seu* Fausto the mechanic a son of his? I had heard the tale of Beiçuda, a real Pompadour of São Miguel. Once on the saint's day this mulatta turned up in church with a hat on. Right away they went and told Aunt Nenen. It was a real act of impudence from that *cabra*. And when she left after mass, a couple of slaves dragged the hat off her head at the church door and tore her fancy dress to shreds.[32]

Here is the whole philosophy of the patriarchal world of the engenhos: as long as the mulatto woman keeps her place, her mistress pretends not to see or hear; but when she dares get dressed up as a lady and go to mass, this is an affront requiring immediate punishment. In *Bangüê* the author describes the attitude of an aunt who is rather disapproving with regard to the sexual escapades of her sons.

> Good as she was, she was also very proud. Whenever she got wind of her son going around with one of the girls of the place, she put the fear up everyone. They said that once a woman came to the house with a child in her arms to ask for her blessing. It was some bastard nephew. She kicked her out, sending her on her way with a series of unprintable insults. And yet she raised the natural child of one of her relations, the *moleque* Arnaldo. She had even seen to his education. The *negro* called her his white mama, and he ate at the table along with the other children.[33]

The protagonist of *Bangüê* is still Carlos de Melo, who has two sons from one of the many Black women on the engenho; and he, too, makes no attempt, save at the end, to acknowledge his responsibility as a father; thus his children are always dirty, sickly, and dressed in rags, just like all the other kids of the senzala.

The lack of the feeling of paternity can be seen as a point of arrival or departure, depending on one's point of view, rather like the problem of the chicken or the egg. Slavery, willed by the white master race, led to the moral depravity of the senzala. Black and mulatto women initiate the young white master into erotic activities at an early age, in which he will continue to indulge throughout adulthood and into old age with every woman of color who comes within his range. If José Lins do Rego refrains from passing judgment on situations that have no direct bearing on himself, he always has time nonetheless to shed a tear for himself. The phrase with which the novel closes, *menino perdido, menino de engenho*, summarizes his point of view, and he has the constant tendency to blame Black women: it was they who seduced him, it was they who sullied his innocence. And yet his innocence was lost the day he arrived on the engenho, when he had seen one of his cousins having a sexual experience with a tranquil cow (the author takes pains to emphasize that the cow was of a tranquil disposition). Carlos de Melo also has similar experiences, but for him the moment of truth comes with the mulatto girl, Luísa, who should have been his nurse. It is she whom Carlos de Melo singles out as being guilty of his downfall, without even a momentary hint at the responsibility of his relatives who, out of all the available Black women, went and chose this young and pretty mulatto girl to look after their nephew who was barely twelve years old.

> She was a sort of dark angel of my childhood. It was she who put me to bed, and when we were alone in the room, she forced me to do all sorts of ignoble things. In my days of innocence that *moleca* dragged me down into the depths of sensuality as you might expect from a mulatta burning with desire. I can't even tell you what she did with me. She took me down to the river to bathe, sullying my childish purity in her bestial excitement.[34]

Naturally he could not leave out the reference to the animal world, a constant leitmotif when Rego writes about Blacks. All told, it may be less serious than it seems, since it must derive from one of those conditioned reflexes embedded in his psyche as a result of the education (or noneducation) received in that patriarchal world from which he never escapes. The author returns to this episode in his autobiography, *Meus verdes anos*; except that this time he does not limit himself to the hypocritical phrase, "I can't even tell you what she did with me." Here he knows exactly, and gives us a full description rich in spicy details.

On the Santa Rosa engenho there was an official prostitute, Zefa Cajá, and Carlos goes with her many times, finally catching a venereal infection from her. Naturally the author resorts to his usual comparisons to describe his encounters with Zefa Cajá. "She caressed me with the amorous voracity of an animal."[35] And yet the venereal infection that Carlos picks up actually becomes a badge of virility and a source of pride which he can flaunt in front of the adults who respond with jocular comments, considering him now a man, and admitting him to their circle when they talk "about certain things." This gives you an idea of the moral level of this sort of world. Gilberto Freyre tells us that on the northeastern engenhos during slavery it was devoutly believed that the best cure for syphilis was to deflower a young Black virgin. Naturally no thought was given to the fact that such a cure—reserved, of course, exclusively for whites—had to be one of the major causes of the spread of the disease.

Also in *Doidinho* the adolescent Carlos finds a Black girl, Paula, who seduces him while he is bathing; and the comment he makes is the same:

> The *negra* was possessed. Once, twice, three times she swept me out of this world in the ardor of her animal vigor. Then I began to wonder what God might think of all my sins. Luísa, Zefa Cajá, Black Paula, the devil gave all three of you a power I could not resist.[36]

José Lins do Rego was morbid and hypersensitive by nature. Unable to resist sensual temptation, he had a constant need to cast the blame on somebody else, and desperately required a god or a devil to allow him more easily to indulge in breast-beating.

This tendency towards self-pity continues in *Bangüê*, by which time Carlos de Melo is an adult and seems to be a responsible human being. Here he has a liaison with a Black woman, Maria Chica, who gives him two sons, or at least he believes one of the two is his. He gives no thought to his responsibilities as a father, save at the very end, when he must now abandon the engenho in defeat, and in a moment of repentance would like to acknowledge his son and take him with him. But this time the Black woman refuses to let him do it and runs away, taking the child with her. Carlos de Melo finds himself alone again, lamenting his fate of being eternally seduced and abandoned.

He is seduced and abandoned by white women, too. In *Menino de engenho* Carlos has an innocent idyll with a young cousin who on the day she leaves seems hardly to notice him. In *Doidinho* he has a brief affair with a female classmate who then leaves him for another. In *Bangüê*, however, he has a long and painful affair with the pretty young wife of a cousin, who is spending a period of convalescence at Santa Rosa; but even she, after having profoundly disturbed him both sexually and intellectually, offering him a different point of view of the patriarchal world, leaves him with no regret, and without a scene, to return to her husband. Then in *Pureza* (*Purity*), one of his minor works, the protagonist who, like Carlos, tells his own story, manages to get himself seduced and then abandoned by the stationmaster's two pretty daughters.

It almost seems that the slow ruin of the world of the engenhos is physically reflected in the declining fortunes of the protagonist, wrapped as they are in an atmosphere of doom that grows thicker each day—like a cloud hanging menacingly over the patriarchal world of the rural Northeast.

This continual obsession with his own sickness, with a physical malaise that blocks all initiative and aspiration, prevents the author-protagonist from seeing the authentic human tragedy around him (we know that Rego was morbidly obsessed by the idea of physical debility). To be precise, we should say that Rego describes in some pages the daily dramas taking place in front of him. He does so, however, without any of the emotional involvement he allows himself when he talks of his own ailments, loves, or those dear to him. It is true that something you see on a daily basis becomes routine and no longer stimulates a reaction; but it is equally true that for Rego this routine became a moral routine. That is to say, it passed from the simple description of the event to the acceptance of that event as a fixed component of a set of standards which, once socially accepted, become automatically just. What surprises one in Rego is not only the absence of a moral category in his description of the life of the people in the senzala, but the lazy, somnolent manner in which he equates this same moral category with the landowners' hypocritical set of ethical norms, which had fixed the system of slavery over the centuries. Possibly this attitude was valid in the literary fiction of *Menino de engenho* or *Doidinho*, where the narration of events is entrusted to Carlos de Melo as a child (who nevertheless assumes the role of adult and critic when commenting on matters of direct concern to him). It is, however, unacceptable in other novels.

If you look at the description of prostitution among the women of the engenho in *Bangüê*, you immediately notice the detached tone of the journalist adopted by the author:

> Now I was going with a very young mulatto girl who had escaped the clutches of the *Sinhozinho* of Santo Antônio. She had told me her story. Her mother and father took little interest in her. They worked in the fields, and she stayed home with the children. The *senhor de engenho* came by her door every day, and paused to talk a while from the top of his horse. One day he fetched her a blow with his whip across her chest. She ran inside. The children had gone down to the river for water. He forced the door. There was no one she could call, and she had no strength to resist him. And what happened, happened.

> She told her father what had happened. Her mother began to scream. Could she expect anything else? She didn't like the *capitão Sinhozinho*, but he was interested in her because he came every day. She got pregnant, but the child died. On one occasion a nasty looking brute turned up and began to beat her. She was well and truly whipped. She began to scream, but her house was in the middle of nowhere. No one heard her shouts. Later she learned it was her *senhor de engenho*'s wife who had sent him.[37]

This is an all-too-familiar situation in the history of the engenhos: the girl from the senzala who cannot say no to her master, at the same time risking reprisal from his wife. These reprisals could amount to something much more than just a flogging. The history of slavery is full of terrible vendettas by landowners' wives who were maddened by jealousy.

And Carlos de Melo takes up with this girl who has sought refuge on his engenho from the wrath of her former mistress:

> We met on the bank of the Água Torta. The cold water of the river helped us. I came out with my knees weak beneath me.
>
> Her name was Adelaide, and I left her before her belly began to swell like Maria Chica's. The young gentlemen were working day and night.
>
> It was very rare to find men of such high moral standards as Uncle Lorenzo. The majority were quite the reverse, exchanging their wives' beds with a mattress for the reed cots of the girls for hire. Beatings followed with regularity, but they had the consolation of being left pregnant by their masters.[38]

The fate of these wretched victims, destined for the lower depths of the world of prostitution, is for the author a mere moment in the life of the estate, fated to be repeated, without anything intervening to change it. The very parents of the women accept the situation as ineluctable, a fixed part of the slave universe, even, as in this case, thirty years after the abolition of slavery:

> Her parents did not blame her for this. They were only unforgiving when their daughters came home empty handed or riddled with disease. But if they came home well dressed with presents for their mother and father, they found the door wide open and a welcome on the mat. Prostitution was even a sign of progress in these parts.[39]

Slavery must have left a deep mark on José Lins do Rego if he can describe a historical situation that we must imagine set in the thirties (*Bangüê* dates from 1934) not only in these terms but without any critical comment whatsoever.

Violence exercised daily on the weak is a part of the routine of the engenho. When Carlos arrives at Santa Rosa, his new playmates show him a picture of a mulatto girl with a mutilated face; the poor creature had been disfigured by her mistress who in a fit of jealousy had had her branded with a red-hot pitchfork. On the same engenho Carlos meets the terrible Aunt Sinhazinha, who is a sort of official torturess, particularly of young children. She raised a little Black girl precisely for this purpose, who slept at the foot of her bed for her to torment whenever the mood took her. The character of Sinhazinha returns with greater violence in *Bangüê*, where Carlos de Melo, now twenty-four years old, tries in vain to save a poor little Black girl from the clutches of that same old crone who used to beat her every day. What is interesting is not so much the character of the old woman, who may well have been completely mad, but the complete lack of reaction, save the partly hysterical one of Carlos, from the others, especially the old coronel José Paulino who had the power to stop the torture, but simply says to his grandson, "Don't get upset over Sinhazinha. It's been going on every day now for over fifty years."[40] Now José Paulino has always been presented to us as a good and just man. Obviously, living around violence makes you believe that blows and whippings distributed over half a century to generations of defenseless little girls are nothing more than a negligible detail, the innocent eccentricity of a dotty old lady.

In *Meus verdes anos*, written in 1956, Rego seems to take a more decisive attitude when he relates an incident similar to that of Sinhazinha. This time the aunt is called Naninha, with whom the author lived for a period of time as a child. Aunt Naninha kept a girl in the house called Virgínia, an orphan, and seemingly subnormal, or made stupid by the frequent and severe beatings she received from her mistress. The violent outbursts of Aunt Naninha were well known throughout the village (while the girl wept, but "wept like an animal, passively, without showing any sign of rebellion"); so one day her husband was obliged to tell her:

> "Naninha, they've come and had a word with me. The fact is that the judge wants to step in and take care of our orphan Virgínia."
>
> I remember the furious look on my aunt's face. All the pride of the slave owner bubbled to the surface in her voice. "This Samuel in our midst should be ashamed of himself. I'll have a word with papa."
>
> Later I saw Aunt Naninha, her eyes red with tears. My uncle wanted to come to a decision to avoid any more gossip in the village. But it was not possible. Virgínia had no father or mother. She was alone. Her only solution was to accept the blows.[41]

This book of memoirs was published in 1956, and one can see an albeit moderately critical position with regard to that aunt who had just about beaten the poor little orphan into insensibility. The reactions of the other characters are interesting: on the one hand, the husband who is concerned not with the beating itself—a human creature brutalized by daily beatings—but rather by the talk it may provoke in the village; the wife on the other hand who feels deeply insulted by the judge who, by taking a mild defense of the unfortunate girl, has betrayed the laws of class loyalty that should link him to his fellow whites. Fortunately—if the word can be used—all is resolved because since the child is an orphan, all she can do is stay where she is and accept her daily thrashing.

In *Menino de engenho*, too, there are plenty of examples of cruelty against Blacks; and when we speak of cruelty, we are speaking of gratuitous cruelty. We do not refer to the violence of punishment inflicted in the name of the order of slavery which, for all it arouses our outrage, was the only order that existed in those parts. The champion of all kinds of cruelty was Major Ursulino, on whose estate the slaves received their first taste of the whip in the morning, before going to work, "at the door of the *senzala*, to warm them up a bit."[42] This sadist had built his sugar mill at the top of a hill so as to make his slaves work even harder, as they were obliged to carry the loads of boiling sugar paste on their heads, while their master enjoyed the spectacle from up above. The slaves detailed for cutting the cane had to work with chains on their feet. Naturally, when abolition came, Major Ursulino found himself without a single slave. There is an episode that deserves quoting in its entirety as an expression of the typical mentality formed by slavery:

> Once a negro from Picos came to the major's house wearing boots and a tie. He had come to speak to the *senhor de engenho*. He went upstairs, offering cigarettes all round. He had come to report some damage caused by some of the cattle on the *engenho* to the sugarcane on the Picos land. He was the steward on that estate, and his master had asked him to bring the message. The major, offended, didn't say a word. He gave orders for the *negro* to be bought from the other estate. But the *negro* was only part slave. Since he belonged to two people, as the result of a legacy, and been divided up along with all the other inherited goods, one of the two heirs had freed that part belonging to him. And so the major bought half the slave. And he brought the insolent cur to his own plantation, where he had him tied to the cart and lashed with a whip of rough leather, but only on the side that belonged to him.[43]

This is a typical slave story, original for the particulars of the half-slave, but quite common as an example of the mentality of the owner class. It was not enough for Blacks to be exploited as beasts of burden to the extreme limits of their physical strength. Nor was it enough for them to be severely punished whenever they transgressed some rule of the slave order. In addition they were to be humiliated whenever they attempted to rise, even in appearance only, to a higher social level, whenever they adopted the manners of complete human beings. So the wife in *Doidinho* has the dress torn from the back of her husband's mulatto mistress, not because she was his mistress, but because she dared to appear in church dressed as a lady. So Aunt Naninha in *Meus verdes anos* is enraged at the judge who had dared to intervene against her right as a slave owner to beat her little servant, because that little girl, before being a girl, a human being, was a thing, a mere possession of the mistress. And so Major Ursulino is offended because a slave appears before him dressed as a human being would dress, and not in rags, the established uniform of the slave.

The end of slavery does not abolish the mentality tied to slavery nor the infamous conventions it generated. Aunt Sinhazinha in *Menino de engenho* and Aunt Naninha in *Meus verdes anos* continue to work out their sadistic fury on all the under-age defenseless Black girls who fall into their clutches. And there is seemingly nothing that can change these good old family habits, because there are no social structures—judges, authorities, laws—that can (or will) step in and put a stop to them. And if such structures do not exist, it is because as yet a certain mentality has failed to emerge, that is, no civic conscience that might induce someone to change the grim order of things.

In *Fogo morto* we saw the episode that tells of the personal drama of Capitão Tomás who fails to capture his runaway slave and so feels like a defeated man, one who falls short in attempting to fulfill his most elementary duties. In *Pureza*, written in 1937, there is a similar story. The protagonist, another alter ego of the author, is a young man from the city who comes to spend a period of convalescence in the country village of Pureza, where he lives quietly with an old Black maid, Felismina, and a moleque called Luís. Felismina is the perfect model of the family slave, even though she is formally a free woman. Having always lived with her master, she continues to look after him even after abolition, which is quite normal. What is abnormal, however, is her indignant refusal of a salary her master tried to offer her, for this would have reduced her to the rank of an ordinary domestic servant; whereas she regarded herself as an integral part of the household, enjoying certain privileges, duties, and social status that this conferred on her in house and kitchen. She is very like the Black women on the engenho of Santa Rosa who continued in service even after slavery was done away with. The moleque Luís has another story: he is fourteen years old, with no parents, and has run away from a nearby engenho. He lives with the protagonist. He is afraid his old coronel might come looking for him, and for this reason he keeps out of sight. And, in fact, one day a man from that estate does turn up looking for the lad. That slavery is over means absolutely nothing. When the hero inquires whether the boy has any parents, or anyone who might act with parental authority, the coronel's man replies no, but adds: "It's as if he did have, dear sir. The boy was raised in the house. As a child he lived in the kitchen of the *engenho*. He belongs to the house."[44] Following the blunt refusal of the protagonist to accept that the boy be considered as a mere "house chattel," another local coronel, who happens to be on good terms with the main character, intervenes as a friendly intermediary. The summary of his viewpoint runs as follows: it is not worth fighting among gentlemen over something of such inherently little worth as a moleque, even though the latter does represent, by his escape, a challenge to the unalterable laws of those parts.

> None of this has the slightest importance. The lad is free, he has no father or mother, he can go wherever he pleases. But, you know, things are different around here. If the *cabras* learn that a *senhor de engenho* can't keep a stable boy in order, they'll soon start to champ at the bit, and soon there'll be nobody to obey you.[45]

Here what is even more apparent than in *Fogo morto* is that the economic question is of minor importance. In the first novel the Black Domingos had a value as a slave. In *Pureza* the moleque Luís has none whatsoever, and from what we understand cannot have been very useful. But what remains is the moral fact: the moleque has run away without asking his master's leave, and the outsider refuses to give him back in the name of a law operative in the metropolis but which carries no weight in the rural backwardness of the Northeast. The story ends with the flight of the boy, who cannot believe that an unarmed outsider with no men behind him can possibly defend him from the ire of the coronel. And we must once again note that when the author writes about Blacks, even of those he sees sympathetically, he lets slip certain comparisons with the animal world:

> Luís, sitting by the house door, kept his eyes down, as though after a beating. I was reminded of a faithful puppy when I saw the *negrinho* like

> that. Maybe it was an insulting comparison for human beings. But I cannot say why the position in which he sat had something purely animal about it—the humility of a guard dog. For *coronel* Zé Joaquim he was no more than this.[46]

Bangüê is the story of the end of the engenho. Carlos de Melo, by now grown up, has returned to Santa Rosa and wants to take his grandfather's place and revive the patriarchal style of the old days. But Carlos de Melo is not José Paulino, and times are not what they were. There are new interests abroad, and new men forging ahead. Near Santa Rosa there is a factory that meets the problem of sugarcane cultivation with large capital outlay and modern technology (one of Carlos's relatives, his Uncle Juca, already works for it). On the estate there is a tenant farmer, a Black called José Marreira, who has become so rich by dint of hard work that he threatens the future of Santa Rosa itself. Carlos de Melo tries to get rid of José Marreira, essentially for reasons of prestige, but he has not enough money to buy up the buildings his tenant has put up on his property. He tries every way he can to send him away, but José Marreira is allied with the men of the factory, and Carlos de Melo finally runs out of hope. It is Carlos who has to go, after selling the plantation that had always been in his family.

Bangüê is the story of a defeat told by the loser. The loser is a white man, Carlos de Melo. The winner is José Marreira, a Black. The loser is a descendant of slave owners. The winner is a son of slaves. These are the basic factors dividing the two characters, but the list could go on forever.

In *Bangüê* we see close up the explosion and exposé of the racial complexes and prejudices that have always been a part of this author's baggage, and now come to light no longer mediated by literary fiction, as in the earlier novels where the situation was described and commented on through the eyes of a child. This time Carlos de Melo is a young man who assumes full responsibility for his opinions; and his creator, José Lins do Rego, must do the same in these pages, which are only partly autobiographical.

From the opening pages, even before the protagonist's return to his grandfather's plantation, one can see the steady emergence of racial prejudice.

> My concerns as a student never measured the extent of my ambitions. Why did my family never have the prestige it deserved from the size of its land holdings? Why did it not own all the land in the valley of the Paraíba? Did they not have the control of thousands of men in their

hands? What they lacked was a leader, someone to put himself at the head of the clan, someone ready and willing to work for all. They spent their time voting along with the others in the university bloc, offering support to outsiders. White as they were, they took orders from mulattoes more able than they.[47]

This reference to mulattoes now in charge of the administration recalls the observations Graça Aranha puts into the mouth of Paulo Maciel, the antihero of *Canaã*.

And thus young Carlos de Melo, so as not to end up as a civil servant (as happened to Rego) taking orders from mulattoes, returns to the family fief to be defeated by a Black man. The reasons for this defeat, if one examines the matter logically, derive from purely emotional factors. The prime mover is the deep antipathy, not to say hatred, that the protagonist bears for his rival, simply because the latter is Black. Carlos de Melo applies himself to cultivating the land of Santa Rosa once more, but he has neither the fiber nor energy of his grandfather; he is a sickly intellectual tormented by doubts. Portions of his land are let to tenant farmers or sharecroppers who pay him back in kind with half their crop. They are all miserably poor except one, José Marreira, who has become rich by working very hard, putting money aside little by little. In terms of pure economic logic, José Marreira's wealth and his continued success coincide with those of Carlos de Melo, whose income also increases proportionately. But economic logic and the patriarchal spirit of ownership do not always coincide, very often finding themselves on opposite sides, as in this case. Carlos de Melo, now the senhor de engenho, finds it inconceivable to his way of thinking that the son of a slave should be as rich, or richer, than he:

I began to notice, however, that José Marreira was getting too rich. Already he was going around well dressed and wearing boots, and eating in restaurants. Rumor had it that he even held the rank of *capitão*. He was no longer *Seu* José; he was moving up. His daughters went to school. And he had the best saddle horse on the estate in his stable. He received the people from Pilar in his house, and gave parties to celebrate baptisms. The local political bigwig was somehow related to him, and he had sent a larger contribution than I on the last patron saint's day. The *moleque* was moving on at quite a rate.[48]

What moves Carlos de Melo to act against José Marreira is a series of wholly visceral reactions. And whenever he speaks of him, he uses terms designed to disparage, certainly in the way they are spoken: *moleque, cabra, negro*.

> I couldn't get José Marreira out of my mind. I went around Santa Rosa, and I could feel his shadow on me. I had allowed that *moleque* to come this far. That *cabra* was already giving himself the airs of a gentleman. He was no longer the creature I had seen at my grandfather's feet, when he had come to report on the work.[49]

Obviously one must make an effort to try to understand the basis of Carlos de Melo's revolt. The patriarchal slave system of the Brazilian Northeast had created, over a period of centuries, a series of both social and moral categories. Slavery, while clearly a basically economic fact, like all forms of violence required some sort of moral alibi as a means of defense. And these alibis, for there were more than one, had been created and had been fully consecrated by the dominant religion. Slavery was the product of a historical situation, of the social will, of a divine order. In a world that had not changed its opinion for more than three centuries, a revolution had occurred without public opinion having been in the least prepared for it. For conservatives like José Lins do Rego, abolition may have been a vaguely utopistic concession, and certainly ill-advised, but nonetheless no more than a concession. In *Menino de engenho* the episode of the slave (or half-slave) who is purchased and whipped because he had dared to appear before the senhor de engenho as an equal, dressed in boots and tie, was included as an example of the cruel malice of Major Ursulino. The bitter resentment of Carlos de Melo is cut from the same cloth: he cannot accept the idea that a Black man, the son of slaves, whom he remembers as working in the fields in rags, should now dress so elegantly and live in comfort.

Far worse is the fact that José Marreira does not flaunt his new prosperity in the presence of Carlos de Melo. In their discussions he shows what amounts to an excess of humility and courtesy, forever repeating that he knows his place and that he would never be so bold as to quarrel with the grandson of his old master. Whenever he goes to see Carlos de Melo on business, if there is ever a difference of opinion, he repeats the following saying to the point of obsession: "*Branco que brigue com branco, camumbembe com camumbembe.*" ("Let whites fight with whites, beggars with beggars.") He is always smiling, agreeable, well mannered. But at the end of the discussion it is always José Marreira who gains ground, without getting flustered, playing his cards correctly:

> Marreira took his leave with the same smile. He would sleep on it and let me know the next day. I saw him get on his horse, a fine gray nag with a gleaming harness. And then he said goodbye, raising his hat to

> me most respectfully. That damned superior air of his! Where the devil had that *moleque* learned all that, those fancy manners of the born gentleman? At one time he had hoed the fields, a day worker, he had driven the carts loaded with home brew when he'd been involved in smuggling *cachaça*. Then he'd become a sharecropper and had worked many years at Santa Rosa, cutting and grinding the cane; he'd never even had a spelling book. And today *Capitão* Zé Marreira was the equal of the grandson of the man who had put him to work in the fields.[50]

The figure of José Marreira has the power to throw Carlos de Melo completely off balance. His education and culture have left him completely unprepared for the idea that a Black man might achieve a position of leadership. Carlos's great problem is that he would like to revive the aristocratic style of life of the so-called golden age of patriarchy, but he fails to notice that the world has changed, that cars now speed along the road that winds around Santa Rosa. His conditioned reflexes lead him to resuscitate instead what we will call the ''civilization of the shout,'' in which the old masters were accustomed to bawl out their orders to the slaves at the top of their voice:

> In the house I hollered at them to bring water for me to wash my feet. That was what my grandfather used to do. The *negra* came into the room with the basin and a towel over her shoulders and washed my feet without looking at me. That was good. I was the absolute master.[51]

This absolute sense of power expressed in the form of a roar leads Carlos de Melo to behave violently even towards people in whose case he ought to know better: ''I was immediately sorry for using such vulgar language in his case. João Miguel was certainly no *cabra*. He had blue eyes and he worked with me because he asked me.''[52]

And instead José Marreira, this dark-skinned Master Don Gesualdo,[53] never loses his temper, always has that agreeable smile on his face which has become a nightmare for Carlos de Melo. With never a false step he manages the double game of allying himself with the people of the factory (for he knows the way the wind is blowing in these changing times) and buying the engenho of Santa Fé after the death of Coronel Lula. (We met him in *Fogo morto* and other novels of the series, where he was presented as a fanatical anti-Black.)

Thus José Marreira comes and tells Carlos de Melo that now they are neighbors, and he is happy to have his old master as a neighbor, particularly since he has never wanted to be anything but a good friend of all white men. This is the last straw, leading to the following outburst from Carlos de Melo, who expresses himself in the usual fashion:

> That wretched *negro*! He had already given me a lot of trouble, caused a lot of problems for the *engenho*, and now he came looking for me as if nothing had happened. He deserved a good whipping. And the worst was I gave him everything he asked for. It was weak and cowardly of me, I admit. I should have kicked the dog out. Hadn't he already sold his property? I should have kicked the dog off my land. And now he was going to be my neighbor.
>
> Santa Fé had suffered a worse fate than the others. It had not even fallen victim to the iron clutches of the factory. The ill-fated *engenho* would now belong to the Marreiras. Senhor Lula's room, the soil trodden by Senhor Lula, the house of Senhor Lula's grandparents would now have a *moleque* for a master, a *camumbembe*. A no-account beggar would walk along those corridors now. And the portraits of Marreira and his wife would hang where those of Senhor Lula's grandparents had hung for generations.[54]

José Marreira settles down on the engenho that had belonged to a notoriously harsh owner of slaves. And the rich Black man can show off in his carriage, which for Coronel Lula had been the very symbol of his superior position as a white lord.

This social rise and new wealth provoke reactions among whites and Blacks. In general the whites are the older relatives of Carlos de Melo, some friends of his grandfather, who feel personally offended at the defeat of the young white man at the hands of a Black neighbor. They propose punitive expeditions, offer their help, not understanding that behind the ex-field worker there is a new world of commercial interests represented by the factory, and they no longer have the necessary strength to settle the matter in the old way, by shooting or whipping. Nor are the Blacks at all happy with the brilliant success of one of their own. This attitude might surprise us, but is, in fact, more easily understandable if you remember that slavery was not only an alibi for whites, but for Blacks as well. The majority ended up by accepting it as something inevitable, a fatality decreed by destiny and sanctioned by one's skin color. The victory of one of them meant that their own passivity was not the only solution, and that, had they reacted, they, too, might have broken out of bondage. We must add that José Marreira, as an ex-field worker, forces his dependents to work very hard indeed, which hardly endears him to them, even though many prefer to work for him because he pays better.

One of the things the peasants say, to offend the workers of Santa Fé, is, "I don't work on a Black plantation."[55] You could not invent a more typically servile reaction, this seeing a form of nobility in the figure of one's master with whom the worker tends to identify himself. When the Santa Rosa workers pass by the rival engenho, they sing popular songs with an obviously racist content:

Branco Deus o fêz
Mulato Deus pintou
Caboclo bufa de porco
Negro o diabo cagou.

Branco dorme na sala,
Mulato no corredô,
Caboclo na cozinha
Negro no cagadô.

God made the white
God painted the mulatto
The *caboclo* [is the] fart of a pig
The Devil shat out the *negro*.

The white sleeps in the room,
The mulatto in the corridor,
The *caboclo* in the kitchen
The *negro* in the shithouse.[56]

But songs cannot turn the clock back nor stop José Marreira's desperate will to succeed. The new estate he bought, Santa Fé, which in the hands of Coronel Lula had become a desert of uncultivated land, is reborn as a prosperous plantation. Marreira himself comes to bring the good news to Carlos de Melo, who is most distressed for it forces him to measure the extent of his defeat:

> When he left I sat thinking about that miracle: Santa Fé now produced two thousand sugarloaves. That beast knew how to make the land produce anything, starting work the minute he woke up, staying in the fields till nightfall, taking advantage of the last minute of light. For him there were really twelve hours in the day. This was his secret. If I had turned over Santa Fé to him, he would have made it as big again as in the days of José Paulino, making his plants grow the length of the valleys of the Paraíba. That *negro*, now so close to me, humiliated me.[57]

So the story of Santa Rosa comes to an end. Carlos de Melo can only leave, having sold the plantation for a good price, admitting in a moment of lucid sincerity, "I was only pretending when I expressed regret over what might befall my *cabras*."[58]

We must give José Lins do Rego credit for two great virtues in these novels of the sugarcane cycle. The first obviously is that he is a grcat writer, one of the finest to have come out of Brazil. The second is his courage in chronicling the end of that world and civilization to which he felt himself so deeply attached. The vision and description of men and events may well be biased and partisan, but the story told, his own, is painfully and sadly exact.

With *Moleque Ricardo* comes the problem of a change in the author's viewpoint. The various novels we have examined so far have two things in common: either they were directly autobiographical, or the main characters came from the same ruling elite as the author. But in *Moleque Ricardo* the hero is, in fact, Black, one of the many moleques on the plantation who flees the countryside for the great urban adventure. Thus the scene changes, too, the background now being provided by the sordid urban slums housing the multitudinous poor of Recife.

We therefore have to deal with the difficult task of transplantation. How will the senhor de engenho, José Lins do Rego, manage to describe the life of the poor, the excluded, the humble, all of those whom hitherto he has observed from the comfortable distance of the patriarchal mansion? We must say that, apart from the literary merits of the book, the writer makes a sincere effort to penetrate this new artistic experience by adopting with reasonable accuracy a new point of view. He is, however, unable to shuck off completely his old persona. Frequently Ricardo gives the impression of being a dark-skinned Carlos de Melo, and not only because of the understandable nostalgia he feels for the plantation where he has lived from birth and where he left his mother and brothers. The fact is that Ricardo has the same existential inability to find himself as his one-time white playmate. He is a failure with women. His marriage is over even before the death of his wife. The links he establishes with fellow workers reveal him as a passive participant, and he lets himself get involved with the struggles of the union without a deep commitment, with all sorts of hesitations and excuses. He shows an obscure fear towards the authentic expression of Négritude represented by the feiticeiro Pai Lucas, and remains an outsider in the city where he lives. That same obsession with sickness and death which plagued José Lins do Rego and Carlos de Melo is here transferred to Ricardo's wife and one of his comrades at work.

In short, we can say that Ricardo is a credible Black figure in the drama of his life, but he is undoubtedly a little odd in that intellectual fear of living which he seems to have inherited from the boy with whom he used to play on the engenho.

We stated earlier that the two poles of Ricardo's life are on the one hand Pai (or Father) Lucas, the feiticeiro, who stands for the cultural origins and roots of his race, and the union, which on the other hand stands for revolutionary change and the wave of the future. And while Ricardo accepts them both in the end, but in different ways, he is always cautious and suspicious in his approach to both. He is as cautious and suspicious as a Carlos de Melo, and as José Lins do Rego was in reality. Lucas, the cult of roots, the renewal of the idea of Black identity, was always a nightmare for the white ruling class; the union, the new and different ideas imported from Europe, Russia, and the United States—both represented a synthesis of fears of the ruling class in general and of José Lins do Rego in particular, who was attached to the past by an almost morbid affection.

Moleque Ricardo was published in 1935, that is, during those years which really represent the start of a new era in Brazilian history. It is difficult for a reader raised in the tradition of European or North American culture to understand what really happened in Brazil in those years, or to appreciate the dimensions of the crisis that erupted in the minds of everyone of that period. Something similar, differing only in form, is happening today in many countries in Africa and Latin America. The classical idea of progress, according to established European patterns, is a tightly organized succession of events, leading to a determined result: the machine is invented, giving rise to industrial civilization. But behind all this is a whole linkage of facts and developments that historically justify the goal attained. The arrival of machinery in Brazil—the creation of a national industry willed by Vargas—was a wise and provident political choice, which, however, had no historical basis in the context of the civilization of the country. Chronologically there are few years between the pompous carriage of Coronel Lula, old José Paulino's horse, and the car belonging to his son, the *neousineiro* Juca; yet they amount to a century's march from one stage of civilization to the next. Brazil accepts the machine for political reasons, so as not to be left on the sidelines, but historically it has no industrial civilization. The result is essentially a crisis of awareness, a period of anxiety and confusion for an entire society finally forced to face up to a reality for which it has been left historically unprepared.

Those who are more culturally aware and sensitive, like José Lins do Rego, perceive this crisis and express it in literary form. This produces the ambiguity of a character like Ricardo, who forever lets himself drift with the tide of events, and who submits to history instead of wanting to take part in it. His is the cultural perplexity of Rego faced with phenomena that lie outside his historical experience,

SPORT OF CAPOEIRA

JOGO DE CAPOEIRA

such as strikes, unions, and class struggle. He might summon up a certain human sympathy for such events, but their real essence and significance escape him.

The same thing can be said with regard to the question of Black culture. The thirties saw the appearance of two phenomena: on the one hand, the affirmation of Black culture and the way it established an autonomous and antithetical position vis-à-vis white culture; on the other hand, the discovery of this same culture by a band of scholars and writers such as Gilberto Freyre, Câmara Cascudo, and Jorge Amado. With regard to the world of Black culture, José Lins do Rego adopts the same attitude he adopted in the case of all social phenomena: a benevolent human sympathy that stops on the threshold of appearances and never seeks to get to the heart of the matter or to understand the reasons for its existence.

Thus Ricardo never lets himself get too involved with Lucas, of whom he is dimly afraid, and is finally drawn into a union struggle towards which he has always shown a marked distrust.

The relationship between Ricardo and Lucas is initially based on fear. For the young man from the plantation, the figure of the witch doctor has something sinister about it.

> He lived alone and people gossiped about him. He was a mysterious creature for all the people of Encruzilhada. Just for this, every time he passed by, Ricardo pretended not to see *Seu* Lucas. Can all they said about him have been true? The gardener went around with no one, because he always had God with him. Every night he left Encruzilhada to go to Fundão, where *Seu* Lucas officiated in a cult. He was the priest of *Xangô, pai-de-terreiro*. What he earned from his flowers he spent on his God, on the *negros* who asked his blessing, on the *negrinhas* who danced in his church. He had been arrested as a *catimbozeiro*, a *negro* evildoer. But none of this had any effect on *Seu* Lucas. He belonged to God, so what could men do to him? He invited Ricardo to go with him, just to see. The *moleque* always refused. On the *engenho* he had always heard of *feitiçaria* with fear. The *negros catimbozeiros* were poison, living for evil, killing people and changing their appearance. Ricardo believed in God and the idea of souls going to the next world. He also believed in the *feitiços*. These were *negros* with the ability to control others. For the folk from the *engenho*, Recife was full of *negros feitiçeiros*. If you wanted to get rid of an enemy, or get a woman, or paralyze someone else's leg, the *negro* would do it for you. God should only spare him from getting mixed up with a *xangô*. When he passed by close to where *Seu* Lucas lived, he crossed the street. Already people were talking of those things, and now the gardener was inviting him to come and see the ceremony of the *catimbó*. In the bakery there were

two views on *Seu* Lucas: Florêncio was against him, but the man in the stovepipe hat insisted that *Seu* Lucas did nothing but good.[59]

Ricardo's initial fear can be explained by the different forms assumed by Black religious expression in the city and countryside. In the countryside there existed a direct relationship between the Blacks and the master, which gave the owner class a great opportunity for exercising power and influence by imposing, among other things, its own religion. We remember Coronel Lula, who forced his slaves to pray together and had banned all religious observance of saints Cosme and Damião as feitiçaria. The official end of slavery had hardly changed a thing and the feiticeiro had continued to exist at the edges of the world of the engenho, which the master wanted to maintain forcibly united and cohesive around the moral principles established by the casa grande. In the city the atmosphere is completely different. Here there is no longer a single senhor de engenho. The worker-master relationship is fragmented among a thousand labor providers—from the larger industries, to the civil service, to the small employer—where what counts is productive capacity, the ratio between energy and output, and nothing else. All one needs to observe is the difference between Ricardo's two employers, Coronel José Paulino on the engenho Santa Rosa, and the Portuguese baker for whom he works in Recife. With José Paulino he did not have a proper labor relationship in the modern sense of the term. He bought the newspapers, washed the horses, and lived on the plantation. The coronel looked after everything and, as we know, had the right to interfere in the private lives of those for whom he felt morally responsible. That is why Ricardo runs away from the plantation, because he knows he *belongs* to Coronel José Paulino. But with Seu Alexandre, the Portuguese baker, the relationship is completely different. Economically he is treated a thousand times better, but he represents no more than a pair of arms obliged to produce bread. When one of the bakery workers falls sick, he is fired on the spot.

That is why in the urban milieu it becomes possible to create a Black religious tradition through the formation of groups and sects. Seu Alexandre is not interested in what Ricardo does when he stops work; and all other employers, big and small, feel the same.

Hence the credibility of Ricardo's fear of Seu Lucas, faced as he is with something that never belonged to his peasant culture.

Ricardo's fear, inspired by magic and witchcraft, is continually mingled with the attraction he feels for this man gifted with supernatural powers. Lucas feels affection for Ricardo and would like him to join his cult.

> But what the pastor wanted was another sheep for his flock and another set of legs for his cult. *Seu* Lucas liked Ricardo. He needed the young man for his god. *Seu* Lucas's god created saints on earth. The spirit of the saints entered the bodies of men, they became flesh and blood, danced and sang. And Ricardo would have made a good saint.[60]

We should remember this passage, this timid and tentative explanation of what is, in fact, the rite of possession of the *macumba*. It is one of the first in all Brazilian literature; and the date is 1935.

In the little world of the down-and-out, the workers, and the poor of the quarter of Recife where Ricardo works, Lucas solemnly exercises his priestly responsibility, filling the institutional void left by the indifferent authorities—political, administrative, and religious—as their legacy to the people. When Florêncio dies, a worker who has been hurt in a strike, it is Lucas who hurries to the dying man's bedside.

> Now *Seu* Lucas gave the orders in the house. Nobody did anything without consulting him. He had come to help the baker die, and this he knew how to do very well, as well as preparing his family for his death. He dressed the dead man, sprinkled perfume over him, and gently closed his eyes. And he sang, to accompany him in his last sleep. *Seu* Lucas's voice filled the *rua* do Cisco with fear . . . Sweet scent and songs were what *Seu* Lucas had brought Florêncio . . . so that he would not go into the next world with the smell of leather and the cackling of vultures about him. The incense of *Seu* Lucas and his holy songs gave this illusion to the *rua* do Cisco. Ricardo listened to the old *negro* and his hymns with fear. Fear. Those groans of a soul surrendering to God made him afraid.[61]

Ricardo stands between a Lucas who fascinates and intimidates him and a labor union in which he has no faith. It is very easy to guess the position of José Lins do Rego with regard to the union, which from his solidly reactionary point of view must have stood for the Antichrist on earth. He can only see the negative side of the union struggle, the cynicism of the precinct captains who exploit the justifiable dissatisfaction of the poor with an eye to their own political advancement. In fact, when Ricardo and the others are finally deported without trial to the island of Fernando de Noronha, Pestana, the union chief, manages to spend only a few hours in jail, moving on to a brilliant political career in the shadow of official power. This kind of episode may well be historically true, but it represents no more than a partial and negative aspect of an important historical phase whose overall significance quite escapes Rego. He does little more than show a benevolent and paternalistic sympathy for the poor and the disinherited.

Lucas himself perceives the negative strength of the union in siphoning off his own best men with alluring and false promises.

> *Seu* Lucas was squatting in his flower bed, tending his roses. Jesuíno was leaving, running into the hands of another. A *cabra* stronger than he had taken his *negro* away from him and given him to others. The pastor must have suffered a great deal. Who knows how bitterly *Seu* Lucas grieved there in his little garden, his hands stained with manure, while he pruned his roses? He had always thought how difficult it would be for a *negro* to abandon his *terreiro*, and yet this one had gone away. For some time he had been cultivating Ricardo, but instead of Ricardo coming in, Jesuíno was going away. The *negro* was deceiving himself. One day he would come back. He'd come back and break into a dance again, until his mouth grew dry with singing. *Seu* Lucas grew thoughtful.
>
> His rose bushes obeyed him. He would transplant them from one point to another and the flowers blossomed with the help of his hands. And now along came Sebastião and carried off the *negro* from his *terreiro*. He hadn't managed to persuade Ricardo, to put a saint into the young man's body; he had not seen him shudder when God visited his body. And Jesuíno was going away. There was a greater strength than his among the people. There was an unknown force greater than his that was moving the people. He gave the people God, he gave them a distant hope in heaven, a heaven that came after every earthly thing. And now there was a new force greater than his that promised and delivered . . . Jesuíno had gone away. He had to change the position of one of his bushes. And he was afraid, he was wavering for the first time. *Seu* Lucas had never been known to waver. . . . But now he began to tremble, now something was telling him that his strength was ebbing away, that there were other forces out there with a grip on the people.[62]

The changes that sadden the old feiticeiro are, in contrast, a source of happiness for Ricardo, who discovers in the struggle and solidarity of his comrades a renewed pleasure in living which the death of his wife, Odete, and the harshness of his existence had taken away from him; and his happiness also results from his not taking the advice of Lucas.

> Jesuíno had gone away. Ricardo would not come. After Odete's death Ricardo would have liked to go to *Seu* Lucas, had been tempted to run to the *terreiro* to put an end to his raving. He immediately thought of the prayers of the old *negro*. One night he was on the point of rushing out of his room to go to Fundão to see *Seu* Lucas, to give his body to him so that he could drive out the fever inside him. But then he was

afraid to go. Maybe the old *negro* would never let him go, and so he stayed home. He suffered terribly, but he didn't go to the *feiticeiro*. It might have been worse: suppose some spirit had entered his body for the rest of his life. Fortunately he got better. His comrades had saved him from that wretched situation. His sleep was free of dreams, of terrible memories. . . . No, he had not completely left *Seu* Lucas. He believed in what his fellow workers said, but he still believed in the prayers of *Seu* Lucas. Bit by bit Ricardo ovecame the fear of Odete with the hopes of Sebastião.[62]

Unfortunately Ricardo's hopes are doomed to disappointment. The strike fails and he and about fifty of his comrades find themselves surrounded by the police. One Black man tries to flee and is killed on the spot by soldiers who are also Black. Racial, like class, solidarity is nothing but a chimera.

The *negro* lay where he fell, flat out on the ground. Soldiers Black like him had killed him, shooting him down as he ran, like a wild beast. The soldiers were everywhere. They were men with the same color of his skin, *negros*, half-castes, mulattoes like him, like Simão, like Deodato, like Florêncio. They had cut down without mercy a *negro* who had tried to escape. And they would have cut us all down the same way.[64]

Nothing remains; there is no more union, no more class solidarity. There barely survives the dubious and tormented faith of Pai Lucas who sees the best of his sons leave in chains, as if they had become slaves once more. His sad song closes the novel, punctuating the night in vain with a queston as to why it all happened, a question for which no one has an answer.

José Lins do Rego is a profoundly pessimistic writer, and his pessimistic vision of the world even extends into the theme of the Carnival. Let us remember once more that the typical Brazilian Carnival, the one we all know, originated in the first years of the twentieth century and not without difficulties and objections. The white portion of the population, the most powerful section, did not look kindly on this noisy and uncontrolled explosion of Black culture that invaded the streets and flowed through the squares. Many years would pass before Carnival would become an expression of multiracial Brazil, with Blacks and whites joining together in song and dance. It is therefore perfectly understandable that Rego should maintain a distant and critical position with regard to a phenomenon that did not yet belong to his cultural world.

Carnival as an antidote to revolution: here are two historical moments that the author does not like, which he does not feel are his;

and they both risk canceling each other out: "Now no one talked any more of revolution, autonomy, or Pestana. People only talked of the Carnival coming up."[65] Carnival by its very nature was antirevolutionary, because its declared aim was to make people forget, if only for a short while, the wretched conditions in which they lived, which are normally the very stuff of revolution. But the author makes no such considerations. He merely describes the explosion of wild joy, which rather frightens him, and still manages to underline the terrible living conditions of the characters:

> The inhabitants of that wretched alley sang all night, singing and dancing in the mud. Carnival was near. And every year, from that same alley, came forth the group known as Paz e Amor [Peace and Love], hysterical men and women cavorting like animals who had grown up in the midst of plenty. Paz e Amor paid no attention to the *urubus* [vultures], the stink of the tannery, the sight of their skinny children. They just threw themselves into the dance. They might shortly die of hunger, they might suffer the pains of hell, but when Carnival came they broke out into a dance. Lcd by a line of torches, and a flag flying in the wind, they came out of their fetid little huts, swaying their bodies in the most animal-like diversion in the world.[66]

We note yet again that unbreakable habit of making comparisons with the animal kingdom, which is the rule every time our author makes a reference to Blacks.

Carnival is a fleeting illusion permitting you to forget for a moment sickness and death:

> There in the midst of the swamplands the voices of the *negras* throbbed as if the earth they pounded was the best in the world. The nearby tannery sent out its noxious fumes, and the *urubus* slept on the palms, but they sang and sang. The *negras* of Paz e Amor sang till their voices cracked with all the strength their lungs allowed. Later they would start to cough like the cigarette girls. Tuberculosis waited until Carnival to complete the work of hunger.[67]

What Rego asserts is undoubtedly true. But for him there is no valid existential possibility outside the magic world of the old plantation, that world he barely glimpsed in his childhood. If we were to indulgc in a little simple psychology, we would say that Rego was afraid of growing up, afraid of living. It was for this that he took refuge in the past, categorically excluding all other ways of life. He fails to see in the passing from the engenho to the *usina* the admittedly painful changes that would lead to broader forms of civilization. He cannot see in the union, despite the intrigues and errors, the premise of new social relationships. Nor can he see in Carnival the unquenchable energies of the people whose high spirits manage to beat back for a while sickness and death. His is an emotional, not logical, position and as such is not conducive to discussion.

There remain two other figures in *Moleque Ricardo* worth a brief mention. Both represent a standard narrative cliché. They are two mulatto women: Isaura, with whom Ricardo falls in love, and Josefa, over whom Seu Alexandre loses his head. They are both the sort of women who drag men down, temptresses who eventually betray them. Seu Alexandre neglects his wife, who has worked like an animal with him all her life, and he now spends all his money on Josefa, who exploits and then finally leaves him. Ricardo, on the other hand, suffers a long time over Isaura, who fuels a passion that ultimately consumes its victim. These are standard figures in Brazilian literature, as is that of Seu Alexandre, the greedy and grasping Portuguese baker. Such characters add nothing new.

And so we arrive at *Usina*, the final catastrophe, the last chapter of failure. *Menino de engenho* and *Doidinho* bore the seeds of this final failure in the partial defeat of a childhood and adolescence by a precocious, animal initiation into sex. *Bangüê* charted the failed attempt to revive the plantation through old-fashioned methods. *Moleque Ricardo* showed the combined failures of the proletarian solution, of the escape from the plantation, and of integration into the new urban world and participation in class struggle. Both novels also depicted the emotional downfall of their protagonists, Black and white. *Usina* offers the failure of the rich and poor in a modern setting, the transformation of the old plantation into a modern industrial and agricultural complex.

We already know the moral position of José Lins do Rego: his rejection of the new, regardless of its form, derives absolutely from his refusal to detach himself from the enchanted world of the past glimpsed in childhood. In *Usina*, however, his problem is to present the theme of failure within a framework of transformation that, however one may wish to consider it, does in fact stand for progress and an improvement over what came before.

There are no limits, however, to the determination of the pessimist. The plot of *Usina* is arranged as follows: Ricardo returns to the plantation, morally destroyed by the painful experience of Fernando de Noronha. He is given a good job in the plantation store and lives a calm and monotonous life. Meanwhile, around him all has changed. Uncle Juca, who has taken over the plantation from Carlos de Melo, has transformed the old engenho, with the help of American capital, into an usina, a complete factory for the production of sugar, and lives exulting in his success as if future progress knew no limits. But there is a fatal contradiction in his character. While on the one hand he lives the exultant life of limitless success with a modern dedication and energy, on the other hand he still retains the atavistic pleasure-seeking habits of the Brazilian landed gentleman. His accumulated wealth, when not immediately reinvested in new machinery, is squandered in a thousand ways: a fancy residence in the city, the latest model cars, travel, expensive mistresses, parties. Then disaster strikes: a devastating drought imperils the crop and brings thousands of starving *sertanejos* onto the plantation, causing serious problems of law and order; ultramodern machinery does not work; the price of sugar falls, bringing with it a tightening of credit. To add to these calamities, the protagonist falls victim to venereal disease (it appears to be a case of syphilis)—reflecting Rego's eternal obsession with sickness and death—and a flood sweeps everything away. Ricardo is finally killed while attempting to help some starving refugees who are trying to loot the store.

It is the end of everything, of all possible solutions suggested by this whole cycle of novels. Even the most historically valid solution, the one that responded to the real demands of the times—transformation and progress—fails because of the unfortunate combination of circumstances and lack of foresight of the protagonist, who finds himself without funds or resources at the hour of need, his health broken.

The author even manages to cast a negative light over the more positive aspects of this social transformation, emphasizing the sufferings of those obliged to endure the consequences of the change. These are the old Black women forced to move out of the houses where they were born and lived, including Aunt Generosa who must give up her place to a new cook. Then there are the field workers who suddenly realize the full wretchedness of their condition. Until that moment they had lived just like the slaves before them, with only one world to contrast with their own, that of their white masters. Now they discover there is another privileged group, the workers in the factory, people who had come out of their own ranks and now lived a much more prosperous existence.

> The children of the factory workers lived a charmed life. If you worked for the factory, you lived like a king compared to the workers in the fields. Most of these workers came from elsewhere, and they had brick houses to live in and received very generous wages. The field hands

> could hardly believe that men like this received six *mil-réis* a day. The workers, who lived around the factory, lived separate from the mob of slaves who lived farther off.[68]

Let us note parenthetically that the author uses the word *escravatura* to describe the farm laborers. And so a class society is being formed which takes the place of a traditional society composed of two unique classes. But the author's visceral pessimism does not allow him to point out the progress being made by those rising up—for the most part these workers came from the working class, whose roots were in the slavery of the not-too-distant past. He prefers to emphasize the sadness of those who remain farm laborers. Nor does he note that in a class society—in which those who belong to a higher class despise those on the step below—such sadness can serve a positive function, as a stimulus to improving one's status. The field worker on the old engenho was resigned to his position, knowing he could never hope to pass into the class of his white masters, the large landowners. But the laborer in the factory might reasonably hope to become a qualified worker, a technician, with a house built of bricks and a higher salary. All this the author does not see, for he is locked into his sentimental position tied to those schemes that for three centuries had stood guard over the rigid system of the casa grande and the senzala.

The transformation of the engenho into an usina and the progressive decline of the latter are underlined by a series of events set in motion by a character from outside, a Black man, a sort of prophet or soothsayer. He is absolutely not a feiticeiro. The author goes out of his way to emphasize the religious unity of Blacks and whites, in contrast to what occurred in the city: "No *feiticeiro* was present in those parts. The God of the Blacks was the same as the whites'. No one knew Xangô and the noisy rites of the *catimbós*."[69] Feliciano, as the Black character in question is called, is a very familiar character in the rural Brazilian world, where the official Catholic religion always found among its followers certain leaders who frequently ended up by taking the place of the official clergy. The activities of these seers generally consisted of promoting and organizing processions and prayer meetings, especially on the occasion of religious festivals. Feliciano enjoys great prestige and his house is a shrine with the images of São Antônio and São Sebastião on his walls. His novenas and processions were always packed with the faithful. Feliciano is the first victim of the new age.

> During the lifetime of old José Paulino, Feliciano enjoyed a certain consideration and was respected by the stewards. The house of the *negro* was the people's church, and the pastor had the right to all forms of

> privilege. Then came the *usina*, which did not respect Feliciano's chapel. He was forced to leave his little brick house by the road and take his saints up the hill where São Antônio and São Sebastião finally found refuge under the fronds of the *catolé*.[70]

Thus these new times begin with a desecration, and the traditions of the people are removed and wiped out:

> The day when the saints of Feliciano were moved into the *caatinga*, women came with white embroidered tablecloths to cover the images, which could not be exposed to the sun. And they formed a procession, intoning hymns as they climbed. They arrived at the *caatinga* just as the sun was slowly setting.[71]

There is a constant contrast between the old times and the new. Ricardo remembers from his childhood the well-tended kitchen garden of Feliciano, his obsequious and cordial relations with old José Paulino, who would never fail to grumble whenever the processions got too noisy, but let everything continue as before. Juca, too, the new master, is nice to Feliciano. He has given orders for him not to be disturbed, but he cannot fail to execute those transformations demanded by progress, whose architect and victim he is. Feliciano, however, is an old Black man who has been a slave and cannot accept the reality of a world that is no longer his. He locks up his saints in the sanctuary in the *caatinga* and refuses to preside over religious ceremonies in spite of the protests of his flock. He spends his time at the store, cursing everything and everybody, and soon the rumor starts to spread that the old man has been possessed by the devil. The faithful would like to break into the sanctuary and rescue the holy images, but are held back by an obscure fear. Then one day the unthinkable happens: the manager of the store loses all patience with the complaints and curses of the old Black man and strikes him.

Following this episode the figure of Feliciano, who has retreated more and more into his madness and obsessions, starts to acquire more sinister dimensions. Everybody, even the men and those who do not believe in him, begins to be afraid of him. Feliciano begins to be persecuted; a frightening legend is circulated about him. It seems the devil comes to his hut every night to dance with him and torment the images of the saints. His old faithful followers ask the parish priest to come and celebrate communion to drive out the devil, but the priest refuses and advises the people to go to Doctor Juca. In his turn Juca assumes an attitude exactly opposite to that of his father, Coronel José Paulino. The latter left Feliciano free to practice his devotions, so long as the situation did not degenerate and was kept under control. Juca does continue to regard Feliciano with some benevolence, but he has no respect for what the old man represents. This is a completely different way of seeing existence and regulating relationships with one's dependents. José Paulino was the senhor de engenho, the old-fashioned patriarch, and everything that happened on his land was his own business. Juca is an *usineiro*, a modern manager of a large industrial concern, living according to the simple logic of profit, which simply excludes from consideration anything that has no economic value. That is why Juca is consistent when he has Feliciano's little temple destroyed—which for him is just a miserable hut—because he needs the land. And he is also consistent when he dismisses the importance of the old shaman's curses and insults, while he still gives the order for him to continue to be fed. For him Feliciano is just an old Black man in his second childhood whom one does not need to take seriously; and certainly a plate of soup is not going to break the usina. What Juca has not understood is that for Feliciano and his followers the saints are very important, much more important than the plate of soup so charitably offered.

And so, Feliciano changes in the eyes of the people. He turns from a holy man into a sorcerer, the devil's disciple. And then one night the old Black man's hut catches fire, everybody runs to it, more than two hundred strong men, but no one has the courage to break down the door, out of fear of the devil living with Feliciano. After the fire, near the ashes of Feliciano, there is no trace of the saints.

> No one had any more doubts: the saints had been freed by the devil. The place where Feliciano's house had stood, the soil covered with ashes, was now sanctified ground.
>
> There God had beaten the devil. The fire had come from hell, but the fire of God, being stronger, had conquered it. The saints had risen to heaven. The night of the fire, a woman from Areia had seen a huge star traveling from one side of the sky to the other, a huge star that changed its position in the sky. All of that was nothing other than the strength of God. At the fair of Itabaiana they said that the altar had risen like a ball; a child had seen it going up into the sky until it was lost from sight.[72]

And so Feliciano's house, or rather his ashes, begins to attract large groups of pilgrims whose numbers swell by the day. Again Juca does not understand, completely underestimates what is happening, and sends one of his guards to drive the people away. The man saves himself by running away, and other bands of armed men sent thereafter are even killed by the aggravated crowd. No one among the people of that place has the courage to attack the faithful camped out on that sacred ground. On Juca's request, the government sends a hundred soldiers who finally manage to expel the *romeiros* after shooting into the crowd, "And the blood of the innocent mingled with the ashes of Feliciano."[73]

The story of Feliciano is over, and the author does not speak of him again. The next chapter begins, however, with the description of the failure of the machinery at the factory, and this series of breakdowns marks the beginning of the end for the whole industrial complex and for Juca and his people. The intention of José Lins do Rego is clear since he linked the two events together. The end of Feliciano represents the end of a world, the world made of ancient traditions, where even the figure of the old shaman was conceded his space and dignity. The old man's chapel was not only a place for the devotions of the poor and ignorant (not only the poor, for later Juca's wife, too, goes to a *curandeira* in a vain attempt to save her sick husband). It is also all that remains of the old days, of the old way of looking at the world. Basically Juca is a heretic for the author, although he never says so outright. He is a man who has destroyed the old order in the name of technology, progress, and the ethics of profit that belong to other countries and come from far away. Those changes, which the gentry accepted in the hopes of making vast profits and to which the poor submitted by force of circumstances, found their last obstacle in Feliciano. For he was the guardian of the temple and custodian of the local gods of the Afro-Brazilian world that had constructed its own identity over three centuries. The sacrilege committed with regard to the little chapel—seen by Juca as a mere technical operation—sets in motion the classic mechanism of the tragedy: the curse that overwhelms the protagonist in the first place, and then the final catastrophe that reestablishes the previously altered balance, thus bringing to an end, dramatically and definitively, that world which the author never wanted to leave.

With the end of the major sugarcane cycle, there is among his minor works, apart from the already cited *Pureza*, a tale that gives a prominent position to Black characters. *Riacho Doce*, a place name, is an anomalous work in the rich canon of José Lins do Rego, a work in which the author abandons his world, in all senses, choosing a totally different setting. The drama begins in a village in Scandanavia, and its heroine is a troubled young woman who moves with her husband, on account of his work, to a village near Maceió, Riacho Doce. This is a rather bold and not entirely successful venture for a writer like Rego, who has never removed himself from his land and his own special world. The attempt to experience a woman's emotions, and those of a northern woman at that, presents considerable difficulties but has allowed the author to see and to imagine an openly racial crisis, which would have been hard to handle with Brazilian protagonists.

In the story told in *Riacho Doce*, Rego deals with the great taboo theme, the one with the power to arouse atavistic complexes and ancient phobias, the tale of a love affair between a Black man and a white woman. During three centuries of slavery the sexual act had been seen only in the context of male dominance of women, in particular the white man's dominance of the Black woman. All forms of dominance and possession took a precise chromatic direction that went from white to black: the white man towards the woman, white or Black, the white man towards the moleque in play, or, for the first childhood sexual initiation, the white man towards the slave. When the opposite occurs, when a Black man loves and possesses a white woman, a series of mechanisms is triggered—from the psychological to the juridical to the social—which tends to reestablish the balance disturbed by the sacrilege committed at the moment of the violation of the taboo.

We must say that Rego has been careful to keep his distance. Edna, his heroine, is Swedish. She is tall and blonde, she belongs to another culture, another race, another religion. Furthermore she lives in a remote country village buried deep in the woods. In short, the author who up till then had restricted himself to the regionalist atmosphere, describing over and again people well known to him, or members of his family circle, has avoided the major risk that one of his female acquaintances should recognize herself in the protagonist; a grave risk, indeed, considering the times and local custom. To have chosen for his heroine a young Swedish woman from the countryside offered distinct advantages. If, in fact, no Brazilian lady—among those who might have committed an indiscretion with a dark-skinned man—could recognize herself in Edna, no reader of either sex could identify, even in a broad sense, with so geographically distant a character. In other words, the reader could participate emotionally in a forbidden affair without feeling directly involved.

Edna is indeed a completely different character, "different" in all senses of the word. As a child she was very unhappy at home, where she had to look after the pigs. Her one positive experience during adolescence was when she struck up a deep friendship with her schoolteacher, an intelligent and sensitive young woman who taught her many things. In the end this friendship became rather too affectionate, leaving Edna deeply disturbed in body and spirit; and this lasts until the schoolteacher is forced to seek a transfer as a result of the puritanical reaction of the village.

Even here the author has been careful to take precautions. The schoolteacher, young and raven-haired with black eyes in a village where all are blond, is called Esther, and she is Jewish, with a tragic family history behind her. *Riacho Doce* was published in 1939 and Rego, like many intellectuals, can hardly have been insensitive to certain ideas that were fashionable at the time over a large portion of the globe. Esther is described as a sensitive young woman; but in the little world of that northern village she is the outsider because she is Jewish, educated, and because she has dark eyes and hair, and because it is for her that Edna conceives this ambiguous and violent passion.

In short, Rego has approached his taboo with the utmost prudence and caution. The encounter between the white woman and the Black man takes place, but the white woman has those characteristics which turn her into a completely rare character, a person who obeys the absurd laws of contradiction. Her passion for a dark-skinned man has its roots in her passion for a woman—who was also of another race, also with a dark skin in comparison with those blond northerners. And what sort of a woman was she to fall in love with another woman, a Jewess, in 1939, with all those nasty things they were saying about Jews in those days? It is worthwhile adding that the term *judeu*, Jew, had a strong, disparaging, and negative connotation, particularly in the Brazilian Northeast; our author used it in this sense when he had described the tragedy of Feliciano in *Usina*: "God had come down to earth to save the saints from the hands of the *judeus*."[74]

Having grown up, Edna marries a Catholic man from the same village, an engineer called Carlos who, a few years later, finds work with a company drilling for oil in the little village of Riacho Doce. For Edna life in this fishing village, with the sun, sea, and the beach, is like the discovery of earthly paradise. It is as if she is living a perpetual dream.

Riacho Doce, however, is a place in the midst of radical transformation, similar to what we saw in *Usina*: the passage from a primitive economic phase, based on fishing and a little agriculture, to an industrial economy. Here again, even though it is not his world, the world of the plantation, the author casts the changes in a negative light. For him the end of the old order never represents progress; it is simply the passing from what we might call the bucolic stage to something that is indisputably worse. The people of Riacho Doce do not look kindly on the installation of an industrial complex, because right in front of them they can see the example of nearby Fernão Velho.

> Now the factory would draw people from over there. Riacho Doce would turn into Fernão Velho, where the people were the slaves of the

> factory whistle, and where the girls would work day and night, making themselves available to the bosses like milk cows. And perdition hung over everyone. Not one fisherman failed to fear for the future of Riacho Doce. They knew what Fernão Velho was like, close by, at the edge of the lagoon. The men were slaves. The women and children were all under the bosses' yoke.[75]

The folk of Riacho Doce are happy with the way they live, however, and do not want any changes.

This is a restatement of the emotional position of José Lins do Rego, who attributes to all his characters that love for the old order of things, which is, on the contrary, entirely his own.

There is a character in *Riacho Doce* whose stream of curses against progress alternate, as in the case of Feliciano from *Usina*, with praises of the good old days. She is an old matriarch who was said to have supernatural powers and whom everyone regards with devoted respect, as part *feiticeira, rezadeira, curandeira*. She is old Aninha, the grandmother of Nô, the handsome mulatto with whom Edna falls in love.

Edna lives a perfectly happy existence at Riacho Doce. If for her this is paradise on earth, for the local fishermen she is a sort of siren when, in her swimsuit—something unheard of at that time—she plunges into the waves and swims out to sea. Nô is the handsomest man in the village. He has worked as a sailor on ocean-going ships and now and again returns to the village, bringing with him tales of the marvels of different countries. On one of these returns he meets Edna, and the two of them conceive a violent passion for each other.

In this portrait of the two main characters, the author has tried to turn them into purely symbolic figures, attempting to remove them from all sense of conditioning by background or upbringing: on the one hand the dark and handsome sailor, the favored grandson of a wise woman, on the other hand the pretty blonde siren from the North. In short, Rego has done his best to turn them both into characters from a fable, outside reality, so as not to shock the sensibility of his public by the violation of the ancient taboo against the embrace of a white woman by a Black man.

But even though Nô and Edna are presented with a history and a past that fall quite outside the norm, they are two human beings, and it is here that the author actually contradicts himself. If, in fact,the character of Nô is rather summarily sketched (Rego has always found himself in great difficulty when obliged to describe personalities outside his personal Amarcord), the figure of Edna is quite different. Her whole manner of life and behavior is a reflection, both real and literary, of so many Brazilian ladies—sensitive, anxious, and dissatisfied—seeking an escape from that complete void of existence in which they find themselves trapped by virtue of their position as married women. Edna obviously has other customs, she is freer, she does not suffer from the atavistic conditioning of skin color; but for the rest she lacks credibility as a Northerner in her passive live-and-let-live attitude, in her lack of other interests. In short, in her submissiveness she is very like the Indian women whom the first colonists took for their own. One has the impression that the author, being unable to tell the tale of a well-bred Brazilian woman for reasons of social discretion, has simply lightened the skin of his heroine and given her a distant and mysterious past.

Quite apart from all this, what is very Brazilian is the reaction of the others, the people in the village and Carlos's colleagues. Old Aninha, Nô's grandmother, reacts as one might expect of her, calling down curses and anathemas on the head of the baggage who seduced her grandson and on the grandson who allowed himself to be seduced. While Edna remains immune to the old woman's attacks, Nô ends by having a fit of hysteria, after which he returns calmly and gently to the fold. The reaction of Carlos and his colleagues, however, is typically racist. They are not as worried by Edna's betrayal of her husband as they are by the fact that she betrayed him with a Black man. Let us not forget that this is 1939, racism is back in style, and many ideas that decency once forbade are once more gaining currency. The first of a series of racist reactions comes in the form of a reprimand from Carlos's superior:

> Doctor Silva was infuriated by his colleague's passivity. He was a man with no energy, no dignity. Could he therefore allow his wife to go with a mulatto, a ne'er-do-well who lived on the beach like a beast in heat, and did he not know what to do about it, as a man should?[76]

Again it is Doctor Silva who tells Carlos he cannot allow their wives to meet socially because of Edna's bad name. Then there is the understandable reaction of Carlos, who, however, is much more upset by the racial aspect of the affair, by the skin color of his wife's lover, than by the adultery itself. Naturally whenever Carlos refers to Nô he always calls him a *negro*, even though Nô is a mulatto, for the darker the skin, the greater the offense according to the racist mentality.

> That was the last straw . . . his wife giving herself to a *negro*. He did not have the courage to confront Edna, to learn that she had been with a man of a different color. What a disaster, a white woman with fair hair and blue eyes loving a Black man, and coupling with him.
>
> When he got home, he did not even have the courage to talk to her. He drank a lot during the evening, and it was late when he went to bed. For him her body stank where it lay stretched out next to him. A

woman who had been his had joined with, had given herself to a *negro* from the village. Edna made him sick.[77]

Carlos's anger boils over into pure racist hate:

He couldn't stand it any more. Everyone regarded him as a poor devil. Even the poorest workers with wives must have thought of him as someone badly done by. He drank, he didn't shave, and his wife, a white woman who was his, gave herself to a shiftless *negro*. She was the shame of her race. He had to do something.[78]

Then just to complete the picture there is the usual comparison with the animal world (how could Rego leave it out on this occasion?):

It was then he began to hear that savage cry, that groaning from an inferior creature, like an animal moaning in pain. And she let herself listen to such things. Her ears were open for such muck. In the room there was the gramophone, a refined selection of records, the music of civilized folk. And she sat there in a daze listening to a worthless vagabond moaning in self-pity.[79]

The novel ends with Nô reduced to a puppet in the hands of his grandmother, the old feiticeira Aninha, and Carlos in prison as the result of an accident at work. Edna, left alone, returns to the sea, seeking in the caress of the waves that embrace which her lover is no longer in a position to give her, and she swims and swims and swims.

Riacho Doce is a novel that comments on itself. We are presented on the one hand with the rhythm of the fable of the northern siren who returns to the waves and the old witch who puts a spell on her grandson. On the other hand we have typical reactions and attitudes of the Brazilian bourgeoisie. All takes place at a precise historical moment when the country, which was still uncertain about its own identity and still open to European influence, was about to clothe its typically petit-bourgeois racial preconceptions in ideological alibis. The later political choices, Brazil's support for the Western democracies against the Axis powers, dampened the spread of certain ideas and prejudices to which *Riacho Doce* gives voice.

We can conclude this chapter on José Lins do Rego by making a sharp and precise distinction between the artist and the man. As an artist and writer, he was one of the finest from Brazil. José Lins do Rego was without doubt the incomparable poet of the world of the casa grande and the senzala, and at the same time the writer who gave voice to those traditional and backward doctrines which refused to acknowledge the changing world beyond the limits of the plantation.

15 JORGE AMADO

The Long March of Hope

> And just before dawn, when shadow still enfolded the fields wet with dew and there rose in the air that powerful smell of earth, Nenén set off for the *caatinga* along the same route taken one day by Jerônimo and his family. The fruits of pain and revolt were growing in those months, red with blood and hunger; harvest time had come.[1]

Even in the vast field of Brazilian literature and the history of Brazil itself, Jorge Amado represents something much more than a writer, however illustrious and famous he may be. Amado is one of those historic figures, in the classic sense of the word, whose presence and influence have made themselves felt in modifying the way of life and thought of his own country. Jorge Amado is the great writer who, without losing any of his art, has managed to be popular, emerging definitively from the tight circle of cultured readers. His novels, taken up by the cinema and still more by television, have become daily topics even for those who have never picked up a book. In other words, Jorge Amado marks a decisive turning point in Brazilian literature.

Amado has also been a politician and fought with conviction for his ideas, bravely challenged the dictatorship of Estado Novo (being imprisoned more than once), been elected deputy for the Brazilian Communist party, vigorously attacked in his writings Hitler and every form of fascism when it was not fashionable to do so, especially in a Brazil that had close contact with the Axis forces. Finally, he has been and is a man able to carry on his political faith, in the noblest sense of the word, in all his writings.

Perhaps this is the secret of the enormous success of Jorge Amado: his works are an act of faith and hope in life. In fact, the Brazilian novel, even when politically and socially committed, always ended up reflecting a constant characteristic of the history of the country: the defeat of man with respect to his own land. The defeat has its remote origins in the very history of the country. Portuguese colonization, essentially commercial and poor in men, had crystallized into huge agricultural, landed estates based on an unalterable dualism of master and slave, thus closing itself to any form of progress or change—to guarantee its own survival—and remained practically the same for centuries. The end of slavery was, as we know, an act more legal than substantial, whose effects were to make themselves felt only towards the thirties when, under President Vargas, the country entered into its industrial phase. Vargas chose the road of capitalism for the country in spite of his populist promises and premises. Amado has always fought for the socialist road towards progress but, despite the enormous ideological differences that have led to enmity between them, they represent, with regard to politicians and writers, the new men, those who believe that after three centuries Brazil can and must change.

This is why we say that the works of Jorge Amado represent the long march of hope. Hope in man and in his destiny, the hope that overcomes the defeat of the individual to realize itself in the victory of those who carry on the fight. The hope of the man who no longer confines himself within the narrow, selfish limits of his own ego but accepts and recognizes himself in his companions, in his brothers. Hope in a tomorrow and in a future no longer the work of Providence or Destiny but the fruit of the struggle of men who finally recognize each other as equals.

Son of the land and son of a *fazendeiro*, like José Lins do Rego, his contemporary (he was born in Bahia in 1912), Amado differs totally from the great Paraiban writer with regard to his basic choice, which is not nostalgic return to the past but vitalistic eagerness projected towards the future. Amado's first novel was written in 1931, before he was twenty years old, and is a still unsure work entitled *O país do carnaval (The Land of Carnival).* It is the story of a young man, Paulo Rigger, who returns to his native land after a journey in Europe: enthusiasm, ambitions, ideals, a great desire to change the world, all crumble bit by bit in the emptiness of human relationships, the incapacity for realization, the endless table talk; and collapse definitively in the face of those preconceptions which the protagonist claimed he wanted to fight against and which he cannot in fact rid himself of. The book ends pessimistically with his affected escape-return to Europe, crossing in anguish and disgust the crazed city of Rio de Janeiro during Carnival—Carnival, the only oneiric reality in which a people that has renounced any more demanding form of expression realizes itself. Hope in spite of everything, despite juvenile romantic pessimism, hope realizes itself in the prayer of Paulo Rigger as he leaves the country of Carnival. The second novel is entitled *Cacau (Cocoa)* and appeared in 1933. A more mature and socially committed work, it has as a background the world of those great cocoa plantations which the writer knows so well, having spent his early youth there. It is the dramatic story of the *alugados* ("the rented" in the literal translation of the term), really and truly slaves in fact, agricultural laborers who hire themselves out to the great landowners, receiving in return for their work their keep and a miserable wage. The wage is, however, so miserable that these poor souls can never pay off their debts to the store of the *fazenda* where they are obliged to buy the provisions necessary for survival—thus their work relationship is but a new form of slavery. *Cacau* is also the story, told in the first person, of the descent into the hell of the cocoa fazenda of a young man of good family who, driven by family need, is forced to accept such a job—the story of two years of hard work and the slow formation of class consciousness, in the name of which the young man refuses the love of the fazendeiro's daughter. This too is an early work which presents social problems in pathetically dramatic forms. Still on the line of social and political commitment is the third novel, *Suor (Sweat)*, written in 1934. It is a choral work with several protagonists, set in a sordid block of houses in Ladeira do Pelourinho in Bahia, where many families live in inhuman conditions. Both *Cacau* and *Suor* are works that, in spite of the dramatic colors of the events, end with words of hope: the tragedy that strikes the lives of the protagonists is destined to pass, the struggle and the sacrifice will tomorrow bring forth their fruits in a better world.

After these three novels, which we could define as opening works, in 1935 Amado presented his first great masterpiece, *Jubiabá*. It is the story of a *pai-de-santo*, of a Black *feiticeiro* called Jubiabá and a Black boy, Antônio Balduíno. The pair may seem at first sight similar to Pai Lucas and Ricardo in *Moleque Ricardo*, written in 1936; seldom have two great writers been so far from each other in their visions of the world as José Lins do Rego and Jorge Amado. *Jubiabá* is a story of struggle and class consciousness in which Antônio Balduíno asserts himself without ever denying his Black cultural origins, represented by the *pai-de-santo* Jubiabá. It is also the painful and delicate story of the love between the Black Antônio Balduíno and the white Lindinalva. *Jubiabá* is a novel that, in spite of some youthful uncertainty still present in the themes chosen by the author, marked a decisive moment in the history of Brazilian literature and had an impact on the social conscience of the country far more violent than can be imagined today. Those were the years when nazism held sway in Europe and many racist theories found favorable echoes in Brazil. They were the years when Vargas chose the road of capitalism and was maneuvering between German and American partners. They were the years, too, when a young man from Bahia openly challenged the regime with a novel in which the Black protagonist (consider the stupendous opening scene where Antônio Balduíno defeats a German in a boxing match) brings to maturity a profound existential crisis, passing from racial to class struggle.

After the violent impact caused by the appearance of *Jubiabá*, Amado continued his literary project wherein art had necessarily to make itself the instrument to denounce social injustice, which appeared more violently and stridently in a country like Brazil, which was seeking to be rightfully recognized as an industrialized nation. In 1936 Amado brought out *Mar morto (Dead Sea)*, a delicate and poetical love story set in the world of fishermen in the port of Bahia. It is also the story of Black religious feeling, personified in the mythical figure of Iemanjá, the siren, the sea-goddess, whose hidden presence dominates the whole novel. The following year, 1937, Amado returned to a most determined political and social commitment, focusing his poetic attention on abandoned children surviving dramatically in a daily struggle against everything and everyone. The title of the novel is *Capitães da areia*, and literally means captains of the sand. It was on the beach, in fact, that these children, these youths without family, found shelter and formed gangs in abandoned and dilapidated buildings. While *Capitães da areia* recalls in part the childhood of Antônio Balduíno of *Jubiabá* (also the continuing presence of certain aspects of Black religious feeling), it asserts its complete autonomy in the pitiless and documented denunciation of the indifference, cruelty, and criminal irresponsibility of the public authorities and the well-to-do classes. The theme of childhood by its very nature obviously lends itself to pathos, but the writer skillfully manages to avoid insisting on facile sentimentality and instead makes of his novel a violent accusation of the collective responsibility of a world that shows itself ever more cruel and pitiless toward the weak and helpless. The ending does not lack a renewed act of political faith in the choice of some of the leading characters to take the road of class struggle and defiance of the regime in power.

Most of these novels are set in the city of Bahia, or Salvador as one may prefer to call it. Only one novel does not have the urban setting as a background and that is *Cacau*, where the action takes place on a cocoa plantation in the interior of Ilhéus. Amado is deeply tied, as a man and as a writer, to two distinct worlds. The first is the city of

Bahia with its splendid baroque churches, its harbor teeming with *saveiros* always full of people, fruit, and various wares, its Mercado Modelo with the multicolored masses that throng in it, the various markets, the narrow, filthy, and beautiful streets, its population of Blacks, mulattoes, and whites, the thousand festivals of Black religion. The second world to which Amado is tied is that of the great cocoa plantations that gravitate around the town of Ilhéus, to the south of Bahia. It is a world he knows very well through first-hand experience, as he is the son of one of those fazendeiros who were the protagonists of the history of the zone, a history made up of violent struggles, gunfights, ambushes, *caxixe*, or apparently legal fraud, of corruption, of gangs of *jagunços*. It is the history of the conquest of a region by determined and cruel men, men seeking to obtain the greatest possible wealth in a war with no holds barred against the land and against their fellow men. It is the history of a struggle with no place for the weak, those inevitably doomed to succumb.

Thus Amado left for a certain time the picturesque world of Bahia to return to the scenes of his childhood. Ten years had passed since the writing of *Cacau*; ten years in which his art and political awareness had ripened. At the same time, however, there is in Amado a clear pride and local patriotism. After all, he is speaking of those countrymen of his who, together with his father or against his father, literally conquered and colonized the region. How then is he to reconcile a *chanson de geste* of the *grapiúna* people with his own distinct political choices, especially in those years when the Vargas dictatorship appeared more and more repressive and violent? Amado achieves his aim perfectly by dividing the history of the region into two novels: the first is set at the beginning of this century during the conflict between fazendeiros for the possession of the land; the second takes place in the same spot right in the middle of the Vargas era, twenty years after the events related in the first novel. *Terras do sem fim*, meaning literally, boundless lands, published in 1942, is a true epic in which events and characters who actually existed are idealized in a plot constructed according to the classical schemes of popular storytelling. There are two powerful family clans: Coronel Horácio da Silveira and all his allies on one side, and on the other, two powerful brothers, the fazendeiros Sinhô and Juca Badaró. In the middle, between the fazendas of the rival groups, is the cause of the dispute, the great forest, the *mata* of Sequeiro Grande. The story is of a long war, interspersed with a series of secondary events and minor characters in which Amado does not conceal his human sympathies for those men who created a country. Sinhô Badaró and Horácio da Silveira, the two rival fazendeiros, are two giants, two men who tower above the others in their stature and the moral force that animates them. Horácio wins, but in the just distribution of rewards in the novel, he is to lose his wife, Ester, and lose her twice, the first time when she dies and the second when he discovers that she was unfaithful to him with another man and never loved him. The Badaró brothers lose but the beautiful and courageous daughter of Sinhô Badaró marries the man she loves, who carries on the family with her.

The story of *São Jorge dos Ilhéus*, published in 1944, is set in the same places twenty or so years after the events described in *Terras do sem fim*. The author himself gives an explanation that illustrates the two novels better than any other comment:

> In these two books I have tried to show, with impartiality and passion, the drama of the cocoa economy, the conquest of the land on the part of feudal *coronéis* at the beginning of the century, and the passing of the land into the greedy hands of the exporters in recent years. The novelist is not to blame if the drama of feudal conquest is epic and that of capitalist conquest merely shabby. Joaquim says that the next stage will be full of heroism, beauty, and poetry, and I believe him.[2]

Joaquim in *São Jorge dos Ilhéus* is a young worker, a militant Communist who struggles to spread the ideas of revolt and the hope that the world may one day change. He is the son of a small farmer, Antônio Vítor, one of the Badarós' workers, who has received a piece of land in return for his services. Joaquim refuses to follow his father's example, to take advantage of the little privilege that comes to him through being the owner of a piece of land. In accordance with his ideas, he understands that running a plantation, small though it may be, against competition forces one to exploit the agricultural workers. Thus he is in conflict with his father who, having laboriously passed from the status of laborer to that of small landowner, does not understand in what sense he is robbing his workers. If anything he complains of his inability to exploit them as well as the great landowners who have more capital available and thus greater bargaining power.

The affairs of Joaquim and his father are, however, but a symbolic story which forms the background to the main drama, the struggle between the great exporters and the fazendeiros for the possession of the land and of power; the imperialist struggle spoken of by the author in the introduction, made up of commercial maneuvers, replaces the feudal battles of the old coronéis, fought out in terms of rifle shots. The plan of the exporters is simple. It consists of keeping the price of cocoa high for all the time that it is in demand on the world markets. At the same time they generously finance the fazendeiros, lending them money at interest, practically acting as banks. When the price of cocoa falls on the world markets, the fazendeiros have no possibility of paying their debts. The exporters, combined in a sort of trust, thus become the owners of the land without striking a blow. It is a typically Brazilian affair, perfectly real, and there was certainly no need for the deeply anticapitalist spirit of Amado to force the truth. The author did nothing but take inspiration from the reality of the facts. One of the aspects of the Brazilian spirit is what we could call negation of the protestant work ethic, something translated onto the practical plane as living from day to day, enjoying well and immediately what one has earned without worrying about the future. This happened historically more than once and is wonderfully well described in *São Jorge dos Ilhéus*. Great and sudden wealth is not used to create more wealth; it is not reinvested to produce more capital. Instead it is squandered and scattered in a long and exhilarating festival that lasts for almost three years and transforms the city of Ilhéus: casinos, the building of elegant houses, luxurious cars, fine clothes, travel, French and Polish prostitutes (even hired love has its own forms of snobbery), a continuous and obsessive ostentation of wealth. It is not only the great fazendeiros who participate in this kind of long carnival; the abundance is for all. The rich spend a lot, the poor spend everything they manage to earn. And when the price of cocoa falls on the world markets, no fazendeiro and no small farmer has the money necessary to pay off the debts to the exporters, who thus become owners of everything.

In *São Jorge dos Ilhéus*, as in *Terras do sem fim*, just deserts are meted out at the end of the novel. Carlos Zude, chief of the exporters, loses his beautiful wife, who leaves him to go and live with a young poet. Another exporter is killed, and all in all the coronéis are merely paying for all the ill they have done their workers. In *São Jorge dos Ilhéus* the writer moves with greater political freedom than in *Terras do sem fim*, where he was personally bound up with the events narrated, to the point of including himself among the characters: "A child, who years after was to write the history of that land, was called by a registar to draw out the names of the citizens chosen to form the jury."[3] In *São Jorge dos Ilhéus*, however, the writer has no problems of personal ties or links of affection for the characters of the events related: the winners are the exporters, mostly foreigners, representatives of that international capitalism against which the writer has always fought, and the commercial coup they carry out finds its place in the classic framework of consumer society. We could therefore say that while *Terras do sem fim* is a reevocative historical novel (and in my opinion the better of the two), *São Jorge dos Ilhéus* is a politically constructed work, its characters and events giving at times the impression of being realized through a precise demonstration.

In 1945 Amado courageously continued his political battle by publishing a book entitled *O cavaleiro da esperança (The Knight of Hope)*, which is the story of a long march, twenty-six thousand kilometers in nearly three years, carried out by Luís Carlos Prestes and his men in an attempt to push the peasant masses into revolt. At the time the book was published, Luís Carlos Prestes, having in the meantime become the leader of the Brazilian Communist party, was in prison. The aim of the book for the writer was to come to his aid.

In 1946 Amado published the book in which he was able to achieve a perfect balance between artistic representation, political and ideological choices, sociological analysis, and historical reevocation. This book, *Seara vermelha (Red Harvest)*, is a work in which the author for the first time moves outside the environment in which he had operated thus far, the city of Bahia and the hinterland of Ilhéus. In this novel Amado tackles the problem of underdevelopment in the agricultural world of the Northeast, viewing through modern eyes and ideological commitment all the aspects of the most backward part of Brazilian society: the part tied up with the great landed estates, which had been cut off from the renewal of the country and left in the bonds of those structures which the end of slavery had in no way altered. *Seara vermelha* is a perfectly constructed work of sociological literature that focuses on and analyzes all the recurring motifs in the literature of the *sertão*, seen through the vicissitudes of a family of *retirantes* driven from the estate on which they worked. The journey of Jerônimo and his family across the arid *caatinga* represents one of the greatest classics among the odysseys of hunger in a succession of episodes that never fall into pathos and are recounted with sober and measured art:

> Wild and inhospitable, the *caatinga* extends. The dry bushes rise for leagues and leagues in the *sertão*, dry and bristling as a desert of thorns. Snakes and lizards drag themselves among the stones in the stifling sun of midday. They are enormous lizards and look as though they have survived since the beginning of the world, still, with no expression in their staring eyes, like primitive sculptures . . . The thorns interlock in the *caatinga*, the impassable desert, the inviolable heart of the Northeast, drought, thorns, and poison, the lack of everything, of the roughest trail, of any tree with good shade and juicy fruit . . . And across the

> *caatinga*, cutting it from every side, travels an innumerable mass of peasants. They are men driven from the land by the great estates and the drought, turned out of their own homes, with no work in the *fazendas*, going in search of São Paulo, the Eldorado of their imaginations . . . The journey began a long time ago and nobody knows when it will end because every year the farmers who have lost their land, the exploited workers, the victims of society and of the *coronéis*, gather together their rags, their children, and their last strength and hit the trail . . . Large families set out and by the time they reach Pirapora, illness and hunger have cut them by half. In the towns near the *caatinga* the most incredible stories, the most terrible misfortunes are related, those no novel could recount without seeming absurd . . . The emigrants are always the same, the names may change but the faces are identical, the same hunger, the same fatalism, the same determination in walking. Crossing the *caatinga*, the stones, the thorns, the snakes, the lizards, they go ever on towards São Paulo where they say there is land for everyone and easy money, or they return from São Paulo where there is neither land nor money . . . The bodies lie along the improvised paths and even they do not modify the desolate landscape where, in the blazing sun, indifferent reptiles sleep. Water is found only where the misery of the *caatinga* ends and the misery of the São Francisco begins.[4]

In addition to the story of the family of Jerônimo and the tragic march towards the South, there is the story of three other members of the same family, the first three children who had long before left home in search of a different destiny. Their stories are symbolic of a northeastern reality that Jorge Amado has done no more than translate into the terms of a novel. One of the sons becomes a *cangaceiro* and is by now famous under the name of Zé Trevoada. His group of bandits joins, after many adventures, a large group of pilgrims following a preacher, the *beato* Estevão, and together they face the forces of the army (the joining of cangaceiros and beatos is another of the constants of the history of the sertão, its most famous example being in the affairs of Canudos and Antônio Conselheiro, of Juazeiro and Padre Cícero). Another son, Jão, joins the military police and falls in combat at the hands of the cangaceiros of his brother in the fight against the people of Estevão. The third, whom everyone calls Nenén, after becoming a soldier as well, matures politically, becomes a Communist and, after a failed revolution, returns to the sertão, to the very spot from which his family left, to preach the message of revolt.

Seara vermelha is a novel but also a work of sociology and politics. The sociological analysis always arrives at the same conclusion: hope is entrusted to a radical change of society possible only through a

Communist revolution. *Seara vermelha* also represents the highest point achieved by Amado in his political novels. In 1952 Amado published *Os subterrâneos da liberdade (The Undergrounds of Liberty)*, in three volumes. This work, through many characters, narrates the history of the Brazilian Communist party during the Vargas era, when persecution was strongest. Most determined was the pressure of the multinationals, eager to corner ample concessions in Brazil with the support of a grasping and corrupt bourgeoisie. The events are interesting—Jorge Amado is a consummate narrator—but the political charge that animates them ends up dominating the whole story. One has the impression that all the other motifs, including the sociological ones, are subordinated to ideological choices.

Evidently Amado was ready to change the literary genre of his work as a writer. And the change came punctually in 1958 with the appearance of the amusing and highly popular *Gabriela, cravo e canela (Gabriela, Clove and Cinnamon)*. What motivated this change that has led to such polemic and criticism, and disconcerted all those who saw the writer by now as an infallible oracle? Going beyond the explanations of the author himself, somewhat vague in fact, and the thousand hypotheses brought out by critics at the time, with the years that have passed we can say that the authentic change was one of historical evolution during the nearly thirty years between the publishing of *O país do carnaval* and *Gabriela, cravo e canela*. The thirties were really decisive years for Brazil, years in which everything truly was possible, years in which the form of development and the future social order of the country were to be decided. Brazil was forced to industrialize and abandon her classic agricultural structure. The great masses for the first time became aware of their strength. The bourgeoisie was disoriented and still tied to frameworks and privileges of feudal origin. Progress and the advent of machines made a large impact. The modern system of communications informed one in a matter of hours of the great crises and great ideological movements sweeping Europe and the United States. In those years everything really was possible and some structural similarities between Brazil and Russia—slavery and serfdom, landed estates and bureaucratic state—made a Communist solution to the problems of Brazil perfectly credible. They were the years of Vargas but also the years of men like Hitler, Stalin, Mussolini. They were years of irreversible and fatal choice.

Amado believed in communism, struggled and suffered exile and prison to assert his political ideal. He sincerely believed, and said so on more than one occasion, that communism of the type realized in the Soviet Union and the countries of eastern Europe was applicable to Brazil. Then came the Second World War with all its consequences. Amado, winner of the Stalin prize, traveled at length in Russia and the eastern countries and saw for himself the reality of the communism he had always dreamt of. Through posthumous self-criticism there came to light the crimes of Stalin, the same Stalin the author had exalted in *Os subterrâneos da liberdade*. In 1954 Vargas died, and if the system did not collapse, at least the man who had represented it disappeared (the man, too, who had been able to shake the hand of and ally himself to Luís Carlos Prestes, the legendary hero for whom Amado had written *O cavaleiro da esperança*). However, in 1956 the invasion of Hungary by the Soviet Union saw the collapse of many illusions and the ratification of the division of the world with the forces of capitalism.

Of the many choices open to him, Amado made perhaps the best: a return to life, to his roots, to mulatto Brazil, to the joy of life. His criticism of the system, of intolerance, of power structures, of the wrong done by man to man, continued as before, but the dogmatic choices were replaced by a mocking and desecrating irony. Jorge Amado is a man with the courage to emerge from his own mythical aura and to participate daily in the evolution of the problems of the common man.

With *Gabriela, cravo e canela* Amado returns to the land of his origin and his adolescence, to Ilhéus at the time of the cocoa boom. Again we find the coronéis always in conflict among themselves; there are the exporters, chief among whom is Mundinho Falcão, an ambitious young man from the capital. There is an infinity of characters in this story, and a whole city changes its face under the stimulus of the prosperity cocoa represents. The environment described in this book is basically the same as that of *Cacau, Terras do sem fim*, and above all *São Jorge dos Ilhéus*, but the moral stance of the author has changed deeply. Here it is no longer a matter of hope for a radical change in the world. Here hope presents itself in a more limited way as a hypothesis of the improvement of the simple world at our disposal. But above all the world of Ilhéus in transformation moves into the background to serve as the setting for the story of Gabriela, the beautiful young mulatto girl who arrives in town one fine morning from the sertão with a group of retirantes driven out by the drought. During the journey she has met and loved a young farmer, Clemente, but refuses to marry and follow him, preferring to try the adventure of city life by herself. Since writing *Suor*, Amado has known how to create courageous, free, and independent women.

Gabriela is one of these in her love of freedom, only she is less idealized, more real, and infinitely more likable. And so Gabriela, a good cook, gets a job in the Vesuvio bar, owned by the Arab Nacib, a naturalized Brazilian. From the second day on Gabriela is Nacib's mistress, spontaneously, sincerely, because she likes Nacib and she likes love. A strange relationship grows up between the two. While Nacib becomes more and more possessive and protective, jealous of the attentions paid to his beautiful cook and mistress by all the rich men of the town, Gabriela continues to love him with splendid simplicity. Nacib manages to get over all his petit-bourgeois preconceptions and marries Gabriela, hoping thus to tie her to him definitively. Instead, the marriage turns out to be a catastrophe for them because Gabriela cannot bear all the obligations the role of married lady involves. Gabriela is unfaithful to Nacib, but without hate, anger, or premeditation; or rather she is not unfaithful to him at all because she still feels free, because love is beautiful, because she feels that she belongs only to herself, because she loves Nacib but there are so many handsome young men around and the life of a married lady is so boring . . . Nacib finds out, the marriage is annulled, and the two separate though they still love each other. Then, one day, Nacib finds himself without a cook and he has an important lunch. They suggest that he contact Gabriela and the whole thing begins again. Gabriela is again cook and mistress, happy to belong to Nacib, to be herself, to love. The fable is a beautiful one with much hidden teaching.

In 1962 Amado produced two more beautiful fables in *Os velhos marinheiros*, the old sailors who are not in fact sailors at all but feel themselves such even though they have never set foot on a boat. This story is another mocking and irreverent criticism of bourgeois respectability, of social conventions, of the absurd laws that regulate the relationships between men and against which Gabriela rebelled before. There are two sailors in the story, protagonists of two different tales. The first is a former model employee who one day abandons family, office, and bourgeois respectability to go to live among prostitutes, tramps, and drunks. His name is Quincas, known as Berro Dágua, that is, Howl of Water, because of the fearful howl he uttered one day when, as a merry drunkard, he gulped down a glass of water believing it to be *cachaça*. Quincas lives his life joyfully, a life as carefree for him as it is a source of care and worry for his family and all his relatives. Death overtakes Quincas in a filthy room where he lives—in fact the tale begins with the death scene: the relatives sigh in relief to be rid of his disturbing presence, a source of continual shame. Equally sincere is the grief of the motley crew formed by his many friends. Here we find the scheme of contrast that is present in almost all the works of the second phase of Jorge Amado's writings and which is clearly delineated here through the two deaths of Quincas: the official death complete with medical certificate and accompanied by the sorrow, equally official, of his relatives; and the real death twenty-four hours later, in the sea as Quincas had always wanted, as the old sailor he had always felt himself to be. In fact during the funeral vigil the relations withdraw and the friends remain, the real ones, companions of sprees and drinking bouts. These friends are drunk enough to convince themselves at a certain point that Quincas cannot be dead. They raise him, support him with his arms around their shoulders and together live through an exhilarating nocturnal adventure that in fact ends up at sea, on a boat where during a sudden squall Quincas disappears in the waves, choosing his own death, the one he had always wanted, the one worthy of an old sailor.

If the story of the double death of Quincas is a graceful fable desecrating the myths of petit-bourgeois respectability, the story of the sea captain (a false captain here, too) Vasco Moscoso is another lovable mockery of the bourgeois cult of qualifications, the myth of efficiency, and professional capacity. Vasco Moscoso is another jolly fellow who has spent everything he inherited on revels and carousing. At a certain point in his life, however, he feels the lack of a title to show off to his numerous friends. A friend of his, a naval officer, procures the diploma of sea captain for him. Here the fun begins because "the cassock is enough to make the priest," no matter what the proverbs may say. Vasco Moscoso falls perfectly into the role of seaman; little by little he creates for himself a past, and acquires seafaring habits and objects. Having become an elderly man, an old sea dog, he retires to a distant suburb of Salvador to live out in peace the legend he has created with no fear of being recognized. Then one fine day, or foul day rather, all the years of effort to build a character for himself risk shipwreck through a banal accident, because Vasco is obliged through a series of fortuitous circumstances to take command of a real ship heading for Belém do Pará. He manages to carry it off brilliantly for the whole voyage, leaving the task of sailing the ship to his officers, but makes a blunder at the end which gives his real identity away: he has the ship tied to the pier with every available piece of rope. That very night, however, unforeseen by old sea dogs and the scientists of the meteorological service alike, a tremendous gale blows up, which tears from their anchorage all the ships except, naturally, one, the one belonging to Captain Vasco Moscoso who, the only one out of so many, has foreseen the hurricane and tied up his ship properly. He makes a triumphant return to official gratitude, the glory of the newspapers and of his birthplace. This time there is not even the contrast between two realities as in the death of Quincas; instead the dreams and fantasies of Vasco find the governor and a brass band on the pier of Bahia harbor.

Still following the line of the two truths in opposition to each other, Amado published in 1964 *Os pastores da noite (Shepherds of the Night)*, three stories about the people of Bahia. The first is a likably male-chauvinist tale that relates the farcical and absurd case of the marriage of Martim, a former corporal in the army who lived by gambling and other shady activities, activities he was forced into because he did not consider it fitting for one who had been a soldier to stoop to work. The second story takes place within the world of Black religion and involves the baptism in a Catholic church of a child whose godfather is Ogun, one of the most important personages of the Black Olympus. And then there is the devil, Exu, who comes to disrupt the party and play tricks until everything is settled and returns to official normalcy. Yet again the two realities coexist perfectly, one sanctioned by the ceremony and documents, and one seen and followed by the few. The third is a tale of the people's occupation of a hill earmarked for building speculation, in which the author returns to the never-forgotten social theme. A thousand stories jumbled together and interwoven, the everyday reality of the poor people living in hastily fashioned huts contrasts with the multiple opposing interests of bankers, authorities, officials, policemen, politicians, journalists, bunglers, and so on. And after great struggles everything resolves itself in the victory of the people and the presence of another reality: a dead man, the only fatality in the battle to occupy the hill, comes back as an *orixá* in every *candomblé*, always incarnated in a beautiful girl with whom he dances the night away.

Jorge Amado has by now taken great strides towards the deepest cultural roots of the Black soul recreated on Brazilian soil: the pantheistic concept of the universe, the immanence of the forces of nature in the daily working out of human events, the annulling of the traditional barrier between real and unreal burst forth again in *Dona Flor e seus dois maridos* (*Dona Flor and Her Two Husbands*, 1966). This novel too begins with a death, as does the tale of "Quincas Berro Dágua." Here the one who dies is Vadinho, the young and handsome husband of Flor. Poor Flor relives in her memory the happy—and the not so happy—hours lived at the side of a man like Vadinho, capable of great tenderness and of violent passion, but also an unfaithful husband, fanatical gambler, and spendthrift (when he had anything to spend). After a strained period of widowhood, the beautiful Flor finds peace by marrying Teodoro, a still youthful chemist, who offers her a life of quiet ease. Yet Flor feels the lack of something, that something represented by the absurd folly of Vadinho. And Vadinho returns, invisible to all but Flor, whose heart and whose feelings as a faithful wife he throws into confusion as he does all the gambling tables. Magic, spells, candomblés are invoked to drive him away, but it appears that Vadinho enjoys high protection in the Black pantheon. In the end Flor lives happily ever after, as in the fairy stories, together with her two husbands.

The two leading characters in *Dona Flor e seus dois maridos* are white and the setting in which the story unfolds is that of the petite bourgeoisie, which is always described with amiable irony. The whole story is, however, a continual contrast between the two forms of reality already encountered in the previous stories: the official reality that culminates in the medical certificate asserting the death of Vadinho, and the reality that lives in the feelings of the protagonists and keeps them close and united beyond what are, for them, mere appearances. What is the truth in this beautiful fable? And then, what sense has truth, what sense can it have when it is applied to the feelings of men?

With *Dona Flor e seus dois maridos* Amado practically achieves perfection in the genre he inaugurated with *Gabriela, cravo e canela*. But Amado is one of those men who live their times intensely and has once already come down from his pillar to abandon the literature of social and political commitment that had made him famous. And the times have changed again: the hard and violent era of Vargas with its exhilarating possibility of definitive and irreversible choices to be made is no more, but also no more is the era of socialist illusions bound up with the creation of Brasília. The military coup d'etat of 1964, which had at the beginning seemed merely incidental, keeps on consolidating its position in technocratic structures bound to the forces of capital and repression. By now it is no longer time for comedy. New forms of intolerance arise in a world on the brink of the ephemeral spring of 1968. And Amado begins his battle over again, publishing in 1969 *Tenda dos milagres (The Tent of Miracles)*, where by miracles are meant the miraculous facts and events that are related in designs on parchment or printed in the workshop. And in the tent, or shop, which is also a center where some friends meet, is always to be found Pedro Archanjo, a mulatto, janitor for the faculty of medicine in Bahia, an adept of candomblé, *capoeira*, and lover of life in all its manifestations. The novel begins in the early years of this century and is a story of the self-awareness and triumph of the Black in Brazil. Pedro Archanjo will remain a man of modest social condition all his life, but what counts is his slow and determined cultural assertion. Starting from the desire to give a more solid content to certain elements of Black life such as Carnival, candomblé, capoeira, and samba, he succeeds in publishing, not without great difficulties, a series of studies clearly defining the determining contribution made to the culture and ethnic formation of Bahia by the Black world. Struggles against the police and against the incomprehension and disdain of reactionary culture, intermingled with loves and adventures, are the constant motif of the half century of activity of the courageous mulatto, who dies on the street in proud poverty.

Tenda dos milagres is a return to the theme already dealt with in 1935 in *Jubiabá* but without the doubling of the characters—Jubiabá, the old *feiticeiro* tied to his African origins, and Antônio Balduíno, young and strong, oriented towards the new social problems, are here united in the character of Pedro Archanjo, young and old in the course of his life, agile capoeira and wise feiticeiro, African in his origins and participator in the new times, white and Black, Brazilian, mulatto. What instead remains unaltered is the framework introduced into the new novels by Jorge Amado, the doubling up of reality. In fact the novel unfolds on two planes distant from each other in time. Pedro Archanjo has by now been dead for many years, and in the Bahia of the Brazilian economic miracle and the miniskirt there arrives the great American Nobel Prize winner Levenson who, before a disconcerted and ignorant audience, speaks of a great scholar of Bahia—Pedro Archanjo, of course. The declarations of the Nobel Prize winner catch the cultural world of Bahia off guard, but the resources of the Establishment are infinite as are the ways of Providence. Newspaper editors, university professors, captains of industry, political figures, the authorities, all take over the figure of Pedro Archanjo and organize his official commemoration in the new climate of nationalistic pride promoted daily by the dictatorship through all the channels of information. According to the reality of the Establishment, Pedro Archanjo is transformed into the consumer product of the totalitarian and consumeristic ideology against which he always fought; Pedro Archanjo becomes the theme of Carnival in 1969 and returns in triumph through the streets of his Bahia, the same streets where, half a century before, defying the bans of the police, he had dared to bring into another Carnival the figure of Zumbi dos Palmares, the hero of Black revolt.

With the next two novels, *Tereza Batista cansada de guerra* (*Tereza Batista Tired of War*, 1972) and *Tieta do Agreste*, published in 1977,

Amado managed to avoid the facile trap the advent of military dictatorship in 1964 offered to such a writer, the most popular in Brazil. He saw with perfect intuition that the coup d'état carried out by the military was the most obvious aspect of an Establishment that had its roots in the new political world order, in the dealings of the multinationals, and in a certain structure of Brazilian society. The evil had to be fought at the source; sending the soldiers back into their barracks would be of no use if the Establishment were able to continue perpetuating its logic through other officials. The pages of *Tenda dos milagres*, with the thousand tricks to absorb and pervert the nature of the figure of Pedro Archanjo, are profoundly significant.

Tereza Batista cansada de guerra is the story of a young and beautiful woman, Tereza, from a small village in the interior and is told according to the patterns of the literature of *cordel*. What did it mean to be a woman in a world like that of Brazilian agrarian civilization which had existed for so long on slavery? It meant being something very like a slave, an object of desire, a piece of goods to be exchanged, a maid at best. For centuries the masters had taken advantage of their female slaves with complete impunity and the situation, as we know, did not substantially change with the end of slavery. A beautiful adolescent, Tereza is sold by her relatives to a rich and brutal businessman, Capitão Justiniano Duarte da Rosa, who for months rapes her and tames her to the point of complete submission as though she were an animal. But the submission of Tereza is only apparent, even if it does last for some years. When she discovers love in the person of a handsome young coward, she does not hesitate to kill her tormentor when he surprises them. Locked up in prison, Tereza is released and taken up by a rich *usineiro*, Emiliano Guedes, already an elderly man. With Emiliano, Tereza leads a life of tranquil ease, warmed by mutual love. Emiliano is very good to her but always remains, in every instant of their life together, the master in the fullest sense of the word. The death of Emiliano sends Tereza back on the streets and into a thousand adventures: prostitute, dancer, and organizer of a strike of prostitutes in Bahia. Finally she finds Januário, an athletic fisherman and good man, to whom she gives herself in complete freedom.

Tereza Batista who from a thousand adventures and a thousand misfortunes is born again eternally virgin and ready to love and live is perhaps a Brazilian symbol—from slavery to hope? Perhaps. Or perhaps the story is a fable of the character of the woman in a slave-owning and male-chauvinist world who, on the long march of suffering and servitude, finally claims the right to choose and give herself in freedom.

The story of Tieta, the beautiful protagonist of *Tieta do Agreste*, is told with the same popular-novel type of rhythm. Even though Tieta is a woman like Tereza—and the two have many points in common—it is no longer the female condition that is the object of Amado's attention. There are other forms of violence, other forms of slavery. A great multinational company has to create a huge factory, the waste from which has a high level of pollution (and Amado took as an example the case of Montedison in Italy); many countries have absolutely refused to grant permission to build the plant on their territory. There exist, however, countries with a desperate need of capital, countries where the weight of public opinion is of little importance. Thus Brazil is chosen and in particular a poor zone in the state of Bahia. The only thing left to decide is whether the site is to be Arembepe (where a factory creating great pollution has, in fact, been built and has destroyed forever a picturesque and beautiful fishing village) or the imaginary village of Sant'Ana do Agreste. The sly tricks of the Establishment carried out in closed environments or luxurious brothels interweave with the return of Tieta, a splendid forty-year-old, to the village of her birth. She had left her village many years before, as an adolescent shepherd girl driven from her home after allowing herself to be seduced by the inevitable traveling salesman. Everyone believes that Tieta is the widow of a rich industrialist from São Paulo, but in fact she is the fortunate proprietress of a deluxe brothel frequented exclusively by men of power.

Once again Amado develops the interweaving of two realities: Tieta wins the battle of progress and Sant'Ana do Agreste is to have electricity and a road while the pernicious *usina*, wanted by some and opposed by others, is diverted towards Arembepe. However, she loses the battle to reinsert herself in the village because her real status as brothel keeper is discovered. Winner and loser, Tieta sets off again on the road to São Paulo, but the memory of her dwells in the minds of those who have known her and her splendid qualities as a human being.

With *Farda, fardão, camisola de dormir* in 1979 Jorge Amado inaugurated a new genre. *Farda* is the military uniform, *fardão* the dress of those elected to the Academia Brasileira de Letras, and *camisola de dormir* is a nightgown. The story is of two men in farda, two soldiers, who at the time of the Estado Novo are in the running for the fardão, a place in the Academy, made vacant by the death of a poet in love with life and with women (the attractive theme of the nightgown comes from the verses of his last poem). An absurd game of a thousand intrigues plotted by the diabolical old men already in the

Academy brings to nought the ambitions of the two soldiers, who die of heart failure. And Amado, an authoritative and respected member of the Academy, passing from one desecration to another, has managed to desecrate himself.

The world of Jorge Amado is a macrocosm of characters who are at times different and contradictory. But the contradiction is above all apparent. Even the passing from the first phase to the second with *Gabriela, cravo e canela* in 1958, which disconcerted critics and admirers so much, neither impaired nor altered the structures and principles to which the author has always remained attached. What many critics forget is that the time factor has changed, with a frightening acceleration, in the last fifty years, subverting not only habits and customs but also moral values themselves. And Amado is a man of his times, a man who lives out the dramas and problems of his times with passion and intensity. And his time is as much 1930 as it is 1980. It is certainly not his fault if in 1930 he was an extremely precocious twenty-year-old writer and in 1980 a youthful old man with no intention of wrapping himself up in his own myth. What did certain critics want him to do? Did the critics want him laboriously to repeat the same themes without realizing that contemporary Brazil is certainly not what it was in the thirties? The historical acceleration we are all involved in and all witnesses of is much more rapid in Brazil just because of the lack of a historical basis with its relative conditioning. Brazil undergoes technical progress much more quickly because it does not have a span of history or structure to be taken into account. The Brazil of atomic plants, computers, heart transplants, and polluted megacities presents problems and structures quite different from the Brazil of the thirties with her *cangaceiros* and *beatos*, even if the preachers and bandits on horseback do exist today. The filthy block of houses at 68 Ladeira do Pelourinho, where Jorge Amado the student stayed in 1928 and where, in 1934, he set *Suor*, is today a charming little hotel and nothing remains of its past but a commemorative plaque. To make up for this, building speculation is destroying the nature of certain quarters of the city, all except the old center. Arembepe is no longer a romantic fishing village—its sky and its sea have been polluted for good and nothing remains of the old days but the memory. The war goes on, the injustice of man to man continues, only the forms have changed and the strike of Antônio Balduíno was only a battle. Lindinalva, seduced and abandoned, has no choice other than the slow death of prostitution, and like her the courageous Marta of *Seara vermelha* will disappear into the brothels. In their place Tereza Batista and Tieta do Agreste will continue to love, to seduce, to fight for the right to live with dignity and in freedom. The war is not finished, said Pedro Archanjo; violence and injustice are reborn after every battle and after every battle it is necessary to see under what mask the eternal enemy is hiding.

Black Man, White Man; From Racial Struggle to Class Struggle

> Antônio Balduíno goes to the house of Jubiabá. Now he regards the *pai-de-santo* as an equal. And he tells him that he has found out what the ABC taught and that he has found the right path. The rich had dried the eye of pity. But they could dry the eye of evil whenever they wanted. And Jubiabá, the *feiticeiro*, bows before him as though he were Oxolufã, old Oxalá, the greatest of saints.[5]

In Jorge Amado the Black world takes on a totally new dimension in a radical change of viewpoint. With Amado the Black definitively ceases to be the "other," the one to be observed with greater or lesser understanding, but always as one belonging to a world different from that of the observer. Amado has no need to go down from the *casa grande* every time he speaks of Blacks; in his novels the Blacks, whites, and mulattoes always move on the one plane so that there is never the impression that any one of them is the "other."

O país do carnaval is, as we know, an extremely youthful work and presents many elements of uncertainty. In this novel there is some indication of the attacks made in Bahia on all those mulattoes who took up intellectual positions and were all the rage in the literary world. Amado himself, who has always defended the value of the mulatto in the creation of the Brazilian world, let slip some unpleasant remarks against the half-breeds, similar in this to writers such as José Lins do Rego and Graça Aranha. In any case, the repulsion felt by Paulo Rigger, the protagonist, for Carnival, from which he flees, is similar to that found in the attitude of Radagásio in *A viagem maravilhosa*.

One of the protagonists of *O país do carnaval* is an old journalist, Pedro Ticiano, a man with a glorious past who carries out his work in Bahia:

> In Bahia, which in other times had been called the Athens of Brazil, there flourished in that epoch the most complete stupidity.
>
> Pedro Ticiano decided to make, in the *buona terra*, a campaign in favor of intelligence. He began by attacking *mulatismo*. A man of courage, he ended up being the terror of the students who claimed to be poets and of the peddlers who wrote the leading articles for the newspapers of Bahia.[6]

Here we remember what José Lins do Rego and Graça Aranha said about the mulattoes and their ability to adapt best to the country and careers in the bureaucracy. We can therefore have an idea of the hostile attitude of many young whites toward their dark-skinned contemporaries. In the novel, Pedro Ticiano represents to some extent the wise old prophet fallen on hard times; and the reason for his professional decline is to be sought in the war against him by the bureaucrats of culture, the mulattoes in fact: "And so he remained in Bahia, poor, having as a prize for his great life the hatred of all the half-breeds writing there."[7]

Let us remember that Amado wrote *O país do carnaval* at an age when one would normally be taking final exams at high school; a great deal of the uncertainty is therefore easily attributed to the influences of his environment. And the environment was certainly not tender toward the representatives of the emerging classes, among whom there were, of course, the mulattoes.

Paulo Rigger, the protagonist, has some literary pretensions and writes a poem on the figure of the Brazilian mulatto girl, a poem in which all the same old clichés are repeated (she always appears as mistress, never as wife, fiancée, or mother). When he then falls in love with a poor girl he is offended when one of his friends, to make fun of him, talks of a *mulatazinha*.

In *O país do carnaval* a scene is described which for the period (1931) and for Brazil must have been an extreme provocation: the meeting, just hinted at, of a Black man and a white woman. The woman is Julie, a Frenchwoman who has been around a lot and is kept by Paulo Rigger, who takes her to his farm. The classic triangle forms in which the part of the other man is allotted to Honório, a gigantic Black man. On the farm Paulo Rigger feels sure of Julie, also because in his fazendeiro mentality he is convinced that "Julie would never dare to encourage one of those brutes, more animals than men."[8] Therefore his surprise is all the more violent and bitter when he finds Julie and Honório in each other's arms (it must also be pointed out that the reaction of Paulo Rigger is extremely civilized given the time and the place; he only drives Honório out and confiscates his house to pay off the debt he had with the fazenda).

There is a constant taboo in the whole of Brazilian literature and it is that of the relationship between Black man and white woman. Even a young revolutionary like Jorge Amado takes certain elementary precautions, and in fact the woman in this case is French (synonym of sinful for the provincial Brazilians) and is really an adventuress and high-class prostitute.

But the true, great novel on Black life, one of the best works ever written in Brazil, remains *Jubiabá*. The old witch doctor Jubiabá and the young, adventurous Antônio Balduíno will remain forever two unforgettable figures, the two poles around which the universe of Black Brazil revolves.

The novel follows the adventures of Antônio Balduíno in his aimless wandering until the death of the woman he loves and the great strike give a sense to his existence. Antônio Balduíno is a little like the pole on which different directrixes converge to resolve themselves in the final catharsis. These directrixes might include: Antônio Balduíno and a white woman, in this case Lindinalva; Antônio Balduíno and the whites, which then turns into Antônio Balduíno and the rich; then there would also be Antônio Balduíno and Jubiabá, but the figure of the old sorcerer is so bound up with the character of his young pupil that it seems difficult to divide them.

Antônio Balduíno meets Lindinalva when he is still a child of twelve and she just a little older. The little Black boy was left without a relative in the world and is taken into the house of a Portuguese *comendador*, a rich businessman, whose daughter is in fact Lindinalva. To Antônio Balduíno, who up to that moment has lived with his companions in the freedom of the hills, the house of the Portuguese seems a prison: he decides to run away, "But since Lindinalva had come to ask him to play he forgot to run away."[9] Lindinalva is to Antônio Balduíno an object of continuous adoration; she reminds him of the images of saints he used to see on calendars. The fondness Lindinalva shows for him arouses the constant jealousy of the Portuguese cook who does nothing but repeat, "The *negro* is a race good only to make slaves of. The *negro* is not born to know anything,"[10] or, "The *negro* is a bad race, the *negro* is not a human being."[11] When Antônio Balduíno is fifteen and Lindinalva by then a young lady, the cook in a fit of jealousy accuses him of looking through the keyhole when Lindinalva has a bath. The Black boy is severely punished but what hurts him most is not being believed, seeing his infantile adoration of Lindinalva turned into something filthy. For Antônio Balduíno it is the end of everything, the birth of his hatred of the whites: "And since they were the only whites he respected, he began to hate them, and with them all the rest."[12]

But that incident also marks for Antônio Balduíno the end of childhood, the night before his escape from the house of the Portuguese:

> That night he dreamt of Lindinalva. He saw her naked and woke up. Then he remembered the vices practiced by the kids of the *morro* and was alone. No, he was not alone. He slept with Lindinalva who smiled at him with that face of hers like a calendar portrait and opened for him

> her white thighs and offered him her adolescent breasts. And from that moment on, whatever woman he slept with, it was always with Lindinalva that the *negro* Antônio Balduíno was sleeping.[13]

The memory of Lindinalva haunts Balduíno for the whole of his life. After some years of vagabond existence with other youths without families, Antônio Balduíno becomes a boxer on the road to success. It is, however, enough for him to read in the newspapers of Lindinalva's engagement to a brilliant lawyer and he goes to pieces. He gets violently drunk and loses the match in a humiliating manner in the third round.

So the Black Antônio Balduíno flees, flees from himself, from Bahia, from the memory of Lindinalva. He returns some years later having done many jobs, including working on a tobacco plantation and as a circus artist. In Bahia he finds Jubiabá and Lindinalva who, seduced by her fiancé and abandoned with a child, has become a prostitute and is about to die. The scene of the death of Lindinalva, despite a certain melodramatic quality, retains a very strong emotional charge. Antônio Balduíno comes to revenge himself and suddenly becomes again the wild boy of so many years before, climbing the trees in the garden to pick fruit to make a little white girl happy.

> And he who had come there for revenge, to possess her and then throw two *mil réis* on the bed . . . He had come to insult her, to tell her that a white woman was worth nothing, that a *negro* like him could do as he liked. Now he goes in search of Pai Jubiabá to see if he can save her. If she gets better, he will disappear forever. But if she dies, what can he do with his life? There is nothing left to him but the sea, the path taken by Viriato the Dwarf, who also had no one in the world. Only then does Antônio Balduíno understand that if Lindinalva dies he will be alone, left with no reason to live.[14]

Lindinalva dies and Antônio, the freest man in Bahia, "throws himself to the foot of her bed like a *negro* slave," a slave for the first time in his life.[15] Only now does he understand that Lindinalva had never left him in all those years, that "she had been white, *negra*, and mulatta, that she had also been that Chinese girl at Beco de Maria Paz, had been fat and slim, had had a masculine voice one night at the port, had lied like the *negra* Joana."[16]

The death of Lindinalva is the moment of truth for Antônio Balduíno, the moment in which he takes the decision that is to change his whole life.

> To help the son of Lindinalva, the *negro* Antônio Balduíno went down into the hold to take the place of Clarimundo, who had been killed by

> the crane. He was to have a job, to be the slave of the hours, of the bosses, of the cranes, and of the ships. But had he not done so, nothing would have been left him but the sea. The enormous shadows of the cranes appear on the sea. And the oily, green sea calls the *negro* Antônio Balduíno. The cranes make slaves, kill men, are the enemies of the *negros* and allies of the rich. The sea makes men free. Just a dive and he will have time to release his laughter. But Lindinalva had stroked his head and had asked him to take care of her son.[17]

Antônio Balduíno's hatred of the whites is born when he runs away from the house of the Portuguese. His hatred was born purely in the guts and then fed on deeper motives. Let us remember that in Bahia there had remained unchanged certain ethnic and social structures inherited from slavery; also the thirties saw the rapid growth and violent transformation of São Paulo while a provincial rhythm of life continued in other parts of the country. Jubiabá is not the only remembrance of the past with his long stories; slavery continues in the institutional structures. And this is something Antônio Balduíno found out as a child:

> They learned their destiny very early: they would grow and go to the docks where they would be bent under the weight of sacks full of cocoa or would go into enormous factories. And they did not rebel because for many years it had been so: the children of the beautiful tree-lined avenues would become doctors, lawyers, engineers, businessmen, rich men. And they would become the servants of these men. It was for this that the *morro* and the inhabitants of the *morro* existed. All these things the *negrinho* Antônio Balduíno had learned when he was little from the daily example of the grown-ups. As in the rich houses there was the tradition of the uncle, the father, the grandfather as famous engineer, successful orator, wise politician, so in the *morro* where so many *negros* and mulattoes lived there was the tradition of slavery to the rich, white gentlemen. And this was the only tradition.[18]

But there is also another tradition, a tradition that few remember, that of the lost freedom of the forest in Africa. Jubiabá is one of the few who keep and nurture the memory; and from his tales, the stories told when the moon is full, Antônio Balduíno arrives at the decision to be a free man, to have himself one day his own ABC illustrating his own life.

But in the stories of Jubiabá there is always a sinister character, the master, the white. And so Antônio Balduíno learns to hate in the white the master who is being renewed in the continuity of slavery. The misfortune suffered in the house of the Portuguese only gives an emotionally more profound character to what Jubiabá had taught him every day.

It is necessary at this point to consider the political position of Jorge Amado, a position completely delineated by 1935 while Brazil was on the brink of the dictatorship of the Estado Novo and the nazism of Hitler held sway in Germany. The opening page of *Jubiabá* is above all a clear and courageous political choice. The opponent whom Antônio Balduíno defeats by technical knockout is not only white, he is a German, he is blond, he is called Ergin and proclaims himself champion of central Europe. What is knocked down is not only a man but also a claimed racial superiority, which Antônio Balduíno derides in simple words, "The white was weak . . . The white wasn't up to it with the *negro* Antônio Balduíno . . . I'm the real man here."[19]

In his wanderings Antônio Balduíno meets other Germans. They are the owners of the tobacco factories; they live in their beautiful homes and are fanatical Nazis while their Black workers survive in inhuman conditions. To their poverty is added the continual humiliation of seeing the few women the bestial work has not yet ruined fall prey to the desires of their masters. Some pray, some lament. Antônio Balduíno hates in his pitiless frankness: "It may be a heresy, my friends . . . but the desire this *negro* here has is to kill all the whites. I killed them and it didn't worry me."[20]

In *Jubiabá* there is also a complete description of a *macumba* and all the explanations. In the period when the novel was written a form of separation still existed between the Black world and the white world; the persecution of any manifestations of Black religion had stopped only a short time before. What is today a spectacle open to the public and included in every tourist trip, was at the time something mysterious, not to be attended for reasons of safety and social order. It was, however, the epoch in which the first scholars and the inquisitive, among them Jorge Amado, began to frequent the Black world and to study it. In the description in question there is also the episode, probably in part autobiographical, of the white who manages to be present at a macumba and who creates great embarrassment among all the Blacks there who feel him to be an outsider and fear that he may be a policeman.

But there arrives for Antônio Balduíno too the moment when he has to recognize in the white someone who may be like him, his brother. He remembered when, as a child, he listened to the talk of the adults, heard the long stories of slavery, and decided to be a free man:

> "The *negro* is still a slave," added a thin man who worked on the docks, "all the poor are still slaves. Slavery is not over yet."
>
> The *negros*, the mulattoes, the whites lowered their heads. Only the head of Antônio Balduíno remained erect. He would not become a slave.[21]

And then Lindinalva dies and to keep the child she has left Antônio Balduíno goes to work on the docks, goes towards the crane that makes men slaves. But one day the great strike breaks out. The bosses do not give in. The bosses are white and Antônio Balduíno is one of the instigators of the strike. But the Blacks, the dockers, are not alone in the strike. There are also the workers in the electricity company, the tram drivers, and they are white. Antônio Balduíno thinks of this while preparing for the struggle. "But now every poor man has become a *negro*, that's what Jubiabá explains."[22] This is also what a Black docker says in his rough way: "We're Black and they're white but right now we're all poor, hungry people."[23]

The racial struggle has definitively been overcome by class struggle, Antônio Balduíno has understood that the real enemy has skin of no defined color and neither has the real friend. Antônio Balduíno, the champion who beat the whites, goes to the docks to dream, to dream of the day when he too will leave, will roam the world, will bring a strike to every port. He dreams of the day when he will say goodbye,

> Goodbye to them all, and he that has been on strike and has learned to love all the mulattoes, all the *negros*, all the whites who on the land and in the holds of the ships on the sea are slaves who are breaking their chains. And the *negro* Antônio Balduíno reaches out his big, calloused hand and waves back to Hans, the sailor.[24]

In the ending of the novel the principal directrixes involved in the story of Antônio Balduíno are resolved: the death of Lindinalva concludes the love-hate relationship he had been dragging around with him since his youth, the great strike and the solidarity of his companions make him a participant in that greater reality which is the class of all the workers.

The third directrix we have mentioned, the one linking Antônio Balduíno and Jubiabá, is without doubt the most complex. The relationship between the two begins in the first years of the Black boy's life. Antônio Balduíno is still a child and is already fascinated by the mysterious figure of Jubiabá. In the evening, when the men meet and the old feiticeiro starts telling stories of the old times, Antônio Balduíno leaves the games of the other youngsters to listen. Another man who fascinates Antônio Balduíno is Zé Camarão, a capoeira fighter, something of a scoundrel, a guitarist who sings the tales of famous bandits, such as Lucas da Feira and Lampião. But his real master in life always remains Jubiabá. It is from him that Antônio Balduíno learns the most important thing, the value of freedom. The only tradition left to the poor people of the morro was that of slavery, the only one they knew.

> Because the tradition of freedom in the forests of Africa had already been forgotten, those who remembered it were rare and they were persecuted and exterminated. In the *morro* only Jubiabá kept it up but Antônio Balduíno did not know this yet. Free men on the *morro* were rare: Jubiabá, Zé Camarão. But both were persecuted: one because he was a *macumbeiro*, the other because he had a record. Antônio Balduíno learned a lot from the heroic stories they told to the people of the *morro*, and forgot the tradition of servitude. He decided to be one of the free, of those who would later have an ABC and songs and would serve as an example for the *negros*, mulattoes, and whites who had become irremediably slaves. It was on Morro do Capa Negro [the Hill of the Castrated Black] that Antônio Balduíno decided to fight. All that he later did resulted from the stories he heard sitting in his aunt's doorway on moonlit nights. Those stories, those songs had been made to show men the example of those who rebel. But the men did not understand or were already deeply enslaved. But a few listened and understood. Antônio Balduíno was one of those who understood.[25]

The relationship between the two is practically never interrupted. When Antônio Balduíno is left alone in the world and is taken into the house of the Portuguese, Jubiabá says goodbye to him and tells him to come back one day when he is a man. Even when he is in the house of the Portuguese, Jubiabá comes to see him every so often and tells him stories, the story of Zumbi dos Palmares and the proud revolt of the slaves against their masters. The long tales of freedom are what accompany Antônio Balduíno throughout his eventful existence and prevent him from giving in, accepting the situation, becoming a slave. When he discovers class struggle he does no more than graft on to something sociologically more valid and more up-to-date from the historical point of view the wonderful tales of his childhood, Zumbi dos Palmares and all those who chose the struggle and freedom.

When Antônio Balduíno runs away from the house of the Portuguese, it is to Jubiabá that he returns. He roams through the city with other boys, steals and begs, sleeps in a different place each night, has different girls, but there is only one fixed point in his life, the pai-de-santo Jubiabá and his stories. He tells story of Morro do Capa Negro where the master had the Blacks castrated who did not produce children to be slaves, the story of the fazenda Corta Mão (Cut Hand), where the master had the female slaves raped and killed by an enormous gorilla, and stories of old Blacks who come to see the feiticeiro and show their backs marked by the lash. Antônio Balduíno listens and remembers. And when Antônio Balduíno flees from Bahia it is from Jubiabá that he asks the last piece of advice before going to "seek in the fairs, in the small towns, the country and the sea his laughter, his way home."[26]

Besides Jubiabá, the other fixed point in the life of Antônio Balduíno is the sea, the sea he fell in love with as a child when he stood enchanted, gazing at it. The sea is freedom, new worlds to discover; the sea is the final solution, death, the last refusal to become a slave, the sea is the supreme renunciation when he chooses the cranes and class struggle, the sea is Jubiabá with the memory of distant Africa and lost freedom.

And when Antônio Balduíno finds Lindinalva again, a consumptive, drunken prostitute, when her voice reminds him of the happy games of childhood and gives him the certainty of innocence forever lost, of all that could have been and never was, the strong and courageous Black man finds again the mysterious roots of his being, his unappeased anguish. "And shaking with fear, shaking with terror, he rushes up the hill and stops only in the house of Jubiabá, crying by the pai-de-santo who caresses him as when he was a child."[27]

Then there arrives the day of the great strike. "My father was a slave and I've been a slave too but I don't want my children to become slaves," says a Black man to his workmates and so begins the desperate battle of the poor against the rich.[28] But this time Antônio Balduíno is alone, Jubiabá is not with him. Jubiabá is in the hills officiating at his macumba. But this time Exu, the devil, who is honored and invited to leave before every ceremony, stubbornly decides to stay and the ceremony cannot begin. Exu seems to go only when Antônio Balduíno arrives but Antônio Balduíno speaks of things that not everyone understands. He talks of a strike, of the city immobilized, of solidarity with those in the struggle, he says there will be no more slaves. And Jubiabá believes that Exu, the devil, has taken possession of Antônio Balduíno. In turn Antônio Balduíno wonders that Jubiabá, the man who knows everything, does not know what a strike is.

> Antônio Balduíno (how many things he learned in that day and that night) explains the strike to Gordo and to Joaquim. And he wonders that

> Jubiabá does not know what strikes are about. Jubiabá knew about saints, stories of slavery, he was free, but he had never taught the strike to the slave people of the *morro*. Antônio Balduíno did not understand.[29]

Jubiabá knows nothing about strikes, but in his intuitive wisdom he has understood many things, things the author does not say but allows us to glimpse. And when the strike finishes, when for the first time the poor, Blacks, whites, and mulattoes, have beaten the rich, have begun to free themselves of slavery, Jubiabá understands that it is not Exu, the devil, who is incarnated in Antônio Balduíno. "And Jubiabá, the *feiticeiro*, bows down before him as though he were Oxolufã, old Oxalá, the greatest of saints."[30]

Jubiabá is a great novel and still greater when read today, more than forty years after it was first published. It is a novel of historical dimensions, a work that marks a turning point in Brazilian literature. In a country where literature was and is the work of the cultured classes, and where in the end the cultured classes inevitably identified with the ruling class, for the first time a young man, little more than twenty years of age, dared to present the public with a story in which the main character is Black—and this explains the greater acceptance Jorge Amado had abroad, at least at the beginning of his career. The principal taboo is not broken and Antônio Balduíno does not make love to Lindinalva. But the story of the gigantic Black man and the white girl with the face of a saint covered in freckles remains one of the most beautiful and sweetest fables ever told.

With *Jubiabá* Jorge Amado worked a revolution, incorporating the Black world definitively into the Brazilian spirit as an active component. If one compares *Jubiabá* to the contemporary *Moleque Ricardo* by José Lins do Rego, one can see that an infinite distance separates the two works: the Black character who in the works of the Paraiban writer always ends up being the "other," with Antônio Balduíno becomes absolutely one of us, a character with whom every reader can proudly desire to identify.

After *Jubiabá* the Black characters in the works of Amado cannot be counted; in fact we would say that there is no sense in counting them since by now what matters is no longer the study of the behavior of the Black characters but rather to establish to what point whatever is Black, in the widest sense of the word, has permeated the Brazilian world. Back in the thirties Gilberto Freyre, with his *Casa grande e senzala*, had tackled with the clarity of a historian and sociologist the problem of the Black presence in Brazil, affirming without the least shadow of doubt its validity and importance.

In the works that came immediately after, in *Mar morto* and in

Capitães da areia, there are some Black characters, but above all there is so much of the Black way of being. *Mar morto* is a story of fishermen set in the port of Bahia. The two main characters, Guma and Lívia, are certainly not Blacks, they are Brazilians tanned by the sun and by infinite intermingling with people with dark skins. And yet the whole novel is a Black story. The real protagonists are the sea and Iemanjá, the goddess of the sea, she of the five names:

> Iemanjá, who is mistress of the seas, of the *saveiros*, of the life of them all, has five names, five sweet names that everyone knows. She is called Iemanjá, has always been called so and this is her real name, mistress of the waters, lady of the oceans. But the boatmen call her Dona Janaína and the *pretos*, who are her favorite children and dance for her and fear her more than do all the others, call her Inaê, with devotion, or make their supplications to the Princess of Aiocá, queen of those mysterious lands that hide behind the blue line that separates them from the other lands. The women of the port, however, who are simple and courageous, the whores, the married women, the girls waiting to get engaged, call her Dona Maria, since Maria is a beautiful name, the most beautiful of all in fact, the most venerated, and so they give it to Iemanjá as a gift, as though they were bringing a crate full of bars of soap to her stone in Dique. She is the siren, the *mãe-d'agua*, mistress of the sea, Iemanjá, Dona Janaína, Dona Maria, Inaê, Princess of Aiocá. She rules the seas, she adores the moon she comes to see on cloudless nights, she loves the music of the *negros*. Every year there is the festival of Iemanjá at Dique and Mont Serrat. And then they call her by all of her five names, they give her all of her titles, they bring her gifts, they sing for her.[31]

The works of Amado, although they are naturally novels, are always based on a real and direct knowledge of habits, ways, customs, events, and even people (there are many people living who have found themselves immortalized in the works of the writer). What he tells us of Black mythology is not the fruit of his artistic imagination but comes instead from a daily experience of life alongside the people, his people. We may therefore make some observations regarding a living reality rather than the free expression of the artist. The cult of Iemanjá has also required cruel sacrifices. The writer tells us of a period in which the fury of the sea frequently destroyed the boats and made impossible any trip out to sea. This meant hunger for the fishermen and their families. The macumbeiro of the place said that Iemanjá was angry and demanded human sacrifices: she was offered children, a blind girl offered herself as a sacrifice, a beautiful little girl was left blindfolded on the rocks so that Iemanjá could carry her away with her. The police intervened and many people ended up in prison. The mother of the little girl went mad and the festival of Iemanjá was prohibited. Then the anger of Iemanjá was placated and the festival started up again, but the human sacrifices were replaced by sacrifices of animals. The writer describes the offering of a horse to the divinity so that she might ride it at her pleasure during the nights of full moon. The animal was blinded with a red-hot iron and dragged into the sea by two boats in the midst of the waves where it was abandoned for Iemanjá to drag down to the bottom of the sea. And on the shore, from the boats full of fishermen, men and women renewed their prayers to the goddess who governed their existence.

Iemanjá has a double role. She is at the same time mother and mistress of the fishermen:

> Iemanjá is so terrible because she is mother and wife. Those waters were born of her on the day in which her son possessed her. Among the people of the port there are not many who know the story of Iemanjá and Orungã, her son. But Anselmo knows it and old Francisco has heard of it too. They avoid telling this story, however, which has the power to unleash the anger of Janaína. It all began when Iemanjá had by Aganju, god of the dry land, a son, Orungã, who became god of the winds, of everything between the earth and the sky. Orungã wandered over these lands living in the midst of the winds but he could not get the image of his mother, the beautiful queen of the waters, out of his mind. She was the most beautiful of them all and all the desires of the son were concentrated on her. And one day he could no longer resist and raped her. Iemanjá fled and in her flight her breasts burst and thus were born the waters and also Bahia de Todos os Santos. And from her womb, impregnated by her son, were born the most feared *orixás*, the ones who send thunder and lightning during the storms.
>
> And so Iemanjá is mother and bride. She loves men as a mother as long as they live and suffer. But on the day they die it is as though they were her son Orungã, crazed with desire, lusting after her body.[32]

A sort of Oedipus myth in Afro-Brazilian version, the cult of Iemanjá is felt very deeply by the coastal peoples and is without doubt the most popular in Brazil. Curiously Jorge Amado speaks to us of Iemanjá represented with long blonde hair. It is more than likely that three centuries of slavery have had their influence in conditioning the canons of beauty of a Black divinity so that she is imagined as similar to one of the beautiful little white ladies, equally unapproachable on the high verandas of the casa grande.

Her occult presence dominates the whole story of *Mar morto*, which is logical seeing that it is a tale of fishermen. Old Francisco, the uncle of Guma, is an old fisherman and one day he saw Iemanjá, or at least so the other fishermen say, because Francisco never answers questions they ask him about it. It happened many years ago when, on a stormy night, Francisco rescued the crew of a trawler and Iemanjá showed herself to him as a reward. The novel ends with the death of Guma who disappears into the sea during a shipwreck to save a friend. His body is never found, as happens to all the brave sailors that Iemanjá carries away with her. The place of Guma at the helm of the boat is taken by Lívia, his beautiful and courageous wife, and when she crosses the bay the old man recognizes in her, for the second time, the goddess of the sea.

> "Isn't it she? Yes, it is. It's Iemanjá coming there." And old Francisco shouts to the others on the quay:
>
> "Look! Look! It's Janaína."
>
> They looked and they saw. Dona Dulce, the schoolmistress looked as well from the window of the school. She saw a strong woman battling. The battle was her miracle. She was beginning to realize herself. From the quays the seamen saw Iemanjá, she of the five names. Old Francisco shouted, it was the second time that he had seen her.
>
> So they say along the quays of the harbor.[33]

As we have already said, in *Mar morto* it is not so much a matter of the Black character as of the Black way of life, the Black culture that has permeated the popular strata of the Brazilian world. There are, however, some secondary episodes that show certain preconceptions against Blacks diffused among the colored people themselves. The first episode refers to a popular song that makes fun of the mulattoes and is sung in fact by a mulatto:

> Sou mulato e não nego
> Ai, meu Deus, de mim tem pena!
> Embora eu queira negá
> Meu cabelo me condena.
>
> I'm a mulatto and don't deny it
> Ah, Lord, have mercy on me!
> Although I'd like to deny it
> My hair condemns me.[34]

Further on two more verses are quoted:

> Inda querendo sê branco
> O cabelo me crimina.
>
> Even if I wanted to be white
> My hair incriminates me.[35]

It is not a question, as it might at first sight seem, of racist expressions, not at least in the sense we use the word racism. The Brazilian soul has more nuances in its expression and they are to be interpreted according to a different mentality. Three centuries of slavery have established codes of life that have also become aesthetic canons: white means master, Black means slave; it is good to be a master, it is sad to be a slave. Therefore, everything that refers to the master, to the white, is positive, while everything that refers to the slave, to the Black, is negative. In a society of widely mixed races such as Brazil—before a new vision of the world reevaluated historically and culturally what is Black—there was therefore established a chromatic scale of values which goes from Black to white. Those most sensitive to this scale of values are in fact the mulattoes, the ones who find themselves in the middle and tend to identify with the whites. In reality just as in literature, it is possible to find phrases or verses by now classic that mock the efforts of the mulatto to forget his Black part, his attempts to identify solely with the white.

In the light of this preconception, this way of thinking, we must interpret the following episode. Guma is a *mulato claro*, a fair-skinned mulatto, and among his friends there is a couple formed by a Black, Rufino, and Esmeralda, a mulatta. The woman is clearly infatuated with Guma and, commenting on Lívia's pregnancy, tries to make some advances:

> Lívia had gone into the kitchen to make some coffee for them all and she began:
>
> "I'm the only one who never finds a man to give me a child. I'm unlucky even in this. A man who stays with me doesn't have children." . . . She was showing some thigh, her legs crossed.
>
> Guma laughed. "All you have to do is ask Rufino."
>
> "Him? It would be the limit if I had a baby by a *negro*! What I need is a baby by someone whiter than I am to improve the family."[36]

Apart from the intention with which the phrase was spoken, the aspiration to unite with those whiter than oneself was as natural as that of finding a rich husband, or at least one with a better economic standing.

There is also another episode that, though it has Blacks as protagonists, is if anything part of those social problems that are a basic motif in all the works of Jorge Amado. The episode occurs in the story of a Black sailor who describes to his friends how the Blacks in Africa, in the French colonies, are mistreated.

> The *negros* were loading a ship and the white man's whip was cracking in the air. All he wanted to see was a *negro* taking his time so that

> he could lash him across the back. At that moment there arrived a *negro* who was the stoker of the ship of the Lloyd Brasiliano—a guy called Bagé—strolling along; he'd been to see a girl. Arriving, he slowed down a *negro* of the place who was going up the plank with a sack on his back, it's a plank they were going up. The *negro* stopped for just an instant, the white man's whip lashed his back and he rolled to the ground. Bagé had never seen how the white man's whip worked before. It was the first time he had visited those lands. When he saw the *negro* writhing in pain, Bagé grabbed the whip from the Frenchman and gave him a punch. The Frenchman lost his balance and landed on his back. The Frenchman tried to fight back but Bagé gave him another thump and broke his snout. Then the *negros* of the place came up out of the hold and sang a samba because they had never seen anything like it before.
>
> The others listened. A *negro* could not resist it and murmured: "I like this Bagé."[37]

Amado evidently does not forget that Brazil is only one of the places where the battle for the freedom of man is fought. It is well worth remembering every so often that injustice is in force in other lands and that there are men who suffer.

Capitães da areia is the story of boys without families who live around the harbor. The novel may remind one in part of the childhood and adolescence of Antônio Balduíno in *Jubiabá*, to which it is related through the determined social commitment that animates it and the Black atmosphere present throughout. The main character is called Pedro Bala and is blond. In the group of boys of which he is leader are represented all the types of human being that populate Brazil. Pedro Bala has never known his father and knows only that he was a docker, was handsome, went on strike, knew how to talk to his workmates, and died in the struggle. Were it not for the color of the skin, it could be the portrait of Antônio Balduíno. The atmosphere of the novel is that of the Black city of Bahia. There is no longer the contrast of races that animated Antônio Balduíno. In *Capitães da areia* the festivals and rites of the Black world are the heritage of all the poor. For this reason the blond Pedro Bala and his friends go to the candomblé of Gantois, which is one of the most famous in Bahia:

> Pedro Bala, Boa-Vida, and Querido-de-Deus went to the *candomblé* of Gantois where Omulu appeared in her most beautiful clothes to tell her poor children with the most beautiful song possible that poverty would soon be over and that she would carry smallpox into the houses of the rich and that the poor would be well fed and happy. The drums resounded in the night of Omulu. And she announced that the day of the

> vendetta of the poor was to arrive. The *negras* danced, the men were joyful. The day of the vendetta was to come.[38]

Amado has by now definitively solved the problem of racial struggle, turning it into class struggle: Black culture, Black religion, the Black world are the common heritage of all the poor, the excluded, all the oppressed who, as such, with no distinctions of race, are naturally in contrast with all those, generally whites, who are in control of the power and of that culture which claims to be the official and the only culture.

Capitães da areia is a realistic novel related in the rhythm of a fable, where violence and misery alternate and are sublimated in poetry. Rereading it today we can see that the author again adopts different standards when he speaks of Black women and of white women. There is the little Black girl whom Pedro Bala, in a moment of frustration and anger, surprises on the beach and forces to have intercourse with him; and there is Dora, the blonde adolescent whom the capitães da areia adopt and who dies in Pedro Bala's arms. Here it is not a matter of an unconscious reflex, of a social taboo: it would have been highly unlikely for a tramp like Pedro Bala to be able to surprise a white girl at night by the docks and equally unlikely for a band of hardened adolescents to grant to a Black girl the role of a princess whom they all serve like so many knights. Again it is the complex of the *sinhazinha*, the beautiful little white missy, like Lindinalva, like blonde-haired Iemanjá. And it is to Iemanjá herself that the lifeless corpse of Dora is offered, accompanied through the waves of the sea by the weeping of the boys and the prayers of a humble and courageous friar, the only one who tries to look after the abandoned children.

And then, inevitably, the boys become men. Each one will choose his own road: one becomes a trickster and another an artist, one kills himself and one feels the call of God, while another hears the call of the sertão and violence. Pedro Bala chooses struggle, the long battle against injustice so that other children may have a better fate, so that men may not die as his father did, killed by the police during a strike. Pedro Bala leaves.

> With upraised fists the boys salute Pedro Bala, who leaves to change the destiny of other children. Barandão shouts in front of everyone, he is now the new leader.
>
> From afar Pedro Bala again sees the *capitães da areia*. Beneath the moon, in an old abandoned warehouse, they raise their arms. They are standing up, destiny has changed.

> In the mysterious night of the *macumbas*, the drums resound like trumpets of war.[39]

So the novel ends. The hope for tomorrow and the decision to fight are accompanied by that drum rhythm which has always been present in all the revolts and in all the Black festivals.

In all the other novels of what is known as the first phase of Jorge Amado there are many Blacks, but by now being Black has no particular meaning in the world of multiracial symbiosis created by the writer from Bahia. Being Black is the same as being tall or short, fat or thin; what counts now is the Black way of being, how it affirms itself, how it is expressed and received. And in this cultural assertion of Négritude one may be Black or white indifferently, Pedro Bala or Antônio Balduíno; the *macumbas* they go to are the same and one and the same is the long battle they are fighting.

In *Terras do sem fim*, in *São Jorge dos Ilhéus*, in *Seara vermelha*, in *Os subterrâneos da liberdade* there are still Blacks, many Blacks, but what counts is no longer their assertion as colored men. What counts now is simply their assertion as men, similar in this to other men of fair skin, united in struggle in a world whose neocapitalistic structures bring forward new forms of slavery.

The only Black character who meaningfully represents Négritude appears in *Terras do sem fim*. He is called Jeremias and is a feiticeiro. Jeremias recalls Jubiabá a little. He too is a man of memories, a representative of times gone by. He lives in the forest of Sequeiro Grande in a hut where he receives all those who turn to him, seeking his powers as sorcerer:

> One day, many years before, when the forest covered much more land, when it spread in all directions, when men had not yet thought of felling the trees to plant cocoa, whose seeds had not yet arrived from the Amazon, Jeremias had hidden in the forest. He was a young *negro*, a runaway slave. The *capitães do mato* were chasing him and he entered the forest where the *índios* lived and never came back out. He came from a sugar plantation where the master had had the backs of his slaves lashed. For many years his back had been tattooed with the sign of the whip. But even when the marks had disappeared, even when he was told that the abolition of slavery had been decreed, he no longer wanted to leave the forest. Many years had passed since his arrival, he had lost track of time, had already lost the memory of those events. He had not, however, forgotten the Black gods his ancestors had brought from Africa and which he had not wanted to replace with the Catholic gods of the *senhores de engenho*. Within the forest he lived in the company of Ogum, of Omulu, of Oxossi and of Oxolufã. From the *índios* he had

> learned the secrets of medicinal herbs. He had mixed with his Black gods some native ones and invoked both the former and the latter when anyone came to ask him for advice or medicine in the heart of the forest. Many people came, people from the city too, and bit by bit they opened a trail right to his hut, a trail blazed by the sick and distressed.
>
> He had seen white men arrive near the forest, had been present at the destruction of other forests, had seen the *índios* flee far away, been present at the birth of the first cocoa plants, seen the formation of the first *fazendas*. He began withdrawing more and more into the heart of the forest and ended up being possessed by a fear that one day men would arrive at the destruction of the forest of Sequeiro Grande. He prophesied endless woe for that day. He told all those who came to consult him that the forest was the home of the gods, that every tree was sacred and that if men laid hands on them, they would be avenged mercilessly.[40]

We have seen that in Jorge Amado there are two phases in Négritude. The first is when the Black world turns in upon itself, seeks in the roots of its being the reasons to go on existing and fighting and closes itself therein, setting itself up as the antithesis of the white world that has enslaved it. Jubiabá and Jeremias are examples of this phase, Jeremias more so than Jubiabá. He is African in the absolute sense, and definitively broke with the world of the whites the day he ran away. In the forest he has rebuilt his home, his cultural roots, his religion. He is another of the men who have absolutely refused compromise. He does not return to the world of the whites at the moment of abolition because he has already achieved freedom by running away. And the day in which Jeremias knows that the white man is preparing to destroy the forest to plant cocoa there, that is the day Jeremias feels that his end has come, since the reason for his being coincides with that of the forest. The only thing left for him to do is to hurl the last curse at those who profane the dwelling of the gods:

> Jeremias rises. This time he has no need of a stick to support his nearly one-hundred-year-old body. He takes two steps towards the door of the hut. Now his blind eyes see the forest perfectly in all its splendor. They have seen it from the remotest days of his past up to this night which marks his end . . . The words of Jeremias were for his gods, the gods who had come from the forests of Africa, Ogum, Oxossi, Iansã, Oxolufã, Omulu, and also Exu who is the devil. He calls them to unleash their rage on those about to disturb the peace of his life. And he said: "The eye of pity is dried up and they look at the forest with the eye of wickedness. Now they will enter the forest but first many of them will die, men and women, children and even birds . . . Their flesh will be manure for the cocoa plants, each tree will be fed with the blood of each of them, of all of them, no one to be spared."

> He shouted once more the names of his beloved gods. He called again upon Exu, entrusting to him his vendetta, while his voice crossed the forest, waking the birds, the monkeys, the snakes, and the wild beasts. He shouted once more and it was a burning curse:
>
> "Each son will plant his cocoa in the blood of his father."
>
> Then for a long time he watched the dawn that was breaking in a twittering of sparrows over the forest of Sequeiro Grande. His body started to give in little by little, his effort had been immense . . . Neither a sigh nor a moan did he utter. In his death agony Jeremias tried only to repeat his curse, his dying mouth twisted with hatred. In the trees the birds sang out the morning. The light of dawn illuminated the forest of Sequeiro Grande.[41]

Jeremias dies in absolute refusal. He has no Antônio Balduíno to whom he can entrust his message of struggle, a struggle that continues even though the terms are changed. And this is the second phase, that of Antônio Balduíno, of the mulatto Guma, of the blond Pedro Bala. The Black way of being, without denying itself, accepts the world in which it finds itself while it also accepts the battle it must necessarily face: The Black condition of whites and Blacks, the struggle of the poor against the rich.

And then there is another form of the Black condition, which in daily life, in a thousand little things, asserts itself, fecundating the white world and being fecundated thereby in turn; the Black condition advances every day laughing, joking, loving. But this is another story.

"Seu corpo rolou, suas ancas partiram, seus pés libertados a dança criaram"

"Her body rolled, her haunches parted, her liberated feet created the dance."[42] No translation is able to do justice to these verses in prose with which Amado describes Gabriela, who lets herself go in the rhythm of the dance, identifying herself in the music and the movement.

With *Gabriela, cravo e canela* in 1958 there begins what the critics call the second phase of Jorge Amado. If with *Jubiabá* and the successive novels racial struggle was replaced by class struggle, in the novels of the second phase the concepts of race and class are in turn overcome. Whites, Blacks, and mulattoes, rich or poor, when they fight, fight for themselves, for their people; or they do not fight, they live and let live. In *Gabriela, cravo e canela* Nacib and Mundinho Falcão, among the main characters, are both men who participate, each in his own way, in the transformation and progress of Ilhéus. Mundinho

Falcão, the youngest of a great Brazilian family, has left a life of ease and luxury in the capital to forget an unhappy love affair and to demonstrate to himself and his brothers that he is capable of doing something without the backing of his family. At Ilhéus Mundinho Falcão begins a prosperous business as an exporter of cocoa and at the same time participates in the political life of the city, allying himself to and leading those groups in favor of the transformation of Ilhéus in a modern sense. The role of Mundinho Falcão is the classic one of an innovating stranger, a man of new ideas, who ends up leading the opposition to the old coronéis (only some of them, since others accept and favor the changes) and defeating them.

Nacib instead operates on another plane, parallel to that of Mundinho Falcão but socially inferior. Having come from Syria as a child, he is a naturalized Brazilian; he has taken over a bar called Vesuvio and successfully started a business. His ambitions are much more modest and his dream is to become rich. His activity inevitably brings him to side with those who want a modern transformation of Ilhéus, and so he becomes the friend of Mundinho Falcão.

We may say that with *Gabriela, cravo e canela* Jorge Amado makes peace with many people. He makes peace with the representatives of capitalism and with the exporters he had described so dismally in *São Jorge dos Ilhéus*. He also makes peace with the coronéis of cocoa, the bloodthirsty protagonists of *Terras do sem fim*, who now either become progressive or, like old Ramiro Bastos, maintain with dignity their role as representatives of a legendary epoch.

With *Gabriela, cravo e canela* we arrive at a new and richer formulation of the Black condition, which is here defined detached from the context of class struggle that risked limiting it to a simple function of confrontation between opposing social forces. Now instead it is considered in itself, in its dignity as a philosophy of life that asserts itself and dominates in Brazil. In fact, in *Gabriela, cravo e canela* the number of Black characters is very limited. Gabriela herself has skin the color of cinnamon; she is a product of the mixed races in Brazil, comes from the sertão, from the lands of drought where Blacks are traditionally not very numerous. What is really Black in the novel is the existential philosophy with which the protagonist, and not she alone, faces life.

But in what does this Black philosophy of life consist? Wishing to be synthetic without being superficial, we can say that it is a form of thought that resolves the transcendental into the immanent—the gods that are identified as expressions of natural forces—and therefore focuses all its interest on the passing instant, on the transient moment to the detriment of the concepts of past and future. It is the modern transposition or, if we prefer, the adaptation to the structures of industrial civilization of the principles that have always governed life in the tropical forest. Life in the tropical forest has the characteristics of immediacy; in the luxuriant monotony of seasons that are always the same, fruit ripens and rots at a speed unknown in temperate climates. What is not consumed today will not be fit to eat tomorrow. It is impossible to tame or dominate the tropical forest by the means with which man, in other climes, has adapted the land to his needs. Yet in the forest a roof of leaves is enough to shelter one from violent storms and the destroyed plants are reproduced with the greatest of ease. No trace remains of the past because the jungle devours everything and little is thought about the future, as it remains the least certain of hypotheses. What counts is the present moment and the chance to live it.

The life of Gabriela is a series of instants in the present, lived in such a way as to make them appear independent of each other. Here she is during the long and desperate journey of the retirantes; it is she who offers herself to the shy Clemente who dares not approach: "Clemente played for Gabriela but did not have the courage to address a word to her. It was she who came, with her dancing steps and her eyes of innocence, to have a word with him."[43] This attitude of Gabriela's is not brazen. She is before sin, that invention, fairly cretinous all in all, that the Europeans carried with them into various continents along with other despicable habits. Gabriela loves Clemente because Clemente is there, because it is the only reasonable thing to do on a journey that may end in death. Then the journey ends and with it Gabriela's love. Her intuition, that of a purely instinctive creature, has told her that Clemente is not a man made to live in the city and she has no desire to go into the forest. When Nacib takes her on as a maid, she instantly forgets Clemente and happily sets off towards a new life.

> Gabriela followed him one step behind with her bundle, having already forgotten Clemente, happy to leave that bunch of *retirantes* and that filthy camp. She walked, laughing with her eyes and mouth, with her bare feet half slipping on the earth, a longing to sing the *sertaneja* songs.[44]

So Gabriela goes with Nacib, spontaneously, with no calculation. In her absolute optimism Nacib is for her a *moço bonito*, a handsome man, while for the others who are not so enthusiastic, he is just "a fat Turk with a face like an ox."[45] She does not think of taking advantage of the situation, accepts presents with a certain embarrassment, refuses the advantageous proposals made to her by the various coronéis. Everything she wants she already has, why want more?

> Happy with Nacib. It was good to sleep with him, with her head resting on his hairy chest, feeling on her hips the weight of the leg of that great big man, a handsome man. His moustache tickled her throat. Gabriela felt a shiver, it was so good to sleep with a man, not an old man, to have a house and food, clothes and shoes. With a young man, sleeping to sleep, a strong and handsome man like Nacib.[46]

Life to the rhythms of dance, the author has given a particular musicality to his phrases when he describes the behavior of Gabriela: "*Gabriela servia para cozinhar, a casa arrumar, a roupa lavar, con homem deitar,*" Again, translation cannot do justice to the original:

> Gabriela was there to cook, to tidy the house, to do the washing, to go to bed with man. Not ugly, old men, not for money. Clemente along the way, Nhôzinho in the country, Zé do Carmo too. In town Bebinho, a young student, such a rich house! He came creeping, on tiptoe, for fear of his mother. The first of all, she was still just a girl, had been her own uncle. She was still a girl, at night her uncle, old and ill.[47]

For Gabriela love is always an end in itself; she never tries to take advantage of a sentimental situation. When the usual friends hint at the possibility of getting Nacib to marry her, he being well off, the owner of a bar, Gabriela marvels at it. It is something she would never have thought of, happy as she is with her position as cook and mistress. She likes the work, she likes Nacib, why on earth change?

Of the two of them, Gabriela and Nacib, the one who suffers doubt and uncertainty is, in fact, Nacib. Gabriela is too beautiful, everyone is after her, they all proposition her when she arrives at the bar. Nacib understands all too well that he cannot compete with the rich coronéis and that the presents he keeps on giving her are nothing compared to what the rich and powerful of the city could give her. So Nacib, with the jealousy that is eating him away, begins to lose Gabriela. He loses her because he does not understand that Gabriela loves him and loves love and that Gabriela does not betray him because she does not belong to him. She belongs only to herself and to love. The canary in a cage that Nacib gives her is freed immediately by the hand of Gabriela, who hates cages, bonds, chains.

The relationship between Nacib and Gabriela recalls a meeting between the two forms of sexuality, the two ways of conceiving of love that are at the basis of the formation of Brazilian civilization. Nacib, the Arab living in a patriarchal agricultural world that is undergoing evolution, has the classic possessive mentality, obsessively jealous and overexcited, traditional to the Latin, Arab, and Lusitanian world: the woman an object, shut up in the house, forbidden to other eyes, the private property of her lord and master. Gabriela, in contrast, a mulatta, has in her blood the innocence and the erotic vitality of her African ancestors, who never tied love to the concept of sin. Love for her is an innocent delight, like picking and eating the marvelous tropical fruit in her garden. Why on earth should it be forbidden? Nacib, however, does not understand this. He cannot understand it, just as Gabriela does not understand why Nacib makes such a fuss when, after they are married, he surprises her with Tonico, a light-hearted dandy:

> One day she realized that he was jealous. Such a great big man, it was funny. So far she had been so careful because she did not want him to suffer. What a silly thing, no explanation at all: why did men suffer so much when a woman they made love to made love to another man? She did not understand it. If Nacib wanted to, he could go to bed with another, sleep in her arms. She knew that Tonico went to bed with other women; Dona Arminda had told her that he had an infinity of them. But if it was so good to go to bed with him, to make love, why demand that it should only be with her? She did not understand. She liked to sleep in the arms of a man. Not just any man. A handsome man like Clemente, like Tonico, like Nilo, like Bebinho, ah! like Nacib. And if the young man wanted to as well, if he looked at her imploringly, if he smiled at her, if he pinched her, why refuse, why say no? If they both wanted it the same? She could not see why not. It was good to sleep in the arms of a man, feel the throbbing of his body, the biting mouth, dying in a sigh. That Nacib got angry, took it so much to heart since they were married, this she understood. There was the law. It was not allowed. Only the man had the right, not the woman? She knew but how was she to resist? She wanted it and did it not remembering that it was not allowed.
>
> She liked certain things, liked them too much: the sun in the morning before it got hot. The cold water, the white beach, the sand, the sea. The circus, the fun-fair. The cinema too. Fruit, *goiaba* and *pitanga*. Flowers, animals, cooking, eating, walking along the road, laughing, chatting. Not with ladies full of themselves, she did not like that. But most of all she liked the handsome young men, being in their arms, moaning, sighing. These were the things she liked. And Nacib. She liked him in a different way. In bed to moan, sigh, kiss, bite, die, and be born again. But also really to sleep, dreaming of the sun, the sand of the beach, the moon in the sky, the lunch to get ready. Feeling on her hips the weight of Nacib's leg. She liked him too much, really too much.[48]

The story of the marriage of Nacib and Gabriela—and of its subsequent annulment—gives Jorge Amado the opportunity to write some of his most amusing pages of social criticism. By now Jorge Amado is no longer fighting against capitalist, bourgeois society. He accepts it and makes fun of it with his biting, desecrating irony. Thus we have a portrait, painted with benevolent ferocity, of the petit-bourgeois world of Ilhéus. Nacib is torn by jealousy and does not know what to do. There is his hard-won position of well-to-do businessman, secretary of the Clube Comercial, his rich relations, the sister who has married an agricultural engineer, a university graduate. How can a man like him marry a retirante like Gabriela? His friends were all too quick to give advice; their reputations were not at stake.

> But how could he marry Gabriela, a cook, mulatta, without family, without virginity, found at the "slave market"? Marriages were to be made with virtuous young ladies, of good family, with a trousseau, a good upbringing and guaranteed virginity.[49]

In spite of everything, this impossible marriage does take place. It takes place because Nacib applies to Gabriela his solid Syrian, Brazilian, bourgeois, business principles, according to the mentality of which marriage represents a fixed point, the definitive means to tie a woman to you. Gabriela, however, does not understand what has changed in her situation, what having become Senhora Saad means, the charm, not in fact all that discreet, of the bourgeoisie of Ilhéus does not tempt her in the least. On the contrary, it is just her new bourgeois condition that is to bring about a crisis in her union with Nacib. Nacib has got the idea into his head of transforming Gabriela into a lady just like all the other ladies in Ilhéus and this, for Gabriela, means the end of so many things she loves: running barefoot along the beach, working in the bar enjoying the admiration and compliments of the men, going dancing with others of her own class, walking, joking, laughing. Now Gabriela has to put on the shoes that hurt her feet, dress with propriety and assume the leaden poses suitable for a married woman. And added to all this is frequenting with other ladies who look down on her and almost never speak a word to her (and when they do, Gabriela does not know how to answer).

There are two very significant episodes, that of the circus and that of the New Year's Ball. In the first there is a circus, one of those nice, poor, popular circuses, that arrives in Ilhéus. Gabriela would, of course, like to go, also because Tuísca, a Black boy who works in the bar and is a friend of hers, has a small part in it. On the same day, however, there is a sort of conference held by a poet, a likable chatterbox and authentic windbag who declaims verses to scrape together a bit of money. All the respectable part of Ilhéus is there, wives and daughters of rich fazendeiros showing off their clothes and culture, pretending to understand. Gabriela is there too, dragged as she has to be by Nacib, death in her soul, her feet aching in the tight shoes, sleepiness and boredom closing her eyelids. And then, as soon as the conference finishes, her barefoot dash along the beach towards the circus, towards fun, towards laughter. And who should she meet in the circus? Who but the handsome Tonico who offers to take her home, along deserted streets where no one can see them and where he can whisper so many sweet things to her.

The second episode, the dance on New Year's Eve, is more significant. In the Brazil of the time (the novel came out in 1958 but it is set in the thirties), popular manifestations typical of the Black world such as dances, festivals, and Carnival were considered vulgar by the so-called good society just because they came from and were the customs of lower classes. Yet, it was considered in good taste to accept typically European traditions, fashionable dances from the United States and even the Argentine tango, since it had spread all over the world. Decades are still to pass before all social classes find and recognize each other and themselves in that Black, popular culture which is to become a unique national expression. On that New Year's Eve, however, a miracle happened at Ilhéus: together with Gabriela, Jerusa, the beautiful niece of Coronel Ramiro Bastos, Mundinho Falcão, the rich exporter, and all the top society danced in the middle of the road.

This is what happened that night at Ilhéus: Gabriela, despite having become the respectable Senhora Saad, had continued to associate with her old friends, who were meeting to dance in preparation for the procession of the *terno de reis.* The terno de reis (*terno* indicates three musical instruments that accompany a group of people dancing in a particular festival, in this case the *reis*, the Three Wise Men), a typical popular manifestation of Bahia, was to proceed through the streets of Ilhéus on New Year's Eve. The best dancer, according to the tradition, was the one chosen to carry the standard and lead the group. And Gabriela had been chosen because she was by far the best. Unfortunately for her, however, Nacib's sister was at Ilhéus for the holidays, together with her husband, the engineer. Bourgeois of the first order, full of airs, they had bitterly criticized Nacib for marrying the cook of his bar. In these conditions it was impossible for Gabriela to take part in the dances of the terno de reis with maids, seamstresses, sailors—the lower classes. Instead she had to go to the sumptuous Clube Progresso where all the top society—with a great display of elegance, men in dinner jackets in spite of the heat, French champagne, deluxe drinks—awaited the arrival of the new year. And along with the new year there arrives the terno de reis dancing in the square. The guests of the Clube Progresso go out to see. The rich watch, the poor dance, the rich offer drinks, Gabriela is itching to dance her dances and not the tangos and waltzes she has had to put up with so far:

> Gabriela could see nothing but the *terno de reis*, the shepherdesses with their lanterns, Nilo with his whistle, Miquelina with the standard. She could not see Nacib, not Tonico, she saw no one. Not even her sister-in-law with her insolent nose. Nilo whistled, the shepherdesses reformed the group, the *bumba-meu-boi* was already moving off. The whistle blew once more, the shepherdesses danced, Miquelina waved the standard into the night.
>
> As pastorinhas ja vão
> noutra parte cantar . . .
>
> The shepherdesses are going
> to sing somewhere else . . .
>
> They were going elsewhere to sing, to dance through the streets. Gabriela took off her shoes, rushed forward, grabbed the standard from the hands of Miquelina. *Seu corpo rolou, suas ancas partiram, seus pés libertados a dança criaram* . . . Her body rolled, her haunches parted, her liberated feet created the dance. The *terno* marched on, her sister-in-law exclaimed: "Oh!"
>
> Jerusa turned and saw Nacib who was about to weep, his face immobile, with shame and sorrow. And so she went forward too, took a lantern from one of the shepherdesses, started to dance. A young man came forward, then another, Iracema took the lantern from Dora. Mundinho Falcão took the whistle from the mouth of Nilo. The English gentleman and his wife threw themselves into the dance. The wife of João Fulgêncio, the merry mother of six, goodness personified, entered the *terno*. Other ladies too, the captain, Josué. All the guests of the Clube were dancing in the middle of the street. At the end of the *terno* even Nacib's sister and her engineer husband danced. In front of them all danced Gabriela, the standard in her fist.[50]

Gabriela, cravo e canela really is the novel of reconciliation. Reconciliation with the idea of economic progress that is not only exploitation of the weakest any longer, reconciliation with capitalism when it is represented by men like Mundinho Falcão, reconciliation with the old coronéis, patriarchs of ancient struggles, reconciliation between rich and poor, all united in the new identity of music and dance.

Reading the novel more attentively, however, one becomes aware of many hidden teachings. The progress Ilhéus is going toward is not only that resulting from greater wealth or more modern structures. The real progress Jorge Amado is talking about is a certain transformation of customs towards civilization. The novel opens with the scene of a double murder, a crime of honor, a fazendeiro who kills his wife and her lover, surprised in adultery. At the end of the story we will learn that for the first time at Ilhéus, after a thrilling trial, a coronel of cocoa is to be sentenced for this type of crime. But the real progess is represented by the reaction of Nacib. He discovers his wife in bed with another and does not kill her even though he is armed. The real progress is the composed reaction of Nacib's friends, who help him, through a legal quibble, to have his marriage declared null and void. The real progress is the new, free union of Nacib and Gabriela, the free Black condition of Gabriela, compatible with the new, free habits of the new times.

If Gabriela is the free expression of a new world in which the idea of new relationships between man and woman is quite compatible with the flexible way in which Blacks have considered relationships between the sexes, we must not forget the presence of another female character who is fighting the same battle as Gabriela but on a diametrically opposite frontier. Malvina, daughter of a rich fazendeiro, young and beautiful, romantic and cultivated, refuses the fate of woman-slave traditional in that world and in that epoch. She falls in love with a married man, an engineer from Rio, and when the man runs away for fear of her father's threats, Malvina courageously and nobly accepts the responsibility for her betrayed love. She too will flee one day, but not to join the man who has disappointed her. She is to flee to São Paulo and live there alone, working and studying, asserting her free and dignified choice of life.

By way of a curiosity we can mention that criticism of customs carried out with the weapon of irony can at times be more dangerous, in every sense, than an attack made in accordance with classical ideological schemes. The appearance of a work as amusing as *Gabriela, cravo e canela*, this ironic portrait of the society of Ilhéus, must have wounded the feelings of many people if Amado had to avoid setting foot in the city of his adolescence for fear of a violent reaction. Only a long time afterwards, almost twenty years later, when *Gabriela* was brought to the television screens in a long *novela*—which had absolutely the greatest success with the public—was Amado able to return to the town, which had become famous through his work.

After *Gabriela, cravo e canela* came a full and clear expansion of the Black condition in all the other novels. In *Os pastores da noite* a whole story is dedicated to a phenomenon of symbiosis between Black religion and Catholicism. The Black Massu has had a child, the mother has disappeared and may be dead. All his friends offer to be godfather at the baptism—there is no problem for the godmother, the choice necessarily falls on Tibéria, respectable proprietress of a brothel. But before all the others, during a *candomblé*, Ogun, god of iron and of metals, has offered to be godfather. It is something new for everyone and a great honor for Massu, who would thus be related to Ogun. But there remain certain practical problems to solve. The baptism will take place in a church: how will Ogun present himself, how will he hold the baby in his arms? Doninha, the great *mãe-de-santo,* is consulted and tries in every way to solve the problem. In the end a solution is found: in every session of candomblé the various orixás descend, that is, they personify themselves in some of their adepts, chosen according to a precise liturgy. The only one in the group who is a son of Ogun is an old gambler at dice, a Black man called Artur da Guima. He is the one chosen to represent Ogun in church and Ogun, when consulted, declares his agreement. And here comes the surprise to be revealed only in the last scene. Before every ceremony it is necessary to make a *despacho,* that is, it is necessary to send away Exu, the devil, after making him a sacrifice so that he does not disturb the occasion. This time, however, there is a hitch. Ogun arrives slightly late to the ceremony and Exu takes his place, incarnating himself in Artur da Guima who, for the occasion, with the complicity of the verger, figures on his baptismal certificate as Antônio de Ogun (Saint Anthony is the Catholic equivalent of Ogun so the symbiosis between the two religions is respected formally too). No one realizes the substitution, not even Doninha the mãe-de-santo, and on the way there Exu pulls every sort of joke, causes confusion on the tram, and has many people arrive from all over. The church is full to the wonder of the priest, a fair-skinned mulatto called Gomes. Exu reveals his identity only in church at the moment of the baptism with Artur da Guima jumping and dancing like a lunatic. But here comes the final coup de théâtre. Ogun, distraught at having arrived late and no longer being able to incarnate himself in Artur da Guima, desperately seeks an adept, a son of his, to do so. And in the end he finds one, one and only one: Father Gomes, Catholic priest, parish priest. How is it possible? Father Gomes, like so many Brazilians, knows little of his origins. He knows that he is the son of a Portuguese businessman and a pious mulatto lady called Josefa. He does not know that his mother was once Josefa de Omulu and his maternal grandfather, a Black African, was Ojuaruá, *obá* of Xangô. He does not know just as he does not know that he is himself destined to Ogun. His true name is Antônio de Ogun. And so, before the amazed congregation, we see Artur da Guima, or rather Exu, dance like a maniac, and Father Gomes, or rather Ogun, first dance and then hurl himself on Artur da Guima, that wretched Exu. Exu abandons Artur and Ogun comes out of the priest in turn to enter Artur. The priest remembers nothing. He thinks he has had a dizzy spell. The baptism takes place according to the rules, with Ogun as godfather. And then later, in the sacristy, the godfather affectionately embraces Father Gomes, Antônio de Ogun embraces Antônio de Ogun. Everything is possible in Bahia.

In the following works, *Os velhos marinheiros* and *Dona Flor e seus dois maridos*, there are many Black characters even though the protagonists are white. But what counts is the existential philosophy with which these white people face life. Quincas Berro Dágua and Vasco Moscoso in their way of acting reject a certain conception of life understood as progress, as continuous becoming, as a strict concatenation of passages leading to a determined end. For them, as for Gabriela, what counts is the present moment, the one that passes and never returns. For all of them what has value is the mockery with which in the end they realize themselves, debunking the structure, the society, and the norm they undergo without accepting it. The false marriage of Gabriela brings her back to the truth of affection; the double death of Quincas frustrates the efforts of his family and the medical certificate; the navigational incompetence of Vasco is rewarded regardless of the technological capacity of the ship's officers. And what is Vadinho, the blond skirt-chasing husband of Flor, but a white, male-chauvinist version of Gabriela, the mulatta? And his return after death with the obliging aid of Exu, completing his marriage to Flor with wedded adultery, what is it but the violation of every established norm, from natural laws to legal formulas, carrying to the limits of the absurd the process begun with the false marriage of Gabriela?

Négritude as a smile, as the joy in living the present moment, as the tragedy of living in a world where those of light skins oppress those of dark skins. Which of them is the truest? To laugh and struggle, sing and study, a man above all, before being member of a race, of a class. Here is the new example, the most complete, Pedro Archanjo Ojuobá, the eye of Xangô.

"Ogun kapê dan meji, dan pelu oniban!"—repeated Archanjo—"Ogun called two snakes and they flung themselves on the soldiers!"[51]

With *Tenda dos milagres* Négritude in the works of Jorge Amado finds a historical dimension. It is set in 1969. The military takeover of 1965, which seemed to be only a drastic and temporary remedy to a situation of emergency has by now structured itself into a Power. The military has chosen its own road, its own very precise profile: alliance with the great multinational industries, accelerated development of the enormous resources of the country, a strong hand internally to curb wage claims. The dream of a Brazilian path to socialism, which had aroused enthusiasm and hope in the sixties, is terminated. It is certainly not similar to the time of Vargas. The country has changed and no longer tolerates certain things. But there are hard moments all the same. The intellectual and political opposition is divided and does not know where to look for a model. The socialist model, even before being destroyed by the military, has destroyed itself through a senseless economic policy. The Communist model, with the crushing intervention of Soviet tanks in Czechoslovakia a bare year before, is impossible to put forward and is counterproductive in a country like Brazil, where the working class is of recent formation. Finally, the division of the world into areas of influence between the Soviet Union and the United States, the new treaty of Tordesillas as they call it, leaves no room for doubt as to the future of Latin America.

But the evil, the worst evil of that time in Brazil is not the dictatorship, which, all in all, is by no means as bad as many other regimes. The evil is having chosen the way of capitalism without that work ethic and pioneering spirit at the basis of Yankee capitalism. The enormous flow of money from the industrialized countries and the rigid withholding of salaries give the impression—the illusion—of easy riches, which becomes concrete in the formation of a new bourgeoisie, in uncontrolled consumption and nationalistic pride continually swelled by official propaganda. The Establishment reveals its incapacity to offer the young an ideal model. The conquest of the interior itself, the praises of which are sung incessantly, takes place according to the directives and interests of the multinationals and uses the poorest and most backward part of the population. Apart from the few who choose the road of revolution, the road of no turning back, the Establishment is able to satisfy for the moment the consumer appetites of the majority, but Brazilian youth has no more dreams.

And here is Amado taking up the fight again after the cheerful and burlesque parenthesis that goes from the innocent and inexhaustible embraces of Gabriela to the almost neurotic and obsessive ones of Vadinho. The miracles described in the book are not those designed by Mestre Lídio in his workshop. The real miracles are the joy of living and the hope of a people that is renewed after every battle and every defeat. The miracle is the history of the Black, white, and mulatto population of Bahia.

The novel, as we have already said, is structured on two different historical planes. The first is that of contemporary Bahia: the economic boom; the luxury and snobbery of the dominant classes; the interests of finance, which coincide with those of commercialized culture, of journalism and of the mass media; and the hidden and obsessive presence of the Establishment. The second plane extends for the whole arc of the life of Pedro Archanjo and is also the story of the suffering and glorious Black way of life. The first plane gives free rein to the author's ironic and desecrating vein. The second allows him to find again that moment of ideal hope which the dull materialism of his times seemed to have destroyed all memory of. The first and second planes then run together in the ending, in the Carnival, where today relives the past, the people on holiday acting out the life and deeds of Pedro Archanjo.

The choice of Carnival also has a precise meaning. Let us not forget that Amado made his literary debut with Paulo Rigger, a cultured white man who fled from Brazil making his way with difficulty through the Black Carnival. Next came Antônio Balduíno, ever present at Carnival dances, and then so many others, up to Vadinho, who has a heart attack right in the middle of Carnival. But the Carnival of Pedro Archanjo is not only a holiday. It is the cultural expression of a people matured through long struggles. Here Amado finds again his best political vein. Certainly no great imagination is required to discover the transparent game. What is the historical reevocation of the Blacks' struggle for freedom—in this case freedom of expression, of words, of religion—if not a transparent parable on the continuous control over freedom of thought exercised by the Establishment at the time of the publication of *Tenda dos milagres*?

The novel refers to a precise historical situation which it would be as well to examine. As noted previously, the end of slavery in 1888 was an act more symbolic than real. In fact, while great masses of Blacks had already become free (and the law of 1871 had practically decreed the end of slavery), at the same time nothing was done to prepare the former slaves to enter into society as active members of a free community. In Brazil genuine racial preconceptions based on a supposed inferiority of the Blacks as human beings have never existed. But, as the structures of society were not modified after 1888, the reproduction was inevitable of the classic framework, which saw in opposition those groups in control of power and wealth and those destined to serve them.

Among the ruling classes, therefore, a precise fear arose, which to us today may seem absurd after a certain evolution of thought, but at the time was well founded, especially in a city like Bahia where there was and is a very high number of Blacks and mulattoes. This fear was based upon numbers: that from the fusion of the two ethnic and social groups—Blacks and whites—a new society might arise in which Black characteristics would predominate. We must remember that at the beginning of this century, culture and civilization were officially represented by what the European world had produced and was producing. Brazil had fallen in line with this concept of culture and was trying in every way to imitate and transplant it. There was, therefore, widespread resentment, witnessed by numerous publications, on the part of white, cultured Brazilian society at being confused with the other side of Brazilian culture, Black and more colorful in a folkloristic sense. The Europe of those years—the great cultural model—had colonized Africa, and had installed there a clear relationship of domination with respect to the Black world, the white man's burden, the light of Christian civilization transforming and illuminating the shadows of barbarism, and so on. Members of Brazilian society, the ruling classes that imitated Europe, found themselves forced to live in formal equality alongside an African society they had brought there themselves and could not do without.

On the Bahia of those years and on the battle waged in the name of civilization against the Black world and its cultural expression, we have rich documentation collected by the scholar Nina Rodrigues from Bahia:

> These religious, cult manifestations are considered in Brazil as the practices of witchcraft and enjoy no protection from the law and are condemned by the dominant religion and by the contempt, frequently only apparent, of the influential classes who, in spite of everything, fear them. During slavery, barely twenty years ago, these manifestations suffered all the violence possible at the hands of the *senhores de engenho*, always arrogant bullies, while the *negros* in the *fazendas* and the plantations were abandoned to the almost unlimited despotism of administrators and bailiffs, as brutal and cruel as they were ignorant.
>
> Today, with slavery over, these manifestations are at the mercy of

the arbitrary bullying of the police, who are certainly no more enlightened than the old masters, and are constantly made the target of public opinion protests, which in their attempt to show strength and culture reveal at every turn the most supine ignorance of sociological phenomena.

It must, unfortunately, be added that the local press also reveals great confusion in the way it deals with the subject while it affirms and spreads the conviction that the sword of the obtuse policeman and the stupid violence of inspectors of equal ignorance have greater efficacy as instruments of catechism and capacity for religious conversion than the whips of the bailiffs.[52]

Nina Rodrigues collected much evidence of this aversion on the part of certain strata of public opinion towards Black cultural and folkloric manifestations. Naturally, the concept of public opinion in Bahia at the beginning of the century is somewhat vague and refers to that restricted group of people, belonging to the wealthier classes, who used the newspapers as a means of spreading their own opinions. Let us begin with some writings on Carnival, the most popular festival in Brazil and in the world, and what is today the best-known expression of Afro-Brazilian folklore. At the beginning of the century, however, Carnival in Brazil was split into two celebrations. On the one side there was the classic, European-style, fancy-dress party. On the other, the Black people began to parade through the streets with their music and their folklore. Against this progressive *africanization*, as it was called with a certain disdain, protests were printed in the newspapers. Let us see, from Bahia, the *Jornal de notícias* of 15 February 1901:

We must unfortunately report that since yesterday the celebrated *africanized groups of canzás and búzios* have begun to exhibit themselves in an infernal confusion, without wit or taste, groups who, far from contributing luster to the Carnival festivities, degrade the name of Bahia with these tasteless and irritating spectacles. Although the attention of the police has already been drawn to this, it seems opportune to us to point out that it would not be a bad idea to prohibit these *candomblés* during the Carnival festivities.[53]

From the same newspaper the following Carnival, 5 February 1902:

If in the Carnival festivities of last year, when enthusiasm exploded at the passing of the victorious *clubes*, these groups of *africanos* aroused clear repugnance, what will happen in the Carnival of 1902 if the police do not take steps to ensure that our streets do not present the appearance of those *terreiros* where fetishism reigns, with their processions of *ogans* and their bands of *canzás* and tambourines?[54]

Let us go on to the following year, 1903, still with the same newspaper on 15 February: "Carnival time is approaching and the drums prepare to sound the sad notes of our debased civilization, transforming festivities like these, so enjoyable in other cities, into real *candomblés*."[55] The news of the twenty-third of the same month, while reporting the increasingly decided assertion of the Black Carnival, voices one of the classic Brazilian fears: the opinion that foreigners might form of their country, with all those Blacks invading the streets and squares:

> The Carnival of this year, despite the patriotic and civilizing appeal made, appeared yet again as a public exhibition of *candomblé*, apart from the odd exception.
>
> If someone from abroad had to judge Bahia from its Carnival, he could not help placing it on the same level as Africa. Furthermore, we must point out, to our shame, that a commission of Austrian scientists are guests of our city and naturally, pen in hand, record all these facts to divulge to the newspapers of cultured Europe their impressions of the journey.[56]

We must point out certain things about these articles: the term *africanos* is used improperly. In fact, in Brazil the word africanos is used to indicate Blacks from Africa. For Blacks born in Brazil, instead, the term *crioulos* is used, even if they are of "pure race," that is, with no percentage of white or Indian blood. At the beginning of this century African Blacks in Brazil were extremely rare, as smuggling had died out about thirty years before. The term africanos is therefore used here in a clearly pejorative way, just as the comparison between Bahia and Africa is pejorative. And if, given the attitude of the time, we can understand the comparison with Africa, considered a land of barbarians and savages, the use of africanos to indicate Blacks is completely unhistorical. Slavery had begun with the discovery of the country and there were, therefore, Blacks with three centuries of Brazilian descent behind them, more than that of many whites.

The term candomblés is also used improperly. Candomblé is an exclusive ceremony that is difficult to witness (let us bear in mind the testimony of Xavier Marques from Bahia in *O feiticeiro*), accompanied by typically Black music and songs. That the same type of music and the same musical instruments were used in the streets during Carnival does not at all mean that candomblé was carried through the streets of Bahia.

From this evidence we can deduce that Bahia was undergoing a process of rejection of the Black presence in its folkloristic manifestations and that the so-called cultured class showed a crass ignorance of the Black world, of those Blacks near whom they had lived for centuries. The appeal for police intervention as the final solution is of such desolating stupidity as to require no further comment.

The repression of Black music and songs had existed since colonial times. The great fazendeiros saw in them the danger of a union of Blacks, who could burst out in revolt. Others instead, like the Conde dos Arcos at the beginning of the last century, considered the same manifestations as the rebirth of the various tribal identities and, therefore, as an element of separation between the various groups of Blacks, united in the misfortune of slavery. These whites were, therefore, in favor of these manifestations and viewed them, on the basis of divide and rule, as a guarantee of slavery. Neither the former nor the latter had understood or foreseen that the various Black identities would fuse together and then fuse again with the white part of the country and in the end originate the multiracial Brazil that so frightened the reporter of the *Jornal de notícias* at the turn of the century.

The presence of Black festivals and ceremonies in Bahia and the other Brazilian cities dates back to the beginning of the nineteenth century. A century later, the cultured classes, those who had studied and traveled, sounded the trumpet call for repression through the press, which should instead have been an expression of freedom of thought. Some accused the adepts of candomblés of being charlatans who exploited the credulity of the ignorant with the sole aim of tricking them out of their money. Others worried about the virginity of the girls during the scenes of possession; still others were indignant because in the site of a candomblé, among a thousand statues and paintings of divinities of all types, there was also a Christ in wood "who attended impassively the fetishistic ceremonies of Tio Yojô"[57] (another proof of the beginning of a symbiosis of the cults).

Among the many articles and letters there are two, written many years apart, in which the Black presence in Bahia is described as something extraneous, not yet established in the country. The letter is published and commented on approvingly in the *Jornal de notícias*, 22 May 1897:

> There are those who are fighting for the disappearance of these religious scenes practiced by African fetishism, *which day by day is sinking its roots in this land*, debilitating and brutalizing the popular spirit which, dragged along by superstition, can only degenerate instead of lifting itself to the high destiny that summons it.[58]

Considering that the first Black slaves arrived in Bahia around 1550, it would seem a trifle anachronistic to speak of roots that are just beginning to sink in, in 1897! Equally anachronistic is the article commenting on a case of lunacy that happened during a candomblé; the text is taken from the *Gazeta do povo*, 16 August 1905:

> But what amazes one above all is the extraordinary resistance and vitality of the beliefs of the Black race. Everything has been tried in vain to wipe them out: the ancient and so prolonged repression, inhuman at times, always violent on the part of the *senhores de engenho* and their bailiffs, the equally violent intervention of the police, the unceasing protests of the press and the urging of the other classes that the evil be uprooted. The *jejenagô* cult, both *terreiros* and *candomblés*, continues to function regularly and every time embeds itself more deeply in the main cities of the state.
>
> The rigorous frequency with which the complaints against the *candomblés* are reproduced every year in the local press at the time of the *nagô* festivities is indicative. These complaints are followed by the severe and precise orders of the police to have done once and for all with this African tradition that nothing can justify in a city like Bahia and that can be uprooted so easily.[59]

Besides the useless repetition of *terreiros* and candomblés (terreiro is the site of the cult, meaning square, and candomblé is the manifestation of the cult, the ceremony), which already indicates a fair dose of ignorance, the final sentence in which it is claimed that nothing can justify an African cult (once more the unhistorical term used in a pejorative way) is truly laughable and shows only the stupid fanaticism of the person who wrote it. The blackest city of Brazil should not have Black traditions and those same traditions could easily be eliminated by the police as though it were a matter of a small group of people and not the majority of the population.

The religious authorities were also worried about the phenomenon and evidence of this, written with far more cultural dignity, comes from a high-ranking Brazilian prelate, Dom João Correia Nery, who describes the cult ritual called *cabula*. He ends with these words:

> As one sees, there are eloquent vestiges of a retrograde and African religion that, transported into Brazil, has mixed with the popular ceremonies of our religion and with other existing associations and sects to form a dangerous amalgam, serving only to offend God and pervert the soul.[60]

Among the many testimonies, apart from the excellent and most useful knowledge he shows of the *cabula*, that of the prelate is the only one not to reveal ignorant fanaticism and to limit itself understandably to speaking of the dangers for the religion he represents.

This brief historical sketch has been necessary because *Tenda dos milagres* is in part a historical novel whose subject is the expansion and establishment of Black culture in the first years of the twentieth century in the city of Bahia. Amado, as in his other novels, mixes reality and imagination, real people and characters created in his artistic fantasy. And if the main character, Pedro Archanjo, is based on figures who really existed, such as Martiniano Eliseu do Bonfim and Manoel Querino, Nina Rodrigues himself is portrayed, in a decidedly altered and negative manner, in the character of a professor in the faculty of medicine, Nilo Argolo d'Ávila de Araújo, from an illustrious family of Bahia, a wicked racist. The titles of the books of the professor Amado created are the same as those Nina Rodrigues published during his fertile scientific activity; but the spirit of the two figures, the real and the fictional, is completely different. All in all, the posthumous fate of Nina is sad. We owe to him a unique and most valid documentation of the Black presence in Brazil, his sociological analyses are still current, his contribution to the culture of his country is fundamental. Side by side with such merit, however, he made the mistake of expressing a series of racist theories on the anthropological inferiority of the Blacks. This choice, which he was not alone in making, has long condemned to ostracism work that deserved a better fate.

It is worthwhile remembering here that those years around the turn of the century were the golden age of European colonization of the world and of Africa in particular. The superiority of the white race was an axiom not to be discussed, which had its basis in the historical superiority of the white man in the technological and industrial field and which, in the end, served as an alibi for the economic exploitation of a large part of the world. Nina was certainly not the only one to express similar theories; his works are thick with quotations from foreign authors, among whom, it should be pointed out, were not a few Italians. Italian and generally European emigration to Brazil had also been encouraged with the aim, often expressed by the Establishment, of diluting and getting rid of the Black presence within a white majority.

Tenda dos milagres is the novelized history of the struggle for self-assertion of the Black way of life from the beginning of this century up to the Second World War, when the end of nazism took from racist theories their strongest support. The arrival of a great North American Nobel Prize winner arouses competition among the great newspapers of Bahia. From this commercialized and commercializing competition (the farce, the eternal farce in Jorge Amado) is born the commemoration of Pedro Archanjo. The reporters are hunting for news; what do they know of the times already gone by?

> Timidity and reticence of the witnesses faced with the oppressive demands of the journalists, greedy for sensational details, for sex, orgiastic and sad, violence for violence's sake; memories of a time and people with no charm for the rat-race press. A time and people still near according to the calendar but so far away in terms of habits, feelings, and life-styles.[61]

And here is the time, still so near and yet so far, of Pedro Archanjo: the setting is the Carnival of 1904, when the chief of police absolutely prohibits the demonstration, thus provoking the defiance of the Blacks, who come out into the streets with their music and their instruments. They are not there only to have a good time. Before beginning Pedro Archanjo asks for the permission and blessing of Majé Bassan, the great mãe-de-santo, who in turn consults the divinities and asks for their protection. The Carnival group is called an *afoxé*—which means spell, miracle—it is a religious group and the theme they have chosen is that of Zumbi dos Palmares, the hero of the Black revolt against the whites. This group does not consist only of Blacks who want to cause confusion, but rather of men who assert their right to exist. The police intervene, they fight and escape through the streets; the chase is unsuccessful. Then Pedro Archanjo laughs contemptuously and his laughter echoes other laughter: the proud laughter of Antônio Balduíno, the warm, sensual laughter of Gabriela. Pedro Archanjo is a mulatto and the choice of Jorge Amado was certainly not made by chance. We remember the by-now-distant times of *O país do carnaval* and the criticism of the mulattoes active in the world of literature. Who knows if among them there was a Pedro Archanjo. The mulatto is the product of a cross between a white man and a Black woman or a Black man and a white woman. Basically Brazil is a mulatto country, with the crossing of many races; Bahia is particularly mulatto, and is the center of ancient traditions, Black and white.

Pedro Archanjo fights for the whole of his existence to assert the cultural and religious dignity of his people. For this purpose he makes use of his position as caretaker in the faculty of medicine (it was Majé Bassan who put him there; many of those in power in the city turn to her for help and she can obtain a lot in return for her favors) to sharpen his limited cultural instruments and confute the racists' theories by making use of the science whites themselves created. Pedro Archanjo fights all his life to be able to give himself a precise identity, to find himself again, and his origins, his roots. At the end of a long journey through books, documents, and struggles he finds a landing place, which is no longer the African village it had been in the dreams and hopes of Jubiabá. His roots are there, in Brazil, in the meeting between a Black man and a white woman so many years before. Naturally in a work by Jorge Amado a moment of farce could not be lacking even in the most serious situations. The caretaker Pedro Archanjo has, among the many enemies he has had to face, always had one who is particularly dangerous, the illustrious pedant Nilo Argolo, the already-mentioned racist. And what does Pedro Archanjo find out? He finds out that the illustrious professor is a distant cousin of his, another descendant of the Black Bomboxé Oubitikô, founder of a great candomblé, who had loved a sweet white girl of the illustrious family of d'Avila.

We have said that Pedro Archanjo is a mixture of Jubiabá and Antônio Balduíno, combining the great Black tradition of the former with the class struggle of the latter. In him there no longer exists the racial struggle because it is already resolved in his mulatto soul, the product of two different cultures, of two different human beings.

Tenda dos milagres is one of the best works of Jorge Amado, the one in which the writer succeeds in achieving a perfect balance between drama and comedy, farce and sorrow. Some figures are completely new in the Brazilian novel and bear witness to the author's clear evolution. Take Rosa de Oxalá, the beautiful Black woman: "Her sandals resounded like music, she had a rose in her hair—her hair was early morning moss—her hips sailing the high seas and a breast that illuminated the sun."[62] The mistress of Lídio, Pedro's friend. Rosa is the woman eternally loved, never possessed, unattainable and hidden as Lindinalva had been for Antônio Balduíno. Such female figures belong to the classic repertoire of literature; the novelty is that for the first time a Black woman takes on the role generally played by white women, preferably blonde and with blue eyes.

Sad and painful is the story of the love of Pedro Archanjo and Rosa de Oxalá. She is a beautiful woman, mistress of a rich man who has taken her off the streets and given her a house and clothes. They have a child together and when the father takes it away from her she claims her freedom as a woman. She meets Lídio and they love each other but she refuses to live with him; her freedom must not be altered. She meets Pedro Archanjo but Pedro is Lídio's best friend—they are like brothers. The love between the mulatto Pedro Archanjo and the Black Rosa de Oxalá is only desperate nostalgia for a different fate, a dream that could not come true.

> Rosa, we are not puppets. We have honor, feelings. We are not degenerates in filthy promiscuity with animals or, worse still, criminals. Yes, Rosa, just this—"degenerate half-breeds in sordid and filthy promiscuity"—is what a professor of medicine, a doctor, a teacher has written. But it is a lie, Rosa, it is a slander by that egghead who knows nothing.[63]

The years pass. Rosa's daughter marries a rich young man and Rosa disappears, abandoning forever her world, Lídio, and Pedro. "I'm not false and a liar because I'm *negra*,"[64] she claims; the slander has sunk in deeply. It is necessary to fight against our very selves, our prejudices against ourselves. The first kiss is the last. Goodbye for ever. And then Pedro Archanjo has become old, his heart is no longer in order. He takes part in a rally in support of the allies in the Second World War. He experiences a dizzy spell and a beautiful girl runs to his aid. It is she, it is Rosa, Rosa's granddaughter, herself Rosa de Oxalá. "She is so much the same and so different. How much blood has been mixed to make her so perfect? She has long silken hair, blue eyes, and an impenetrable mystery in her slim and shapely body."[65] He takes a few more steps, then dies a sudden death pronouncing once more the name of Rosa.

The most interesting part of the novel always remains that of the struggle, however, the cultural affirmation that comes progressively through studies, the publication of books, and the ever more frequent fighting against the forces of repression, the eternal and sad fable of Power, which in order to exist must necessarily be oppressive. While in the halls of the universities and the pages of the newspapers cultural representatives enunciate their theories on the superiority of the white race and the congenital inferiority of the Black race, through the streets and the squares, in the woods and the fields, groups of fanatical policemen mercilessly carry out an attack with no quarter given against candomblés and pais-de-santo, against a whole people who ask only the right to exist in the way that suits them best.

The moment of truth arrives when Majé Bassan, the great mãe-de-santo, dies and leaves Pedro Archanjo a story she whispers to him before dying. Pedro Archanjo has a high rank in the candomblé, his name is Ojuobá, the eyes of Xangô. Pedro is destined to see and understand more than the others. Therefore he accepts serenely the story of Majé Bassan, the story of a festival of Ogun when the soldiers arrived to destroy everything. But Ogun had provided two poisonous snakes that at his call arose and hurled themselves on the soldiers who fled and never returned. Pedro Archanjo waits while the delegado, the police commissioner, Pedrito Gordo kills and destroys as he likes. When the time for the festival of Oxossi arrives, Procópio, the pai-de-santo, prepares to celebrate his candomblé although he has received an unmistakable death threat from Pedrito Gordo. At the climax of the ceremony with few people present, among them Pedro Archanjo, Pedrito Gordo arrives with his men, foremost among whom is a gigantic Black man, Zé Alma Grande, a former adept of the candomblé, from which he had been driven away by Majé Bassan, under the name of Zé de Ogun. Pedrito Gordo orders Zé Alma Grande to take Procópio.

The *negro* advanced, bigger than a house. Ojuobá perceived with the eyes of Xangô an instant of hesitation in the step of the delinquent at the moment of penetrating the holy grounds of the Terreiro. Samuel Cobra Coral and Zacarias da Goméia took up their positions, ready to stop any form of protest. Procópio carried on with the dance. He was Oxossi, the hunter, lord of the forest, king of Ketu.

They relate that in that precise moment, Exu, returning from the horizon entered the hall. Ojuoba said, "Laroiê, Exu!" It all happened very quickly. When Zé Alma Grande took another step towards Oxossi, he found Pedro Archanjo in front of him. Pedro Archanjo, Ojuobá, Exu himself according to the opinion of many. The voice resounded imperiously in the terrible anathema, in the final curse!

"*Ogun kapê dan meji, dan pelú oniban*!"

As big as a house, with the eyes of a murderer, arms like cranes, the hands of death, the terrified *negro* Zé Alma Grande halted to hear the spell. Zé de Ogun gave a cry and a jump, hurled his shoes away, spun round in the hall, became an *orixá*; when he received the saint his strength was doubled. "Ogunhê!" he yelled and all those present answered: "Ogunhê, Ogun my father!"

"*Ogun kapê dan meji, dan pelú oniban*!" repeated Archanjo: "Ogun called two snakes and they hurled themselves on the soldiers!"

The arms of the *orixá* rose, the pincerlike hands were two snakes: Zé Alma Grande, Ogun in fury, flung himself on Pedrito.

"Have you gone mad, Zé?"

Samuel Cobra Coral had no other choice. They put themselves between the commissioner and the Demon. With his right hand Zé Alma Grande seized Samuel Cobra Coral. He lifted him into the air and swung him like a child's toy. Then, with all his strength, he threw him to the ground, head first. The head was buried to the neck, the backbone shattered, the base of the skull cracked, the corpse fell at the commissioner's feet. Zacarias da Goméia was about to shoot. He had no time. He was kicked in the genitals and fainted howling, never again good for any type of action.

The streets, crowded with people, saw the commissioner Pedrito Gordo, the wild beast of the police force, the swaggering bully, the sinister chief of a band of killers, the evil with no soul, the terror of the people, in sorry flight chased by an *orixá* of *candomblé*, by the warrior Ogun unleashed in serpents. The whole city laughed. It was a joke, the comic news in the opposition newspapers, the song of the troubadours:

> Mestre Archanjo já acabou
> Com a farromba de Pedrito
>
> Mestre Archanjo has already wiped out
> That braggart Pedrito.[66]

This is a classic example of Négritude. Amado has placed himself clearly in the middle of the events, adopting wholly the attitudes of the protagonists. But it is only a moment. The Black condition must rid itself of itself if it wants to survive. Antônio Balduíno separated himself from Jubiabá, from the impossible dream of a return to the African forest. Pedro Archanjo must abandon a part of himself in order to fulfill himself as a man, as a mulatto, as white and as Black. The dances in the terreiro, the participation in the candomblés, the songs, the violent struggle to survive and, at the same time, the studies, the science of the whites: his two souls, one of which will end up killing forever a part of the other.

The explanation arrives and, if we analyze it carefully, it is not merely the imaginary story of the old man Pedro Archanjo and his struggle for the assertion of Négritude. It is perhaps also the struggle of Jorge Amado on the threshold of old age, the memory of the motives that led him to fight, the motives he perhaps no longer believes in, even if he still believes in life, in the struggle, because the struggle is song, is dance, is laughter.

The explanation appears during a conversation between Pedro Archanjo and Fraga Neto, a university professor. Fraga Neto is one of those classic intellectuals (and how could such a specimen be lacking in the gallery of Jorge Amado?) who, although an excellent person and sincere friend Pedro Archanjo, takes an interest in candomblés and in Black religion with the detachment of a white scientist who sees in it all something interesting, pleasantly folkloric, but nothing more than that. It is a way of seeing things that is quite common today. Amado could not fail to be aware of the inverted racism such an intellectual position involves: the interest in the Blacks, in the *índios*, or in any other ethnic group not for the value their civilizations represent in themselves but for the difference they represent—and therefore the interest—from our society, which thus remains the norm, the only one, the right one, the one everyone must imitate, towards which all must tend.

With a certain intellectual petulance, Fraga Neto insists on knowing how Pedro Archanjo can believe simultaneously in the truths of science and in candomblés, ''*aquele bisbilhoterio queria a chave da advinha mais difícil, do cabuloso enigma* . . . that sly one wanted the key to the most difficult sorcery, to the mysterious enigma.''[67] Slow and painful, full of bashful reticence, is the confession of Pedro Archanjo:

''I am a half-breed. I have something of the *negros* and something of the whites, I am white and *negro* at the same time. I was born in the *candomblé*, grew up with *orixás* and took on a high position in the Terreiro when still young. Do you know what Ojuobá means? I am the eyes of Xangô, my illustrious professor. I have a compromise, a responsibility . . . For years I believed in my *orixás* as Brother Timóteo believe in his saints, in Christ, in the Virgin. At that time all that I knew I had picked up in the streets. Then I looked for other sources of knowledge, I attained new values, I lost the faith . . . All that had been my land, the earth in which I had planted my feet, everything was transformed into a simple game of riddles. What had been the mysterious descent of the saints was reduced to a state of trance that any freshman in the faculty can analyze and demonstrate. For me, Professor, there exists only matter. But this does not make me stop going to the Terreiro and exercising the functions of my position of Ojuobá, does not stop me from carrying out my duty . . . We are in the middle of a hard and bitter struggle. See with what violence they want to destroy all that we, *negros* and mulattoes, possess, our goods, our philosophy . . . If I had proclaimed my materialism to the four winds, if I had abandoned the *candomblé*, if I had said that it was all nothing but an infantile trick, the result of primitive fear, of ignorance, of poverty, who would I have helped? I would have helped, Professor, Commissioner Pedrito and his gang of murderers, I would have helped to destroy a festival of the people. I prefer to continue going to the *candomblé*. Apart from anything else, I like it. I like to sing and dance before the drums . . . I think that the *orixás* belong to the people . . . Terreiro de Jesus, everything is mixed together in Bahia, Professor . . . I am a mixture of races and of men. I am a mulatto, a Brazilian. Tomorrow it will be as you say and as you wish. Certainly it will be like that; man goes on. On that day everything will be completely mixed and what is today the struggle and mystery of poor people, of *negros* and half-breeds, banned music, illegal dances, *candomblé*, samba, *capoeira*, all this will be the festival of the Brazilian people . . . I bear all this in my blood, Professor. The ancients still live in me, regardless of my will, because I was one for a long time. Now I will ask you, Professor: is it easy or difficult to reconcile theory and life, what you read in books and the life that you live every second?''

"When one tries to apply theories to iron and flame they burn our hands. Is that what you mean?"

"If I proclaimed my truth to the four winds and said that it was all only a game, I would put myself on the side of the police and get on in life, as they say. Listen, my friend, one day the *orixás* will dance on the stages of the theaters. I do not want to get on, I keep going, my friend."[68]

The question of Professor Fraga Neto and the answer of Pedro Archanjo may also be interpreted, as we have already mentioned, as a confession by Jorge Amado who, in the arc of the struggle between Négritude and the Establishment, reviews the history of the struggle against every form of power exercised by man upon man.

Thus ends the long fable of Pedro Archanjo, the most complete story of the Black condition in Brazil ever written. It ends with a last piece of mockery, the final farce against the offensive and suffocating Establishment. In the great hall are met in squalid and hypocritical solidarity all the men of the Establishment: governor, deputies, newspaper editors, university professors, all there to commemorate Pedro Archanjo, to get their hands on the much-advertised heritage of the man who had always fought against them. In a progressive crescendo each one of those present—except a young woman, a student—takes over his part of Pedro Archanjo, who ends up becoming a character increasingly different from what he really was. The worst moment is at the end with the speech of Professor Baptista, president of the Association for the Defense of Tradition, of the Family and of Property, a foul reactionary, one who informs on his colleagues, a spy for the military. And when everything seems to be extinguishing itself in the monotonous and threatening words of the miserable Baptista, here is the coup de théâtre that overturns the situation, that avenges Pedro Archanjo and pours scorn on the Establishment. Major Damião appears, a major in a manner of speaking, lawyer and defender of the poor, a most popular figure in Bahia, a person who actually existed, godson of Pedro Archanjo, who asks to be allowed to speak. In a magnificent speech, in "words that were bombastic, baroque, utterly Bahian,"[69] he recalls the deceased and shows to them all a poor mulatto woman, pregnant, a widow, mother of seven children, without a penny, descendant of Pedro Archanjo. For her, only for her and for Pedro Archanjo, he asks for donations, appealing to the well-known generosity of that magnificent elite of intellectuals and potentates gathered together there. After emptying the hat full of money into the lap of the poor woman, the old major disappears to merrily continue his interrupted drinking bout. Professor Fraga Neto goes up to the woman and asks her about her relationship to Pedro Archanjo, given that he never knew he had left any descendants. And here is the stupefying answer:

> "Sir, I know nothing about it. I've never met this Pedro Archanjo, don't know who he is, and have heard of him for the first time today. But all the rest is true: the necessities, the little ones, there are four of them not seven, my man isn't dead but he's left me without a bean . . . So I went to the Major to ask his help. I found him in the Triunfo bar. He told me he was broke but would take me to a place where he could get me some help. He brought me here." . . . She smiled and left. Although she was pregnant she rolled her hips with the same elastic step as the late Pedro Archanjo.
>
> Professor Fraga Neto smiled too, shook his head . . . In that commemoration it had all been farce and trickery, a series of absurdities. Perhaps the only true thing had been the invention of the Major, the mulatto woman pregnant and hungry, needy and vivacious, false relative, true relative, people of Archanjo, universe of Archanjo. He repeated from memory, "The invention of the people is the only truth, no power will ever succeed in denying and corrupting it."[70]

The invention of the people against the Establishment, Carnival—the most beautiful of inventions—against the Establishment the Carnival of Antônio Balduíno, of Gabriela, and of Vadinho; the long Carnival of Pedro Archanjo from the end of the last century past his own death, Pedro Archanjo again in triumph among his people . . . "*Todos pobres, pardos e paisanos* . . . All poor, mulattoes and without uniforms."[71]

16 CONCLUSIONS AND HYPOTHESES

What can we conclude at the end of what must necessarily be a partial study such as this? The first and most important conclusion is the one we referred to at the outset: all literature on the subject of Blacks—with the one exception of Jorge Amado—reflects the typical thinking patterns of the land- and slave-owning class. The great Brazilian novel is born in the second half of the nineteenth century when slavery was about to come to an end, thanks to the pressures from the new economic institutions that were finally establishing themselves throughout the country. Slavery, however, had lasted in Brazil for about three centuries; it had been born with the colonization of the country, and had established the most solid tradition in a country devoid of traditions.

It is difficult to measure the full impact of slavery on the formation of the Brazilian soul. Forms of bondage inflicted by man on man have always existed to some extent in different countries, but have never achieved the importance they did in Brazil, which geographically is one of the largest countries in the world and whose economic history for three hundred years was based on slavery. There exist numerous documents written by foreigners—travelers and diplomats, English for the most part—that testify to the impossibility of survival for a citizen (we are referring here to the standard well-to-do nineteenth-century bourgeois) without some use of slave labor. A diplomatic representative or an English merchant was forced to use slaves in spite of the prohibition of his government. A whole series of menial tasks—house servants, coachmen, grooms, gardeners, nurses, and nannies—was undertaken solely by slaves. It was impossible to find free men who would lower themselves to such forms of labor. In the larger country houses, especially in the *fazendas* in the interior, even the skilled workers—the smiths, carpenters, and shoemakers—were slaves. This explains one of the most important characteristics of Brazilian society: its immobility. A class society finds the roots of its dynamism and growth in the will to change through the improvement of one's personal lot, in the upward mobility of the lower towards the upper classes, in the craftsman who wants to become a manufacturer, in the servant who wants to become a master. In Brazil this was practically and legally impossible.

We must therefore understand the reticence and fear of these writers who confronted the question of the Black presence, and with it slavery. They were dealing with the institution that had been the basis of their civilization for three centuries, which had been present in their lives from birth to death, and which had been broadly codified and supported by the dominant legal system and prevailing morality. The Church itself, in fact, apart from naturally using slaves, had several times issued a series of guidelines intended to regulate the just relationship between the master and those who belonged to him. It had never actually questioned slavery, but had rather officially blessed and baptized it with an index of Christian regulations to which the masters were supposed to refer. This was the catechism of the good *fazendeiro* in which one would not find even the most oblique reference as to whether it was or was not just to own a fellow human being. At the most the good master was advised not to beat those slaves who had not been disobedient or not to separate married couples for reasons of economic convenience.

The difference between this and other countries where slavery was practiced lies in the extent of the slave phenomenon in Brazil. If you compare another large country like the United States, you will see that slavery represents only a fraction of the national economy; whereas in Brazil the whole economy, we must repeat again, was rooted in the system of slavery.

The first conclusion to be drawn, therefore, is that all literature on the Black question reflects the slave-owning mentality and is impregnated by a series of conditioned reflexes that writers simply cannot slough off, or of which they are unaware.

From this stem all the other conclusions, beginning with the fear of accepting—or really the refusal to accept—the Black for what he is, in his reality and dignity as a human being. This occurs even when the intentions of the author are openly and sincerely abolitionist. Thus we have the false slave Isaura of Bernardo Guimarães serving as a pretext for a romantic tale with a happy ending and nothing more. There is the false mulatto Raimundo of Aluísio Azevedo, another pretext for a violent criticism of the society of the Maranhão and its narrow-minded prejudices. And then there are the attacks on slavery from Joaquim Manoel de Macedo, but only insomuch as the institution might be harmful to the ruling class. And finally there are all those Blacks and slaves whose function is no more than to put into relief the drama of the white protagonists, starting with the realist and positivist work of Júlio Ribeiro, passing through most of the Modernists, and ending with the poetic evocations of José Lins do Rego.

We thus have a series of monotonously repeated stereotypes that is the logical consequence of the above premises. There is, for example, the characterization of the monkeylike *moleques*, those Black youngsters who literally ape, in caricatural fashion, the attitudes of their white masters out of the simple force of habit acquired from living in the presence of the members of the white ruling class. An example is the sympathetic Tobias of *A moreninha* who serves as a go-between in the amorous intrigues of his white masters, and another is the less agreeable André of *A escrava Isaura* who includes himself among the various suitors of the fair slave girl. But the prince of the moleques is still Prudêncio of *Memórias póstumas de Bráz Cubas* with his dazzling imitation of his master's behavior. Every blow he has received from his master, growing up, he returns with interest to his own slave, as if unloading on the more unfortunate every injury received. The eternal and bitter fable of Machado de Assis, without ever saying so directly, serves as a searing indictment of slavery.

In the creation and repetition of such stereotypes, all of which conform to the concepts of the slave universe, a distinction is necessarily made between the good and the bad. The good slaves are those who, one way or another, accept their servile condition and end up as accomplices of the system. The bad ones are naturally those who have the utter cheek to express their dissatisfaction with being slaves. The former, the good *negros*, are the most convenient alibi for the master's conscience. These are the slaves who defend the estate against the treacherous *quilombolas* in *O reino encantado* and those who aid their masters in *As vítimas-algozes*. They are the many like Thebas who, as in the novel of the same name by Nuto Sant'Ana, stay slaves because they have a servile mentality, because when they are unjustly whipped or vilified—according to the so-called justice system of the slave order—they always try to redeem themselves without daring to violate the order that has robbed them forever of their dignity as human beings.

But where the hypocrisy of the slave-owner mentality that has informed the Brazilian novel reaches its apex is in the creation of the figure of the *mãe preta*, the Black mammy, the nursemaid. The mãe preta is the slave who serves as a mother, beginning with the nursing of the newborn, for her white master's children and it is natural that she should love them. Often such a woman has been denied her own natural children, who are sold off (as in the case of the character of Mônica in *O mulato*), and consequently she showers even greater affection on her adoptive children. This figure, who must have been very common in Brazilian life, becomes a perfect excuse for that slavery "so sweet and so Brazilian," as Gilberto Freyre describes it, writing in the Brazil of 1978. Sometimes she is accused of transmitting diseases to the little ones whom she nurses—syphilis in *As vítimas-algozes* by Manoel Macedo, rheumatic fever to Amâncio in *Casa de pensão* by Aluísio Azevedo—but in essence she remains the good character par excellence. In particular the novels of José Lins do Rego are full of these affectionate Black servants—all called *tias* and *vovós* in their new and enforced relationship with their masters' children—who have never gone away from the house that became theirs, even when they were no longer slaves. By staying, they are proof in their very presence of the goodness of the good old days. Slavery cannot have been so bad after all if they chose to stay on the estate, all the more so since nobody wonders where they might possibly go, or what really happened after the 13th of May 1888.

Next to the character of the mãe preta is that of the *mucama*, the companion of the white mistress, and also decidedly among the good. The mucama, in fact, is chosen from among those female slaves whose qualities show that they are best suited to live in the presence of white ladies. They led an undoubtedly privileged life, never sleeping in the *senzala*, and could easily ask favors of their mistresses. It was the custom occasionally to offer them as a present to the young daughters of the family when they were in both cases still children. They would thus be educated together, and sometimes ended up by becoming close friends. Even more than her male equivalent, the moleque, the mucama was the slave who was the most intimate with the white world. It is natural that she is always described as a good person, and so she is always presented, with the exception of Lucinda from *Lucinda, a mucama* in the series *As vítimas-algozes* by Manoel Macedo (but in this case we are dealing with a *roman à thèse*). Lúcia from *Rei negro* by Coelho Neto, poor and unhappy Lúcia, is the classic mucama, so lovely and so white, so assimilated into the white world that her own mistress, never slow to reveal her ingrained insensitivity, complains that she is being given as a bride to such a black *negro* as Macambira. Even in *A menina morta* by Cornélio Penna there are many mucamas by the side of their little mistress throughout the long nightmare of the events of that novel.

Mucamas and mães pretas are at the head of the procession of good characters as conceived in that expression of the world of the slave-owner which the Brazilian novel essentially is. They are a part of the order of the many slaves who most effectively contribute to the maintenance of slavery itself. We remember the phrase with which Thebas, the good slave of *Thebas, o escravo* by Nuto Sant'Ana, is rewarded after saving his little mistress's life: "He was a white *preto*, he was a man," a *preto branco*, no higher accolade could be conferred on a Black man for his ability to approximate the human model offered by his white masters.[1]

And then there are the bad characters, those who represent a contrast to the universe erected and willed by their masters, or who simply irritate the whites as a result of the way they are, their way of being. Beginning with the women, we have a further illustration of the hypocrisy whereby the white attempted to defend his own conscience. Hence the rumors of lustful Black and mulatto women who drag to perdition all men who happen to cross their path. Naturally there is never a reference to the heavy responsibilities of the white masters who by their arrogance reduced their female slaves to mere objects of pleasure and speeded up the breakdown of the family by separating married couples. A bad *negra* is Esméria,who seduces her good master Borges in *Pai Rayol, o feiticeiro* by Manoel Macedo. The endless series of misdeeds committed by Julinho in Coelho Neto's *Rei negro* is in part justified by the uncontrollable sensuality that Black women and men alike display on every page. Beyond the world of slavery is the standard figure of the man-eating mulatta in the character of Rita Baiana in *O cortiço* by Aluísio Azevedo; in this case her victim is Jerônimo, an honest Portuguese worker who is dragged into dishonor. In *A viagem maravilhosa* by Graça Aranha we have the Black Balbina who indulges in a passionate physical affair with Radagásio, her master and half-brother (both having shared the same wet-nurse as babies). And so in book after book one comes across these lustful and voluptuous Black and mulatto sirens. The list goes on and on monotonously.

The palm for this type of accusation goes to José Lins do Rego, whose artistic ability to recreate lost worlds is equaled only by his morbid capacity to cry over his fate, without a trace of a sense of humor. Both in *Menino de engenho* and *Doidinho*, as well as in *Meus verdes anos*, we find Black and mulatto women who with their aggressive sexuality rob the young boy of his innocence and contrive to turn the *menino de engenho* into the *menino perdido* (lost boy). But even putting to one side the considerable responsibilities of his relatives and mentors—those adults who treat as a joke the fact that the twelve-year-old boy has contracted a venereal infection, paying him compliments—the protagonist had plenty of other ways to lose his innocence. Indeed, if in the evening he was put to bed by the pretty young mulatto maid whom the moral indifference of his relatives had provided for him as a nurse, and who then initiated him into various types of erotic play (here we must add a comment on the typical structure of the slave society with its provision of totally useless services, as if a twelve-year-old boy could not put himself to bed), during the day he ran wild with the other moleques in the fields, deflowering she-goats and mother hens. In short, the nocturnal mulatta served as the complement to the daily hen, and yet the hero blames the servant. Such ingratitude! Probably in his mania for self-pity the author could not bring himself to blame the hen for seducing him (not to speak of the homosexual relations he had with the other boys).

But the ultimate bad character in Brazilian literature, public enemy number one, remains the *feiticeiro*, the sorcerer, and his female counterpart, the witch. Here all the novelists reveal the patterns of their ways of thought, which are those of slave owners, even when they go out of their way to assert the opposite. This is because the sorcerer, or wise man, is unassimilated, and thus the single authentic threat to the slave order. The feiticeiro is the one who has retained his own Black identity, his language, his religion, and its secrets. He has remained aloof from his companions who have bowed to the yoke of slavery, and he has kept intact his dignity as a free man, even though he lives in chains. He also exercises a mysterious power over his fellow Blacks and masters. He is a slave like all the rest, but his soul has remained free; his soul is what his white masters want, but they will never have it. The feiticeiro is the one true alternative to the Establishment, to the steward's whip, the harangues of the fazendeiro, the priest's sermons, the police forays, and the decrees of the authorities.

And for this the majority of writers—all of them, in fact, with the exception of Xavier Marques and Jorge Amado—insist on presenting us with a portrait of these feiticeiros that is both sinister and full of holes. The portrait is sinister because the writers were all members of the ruling class, and full of holes because they never really made an effort to understand what Black culture truly was in the broadest sense of the term. These men who all considered themselves as cultured, and who represented the avant-garde of the nation, reacted to the figure of the feiticeiro just like the most illiterate slave, in fear and trembling at what they did not know, rejecting and denying. And yet we know—and here our authority is above all Xavier Marques—that many members of respectable white society availed themselves of soothsayers and sibyls, as long as it was kept secret.

There is a long and monotonous series of such types, the first of whom chronologically is Joaquim Manoel de Macedo's creation, Pai Rayol,

> a man of short stature, whose body was much more developed than his legs. He had a big head and his squinting eyes gleamed, and when he fixed you with his stare it was impossible to turn away, in part because of the strange effect of that double squint, in part because of a mysterious, diabolical force flowing from within. On his cheeks he had terrible scars from cuts inflicted in childhood. One knife slash had split his upper lip in two, leaving two white, shining and pointed teeth quite open to view. They were canines and pointed threateningly at the observer. And finally he had very long arms, ending in huge hands that came down to his knees, completing this repugnant picture of a singularly unprepossessing figure.[2]

This is the first of a series of similar monsters (the author's description dwells on a thousand repugnant details, which we have obviously had to abbreviate), and the appearance of the character is decidedly simian.

Then there is Balbina, the feiticeira of José do Patrocínio's *Motta Coqueiro* (and we recall that the author, a very dark-skinned mulatto, had a long history of fighting against slavery): "She was a tall, corpulent *negra* with evil, bloodshot eyes, a big nose, and swollen lips."[3] Straight away we have the mad and seemingly possessed Frei Simão, the monster of Pedra Bonita, part quilombola, part Sebastianist, described by Araripe Júnior in *O reino encantado*. Then there is the ugliest of all, Joaquim Cambinda, in Júlio Ribeiro's *A carne*:

> He was terrifying, that *negro*—bald, lipless, with enormous jawbones, and yellow eyes furrowed by blood red lines that stood out against his dark skin. He resembled a dusky hyena, slow, cowardly, fierce, repellent. His hands were dry and hooked; his toes were twisted in on themselves, with no nails, frightening.[4]

In Machado de Assis there are no magicians, just a fortune-teller, a *cabocla* to whom the wife of the banker Santos goes in *Esaú e Jacó*; one more proof of how members of the upper classes could be numbered among the initiates of occult practices. The same thing happens among the whites and the rich in Bahia, according to Xavier Marques in *O feiticeiro*, the first work to look at the question of Black religious belief with a cultural sophistication and awareness on a much higher level.

After this brief parenthesis the list of bad characters begins again. In Coelho Neto's *Rei negro* there is old Balbina (the same name as the feiticeira of José do Patrocínio):

> Balbina, the old *negra* reputed to be a *mandingueira*, always dirty and dressed in rags, she stank of sheep and pig fat. You could hardly see her red, bloodshot eyes, which were always darting out suspicious glances.[5]

The eyes always seem the focal point of these descriptions. Apart from the magnetic squint of Pai Rayol, Coelho Neto's Balbina and the one of José do Patrocínio must have suffered from acute conjunctivitis, judging from their continuously bloodshot eyes. But our authors, men of education and culture, always emphasize this detail as a sign of evil. And they claimed that they did battle in the name of culture and progress!

The list of these grotesques continues, from the squinting, magnetic eyes of Pai Rayol to those that fortunately are simply magnetic of Pai Jerônimo (toothless mouth, blackened gums, an elongated head, twisted feet, hands like old iron, arthritic limbs) described by Graça Aranha in *A viagem maravilhosa*. He is the magician to whom the treacherous Balbina goes (a decidedly unfortunate name that seems to be applied to a host of untrustworthy characters) for him to do a *feitiço* against her mistress.

From the magnetic eyes of Pai Jerônimo we pass to the sibylline eyes of old Dadate in the fearful evocation by Cornélio Penna in *A menina morta*: she was "unable to escape those sibylline eyes that wandered all over her, like those of a strange, voracious animal lying in wait."[6] This old paralytic—with the myth of her evil powers and her great toothless mouth—is the one who hears the pounding hoofbeats of the black goat that only she sees.

In Lima Barreto, in contrast, the two sorcerers we come across are of small importance. They are a man and a woman who work as healers in rural areas, and their clientele includes rich and poor, Blacks and whites.

In José Lins do Rego the true feiticeiro is not really Pai Lucas of *Moleque Ricardo*, who is described more as a parish priest than as a proper magician or shaman. The true witch is Maria Gorda from *Menino de engenho*, an eighty-year-old woman with drooping breasts and puffy lips, sitting on the step outside her hut, muttering her incomprehensible language, smoking her pipe and dancing with the devil at the festival of São João. Or it is old Feliciano from *Usina*, who with his curses, his madness, and his death puts into relief the final slow agony of the patriarchal system; or even old Aninha of *Riacho Doce*, who drives her beloved but disobedient grandson mad.

In Jorge Amado the same characters continue to appear (they all correspond to figures taken from real life) except that the author revolutionizes all the old principles, whereby what was formerly taken as negative is now seen in a positive light. Hence the mulatto women, Gabriela (from the novel of the same name) and Ana Mercedes (from *Tenda dos milagres*), continue to seduce and abandon their gentlemen lovers; but it all takes place in an atmosphere of sport and fun, without brooding and tragedy, in a spirit of vital enthusiasm. Gabriela is sex and femininity at their purest. Ana Mercedes is more sophisticated, using her gifts to advance her career; but all this is secondary with respect to the new—and decidedly more fascinating—concept of life and human relationships which the two women represent.

There is no need to underline the difference between the various feiticeiros listed above with all their horrifying characteristics, which seem to come straight from children's fairy stories (at least in most cases), and Jubiabá and Pedro Archanjo.

There are in the novels listed above repeated situations and characteristics that Jorge Amado turns upside down, at least in the latter part of his career. We have seen, for example, that the majority of the white, wealthy protagonists do not work, which is perfectly normal in a society based on slave labor. The first flurries of change occur only in those novels that reflect a certain shift in society towards the end of the nineteenth century. Thus Machado de Assis has given us a masterly gallery of drones, and introduces the new men, such as the unscrupulous Palha of *Quincas Borba* or the banker Santos of *Esaú e Jacó*. On another level we have the prototype of a society in the process of transformation in João Romão of *O cortiço* by Aluísio Azevedo, who has also left us an unforgettable series of portraits of parasites. In the vast majority of other writers the question of work and working does not even come up. In Jorge Amado's early novels work is seen through the lens of class struggle: slavery for the various Antônio Balduínos and illicit wealth for fazendeiros and capitalists. But in a later phase work is seen as progress (Mundinho Falcão and Nacib, for example) or the denial of work in farcical terms (Vasco Moscoso, Quincas, Vadinho and company). In José Lins do Rego, work is just one more moment in the defeat of the central figures repeated in *Moleque Ricardo*, *Bangüê*, and *Usina*.

Another common characteristic in these novels is the lack of a sense of paternity and paternal responsibility, and this, too, is a consequence of a historical situation. The owners had always had children from their female slaves throughout the centuries (children who remained slaves, by the way), and the promiscuity of the senzala impeded the establishment of regular family relationships. Even among contemporary authors there are plenty of examples of the sort. In *Bangüê* Carlos de Melo has sons by a Black woman, thus following in the footsteps of his uncle and grandfather. Pedro Archanjo is a real stallion, and completely indifferent to his numerous progeny.

The repetition of facts and situations is a constant throughout the treatment of Blacks in Brazilian literature, simply because, as we have had cause to restate time and again, the system founded on slavery is the least dynamic one could ever possibly imagine. This is a society crystallized in fixed and unchangeable forms and structures. There is enough material to write a separate study on the question, but this is not the intention of the present work, which is solely that of analyzing historically how a society born out of slavery has represented Blacks, and the contradictions into which it has fallen.

After Jorge Amado, literature dealing with the Black theme continues to develop, but has been unable to renew its perspectives or its energies. Amado fought and won a precise battle for the dignity of men, incorporating the Black as an active element in Brazilian civilization. Today the *orixás* dance on theater stages, as Pedro Archanjo had prophesied. But those prejudices which were once expressed so violently and unequivocally have nowadays taken on more subtle and less identifiable forms. It is true that today the orixás dance in the public theaters, but they risk being confined to the ghetto of folklore. The new course that Brazilian politics has taken over the last fifteen years has tended to reevaluate everything that is national, which includes the Black and the multiracial civilization that Brazil has produced, the only truly multiracial tradition in the world. But within this civilization there are still many battles yet to be fought, and many little prejudices that remain to be defeated. In a class society the great models continue to be white and in the upward movement from one class to another color continues to play its part. There are valuable works by numerous scholars who have dealt with the question, but the scholar has a great advantage over the novelist. He writes for a limited public and he does not have to please it. The limited public that reads a critical work likes to be provoked, but the larger public that reads a novel likes to be comforted in its conscious and subconscious aspirations. And the public at large continues to be white, or to have white cultural models. For this reason today we have no novels in which a young Black or a dark mulatto harbors diplomatic ambitions, or wants to marry a white woman from the higher social ranks, or wants to become a gynecologist in a major clinic; not to mention novels where the heroine is Black who wants to assert herself socially or marry a white man from high society. In the absence of another Jorge Amado such novels do not exist.

The Brazilian novel has preferred instead to stay close to familiar ground, to base itself on acquired models and battles won. There are so many examples that we can only quote a few. Let us take one of the most famous and popular Brazilian writers, Érico Verissimo, the author of a series of historical novels published under the general title of *O tempo e o vento (Time and the Wind)*. These novels tell the history of Rio Grande do Sul, a region that, because of its geographical position and temperate climate, similar to that of southern Europe, and its ethnic groups, including many Italian and German colonists, was among those that least needed a slave work force to develop it. (It is certainly not by chance that Rio Grande do Sul is among the most developed regions.) In the second volume of the series, entitled *O continente*, published in 1949, Verissimo relates an episode, which is secondary to the main narrative thrust of the book, in which the main character, Licurgo, frees his slaves. He makes this gesture for purely political rather than humanitarian reasons: Rio Grande do Sul is a modern and progressive state with respect to the northern states and the central power, and the liberation of the slaves is intended to hasten the end of the Empire and the establishment of the Republic.

In all the dynamics of the event we see quite clearly that for Licurgo the freedom of his slaves takes second place to the political value of his gesture. He is completely uninterested in the fate of those men. What counts for him is the effect his action might have, along with all the repercussions, on the political scene. There is, furthermore, a distinct contrast between the ideology, in itself noble and generous, that drives him on and his own mentality as an owner of both land and men.

> At the very moment he said these things, Licurgo knew he was not sincere. He wasn't saying what he thought. It was inconceivable to him that these dirty *negros* should one day come and dance in the rooms of his house in intimate contact with his family.[7]

The ceremony itself at which Licurgo distributes the *cartas de alforria* is more boring and irritating than solemn. The slaves get mixed up, many of them do not understand what is going on, some do not even know their own name, so used are they to being called by a nickname. They all stop and kiss Licurgo's hand and the dress of Bibiana, his grandmother and the matriarch of the house. There is a moment when Licurgo can barely restrain himself from revealing his true nature as lord and master, and that is when a slave appears whose nature, in contrast with all the others', is quite the reverse of servile.

> There was, however, one of them who came in with his head held high. He cast an arrogant glance around him, with a challenging air. He received the paper and, without the slightest gesture or even a word of thanks, turned on his heel and went back out into the courtyard, as impassive as a king who has just received an homage that was his by right. Licurgo stared after him with a furious look. It was João Batista! He deserved four lashes across his face. He had always been proud and provocative. He was a good cowherd and horse trainer, a tireless worker, but he had always had this high-hatted attitude, and more than once Licurgo had been tempted to give him a thrashing and take him down a peg.[8]

Verissimo was very skillful in outlining the characteristic mentality of the landowning class, even when he was dealing, as in the case of Licurgo and others from Rio Grande do Sul, with people used to working, in contrast to their contemporaries from the North. This whole area of the Rio Grande, even before the arrival of Italian and German immigrants, was characterized by a typically colonialist situation in which the owners worked in the fields alongside their workers. This is totally different from the attitude of the other fazendeiros in Brazil, who handed over the running of their estates to their managers and bailiffs, while they themselves lived far away in the big coastal cities. In spite of his completely different background, Licurgo is most uneasy as a result of the conditioned reflexes typical of his class and the liberal and republican ideas he professes. The proud and dignified demeanor of João Batista angers him profoundly because a man of his mentality and upbringing can never consider the Black man as a complete human being. And yet the stupidity and clumsiness of the others get on his nerves, because they drag the ceremony out and make it boring and "what was worse, the Sobrado was already starting to stink like the *senzala*."[9] And when the ceremony ends with the applause and embraces and toasts from his friends and colleagues in the party, it is the voice of old Bibiana which brings the affair to an end with the ultimate comment of the conservative and reactionary slave owner, "Now open the windows and get rid of this goat stink."[10]

Among contemporaries closer to our own period we should recall Adonias Filho, a writer with the rare ability to create images and an atmosphere pregnant with force and violence. One of his favorite themes is the creation of a Brazilian mythology that unites the typical themes of the *sertão*, ancient regional themes, with the loose and violent rhythms of the western movie. In his earliest works Blacks figure among the main characters. In *Corpo vivo (Living Body)*, which dates from 1962, there is the Black man, Setembro, who saves the hero when he is still a child, ultimately sacrificing his life for him. In *O forte* (*The Fort*, 1965), which is the history of the city of Bahia as seen through the vicissitudes of the fort itself, the fortress defending the city, the protagonist is a Black man by the name of Olegário, a choral character who narrates the chapters of the city's history in which Blacks appear at the center of struggle and desperate revolt. In *Léguas da promissão* (*Leagues of the Promise*, 1968), a series of tales set, as are all his novels, against the background of the cocoa-producing area of the country, there is a story rich in symbolism. It is entitled "Simoa," and in it a group of Blacks sets out on a desperate flight to escape the war that has broken out between the hunters and the cocoa planters for control of the forest. They are guided by Simoa Iemanjá, queen and goddess, the mistress of the waters, towards their fated destiny, towards her kingdom, the sea.

The theme of the sea and the mythical return to one's origins occurs again in *Luanda Beira Bahia* (1971). This long pilgrimage of love and death takes the protagonists from Bahia to Luanda in Angola and to Beira in Mozambique, to end once and for all in the waters off that third coastline of Africa which is Brazil. And finally there is another journey, this time through the forests of Ilhéus, in search of a tomb, and on that trek we meet four old women, four Fates, four moments of the past: all this in *As velhas* (*The Old Women*, 1975). The strongest among them, Zonga, an old Black woman almost six feet tall, embodies a living memory of slavery suffered and liberty regained.

Adonias Filho is an author who responds to the fascination of myth, and has the ability to transform reality into legend, the real into the fable. Obviously he cannot offer us a new prophetic vision of the place of the Black in Brazilian society, but he has nevertheless been able to give us a marvelous portrait gallery of characters that definitively incorporates the Black in the very roots of his land, in the very mythological depths of Brazil. Here he now stands beside the Indian, who hitherto always assumed the place of honor in the works of novelists and poets.

The myth of the return to Africa, the memory of origins that Jubiabá kept alive, the journey described by Adonias Filho in *Luanda Beira Bahia*, become reality in *A casa da água* by Antônio Olinto (1969). *A casa da água* is a novel based on fact, facts the author had already written about in another work, *Brasileiros na Africa (Brazilians in Africa)*. It is the story of those Blacks who after abolition no longer wanted to stay in Brazil and returned to Africa, in this case Nigeria, where they found a place for themselves in African life, while preserving many of the customs acquired in Brazil, notably the Portuguese language. The connecting thread of the story is provided by the main figure, Mariana, who leaves Brazil together with her family headed by her grandmother who had been sold into slavery as a child and taken away to Brazil. The book describes the long return journey, the forced stop in the middle of the ocean for lack of wind (something that really happened and lasted six months), and finally the arrival in the promised land. They then discover that the fatherland of their dreams is not the paradise they have talked about for so many years but simply another land where you have to work hard and adopt new habits. The challenge to Mariana in Nigeria is essentially quite similar to that of her grandmother in Brazil: to reconstruct her own identity without forgetting her roots. The writer follows Mariana through her life, into marriage and economic success, following the discovery and development of a well on their land, *a casa da água*, which explains the title of the novel (the house of the water). Then come the children, their social climb through politics, and a total involvement in the country's life through rediscovered roots.

Among contemporary Brazilian writers, the most complex and interesting figure is undoubtedly Guimarães Rosa with his striking linguistic creations and his series of legendary characters. The world of Guimarães Rosa is confined to that of the sertão with its cowherds, struggles, myths, and legends. There are far fewer Blacks in the sertão than elsewhere, precisely because the earth is much poorer, the territory far more broken up, and the sort of life much more suitable for free men rather than slaves. There are Blacks on the sertão, however, and along with them racial prejudices, far harder to root out because they are so deeply embedded in the popular imagination. One example is the novella *Dão-Lalalão*, which comes from the *Corpo de baile* cycle (*Corps de Ballet*), published in 1965. The main character, Soropita, is an ex-gunfighter who has withdrawn into the country to live quietly with his wife, Doralda. The only problem is that Doralda, whom Soropita loves passionately, is an ex-prostitute; and thus her husband is prey to a continuous and obsessive jealousy, an obsession with no solution and no end, because it is rooted in the past, referring to moments and persons who cannot be canceled out because they have happened. Soropita lives in fear lest one day some old client of Doralda should turn up and recognize her at this little hermitage where they have shut themselves away. The situation comes to a head through a succession of monologues and broken phrases with which the protagonist gives vent to his paranoia when a friend of Soropita arrives at his farm accompanied by some others, including a Black man called Iládio. What drives Soropita mad is that his wife, during the years spent as a prostitute, might have been with a Black man. Obsessed by this idea, he tortures her and himself with a thousand questions while forging in his fevered imagination a thousand images of the Black man with his wife. Every gesture, every move, every word of Iládio, who is quite oblivious to what is going on, is interpreted as a justification of Soropita's paranoia. When the tragedy is about to explode, when Soropita is actually about to murder Iládio, it is only the latter's screams that manage to bring Soropita back to reality. The tale comes to an end with no blood on the floor.

The technique whereby Guimarães Rosa constructs his tales is something too complex to explain in a few words. We will merely say that one of the devices he uses to bring the story alive is the monologue and the subjective impressions of each character. Thus Iládio becomes from time to time:

> The *negro* Iládio, Beelzebub, sulphur stink, huge and mounted on his black beast, go and bang on your cauldrons in Hell! You, *negro*, hiding behind that poor woman, monkey stink . . . Soropita shouted his orders to that great slave from the foot of his horse. Like an evil thought the *negro* disappeared for a thousand years. And the vultures overhead fed on his name.[11]

A single episode is inadequate as an analysis of a writer like Guimarães Rosa. What we can say is that this writer has been able to translate into artistic terms the clear racial prejudices broadly spread among the people of the sertão.

To look back at the past, once the passing of time has provided the solution to many problems, can be handled in two separate ways. Either one can see the event as an episode in contemporary history and apply to it one of our modern political approaches—as Jorge Amado did in *Tenda dos milagres*—or one can write a standard historical novel in which the facts are set down without reference to political solutions. The second solution is that chosen by Josué Montello in his *Os tambores de São Luís* (*The Drums of São Luis*, 1975). In this novel the author narrates a long chapter in the history of slavery from his native Maranhão, which as we know from the work of Aluísio Azevedo, Graça Aranha, and Dunshee de Abranches was always one of the most backward and traditional parts of Brazil. Montello, without ideological bias, tells the long story of the life of a man, a Black man named Damião, from his childhood to old age, from the freedom of the *quilombo* to a return to the horrors of slavery. Damião's life subsequently passes back to freedom again and he enjoys a long life devoted to study and work; his story serves as a connecting thread which links together the main stages of the Black struggle for emancipation.

Montello's novel is undoubtedly very interesting, but from the historical and ideological point of view it is an attempt at reconciliation carried forward with great earnestness and skill. Certainly the author does not hide, nor could he, the reality of certain facts already exposed in their time by Azevedo and de Abranches, but he shrewdly emphasizes those who opposed the authors of those crimes. Young Damião manages to survive the horrendous experience of slavery, but is bought out and turned towards ecclesiastical studies by the Bishop of São Luís do Maranhão. The sinister figures of the priests described by Azevedo vanish behind the gentle, human figure of the bishop, while the other priests and seminarists hostile to Damião are relegated to the background. Damião does not become a priest thanks to the determined racist opposition of the Curia, which did not want Blacks to be ordained; but this decision rather favors the private choice of Damião, who does not have a conspicuous vocation for the religious life. The trial of a lady from polite society accused of murdering a slave boy with a pitchfork emphasizes the noble figure of the lawyer for the prosecution who with this act risks his political career. And another who risks his political career is the prefect who tries in vain to resist the despotic power of Donana Jansen, the terrible slave-owner whose name is now historically associated with excessive wealth and fearful crimes committed against Blacks. The people of São Luís are shown to be narrow-minded and wretched in their racism, and yet in their very midst Damião manages to live and gather around him friends and family.

As frequently happens with many Brazilian authors, Montello gives us some of his most interesting pages on slavery precisely when he is talking about other matters, in other words when he expresses his prejudices, which derive from the caste of Maranhão gentlemen to which he belongs. In one of his most fascinating books, *Noite sobre Alcântara* (*Night Falls on Alcântara*, 1978) the slow death throes of the city of Alcântara are described. Today the city is more of a museum, but it was once the old capital of Maranhão. Cut off from any form of progress, this town was unable to survive the disappearance of the old slave-owning regime, and the book describes a series of characters who live the barely credible drama of the daily end of a civilization. What amazes the reader in this novel is the tone of absolute normality in which the tale is narrated, and which must have been quite familiar to the author. The main character, who is followed throughout his life, is an intelligent and cultured young man, a veteran of the Paraguayan war. This man does absolutely nothing throughout his life, save write the occasional political article in which he propagandizes certain liberal ideas, and seduce whatever girls might be available. He makes no attempt to revive his abandoned fazenda, to produce, to invest, to transform, to postpone the inevitable decline. He never travels, he does not enjoy himself, he has not even the courage to get up and leave. And so he arrives at his own end, without having worked a day in his life. We might include him among the victims of slavery, that institution he fights on the ideological level, but from which he cannot free himself, so intimately tied is it to his very way of being; and without it he can do no more than abandon himself to death together with Alcântara itself. Again it is the tone of complete normality with which Montello describes the events that attracts the reader's attention. Such a tone might be more grotesque than tragic, but derives from that distant memory of a certain ruling caste or elite to which this Maranhão author seems to be intimately linked.

An amusing historical fiction (perhaps the only amusing story written about slavery) is *Xica da Silva* (1976) by João Felício dos Santos, the writer who has also brought to the cinema real historical figures such as Ganga-Zumba (one of the heroes of Palmares), João Abade (another Black, a defender of Canudos), and others. Xica da Silva was a beautiful Black woman who lived in the second half of the eighteenth century in Diamantina, the diamond city in the state of Minas. She became the mistress and then wife of a very rich diamond merchant and in her own province achieved almost regal powers, which she used and abused with the primitive enthusiasm of a tropical Pompadour. *Xica da Silva* is not a book that deals with the problem of slavery, which at the time was the basis of the wealth and economic stability of the country. It is nevertheless an amusing account of the life and misdeeds of an amiable black-skinned female rogue who achieved in her time the power to command and humiliate any number of white men, and who persuaded her lover to create for her an artificial lake on which she could take boat trips, the sea being too far away and out of reach.

This list of contemporary authors is necessarily incomplete, and it is not at this moment worth hunting around for new themes with which we have not had time to deal. Let us close instead with the one literary example that comes from the other side, a dazzling document detailing the outermost limits of social alienation and exploitation that one can still discover in our time. *Quarto de despejo* is the diary of Carolina Maria de Jesus, the story of a *favelada*, published in 1960. Carolina Maria de Jesus is a woman who lives alone with her children in a society still openly male chauvinist, and she lives in a *favela* because she is poor and her house is a hut; and she is a woman in a world where the levers of power are in the hands of white males, all of them descendants of slave-owners. A woman, Black and poor, de Jesus puts down in her diary day after day the simple events of her life. The language is poor and she makes many mistakes. Verbs are conjugated in the singular even when the subject is plural; "e's" and "o's" are often replaced by "i's" and "u's," following the rules of pronunciation rather than spelling. Many sentences clearly reflect the radiophonic language of the mass media (television had not yet made its appearance in the favela, but the radio was an indispensable means of communication, sometimes the single form of social participation for those on the margin of society).

De Jesus does not boast a political commitment in the sense we usually give to the term. Her criticisms of those politicos who never keep their promises, and who turn up in the favela just before election time, are familiar enough and even commonplace. De Jesus never went beyond the second grade of her elementary school, and what she has managed to teach herself since is essentially minimal. Her political commitment in the historical and more profoundly human sense of the term is, on the contrary, enormous. This is an exceptional document of the dignity of a human being who refuses the ultimate outrage of being discarded from society, who will not accept the humiliation to which she seems condemned by the lack of any real benefit from the consumer society, the world of middle-class prosperity.

In her ungrammatical and incomplete sentences we sense the return of the old ghosts we came across in the works of the masters of the Brazilian novel. Now we know what Maria Gorda was muttering at the threshold of her stinking cabin, those phrases that the young master Carlos de Melo from *Menino de engenho* could never quite understand. Perhaps they were the same phrases old Balbina in *Rei negro* repeated to Macambira, or the dark muttering of old Dadate in *A menina morta*. Now we might better understand the feminine and feminist pride of Teresa Batista and Tieta do Agreste.

The *quarto de despejo* is the place where they throw everything old, useless, and dirty. The huge favela of Canindé is the quarto de despejo of the city of São Paulo, where men and filth are dumped every day.

And every day Carolina sifts through the garbage for something that will allow her and her children to survive.

What strikes us in de Jesus's work is her awareness, which she reminds us of and expresses so powerfully, of the social exclusion and indignity that are part and parcel of her daily life. The account of the monotonous repetition of the events of her existence is not an end in itself, nor is it guilty of pathos. Behind every fact there is a comment and a judgment. Carolina knows that she and her fellow favelados endure a subhuman existence because this injustice has been decreed by other men.

Let us see the points that make de Jesus's book something unique of its kind. In the first place the author is proud that she is an independent woman in her poverty, without having to depend on any man. She lives alone with her three children (she makes merely a passing reference to the father of her youngest daughter), and she alone is responsible for raising and feeding them. She notes that the majority of women with a husband live with a false sense of security. A man's presence does not improve the situation, and they are often forced to beg and are frequently beaten by their men. Carolina, in contrast, fights her daily battles on her own. She gets up at dawn to go and get her water ration (there are very few water faucets in the favelas where one can renew one's supply, and there is always a long line). Then she begins her search for torn paper, bottles, or bits of old iron which she sells to dealers. And so it goes day after day. Her economy is characterized by immediacy; the little she manages to make serves to provide the daily necessities for herself and her children. Sometimes she is lucky enough to find among the piles of garbage a pair of old shoes or some food.

The favela is right next door to a respectable middle-class neighborhood where the houses are made of stone. The inhabitants of this district hate the people of the favela because of their noise and the stench with which they infect the air. But the most impressive part of the book is not the detailing of squabbles with the people of the bourgeois district but rather the denunciation of the root structure of the consumer society. The larger merchants and small shopkeepers hoard food supplies in anticipation of a rise in prices, and wait for the food to go rotten so that they can throw it away. Whole crates of canned sausage gone bad are dumped on the favela garbage heap, and many eat it and some die. Old dried cod, which no one buys, but which is still edible, is sprinkled with disinfectant before being thrown away so that no one can use it. Cakes, rice, and other foodstuffs actually get thrown in the river. Lucky fish, comments Carolina, they don't work and they eat like kings! At the tomato canning plant Carolina sometimes finds a few tomatoes that have fallen from the trucks, but only when the boss is not around, because he prefers the vegetables to be crushed under the wheels of the vehicles rather than be gleaned by the favelados. Generally Carolina has better luck at the butcher's, where she manages to scrape together the odd bone with a little fat on it. And so it goes day in, day out, every day of the year. And this includes the thirteenth of May, the national holiday, the anniversary of the freedom of the slaves: "And so on the day of May 13, 1958, I was struggling against today's slavery—hunger!"[12]

Hunger is the dominant theme, the perennial nightmare of the book:

> You have to know hunger to be able to describe it. Brazil should be governed by somebody who has already suffered hunger. Hunger is a teacher, too. Those who suffer from hunger learn how to think of their neighbor and their children.[13]

The story of Carolina Maria de Jesus and the favela Canindé is written in such simple sentences as this, offering many judgments expressed without hate, but also without resignation. The favela is a world that contains everything. "The one thing that you won't find in the *favela* is solidarity."[14] Poverty and degradation do not improve people: daily violence, the prostitution of minors, all forms of perversion, that is the panorama of the favela against which Carolina rebels, and runs to the police every time. The one consolation for Carolina, her one luxury, is listening to the radio which, along with reading, helps to keep alive her hope and her awareness of the injustice she endures every day.

The long lines to get help from an immovable and insolent bureaucracy, her encounters with men, the rare celebrations on the eve of elections, alternate with her obsessive search for food. If you do not find food, you die amid the general indifference. Meanwhile her diary bears witness to the simple culture of Carolina within the daily squalor:

> And I thought of Casimiro de Abreu who says: "Laugh, child. Life is beautiful."
>
> Maybe life was good in those days. Because nowadays it's better to say: "Weep, child. Life is bitter."[15]

Carolina is a Black woman, with a simple pride in being Black. The Black's hair is better, she says, it doesn't fly away like the whites'. It stays put on your head even in the wind. And if someone says to her, "It's a pity you are Black," Carolina replies that she is proud to be Black and to be a woman.

And one day a reporter comes and gets Carolina's book published, and she becomes rich and famous and goes to tea with the Matarazzos, the great São Paulo family. She goes to live in a *casa de alvenaria*, a house of stone and brick, not a smelly little hut.

And so in 1960 Carolina Maria de Jesus will cross that small and infinite space, which is both of the present and centuries old, that separates the favela from the casas de alvenaria, the *mucambos* from the *sobrados*, the senzala of her slave forefathers from the *casa grande* of the new masters, the *maloca*—as they call her shack, referring back to the old Indian term—from a civilized dwelling.

History—and not only in Brazil—repeats itself.

NOTES

CHAPTER 1

1. Horácio de Almeida in Maria Firmina dos Reis, *Ursula* (Rio de Janeiro: Olímpica, 1975), viii.
2. José de Alencar, *O demônio familiar* (Rio de Janeiro: MEC, 1957), 165.
3. Ibid., 168.
4. José do Patrocínio, *Motta Coqueiro* (Rio de Janeiro: Gazeta de Notícias, 1877), 35.
5. Ibid., 41.

CHAPTER 2

1. Astrojildo Pereira, *O romance brasileiro* (Rio de Janeiro: O Cruzeiro, 1952), in Joaquim Manoel de Macedo, *A moreninha* (Rio de Janeiro: Clássicos Brasileiros, 1970), 9.
2. Macedo, 34.
3. Ibid., 190.
4. Joaquim Manoel de Macedo, *As vítimas-algozes* (Rio de Janeiro, Paris: Garnier, 1878), 1:29.
5. Ibid., 30.
6. Ibid., 66.
7. Ibid., 67.
8. Ibid.
9. Ibid., 40.
10. Ibid., 53.
11. Ibid., 54.
12. Ibid., 2:134.
13. Ibid., 133.
14. Ibid., 1:131.
15. Ibid., 156.
16. Ibid.
17. Ibid., 123.
18. Ibid., 129.
19. Ibid., 172.
20. Ibid., 179.
21. Ibid., 269.
22. Ibid., 270.

CHAPTER 3

1. Araripe Júnior, *O reino encantado* (Rio de Janeiro: Gazeta de Notícias, 1878), 9.
2. Ibid., 12.
3. Ibid., 29.

4. Ibid., 23.
5. Ibid., 33.
6. Ibid., 36.
7. Ibid.
8. Ibid., 72.
9. Ibid., 149.

CHAPTER 4

1. Bernardo Guimarães, *A escrava Isaura* (Rio de Janeiro: Melhoramentos, n.d.), 183.
2. Ibid., 10.
3. Ibid.
4. Ibid., 12.
5. Ibid., 23.
6. Ibid., 24.
7. Ibid., 56.
8. Ibid., 57.
9. Ibid., 58.
10. Ibid., 18.
11. Ibid., 95.
12. Ibid., 44.
13. Ibid., 89.
14. Ibid., 99.
15. Ibid., 120.
16. Ibid., 86.
17. Ibid., 88.
18. Ibid., 86.
19. Ibid.
20. Donald Pierson, *Brancos e pretos na Bahia* (São Paulo: Nacional, 1971), 131.
21. Guimarães, 16.

CHAPTER 5

1. Luciana Stegagno Picchio, *La letteratura brasiliana* (Florence-Milan: Sansoni Accademia, 1972), 249.
2. Ibid.
3. "A candle is not the sun and yet a candle illuminates. . . . Kings, though gorged with riches, do not always scorn the puny gifts of poor peasants." Júlio Ribeiro, *A carne* (Rio de Janeiro: Clássicos Brasileiros, 1977), 15.
4. Ibid., 81.
5. Ibid., 141.
6. Ibid., 49.
7. Ibid., 50.
8. Ibid., 54.
9. Ibid., 58.
10. Ibid., 59.
11. Ibid., 60.
12. Ibid., 102.
13. Ibid., 103.
14. Ibid., 105.

15. Ibid., 106.
16. Ibid., 77.
17. Ibid.
18. Ibid., 223. According to the September 28, 1871, Law of the *Ventre Livre*, slaves' children born after that date were free.
19. Ibid., 225.
20. Ibid., 260.

CHAPTER 6

1. Dunshee de Abranches, *O cativeiro* (Rio de Janeiro: n.p., 1941), 228.
2. Ibid., 69.
3. Capistrano de Abreu, in Astolfo Serra, *A Balaiada* (Rio de Janeiro: Bedeschi, 1946), 9.
4. De Abranches, 101. *Bemtevi* [tyrant flycatcher] is a forest bird that by its chirping indicates the presence of a human. The name means "I saw you clearly," and, it was said, this characteristic facilitated the task of the slave hunters.
5. Ibid., 137.
6. Graça Aranha, *O meu próprio romance* in *Obra completa* (Rio de Janeiro: MEC INL, 1969), 561.
7. De Abranches, 143.
8. Ibid., 41.
9. Ibid., 15.
10. Ibid., 134.
11. Graça Aranha, 557.
12. De Abranches, 154.
13. Aluísio Azevedo, *O mulato* (São Paulo: Martins, 1969), 113.
14. Ibid., 127.
15. Ibid., 56.
16. Ibid., 37.
17. Ibid., 64.
18. Ibid., 92.
19. Ibid., 222.
20. Ibid., 46.
21. Ibid., 49.
22. Ibid., 222. The famous engineer André Rebouças, invited to a ball at the court of the Emperor, found no lady willing to dance with him because he was a mulatto. So the Empress rose and invited him to dance.
23. De Abranches, 47. The expression *coçar a orelha em pequena*, to scratch one's ear when young, was a pejorative term used to indicate Blacks, male or female. It probably derives from a comparison with monkeys.
24. De Abranches, 49.
25. Azevedo, 103.
26. Ibid., 34.
27. Raymundo Faoro, *Machado de Assis: a pirâmide e o trapézio* (São Paulo: Nacional, 1974), 281.
28. Aluísio Azevedo, *Casa de pensão* (São Paulo: Martins, 1972), 13.
29. Ibid., 21.
30. Ibid., 26.
31. Ibid.

32. Ibid., 38.
33. Ibid.
34. Ibid., 215.
35. Ibid., 66.
36. Ibid., 286.
37. Ibid., 132.
38. Ibid., 131.
39. Ibid., 228.
40. Aluísio Azevedo, *O cortiço* (São Paulo: Martins, 1965), 43.
41. Ibid., 33.
42. Ibid., 248.
43. Ibid., 244.
44. Ibid., 19.
45. Ibid., 20.
46. Ibid., 21.
47. Ibid., 22.
48. Ibid., 165.
49. Ibid., 170.
50. Ibid., 65.
51. Ibid., 68.
52. Ibid., 87.
53. Ibid., 89.
54. Ibid., 187.
55. Ibid.
56. Ibid., 105.
57. Ibid., 216

CHAPTER 7

1. Machado de Assis, *Memórias póstumas de Brás Cubas* in *Obra completa* (Rio de Janeiro: Aguilar, 1962), 1:637.
2. Luciana Stegagno Picchio, *La letteratura brasiliana* (Florence-Milan: Sansoni Accademia, 1972), 271.
3. De Assis, *A mão e a luva* in *Obra Completa* 1:246.
4. Lúcia Miguel Pereira, *Machado de Assis* (Rio de Janeiro: Olympio, 1955), 151.
5. Agrippino Grieco, *Viagem em torno a Machado de Assis* (São Paulo: Martins, 1969), 69.
6. De Assis, *Dom Casmurro*, in *Obra completa*, 1:925.
7. Pereira, 154.
8. Machado de Assis, *Contos esquecidos* (Rio de Janeiro: Clássicos Brasileiros, 1966), 48.
9. Augusto Meyer, in Machado de Assis, *Antologia machadiana* (Rio de Janeiro: Lia, n.d.), 10.
10. Raymundo Faoro, *Machado de Assis: a pirâmide e o trapézio* (São Paulo: Nacional, 1974), 346.
11. Pereira, 156.
12. Meyer, 241.
13. Faoro, 183.
14. Ibid., 78.
15. Ibid., 128.

16. De Assis, *Ressurreição*, in *Obra completa*, 1:115.
17. Ibid., 1:116.
18. Ibid.
19. De Assis, *A mão e a luva*, 1:215.
20. Ibid., 1:221.
21. De Assis, *Iaiá Garcia*, in *Obra completa*, 1:400.
22. De Assis, *Memórias póstumas de Brás Cubas*, 1:540.
23. Machado de Assis, *Quincas Borba*, in *Obra completa*, 1:710.
24. Otto Maria Carpeaux, *Machado para a juventude* (Rio de Janeiro: Lia, n.d.), 17.
25. De Assis, *Contos recolhidos* (Rio de Janeiro: Clássicos Brasileiros, 1966), 247.
26. Machado de Assis, *Contos sem data* (Rio de Janeiro: Clássicos Brasileiros, 1966), 53.
27. Ibid.
28. De Assis, in *Obra completa*, 2:335.
29. Ibid.
30. Ibid., 2:339.
31. De Assis, *Ressurreição*, 1:118.
32. De Assis, *Quincas Borba*, 1:719.
33. Ibid., 1:757.
34. De Assis, *Esaú e Jacó*, in *Obra completa*, 1:1072.
35. De Assis, *Helena*, in *Obra completa*, 1:286.
36. De Assis, *Contos esquecidos*, 100.
37. De Assis, *A mão e a luva*, 1:268.
38. De Assis, *Memórias póstumas de Brás Cubas*, 1:559.
39. Faoro, 354. *Encilhamento*: the term refers to a great speculative movement on the stock exchange in the early years of the republic.
40. Ibid., 359.
41. Grieco, 105.
42. Faoro, 326.
43. De Assis, *Ressurreição*, 1:184.
44. De Assis, *Helena*, 1:367.
45. De Assis, *Iaiá Garcia*, 1:392.
46. Faoro, 327.
47. De Assis, *Iaiá Garcia*, 1:503.
48. Ibid.
49. De Assis, *Memórias póstumas de Brás Cubas*, 1:524.
50. Ibid., 580.
51. Ibid., 618.
52. Ibid.
53. De Assis, *Quincas Borba*, 1:642.
54. De Assis, *Esaú e Jacó*, 1:969.
55. De Assis, *Memorial de Aires*, in *Obra completa*, 1:1114.
56. Ibid.
57. Ibid.
58. Ibid., 1136.
59. Ibid., 1116.
60. Ibid. Together with the abolition of slavery was also decreed the destruction of all laws, acts of buying and selling, and the like pertaining to slavery.
61. De Assis, *A semana*, in *Obra completa*, 3:583.
62. Ibid., 352. Valongo refers to the slave market of Rio de Janeiro. The law of September 28, 1871, freed slaves' children born after that date.

63. Ibid., 367.
64. Ibid., 490.
65. Ibid., 2:360.
66. De Assis, *Memorial de Aires*, 1:1198.
67. De Assis, *Relíquias de Casa Velha*, in *Obra completa*, 2:659.
68. Ibid.
69. Ibid., 666.
70. Ibid., 667.
71. Ibid.
72. Ibid.

CHAPTER 8

1. Canudos was a city of the interior in the state of Bahia; founded by the mystic Antônio Conselheiro and his followers; the laws of the Republic were neither recognized nor respected there. It was wiped out by the army in 1897 after four bloody military expeditions.
2. The Recôncavo of Bahia is the vast hinterland surrounding the city of Salvador da Bahia.
3. Xavier Marques, *O feiticeiro* (São Paulo–Brasília: GRD INL, 1975), 17.
4. Ibid., 18. The *terreiro* is a threshing floor or space where candomblé is held. The *peji* is the altar, the seat of the *orixás*, the saints of candomblé.
5. Ibid., 246.
6. Ibid., 10.
7. Ibid., 29.
8. Ibid., 186. The word *tio*, uncle, may be used instead of *pai*, as a term of respect.
9. Ibid., 218.
10. Ibid., 72.
11. Ibid. *Malês* and *hauçás* are Black populations of Brazil that were involved in bloody revolts.
12. Ibid., 122.
13. Ibid., 118.
14. Ibid., 245.

CHAPTER 9

1. Graça Aranha, *Canaã* in *Obra completa* (Rio de Janeiro: MEC INL, 1969), 88.
2. Ibid., 60.
3. Ibid., 148.
4. Ibid., 187.
5. Ibid., 136.
6. Ibid., 210.
7. Ibid.
8. Ibid., 211.
9. Ibid., 110.
10. Ibid., 51.
11. Ibid., 48.
12. Ibid., 53.
13. Ibid., 50.
14. Ibid., 219.

15. Graça Aranha, *A viagem maravilhosa* in *Obra completa* (Rio de Janeiro: MEC INL, 1969), 417.
16. Ibid., 229.
17. Ibid., 255.
18. Ibid.
19. Ibid., 293.
20. Ibid., 351.
21. Ibid., 352.
22. Ibid., 266.
23. Ibid., 267.
24. Ibid., 289.
25. Ibid., 306.
26. Ibid., 241.
27. Ibid., 333.
28. Ibid., 403.
29. Ibid., 452.
30. Ibid., 454.
31. Ibid., 297.
32. Ibid.
33. Ibid., 360.
34. Ibid., 299.
35. Ibid., 440.
36. Ibid., 475.
37. Ibid., 433.
38. Ibid., 422.
39. Ibid., 426.
40. Ibid., 445.
41. Ibid., 487.
42. Ibid., 488.

CHAPTER 10

1. Sérgio Buarque de Hollanda in Lima Barreto, *Clara dos Anjos* (São Paulo: Brasiliense, 1969), 10.
2. Francisco de Assis Barbosa, *A vida de Lima Barreto* (Rio de Janeiro: Olympio MEC, 1975), 91.
3. Ibid., 92.
4. Ibid., 217.
5. Ibid., 37.
6. Ibid.
7. Afonso Henrique de Lima Barreto, *Triste fim de Policarpo Quaresma* (São Paulo: Brasiliense, 1972), 48.
8. Ibid., 183.
9. Ibid., 109.
10. Ibid., 214.
11. Ibid., 167.
12. Machado de Assis, *A semana* (Rio de Janeiro: Jackson, 1937), 427.
13. Barreto, *Triste fim de Policarpo Quaresma*, 169.
14. Ibid., 201.
15. Ibid., 202.

16. Afonso Henrique de Lima Barreto, *Vida e morte de M. J. Gonzaga de Sá* (Rio de Janeiro: Mérito, 1949), 79.
17. Afonso Henrique de Lima Barreto, *Recordações do escrivão Isaías Caminha* (São Paulo: Brasiliense, 1968), 70.
18. Ibid., 145.
19. Ibid., 155.
20. Ibid., 187.
21. Barreto, *Clara dos Anjos*, 95.
22. Ibid., 96.
23. Barreto, *Triste fim de Policarpo Quaresma*, 110.
24. Ibid., 111.
25. Ibid.
26. Ibid., 133.
27. Ibid., 194.
28. Barreto, *Recordações do escrivão Isaías Caminha*, 45.
29. Ibid., 53.
30. Ibid., 240.
31. Ibid., 273.
32. Ibid., 92.
33. Ibid., 128.
34. Ibid., 269.
35. Barreto, *Triste fim de Policarpo Quaresma*, 39.
36. Ibid., 179.
37. Ibid., 193.
38. Ibid., 194.
39. Ibid.
40. Ibid., 180.
41. Ibid., 67.
42. Barreto, *Clara dos Anjos*, 111.
43. Ibid., 75.
44. Ibid., 57.
45. Ibid., 35.
46. Ibid., 48.
47. Ibid., 82.
48. Ibid., 98.
49. Ibid., 62.
50. Ibid., 166.
51. Ibid., 165.

CHAPTER 11

1. Henrique Maximiniano Coelho Neto, *Rei negro* (Rio de Janeiro: Clássicos Brasileiros, 1970), 161.
2. Ibid., 196.
3. Ibid., 130.
4. Ibid., 37.
5. Ibid., 36.
6. Ibid., 29.
7. Ibid.
8. Ibid., 27.

9. Ibid., 31.
10. Ibid., 32.
11. Ibid.
12. Ibid., 168.
13. Ibid., 85.
14. Ibid., 81.
15. Ibid., 31.
16. Ibid., 133.
17. Ibid., 134.
18. Ibid., 125.
19. Ibid., 193.
20. Ibid., 22.

CHAPTER 12

1. Luciana Stagagno Picchio, *La letteratura brasiliana* (Florence-Milan: Sansoni Accademia, 1972), 492.
2. Mário de Andrade, *Macunaíma* (São Paulo: Martins, 1972), 9.
3. Ibid., 47.
4. Ibid., 73.
5. Sabino de Campos, *Catimbó* (Rio de Janeiro: Valverde, 1946), 256.
6. Ibid., 267.
7. Ibid., 298.
8. Ibid., 331.
9. Ibid., 370.
10. Ibid., 110.
11. Sabino dos Campos, *Lucas, o demônio negro* (Rio de Janeiro: Pongetti, 1957), 37.
12. Ibid., 51.
13. Ibid., 121.
14. Ibid., 154.
15. Ibid., 167.
16. Monteiro Lobato, *Negrinha* (São Paulo: Brasiliense, 1968), 3.
17. Ibid., 5.
18. Ibid., 43.
19. Nuto Sant'Ana, *Preto Eusébio* (São Paulo: Brasil, 1932), 52.
20. Ibid., 88.
21. Nuto Sant'Ana, *Thebas, o escravo* (São Paulo: Brasil, 1939), 33.
22. Ibid., 68.
23. Ibid., 105
24. Ignácio Raposo, *Mestre Cuia* (São Paulo: Brasil, 1937), 238.
25. Ibid.
26. Lúcia Miguel Pereira, *Amanhecer* (Rio de Janeiro: Olympio, 1938), 85.
27. Ibid., 148.

CHAPTER 13

1. Mário de Andrade in Cornélio Penna, *Romances completos* (Rio de Janeiro: Aguilar, 1958), 174.
2. Luciana Stegagno Picchio, *La letteratura brasiliana* (Florence-Milan: Sansoni Accademia, 1972), 480.

3. Paulo Prado, *Retrato do Brasil* (São Paulo: DP & C, 1928), 33.
4. Ibid., 139.
5. Ibid., 158.
6. Ibid., 192.
7. Ibid., 194.
8. Penna, 227. *Fruto* and *espírito*—the difference in the pronunciation of many words by the Blacks has brought about a transformation of the Brazilian language, making it more melodious and richer in words than the Portuguese spoken in Portugal.
9. Penna, 227.
10. Ibid., 419.
11. Ibid., 1137.
12. Ibid., 803.
13. Ibid., 760.
14. Ibid., 734.
15. Ibid.
16. Ibid. *Angu* and *fubá* are types of a dish made with flour, manioc, or rice and water.
17. Penna, 734.
18. Ibid., 746.
19. Ibid., 866.
20. Ibid., 1168.
21. Ibid., 1225.
22. Ibid., 1123.
23. Ibid.
24. Ibid., 1209.
25. Ibid., 1026.
26. Ibid., 1280.
27. Ibid.
28. Ibid., 1281.

CHAPTER 14

1. Luciana Stegagno Picchio in José Lins do Rego, *Menino de engenho* and *Moleque Ricardo*, trans. by Antonio Tabucchi as *Il treno di Recife* (Milan: Longanesi, 1974), 15.
2. José Lins do Rego, *Fogo morto* (Rio de Janeiro: Olympio, 1972), 18.
3. Ibid., 20.
4. Ibid., 21.
5. Ibid.
6. Ibid., 12.
7. Ibid., 79.
8. Ibid., 53.
9. José Lins do Rego, *Meus verdes anos* (Rio de Janeiro: Clássicos Brasileiros, 1970), 57.
10. Do Rego, *Fogo morto*, 140.
11. Ibid., 145.
12. Ibid., 155.
13. Ibid., 156.
14. Ibid., 159.
15. Ibid., 146.
16. Ibid., 160.

17. Ibid., 165.
18. José Lins do Rego, *Menino de engenho* (Rio de Janeiro: Olympio, 1969), 90.
19. Ibid.
20. Ibid., 88.
21. Ibid., 54.
22. Ibid., 56.
23. Ibid., 57.
24. Ibid., 59.
25. Ibid., 58.
26. Ibid.
27. José Lins do Rego, *Doidinho* (Rio de Janeiro: Olympio, 1969), 168.
28. Do Rego, *Menino de engenho*, 57.
29. Ibid., 44.
30. Ibid., 115.
31. Do Rego, *Doidinho*, 50.
32. Ibid., 115.
33. José Lins do Rego, *Bangüê* (Rio de Janeiro: Olympio, 1969), 108.
34. Do Rego, *Menino de engenho*, 102.
35. Ibid., 115.
36. Do Rego, *Doidinho*, 67.
37. Do Rego, *Bangüê*, 110.
38. Ibid., 111.
39. Ibid.
40. Ibid., 19.
41. Do Rego, *Meus verdes anos*, 217.
42. Do Rego, *Menino de engenho*, 69.
43. Ibid., 89.
44. José Lins do Rego, *Pureza* (Rio de Janeiro: Olympio, 1970), 39.
45. Ibid., 53.
46. Ibid., 40.
47. Do Rego, *Bangüê*, 7.
48. Ibid., 136.
49. Ibid., 137.
50. Ibid., 154.
51. Ibid., 161.
52. Ibid., 143.
53. Master Don Gesualdo is the eponymous hero of Giovanni Varga's Sicilian novel (published in 1889) and symbol of the self-made man.
54. Do Rego, *Bangüê*, 170.
55. Ibid., 175.
56. Ibid., 176.
57. Ibid., 177.
58. Ibid., 210.
59. José Lins do Rego, *Moleque Ricardo* (Rio de Janeiro: Olympio, 1961), 34.
60. Ibid., 92.
61. Ibid., 113.
62. Ibid., 182.
63. Ibid., 184.
64. Ibid., 188.
65. Ibid., 90.

66. Ibid., 57.
67. Ibid., 99.
68. José Lins do Rego, *Usina* (Rio de Janeiro: Olympio, 1961), 302.
69. Ibid., 297.
70. Ibid.
71. Ibid.
72. Ibid., 335.
73. Ibid., 338.
74. Ibid.
75. José Lins do Rego, *Riacho Doce* (Rio de Janeiro: Olympio, 1961), 436.
76. Ibid., 517.
77. Ibid., 527.
78. Ibid., 529.
79. Ibid.

CHAPTER 15

1. Jorge Amado, *Seara vermelha* (São Paulo: Martins, 1969), 341.
2. Jorge Amado, *São Jorge dos Ilhéus* (São Paulo: Martins, 1968), 13.
3. Jorge Amado, *Terras do sem fim* (São Paulo: Martins, 1968), 270.
4. Amado, *Seara vermelha*, 59.
5. Jorge Amado, *Jubiabá* (Lisbon: Livros do Brasil, 1977), 323.
6. Jorge Amado, *O país do carnaval* (São Paulo: Martins, 1970), 26.
7. Ibid., 26.
8. Ibid., 41.
9. Amado, *Jubiabá*, 54.
10. Ibid.
11. Ibid., 58.
12. Ibid., 59.
13. Ibid.
14. Ibid., 278.
15. Ibid., 279.
16. Ibid., 280.
17. Ibid.
18. Ibid., 33.
19. Ibid., 14.
20. Ibid., 154.
21. Ibid.
22. Ibid., 285.
23. Ibid., 287.
24. Ibid., 328.
25. Ibid., 34.
26. Ibid., 137.
27. Ibid., 277.
28. Ibid., 290.
29. Ibid., 307.
30. Ibid., 323.
31. Jorge Amado, *Mar morto* (São Paulo: Martins, 1970), 78.
32. Ibid., 84.
33. Ibid., 264.

34. Ibid., 94.
35. Ibid.
36. Ibid., 175.
37. Ibid., 204.
38. Jorge Amado, *Capitães da areia* (São Paulo: Martins, 1970), 98.
39. Ibid., 292.
40. Amado, *Terrras do sem fim*, 120.
41. Ibid., 123.
42. Jorge Amado, *Gabriela, cravo e canela* (São Paulo: Martins, 1969), 384.
43. Ibid.,; 113.
44. Ibid., 157.
45. Ibid., 237.
46. Ibid., 234.
47. Ibid., 235.
48. Ibid., 400.
49. Ibid., 256.
50. Ibid., 384.
51. Jorge Amado, *Tenda dos milagres* (Mira-Sintra: Europa-America, 1978), 290.
52. Nina Rodrigues, *Os africanos no Brasil* (São Paulo: Nacional, 1977), 238.
53. Ibid., 158.
54. Ibid.
55. Ibid.
56. Ibid.
57. Ibid., 243.
58. Ibid., 240.
59. Ibid., 245.
60. Ibid., 260.
61. Amado, *Tenda dos milagres*, 78.
62. Ibid., 99.
63. Ibid., 103.
64. Ibid., 245.
65. Ibid., 340.
66. Ibid., 289.
67. Ibid., 296.
68. Ibid. Terreiro de Jesus is the great square where the cathedral of Bahia rises. The term *terreiro*, which means space, is generally used to indicate the place where *candomblé* is carried out. Terreiro de Jesus is a clear manifestation of the symbiosis between the Roman Catholic religion and that of African origin.
69. Amado, *Tenda dos milagres*, 347.
70. Ibid., 350.
71. Ibid., 353.

CHAPTER 16

1. Nuto Sant'Ana, *Thebas, o escravo* (São Paulo: Brasil, 1939), 33.
2. Joaquim Manoel de Macedo, *As vítimas-algozes* (Rio de Janeiro–Paris: Garnier, 1878), 1:141.
3. José do Patrocínio, *Motta Coqueiro* (Rio de Janeiro: Gazeta de Notícias, 1877), 31.
4. Júlio Ribeiro, *A carne* (Rio de Janeiro: Clássicos Brasileiros, 1977), 106.
5. Coelho Neto, *Rei negro* (Rio de Janeiro: Clássicos Brasileiros, 1970), 31.

6. Cornélio Penna, *A menina morta* in *Romances completos* (Rio de Janeiro: Aguilar, 1958), 1225.
7. Érico Verissimo, *O tempo e o vento* (Porto Alegre: Globo, 1967), 569.
8. Ibid., 630.
9. Ibid.
10. Ibid., 631.
11. Guimarães Rosa, "Noites do sertão," *Corpo de baile* (Rio de Janeiro: Olympio, 1965), 78.
12. Carolina Maria de Jesus, *Quarto de despejo* (São Paulo: Edibolso, 1976), 29.
13. Ibid., 28.
14. Ibid., 13.
15. Ibid., 33.

GLOSSARY

ABC	Poem of folk origin in which each strophe begins with a different letter of the alphabet, beginning with A. In general it relates the deeds of famous bandits or important persons.
Afoxé	Black Carnival group; spell, miracle (lit.).
Africano(s)	Black(s) from Africa.
Aganju	Black divinity, husband and brother of Iemanjá, the goddess of the sea.
Agregado	One living with a family not his own; laborer.
Aiocá	One of the names of Iemanjá, the sea goddess.
Alentejano	Native or inhabitant of Alentejo, a region of Portugal.
Alforria	Freedom granted to slaves.
Alugado	Agricultural laborer who hires himself out in conditions of semislavery.
Amaca	Hammock.
Amarcord	Title of a film by Fellini; it means "I remember."
Amigação	Union of a man and woman who are not married.
Angu	Traditional dish made of flour, manioc, and water.
Azulejo	Shiny tile with colored designs, generally blue.
Bacalhau	Codfish; synonym for a whip ending in strips of twisted leather.
Bacurau	Type of nocturnal bird; popular word for individuals who go out at night.
Balaiada	Maranhão civil war (1838–1840).
Balaio	Straw basket; synonym for rebel of the *balaiada*. The *balaios* took their name from their leader, a craftsman who made *balaios*.
Bandeira	Flag; synonym for those bands that, at the beginning of the eighteenth century, searched the interior for slaves and diamonds, setting out from São Paulo.

Bangüê	Oven for making sugar; by extension *engenho* of rustic type complete with oven.
Beato	A sort of holy man or preacher still common in the interior.
Benguela	Also *banguela*. Name given to Blacks from the port of Angola bearing the same name; also, toothless.
Bisonho	Crude, inexpert.
Boa terra	Good land, a way of describing one's own region.
Botequim	Small bar.
Bugio	Type of monkey.
Bumba-meu-boi	Dance very popular among the cowherds of the Northeast.
Búzio	Seashells of various sizes and uses: as a trumpet (those of greatest proportions), ornament, votive offering, divination.
Caatinga	Undergrowth of thorny bushes, typical of the Northeast.
Caboclo	Peasant or cowherd of the interior, deeply sunburnt. Generally the result of a cross between white and Indian.
Cabra	Goat. Used also as a synonym in a pejorative sense for a man of little value, and to mean dark mulatto.
Cabula	Afro-Brazilian cult.
Cachaça	Popular Brazilian alcoholic beverage made from sugarcane, similar to rum.
Cafuzo	Mixture of Black with Indian. Very dark.
Caixeiro	Employee of a commercial enterprise.
Camumbembe	Man of low social status, penniless, ragamuffin; generally dark-skinned.
Candomblé	Important Afro-Brazilian cult.
Cangaceiro	Bandit.
Cangaço	Banditry.
Canhoto	Left-handed. Also synonym for the devil.
Canzá	Musical instrument also called *reco-reco*, a percussion instrument that produces a scratching sound.
Capitão	Captain. Honorary title of the National Guard.
Capitão da areia	Captain of the sand, synonym for abandoned child who lives on the beach.

Capitão do mato	Captain of the undergrowth, synonym for slave hunter.
Capoeira	The feminine form (*a capoeira*) indicates a typical martial art–dance of Afro-Brazilian origin. The masculine (*o capoeira*) is a synonym for wrestler or ruffian, or simply a practitioner of capoeira.
Carapinha	African hair.
Carta de alforria	Document of freedom for slaves.
Casa do tronco	Type of rustic jail where slaves were punished.
Casa grande	The house of the master on the plantation.
Castelhano	Synonym for Spanish, language or man.
Catimbó	Northeastern cult of multiple origin, more similar to European-style witchcraft than to the various Afro-Brazilian cults.
Catimbozeiro	Adept of *catimbó*.
Catinga	Smell; generally used to indicate the odor of Blacks or animals.
Catolé	Also *catulé*. Type of palm.
Caudilho	Term of Spanish origin meaning political or military leader.
Caxixe	Swindle involving the forgery of documents, also business done regarding cocoa-producing land.
Ceará	State in the Northeast of Brazil.
Cearense	Inhabitant of Ceará, or anything of Ceará, such as a dance or custom.
Chorado	Type of music; literally, wept. Also used to designate music played in a mournful fashion.
Comarca	Region, district.
Comendador	Holder of a *comenda*, an honorary title.
Cometa	Comet; synonym for traveling salesman.
Conselheiro	Adviser, one who gives advice; high-ranking state official.
Conto	Old Brazilian coin.
Convidado	Guest.
Cordel	String to which wandering storytellers attached their sheets of paper. *Literatura de cordel* is a synonym for the popular literature of the Northeast.
Coronel	Colonel. Honorary title of the National Guard; used to indicate the great landowners.
Cortiço	Great block of popular housing typical of the ur-

	ban agglomerations of the second half of the nineteenth century and the early twentieth century.
Crioulo	Old term for Blacks born in Brazil. Now used to indicate Blacks in general.
Curandeiro	One who treats illnesses with primitive medicine, herbs, and prayer.
Delegado	Police commissioner.
Despacho	Offering made to Exu, the devil, to send him away. Offering placed at crossroads to do harm to a particular person.
Diabo	Devil.
Encilhamento	Great movement of speculation on the stock exchange in Brazil in the early years of the Republic.
Engenho	Sugarcane plantation generally provided with a mill.
Escravatura	Slavery.
Espírito	Spirit.
Exu	Afro-Brazilian divinity, represents the forces of evil and mischief.
FAB	*Força Aérea Brasileira*, Brazilian Air Force.
Fado	Portuguese folk song, sad and fatalistic.
Farda	Military uniform.
Fardão	Uniform of the members of the Brasilian Academy of Letters.
Farofa	Food made by frying manioc flour.
Favela	Group of huts in or near a city, shanty town.
Favelado	Inhabitant of a *favela*, synonym for extremely poor person.
Fazenda	Great farm.
Fazendeiro	Great landowner, proprietor of a *fazenda*.
Feitiçaria	Witchcraft.
Feiticeira	Witch (fem.).
Feiticeiro	Sorcerer, witch-doctor.
Feitiço	Spell, action not necessarily malevolent performed by a *feiticeiro* or *feiticeira*.
Fidalgo	Nobleman, person of rank.
Filha-de-santo	Daughter of a saint, adept of *candomblé*.

Forro	Ex-slave now freed.
Fruto	Fruit.
Fubá	Typical dish of flour, rice, and water.
Gaúcho	Inhabitant of Rio Grande do Sul, or something that originated in or is associated with that region.
Goiaba	Guava.
Grapiúna	Inhabitant of the zone of Ilhéus.
Guarda-livros	Accountant.
Hauçá	Hausa people and language. Ethnic group from the Sudan and northern Nigeria brought as slaves into the area of Bahia; protagonists of many revolts.
Iaiá	Lady, or mistress, in the language of the Blacks in the time of slavery.
Iansã	Afro-Brazilian divinity, queen of winds, lightning and storms. Corresponds to Saint Barbara.
Iemanjá	Also *Yemanjá*. The most important Afro-Brazilian divinity. Queen of the seas. Her cult is assimilated into that of the Virgin Mary.
Inaê	One of the names of *Iemanjá*.
Índios(as)	Indians, masc. and fem.
Ioiô	Diminutive of sir, gentleman, or master in the language of the Blacks during slavery.
Jagunço	Follower of Antônio Conselheiro at Canudos. Today, violent man, hooligan. Also used to refer to inhabitants of the *sertão*.
Janaína	One of the names of *Iemanjá*.
Jangada	Small sailing boat of the northeastern fishermen, similar to a raft.
Jangadeiro	Fisherman, one who uses a *jangada*.
Jeje	Language of the slaves from Benin.
Jeje-nagô	Language and culture formed by the union of peoples speaking *jeje* and *nagô*.
Judeu	Jew; also a synonym for miserly person.
Maconha	Drug, type of opiate, derived from *canhamo*, hemp (cannabis sativa).

Macumba	Important Afro-Brazilian cult.
Macumbeiro	Adept of *macumba*.
Mãe-de-santo	Chief priestess of Afro-Brazilian cult, *macumba* or *candomblé*.
Mãe preta	Black mammy, wet nurse to the whites.
Mãe d'agua	Water divinity.
Malês	Black Muslims from the region of Bahia.
Maloca	War house of the Indians, today synonym for hut.
Mameluco	Mixture of Indian and white.
Mandinga	Spell; also individual belonging to the Mandinga African ethnic group.
Mandingueiro	Witch-doctor who practices *mandinga*.
Maranhão	Brazilian state.
Maranhense	Inhabitant of Maranhão, or anything originating in or of the Maranhão.
Mata	Forest.
Mato	Undergrowth, open zone.
Maxixe	Popular dance originating in Rio de Janeiro.
Menino	Boy.
Mestre	Master, one who teaches an art or craft, skilled craftsman.
Mil-réis	Old Brazilian currency replaced by the *cruzeiro*.
Minas	Name given to Blacks from Ghana. Also the short form of the Brazilian state of Minas Gerais.
Mineiro	Inhabitant of the region of Minas, or Minas Gerais.
Minhoto	Inhabitant of the region of Minho in Portugal.
Moleca	Black girl, female form of *moleque*.
Moleque	Also *muleque*. Black boy.
Moquear	To dry meat or fish to conserve it.
Morro	Hill.
Mourejar	To work hard, like a Black (*mouro*).
Muamba	Spell; synonym of *feitiço, despacho*.
Mucama	Black or mulatto female slave used as a maid or companion by a white lady.
Mucambo	Also *mocambo*, hut.
Nagô	Slaves from the Sudan. Language spoken by the Blacks in Bahia.
Namoro	Courting.

Negralhada	Group of Blacks, term of abuse. (Also, *negrada.*)
Negro	Color black. Commonly used to indicate colored person.
Negro novo	Black just arrived from Africa. *Novo* means new.
Neousineiro	New owner of a sugar factory.
Nhanhã	Diminutive of lady, madam, in the language of the Black slaves.
Nhonhô	Diminutive of sir, master, gentleman in the language of the Black slaves.
Nobreza	Nobility.
Novela	Story, tale, or soap opera.
Novena	Punishment of flogging carried out over nine days.
Oba	Priest of Xangô, god of thunder and lightning.
Ogã	Also *ogan*. Important personage in the cult of *candomblé*.
Ogun	God of iron in Afro-Brazilian cult. Corresponds to Saint Anthony in Bahia and Saint George in Rio de Janeiro. Also called *Ogum*.
Omulu	Also *Omolu*. Smallpox divinity. Corresponds to Saint Lazarus or Saint Benedict.
Orixá(s)	God(s) of Afro-Brazilian cults.
Orungã	Son of Iemanjá. Raped his mother thus giving origin to other gods.
Oxalá	Father of humanity, one of the chief Afro-Brazilian divinities.
Oxolufã	Old form of *Oxalá*, patron of fecundity and procreation.
Oxossi	God of hunting, son of Iemanjá. Corresponds to Saint George in Bahia and Saint Sebastian in Rio de Janeiro.
Pai	Father. Title of respect used by old and important Blacks.
Pai-de-santo	Chief priest of Afro-Brazilian cult. Also *pai-de-terreiro*.
Palmares	Region in the Northeast of Brazil rich in palms. In one of these zones Black runaway slaves organized resistance under a legendary leader called Zumbi dos Palmares.

Palmatória	Punishment and instrument of punishment, cane with holes used to deal violent blows to the hands.
Paraíba	State in the Northeast of Brazil.
Paraibano	Inhabitant of Paraíba, something originating in or of Paraíba.
Parati	Town on the coast renowned for its beauty and its *cachaça. Parati* is a synonym for *cachaça*.
Pataca	Old coin of little value.
Paulista	One from São Paulo, city or state.
Paulistano	Inhabitant of the city of São Paulo.
Peji	Altar of Afro-Brazilian cult.
Pitanga	Type of fruit.
Portuga	Pejorative term for Portuguese.
Prefeito	Chief of the administration in a city.
Preto	Color black. Commonly used to indicate a person of color.
Quilombo	Refuge for Black fugitives from slavery; often organized along traditional African lines, similar to Maroons of the Guyanas.
Quilombola	Black belonging to a *quilombo*.
Retirante	One driven out by a natural disaster, generally drought or flood.
Rezadeira	Woman whose prayers have healing powers.
Romeiro	Pilgrim.
Rua	Road, street.
Ruim	Bad, useless.
Saci	Also *saci-pererê*. Black elf of the woods.
Samba	Popular dance and music of African origin.
Saveiro	Sailboat typical of Bahia.
Sebastianista	*Sebastianistas* are those who believed in the return of the mythical king Dom Sebastião of Portugal. Also used for the followers of Antônio Conselheiro in the war of Canudos. When the Republic was set up those in Rio de Janeiro attached to the old imperial regime were called *sebastianistas*.
Senhor	Sir, gentleman.
Senhora	Madam, lady.

Senhor de engenho	Proprietor of a great sugarcane plantation.
Senzala	Slave quarters or house.
Sertanejo(a)	Inhabitant of the *sertão*; adj. "of the sertão" e.g., *canções sertanejas* = songs of the sertão.
sertão	Uncultivated arid zone of the interior.
Seu	A colloquial reduced form of *senhor*, sir, gentleman, Mr.
Sinhá	Diminutive of *senhora* in the language of the Black slaves.
Sinhazinha	Diminutive of *sinha*.
Sinhô	Diminutive of *senhor*.
Sinhô-moço	Young gentleman.
Sinhozinho	Diminutive of *sinhô*.
Sobrado	Gentlemanly residence of one or more stories in the city.
Subúrbio	Outskirts of a big city.
Tabelião	Notary.
Tapuio	Synonym of Indian.
Terno de reis	Folkloristic procession on the occasion of the holiday of the Three Kings, the Three Wise Men.
Terreiro	Large open space, or location where a *candomblé* ceremony is held. Synonym of *candomblé*.
Tia	Aunt, elderly person.
Tio	Uncle, elderly person.
Tronco	Form of punishment for slaves consisting of a great board or trunk with two holes where the feet of the offender were placed.
Tupi-guarani	Important Indian language of Brazil.
Ufanista	Nationalist (from *ufanar*, to be proud of).
Urubu	Type of vulture.
Usina	Factory, or sugar factory.
Usineiro	Sugar factory owner.
Venda	Shop, store.
Ventre Livre	"Free Womb"; law freeing all slaves born after 1871.
Vovô	Grandfather.
Vovó	Grandmother.

Xangô God of thunder and lightning. Corresponds to Saint Jerome. General term used in certain areas of the Northeast to indicate everything referring to Afro-Brazilian cults.

Yojô African or africanized word meaning ''master''; see *Ioiô*.

Zumbi Ghost, spirit from the other world. Name or nickname of the hero of a great Black revolt, Zumbi dos Palmares.

BIBLIOGRAPHY

Abranches, Dunshee de. *O cativeiro*. Rio de Janeiro: n.p., 1941.

Adonias Filho. *Corpo vivo*. Rio de Janeiro: Civilização Brasileira, 1966.

——. *O forte*. Rio de Janeiro: Civilização Brasileira, 1965.

——. *Léguas da promissão*. Rio de Janeiro: Civilização Brasileira, 1968.

——. *Luanda Beira Bahia*. Rio de Janeiro: Civilização Brasileira, 1971.

——. *As velhas*. Rio de Janeiro: Civilização Brasileira, 1977.

Albuquerque, Leda Maria. *Zumbi dos Palmares*. São Paulo-Brasília: IBRASA INL, 1978.

Alencar, José de. *O demônio familiar*. Rio de Janeiro: MEC, 1957.

Almeida, José Americo de. *A bagaceira*. Rio de Janeiro: Olympio, 1978.

Amado, Jorge. *Capitães da areia*. São Paulo: Martins, 1970.

——. *Dona Flor e seus dois maridos*. São Paulo: Martins, 1966.

——. *Farda, fardão, camisola de dormir*. Rio de Janeiro: Record, 1979.

——. *Gabriela, cravo e canela*. São Paulo: Martins, 1969.

——. *Jubiabá*. Lisbon: Livros do Brasil, 1977.

——. *Mar morto*. São Paulo: Martins, 1970.

——. *O país do carnaval, Cacau, Suor*. São Paulo: Martins, 1970.

——. *Os pastores da noite*. São Paulo: Martins, 1966.

——. *Os subterrâneos da liberdade*. São Paulo: Martins, 1968.

——. *Os velhos marinheiros*. São Paulo: Martins, 1965.

——. *São Jorge dos Ilhéus*. São Paulo: Martins, 1968.

——. *Seara vermelha*. São Paulo: Martins, 1969.

——. *Tenda dos milagres*. Mira-Sintra: Europa-America, 1978.

——. *Tereza Batista cansada de guerra*. São Paulo: Martins, 1973.

——. *Terras do sem fim*. São Paulo: Martins, 1968.

——. *Tieta do Agreste*. Rio de Janeiro: Record, 1977.

Amaral, Amedeu. *Letras floridas*. São Paulo: Hucitec, 1976.

Andrade, Manuel Correia de. *A guerra dos cabanos*. Rio de Janeiro: Conquista, 1965.

Andrade, Mário de. *Macunaíma*. São Paulo: Martins, 1972.
Aranha, Graça. *Obra completa*. Rio de Janeiro: MEC INL, 1969.
Araripe Júnior, Tristão de. *O reino encantado*. Rio de Janeiro: Gazeta de Notícias, 1878.
Archer, Maria de. *Brasil, fronteira da África*. São Paulo: Felman Rego, 1963.
Arinos, Afonso de. *Obra completa*. Rio de Janeiro: MEC INL, 1969.
Assis, Machado de. *Antologia machadiana*. Rio de Janeiro: Lia, n.d.
——. *Contos esquecidos*. Rio de Janeiro: Clássicos Brasileiros, 1966.
——. *Contos recolhidos*. Rio de Janeiro: Clássicos Brasileiros, 1966.
——. *Contos sem data*. Rio de Janeiro: Clássicos Brasileiros, 1966.
——. *Obra completa*. Rio de Janeiro: Aguilar, 3 vol., 1962.
——. *A semana*. Rio de Janeiro: Jackson, 1937.
Azevedo, Aluísio. *Casa de pensão*. São Paulo: Martins, 1972.
——. *O cortiço*. São Paulo: Martins, 1965.
——. *O mulato*. São Paulo: Martins, 1969.
Barbosa, Francisco de Assis. *A vida de Lima Barreto*. Rio de Janeiro: Olympio MEC, 1975.
Barbosa, Waldemar de Almeida. *Negros e quilombos em Minas Gerais*. Belo Horizonte: n.p., 1972.
Barreto, Afonso Henrique de Lima. *Clara dos Anjos*. São Paulo: Brasiliense, 1969.
——. *Recordações do escrivão Isaías Caminha*. São Paulo: Brasiliense, 1968.
——. *Triste fim de Policarpo Quaresma*. São Paulo: Brasiliense, 1972.
——. *Vida e morte de M. J. Gonzaga de Sá*. Rio de Janeiro: Mérito, 1949.
Bastide, Roger. *O candomblé da Bahia*. São Paulo: Nacional, 1978.
——. *Psicanilise do cafuné*. São Paulo: Guaira, 1941.
——. *As religiões africanas no Brasil*. São Paulo: Livraria Pioneira, 2 vol., 1971.
Bastide, Roger, and Florestan Fernandes. *Brancos e pretos em São Paulo*. São Paulo: Nacional, 1971.
Bastos, Abguar. *Os cultos mágicos-religiosos no Brasil*. São Paulo: Hucitec, 1979.
Benci, Jorge. *Economia cristã dos senhores no governo dos escravos*. São Paulo: Grijalbo, 1977.
Bethell, Leslie. *A abolição do tráfico dos escravos no Brasil*. Rio de Janeiro: Expressão e Cultura, 1976.
Calmon, Pedro. *Espírito da sociedade colonial*. São Paulo: Nacional, 1935.

——. *História do Brasil*. Rio de Janeiro: Olympio, 7 vol., 1959.
Caminha, Adolfo. *Bom crioulo*. Rio de Janeiro: Olivé, n.d.
Campos, Sabino de. *Catimbó*. Rio de Janeiro: Valverde, 1946.
——. *Lucas, o demônio negro*. Rio de Janeiro: Pongetti, 1957.
Cardoso, Ciro Flammarion. *Agricultura, escravidão e capitalismo*. Petrópolis: Vozes, 1979.
Cardoso, Fernando Enrique. *Capitalismo e escravidão no Brasil meridional*. Rio de Janeiro: Paz e Terra, 1977.
Carneiro, Edison. *Antologia do negro brasileiro*. Porto Alegre: Globo, 1950.
——. *Candomblés da Bahia*. Rio de Janeiro: Conquista, 1961.
——. *Folguedos tradicionais*. Rio de Janeiro: Conquista, 1974.
——. *A insurreição praieira*. Rio de Janeiro: Conquista, 1960.
——. *Negros bântus*. Rio de Janeiro: Civilização Brasileira, 1937.
——. *O quilombo de Palmares*. São Paulo: Brasiliense, 1958.
——. *Religiões negras*. Rio de Janeiro: Civilização Brasileira, 1936.
Carpeaux, Otto Maria. *Machado para a juventude*. Rio de Janeiro: Lia, n.d.
Cascudo, Luís da Câmara. *Antologia do folclore brasileiro*. São Paulo: Martins, 1971.
——. *Dicionário do folclore brasileiro*. São Paulo–Brasília: Melhoramentos INL, 1979.
——. *Literatura oral*. Rio de Janeiro: Olympio, 1952.
——. *Made in Africa*. Rio de Janeiro: Civilização Brasileira, 1965.
Castro, Josué. *Geografia da fome*. São Paulo: Brasiliense, 1967.
Chacon, Vanireh. *História das idéias socialistas no Brasil*. Rio de Janeiro: Civilização Brasileira, 1965.
Coelho Neto, Henrique Maximiniano. *Rei negro*. Rio de Janeiro: Clássicos Brasileiros, 1970.
Conrad, Robert. *Os últimos anos da escravatura no Brasil*. Rio de Janeiro: Civilização Brasileira, 1975.
Costa, Emília Viotti da. *Da senzala à colônia*. São Paulo: Difusão Européia do Livro, 1970.
Coutinho, Afrânio. *A literatura no Brasil*. Rio de Janeiro: Sul Americana, 6 vol., 1970.
Degler, Carl N. *Nem preto nem branco*. Rio de Janeiro: Labor do Brasil, 1976.
Dornas Filho, João. *A escravidão no Brasil*. Rio de Janeiro: Civilização Brasileira, 1939.
Duque-Estrada, Osório. *A abolição*. Rio de Janeiro: Livraria Anglo Brasileira, 1918.
Etzel, Eduardo. *Escravidão negra e branca*. São Paulo: Global, 1976.

Faoro, Raymundo. *Machado de Assis: a pirâmide e o trapézio*. São Paulo: Nacional, 1974.
——. *Os donos do poder*. São Paulo: Globo, 1975.
Fernandes, Florestan. *A integração do negro na sociedade de classes*. São Paulo: Ática, 2 vol., 1978.
——. *O negro no mundo dos brancos*. São Paulo: Difusão Européia do Livro, 1972.
——. *A revolução burguesa no Brasil*. Rio de Janeiro: Zahar, 1975.
Ferreira, Athos Damasceno. *Menininha*. Porto Alegre: Globo, 1941.
——. *Moleque*. Porto Alegre: Globo, 1938.
Figueiredo, Ariosvaldo. *O negro e a violência do branco*. Rio de Janeiro: Alvaro, 1977.
Franco, Maria Sylvia de Carvalho. *Homens livres na ordem escravocrata*. São Paulo: Ática, 1974.
Freitas, Décio. *Os guerrilheiros do imperador*. Rio de Janeiro: Graal, 1978.
——. *Palmares*. Porto Alegre: Movimento, 1973.
Freitas, Mário Martins. *Reino negro de Palmares*. Rio de Janeiro: Biblioteca do Exército, 1954.
Freyre, Gilberto. *Casa grande e senzala*. Rio de Janeiro: Olympio, 2 vol., 1969.
——. *O escravo nos anúncios dos jornais brasileiros do século XIX*. São Paulo: Nacional, 1979.
——. *Ingleses no Brasil*. Rio de Janeiro: Olympio, 1977.
——. *Interpretação do Brasil*. Rio de Janeiro: Olympio, 1947.
——. *O mundo que o português criou*. Lisboa: Livros do Brasil, n.d.
——. *Novos estudos afro-brasileiros*. Rio de Janeiro: Civilização Brasileira, 1937.
——. *Sobrados e mucambos*. Rio de Janeiro: Olympio, 1968.
——. *Vida social do Brasil nos meados do século XIX*. Rio de Janeiro: Artenova, 1977.
Furtado, Celso. *Formação econômica da América Latina*. Rio de Janeiro: LIA, 1970.
——. *Formação econômica do Brasil*. São Paulo: Nacional, 1977.
Gerson, Brasil. *A escravidão no império*. Rio de Janeiro: Pallas, 1975.
Gorender, Jacob. *O escravismo colonial*. São Paulo: Ática, 1978.
Goulart, José Alipio. *Da palmatória ao patíbulo*. Rio de Janeiro: Conquista, 1971.
Goulart, Maurício. *Escravidão africana no Brasil*. São Paulo: Martins, 1949.
Grieco, Agrippino. *Viagem em torno a Machado de Assis*. São Paulo: Martins, 1969.

Guimarães, Bernardo. *A escrava Isaura*. Rio de Janeiro: Melhoramentos, n.d.

Ianni, Octávio. *Escravidão e racismo*. São Paulo: Hucitec, 1978.

——. *As metamorfoses do escravo*. São Paulo: Difusão Européia do Livro, 1962.

——. *Raças e classes sociais no Brasil*. Rio de Janeiro: Civilização Brasileira, 1972.

Jesus, Maria Carolina de. *Quarto de despejo*. São Paulo: Edibolso, 1976.

La Porta, Ernesto. *Rituais afro-brasileiros*. Rio de Janeiro: Atheneu, 1979.

Lobato, Monteiro, *Negrinha*. São Paulo, Brasiliense, 1968.

Macedo, Joaquim Manoel de. *A moreninha*. Rio de Janeiro: Clássicos Brasileiros, 1970.

——. *As vítimas-algozes*. Rio de Janeiro, Paris: Garnier, 2 vol., 1878.

Macedo, Sérgio. *Crônica do negro no Brasil*. Rio de Janeiro: Record, 1974.

Machado Filho, Aires da Mata. *O negro e o garimpo em Minas Gerais*. Rio de Janeiro: Civilização Brasileira, 1975.

Magalhães, Elyette Guimarães de. *Orixás da Bahia*. Salvador: Artes Graficas, 1977.

Magalhães Júnior, Raymundo. *Machado de Assis desconhecido*. Rio de Janeiro: Civilização Brasileira, 1955.

Mario, Armando Souto. *Quebra-quilos*. São Paulo: Nacional, 1978.

Malheiro, Perdigão. *A escravidão no Brasil*. São Paulo: Cultura, 1944.

Marchant, Alexander. *Do escambo à escravidão*. São Paulo: Nacional, 1943,

Marques, Xavier. *O feiticeiro*. São Paulo–Brasília: GRD INL, 1975.

Meyer, Augusto. *Machado de Assis*. Rio de Janeiro: Livraria São José, 1958.

Montello, Josué. *A noite sobre Alcântara*. Rio de Janeiro: Olympio, 1978.

——. *Os tambores de São Luis*. Rio de Janeiro: Olympio, 1978.

Moraes, Evaristo de. *A escravidão africana no Brasil*. São Paulo: Nacional, 1933.

Morais Filho, Nascimento. *Fragmentos de uma vida*. São Luis: n.p., 1975.

Morel, Edmar. *Vendaval da libertade*. Rio de Janeiro: Civilização Brasileira, 1967.

Moura, Clovis. *O negro*. Rio de Janeiro: Conquista, 1977.

——. *Rebeliões da senzala*. São Paulo: Zumbi, 1959.

Nabuco, Joaquim. *O abolicionismo*. São Paulo: Nacional, 1938.

Nascimento, Abdias do. *O genocídio do negro brasileiro*. Rio de Janeiro: Paz e Terra, 1978.
Olinto, Antônio. *Brasileiros na África*. Rio de Janeiro: GRD, 1964.
——. *A casa da água*. Rio de Janeiro: Bloch, 1969.
Patrocínio, José do. *Motta Coqueiro*. Rio de Janeiro: Gazeta de Notícias, 1877.
Penna, Cornélio. *Romances completos*. Rio de Janeiro: Aguilar, 1958.
Pereira, Lúcia Miguel. *Amanhecer*. Rio de Janeiro: Olympio, 1938.
——. *Machado de Assis*. Rio de Janeiro: Olympio, 1955.
Pierson, Donald. *Brancos e pretos na Bahia*. São Paulo: Nacional, 1971.
Prado Júnior, Caio. *Formação do Brasil contemporâneo*. São Paulo: Brasiliense, 1953.
——. *História econômica do Brasil*. São Paulo: Brasiliense, 1974.
Prado, Paulo. *Retrato do Brasil*. São Paulo: DP & C, 1928.
Queiros, Rachel de. *3 Romances*. Rio de Janeiro: Olympio, 1948.
Queiroz, Maria Isaura Pereira de. *O campesinato brasileiro*. Petrópolis: Vozes, 1973.
Queiroz, Suely Robles Reis de. *Escravidão negra em São Paulo*. Rio de Janeiro: Olympio, 1977.
Queiroz Júnior, Teófilo de. *Preconceito de cor e a mulata na literatura brasileira*. São Paulo: Ática, 1975.
Querino, Manoel de. *A Bahia de outrora*. Salvador: Progresso, 1955.
Quintas, Amaro. *O sentido social da revolução praieira*. Rio de Janeiro: Civilização Brasileira, 1967.
Rabassa, Gregory. *O negro na ficção brasileira*. Rio de Janeiro: Tempo Brasileiro, 1965.
Ramos, Arthur. *As culturas negras*. Rio de Janeiro: Livraria, n.d.
——. *As culturas negras no novo mundo*. São Paulo: Nacional, 1979.
——. *Estudos de folclore*. Rio de Janeiro: Livraria, 1951.
——. *O folclore negro do Brasil*. Rio de Janeiro: Livraria, 1954.
——. *O negro brasileiro*. Rio de Janeiro: Civilização Brasileira, 1934.
——. *O negro na civilização brasileira*. Rio de Janeiro: CEB, 1971.
Raposo, Ignácio. *Mestre Cuia*. São Paulo: Brasil, 1937.
Raymundo, Jaques. *O negro brasileiro*. Rio de Janeiro: Record, 1936.
Rego, José Lins do. *Bangüê*. Rio de Janeiro: Olympio, 1969.
——. *Doidinho*. Rio de Janeiro: Olympio, 1969.
——. *Menino de engenho*. Rio de Janeiro: Olympio, 1969.
——. *Meus verdes anos*. Rio de Janeiro: Clássicos Brasileiros, 1970.
——. *Moleque Ricardo*. Rio de Janeiro: Olympio, 1961.
——. *Pureza*. Rio de Janeiro: Olympio, 1970.

——. *Riacho Doce*. Rio de Janeiro: Olympio, 1961.

——. *Usina*. Rio de Janeiro: Olympio, 1961.

Reis, Maria Firmina dos. *Ursula*. Rio de Janeiro: Olímpica, 1975.

Ribeiro, Darcy. *Le Americhe e la civiltà*. Torino: Einaudi, 3 vol., 1975.

Ribeiro, João. *O elemento negro*. Rio de Janeiro: Record, 1939.

Ribeiro, Júlio. *A carne*. Rio de Janeiro: Clássicos Brasileiros, 1977.

Rodrigues, José Honorio. *Brasil e África*. Rio de Janeiro: Civilização Brasileira, 2 vol., 1964.

Rodrigues, Nina. *O animismo fetichista dos negros bahianos*. Rio de Janeiro: Civilização Brasileira, 1935.

——. *Os africanos no Brasil*. São Paulo: Nacional, 1977.

Rosa, João Guimarães. "Noites do sertão," *Corpo de baile*. Rio de Janeiro: Olympio, 1965.

Sant'Ana, Nuto. *Preto Eusébio*. São Paulo: Brasil, 1932.

——. *Thebas, o escravo*. São Paulo: Brasil, 1939.

Santos, João Felicio dos. *Ganga Zumba*. Rio de Janeiro: Clássicos Brasileiros, 1978.

——. *João Abade*. Rio de Janeiro: Agir, 1958.

——. *Xica da Silva*. Rio de Janeiro: Civilização Brasileira, 1976.

Santos, Joaquim Felicio dos. *Memórias do distrito Diamantino*. Petrópolis: Vozes, 1978.

Santos, Juana Elbein dos. *Os Nàgô e a morte*. Petrópolis: Vozes, 1976.

Sayers, Raymond. *O negro na literatura brasileira*. Rio de Janeiro: O Cruzeiro, 1958.

Scarano, Julita, *Devoção e escravidão*. São Paulo: Nacional, 1978.

Seljam, Zora. *3 Mulheres de Xangô*. São Paulo–Brasília: IBRASA INL, 1978.

Serra, Astolfo. *A balaiada*. Rio de Janeiro: Bedeschi, 1946.

Skidmore, Thomas E. *Preto no branco*. Rio de Janeiro: Paz e Terra, 1976.

Sodré, Nelson Werneck. *História da burguesia brasileira*. Rio de Janeiro: Civilização Brasileira, 1976.

Stegagno Picchio, Luciana. *La letteratura brasiliana*. Florence–Milan: Sansoni Accademia, 1972.

Tavares, Odorico. *Bahia*. Rio de Janeiro: Clássicos Brasileiros, 1978.

Valente, Waldemar. *Sincretismo religioso afro-brasileiro*. São Paulo–Brasília: Nacional INL, 1976.

Veríssimo, Érico. *O tempo e o vento*. Porto Alegre: Globo, 3 vol., 1967.

Williams, Eric. *Capitalismo e escravidão*. Rio de Janeiro: Americana, 1975.

INDEX

ABOUT THE AUTHOR

Giorgio Marotti is Professor of Brazilian Literature at the University of Rome. Since 1973, he has been a researcher specializing in South America for Italy's National Council for Research (CNR). During his tenure with the CNR, Marotti produced his two principal works, *Canudos, storia di una guerra* (1978), a historical, literary analysis of the fratricidal war which is the subject of Euclides da Cunha's classic, *Os sertões*, and the work that is translated in the present volume, *Il negro nel romanzo brasiliano* (1982). Other works by Marotti are *O sertão* (1972) and *Jorge Amado* (1972).

After obtaining a degree in Philosophy from the University of Rome in 1962, Marotti traveled extensively throughout Europe and Africa. He taught in Zaire with UNESCO sponsorship, and in Rio de Janeiro after receiving a scholarship from the Brazilian government in 1965. In 1969, Marotti was appointed headmaster of a high school in the Kasai region of Zaire, and in 1970 returned to Brazil. For three years, he taught Italian language and literature there while researching Brazilian literature. Marotti has resided in Rome since 1973.

Maria Ornella Marotti has been an Assistant Professor of American Literature at the University of Rome since 1981. She has also been a visiting lecturer in English at the University of California, Santa Barbara. Her essays, on the Mark Twain papers, Saul Bellow, American autobiography, and women's fiction, have been published both in Italy and the United States. She has translated several works of drama from English into Italian.

Born in Manchester, England in 1939, Harry Lawton obtained a B.A. in French and Italian (1960) and a B. Litt. in Italian (1963) from St. Edmund Hall, Oxford. He went on to join the Department of Romance Languages of the University of Michigan, Ann Arbor (1963–1965), and in 1967 he took the post of Lecturer in Italian at the University of California, Santa Barbara, which he holds at present. He also holds a partial position in the UCSB film studies program. Lawton specializes in twentieth-century Italian poetry and fiction and Italian and world cinema.